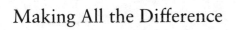

Making All the Difference

MARTHA MINOW

Making All the Difference

INCLUSION, EXCLUSION, AND AMERICAN LAW

Cornell University Press

Ithaca and London

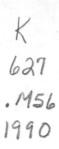
International Standard Book Number 0-8014-2446-1
Library of Congress Catalog Card Number 90-1754
Printed in the United States of America
Librarians: Library of Congress cataloging information appears on the last page of the book.

∞The paper in this book meets the minimum requirements
  of the American National Standard for Information Sciences—Permanence
  of Paper for Printed Library Materials, ANSI Z39.48-1984.

To Burton Minow

Contents

Acknowledgments

Many people have made all the difference for me. I think I wrote the book for this chance to tell them.

I dedicate this book to my uncle, Burton Minow. He has taught me many of the themes important to it. I quote him in Chapter 3: "The point I'm trying to make is that we would prefer to have people laugh with us than at us." Uncle Burt also teaches me, despite my reluctance, about baseball; he teaches me, more successfully, about poetry, about ethics, about patience and courage, and about greeting each day with humor, no matter what is dished out.

I want to thank my parents. I'm glad they decided to have children. I'm especially glad that it is in relationship to them that I became who I am still becoming. Newton Minow always teaches me with his passion for watering wastelands and for turning law to serve justice. He also has taught me to discard the jargon I somehow absorbed in university life and to think about what my work might mean for people beyond these ivy-covered walls. Josephine Baskin Minow's gift for relationships and her lifelong commitment to children and families in need—whether need due to domestic violence or to political oppression—infuse my questions and, I hope, my answers. And together, they have sent a constant supply of relevant clippings from more magazines and newspapers than I knew existed.

My grandmother Doris Minow's *rachmanas* and practical wisdom and her gift for knitting together a far-flung family are inspirations I want to acknowledge. In addition, I owe many ideas in this book to her own efforts to demand that a school system respond to a different child. That story was my first understanding that people can make the difference for one another by remaking the institutions that surround them.

Thanks to Nell Minow for her constant encouragement, her anecdotes, her eloquent comments on this manuscript, her movie recommendations, and her willingness to grant me access to the best mental filing cabinet I've ever seen. Thanks, Nell, for reminding me as only an older sister could of the first poem I ever learned, and clearly took to heart:

I met a little elf-man once
Down where the lilies grow
I asked him why he was so small
And why he did not grow
He slightly smiled and with his eye
He looked me through and through
"I'm quite as big for me," he said,
"As you are big for you."
[John Kendrick Bangs]

I also thank David Apatoff for his most challenging questions and for the help of his time and acumen. I'm glad that Benjamin and Rachel Apatoff remind me that we are all "big enough now" and that we should all "live life and enjoy it." Thanks to Mary Minow for her love of books, and for her days as a nursing home volunteer; her journeys to work with people in need in other countries; her vision of a library as a place where everyone can find a home; and her good judgment in bringing James Robenolt to the family. Also, thanks to Mary's skills as a research librarian and her generous gift of time, some of the references in this book are more accurate and complete than they would otherwise have been. Gale and Pete Adland, and Ari, Jesse, and Naomi teach me about how to live day by day with differences and with delight. Anne Rayman and Bob Singer, along with Adam and Rachel, have made every get-together a holiday; special thanks to Anne for her insights about the worlds of hearing-impaired adolescents. Max and Lila Singer make me feel welcome in ways that convince me that family, in its best meanings, can indeed reach beyond biological ties.

Mary Joe Frug, Mary Ann Glendon, Randy Kennedy, Frank Michelman, Avi Soifer, and Kathleen Sullivan offer that most rare and delicious form of sustenance: daily collegiality that integrates friendship and intellectual exchange. Their own work and their willingness to enter my obsessions regularly made all the difference. The five years of work behind this book would have stretched to many more without the attentive, inventive, and thorough help of David Fernandez, Maura Kelley, Becky Tannenbaum, George Taylor, Sarah Walzer, and Stephen Wieder. The book simply could not have come to fruition without Karol Dean's remarkable skills, good humor, and friendship. Wendi Brown's negotiation talents, computer skills, and sense of perspective were also crucial and much appreciated. Andy Bracker, Chris Branson, and Claire Ancona-Berk made the final stages a chance for new ideas and for breathing life into old ones. And I thank Harvard Law School not only for financial support and a comfortable work setting but also for offering me a vivid laboratory for studying varied treatments of difference. Many, many Harvard law students offered challenging questions and help.

Kate Bartlett and Judith Wegner invited me in 1983 to participate in a symposium on special education. They deepened this opportunity by prodding me to say more fully what I thought I meant. Martha Fineman, Dirk Hartog, Stanley Kutler, and David Trubek created hospitable and stimulating communities of scholars during several summers I spent at the University of Wisconsin, studying and debating the history of family law. Robert Cover's work as a teacher and scholar continues to challenge me and point toward deeper understandings; a pivotal turning point for me occurred as I struggled to respond to his "Violence and the Word" (*Yale Law Journal* 95 [1986], 1601) in what appears here as parts of Chapter 9.

A number of journals that invited me to contribute articles have kindly permitted me to use parts of them in this book. Portions of Chapters 1, 2, and 3 originally appeared in "Learning to Live with the Dilemma of Difference: Bilingual and Special Education," *Law and Contemporary Problems* 48 (Spring 1985), 157 (copyright 1985, Duke University School of Law). Portions of Chapters 4, 5, and 7 originally appeared in "When Difference Has Its Home," *Harvard Civil Rights–Civil Liberties Review* 22 (Winter 1987), 111 (copyright © Martha Minow, 1987). Portions of Chapter 6 appeared originally in "Law Turning Outward," reprinted from *TELOS* 73 (1987), 79. Portions of Chapters 2, 8, and the Afterword originally appeared in "Foreword: Justice Engendered," *Harvard Law Review* 101 (November 1987; copyright © 1987 by the Harvard Law Review Association). Portions of Chapter 8 appeared originally in "Feminist Reason: Getting It and Losing It," reprinted from *Journal of Legal Education* 38 (1988), 47. Portions of Chapter 9 appeared originally in several of my articles: "Forming underneath Everything That Grows," reprinted from *Wisconsin Law Review* (1985), 819 (copyright © 1985 by the University of Wisconsin); "Consider the Consequences," reprinted from *Michigan Law Review* 84 (February–April 1986), 900; "Are Rights Right for Children?" reprinted from the *American Bar Foundation Research Journal* 1 (Winter 1987), 203; "Interpreting Rights: An Essay for Robert Cover," reprinted by permission of The Yale Law Journal Company and Fred B. Rothman & Company from *The Yale Law Journal* 96, no. 8 (1987). Portions of Chapter 10 appeared originally in "Beyond State Intervention in the Family: For Baby Jane Doe," reprinted from *University of Michigan Journal of Law Reform* 18 (1985), 933.

Gracious audiences at the University of Toronto Law School, Harvard Law School, Yale Law School, New York University, Columbia University, Duke Law School, the 1986, 1987, and 1989 Law and Society Association meetings, and the American Political Science Association meetings in 1986, 1987, and 1988 gave me chances to try out many of the book's ideas and to carry home to the word processor the helpful conversations that ensued.

I thank the boards of the W. T. Grant Foundation and the Judge Baker Children's Center for offering me, in the privilege of our shared work, continuing education in the fields of research affecting children. I hope Saul Touster sees here some consequences of his commitment to restore professional ethics through encounters with literature. Susan Wolf's comments deepened my understanding of the debates over medical treatment decisions. Dennis Thompson's helpful words about the unusual challenges of writing a book came at an important moment.

Peter Agree deserves many thanks for asking me if I wanted to write a book; Patricia Sterling and all the folks at Cornell University Press made a real difference and improved the result.

A remarkable community of women gathers monthly under the name of "Fem-Crits and Friends" in a sequence of crowded Cambridge living rooms. The comfort, challenges, and conversations of this community make me a different and, I think, better person; thanks to you all. In addition, Sally Burns, Ellen Wright Clayton, Nancy Cott, Brenda Cossman, Dirk Hartog, Alice Kessler-Harris, Jenny Nedelsky, Debra Ratterman, Elizabeth Schneider, Deborah Stone, Cass Sunstein, Carol Weisbrod, and Joan Williams shared their ideas, their questions, and their support with generosity and welcome insight. Zipporah Wiseman's constant friendship many times made all the difference. Vicky Spelman gave me a thread, a pulley, a rubber ball, and a pipe that each became important parts of this work. The pipe is ordinary curved copper, but it reminds me daily that there are ways out just when it seems that there is a dead end. And thanks to Joe Singer's own footnotes, his grocery shopping, and his gift for mutual reliance on relationships, I am always coming home.

MARTHA MINOW

Cambridge, Massachusetts

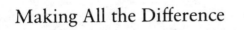

Making All the Difference

Making a Difference

Doesn't everything divide us?
                    —Quoted in Faith Conlon et al.,
                    The Things That Divide Us

The children's television show *Sesame Street* instructs with anima-
tion, skits, and songs. One song asks, "Which one of these things is not like
the others?" The screen depicts a group of items, perhaps a chair, a table, a
cat, and a bed. By asking young viewers to pick out the items that do not
belong with the rest of the group, the song helps them sharpen their vocabulary, perception, and analysis of objects in the world.

I often tell people that if you master this *Sesame Street* episode, you have
started to think like a lawyer. For much of legal reasoning demands famil-
iarity with legal terms, practice in perceiving problems through categories,
and acceptance of the consequences assigned to particular legal categories.
Consider a collision of two automobiles at an intersection of two busy
streets. The traditional law of accidents, known as tort law, asked who was
at fault in the accident. An answer to this question would also yield an
answer to the question of who should pay for it. The law then defined fault: a
person would be at a fault whose own actions or failures to act caused the
injury, and whose actions or failures to act were "negligent." Negligence, in
turn, was defined as a failure in a duty to take adequate care, with the duties
of care specified according to who the actor was and what he or she was
doing. A driver of an automobile would be negligent for failing to drive at the
legal speed or failing to observe traffic signals. Legal analysis would fit the
facts about the collision into this latticework of definitions. Arguments could
then be channeled into the specific issues focused by the legal terms: was the
driver of the blue car negligent? Or was there a separate cause, such as the
second driver's own negligence, or perhaps a child who ran into the street
and led the first driver to swerve to avoid her? Each of these questions could

Epigraph: From *The Things That Divide Us*, edited by Faith Conlon, Rachel da Silva, and
Barbara Wilson, copyright 1985. Published by The Seal Press, 3131 Western Ave., Suite 410,
Seattle.

be answered yes or no, and each answer would signal consequences about who should be held liable and who must pay.

The fault-based approach highlights the way legal analysis simplifies the world. The categories of negligence and cause might seem infinitely malleable. Certainly, in the abstract, we could debate a variety of duties people may owe to one another when driving cars; we could also identify an infinite chain of causes and effects, preceding the births of the drivers and extending long into the future. But legal analysis contracts such discussions by sharpening the definitions and by referring back to precedents: prior judicial decisions ruling on the meanings of negligence and causation in similar contexts. The lawyers turn to these precedents to engage directly in a *Sesame Street* analysis: which of the precedents does the current case resemble? Is it like the prior decision declaring it nonnegligent conduct for a driver cruising at the legal speed to fail to slow down at the intersection? Or does it more comfortably belong with the case declaring it negligent conduct for the driver to fail to slow down at the intersection when it was raining? Legal analysis is a process of perceiving and selecting traits of a given conflict, and analogizing and distinguishing prior decisions. Legal rules announced in statutes and in judicial opinions provide definitions and categories; legal precedents appearing in prior court judgments provide constellations of fact patterns and competing normative rules that allow advocates to fit a new case to the rule—or to an exception. And the basic method of legal analysis requires simplifying the problem to focus on a few traits rather than the full complexity of the situation, and to use those traits for the comparison with both the governing rule and the precedents that could apply.

When framed for judicial resolution, this legal analysis casts the problem in either/or terms: the plaintiff was either negligent or not; the plaintiff either wins or loses. A premise of the judicial system is that the truth will best emerge and justice will be served if two adversaries fully and aggressively present the competing versions of the case. The judge then selects the winning side. There are, however, other ways to analyze and judge the event.[1] One alternative would reject the idea that cause can be located in one actor, trying instead to apportion the contribution of fault manifested by both drivers and allocating the costs from the accident accordingly.[2] This approach could even subtract from the total damages that portion of the damages that would be the fault of neither one. Another approach would reject altogether the idea

---

[1]Beyond the approaches described in the text, we might view the accident as fated: the losses fall where they fall. This approach has characterized law in contexts where particular actors are thought to owe no duty to others arising from their own conduct; it has become unpopular, and unlikely, in this era in which victims have trouble protecting themselves from the onslaught of complex technologies beyond their control.

[2]One rule, still used in many jurisdictions, assessed the fault of the different drivers only to defeat the lawsuit of a complainant whose "contributory negligence" was demonstrated; see *Restatement (Second) of Torts* (St. Paul, Minn.: American Law Institute, 1965), sec. 467. A more recent version, "comparative negligence," provides for the assessment and allocation described in the text. See Victor E. Schwartz, *Comparative Negligence*, 2d ed. (Indianapolis, Ind.: A. Smith, 1986).

that liability and payment should rest on fault, and instead tax all drivers (or demand their own private purchase of insurance) to create a pool of money for distribution based on the predictable level of accidents in the particular community.[3] These alternative theories have indeed become prevalent for handling automobile accidents in many communities. Together with the fault theory, they exemplify the tools of legal analysis: specially crafted categories, narrowing and simplifying a problem, are used to assign consequences to people in a real-world dispute, once the facts of their dispute are sorted into the legal categories. Yet in contrast to the fault theory, both the alternative rule of comparative negligence and the insurance-based scheme removing car accidents entirely from the fault-based tort system begin to alter the basic dualistic, win/lose quality of traditional legal analysis.

Except for its specialized vocabulary, legal analysis looks a lot like other kinds of analysis—as the comparison with the *Sesame Street* song should suggest. When we analyze, we simplify. We break complicated perceptions into discrete items or traits. We identify the items and call them chair, table, cat, and bed. We sort them into categories that already exist: furniture and animal.[4] It sounds familiar. It also sounds harmless. I do not think it is.

I believe we make a mistake when we assume that the categories we use for analysis just exist and simply sort our experiences, perceptions, and problems through them. When we identify one thing as like the others, we are not merely classifying the world; we are investing particular classifications with consequences and positioning ourselves in relation to those meanings. When we identify one thing as unlike the others, we are dividing the world; we use our language to exclude, to distinguish—to discriminate. This last word may be the one that most recognizably raises the issues about which I worry. Sometimes, classifications express and implement prejudice, racism, sexism, anti-Semitism, intolerance for difference. Of course, there are "real differences" in the world; each person differs in countless ways from each other person. But when we simplify and sort, we focus on some traits rather than others, and we assign consequences to the presence and absence of the traits we make significant. We ask, "What's the new baby?"—and we expect as an answer, boy or girl. That answer, for most of history, has spelled consequences for the roles and opportunities available to that individual. And when we respond to persons' traits rather than their conduct, we may treat a given trait as a justification for excluding someone we think is "different." We feel no need for further justification: we attribute the consequences to the

---

[3]Commonly called "no-fault" insurance, this approach originated in the work of Robert Keeton in Massachusetts; see his *Basic Text on Insurance Law* (St. Paul, Minn.: West, 1971). One virtue is that it can remove automobile accident cases from court and eliminate the costs of litigation by devising an administrative scheme to handle the disbursement process.

[4]There may be similarity as well as difference: e.g., the chair, table, cat, bed each have four legs. And there may be differences that demand new categories for each item—based on color, size, age, physical location, symbolic significance, and a variety of still more distinguishing traits. Thus, the selected traits may submerge from view other traits that provide different axes for comparison.

differences we see. We neglect the other traits that may be shared. And we neglect how each of us, too, may be "different."

Presuming real differences between people, differences that we all know and recognize, presumes that we all perceive the world the same way and that we are unaffected by our being situated in it. This presumption also ignores the power of our language, which embeds unstated points of comparison inside categories that falsely imply a natural fit with the world. The very term "working mother" reveals that the general term "mother" carries some unstated common definition—that is, a woman who cares for her children full time without pay. Even if unintended, such unstated meanings must be expressly modified if the speaker means something else.[5] Labels of difference often are assigned by some to describe others in ways they would not describe themselves, and in ways that carry baggage that may be difficult to unload.

If you have ever felt wronged by a label of difference assigned to you, you may know what I mean. People often feel unrecognized, excluded, or degraded "because" of their gender, religion, race, ethnicity, nationality, age, height, weight, family membership, sexual orientation, or health status. The expansiveness of this list does not trivialize the issue, even though it does suggest that there are many more differences that people make significant than any of us may note self-consciously. Organizing perceptions along some lines is essential, but which lines will we use—and come to use unthinkingly? Human beings use labels to describe and sort their perceptions of the world. The particular labels often chosen in American culture can carry social and moral consequences while burying the choices and responsibility for those consequences. The labels point to conclusions about where an item, or an individual, belongs without opening for debate the purposes for which the label will be used. This is what worries me about any mode of analysis that asks, "which one of these is not like the others?"

Labels and Morals

An animal behaviorist, Harold A. Herzog, Jr., has examined the impact of the labels we use in our moral responses to, of all things, mice. At the University of Tennessee a clean and well-run facility for animals houses some 15,000 mice used each year in experiments. The university requires approval by an animal care committee for any experiment using the mice, and both the federal Department of Agriculture and the American Association for the Accreditation of Laboratory Animal Care inspect and monitor the standards of care provided. Yet it is only the experimental mice, Herzog notes, who are

---

[5]See George Lakoff, *Women, Fire, and Dangerous Things: What Categories Reveal about the Mind* (Chicago: University of Chicago Press, 1987), pp. 80–81. As another example, the term "surrogate mother" obscures the fact that it applies to the person who is actually the biological mother.

protected by these concerns for animal care. At any given time, some mice escape; these become "pests" and are routinely captured and destroyed. The staff at the center use "sticky" traps, something like flypaper, to catch these "pests" overnight, and those that are not dead by morning are gassed. Herzog observes that these traps would never be used for the "good" experimental mice, yet no animal care committee, no public or private agency, reviews this "pest removal" process. "Once a research animal hits the floor and becomes an escapee, its moral standing is instantly diminished."[6] Similarly, some mice are used as food for other research animals, and a mouse labeled "snake food" also falls outside the attention of an animal care committee. The role, and label, of the creature determines variations in how the very same animal may be perceived and treated.

Perhaps most ironically, Herzog reports an incident from his family life. His young son had a pet mouse, Willie. When Willie died, the family gave him a burial, with a tombstone and a funeral. "At the same time that we were mourning Willie's demise, however, my wife and I were setting snap traps each night in a futile attempt to eliminate the mice that inhabit our kitchen."[7] The mere change in label from pet to pest transformed the moral status of the different mice. Herzog explains that he is not opposing the use of mice in research; nor is he criticizing the treatment of mice at his university; and he acknowledges that countless mice are consumed by their natural predators outside of human laboratories and homes. He concludes that the roles and labels humans assign to animals "deeply influence our sense of what is ethical."[8]

The interaction between labels and moral judgments is, if anything, more pronounced when the labels are about people. To the ridicule or indifference of others, groups of women, members of racial minorities, and disabled persons have often struggled to remake the labels assigned to them—and to shake free of the negative associations those labels have carried. Which would, should, we use: ladies or women? blacks or African Americans? Hispanics or Chicanos? Puerto Ricans or Latinos? handicapped or physically challenged? exceptional or disabled? In the struggle for terms of self-description, we are caught invariably in our membership in a larger society whose language we share, even if we resist the words used by others to describe us. Negative labels are especially a problem for members of minority groups or groups with less influence in the society. For this very reason, the

---

[6]Harold A. Herzog, Jr., "The Moral Status of Mice," *American Psychologist* 43 (June 1988), 473, 474.

[7]Ibid., p. 474.

[8]Labels not only influence but also reflect our sense of what is ethical. Herzog (ibid.) explains, "I suspect that there is an interaction between our labels (i.e., pest, pet, food, subject) and how we treat animals. Labels are, in part, the result of the role that the animal occupies relative to humans; conversely, the label influences the behavior and emotions directed toward the animal. . . . Moral codes are the product of human psychology, not 'pure' reason. Because ethical judgments are inextricably bound in a complex matrix of emotion, logic, and self-interest, a better understanding of the *psychology* of how humans arrive at moral decisions will be critical to progress in the area of animal welfare."

efforts to rename oneself may be circumscribed by the attitudes and authority of those who have defined the difference.

The tendency to build social divisions based on selected traits is not, however, restricted to those who have enjoyed more privilege or those who have been in the majority. Holly Near and Adrian Torf wrote a song called "Unity" that brings a shock of recognition to many audiences:

> One man fights the KKK
> But he hates the queers
> One woman works for ecology
> It's equal rights she fears;
> Some folks know that war is hell
> But they put down the blind.
> I think there must be a common ground
> But it's mighty hard to find.[9]

Athol Fugard, John Kani, and Winston Ntshona wrote a play, *The Island,* set in a prison on Robben Island off the shore of South Africa. In the play, two political prisoners live a wretched existence of grueling physical toil and brutal treatment, but they are deep friends and mutually supportive—until one of the prisoners learns that he is to be released. The sheer idea of an endpoint to his incarceration distinguishes him from his cellmate, and the two are no longer equal. The other prisoner feels jealous, desperate, even brutal; his fellow prisoner's better fortune seems to confirm rather than challenge his despair.[10] Both *The Island* and the song "Unity" depict recognizable patterns of subjection and domination in which people participate— as victims, as perpetrators, and as perpetuators of prejudice.

Language and labels play a special role in the perpetuation of prejudice about differences. After Martin Luther King was killed in 1968, a third grade teacher in Iowa decided she had to teach her students, who were all white, about discrimination. Jane Elliott created a two-day experiment: on the first day she gave children with brown eyes special privileges and permission to discriminate against their "inferior" blue-eyed classmates. On the second day the students reversed roles. The teacher was stunned by how readily the "superior" students on each day took to their privileges and delighted in degrading their classmates. Equally noteworthy was the reaction of the "inferior" students: they demonstrated physical and emotional signs of de-

---

[9]© 1982 Hereford Music (ASCAP), words by Holly Near, music by Holly Near & Adrian Torf. All Rights Reserved. Used by permission. Available on *Speed of Light* by Holly Near. Distributed by Redwood Records 1-800-888-SONG.

[10]*The Island,* in Athol Fugard, John Kani, and Winston Ntshona, *Statements 45* (New York: Theater Communications Group, 1986). The prison authorities arrange for them both to participate in a dramatic production of Antigone. The prisoner without a release date is assigned to play Antigone, and initially objects to another humiliation: playing a woman. Yet in the course of speaking Antigone's lines he actually finds a voice for his own objections to the injustice he faces.

feat and passivity, even performing more poorly in classroom assignments.[11] Name-calling by school children may seem juvenile, but it reappears in the shorthand of corporate boardrooms, which labels those who are "unsound" or "not one of us." The familiar wartime device of naming people on the enemy side so that they are no longer fully human gave us "Jap," "Kraut," and "Gook."

The systematic genocide orchestrated by the Nazis followed policies of labeling Jews, gypsies, political dissidents, and homosexuals. As one survivor remembered: "We had to wear yellow stripes. People treated us like animals. When people saw the yellow they did not see the human being who wore it. Maybe people are really all animals and only human on a very thin surface."[12] Genocide and war are not due only to labeling, but putting labels on other people does compress moral sensibilities and make it easier to deny any bonds of commonality.

Perhaps we know only by comparing, by drawing distinctions from and similarities to what we already know. But when we use our terms of comparison to shut off any understanding of our connections with one another as human beings, we risk becoming something less than human ourselves.

Boundaries

The questions I am raising here may seem both impractical and disturbing. They attack what has counted as analysis, and what may be an inevitable human need to sort through overwhelmingly complicated experience. And aren't people really different, anyway? Don't we need the boundaries of difference to make sense of perceptions, experience, identities, and human obligations?

Boundaries based on difference have been critical to what has counted as legal analysis, and boundaries also figure prominently in legal assumptions about the self and about society. Traditional legal rules presume that there is a clear and knowable boundary between each individual and all others. Tort law describes the violations when one individual crosses another's boundaries. Rules of contract contemplate distinct parties, able to formulate their preferences and express their wills in the form of a knowing and voluntary exchange. Constitutional law recognizes the rights of each distinct individual, not groups; constitutional law also establishes three distinct and bounded branches of government. Each of these legal rules may seem to

---

[11]William Peters, *A Class Divided: Then and Now,* exp. ed. (New Haven, Conn.: Yale University Press, 1987). The experiment was repeated and filmed for a television documentary, "A Class Divided" in 1970; at a reunion fourteen years later the students reported the long-lasting impression the experiment had made in their lives.

[12]Frau Dr. Jolana Roth, quoted in Claudia Koonz, *Mothers in the Fatherland: Women, the Family, and Nazi Policies* (New York: St. Martin's Press, 1987), p. 424. See also Vasily Grossman, *Life and Fate* (New York: Harper & Row, 1980), pp. 80–93.

avoid labels because it emphasizes the importance of each individual. And yet, these rules contribute to labeling by favoring a view of certain and clear boundaries rather than of relationships.

Legal doctrines within each field of law also tend to establish categories, conceived as bounded rather than open-ended or determined through inter-action with events. The lawyer makes an argument to fit a problem inside or outside a category, such as negligence; the adversary makes opposing argu-ments. The parties' lawyers themselves are bounded, distinct; their job in court is to disagree, not to agree.[13] Judges determine whether "the doctrine applies," whether the problem "falls within the statute or rule," and whether the precedent is "on all fours," perched squarely on top of the pending dispute. These descriptions of legal reasoning treat the categories of law as given receptacles, ready to contain whatever new problem may arise. Miss-ing from these descriptions is the possibility that our very process of sorting may stretch some categories, contract others, or even require us to invent a new box for what we cannot yet classify.

Legal rules in Western societies historically have drawn a boundary be-tween normal and abnormal, or competent and incompetent people. Chil-dren and mentally disabled persons present classic instances of the legally incompetent individual; for most purposes, they still remain labeled legally incompetent and subject to restraints by law. During different periods of history, women, slaves, sailors, Jews, and clergy also took their places across the line of legal competency and suffered legal disabilities curbing their rights and powers under law. In hindsight, after many changes, we can question whether any of these groups ever belonged on the other side of the line defining sufficient capacity or competence to enjoy legal rights. But beyond the historic assignments of difference that we might now view as error, the traditional creation of two classes of people ignores the possibility that people exhibit a range of capacities and abilities. The traditional view also neglects the possibility that certain kinds of incapacity could be remedied by different social practices; certain kinds, indeed, were created by them.[14]

Finally, law has long sought to define the boundaries of each person's obligations to others. Anglo-American law during the past 150 years estab-lished limits to these obligations at the duty to do no harm to others.[15] For example, there is no duty to rescue a drowning stranger, and a rescuer may

[13]Where the opponents do not sufficiently disagree, the court may dismiss the case as collusive or insufficiently adverse. See Laurence Tribe, *American Constitutional Law* (Mineola, N.Y.: Foundation Press, 1988), pp. 93–95.

[14]For example, the legal disabilities assigned to women largely followed from other legal rules depriving them of control over their own property, labor, and person; see Chapters 5 and 9.

[15]See Joel Feinberg, *Reason and Responsibility* (Encino, Calif.: Dickenson, 1975); Joel Feinberg, "Legal Paternalism," in *Paternalism*, ed. Rolf Sartorius (Minneapolis: University of Minnesota, 1983). See also Alan Dershowitz, "Toward a Jurisprudence of 'Harm' Prevention," in *The Limits of Law*, Nomos vol. 15, ed. James Roland Pennock and John William Chapman (New York: Lieber-Atherton, 1974), p. 135.

even incur liability for a job incompletely done.[16] Yet legal rules treat certain special relationships differently: parents bear obligations to children, trustees to wards, and professionals to clients. These exceptional relationships also mark the people who are often labeled legally incompetent or abnormal. When law recognizes relationships of assigned rather than chosen obligation, it also classifies some people as marginal. The traditional rules that made husbands responsible for their wives also removed married women from the world of individual rights.

Law's usual boundaries distinguish the self from others, the normal group from the abnormal, and autonomous individuals from those in relationships of dependency. With this vocabulary, law has organized perceptions of individuals and of groups and has helped to implement norms curbing responsibility to anyone outside one's own family. This vocabulary that neatly defines persons and their roles and obligations has its costs. One is that legal rules often falter when conflicts arise within ongoing relationships. Conflicts within the family, disputes within schools, and disagreements over the treatment of anyone considered incompetent or abnormal often strain the resources of judges and administrators and provoke intense public controversy. Families and communities fight over educational and medical decisions for disabled children, and existing legal rules provide few answers. Some argue that there is no vocabulary for embedding rights within relationships without disturbing or disrupting those relationships. Others protest that without rights, relationships of unchecked power endanger the well-being and security of the more vulnerable parties.

Another cost of its bounded vocabulary is that law ends up contributing to rather than challenging assigned categories of difference that manifest social prejudice and misunderstanding. Especially troubling is the meaning of equality for individuals identified as different from the norm. What should equality mean when schools and public institutions make decisions about people who differ by race, physical capability, mental ability, language proficiency, ethnic identity, gender, or religion? Does equality mean treating everyone the same, even if this similar treatment affects people differently? Members of minorities may find that a neutral rule, applied equally to all, burdens them disproportionately. Instructing a class entirely in English carries different consequences for students proficient in English and students proficient in Spanish instead.

Because of its preoccupation with boundaries, law has neglected ongoing relationships between people, and law has failed to resolve the meaning of equality for people defined as different by the society. Both these problems concern people who are often marginal: children, disabled persons, members of ethnic and religious and racial minorities. Women of any background may be neglected by legal rules, given their traditional exclusion from the public

[16]See Leon Sheleff, *The Bystander* (Lexington, Mass.: Lexington Books, 1978); *The Good Samaritan and the Law,* ed. James Ratcliffe (Garden City, N.Y.: Anchor Books, 1966).

processes for defining the rules of marriage and divorce, the workplace, and violence, domestic or otherwise. Law has treated as marginal, inferior, and different any person who does not fit the normal model of the autonomous, competent individual. Law has tended to deny the mutual dependence of all people while accepting and accentuating the dependency of people who are "different." And law has relied on abstract concepts, presented as if they have clear and known boundaries, even though the concepts await redefinition with each use. Even the institutions of government are treated as separate and bounded by governing legal rules. This view restrains some efforts by government officials to respond to people's needs. If courts, in particular, are denied power to respond to people's vulnerabilities, abuses of public and private power may persist without relief.

These characteristics of law reflect the powerful human need to set boundaries in order to avoid being overwhelmed by perceptions, obligations, and connections with others. But many different sets of categories can be used to organize the world. Anglo-American law has historically used categories to assign people to different statuses. The price of these legal categories has been borne disproportionately by the most marginal and vulnerable members of the society. Labeling them will only hide human responsibility for their treatment, not solve the problems of organizing perceptions and responsibilities. Naming differences to distinguish people isolates those who do the naming as well, and naming differences may deny the humanity of those who seem different.

Moreover, the whole concept of a boundary depends on relationships: relationships between the two sides drawn by the boundary, and relationships among the people who recognize and affirm the boundary. From this vantage point one can see that connections between people are the preconditions for boundaries; the legal rules erecting boundaries between people rely on understanding social agreements and the sense of community.[17]

Once we understand the relationships that are critical to setting and respecting boundaries, we can examine more honestly which boundaries express and promote the kinds of relationships we know and desire. For example, the tort rules governing automobile accidents all depend upon relationships. The rules defining fault in terms of negligence and direct causation express patterns of relationships between people, patterns of presumed independence and bounded separateness respected by the government and by the people living in the community.[18] The modified rule that compares the negligence or fault of the two drivers embodies a conception of

[17]For a thoughtful exploration of the flawed conception of boundaries as applied both to the self and to legal rights, see Jennifer Nedelsky, "Law, Boundaries, and the Bounded Self" (University of Toronto Faculty of Law, unpublished manuscript, 1989). The development of an individual sense of autonomy depends upon a close psychological relationship with another person, whose presence and acts of mirroring critically contribute to the individual's sense of self (see Chapter 7).

[18]This fault approach may be understood as an effort to hold people responsible for their own actions, and to induce people to change their behavior in anticipation of possible future fault.

their relationship as mutual rather than one-directional: it takes two drivers to create an accident, and each contributes to what counts as its cause.[19] The insurance approach takes this understanding of relationships one step further: here, the conception of relationships expands to include all members of the driving community, who share the risk of accidents. The insurance scheme distributes the costs of accidents throughout the group that shares the risk, the group that contributes to the insurance pool.[20] Law then expresses and organizes a different sense of boundaries but retains the power and the commitment to provide clarity and resolution to conflicts between people that are bound to arise. The choice is not between boundaries and connections; it is a question of what kinds of boundaries and connections to construct and enforce. The choice is not between individualism and relationships; it is a question of which kinds of relationships we should sponsor, especially in light of the distribution of shared risks.

Similar contrasting approaches can be adopted in the legal treatment of difference. We can treat differences as the private, internal problem of each different person, a treatment that obviously depends on communal agreements and public enforcement. We can treat differences as a function of relationships and compare the contributions made by different people to the costs and burdens of difference. Or we can treat differences as a pervasive feature of communal life and consider ways to structure social institutions to distribute the burdens attached to difference.[21]

Overview of This Book

These are the issues for this book: how does and how could law treat differences and boundaries between people? The legacy of statuses assigned by law to differentiate people and the continuing struggles to alter that legacy

---

[19]This contributory fault approach more finely tunes the relationship between fault and liability by communicating to both parties that they may share responsibility for any meetings by accident.

[20]Eligibility rules for insurance can provide a basis for changing the conduct and practices of the applicant: the insurance companies can refuse to insure drivers who have repeated accidents or whose cars fall below a specified standard of safety. Thus, the insurance route does not take the level of accidents as a given but permits methods of trying to alter the behaviors that contribute to it.

[21]Traditional legal rules governing challenges to race and gender discrimination in fact have borrowed from torts the notion of fault, requiring demonstration that the perpetrator caused the harm—and (unlike the requirements of the negligence standard) actually intended it. With lawsuits initiated by groups of people, the law expanded in the field of employment discrimination to permit a presumption of discrimination based on statistical measures of the disparate impact on the minority group of the defendants' employment practices. To some extent, affirmative action programs, whether voluntary or court imposed, represent both corrective action and an insurance concept, distributing the costs of past discrimination throughout the community rather than assigning them solely to the past victims. See, e.g., Kathleen Sullivan, "Sins of Discrimination: Last Term's Affirmative Action Cases," *Harv. L. Rev.* 100 (1986), 78. The focus of this book is less on the doctrinal developments in discrimination law than on the legal conceptions of difference.

are of central concern. Chapter 1 presents what I have called "the dilemma of difference," the conundrum of equality in a legal and social world that has made certain traits signify important differences in people's statuses and entitlements. What does, and what should, equality mean for a handicapped child's education? Should she enroll in a special school for handicapped children, or a mainstream school where she will be "different" from the other students? In the mainstream school, what kinds of programs does she need, and what kinds does she deserve, to be treated equally? Similar questions arise about education for students whose primary language is not English. Another example appears in the employment problems women experience when they become pregnant and become mothers: what kinds of accommodation do they deserve to assure equality? Does accommodation undermine equality by treating them differently?

Chapter 2 examines the assumptions built into the legal analysis of such dilemmas of difference which make the dilemmas intractable. These are assumptions about the sources of difference, about the perspective that matters for perceiving and judging the world, and about what is immutable and what is mutable in the institutional arrangements of society. Such assumptions about knowledge, categories, and boundaries usually remain implicit and unexamined. Making them explicit permits debate and the exploration of alternatives.

Chapter 3 pursues the alternative approaches enabled by a focus on the relationships within which we define and construct difference. If difference is no longer presumed inherent in the "different" person but is instead a feature of a comparison drawn between people, the relationships behind the comparisons become salient and crucial. A student in a wheelchair is different only in relation to those who are mobile on foot, and this difference is significant only in relation to institutions that have made this difference matter by placing steps before each entrance and by using doorways too narrow to be navigated by someone in a wheelchair. The meanings of many differences can change when people locate and revise their relationships to difference. The student in a wheelchair becomes less "different" when the building, designed without him in mind, is altered to permit his access.

Not all differences are so easy to reconceive, and even this one may invite objections about costs and inefficiencies. The second part of the book pursues the enduring attitudes about difference which persist in contemporary and in historical legal thought. By examining in detail the judicial struggle over a neighborhood's objections to a group home for mentally retarded persons, Chapter 4 unearths three contrasting approaches to difference that currently appear in legal arguments. The first assumes that difference is inherent in some people, and those "abnormal" people deserve distinctive legal treatment. The second starts with a guarantee of equal rights to everyone but defines equality in terms of sameness. Seeing real differences between people as reason for different treatment, the "equal rights" approach launches inquiries into what differences are "real"; it thereby preserves a two-class system, prescribing one legal treatment for people who are the same and another for people who are "really" different. The third approach conceives of difference as a function of social relationships and invites a challenge to the patterns of relationships and knowledge that assign the burden of differences between people to only some people. All three approaches appear in contemporary judicial opinions, which suggests the power of continuity alongside change in legal thought.

Chapter 5 delves into the histories of the first two legal approaches to difference. Both medieval law and the subsequent revolution of liberal legalism contributed to the origins and development of the "abnormal-persons" approach. Developments in the social sciences, along with political struggles for racial and gender equality, helped to forge rights analysis. Chapter 5 also explores the promises and the limitations of rights analysis in a lengthy lawsuit over an institution for mentally retarded persons in Pennsylvania.

Chapter 6 examines rights analysis in conjunction with other contemporary legal theories and finds that they share the same limitations in their treatment of difference. "Social contract" and "natural rights" theories inform legal rights analysis with commitments to check power and to affirm individuality, but, perpetuating assumptions about two classes of people, normal and abnormal, they fail to offer ways out of dilemmas of difference. Contrasting legal theories known as "legal process" and "law and economics" diverge from rights analysis in many respects but nonetheless share similar limitations in the legal treatment of difference. The chapter concludes with a consideration of "critical legal studies," whose advocates offer some avenues for rethinking difference while failing to break free from the limiting assumptions of the schools of thought they criticize.

Chapter 7 locates the history of the "social relations" approach in century-long innovations across science, social science, and philosophy and in literary studies. In each of these fields, scholars in this century have argued for a shift in paradigms by focusing on relationships between things rather than the discrete things themselves. The theory of relativity and the uncertainty principle in physics are familiar examples; psychologists' conceptions of object relations and sociologists' view of the social construction of meaning provide other instances. Even controversies within fields, such as the debate contrasting structuralism and interpretive methods in anthropology, demonstrate a convergence in their shared focus on relationships between the objects studied, and relationships between the observed and the observer. American pragmatism offered philosophy an analogous shift in focus. Its emphasis on the relationships between knowledge and its use and between theory and context mirrors the developments in other fields. Literary theories of structuralism, deconstruction, reader response, and hermeneutics similarly share a renewed interest in relationships within texts, between texts, and between text and reader. Feminist work in each of these fields identifies hidden assumptions about the norm—the male norm—at work in prevailing theories about the world and richly conveys the relationships between knower and known, theory and context, parts and wholes, and self and other which often lie buried in the usual understandings. The chapter returns in the end to the legal treatment of difference and the problems involved in relational approaches.

Chapter 8 launches Part III of the book by pursuing objections to and refinements of relational approaches. It first criticizes contemporary feminist theory for recreating the problem feminism sought to address: the adoption of unstated reference points that hide assumptions of "the norm" from view and shield it from challenge. In critiques of the "male" point of view and in celebrations of "the female," feminists run the risk of treating particular experiences as universal and of ignoring differences of race, class, religion, ethnicity, nationality, and disability. Chapter 8 also reviews the social and legal reforms launched at the turn of this century by Progressive reformers. Many of these reforms embodied the ideas of such women as Jane Addams, who sought to bring to public life the norms of caretaking associated with the private sphere of the family. By examining the rise and fall of the juvenile court, protective labor legislation, and child and maternal health reforms, this chapter offers cautionary tales about reforms founded on commitments to relationships without full participation by those targeted for help.

Chapter 9 seeks to learn from the warnings raised in Chapter 8 and returns to rights in an effort to salvage their promise for checking power and affirming individuality. Yet, mindful of the shortcomings of rights analysis in past treatments of difference, Chapter 9 connects rights to relationships—between people, between individuals and communities, and between texts and consciousness. By focusing on the legal treatment of families and family members, a conception of rights in relationships can counter forms of both public and private power that have in the past oppressed individuals and assigned the burdens of differences to women and children. The legal tradition, known as legal realism, that brought pragmatism to law offers a route for integrating relational insights into analyses of power. The chapter pursues this route while probing the special problems posed by rights for children.

Chapter 10 uses the debates over medical treatment for severely disabled newborns as a setting for trying out the relational methods developed in the book. The techniques of literary criticism provide a basis for finding similarities between adversarial positions; psychological methods offer insight into the fears and other intense emotions aroused by these debates. The problems of knowledge—and especially the impact of the knower on the known—become central in evaluating parents and other possible decisionmakers, who, under examination, all bring their own situated perspectives to the medical treatment decision. Perhaps most critically, the chapter considers the relationship between the disabled newborn and the family and community after the medical treatment as a source and resource for remaking the meaning of difference. The chapter closes with a case study involving an unusual medical treatment decision for a child with Down's syndrome.

Chapter 11 turns to what may seem an unexpected topic: the powers of the branches of government. Yet this topic also offers a context for applying the relational strategies developed in the book and for reconsidering the relationship between law and people who are "different." The constitutional doctrine of separation of powers has helped to sustain criticism of judicial initiatives on behalf of such people. The chapter reexamines the separation of governmental powers in terms of the relationships necessary to construct and monitor their boundaries, drawing an analogy with individual persons who also need continuing relationships to construct and maintain boundaries of the self. Two case studies of complex litigation—one involving disputes over the tribal status of a Native American community, and one authorizing deinstitutionalization of mentally retarded persons—provide occasions to examine the reach of and restraints on innovative judicial action. Alternatives to either/or problem-solving figure prominently in both the courts' own work and in their efforts in evaluation.

To Keep in Mind

Given my interests, it should not be surprising that there are complex relationships between the chapters and themes in this book. I advocate a shift in the paradigm we use to conceive of difference, a shift from a focus on the distinctions between people to a focus on the relationships within which we notice and draw distinctions. But I do not reject all that the prior frames of thought have offered; I suggest a dialectical approach connecting a renewed interest in relationships to the prior frameworks that emphasized rights and distinctions between people.

The book offers an introduction to the legal treatment of difference in a variety of contexts; the relationships across apparently different problems and apparently different legal precedents are as important as their distinctions. I also engage in debate with other theorists about the role of rights and the limits of individualism in political and legal theory. Here, I reject both the claim that we must abandon rights as illusory or insufficient and the claim that we must preserve existing forms of rights as protections for individual autonomy. Embedding rights within relationships, I argue, offers another and more promising alternative. I advocate self-consciousness about the concepts we use and their effects on what we think we know and who we are. And I am interested in the relationships behind what we think of as distinct or different, even as I acknowledge that this interest can seem unfamiliar and uncomfortable.

Thus, the laws governing the treatment of disability, race, ethnicity, religion, gender, family, and children each have distinct histories, and yet comparisons among them show deeper patterns of thought about difference, about relationships, and about law and society. Contrasts between theories of law are important, but connections between them show many assumptions that they share, especially about the people whose fates they have ignored. The conception of caretaking and mutual obligation advocated by some feminists—and some Progressive-era reformers—can be made compatible with conceptions of rights, individual boundaries, and restraints on both public and private power.

A scholar's—and a reader's—focus on people who are "different" or who seem marginal is itself a way to remake the meaning of difference. Making central what has been marginal remakes the boundaries of knowledge and understanding and sheds new light on the whole; we are constituted by what and how we know even as we constitute what we know as we know it.

Strategies for remaking difference include challenging and transforming the unstated norm used for comparisons, taking the perspective of the traditionally excluded or marginal group, disentangling equality from its attachment to a norm that has the effect of unthinking exclusion, and treating everyone as though he or she were different.

Instead of making differences, let us make all the difference.

PART I

DILEMMAS OF DIFFERENCE

CHAPTER I

The Dilemma of Difference

Now suddenly she was Somebody, and as imprisoned in her
difference as she had been in anonymity.
                              —Tillie Olsen, "I Stand Here Ironing"

To gain the word
to describe the loss
I risk losing everything.
                              —Cherríe Moraga, *This Bridge Called My Back*

All the teachers in the San Francisco public schools during the
1960s taught their classes in English, just as they always had. But by the end
of the decade a group of parents sought out a lawyer to object that this
instruction deprived their children of the chance for an equal education.
Their children, who spoke primarily Chinese, were falling far behind in
classes taught only in English. The parents pushed the courts to consider
whether according the same treatment to people who differ—to the students
who speak English and those who speak Chinese—violates commitments to
equality.

Ultimately, the Supreme Court of the United States heard the case. In 1974
the Court concluded that "the Chinese-speaking minority receives less benefits than the English-speaking majority" from the schools and that therefore
the school system "denies them a meaningful opportunity to participate in
the educational program."[1] The Court directed the school system to take

---

First epigraph: From Tillie Olsen, *Tell Me a Riddle* (New York: Laurel/Dell, 1961), copyright
© 1961 by Tillie Olsen. Reprinted by permission of Delacorte Press/Seymour Lawrence. Second
epigraph: From *This Bridge Called My Back: Writings by Radical Women of Color*, edited by
Cherríe Moraga & Gloria Anzaldúa. Reprinted with permission of Kitchen Table: Women of
Color Press, P.O. Box 908, Latham, N.Y. 12110.

[1]Lau v. Nichols, 414 U.S. 563 (1974). The suit followed earlier judicial orders to desegregate
the school system. Some instruction aimed at students lacking English proficiency began in
1967, but by 1970 less than half the students in this situation had received any help. 483 F.2d
791, 797 (9th Cir. 1973).

affirmative steps to rectify the language deficiency.[2] "Special," not similar, treatment was the legal solution to the question of equality. The decision encouraged bilingual education programs that separated the students lacking English proficiency from their peers for part of the school day or provided months or even years of specialized schooling.

Also during the 1970s, parents and lawyers challenged traditional educational practices for children with physical or mental disabilities, claiming that those children were being denied equal treatment. Here, though, the challengers objected to the exclusion of disabled children from the public school classrooms attended by their peers. Borrowing rhetoric and legal analysis from the crusade for racial desegregation, advocates for the rights of handicapped students urged their integration into mainstream classrooms, along with services to facilitate such programs.[3]

Perhaps ironically, then, educational policymakers and law reformers during the 1970s and 1980s switched allegiance to bilingual programs that pull students at least part time from the mainstream classroom, while simultaneously sponsoring special education programs that integrate handicapped students into either the mainstream classroom or the "least restrictive alternative." The apparent contrast between these two responses to students who differ from their peers, however, suggests a deeper similarity. Schools, parents, and legal officials confront in both contexts the difficult task of remedying inequality. With both bilingual and special education, schools struggle to deal with children defined as "different" without stigmatizing them. Both programs raise the same question: when does treating people differently emphasize their differences and stigmatize or hinder them on that basis? and when does treating people the same become insensitive to their difference and likely to stigmatize or hinder them on *that* basis?

I call this question "the dilemma of difference." The stigma of difference may be recreated both by ignoring and by focusing on it. Decisions about education, employment, benefits, and other opportunities in society should not turn on an individual's ethnicity, disability, race, gender, religion, or membership in any other group about which some have deprecating or hostile attitudes. Yet refusing to acknowledge these differences may make them continue to matter in a world constructed with some groups, but not others, in mind. The problems of inequality can be exacerbated both by treating members of minority groups the same as members of the majority and by treating the two groups differently.

The dilemma of difference may be posed as a choice between integration

---

[2]The Supreme Court remanded the case for fashioning appropriate relief under section 601 of the Civil Rights Act of 1964, 42 U.S.C. sec. 2000d, and regulations adopted under that statute by the Department of Health, Education and Welfare. That remand, and further regulatory activity by the department, produced guidelines for bilingual education for all schools receiving federal assistance (see below).

[3]The landmark litigation efforts of Mill v. Board of Education, 348 F. Supp. 866 (D.D.C. 1972) and Pennsylvania Ass'n for Retarded Children (PARC) v. Pennsylvania, 343 F. Supp. 279 (E.D. Pa. 1972) also inspired legislative reforms at the state and federal levels.

and separation, as a choice between similar treatment and special treatment, or as a choice between neutrality and accommodation. Governmental neutrality may be the best way to assure equality, yet governmental neutrality may also freeze in place the past consequences of differences. Do the public schools fulfill their obligation to provide equal opportunities by including all students in the same integrated classroom, or by offering some students special programs tailored to their needs? Special needs arise from "differences" beyond language proficiency and physical or mental disability. Religious differences also raise questions of same versus different treatment. Students who belong to religious minorities may seek exemption from courses in sex education or other subjects that conflict with their religious teachings. Religiously observant students may ask to use school time and facilities to engage in religious activities, just as other students engage in other extracurricular activities. But the legal obligation of neutrality is explicit here, in a polity committed to separating church and state. Do the schools remain neutral toward religion by balancing the teaching of evolution with the teaching of scientific arguments about creation? Or does this accommodation of a religious viewpoint depart from the requisite neutrality?

The difference dilemma also arises beyond the schoolhouse. If women's biological differences from men justify special benefits in the workplace—such as maternity leave—are women thereby helped or hurt? Are negative stereotypes reinforced, in violation of commitments to equality? Or are differences accommodated, in fulfillment of the vision of equality? Members of religious groups that designate Saturday as the Sabbath may desire accommodation in the workplace. Is the commitment to a norm of equality advanced through such an accommodation, or through neutral application of a Saturday work requirement that happens to burden these individuals differently from others?

These knotty problems receive diverse labels and inconsistent treatment in the legal system. The dilemma of difference—sometimes treated as a constitutional question of equal protection, due process, or religious freedom; sometimes treated as a problem of statutory interpretation in civil rights, education, employment, housing, or income maintenance benefits—produces heated legal controversies that reverberate beyond courtrooms and legislatures. They occupy the attention of students and teachers, parents and neighbors, mass media and scholars. These controversies enact the political dramas of a diverse society committed to equality and to pluralism.

I suggest that the dilemma of difference is not an accidental problem in this society. The dilemma of difference grows from the ways in which this society assigns individuals to categories and, on that basis, determines whom to include in and whom to exclude from political, social, and economic activities. Because the activities are designed, in turn, with only the included participants in mind, the excluded seem not to fit because of something in their own nature. Thus, people have used categories based on age, race, gender, ethnicity, religion, and disability to decide formally and informally who is eligible to enroll in a given school, who is excluded from a particular sports activity, who may join a particular club, who may adopt a given child, and a variety of other questions.

An organization that holds its meetings in a club that excludes women, non-Christians, or nonwhites, for example, reflects the assumptions held by its conveners about who will be members. Yet if the organization tries to remedy the historical exclusion by heralding that the former blackballing category is now a basis for inclusion, the dilemma of difference becomes palpable. This solution still focuses on a category rather than treating persons as unique individuals, each one an intersection of countless categories; moreover, this solution reemphasizes the particular category that has mattered in the past. Racially segregated schools thus are changed by a focus on the racial identity of the individual students and an enrollment design to balance the composition of the school on this, and only this, basis. Similarly, when an organization that has excluded women in the past seeks to change by soliciting women members, it runs the risk of treating such new members as eligible and welcome only because they are women. Besides reducing people to one trait, this solution risks new harms if the category itself still carries stigmatizing or exclusionary consequences in other contexts.

The dilemma persists when legal reasoning itself not only typically deploys categorical approaches that reduce a complex situation, and a multifaceted person, to a place in or out of a category but also treats those categories as natural and inevitable. A complex legal dispute becomes focused on a narrow question: for example, does an employer's refusal to hire a woman fall within the statutory exemption from the antidiscrimination statute as a business necessity?[4] Both the social and legal constructions of difference have the effect of hiding from view the relationships among people, relationships marked by power and hierarchy. Within these relationships, we each become who we are and make order out of our own lives. Yet, by sorting people and problems into categories, we each cede power to social definitions that we individually no longer control.

Difference, after all, is a comparative term. It implies a reference: different from whom? I am no more different from you than you are from me. A short person is different only in relation to a tall one; a Spanish-speaking student is different in relation to an English-speaking one. But the point of comparison is often unstated. Women are compared with the unstated norm of men, "minority" races with whites, handicapped persons with the able-bodied, and "minority" religions and ethnicities with majorities.[5] If we identify the unstated points of comparison necessary to the idea of difference, we will

---

[4]See Robinson v. Lorillard Corp., 444 F.2d 791 (4th Cir. 1971).

[5]Minority itself is a relative term. People of color are numerically a majority in the world; only in relation to white Westerners are they minorities, and that may soon be in terms of power rather than numbers, given projections of possible population distributions in California, Texas, and Florida. We often describe a trait in language that seems to assign the trait to only one of the persons being compared. The choice of terms to describe an individual or a group unavoidably reflects one perspective among others. Throughout this book, terms appear that may not be those most preferred by members of the identified group; some prefer "physically challenged" to "handicapped," "developmental disability" to "mentally retarded," "Latino" to "Hispanic," and "African American" to "black." It is my hope that the arguments in the book support

then examine the relationships between people who have and people who lack the power to assign the label of difference. If we explore the environmental context that makes some trait stand out and some people seem not to fit in, we will have the opportunity to reconsider how and for what ends we construct and manage the environment. Then difference will no longer seem empirically discoverable, consisting of traits inherent in the "different person." Instead, perceptions of difference can become clues to broader problems of social policy and human responsibility.[6]

This switch in the focus of attention from the "different person" to the social and legal construction of difference challenges long-established modes of reasoning about reality and about law. Yet this new focus is enabled by the flowering of theoretical works in a striking array of fields, ranging from literary theory to sociology, feminist theory to metaphysics and biology. Thus, an exploration of the dilemma of difference also means a journey through historical shifts in patterns of knowledge in law and in many other fields.

Dilemmas of Difference in Education

The U.S. education system offers clear examples of the dilemma. Historically, school programs for children who are not native speakers of English have often ignored the difference between those children and their peers; more recently, through bilingual education programs, their difference has spelled important consequences for their schooling. School programs for children with disabilities currently emphasize their similarities with other children, yet historically—and sometimes in the present—it is their differences that have mattered.

Each program recapitulates aspects of the racial desegregation saga. The legal argument against racially segregated schooling challenged the Jim Crow laws and the principle of "separate but equal," approved when the U.S. Supreme Court accepted racially segregated railway cars in 1896. At that time, the justices confronted claims that racial segregation treated difference as a question of status carrying a social meaning of inferiority. The Court reasoned that "laws permitting, and even requiring, [racial] separation in places where [the races] are liable to be brought into contact do not necessarily imply the inferiority of either race to the other, and have been generally, if not universally, recognized as within the competency of the state legislatures in the exercise of their police power." So long as the railway provided equal accommodations, continued the Court, separation by race itself carried no stigma.[7]

---

collective processes through which the naming of groups will come to express more fully the choices of those affected, while teaching others about shared humanity.

[6]See Harlan Hahn, "Public Policy and Disabled Infants: A Sociopolitical Perspective," *Issues in Law & Med.* 3 no. 1 (1987), 3.

[7]Plessy v. Ferguson, 163 U.S. 537 (1896); id. at 544, 551–52.

The National Association for the Advancement of Colored People (NAACP) waged a litigation campaign that took the Court at its word: the lawyers challenged the alleged equality of separate facilities, rather than the "separate but equal" principle itself. This strategy proved successful in attacking graduate level public universities and colleges, where separate facilities for blacks were either nonexistent or a sham.[8] When the NAACP turned to public elementary schools, however, the lawyers wanted to question the principle itself, as well as to demonstrate that the schools provided for black children lacked facilities and resources comparable to those for whites. The lawyers sought the help of social psychologist Kenneth Clark, who developed studies showing that the low self-images of black children undermined their motivation to learn. Evolving social science teachings that attacked traditional theories of racial difference also supplied ammunition for the NAACP attack on segregated schooling. Evidence and arguments along these lines, together with carefully framed arguments from the precedents won in prior NAACP suits, ultimately convinced the Supreme Court in Brown v. Board of Education.[9]

Judicial efforts to implement the mandate of *Brown* after 1954 met with resistance. Even where urban public schools survived violence, white families fled to suburban or private schools. Courts ordered racial balance remedies for the students left in the public school systems, but these judicially sponsored remedies failed to improve the educational opportunities for many black students. The lawyers had linked integration and equality, but in practice, integration proved difficult and equality often elusive. Whites continued to stigmatize those blacks who did enroll in integrated schools. White flight from city schools reduced the political and economic resources for improving education. Even in schools that did achieve racial balance, "ability tracking" programs in effect resegregated students on the basis of race within the same school.

Resenting their continued segregation and powerlessness, the new generation of black leaders who started the Black Power movement favored community control of local, segregated schools. They vocally rejected assimilation as a threat to black culture and black self-consciousness. They sought to raise the status, power, and pride of their communities through self-governance.[10] Judges and scholars soon perceived these demands for community control and developed new legal and political proposals to remedy race discrimination by emphasizing black empowerment and redistributing authority over schooling. The Atlanta Plan, often cited as a model, emphasized hiring blacks to fill administrative positions in the school system, including the post of superintendent.[11] Derrick Bell, Jr., the first black law

[8]Missouri ex rel. Gaines v. Canada, 305 U.S. 337 (1938); Sweatt v. Painter, 339 U.S. 629 (1950); McLaurin v. Oklahoma State Regents for Higher Educ., 339 U.S. 637 (1950).

[9]347 U.S. 483 (1954).

[10]Diane Ravitch, "The Evolution of School Desegregation Policy, 1964–1979," in *Race and Schooling in the City,* ed. Adam Yarmolinsky, Lance Liebman, and Lorraine S. Schelling (Cambridge, Mass.: Harvard University Press, 1981), pp. 9, 15.

[11]See Barbara Jackson, "Urban School Desegregation from a Black Perspective," in *Race and Schooling in the City,* pp. 204, 209–11.

professor at Harvard, campaigned for judicial remedies that would address the quality of education rather than racial integration.[12]

Kenneth Clark, the social psychologist who had provided critical work in the *Brown* litigation, warned in 1970 that community control "may further isolate the poor and the minority groups from the majority society and bring the customary consequences of racial and class isolation—eroded facilities, inadequate teaching and administrative staffs, and minimum resources. . . . Community controversy therefore requires a commitment of the city as a whole, genuine delegation of power, and continued efforts to relate the community to the larger society. Perhaps paradoxically, the lower-status community will never have genuine power until its isolation is ended."[13] This paradox expresses a version of the dilemma of difference: continued power-lessness for blacks may result even from self-chosen segregation, but power-lessness may also emerge from efforts to integrate with a larger community that still assigns a lower status to blacks. Acknowledging and organizing around difference can perpetuate it, but so can assimilation. Separation may permit the assertion of minority group identity as a strength but not change the majority's larger power. Integration, however, offers no solution unless the majority itself changes by sharing power, accepting members of the minority as equal participants and resisting the temptation to attribute as personal inadequacies the legacy of disadvantage experienced by the group.[14] Neither separation nor integration can eradicate the meaning of difference as long as the majority locates difference in a minority group that does not fit the world designed for the majority.

The dilemma of difference was not a new discovery in the wake of *Brown*. W. E. B. Du Bois and Booker T. Washington had carried on a debate, at times enacting both sides of the dilemma, more than half a century before. They disagreed over whether black reformers should seek to integrate blacks within the dominant culture or should instead attempt to alter that culture by celebrating the distinct traditions of African and African-American experience.[15] Each position received periodic acclaim followed by blame as a cause of continuing racial oppression. Continued attachment to a separate racial identity, with separate schools and culture, could perpetuate rather than alter the historic degradation of blacks. Integration, however, could do the same

[12]Derrick Bell, "Brown v. Board of Education and the Interest-Convergence Dilemma," *Harv. L. Rev.* 93 (1980), 518; Derrick Bell, "Waiting on the Promise of Brown," *Law & Contemp. Probs.* 1975 (Spring 1975), 341; Derrick Bell, "Serving Two Masters: Integration Ideals and Client Interests in School Desegregation Litigation," *Yale L.J.* 85 (1976), 470. See generally Willis D. Hawley, "The New Mythology of School Desegregation," *Law & Contemp. Probs.* 1978 (Autumn 1978), 214, which criticizes scholarly disenchantment with desegregation.

[13]Kenneth Clark, Introduction to *Community Control and the Urban School*, ed. Mario D. Fantini, Marilyn Gittell, and Richard Magat (New York: Praeger, 1970), p. xi.

[14]See also Hahn, "Public Policy," pp. 4–6: the nondisabled majority tends to view disability as a personal misfortune rather than as an interaction between an environment designed with the majority in mind and the minority, who do not fit the design.

[15]Merle Eugene Curti, *The Social Ideas of American Educators* (New York: Scribner, 1935), pp. 288–309, compares Washington and Du Bois. Cf. W. E. B. Du Bois, *The Souls of Black Folk: Essays and Sketches* (New York: Dodd, Mead, 1979); and Booker T. Washington, *Up from Slavery: An Autobiography* (Garden City, N.Y.: Doubleday, 1963).

and even further undermine black students by isolating them within an unwelcoming community. Even when well-intentioned people ignore differences, they reproduce them.

Recently, a scholarly and political debate has erupted over "Black English." Some claim that a distinct dialect, rather than poor language skills, explains some black students' difficulties in school.[16] Even performance in mathematics classes may be undermined, one teacher has argued, by the different meanings some black students associate with basic verbal instructions.[17] Others argue that any effort to acknowledge or respond to Black English perpetuates negative stereotypes and confines blacks to less than full participation in the dominant language and culture of this society. In this context, the struggle for racial justice echoes as well as foretells conflicts over differences in children's languages and disabilities. The history of these battles further illuminates the dilemma of difference.

Bilingual Education

There is no neutral history of bilingual education because the telling of its history is inescapably part of the politics it has engendered. With that caveat, it remains fair to note that public schools supplanted the language and culture of immigrant groups—after early immigrants themselves had supplanted the language and culture of the natives of this continent. English became the dominant language of public life, including the legislatures and courts, the marketplace, and the public schools.

Decisions to exclude languages other than English from the public schools did not, however, go uncontested. Immigrant subcommunities maintained the language of their home countries through local newspapers, cultural entertainment, and religious activities, and their members periodically pushed for recognition of their language and culture within the schools. In some places politically sophisticated immigrants successfully elected school boards that implemented courses in the group's language, while also directing teachers to instruct the children in English.[18] Opponents fought back. By the turn of this century some communities had adopted statutes forbidding the teaching of any non-English language, even in a private school, to students below the eighth grade. The minority groups then enlisted the judiciary's help. In a now famous 1923 decision, Meyer v. Nebraska, the United States Supreme

[16]Martin Luther King Jr. Elementary School Children v. Ann Arbor School District Board, 473 F. Supp. 1371, 1382 (E.D. Mich. 1979) (holding that teachers of standard English should be sensitive to the language differences of students who speak "Black English").

[17]See Eleanor Wilson Orr, *Twice as Less: Black English and the Performance of Black Students in Mathematics and Science* (New York: Norton, 1987), arguing that a coherent, separate dialect of Black English leads some children to systematically mistranslate instruction in science and mathematics.

[18]David B. Tyack, *The One Best System: A History of American Urban Education* (Cambridge, Mass.: Harvard University Press, 1974), pp. 106–9, discusses German programs in Cincinnati and St. Louis, 1840–90. See generally Heinz Kloss, *The American Bilingual Tradition* (Rowley, Mass.: Newbury House, 1977), describing bilingualism in the nineteenth century.

Court concluded that such legislation violated the Constitution, although states did have power to "foster a homogeneous people with American ideals, prepared readily to understand current discussions of civic matters."[19] The decision in *Meyer* became an important milestone in the nation's commitment to pluralism, even though the Court simultaneously encouraged assimilation. The decision did not place foreign languages on an equal footing with English, nor did it entitle children to instruction in a foreign language. The Court simply forbade laws proscribing such instruction.

Opposition to "foreign language" instruction repeatedly escalated in the name of patriotism during wartime, especially during World War I.[20] Public schools permitted foreign language instruction only through elective courses for students already proficient in English.[21] After World War II, however, minority groups mustered new reasons for instruction in their mother tongues for children not proficient in English. Immigration increased. Cold War competition with the Soviet Union fueled a campaign for excellence and school achievement, and justified federally funded programs that could raise student performance. Perhaps most important, the civil rights movement of the 1950s and 1960s shaped political and legal rhetoric while strengthening a moral claim demanding that majorities respect the rights and needs of minority groups. Rather than aspiring to merge in the melting pot, new groups of immigrants by the 1970s were claiming ethnic pride and demanding that language and cultural education respect the heritage of minority groups.

Minority and majority groups gave heightened significance to language and cultural differences. It is the story of a political struggle over cultural dominance and tolerance perhaps even more than a struggle over educational policy.[22] As a conflict about social status and cultural integrity, the bilingual education battle united concerns for group and individual identities. The movement for bilingual education borrowed from the arguments made by lawyers and educators for racial desegregation: when their identities are devalued in the society, children know it, and that message damages their self-esteem and ability to succeed. One side of the difference dilemma appears: a majority's failure to acknowledge a minority's difference communicates disapproval and nonacceptance and thus reinforces that difference.

[19]262 U.S. 390, 402 (1923).

[20]Theodore Roosevelt, a noted patriot, opposed bilingualism: "We cannot tolerate any attempt to oppose or supplant the language and culture that has come down to us from the builders of this republic with the language and culture of any European country. The greatness of this nation depends on the swift assimilation of the aliens she welcomes to her shores" (quoted in Stephen Wagner, "The Historical Background of Bilingualism and Biculturalism in the United States," in *The New Bilingualism: An American Dilemma*, ed. Martin Ridge [Los Angeles: University of Southern California Press, 1981], p. 37).

[21]Theodore Andersson and Mildred Boyer, *Bilingual Schooling in the United States*, 2d ed. (Austin, Tex.: National Educational Laboratory Publishers, 1978), pp. 21–22.

[22]Rachel Moran, "Bilingual Education as a Status Conflict," *Calif. L. Rev.* 75 (1987), 321, 341, 354–58, describes bilingual education battles as a status conflict. The respectful attitudes toward bilingualism and, indeed, multilingualism, in other countries underscores the culturally contingent battle in the United States, whose majorities have had the luxury of presuming that anyone they want to communicate with will speak their own language.

Leonard Covello, the first New York City public school principal of Italian heritage, recalled his public school experience at the turn of the century: "The Italian language was completely ignored in the American schools. In fact, throughout my whole elementary school career, I do not recall one mention of Italy, or the Italian language or what famous Italians had done in the world, with the possible exception of Columbus. . . . We soon got the idea that 'Italian' meant something inferior, and a barrier was erected between children of Italian origin and their parents. This was the accepted process of Americanization. We were becoming Americans by learning how to be ashamed of our parents."[23]

Advocates of bilingual education link this shame about family, ethnicity, and ultimately oneself to the poor academic achievement of many children for whom English is a second language. The advocates contend that to force a child to give up a family language while attending school is worse than cruel; it is devastating to a child's self-respect. It disparages not only the language used in the family but also the value system and culture of the home; in such a context children often perform poorly in school. Supporters of bilingual education therefore argue for educating children in the language used in their homes, at least until they have mastered English, in order to nurture self-respect and self-confidence.[24]

Yet this view is challenged by others, including some members of minority communities, who warn that accentuating difference may replicate patterns of exclusion and hierarchy. Author Richard Rodriguez offers this assessment: "Without question, it would have pleased me to hear my teachers address me in Spanish when I entered the [parochial school] classroom. I would have felt much less afraid. I would have trusted them and responded with ease. But I would have delayed—for how long postponed?—having to learn the language of public society. I would have evaded—and for how long could I have afforded to delay?—learning the great lesson of school, that I had a public identity. And [w]hat I needed to learn in school was that I had the right—and obligation—to speak the public language of *los gringos*."[25]

Both Rodriguez and Covello understood schooling as a process of transferring loyalties and transforming identities. One argues that to do so undermines the self-esteem of the "different" child. The other maintains that to do otherwise risks perpetuating exclusion on the basis of that difference. Acknowledgment of difference can create barriers to important parts of the school experience and delay or derail successful entry into the society that

[23]Quoted in Charles E. Silberman, *Crisis in the Classroom: The Remaking of American Education* (New York: Random House, 1970), p. 58.

[24]Martin Ridge, "The New Bilingualism: An American Dilemma," in Ridge, *The New Bilingualism*, pp. 259, 260. A Hispanic school administrator explained, "You tell the child, 'Your language is second-rate and you shouldn't speak it. Your culture is second-rate and you need to be something else.' . . . What you are in fact saying to the kids is 'You are second-rate' " (José Gonzales, associate superintendent of the Chicago Board of Education, quoted in Alfredo S. Lanier, "Teaching with Subtitles," *Chicago*, June 1984, pp. 163, 191).

[25]Richard Rodriguez, *Hunger of Memory: The Education of Richard Rodriguez* (New York: Bantam Books, 1983), p. 19.

continues to make difference matter. Failure to acknowledge difference can leave the child scarred by silent nonrecognition and implicit rejection.

Moreover, when students in the majority avoid the experience of not being understood, or of not understanding what others say, they fail to learn about the limits of their own knowledge. They miss a chance to discover the importance of learning another language. By their very comfort in the situation, they neglect the perspective of any student they consider different from themselves.

Special Education

Education for handicapped children has a different history, but here too the dilemma of difference appears and reappears. "Disabilities" have their own histories. Some traits have undergone changes in name and medical explanation. Some, such as "learning disabilities," have been identified only recently; others, such as epilepsy, have receded in significance, thanks to changes in medical knowledge and public attitude. Alongside these shifting definitions, however, is the more general picture of official treatment of children labeled at any given time as disabled. Public schools have historically excluded from mainstream classrooms—or from schooling altogether—any child with physical or mental disabilities. During the past several decades parents and professionals have pushed to expand and improve the educational opportunities for exceptional children by recognizing what these children share with other students, as well as how they differ.

Before state and local laws made schooling compulsory, public schools were available in many areas but excluded children whom teachers identified as ineducable. Until the Civil War, parents and officials often hid children— children whom we now would treat as "having special needs"—away from the community, in attics or poorhouses. Humanitarian reformers, led by physicians in both Europe and the United States, built special institutions for deaf and blind individuals during the early part of the nineteenth century.[26] After the Civil War, as many communities adopted compulsory education laws and enforced them, exceptional children began to present themselves to school officials in increasing numbers. Educators responded by creating within the public school system separate day schools and separate classrooms within existing schools for children whom they identified, in the language of the day, as "deaf," "feebleminded," "crippled," or otherwise disabled. Some recent critics have noted how the creation of separate educational programs for disabled students coincided with rising waves of immigration, offering ways to segregate and control immigrant children.[27] Ability

[26]Samuel Alexander Kirk and James J. Gallagher, *Educating Exceptional Children*, 3d ed. (Boston, Mass.: Houghton Mifflin, 1979), pp. 4–5.
[27]Seymour Bernhardt Sarason and John Doris, *Educational Handicap, Public Policy, and Social History: A Broadened Perspective on Mental Retardation* (New York: Free Press, 1979), p. 245.

tracking and separate schools or programs for disabled children became the norm for most of the first half of this century.

Not until the 1960s did this practice of tracking and sorting students on the basis of ability and disability strike parents and law reformers as a new form of illicit segregation. Some courts declared such tracking systems illegal where they produced patterns of racial and ethnic segregation.[28] Like the lawyers who enlisted the collaboration of social scientists in the context of racial segregation, advocates for handicapped children in the 1970s worked with psychological experts to identify a psychological detriment to children labeled as different and inferior. Together, the reformers pushed to expand special educational services and at the same time to integrate exceptional children with their "normal peers to whatever extent is compatible with potential for fullest development."[29] Building on Brown v. Board of Education, the educators pointed to the stigma of separate treatment, the risks of misclassification and labeling in inducing stigma and creating low self-esteem, and the abusive use of separate classes to perpetuate racial and ethnic discrimination. Translated into legal arguments, these became alleged violations of the constitutional guarantee of due process: a negative label should be understood as a deprivation of liberty. The lawyers demanded the protections of individualized hearings and official accountability. Moreover, the imposition on the child's liberty represented by compulsory schooling itself should require, according to the reformers, some governmental service—some actual educational benefit—in exchange. These legal arguments assimilated the handicapped child within the model of the normal child by asserting that all children are entitled to basic legal rights and basic educational opportunities. The legal arguments also integrated disabled children, at least conceptually, within the larger community.

Two landmark federal district court cases produced victories in the form of stipulated "consent decrees,"[30] through which the school systems agreed to provide appropriate services and programs for disabled children while including them as much as possible within the mainstream school classrooms.[31] Relying in part on these judicial decisions, reformers successfully

[28]See Hobson v. Hansen, 269 F. Supp. 401 (D.D.C. 1967), aff'd sub nom. Smuck v. Hobson, 408 F.2d 175 (D.C. Cir. 1969) (en banc); Larry P. v. Riles, 343 F. Supp. 1306, 1309 (N.D. Cal. 1972), aff'd 502 F.2d 963 (9th Cir. 1974).

[29]Kirk and Gallagher, *Educating Exceptional Children*, p. 7.

[30]A consent decree (or consent judgment) is a settlement agreement issued and enforced by a court; it carries the same effect as a court-ordered remedy; see John J. Cound, Jack H. Friedenthal, and Arthur R. Miller, *Civil Procedure: Cases and Materials*, 3d ed. (St. Paul, Minn.: West, 1980), p. 753. If the parties represent interests of absent individuals, the court evaluates the fairness of the agreement; see Paul D. Carrington and Barbara Allen Babcock, *Civil Procedure: Cases and Comments on the Process of Adjudication* (Boston, Mass.: Little, Brown, 1983), p. 123. In a federal class action suit, the court must approve any settlement or dismissal and ensure notice to all class members affected by the decision; see Fed. R. Civ. P. 23(e).

[31]Pennsylvania Ass'n for Retarded Children (PARC) v. Pennsylvania, 334 F. Supp. 1257 (E.D. Pa. 1971) (per curiam, 343 F. Supp. 279 (E.D. Pa. 1972); Mills v. Board of Educ. 348 F. Supp. 866 (D.D.C. 1972).

persuaded state and federal legislatures to secure these rights for handicapped children through statutes and appropriations.[32]

Even in this story of successful reform, however, the dilemma of difference reappears in a striking form. Recognizing the special needs of disabled children can run counter to granting them entry to the educational worlds of other children. Using ever more sophisticated methods to recognize varieties of handicapping conditions, school personnel and parents identify increasing numbers of children as different and therefore entitled to some specialized instruction and services. Yet making differences matter singles out the disabled child. Until every student is identified as different and thus entitled to special education, the tendency to create a "normal" group and to label others as "deviant" will remain pronounced and take on forms of childish cruelty in the school setting. For this reason, the legal commitment to treat special-needs children like other children cautions against separate tracking or segregated schooling. At the same time, integrating those children in the mainstream classroom may perpetuate both their stigmatization and their difficulties in achieving educational success.

Laws and Programs

The paradoxes in treating difference mark not only the history of bilingual and special education but also present-day practice. The dilemma of difference helps to explain points of confusion and contention in the welter of legal authorities. As already noted, federal and state litigation and legislation have produced contrasting educational models for children lacking English proficiency and for those subject to the label of disability.

For bilingual education, the Supreme Court decision in Lau v. Nichols linked affirmative obligations to provide language instruction to the basic civil rights command against discrimination. The Court remained neutral, however, about how schools should fulfill these obligations: "Teaching English to the students of Chinese ancestry who do not speak the language is one choice. Giving instruction to this group in Chinese is another. There may be others."[33] Congress, as a partial response, adopted the Bilingual Education Act, as amended by the Equal Educational Opportunity Act, which directs instruction in the mix of languages that "shall, to the extent necessary, be in all courses or subjects of study which will allow a child to progress effectively through the educational system."[34] Rather than specifying how much integration, how much separate instruction, and how much preservation of the child's native language and culture, the statute directs only that critical choices are to be resolved with reference to undefined and uncertain terms: "to the extent necessary" for the child "to progress effectively through

[32]See Jeffrey Zettel and Alan Abeson, "The Right to a Free Appropriate Public Education," in *The Courts and Education,* ed. Clifford P. Hooker (Chicago: University of Chicago Press, 1978).
[33]414 U.S. 563 (1974); id. at 564–65.
[34]20 U.S.C. sec. 3221–61 (1982); 20 U.S.C. sec. 3223 (a)(4)(A)(i)(1982).

the educational system." These phrases are especially ambiguous because the meanings of "necessary" and "effective progress" could themselves change with the introduction of bilingual education.[35] Administrative efforts to develop clear guidelines included lengthy hearings but ended in federal preference for local flexibility.[36]

In the face of this remedial ambiguity, federal courts and agencies developed a range of possible programs, which differ in both the mix of services and the setting in which the services are offered.[37] The programs fall into two major types, and the selection among all the options presents the dilemma of difference in stark form.

The first type of program, "English as a Second Language Instruction" (ESL), has been defined by the federal government as "[a] structured language acquisition program designed to teach English to students whose native language is not English."[38] Typically, ESL provides intensive instruction in English, with the goal of enabling the student to speak and understand English as quickly as possible. ESL employs the "pull out" method: the language-minority student spends most of the school day in the mainstream

[35]The Equal Educational Opportunity Act also leaves undefined such critical terms as "appropriate" and "equal participation" and thereby preserves unresolved the question of whether to avoid discrimination by constructing separate programs or by integrating the different child into the mainstream class. See 20 U.S.C. sec 1703 (1982): "No state shall deny equal educational opportunity to an individual on account of his or her race, color, sex, or national origin by . . . the failure by an educational agency to take appropriate action to overcome language barriers that impede equal participation by its students in its instructional programs."

[36]See Howard F. Nelson, "Assessment of English Language Proficiency: Standards for Determining Participation in Transitional Language Programs," *J. Law & Educ.* 15 (1986), 83, 86, 89–90.

[37]Stephan R. Goldstein and E. Gordon Gee, *Law and Public Education: Cases and Materials*, 2d ed. (Indianapolis, Ind.: Michie, 1980), p. 801, describes these variants: (1) segregated non-English-speaking students taught by instructors using both English and the children's native language; (2) segregated students taught in their own language and instructed in English as a second language; (3) students integrated in classrooms where both English and another language are used; (4) minority students placed in mainstream classrooms with supplementary instruction in English as a second language.

[38]Office for Civil Rights, U.S. Dep't of Health, Education and Welfare, *Task Force Findings Specifying Remedies for Eliminating Past Educational Practices Ruled Unlawful under Lau v. Nichols*, reprinted in *Bilingual Education: A Reappraisal of Federal Policy*, ed. Keith A. Baker and Adriana A. de Kanter (Lexington, Mass.: Lexington Books, 1983), pp. 213, 331. Developed during the Carter administration, these "Lau Remedies" became incorporated in compliance agreements between the federal government and some 500 school districts receiving federal funds contingent on satisfying federally specified conditions. See Lori Orum and Raul Yazguirre, "Secretary Bennett's Bilingual Education Initiative: Historical Perspectives and Implications," *La Raza L.J.* 1, (1986), 213, 331. After a court challenge to the Lau Remedies, the guidelines were modified and published as proposed regulations in 1980, but the Reagan administration withdrew them. Congress amended the Bilingual Education Act in 1984 to authorize funding, limited to 4 percent of the total federal education appropriations, for a limited number of special alternative programs that would not require instruction in students' native languages (20 U.S.C. sec. 3221–62). William Bennett, Reagan's secretary of education, issued new regulations allowing school districts "broad discretion" in methods of instruction, including essentially English-only programs (51 Fed. Reg. 22, 422 [June 19, 1986]). On June 28, 1988, Reagan signed into law the Hawkins-Stafford Elementary and Secondary Education Improvement Amendments of 1988, which removed the 4 percent cap and relaxed the restrictions on methods of instruction authorized for funding under the act (P.L. 100–297). The Reagan administration did not, however, seek modifications of the 500 compliance agreements based on the Lau Remedies.

class setting without language assistance and is pulled out during part of the day for ESL instruction. ESL does not, then, conduct native-language instruction in, say, math or social studies during the time before the student gains mastery of English. Nor does ESL expose the English-speaking students to the language or culture of the non-English-speaking students. Through a variant of ESL known as "transitional bilingual education," the school may temporarily conduct instruction in math, social studies, and other subjects in the children's home language until their proficiency in English improves enough to enable their participation in the regular classroom. Despite designs to treat either ESL or transitional bilingual education as temporary, many schools find such programs stretching on because the children often fall behind the mainstream class in other subjects or continue to perform less successfully as a result of the prior language barrier.

The second major type of program, commonly called "bilingual-bicultural education," combines ESL training, instruction in other subjects conducted in the child's native language, *and* instruction in the cultures and histories of both the United States and the nation or ethnic group associated with the student's native language. Programs are also distinguished by whether they emphasize "surface" culture, such as crafts and music, or "deep" culture, such as attitudes about family, health, and gender roles.[39]

Congress did not oblige local school authorities to adopt bilingual-bicultural programs in implementing equal opportunity requirements but preserved local discretion on this issue.[40] The ambiguous language in federal legislation permits both the use of the child's native language and the integration of bicultural instruction.[41] Federal courts have imposed contrasting interpretations of the statutory requirements in different contexts.[42] The

---

[39]Frank Gonzales, "Reinforcing Culture in Three Bilingual Education Programs," in *Early Childhood Bilingual Education: A Hispanic Perspective*, ed. Teresa Escobedo (New York: Teachers College Press, 1983), pp. 93, 96–99.

[40]See also Gomez v. Ill. State Board of Educ., 811 F.2d 1030 (CA 1987) (holding that state's failure to test plaintiffs for English proficiency or to provide bilingual or compensatory education constitutes a cognizable claim under the Equal Educational Opportunity Act). See 20 U.S.C. sec. 3222 (1982) (federal grant program). State legislation also generally does not specify the form of bilingual program. See e.g., Tex. Educ. Code Ann. sec. 21.451 (Vernon Supp. 1973). But see Mass. Ann. Laws ch. 71A sec.1–9 (Law Co-op 1978) (requiring a transitional program but including instruction in the history and culture of non-English-speaking students).

[41]20 U.S.C. sec. 3223 (a)(4)(A)(i) (1982). Amy Gutmann, *Democratic Education* (Princeton, N.J.: Princeton University Press, 1987), p. 86, argues for local decision-making rather than federal prescription of "a pedagogical approach of disputed and unproven efficacy," especially given diverse views of ethnic communities about the value of bilingual education: "If bilingualism also is valued for enabling ethnic communities to preserve their cultural heritage and identity, then those communities—rather than the federal government—should be empowered to decide whether and how they wish to preserve their culture through bilingual education." Although this position is appealing, it neglects the political reality that many minority communities lack clout in the local setting and can only be heard by banding together in national politics.

[42]Cf. Cintron v. Brentwood Union Free School Dist., 455 F. Supp. 57, 62–64 (E.D. N.Y. 1978) (requiring bilingual and bicultural instructional methods) with Rios v. Read, 480 F. Supp. 14, 22 (E.D. N.Y. 1978) (requiring temporary bilingual instruction) and Guadalupe Org., Inc. v. Tempe Elementary School Dist., 587 F.2d 1022, 1030 (9th Cir. 1978) (approving nonbilingual-bicultural program to meet the needs of language-minority students).

legal ambiguity permits continued political battles among interest groups over which of the permissible types of programs for minority-language students should or will be used in specific schools.[43]

The contrast between ESL alone and bilingual-bicultural instruction illustrates a difficult choice between assimilation and preservation of group differences. It is especially difficult because it is also bound up with confusion about what constitutes equal opportunity.[44] ESL proposes short-term segregation during part of the school day and long-term integration, abandoning minority identity within the school context. Its critics argue that the program reconfirms the association of difference with inferiority by refusing to recognize the positive experiences of minority difference and by failing to instruct either minority or majority children in the minority language and culture. Bilingual-bicultural programs, in attempting to meet this criticism, encounter the other side of the dilemma: by reinforcing minority difference and prolonging separation, such programs risk reconfirming the identification of difference with alien and inferior status. They also risk failing to prepare their students for a society in which mastery of English language and comfort with dominant American culture are made preconditions for success. Nathan Glazer put it this way: "One will never do as well in the United States living in Spanish, or French, or Yiddish, or Chinese, as one will do living, learning, and working in English. . . . [It] is therefore a naive argument to say that putting bilingual/bicultural education into the public school curriculum will make a significant difference in affecting the general respect in which a given culture and language are held."[45]

Failing to acknowledge the way in which all children in this sense are similarly situated to the school criteria for success could produce educational programs that reinforce the differences of already stigmatized and isolated groups. Should schools create an enclave of Spanish language and Chicano culture, for example, in order to bolster the student's self-esteem and ability to perform well in school? Or should schools instead create limited, transitional programs to give Chicano students basic language skills and then incorporate those students as quickly as possible into classrooms designed

---

[43]See Shirley M. Hufstadler, "Is America Over-Lawyered?" *Clev. St. L. Rev.* 31 (1982), 371, 380–81. See also William Bennett, "On Bilingual Education," *La Raza L.J.* 1 (1986), 213, discussing Reagan administration's preference for English-only instruction and primary goal of English proficiency.

[44]Debates over the alternative programs are also confused because studies of their effects are inadequate, inconsistent, and largely unreliable. Christine Rossell and J. Michael Ross, "The Social Science Evidence on Bilingual Education," *J. Law & Educ.* 15 (1986), 385, reviews previous research and shows it wanting. The authors conclude that transitional programs have proved no more effective than simply submerging the child in the mainstream classroom; they recommend (p. 413) bilingual maintenance programs and instruction in the mainstream classroom by bilingual, same-ethnic-group teachers. An intriguing book by Kenji Hakuta, *Mirror of Language: The Debate on Bilingualism* (New York: Basic Books, 1986), suggests that although children educated bilingually may not retain mastery in both languages, they may nonetheless acquire cognitive skills and develop talent for creative problem solving, perhaps as a result of their early experiences in translating between two languages.

[45]Nathan Glazer, "Pluralism and Ethnicity," in Ridge, *The New Bilingualism*, pp. 51, 55, 63.

for the rest of the students? Either approach may fail to provide sufficient English proficiency among those who start off with another language; both approaches risk recreating negative meanings of difference for students in the short term and the long term. As if it were not already complicated enough, the dilemma recurs in a new form within schools where some students present a third language or culture—and experience the bilingual-bicultural school as excluding *them* as different, and devaluing *their* heritage.[46] The underlying attitudes about difference, in short, may be the most critical source of the difference dilemma, whatever programmatic solution is tried.[47]

Similar tensions appear in the legal and educational frameworks for the education of handicapped children. One federal statute, Section 504 of the Rehabilitation Act of 1973, forbids discrimination on the basis of handicap by programs receiving federal assistance, and yet the statute also requires that a protected individual be "otherwise qualified" for the program at issue before this antidiscrimination principle applies.[48] Thus, the statute itself does not clearly indicate whether it applies to students qualified to participate in a given school program unless their handicap disqualifies them or to persons qualified even given their handicap. Underlying this ambiguity is the difficult choice between integrating disabled persons into programs designed without them in mind and excluding them from such programs and sorting them into specialized ones designed for them. A third alternative would be to foster integration with such accommodation as may be necessary to facilitate the disabled person's participation in the mainstream program. This alternative could entail considerable financial expenditure, and perhaps modification of the rules and practices of the program that would be resisted by other students and by those in charge.

As so often happens, the legal solution to this problem is itself ambiguous. In a lawsuit brought by a deaf student to challenge exclusion from a college nursing program, the Supreme Court concluded that Section 504 did not require the school to undertake affirmative steps to accommodate that student's special needs, but the Court also reasoned that refusal to modify an existing program to accommodate a disabled person's needs could amount to illegal discrimination.[49] The Court left interpretation of the law's requirements to case-by-case analysis.[50]

For students in public elementary and secondary schools, the federal government has provided a more explicit statutory framework. The Education for All Handicapped Children Act offers financial incentives to encour-

---

[46]Margaret Bellamy, "Educating Minority Language Students" (unpublished paper, 1988, in author's possession).

[47]Research on successful bilingual education in Canada, which involves students from middle-class and majority backgrounds, suggests an important comparison. See Hakuta, *Mirror of Language*, p. 239.

[48]29 U.S.C. sec. 794 (1982).

[49]442 U.S. 397, 411–12 (1979).

[50]See Note, "Employment Discrimination against the Handicapped and Section 504 of the Rehabilitation Act: An Essay on Legal Evasiveness," *Harv. L. Rev.* 97 (1984), 997, 1009.

age states to provide special services for handicapped children.[51] To obtain grants under the act, an applicant state must submit a yearly plan that details how the state intends to meet the act's objectives: (1) identifying all handicapped children needing special education and related services;[52] (2) protecting the rights of children and their parents to freedom from discrimination in the evaluation and placement process and confidentiality in the handling of personally identifiable data; and (3) mainstreaming, or integration of handicapped children with nonhandicapped children. Though leaving to each participating state the task of formulating actual programs to achieve these goals, the statute specifies a set of substantive and procedural rights that the state must endorse. The procedural rights include the right to be notified about the benefits available for disabled children, the right of parents to participate in the process of identifying the child's needs and devising the child's educational plan, and the right to have administrative and judicial reconsideration of the child's diagnosis and educational plan.[53]

In these procedural rights, the due-process origins of the legal framework are evident, but so are the competing goals behind the special education movement. On the one hand, procedural protections represent restraints against labeling a child as disabled—as different—because history shows the stigmatizing and often segregative consequences of such labeling. On the other hand, the procedural protections represent means by which parents may secure special attention for their child: special consideration of the child's needs, an educational program drawn up specifically for that child, and review by administrators and courts to assure that such specialized attention and individualized programs are in fact delivered. Captured within the single framework of the statutory scheme, then, are both the goal of restraining school officials from identifying a student as "different" and the goal of enabling parents to secure the label of "different" when they believe that doing so will help the child obtain useful educational assistance.

These two goals, of course, manifest the two sides of the difference dilemma. Identifying a child as handicapped entitles her to individualized educational planning and special services but also labels the child as handicapped and may expose her to attributions of inferiority, risks of stigma, isolation, and reduced self-esteem. Nonidentification frees a child from the risks associated with labeling but also denies him specialized attention and services. As school districts encounter parents clamoring for services for their children despite the problems of labeling, the procedural dimensions of the

[51]20 U.S.C. sec. 1411–20 (1982) (grant programs). The act defines "handicap" broadly, and its interpretive regulations focus on whether a child needs special education and related services because of an impairment (which may be a health condition that "adversely affects a child's educational performance"); see 34 C.F.R. sec. 300.5 (a)(1984).

[52]"Related services" are noneducational services that may be essential if a handicapped student is to benefit from education: transportation, speech or sign language instruction, psychological services, physical therapy, diagnostic medical services, and other medical or nursing services needed for the child to attend school.

[53]20 U.S.C. sec. 1412 (5)(c); 20 U.S.C. 1417 (c)(1982); 20 U.S.C. sec. 1412 (5)(B)(1982); 20 U.S.C. sec. 1412 (4),(5)(C), 1415 (e).

law give parents leverage to express their preference for whatever individualized attention or special programs their children can receive.[54] Indeed, the identification of increasing numbers of children as having special needs may overcome the risks of stigma and isolation by converting the minority to a majority. One observer has commented that "the labeling process is designed to secure funding,"[55] which parents may want despite the negative associations of the label. "Magnet labeling," attracting participation because of the benefits that can follow, is bound to threaten the definitional and budgetary constraints in serving the disabled.

This is not merely a theoretical problem. Advocates for children with traditional disabilities—such as certain visual impairments—have already objected that the Education for All Handicapped Children Act is inclusionary in two negative senses: it dilutes the claims of specified disability groups to special services by enabling many others to compete for limited funds; and it pushes the mainstreaming of students and thereby diminishes the schools' opportunity to employ specialized teachers, trained to deal with a particular disability.[56]

Moreover, given the guarantee of individual assessment and diagnosis for any child, and substantive ambiguities in defining disabilities, a new category of "learning disability" has become a growth area for special education and for budgetary allocations. Increasing recognition by educators of perceptual and psychological conditions that impair learning can be used to identify handicapping conditions for increasing numbers of students.[57] The category of learning disabilities already comprises the largest number of students served by special education.[58] Not only does such labeling secure special

[54]A study of Massachusetts practice, under a state law that was in fact the model for the federal legislation, shows that parents can obtain sufficient leverage and incentive to file lawsuits against school systems and obtain favorable settlements, securing special treatment for their children. See *Final Report: Implementing Massachusetts' Special Education Law: A Statewide Assessment*, ed. James McGarry (Boston: Massachusetts Department of Education, Division of Special Education, 1982), pp. 9–11, 27–28. See also Joel F. Handler, *The Conditions of Discretion: Autonomy, Community, Bureaucracy* (New York: Russell Sage Foundation, 1986).
[55]Kenneth Howell, *Inside Special Education* (Columbus, Ohio: Merrill, 1984), p. 281.
[56]See Alan Gartner and David B. Lipsky, "Beyond Special Education: Toward a Quality System for All Students," *Harvard Education Review* 57 (1987), 376: economic incentives sometimes favor mainstreaming to avoid the higher costs of special schools, and sometimes favor special schools for which the state reimburses local districts. Amanda Trask, "Deaf Children and the Least Restrictive Environment: Mainstreaming Is Not the Answer" (unpublished paper, 1987), argues that mainstreaming is motivated by cost concerns rather than educational appropriateness.
[57]Close study suggests individual variations that are often ignored by uniform educational programs, to the detriment of particular students. See Helvine D. Levine, *The Difference That Differences Make: Adolescent Diversity and Its Deregulation*, Report Prepared for Youth and America's Future (New York: William T. Grant Foundation Commission of Work, Family, and Citizenship, 1988).
[58]According to present criteria, more than 80 percent of the student population could be classified as learning disabled. See Gartner and Lipsky, "Beyond Special Education," pp. 376, 382, citing James Ysseldyke, "Classification of Handicapped Students," in *Handbook of Special Education: Research and Practice*, vol. 1, *Learner Characteristics and Adaptive Education*, ed. Margaret C. Wang, Maynard C. Reynolds, and Herbert J. Walberg (New York: Pergamon Press,

attention and services for the child; it may also help parents and teachers remove a difficult child from the mainstream classroom simply because he is hard to teach.[59]

These problems emerge because the ambiguity in the definitions of disability encourage both parents and teachers to push for labeling—and to push to restrain it. Parents may want their child treated as different in order to secure help to overcome obstacles to success in school, even though this different treatment may expose the child to ridicule or stigma; teachers may respond by preferring to treat the child as the same as other children—to save money, to avoid conflict, and to reduce the risk of stigma. Or the roles may be reversed. Parents may want their child mainstreamed, and seek to reduce any signs of difference for a child who has a disability such as blindness, deafness, or motor impairment; teachers may prefer to segregate such students for economies of scale, for the ease of teaching a more homogeneous class, or for fear of the stigma that can come when the "different" child is not invited to birthday parties or experiences even more serious exclusionary activities within the society of the classroom.[60]

These aspects of the difference dilemma, enacted by parents and teachers through the procedural dimensions of the Education for All Handicapped Children Act, are replicated in the substantive dimensions of the act, ambiguous as they are. The act specifies that a participating state must guarantee

---

1987). Children's Hospital–Boston, *Report of Findings from the Collaborative Study of Children with Special Needs: Rochester City School Dist. 19* (May 1984), cites learning problems for over 70 percent of the children. William M. Cruickshank, "Myths and Realities in Learning Disabilities," *Journal of Learning Disabilities* 10 (1977), 51, reports an elementary school principal's estimate that 83 percent of her center-city pupils functioned as if they were perceptually handicapped. The patterns of labeling reflect economic incentives more than any rational basis of individualized treatment; pressure to raise test scores, special education requirements, shrinking budgets, and persistent attitudes about the inherent abnormality of students who do not fit into the mainstream classroom contribute to the labeling and segregation of many minority, poor, and unconventional students into virtually permanent special education programs (p. 383). See also Division of Innovation and Development, Office of Special Education Programs, Office of Special Education and Rehabilitative Services, *Fourth Annual Report to Congress on the Implementation of Public Law 94–142: The Education for All Handicapped Children Act* (Washington, D.C.: U.S. Department of Education, 1982), p. 103; State Program Implementation Studies Branch, Office of Special Education and Rehabilitative Services, *Second Annual Report to Congress on the Implementation of Public Law 94–142: The Education for All Handicapped Children Act* (Washington, D.C.: U.S. Department of Education, 1980), 161.

[59]Howell, *Inside Special Education*, p. 81.

[60]Parent participation in the student's classification and placement may actually be reduced by the routinized processes of special education programs. See Handler, *Conditions of Discretion*, pp. 68–69. Yet some parents' active involvement may create new dilemmas of difference. For example, a group of Hasidic Jews in one New York community pushed for the creation of a local school district so that their handicapped children would not be forced to attend public schools outside the community in order to obtain public assistance. The parents feared that the children would face ostracism because of their religious costume and dress. School board groups challenged this plan as a violation of the institutional separation of church and state. See "Suit Contests Hasidic District," *New York Times*, Jan. 21, 1990, p. 28. Here, the dilemma is whether to risk recreating the religious difference of disabled children by acknowledging or by ignoring it.

every handicapped child a "free appropriate public education" and an education in the "least restrictive environment" possible. This "least restrictive" requirement means mainstreaming the child in a classroom with nonhandicapped children if possible or, if not, placing him in the closest approximation that can serve his needs.[61] Whether to mainstream an exceptional child presents the issue of whether to respond to difference by separation or by integration, and the analogy to bilingual education is direct.

Consider the example of a child with a severe hearing impairment. She may experience the pain of isolation and misunderstanding amid a class of hearing students, but she may have a similar experience of stigma and alienation if segregated in a separate class for deaf children. If mainstreamed, she may lack the continuous, specialized instruction tailored for her needs; if segregated, she will lack the opportunity to develop day-to-day relationships with hearing children and the chance to challenge their stereotypes and her own about her disability. Failing to accommodate the handicapped student could perpetuate the negative consequences of her disabilities without equipping her to handle them in other environments that fail to accommodate her.

These problems perhaps take a different shape for severely mentally disabled young people, for whom parents and school officials battle over the appropriateness of residential treatment. Yet here too we face questions of how to respect and acknowledge differences without preserving the historical negative consequences. How should this society prepare a young person for as much self-sufficiency and integration in the general community as possible without undermining his or her chances for developing self-esteem and a sense of being valued within a subcommunity, responsive to special needs?

As with the education of children whose primary language is not English, the dilemmas faced in educating disabled students reveal the difficulties of redressing minority status as long as members of the larger society deprecate individuals who have traits different from their own. The majority presumes that anyone who differs from them is inferior and thereby creates an environment that tells minority children they are inferior. Shielding a minority or disabled child from community dislike may allow her to develop a sense of self-esteem but disable her from coping with that community—or from recognizing hostility when it comes her way. The black poet Audre Lorde recalls racial tension on the streets of New York when she was growing up:

> As a very little girl, I remember shrinking from a particular sound, a hoarsely sharp, guttural rasp, because it often meant a nasty glob of grey spittle upon my coat or shoe an instant later. My mother wiped it off with the little pieces of newspaper she always carried in her purse. Sometimes she fussed about low-class people who had no better sense nor manners than to spit into the wind no matter where they went, impressing upon me that this humiliation was totally random. It never occurred to me to doubt her. It was not until years later once in conversation I said to her: "Have you noticed people don't spit into the wind so much the way they used to?" And the look on my mother's face told me that I

---

[61] 20 U.S.C. sec. 1401 (1982); 20 U.S.C. 12 (5)(b)(1982).

had blundered into one of those secret places of pain that must never be spoken of again.[62]

Catharine MacKinnon commented on this incident: "Which is worse: to protect the child from knowing that she is the object of degradation by some members of the community, or to alert her and prepare her to deal with that attitude when it comes her way?"[63] Experience with community hostility may injure the child's sense of self, yet such experience could also itself be the best educator and strengthen the child to deal with a world where her difference has been made to matter.

Similar questions have arisen in child custody battles when one parent is a member of a minority group or leads a life-style lacking respect in the community. In one case a father challenged the granting of custody to the mother, who was a lesbian. The judge rejected this challenge: "It is just as reasonable to expect that [children] will emerge better equipped to search out their own standards of right and wrong, better able to perceive that the majority is not always correct in its moral judgments, and better able to understand the importance of conforming their beliefs to the requirements of reason and tested knowledge, not the constraints of currently popular sentiment or prejudice."[64] Clearly, the difference dilemma can appear in many settings.

The Difference Dilemma in Other Contexts

The risk of recreating difference by either noticing it or ignoring it arises with decisions about employment, medical treatment, and legal processes as well as education. Such decisions should not turn on an individual's race, gender, religion, or membership in any other group toward which some have deprecating or hostile attitudes. Yet refusing to acknowledge these differences may make them continue to matter in a world constructed with some groups but not others in mind. A current example is the issue of gender difference in the distribution of property following divorce. A legislative reform movement has advanced the idea of equality: equal division of assets and duties following divorce. Yet this approach may fail to address the practical difference between a woman who acts as the primary caretaker of the couple's children—and must provide for them as well as herself—and the man who has established himself as the family's "breadwinner" in a marketplace that has historically valued men's work more than women's. But the alternative of identifying women's greater economic needs and difficulties in meeting them while caring for children is disturbing as well, for it may lock women into the stereotyped role that many wish to challenge. Still other

[62]Audre Lorde, *Zami: A New Spelling of My Name* (Freedom, Calif.: Crossing Press, 1982), pp. 17–18.
[63]Lecture by Catharine MacKinnon, Harvard Law School, January 1983.
[64]M.P. v. S.P., 169 N.J. Super. 425, 438 A.2d 1256, 1263 (1979).

women—and men—may prefer to maintain the traditional gender-based assignment of family roles and may value the differences in these roles. But whose values about gender difference should guide the couple in dispute at the time of divorce? Here as in other contexts, traits of difference, if employed to distribute benefits and burdens, can carry meanings uncontrolled and unwelcomed by those to whom they are assigned. Yet denying those differences may ignore qualities that matter much to those who have them. Ignoring differences undermines the value they may have to those who cherish them as part of their identity.

Consider the problem by viewing women's relationship to the workplace. Women's biological differences from men may be deployed to justify special accommodations at the workplace, such as safety protections against chemical damage to their reproductive systems, or maternity leave following childbirth. Special benefits for women, however, can reinforce the negative stereotypes that have been used to exclude women from the workplace or hold them back from direct competition with men. Although less than 10 percent of American families fit the traditional image of the father who earns a living and the mother who stays at home to care for the children,[65] women who become pregnant or who have major child-care responsibilities are people with a "difference" in most work settings. Traditional legal rules about what counts as discrimination in employment and in unemployment benefits implement a commitment to neutrality: no differences should be permitted on the basis of gender. But this very commitment to neutrality poses a dilemma for women who face a world of paid employment designed without women in mind. If women seek to have their special needs acknowledged, they depart from the demand for neutrality, yet women's differences reappear in the face of neutral rules that lack any accommodation for pregnancy, motherhood, or child-rearing responsibilities. For example, a state law denying unemployment benefits to a woman out of work because of pregnancy may withstand a sex discrimination challenge if the rule also denies benefits to others who leave their jobs "voluntarily," or for reasons unrelated to the employer's action. The Supreme Court affirmed one such statute in the face of a sex discrimination challenge, reasoning that the state's rule "incidentally disqualifies pregnant or formerly pregnant claimants as part of a larger group."[66]

---

[65]Family Policy Panel, Economic Policy Council of UNA-USA, *Work and Family in the United States: A Policy Initiative* (New York: United Nations Association–United States of America, 1985). My own understanding of this topic has been assisted by the work of Nancy Dowd, "The Work-Family Conflict: Restructuring the Workplace" (Rockefeller Foundation Proposal, Feb. 13, 1987); Mary Joe Frug, "Securing Job Equality for Women: Labor Market Hostility to Working Mothers," *B.U.L. Rev.* 59 (1979), 55; Lucinda Finley, "Transcending Equality Theory: A Way Out of the Maternity and the Workplace Debate," *Colum. L. Rev.* 86 (1986), 1118.

[66]Wimberly v. Labor and Industrial Relations Comm'n of Missouri, 107 S.Ct. 821 (1987). The Court rejected a challenge to the Missouri law despite a federal statute forbidding discrimination in unemployment compensation "solely on the basis of pregnancy or termination of pregnancy"; see 26 U.S.C. sec. 3304 (1)(12)(1982). See also General Electric Co. v. Gilbert, 429 U.S. 125 (1976) (concluding that an employer who excludes pregnancy from medical benefits has not violated a statutory ban on sex discrimination because women, as well as men, may be

This conclusion treats women like men; it ignores any difference between them.[67] Yet because women do differ from men, who are treated as the norm, this decision leaves women to shoulder the burdens of their difference. And responding to such burdens becomes a dilemma in itself when women remember the disadvantages historically that have resulted from official recognition of women's differences from men. Traditional rules denied married women the power to enter into contracts or to hold, sell, or give away property; withheld the prerogative of voting, serving on juries, or otherwise exercising political rights; denied them entry to the professions; and refused them legal custody of their children.[68] Even after political struggles persuaded courts and legislatures to reverse many of these legal restrictions, images of women's differences continued to justify excluding women from activities engaged in by men and restricting women's choices about their own lives.[69] Perhaps, then, it should come as no surprise that advocates for women's rights themselves split intensely over whether to favor maternity leave policies, which acknowledge a gender difference, or whether instead to oppose any policy that abandons neutrality on the issue of gender.

Neutrality as a solution to the dilemma of difference is the elusive goal that itself may exacerbate the dilemma, especially when the government is the decision-maker. Governmental neutrality may freeze in place the past consequences of differences, yet any departure from neutrality in governmental standards uses governmental power to make those differences matter and thus symbolically reinforces them. If the government delegates discretion to employers, legislators, and judges, it disengages itself from directly endorsing the use of differences in decisions but still allows those other decision-makers to give significance to differences. Official rules constraining public or private discretion could alter the ways decision-makers use differences, but the very specificity of such rules might underscore the salience of those differences.

The commitment to neutrality as a solution to difference is, however, deeply embedded in our legal system. The Constitution is perhaps most

---

nonpregnant); and Geduldig v. Aiello, 417 U.S. 484 (1974) (same reasoning, under constitutional equal protection). Congress rejected the Court's statutory view and adopted the Pregnancy Discrimination Act, which amended the Title VII sex discrimination ban to expressly include discrimination on the basis of pregnancy within impermissible sex discrimination; see 42 U.S.C. sec. 2000e(k) (1982).

[67]This conclusion also presumes that the individual worker, rather than the workplace structure, is responsible for the choice between staying at work and leaving work for childbirth and child-care reasons. A shift in perspective could locate the problem in workplace arrangements that give the individual worker no alternative way to manage childbearing and child-rearing duties alongside workplace responsibilities. The meanings of "voluntary" and "unrelated to work" could thus shift depending on what conception of work and family relationships are treated as the norm.

[68]See generally William Blackstone, *Commentaries on the Laws of England* (Philadelphia: Abraham Small, 1822), 1:433–36; Norma Basch, *In the Eyes of the Law: Women, Marriage, and Property in Nineteenth-Century New York* (Ithaca: Cornell University Press, 1982); Eleanor Flexner, *Century of Struggle: The Women's Rights Movement in the United States* (Cambridge, Mass.: Belknap Press of Harvard University Press, 1975).

[69]See Mary Becker, "From Muller v. Oregon to Fetal Vulnerability Policies," *U. Chi. L. Rev.* 53 (1986), 1219.

explicit about seeking neutrality in its treatment of religion—yet nowhere in the Constitution is the dilemma of difference more palpable. The First Amendment guarantees free exercise of religion, unburdened by the government; it also forbids, under the establishment clause, any governmental action motivated by a desire to advance one religion or, indeed, any religion. In essence, the framers of the amendment understood that dominant groups might organize society in ways that would cramp the religious practices of minorities, and the framers also understood that any governmental action favoring a religion could so accentuate that trait as to disadvantage anyone who did not subscribe to that religion.[70] The First Amendment thus grasps the dilemma of difference but does not resolve it. To be truly neutral, the government must walk a perhaps nonexisting path between promoting or endorsing religion and failing to make room for religious exercise. Accommodation of religious practices may look nonneutral, but failure to accommodate may also seem nonneutral by burdening the religious minority whose needs were not built into the structure of mainstream institutions.

An example of the problem in attaining neutrality toward religion interestingly mirrors the treatment of pregnancy in the context of unemployment benefits. Should a state be allowed to deny unemployment benefits to a person who loses her job because of her religious observances? Several cases of this sort have reached the courts. Typically, an employer's seemingly neutral rule imposes a special burden on a member of a minority religious group that commands observance of a different Sabbath, or directs its adherents to wear particular clothing. For example, a woman who is a Seventh Day Adventist sought unemployment benefits after she was discharged for refusing to work on Saturdays, her religious Sabbath. The state argued that the employee's refusal to work amounted to misconduct related to her work and rendered her ineligible for unemployment benefits under a statute limiting compensation to persons who become "unemployed through no fault of their own." Moreover, the state argued that if its unemployment benefits scheme were to accommodate an individual's religious beliefs and practices, it would violate the Constitution's ban against establishing or even favoring

---

[70]I do not mean to invoke adherence to original intent in the application of the Constitution to new circumstances. Scholarly and judicial views of the relationship between the First Amendment's ban on governmental establishment and protection of the free exercise of religion have changed over time; in 1818, twenty years after Connecticut's adoption of the Constitution, even its framers were still deeply divided over the meaning of disestablishment and religious freedom. See Carol Weisbrod, "On Evidence and Intentions: The More Proof, The More Doubt," *Conn. L. Rev.* 18 (1986), 803, 819. One group approved state support of Christianity; another sought separation between church and state while still adhering to the idea of a nonsectarian Christian nation; still others rejected the idea of the Christian nation itself as too nearly endorsing particular religious views (pp. 822–24). As applied to schools, contemporary constitutional commitments to disestablish religion turn earlier understandings on their head. Prerevolutionary colonies deliberately created schools to promote religious practice and exercise. The public schools' more restrictive treatment of religion was probably adopted less to promote separation of church and state than to prevent the teachers of one sect from indoctrinating children whose parents belonged to other sects. See Donald Boles, *The Bible, Religion, and the Public Schools* (New York: Crowell-Collier, 1963), p. 21.

religion.[71] The Supreme Court rejected these arguments, however, and concluded instead that the state's position unlawfully burdened the employee's
right to free exercise of her religion. By requiring accommodation for her free
exercise, despite charges of establishing religion, the Court's solution thus
framed the difference dilemma as a dilemma of neutrality: how can the
government's means be neutral in a world that is not itself neutral?

Lawsuits challenging the teaching of evolution and the teaching of creationism in public schools also highlight the dilemma. A long-standing debate about the incompatibility of evolutionary theory and fundamentalist
Christian religious beliefs has spawned several famous lawsuits and even
inspired books and a movie.[72] After the state of Louisiana adopted a statute
requiring public schools to teach creation science whenever they teach the
theory of evolution, a group of parents challenged the statute as a violation
of the establishment clause. Community members subscribing to fundamentalist religious beliefs, however, have argued that public school instruction in
evolution alone is not neutral, because it gives a persuasive advantage to
views that undermine their own religious beliefs. Relying on similar arguments, the state avowed a neutral, nonreligious purpose for its statute. The
case ultimately reached the U.S. Supreme Court, which rejected the state's
arguments and struck down the statute as a violation of the First Amendment.[73]

Yet the Court itself divided on the question, as revealed in a hot dispute
between the majority and dissenting opinions. Justice William Brennan's
opinion for the majority concluded that the "Balanced Treatment Act"
requiring instruction in creation science whenever evolution was taught was
actually intended to "provide persuasive advantage to a particular religious
doctrine that rejects the factual basis of evolution in its entirety."[74] By
contrast, the dissenting opinion by Justice Antonin Scalia, which was joined
by Chief Justice William Rehnquist, expressly tangled with the neutrality
problem. The dissent noted the difficult tensions between antidisestablish-
ment and free-exercise concerns, and between neutrality through indiffer-

[71]Hobbie v. Unemployment Appeals Commission, 107 S.Ct. 1046 (1987); id. at 1048 (quoting Fla. Stat. sec. 443.021 [1985]; id. at 1051 n.11. See also Sherbert v. Verner, 374 U.S. 398
(1963).

[72]See Ray Ginger, *Six Days or Forever? Tennessee v. John Thomas Scopes* (Boston: Beacon
Press, 1958); and Epperson v. Arkansas, 393 U.S. 97 (1968). The play *Inherit the Wind* and the
film based on it, inspired by the Scopes trial, dramatized the threat to their religious beliefs that
some fundamentalists perceived in the theory of evolution—and the threat to the freedom of
expression represented by a law that would protect those fundamentalists. The actual conflict
was more complicated: for example, Clarence Darrow, who defended the dismissed teacher, was
a close ally and friend of William Jennings Bryan, the lawyer for the state. And Bryan, unlike
most of the fundamentalists, was a committed social reformer; he worried that the theory of
evolution contradicted not only the Bible's story of creation but also social reforms that
challenged the status quo. See Willard H. Smith, *The Social and Religious Thought of William
Jennings Bryan* (Lawrence, Kan.: Coronado Press, 1975), pp. 167–68; David D. Anderson,
William Jennings Bryan (Boston: Twayne, 1981), p. 183.

[73]Edwards v. Aguillard, 107 S.Ct. 2573, 2576 (1987).

[74]Id. at 2582; accord id. at 2587 (Powell, J., concurring).

ence and neutrality through accommodation. Acknowledging precedents construing the establishment clause as forbidding state action designed either to advance or to inhibit religion, the dissent concluded that "a State which discovers that its employees are inhibiting religion must take steps to prevent them from doing so, even though its purpose would clearly be to advance religion."[75] Moved by the state's attempt to avoid undermining the different views of fundamentalist Christian students, the dissent would have permitted the state requirement that "creation science" be taught alongside evolution. Even though the majority concluded to the contrary that the statute gave an illegal preference to a particular religious view, the justices on both sides of the fence shared this understanding: the commitment to neutrality could be jeopardized either by acts undermining the views of the minority or by acts promoting those views.[76]

In a variety of discrimination-law contexts, arguments over the meanings of religious, ethnic, and racial identities reflect the dilemma of difference. Statutes forbidding racial discrimination, like all statutes, present questions of scope: who exactly should be eligible to claim their protections? Following the Civil War, constitutional amendments and reform legislation sought to eradicate both slavery and its consequences. These reforms still bear the imprint of the slavery experience and use it as the paradigm of the form of illicit discrimination to be banned. The status of the free, white citizen, then, stands as the measure for nondiscrimination. When individuals claim to be members of minority races in order to secure special legal protections, they risk fueling negative meanings of that identity, meanings beyond their control. Although racial identification under federal civil rights statutes provides a means of legal redress, it can also recreate stigmatizing associations, thereby stimulating prejudice and the punitive consequences of difference.

When members of a Jewish congregation whose synagogue was defaced by private individuals used racial grounds to allege violations of the federal guarantee against interference with property rights,[77] the difference dilemma

---

[75]107 S.Ct. at 2595 (Scalia, J., dissenting).

[76]Philosopher Amy Gutmann (*Democratic Education*, p. 103) has argued that "teaching creationism as science—even as one among several reasonable scientific theories—violates the principle of nonrepression in indirectly imposing a sectarian religious view on all children in the guise of science." She also notes: "The religions that reject evolution as a valued scientific theory also reject the secular standards of reasoning that make evolution clearly superior as a theory to creationism" (p. 102). Gutmann concludes that "the case for teaching secular but not religious standards of reasoning does not rest on the claim that secular standards are neutral among all religious beliefs. The case rests instead on the claim that secular standards constitute a better basis upon which to build a common education for citizenship than any set of sectarian religious beliefs—better because secular standards are both a fairer and a firmer basis for peacefully reconciling our differences" (p. 103). Although I respect her larger enterprise in articulating a democratic theory of education that seeks both to empower citizens to make educational policy and to constrain their choices in accord with democratic commitments against repression and discrimination (p. 14), this resolution of the conflict between religious and secular views seems too quick a conclusion as to what counts to many people as unacceptable repression or discrimination.

[77]42 U.S.C. sec. 1982 (1982) guarantees all citizens "the same right . . . as is enjoyed by white citizens . . . to inherit, purchase, lease, sell, hold, and convey real and personal property."

appeared on the face of the complaint launching the lawsuit. The petitioners argued that Jews are not a racially distinct group, yet they claimed that Jews should be entitled to protection against racial discrimination because others treat them as though they were distinct.[78] The petitioners thus demonstrated their reluctance to have a difference identified in a way that they themselves could not control; they simultaneously expressed their desire for protection against having that difference assigned to them by others. To gain this protection, though, the petitioners had to identify themselves through the very category they rejected as a definition of themselves.

Both the district court and the court of appeals refused to allow the petitioners to be included in the protected group on the basis of the attitudes of others, without some proof of well-established traits internal to the group itself. "Although we sympathize with appellant's position," reasoned the court of appeals, "we conclude that it cannot support a claim of racial discrimination solely on the basis of defendants' perception of Jews as being members of a racially distinct group. To allow otherwise would permit charges of racial discrimination to arise out of nothing more than the subjective, irrational perceptions of defendants." One member of the appeals panel did dissent from this point. He argued: "Misperception lies at the heart of prejudice, and the animus formed of such ignorance sows malice and hatred wherever it operates without restriction."[79]

Is the cause of individualized treatment advanced by allowing groups to claim the legal protections of group membership, however erroneously that membership is assigned by others? Conversely, will not denial of legal protection for such claims against assigned difference put the courts in the position of ignoring differences and thereby failing to halt their power in community attitudes? The Supreme Court resolved the question by turning to the intention of the legislators who adopted the antidiscrimination statutes shortly after the Civil War. Because those legislators and their nineteenth-century contemporaries viewed Jews as members of a distinct race, the Court permitted Jews in the 1980s to claim legal protection against racial discrimination.[80] The Court thus used a historical test for membership in a minority race and deferred to the categorical thinking about race that prevailed in the 1860s, despite the considerable changes in scientific and moral understandings about racial labels since that time. In so doing, the Court may have reinvigorated an old mode of thinking about racial difference—categorical thinking about abnormal persons—even as it enabled a group to challenge private discrimination on that basis. Trapped in the dilemma of difference, the Court perpetuated attributions of difference in the course of permitting challenges to discrimination on that basis.

---

[78]Shaare Tefila Congregation v. Cobb, 107 S.Ct. 2019, 2021 (1987).

[79]785 F.2d 523, 527 (4th Cir. 1986); id. at 529 (Wilkinson, J., concurring in part and dissenting in part). Judge Wilkinson explained: "It is an understatement to note that attempts to place individuals in distinct racial groups frequently serve only to facilitate continued discrimination and postpone the day when all individuals will be addressed as such" (id. at 533).

[80]Shaare Tefila, 481 U.S. 615 (1987).

The dilemma for decision-makers—courts, states, employers—is how to help overcome past hostilities and degradation of people on the basis of group differences without employing and, in that sense, legitimating those very differences. Put in these terms, the dilemma of difference appears in debates about affirmative action in employment and educational practices. How can historical discrimination on the basis of race and gender be overcome if the remedies themselves use the forbidden categories of race and gender? Yet without such remedies, how can historical discrimination and its legacies of segregation and exclusion be transcended? Should nonneutral means be risked to achieve the ends of neutrality?[81] A similar conundrum arises over how to acknowledge victimization without repeating the victimization in the process of acknowledging it.[82] This difficulty is pronounced in the legal treatment of people defined as victims of violent assault, rape, or child abuse.[83] Demanding that those who have been injured by others present their injuries in the often brutalizing process of adversarial litigation may inflict new injuries. Yet new injuries can also be induced if the legal system denies access to this process and directs such people to less established alternatives, such as mediation, or away from the legal system altogether.

The Challenge of Difference

In many areas, then, we confront historical practices giving particular significance to traits of difference along lines of race, ethnicity, disability, gender, and religion—traits that are largely or entirely beyond the control of the individuals who are identified by them.[84] Even the meanings of these traits are beyond the control of any individual, although groups of people may organize to challenge negative meanings assigned to a trait they share. Social, political, and legal reform efforts to challenge exclusion and degradation on the basis of assigned traits continually run up against the danger either of recreating differences by focusing upon them or of denying their enduring influence in people's lives. This dilemma of difference burdens people who have been labeled different with the stigma, degradation, or

---

[81]See generally Kathleen M. Sullivan, "Sins of Discrimination: Last Term's Affirmative Action Cases," *Harv. L. Rev.* 100 (1986), 78.

[82]Lucie White, "To Learn and to Teach: Lessons from Driefontein on Lawyering and Power," *Wis. L. Rev.* 1988 (1988), 699.

[83]People who object to their own victimization sometimes encounter renewed humiliation in the very processes established to receive their complaints. See, e.g., Susan Estrich, *Real Rape* (Cambridge, Mass.: Harvard University Press, 1987), pp. 3–4, 42: rape prosecutions revictimize women by requiring invasive physical examination to corroborate their stories, by delving into their sexual histories, and by blaming them for not resisting enough.

[84]The Supreme Court has described these traits as identifying groups that are "discrete and insular." See United States v. Carolene Products Co., 304 U.S. 144, 152 n.4 (1938). And judicial protection for such groups has been justified on the grounds of their political powerlessness and the involuntary nature of their membership. See John Ely, *Democracy and Distrust: A Theory of Judicial Review* (Cambridge, Mass.: Harvard University Press, 1980).

simple sense of not fitting in while leaving the majority free to feel unresponsible for and uninvolved in the problems of difference.

Legal responses to the dilemma of difference recreate rather than resolve it. The right to be treated as an individual ignores the burdens of group membership; the right to object to the burdens of group membership reinvokes the trait that carries the negative meanings. Particularly intractable versions of the dilemma complicate decisions over medical treatment for severely disabled persons, whether young or old. Denying them treatment that would be available to someone less disabled, or to someone of a different age, seems to punish on the basis of a difference beyond the person's control. Yet extending medical treatment, including extraordinary measures, with deliberate disregard of the individual's age or disability may fulfill a principle of neutrality at the cost of ignoring that individual's actual situation. Since the individual is usually unable to speak to the decision, the problem is especially pronounced; there is no recourse to the person's own views to help establish a ground for respecting the individual. Similarly, decisions about housing, education, and employment for individuals with severe mental disabilities add to the dilemma of difference the difficulty of learning what the individuals most affected would themselves want. Decisions about the treatment of AIDS and people at risk of acquiring the AIDS virus also head directly into the difference dilemma. Identification of people at risk exposes them to discrimination; nonidentification puts them in danger of unwittingly catching the virus or passing it on to others.

Once we notice the difference dilemma, it is easy to see it in unexpected places. But more intriguing than its pervasiveness, I believe, are its sources. Why do we encounter this dilemma about how to redress the negative consequences of difference without reenacting it? What is, or should be, the meaning of difference?

CHAPTER 2

Sources of Difference

Is my understanding only blindness to my own lack of
understanding?
　　　　　　　　—Ludwig Wittgenstein, *On Certainty*

When you presume, you are not treating me as the person I
am; when you do not presume, you are treating me as the
person I am in a minimal sense; when you recognize and
respond to the person I am, you are treating me as the person I
am in a maximal sense.
　　　　　—Elizabeth V. Spelman, "On Treating Persons as Persons"

Dilemmas of difference appear unresolvable. The risk of nonneutrality—the risk of discrimination—accompanies efforts both to ignore and
to recognize difference in equal treatment and special treatment. Difference
can be recreated in color or gender blindness and in affirmative action;[1] in
governmental neutrality and in governmental preferences; and in discretionary decisions and in formal constraints on discretion. Why does difference
seem to pose choices each of which undesirably revives difference or the
stigma or disadvantage associated with it?

First epigraph: Reprinted by permission of Basil Blackwell, Inc., from *On Certainty*, by
Ludwig Wittgenstein. Second epigraph: Reprinted by permission of University of Chicago Press
from "On Treating Persons as Persons," by Elizabeth V. Spelman, *Ethics* 88 (1978).

[1] Affirmative action programs seek to aid disadvantaged groups by giving them special treatment. Some plans are voluntary, adopted by schools and employers to alter the composition of
their communities to better reflect the larger population. Some are imposed by courts or agencies
as remedies for demonstrated past discriminatory practices. A dilemma of difference may arise if
the special treatment highlights the historic differences and reintroduces stigma for those who
participate in the program; thus, minority members or white women may become stigmatized as
merely affirmative action hires, presumed unqualified without the special treatment. This result
may reflect misunderstanding of the program and a faulty view that the prior selection procedures were themselves free from bias, yet the risk of aggravating stigma persists. See, e.g.,
William Van Alstyne, "Rites of Passage: Race, the Supreme Court, and the Constitution," *U.
Chi. L. Rev.* 46 (1978), 775, 778: affirmative action plans fail to alleviate discrimination and
instead contribute to "racism, racial spoils systems, racial competition and racial odium."

In this last question lies a clue to the problem. The possibility of reiterating difference, whether by acknowledgment or nonacknowledgment, arises as long as difference itself carries stigma and precludes equality. Buried in the questions about difference are assumptions that difference is linked to stigma or deviance and that sameness is a prerequisite for equality. Perhaps these assumptions themselves must be identified and assessed if we are to escape or transcend the dilemmas of difference.

If to be equal one must be the same, then to be different is to be unequal or even deviant.[2] But any assignment of deviance must be made from the vantage point of some claimed normality: a position of equality implies a contrasting position used to draw the relationship—and it is a relationship not of equality and inequality but of superiority and inferiority.[3] To be different is to be different in relationship to someone or something else—and this point of comparison must be so taken for granted, so much the "norm," that it need not even be stated.

At least five closely related but unstated assumptions underlie difference dilemmas. Once articulated and examined, these assumptions can take their proper place among other choices about how to treat difference, and we can consider what we might do to challenge or renovate them.

Five Unstated Assumptions

First, we often assume that "differences" are intrinsic, rather than viewing them as expressions of comparisons between people on the basis of particular traits. Each of us is different from everyone else in innumerable ways. Each of these differences is an implicit comparison we draw. And the comparisons themselves depend upon and reconfirm the selection of particular traits as the ones that assume importance in the comparison process. An

---

[2]See Carol Gilligan, "In a Different Voice: Women's Conceptions of Self and Morality," *Harvard Education Review* 47 (1977), 418, 482 (1977); Audre Lorde, "Age, Race, Class and Sex: Women Redefining Difference," in *Sister Outsider: Essays and Speeches* (Trumansburg, N.Y.: Crossing Press, 1984), pp. 114, 116.

[3]See Catharine MacKinnon, *Feminism Unmodified: Discourses on Life and Law* (Cambridge, Mass.: Harvard University Press, 1987); and Ruth Colker, "Anti-Subordination above All: Sex, Race, and Equal Protection," *N.Y.U. L. Rev.* 61 (1986), 1003, both criticizing equal rights debates for failing to focus on issues of superiority and subordination. MacKinnon charges the debates with focusing on women's similarities and their differences from men, while treating maleness as the unquestioned norm. "Why should you have to be the same as a man to get what a man gets simply because he is one? Why does maleness provide an entitlement . . . so that it is women . . . who have to show in effect that they are men in every relevant respect?" (p. 37). MacKinnon urges instead what she calls the "dominance approach"—which presumes that "the question of equality . . . is at root a question of hierarchy"—and then equal distribution of power (p. 40). Colker similarly views hierarchy, not difference, as the root problem: "Facially differentiating and facially neutral policies are invidious only if they perpetuate racial or sexual hierarchy" (pp. 1007–8). Both MacKinnon and Colker maintain that talk of "sameness" or "neutrality" obscures the hierarchy that is already in place; therefore, eliminating the hierarchy is the ultimate goal for movements for equality.

assessment of difference selects out some traits and makes them matter; indeed, it treats people as subject to categorization rather than as manifesting multitudes of characteristics.[4]

Second, we typically adopt an unstated point of reference when assessing others. It is from the point of reference of this norm that we determine who is different and who is normal. The hearing-impaired student is different in comparison to the norm of the hearing student—yet the hearing student differs from the hearing-impaired student as much as she differs from him, and the hearing student undoubtedly has other traits that distinguish him from other students. Unstated points of reference may express the experience of a majority or may express the perspective of those who have had greater access to the power used in naming and assessing others. Women are different in relation to the unstated male norm. Blacks, Mormons, Jews, and Arabs are different in relation to the unstated white Christian norm. Handicapped persons are different in relation to the unstated norm of able-bodiedness or, as some have described it, the vantage point of "Temporarily Able Persons."[5]

The unstated point of comparison is not general but particular, and not inevitable but only seemingly so when left unstated.[6] The unstated reference point promotes the interests of some but not others; it can remain unstated because those who do not fit have less power to select the norm than those who fit comfortably within the one that prevails.

A reference point for comparison purposes is central to a notion of equality. Equality asks, equal compared with whom? A notion of equality that demands disregarding a "difference" calls for assimilation to an unstated norm. To strip away difference, then, is often to remove or ignore a feature distinguishing an individual from a presumed norm—such as that of a white, able-bodied, Christian man—but leaving that norm in place as the measure for equal treatment. The white person's supposed compliment to a black friend, "I don't even think of you as black," marks a failure to see the implicit racism in ignoring a "difference" and adopting an unstated and potentially demeaning point of comparison.[7] As historian J. R. Pole has explained, constitutional notions of equality in the United States rest on the idea that people are equal because they could all take one another's places in work, intellectual exchange, or political power if they were disassociated from their

---

[4]See Gordon W. Allport, *The Nature of Prejudice* (1954; Cambridge, Mass.: Addison-Wesley, 1958), pp. 19–27: prejudice is founded on categorical thinking and overgeneralization.

[5]See Nancy Mairs, "Hers," *New York Times,* July 9, 1987, p. C2.

[6]Whites tend to cite the race of an individual only if that person is not white, since the unstated race is understood to be white. Marilyn Frye, *The Politics of Reality: Essays in Feminist Theory* (Trumansburg, N.Y.: Crossing Press, 1983), p. 117, comments: "As feminists we are very familiar with the male version of this: the men write and speak and presumably, therefore, also think as though whatever is true of them is true of everybody. White people also speak in universals. . . . For the most part, it never occurred to us to modify our nouns accordingly; to our minds the people we were writing about were *people*. We don't think of ourselves as *white*."

[7]See Karen Russell, "Growing Up with Privilege and Prejudice," *New York Times Magazine,* June 14, 1987, pp. 22, 24.

contexts of family, religion, class, or race and if they had the same opportunities and experiences.[8] This concept of equality makes the recognition of differences a basis for denying equal treatment. In view of the risk that difference will mean deviance or inequality, stigmatization from difference, once identified, is not surprising.

Third, we treat the person doing the seeing or judging as without a perspective, rather than as inevitably seeing and judging from a particular situated perspective. Although a person's perspective does not collapse into his or her demographic characteristics, no one is free from perspective, and no one can see fully from another's point of view.[9]

Fourth, we assume that the perspectives of those being judged are either irrelevant or are already taken into account through the perspective of the judge. This assumption is a luxury of those with more power or authority, for those with less power often have to consider the views of people unlike themselves. As a novelist has wryly observed, horses "have always understood a great deal more than they let on. It is difficult to be sat on all day, every day, by some other creature, without forming an opinion about them. On the other hand, it is perfectly possible to sit all day, every day, on top of another creature and not have the slightest thought about them whatsoever."[10] Moreover, this assumption treats a person's self-conception or world view as unrelated to how others treat him or her.

Finally, there is an assumption that the existing social and economic arrangements are natural and neutral. If workplaces and living arrangements are natural, they are inevitable. It follows, then, that differences in the work and home lives of particular individuals arise because of personal choice. We presume that individuals are free, unhampered by the status quo, when they form their own preferences and act upon them.[11] From this view, any departure from the status quo risks nonneutrality and interference with free choice.[12]

These interrelated assumptions, once made explicit, can be countered with some contrary ones. Consider these alternative starting points. Difference is relational, not intrinsic. Who or what should be taken as the point of reference for defining differences is debatable. There is no single, superior

[8]J. R. Pole, *The Pursuit of Equality in American History* (Berkeley: University of California Press, 1978), pp. 293–94.

[9]See Kenneth L. Karst, "The Supreme Court, 1976 Term—Foreword: Equal Citizenship under the Fourteenth Amendment," *Harv. L. Rev.* 91 (1977), 54 n.304, commenting on the effects of the absence of a woman justice on the Supreme Court that decided that pregnancy is sex-neutral.

[10]Douglas Adams, *Dirk Gently's Holistic Detective Agency* (New York: Simon & Schuster, 1987), p. 4.

[11]For critiques of this view, see John Elster, *Sour Grapes* (Cambridge: Cambridge University Press, 1983); Cass R. Sunstein, "Legal Interference with Private Preferences," *U. Chi. L. Rev.* 51 (1986), 1129.

[12]See, e.g., Alexander M. Bickel, *The Supreme Court and the Idea of Progress* (New York: Harper & Row, 1970). But J. Skelly Wright, "Professor Bickel, the Scholarly Tradition, and the Supreme Court," *Harv. L. Rev.* 84 (1971), 769, criticized the value-neutrality approach for its insensitivity to the powerless.

perspective for judging questions of difference. No perspective asserted to produce "the truth" is without a situated perspective, because any statement is made by a person who has a perspective. Assertions of a difference as "the truth" may indeed obscure the power of the person attributing a difference while excluding important competing perspectives. Difference is a clue to the social arrangements that make some people less accepted and less integrated while expressing the needs and interests of others who constitute the presumed model. And social arrangements can be changed. Arrangements that assign the burden of "differences" to some people while making others comfortable are historical artifacts. Maintaining these historical patterns embedded in the status quo is not neutral and cannot be justified by the claim that everyone has freely chosen to do so.

Let us consider the usual assumptions and these alternatives in the context of contested legal treatments of difference. Making the usually unstated assumptions explicit can open up debate about them and also reveal the many occasions when lawyers and judges have mustered alternative views.

Assumption 1: Difference Is Intrinsic, Not a Comparison

Can and should questions about who is different be resolved by a process of discovering intrinsic differences? Is difference something intrinsic to the different person or something constructed by social attitudes? By posing legal claims through the difference dilemma, litigants and judges treat the problem of difference as what society or a given decision-maker should do about the "different person"—a formulation that implicitly assigns the label of difference to that person.

The difference inquiry functions by pigeonholing people in sharply distinguished categories based on selected facts and features. Categorization helps people to cope with complexity and to understand one another.[13] Devising categories to simplify a complicated world may well be an inevitable feature of human cognition.[14]

When lawyers and judges analyze difference and use categories to do so, they import a basic method of legal analysis. Legal analysis, cast in a judicial mode, typically asks whether a given situation "fits" in a category defined by a legal rule or, instead, belongs outside it. Questions presented for review by the Supreme Court, for example, often take the form "Is this a that?"[15] For

[13]George Lakoff, *Women, Fire, and Dangerous Things: What Categories Reveal about the Mind* (Chicago: University of Chicago Press, 1987), p. xi.

[14]See Jerome S. Bruner, "Art as a Mode of Knowing," in *On Knowing: Essays for the Left Hand*, ed. Jerome S. Bruner (Cambridge, Mass.: Belknap Press of Harvard University Press, 1979), pp. 59, 69: "There is, perhaps, one universal truth about all forms of human cognition: the ability to deal with knowledge is hugely exceeded by the potential knowledge contained in man's environment. To cope with this diversity, man's perception, his memory, and his thought processes early become governed by strategies for protecting his limited capacities from the confusion of overloading. We tend to perceive things schematically, for example, rather than in detail, or we represent a class of diverse things by some sort of averaged 'typical instance.'"

[15]See Martin P. Golding, *Legal Reasoning* (New York: Knopf, 1984), p. 104.

example, are Jews a race? Is a contagious disease a handicap? Other questions take the form "Is doing *x* really doing *y*?" For example, is offering a statutory guarantee of job reinstatement after maternity leave really engaging in gender discrimination? Is denying unemployment benefits to someone who left work because of pregnancy also really discriminating on the basis of gender? As Martin Golding has explained, these may appear to be simple factual questions with clear answers, but they are also "questions about the application of a name, to which any answer is arbitrary."[16] Edward Levi, a leading expositor of the nature of legal reasoning, has explained the three steps involved: "Similarity is seen between cases; next the rule of law inherent in the first case is announced; then the rule of law is made applicable to the second case. . . . The finding of similarity or difference is the key step in the legal process."[17]

Again, as critics have noted for nearly a century, these patterns of legal analysis imply that legal reasoning yields results of its own accord, beyond human control.[18] But differences between people and between problems and between legal concepts or precedents are statements of relationships; they express a comparison with another person, problem, concept, or precedent. A difference cannot be understood except as a contrast between instances, or between a norm and an example.[19] Assessing similarities and differences is a basic cognitive process in organizing the world; it depends on comparing a new example with an older one. Legal analysis depends on the process of comparing this case with other cases, a process of drawing similarities and differences. Ann Scales has noted: "To characterize similarities and differences among situations is a key step in legal judgments. That step, however, is not a mechanistic manipulation of essences. Rather, that step always has a

[16]Ibid. See also Charles Taylor, "Overcoming Epistemology," in *After Philosophy: End or Transformation?* ed. Kenneth Barnes, James Bohman, and Thomas McCarthy (Cambridge, Mass.: MIT Press, 1987). Taylor compares theories of knowledge that treat language as a violent interference with reality and an obstacle to truth, and theories of knowledge that conceive of emphatically self-critical reason as capable of reaching more and more correct insights about the world.

[17]Edward Hirsch Levi, *An Introduction to Legal Reasoning* (Chicago: University of Chicago Press, 1949), p. 2. But Levi also emphasizes that the rules are not fixed, and "the classification changes as the classification is made. The rules change as the rules are applied" (pp. 3–4). Analysis of sameness and difference characterizes both reasoning by analogy and precedential reasoning. Other modes of contemporary legal reasoning include policy analysis, weighing costs and benefits, and evaluating proposed action in terms of consequences.

[18]See Grant Gilmore, *The Ages of American Law* (New Haven, Conn.: Yale University Press, 1977), discussing Cardozo and uncertainty; Felix Cohen, "Field Theory and Judicial Logic," *Yale L.J.* 59 (1950), 238, 244–49; Joseph William Singer, "Legal Realism Now: Review of Laura Kalman, Legal Realism at Yale: 1917–1960," *Calif. L. Rev.* 76 (1988), 467; Joseph William Singer, "The Player and the Cards: Nihilism and Legal Theory," *Yale L.J.* 94 (1984), 1.

[19]See Mary Douglas, *How Institutions Think* (Syracuse, N.Y.: Syracuse University Press, 1986), pp. 58–59: "It is naive to treat the quality of sameness, which characterizes members of a class, as if it were a quality inherent in things or as a power of recognition inherent in the mind. . . . Sameness is not a quality that can be recognized in things themselves; it is conferred upon elements within a coherent scheme."

moral crux."[20] The very act of classification remakes the boundaries of the class, moving the line to include rather than exclude this instance. Indeed, many categories used to describe people's differences are invented only at the moment when summoned into the service of defining someone.[21] Acknowledging this means acknowledging that difference is not discovered but humanly invented.

Sometimes, courts have made such acknowledgments. For example, when asked whether Jews and Arabs are distinct races for the purposes of civil rights statutes, the Supreme Court in 1987 reasoned that objective, scientific sources could not resolve this question, essentially acknowledging that racial identity is socially constructed.[22] Yet, oddly, the justices then turned to middle and late nineteenth-century notions of racial identity, prevalent when the remedial statutes were adopted, rather than examining contemporary assumptions and current prejudices. The problem for the litigants was whether to invoke categories that had been used to denigrate them in order to obtain legal protection. As these cases illustrate, groups that seek to challenge assigned categories and stigma run into this dilemma: "How do you protest a socially imposed categorization, except by organizing around the category?"[23] Moreover, a label of difference accentuates one over all other characteristics and may well carry a web of negative associations. Perceptions and assessments of difference pick out the traits that do not fit comfortably within dominant social arrangements, even when those traits could easily be made irrelevant by different social arrangements or different rules about what traits should be allowed to matter.

Legislatures on occasion demonstrate an understanding of the labeling process that assigns some people to categories based on traits that may be only imagined by others. The federal Rehabilitation Act forbids discrimination against handicapped persons—and also against persons perceived by others to be handicapped.[24]

Some have argued that the assignment of differences in Western thought entails not just relationships and comparisons but also the imposition of

[20]Ann C. Scales, "The Emergence of Feminist Jurisprudence: An Essay," *Yale L.J.* 95 (1986), 1373, 1386–87. See Douglas, *How Institutions Think*, p. 63: "Institutions bestow sameness. Socially based analogies assign disparate items to classes and load them with moral and political content."

[21]See Ian Hacking, "Making Up People," in *Reconstructing Individualism: Autonomy, Individuality and Self in Western Thought*, ed. Thomas C. Heller, Morton Sosna, and David E. Wellbery (Stanford, Calif.: Stanford University Press, 1986), pp. 222, 228–29, identifies the process by which categories are invented as persons are assigned to them.

[22]See Shaare Tefila Congregation v. Cobb, 107 S.Ct. 2019 (1987); and Saint Francis College v. Al-Khazraji, 107 S.Ct. 2022 (1987). For a thoughtful exploration of the history of the social construction of racial identity, see Neil Gotanda, "Towards a Critique of Colorblind: Abstract and Concrete Race in American Law" (unpublished draft, 1987).

[23]Steven Epstein, "Gay Politics, Ethnic Identity: The Limits of Social Constructionism," *Socialist Review*, May–Aug. 1987, pp. 9, 19.

[24]See School Board v. Arline, 107 S.Ct. 1123, 1130 (1987) (interpreting 29 U.S.C. sec. 706 [7][B]ii, 794).

hierarchies.[25] To explore this idea, we need the next unstated assumption: the implicit norm or reference point for the comparison through which difference is assigned.

Assumption 2: The Norm Need Not Be Stated

To treat someone as different means to accord him treatment that is different from the treatment of someone else; to describe someone as "the same" implies "the same as" someone else. When differences are discussed without explicit reference to the person or trait on the other side of the comparison, an unstated norm remains. Usually, this default reference point is so powerful and well established that specifying it is not thought necessary.[26]

When women argue for rights, the implicit reference point used in discussions of sameness and difference is the privilege accorded some men—typically, white men who are well established in the society. It is misleading to treat the implicit norm as consisting of all men, as rhetoric for women's rights tends to do, for that obscures historical racial and class differences in the treatment of men themselves. But the reference point of privileged men can present powerful arguments for overcoming the exclusion of women from activities and opportunities. Reform efforts on behalf of women during the nineteenth and twentieth centuries asserted women's fundamental similarities to the men who were allowed to vote, sit on juries, engage in business, and participate in essential political and economic institutions. Declarations of rights in the federal Constitution and other basic legal documents used universal terms, and advocates for women's rights argued that women fit those terms as well as privileged men did.[27] Unfortunately for the reformers, embracing the theory of "sameness" meant that any sign of

---

[25]This has been a theme emphasized in the work of deconstructive critics. See, e.g., Jacques Derrida, "Différance," in *Speech and Phenomena and Other Essays on Husserl's Theory of Signs,* trans. David Allison (Evanston, Ill.: Northwestern University Press, 1973), pp. 129–60; Collette Guillaumin, "The Question of Difference," trans. Helene Wenzel, in *Feminist Issues* 2 (1982), 33–52; Barbara Johnson, Translator's Foreword to Jacques Derrida, *Disseminations,* trans. Barbara Johnson (Chicago: University of Chicago Press, 1981), p. viii. For feminist works, see Alice Jardine, "Prelude: The Future of Difference," in *The Future of Difference,* ed. Hester Eisenstein and Alice Jardine (Boston: G. K. Hall, 1980), pp. xxv, xxvi; Frances Olsen, "The Sex of Law" (unpublished manuscript, 1984); Patricia Collins, "Learning from the Outsider Within: The Sociological Significance of Black Feminist Thought," *Social Problems* 33 (Dec. 1986), S14. On critical legal theory, see Duncan Kennedy, "Form and Substance in Private Law Adjudication," *Harv. L. Rev.* 89 (1976), 1685; Pierre Schlag, "Cannibalistic Moves: An Essay on the Metamorphosis of the Legal Distinction," *Stan. L. Rev.* 40 (1988), 929.

[26]Donald A. Schon, *The Reflective Practitioner: How Professionals Think in Action* (New York: Basic Books, 1983), p. 53, quotes Geoffrey Vickers: "We can recognize and describe deviations from a norm very much more clearly than we can describe the norm itself."

[27]E.g., Bradwell v. State, 83 U.S. 130 (1872) (Myra Bradwell arguing unsuccessfully that the privileges and immunities clause protected her from gender bias in rules governing admission to the bar); and United States v. Susan B. Anthony, transcript of 1872 argument following Anthony's arrest for illegally voting, reprinted in *Feminism: The Essential Historical Writings,* ed. Miriam Schneir (New York: Vintage Books, 1972), pp. 132–36.

difference between women and the men used for comparison could be used to justify treating women differently from those men.

A prominent "difference" assigned to women, by implicit comparison with men, is pregnancy—especially pregnancy experienced by women working for pay outside their homes. The Supreme Court's treatment of issues concerning pregnancy and the workplace highlights the power of the unstated norm in analyses of problems of difference. In 1975 the Court accepted an appeal to a male norm in striking down a Utah statute that disqualified a woman from receiving unemployment compensation for a specified period surrounding childbirth, even if her reasons for leaving work were unrelated to the pregnancy.[28] Although the capacity to become pregnant is a difference between women and men, this fact alone did not justify treating women and men differently on matters unrelated to pregnancy. Using men as the norm, the Court reasoned that any woman who can perform like a man can be treated like a man. A woman could not be denied unemployment compensation for different reasons than a man would.

What, however, is equal treatment for the woman who is correctly identified within the group of pregnant persons, not simply stereotyped as such, and temporarily unable to work outside the home for that reason? The Court first grappled with these issues in two cases that posed the question of whether discrimination on the basis of pregnancy—that is, employers' denial of health benefits—amounted to discrimination on the basis of sex. In both instances the Court answered negatively, reasoning that the employers drew a distinction not on the forbidden basis of sex but only on the basis of pregnancy; and since women could be both pregnant and nonpregnant, these were not instances of sex discrimination.[29] Only from a point of view that regards pregnancy as a strange occurrence, rather than an ongoing bodily potential, would its relationship to female experience be made so tenuous; and only from a vantage point that regards men as the norm would the exclusion of pregnancy from health insurance coverage seem unproblematic and free from gender discrimination.

Congress responded by enacting the Pregnancy Discrimination Act, which amended Title VII (the federal law forbidding gender discrimination in employment) to include discrimination on the basis of pregnancy within the range of impermissible sex discrimination.[30] Yet even under these new statutory terms, the power of the unstated male norm persists in debates over the definition of discrimination. Indeed, a new question arose under the Pregnancy Discrimination Act: if differential treatment on the basis of pregnancy is forbidden, does the statute also forbid any state requirement for pregnancy

[28]The case was decided on due process grounds. See Turner v. Department of Employment, 423 U.S. 44 (1975) (per curiam); see also Cleveland Board of Educ. v. LaFleur, 414 U.S. 632 (1974) (invalidating a local school board rule requiring pregnant teachers to take unpaid maternity leaves as a violation of due process).

[29]See General Electric Co. v. Gilbert, 429 U.S. 125 (1976) (Title VII); Geduldig v. Aiello, 417 U.S. 484 (1974) (equal protection).

[30]Pub. L. No. 95-555, 92 Stat. 2076 (1978) (codified at 42 U.S.C. sec. 2000e [k][1982]).

or maternity leaves—which are, after all, distinctions drawn on the basis of pregnancy, even though drawn to help women?

A collection of employers launched a lawsuit in the 1980s arguing that even favorable treatment on the basis of pregnancy violated the Pregnancy Discrimination Act. The employers challenged a California statute that mandated a limited right to resume a prior job following an unpaid pregnancy disability leave.[31] The case—California Federal Savings & Loan Association v. Guerra, which became known as "Cal/Fed"[32]—in a real and painful sense divided the community of advocates for women's rights. Writing briefs on opposing sides, women's rights groups went public with the division. Some maintained that any distinction on the basis of pregnancy—any distinction on the basis of sex—would perpetuate the negative stereotypes long used to demean and exclude women. Others argued that denying the facts of pregnancy and the needs of new mothers could only hurt women; treating women like men in the workplace violated the demands of equality. What does equality demand—treating women like men, or treating women specially?

What became clear in these arguments was that a deeper problem had produced this conundrum: a work world that treats as the model worker the traditional male employee who has a full-time wife and mother to care for his home and children. The very phrase "special treatment," when used to describe pregnancy or maternity leave, posits men as the norm and women as different or deviant from that norm. The problem was not women, or pregnancy, but the effort to fit women's experiences and needs into categories forged with men in mind.[33]

The case reached the Supreme Court. Over a strenuous dissent, a majority of the justices reconceived the problem and rejected the presumption of the male norm which had made the case seem like a choice between "equal treatment" and "special treatment." Instead, Justice Marshall's opinion for the majority shifted from a narrow workplace comparison to a broader comparison of men and women in their dual roles as workers and as family members. The Court found no conflict between the Pregnancy Discrimination Act and the challenged state law that required qualified reinstatement of women following maternity leaves, because "California's pregnancy disability leave statute allows women, as well as men, to have families without losing their jobs." The Court therefore construed the federal law to permit states to require that employers remove barriers in the workplace that would

[31]California Fair Employment and Housing Act, Cal. Gov't Code Ann. sec. 12945 (b)(2)(West 1980).

[32]107 S.Ct. 683 (1987).

[33]See generally Lucinda M. Finley, "Transcending Equality Theory: A Way Out of the Maternity and the Workplace Debate," *Colum. L. Rev.* 86 (1986), 1118; Nadine Taub and Wendy W. Williams, "Will Equality Require More than Assimilation, Accommodation, or Separation from the Existing Social Structure?" *Rutgers L. Rev./Civ. Rts. Devs.* 37 (1985), 825. Several scholars have demonstrated the pull of unstated norms in the context of employment and public regulation. See Jack M. Beermann and Joseph William Singer, "Baseline Questions in Legal Reasoning: The Example of Property in Jobs," *Ga. L. Rev.* 23 (1989), 911; Cass Sunstein, "Lochner's Legacy," *Colum. L. Rev.* 87 (1987), 873.

disadvantage pregnant people compared with others. Moreover, reasoned the majority, if there remains a conflict between a federal ban against sex-based discrimination and a state law requiring accommodation for women who take maternity leaves, that conflict should be resolved by the extension to men of benefits comparable to those available to women following maternity or pregnancy leaves.[34] Here, the Court used women's experiences as the benchmark and called for treating men equally in reference to women, thus reversing the usual practice. The dissenters, however, remained convinced that the federal law prohibited preferential treatment on the basis of pregnancy; they persisted in using the male norm as the measure for equal treatment in the workplace.[35]

There remains a risk of using the child-rearing couple as a new unstated reference point and failing then to recognize the burdens of workers who need accommodation to care for a dependent parent or to take care of some other private need. A new norm may produce new exclusions and assign the status of "difference" to still someone else. Unstated references appear in many other contexts. The assumption of able-bodiedness as the norm is manifested in architecture that is inaccessible to people who use wheelchairs, canes, or crutches to get around. Implicit norms often work subtly, through categories manifested in language. Reasoning processes tend to treat categories as clear, bounded, and sharp edged; a given item either fits within the category or it does not. Instead of considering the entire individual, we often select one characteristic as representative of the whole. George Lakoff has illustrated this phenomenon with the term "mother." Although "mother" appears to be a general category, with subcategories such as "working mother" and "unwed mother," the very need for modifying adjectives demonstrates an implicit prototype that structures expectations about and valuations of members of the general category, yet treats these expectations and valuations as mere reflections of reality.[36] If the general category is religion but the unstated prototype is Christianity, a court may have trouble recognizing as a religion a group lacking, for example, a minister.[37]

Psychologist Jerome Bruner wrote, "There is no seeing without looking, no hearing without listening, and both looking and listening are shaped by expectancy, stance, and intention."[38] Unstated reference points lie hidden in

[34]107 S.Ct. at 694, 695.

[35]See 107 S.Ct. at 698 (White, J., dissenting).

[36]See Lakoff, *Women, Fire, and Dangerous Things*, pp. 39–84.

[37]We tend to think metaphorically, allowing one concept to stand for another, or synecdochically, letting a part stand for a whole. These ways of thinking often obscure understanding either because they keep us from focusing on aspects of a thing that are inconsistent with the metaphor we choose, or because we fail to remember that we have made the substitution. See Howard Gardner, *The Mind's New Science: A History of the Cognitive Revolution* (New York: Basic Books, 1985), pp. 372–73; George Lakoff and Mark Johnson, *Metaphors We Live By* (Chicago: University of Chicago Press, 1980), pp. 10–13, 35–40; *Judgment under Uncertainty: Heuristics and Biases*, ed. Daniel Kahneman, Paul Slovic, and Amos Tversky (New York: Cambridge University Press, 1982), pp. 23–98.

[38]Jerome S. Bruner, *Actual Minds, Possible Worlds* (Cambridge, Mass.: Harvard University Press, 1986), p. 110, paraphrasing Robert Woodworth. Similarly, Albert Einstein said, "It is the

legal discourse, which is full of the language of abstract universalism. The U.S. Constitution, for example, included general language to describe persons protected by it, even when it excluded black slaves and white women from its intended reach.[39] Legal language seeks universal applicability, regardless of the particular traits of an individual, yet abstract universalism often "takes the part for the whole, the particular for the universal and essential, the present for the eternal."[40] Legal reasoning feels rational, according to one theorist, when "particular metaphors for categorizing likeness and difference in the world have become frozen, or institutionalized as common sense."[41] Making explicit the unstated points of reference is the first step in addressing this problem; the next is challenging the presumed neutrality of the observer, who in fact sees inevitably from a situated perspective.

Assumption 3: The Observer Can See without a Perspective

This assumption builds on the others. Differences are intrinsic, and anyone can see them; there is one true reality, and impartial observers can make judgments unaffected and untainted by their own perspective or experience.[42] The facts of the world, including facts about people's traits, are knowable truly only by someone uninfluenced by social or cultural situations. Once legal rules are selected, regardless of prior disputes over the rules themselves, society may direct legal officials to apply them evenhandedly and to use them to discover and categorize events, motives, and culpability as they exist in the world. This aspiration to impartiality in legal judgments, however, is just that—an aspiration, not a description. The aspiration even risks obscuring the inevitable perspective of any given legal official, or of anyone else, and thereby makes it harder to challenge the impact of perspective on the selection of traits used to judge legal consequences.

The ideal of objectivity itself suppresses the coincidence between the viewpoints of the majority and what is commonly understood to be objective or unbiased. For example, in an employment discrimination case the defendant, a law firm, sought to disqualify Judge Constance Baker Motley from sitting on the case because she, as a black woman who had once represented plaintiffs in discrimination cases, would identify with those who suffer race

---

theory which decides what we can observe" (quoted in Daniel Bell, *The Coming of Post-Industrial Society: A Venture in Social Forecasting* [New York: Basic Books, 1973], p. 9).

[39]Nancy Cott, "Women and the Constitution" (unpublished paper). Cott notes that only the post–Civil War amendments introduce the particularizing language of race and gender, attempting to secure actual universal reach where the previous universal language of the Constitution had not intended to do so.

[40]Carol C. Gould, "The Woman Question: Philosophy of Liberation and the Liberation of Philosophy," in *Women and Philosophy: Toward a Theory of Liberation,* ed. Carol C. Gould and Marx Wartofsky (New York: Putnam, 1976).

[41]Gary Pellar, "The Metaphysics of American Law," *Calif. L. Rev.* 73 (1985), 1151, 1156.

[42]See Alison Jaggar, *Feminist Politics and Human Nature* (Totowa, N.J.: Rowman & Allenheld, 1983), p. 356.

or sex discrimination. The defendant assumed that Judge Motley's personal identity and her past political work had made her different, lacking the ability to perceive without a perspective. Judge Motley declined, however, to recuse herself and explained: "If background or sex or race of each judge were, by definition, sufficient grounds for removal, no judge on this court could hear this case, or many others, by virtue of the fact that all of them were attorneys, of a sex, often with distinguished law firm or public service backgrounds."[43]

Because of the aspiration to impartiality and the prevalence of universalist language in law, most observers of law have been reluctant to confront the arguments of philosophers and psychologists who challenge the idea that observers can see without a perspective.[44] Philosophers such as A. J. Ayer and W. V. Quine note that although we can alter the theory we use to frame our perceptions of the world, we cannot see the world unclouded by preconceptions.[45] What interests us, given who we are and where we stand, affects our ability to perceive.[46]

[43]Blank v. Sullivan & Cromwell, 418 F. Supp. 1 (S.D. N.Y. 1975); accord Commonwealth v. Local Union 542, Int'l Union of Operating Eng'rs, 388 F. Supp. 115 (E.D. Pa. 1974) (Higginbotham, J.) (denying defendant's motion to disqualify the judge from a race discrimination case because of the judge's racial identity as a black person). Judge Higginbotham noted that "black lawyers have litigated in federal courts almost exclusively before white judges, yet they have not urged the white judges should be disqualified on matters of race relations (id. at 177).

[44]Science shares both this aspiration of impartiality and the preference for universalist language. See, e.g., Karl Popper, *Realism and the Aim of Science*, ed. W. W. Bartley III (Totowa, N.J.: Rowman and Littlefield, 1983). Popper stated his view of the aspiration frankly: "It is the aim of science to find satisfactory explanations," and such explanations should be "in terms of testable and falsifiable universal laws and initial conditions" (pp. 132, 134). However, considerable critical attention has focused on the aim of science to derive impartial universal laws from objective observations. For instance, Paul Feyerabend, *Against Method*, rev. ed. (London: Verso, 1988), challenges the notion of *objective* observations, arguing that all facts are value-laden or "contaminated." And Thomas Kuhn's seminal book *The Structure of Scientific Revolutions*, 2d ed. (Chicago: University of Chicago Press, 1970), calls into question the impartiality of scientific endeavors. Kuhn demonstrates that competing scientific theories are usually incommensurable; therefore, there is often no logical or objective basis for choosing between them. This suggests that something other than logic plays a significant part in charting the course science pursues. Bringing a different angle to the critique of science, Evelyn Fox Keller, *Reflections on Gender and Science* (New Haven, Conn.: Yale University Press, 1985), argues that the aspiration of science to generate universal laws in an impartial fashion reflects not merely a search for truth. She maintains that the quest for objectivity and universality is largely a projection onto science of a need to dominate and control the world.

[45]A. J. Ayer, *Philosophy in the Twentieth Century* (New York: Random House, 1982), p. 157; W. V. Quine, *Ontological Relativity and Other Essays* (New York: Columbia University Press, 1969). See also Thomas Nagel, *The View from Nowhere* (New York: Oxford University Press, 1986); Hilary Putnam, *Reason, Truth, and History* (New York: Cambridge University Press, 1981); William James, *Psychology* (New York: Holt, 1892). The idea is even more pronounced in Kuhn, *Structure of Scientific Revolutions*, pp. 23–25; Kuhn argues that scientific inquiry has pursued truth within a paradigm of rational organization of fact gathering that is so taken for granted that it restricts the scientists' vision according to its own premises.

[46]William James, *On Some of Life's Ideals: A Certain Blindness in Human Beings* (New York: Holt, 1900; rpt. Folcroft, Pa.: Folcroft Library Editions, 1974); Luce Irigaray, *Ethique de la différence sexuelle* (Rotterdam: Erasmus Universiteit Rotterdam, 1987), pp. 19–20, quoted in Stephen Heath, "Male Feminism," in *Men in Feminism*, ed. Alice Jardine and Paul Smith (New York: Methuen, 1987): "I will never be in a man's place, a man will never be in mine. Whatever

The impact of the observer's unacknowledged perspective may be crudely oppressive. When a municipality includes a nativity creche in its annual Christmas display, the majority of the community may perceive no offense to non-Christians in the community. If the practice is challenged in court as a violation of the Constitution's ban against establishment of religion, a judge who is Christian may also fail to see the offense to anyone and merely conclude, as the Supreme Court did in 1984, that Christmas is a national holiday.[47] Judges may be peculiarly disabled from perceiving the state's message about a dominant religious practice because judges are themselves often members of the dominant group and therefore have the luxury of seeing their perspectives mirrored and reinforced in major social and political institutions. Similarly, members of a racial majority may miss the impact of their own race on their perspective about the race of others.[48]

The power of unacknowledged perspectives permeated a recent Supreme Court analysis of the question of whether a federal statute exempting religious organizations from rules against religious discrimination in employment decisions violates the establishment clause of the First Amendment. A majority for the Court endorsed this legislative grant of discretion to religious organizations, and rejected a discharged employee's claims that such accommodation of religion unconstitutionally promotes religious organizations at the price of individual religious liberty. The majority reasoned that the preference for religion was exercised not by the government but rather by the church.[49] Here, the justices suggested that the government could remain neutral even while exempting religious organizations from otherwise universal prohibitions against discriminating on the basis of religion in employment decisions.

Justice Sandra Day O'Connor pointed out in her concurring opinion that allowing a private decision-maker to use religion in employment decisions inevitably engaged the government in that discrimination. For her, the question for the Court was how an "objective observer" would perceive a government policy of approving such religion-based employment decisions. She challenged the justices in the majority to admit that the law was not neutral and to explore the meaning of this nonneutrality to someone not involved in the dispute. The aspiration to impartiality infuses her analysis, yet the meaning of objectivity almost dissolves in application: "To ascertain whether the statute [exempting religious organizations from the ban against religious

---

the possible identifications, one will never exactly occupy the place of the other—they are irreducible the one to the other."

[47]Lynch v. Donnelley, 465 U.S. 668 (1984). Subsequently, the Court has emphasized that context matters in the assessment of establishment clause challenges to public displays of a crèche. See County of Allegheny v. American Civil Liberties Union, 109 S.Ct. 3086 (1989).

[48]See Charles R. Lawrence III, "The Id, the Ego, and Equal Protection: Reckoning with Unconscious Racism," *Stan. L. Rev.* 39 (1987), 317, 380.

[49]See Corporation of the Presiding Bishop of the Church of Jesus Christ of Latter-Day Saints v. Amos, 107 S.Ct. 2862, 2869 n.15 (1987). The case arose in the context of nonprofit religious activities.

discrimination in employment] conveys a message of endorsement, the relevant issue is how it would be perceived by an objective observer, acquainted with the text, legislative history, and implementation of the statute."[50]

What could "objective" mean here? First, it acknowledges the limited perspective of the government representatives. Second, it rejects the viewpoint of the religious group as too biased or embedded in the problem.[51] So at a minimum, "objective" means "free from the biases of the litigating parties." But is there anyone who has no perspective on this issue? Justice O'Connor described a judge as someone capable of filling the shoes of the "objective observer," yet she acknowledged that she was answering from her own perspective: "*In my view* the objective observer should perceive the government action as an accommodation of the exercise of religion rather than as a government endorsement of religion."[52] Although at other times, Justice O'Connor has indicated a sensitive awareness of perspectives other than her own, here she failed to consider that no one can achieve a perspective free from a particular viewpoint. Her conclusion in this case—like her rejection of a religious-freedom challenge to a military regulation punishing servicemen for the wearing of religious headgear[53]—did not consider the possibility that her own perspective matches the perspective of a majority group and neglects the perspective of a minority. The comfort of finding one's perspective widely shared does not make it any less a perspective, especially in the face of evidence that other people perceive the world from a different perspective.

Justice Antonin Scalia's dissenting opinion in an affirmative action case reveals both considerable shrewdness about the effect of the observer's hidden perspective and surprising unawareness about the impact of his own perspective. He predicted that the majority's approval of an affirmative action employment plan would lead many employers to engage in voluntary affirmative action plans that employ only minimally capable employees rather than risk litigation challenging their employment practices as discriminatory: "This situation is more likely to obtain, of course, with respect to the least skilled jobs—perversely creating an incentive to discriminate against precisely those members of the nonfavored groups *least* likely to have profited from societal discrimination in the past."[54] Justice Scalia thus implied,

[50]See id. at 2874 (O'Connor, J., concurring).

[51]Cf. William James (*On Some of Life's Ideals*, p. 6): "The subject judged knows a part of the world of reality which the judging spectator fails to see, knows more while the spectator knows less; and, wherever there is conflict of opinion and difference of vision, we are bound to believe that the truer side is the side that feels the more, and not the side that feels the less."

[52]107 S.Ct. at 2875 (O'Connor, J., concurring) (emphasis added).

[53]See Goldman v. Weinberger, 106 S.Ct. 1310 (1986) (rejecting claim by an Orthodox Jew, serving as military psychologist, of a religious exemption from Air Force dress regulations to permit him to wear a yarmulke); Frank I. Michelman, "The Supreme Court, 1985 Term—Foreword: Traces of Self-Governance," *Harv. L. Rev.* 100 (1986), 1.

[54]Johnson v. Transportation Agency, 107 S.Ct. 1442, 1475 (1987) (Scalia, J., dissenting) (original emphasis).

without quite saying, that the perspective of the justices had influenced their development of a rule promoting affirmative action plans in a setting that could never touch members of the Court or people like them.[55]

Yet in another respect his opinion manifests, rather than exposes, the impact of the observer's perspective on the observed. He provided a generous and sympathetic view of the male plaintiff, Johnson, but demonstrated no comparable understanding of Joyce, the woman promoted ahead of him; his description of the facts of the case offered more details about Johnson's desires and efforts to advance his career. In effect, Justice Scalia tried to convey Johnson's point of view that the promotion of Joyce represented discrimination against Johnson.[56] Unlike the majority of the court, Justice Scalia provided no description of Joyce's career aspirations and her efforts to fulfill them; he thus betrayed a critical lack of sympathy for those most injured by social discrimination in the past.[57] Most curious was his apparent inability to imagine that Joyce and other women working in relatively unskilled jobs are, even more so than Johnson, people *"least* likely to have profited from societal discrimination in the past."[58] Operating under the apparent assumption that people fall into one of two groups—women and blacks on the one hand; white, unorganized, unaffluent, and unknown persons on the other[59]—Justice Scalia neglected the women who have been politically powerless and in need of the Court's protection. Although his opinion reveals that the Court may neglect the way it protects professional jobs from the affirmative action it prescribes for nonprofessionals, he himself remained apparently unaware of the effects of his own perspective on his ability to sympathize with some persons but not others.

A classic instance of unselfconscious immersion in a perspective that harms others appears in the Supreme Court's majority opinion in Plessy v. Ferguson,[60] which upheld the rationale of "separate but equal" in rejecting a challenge to legislated racial segregation in public railway cars. This is the decision ultimately overturned by the Court in Brown v. Board of Education.[61] A majority of the Court reasoned in *Plessy* that if any black people felt that segregation stamped them with a badge of inferiority, "it is not by reason of anything found in the [legislation], but solely because the colored race

[55]Justice Scalia ignored, however, the calls for diversifying the judiciary. See, e.g., Charles Halpern and Ann MacRory, "Choosing Judges," *New York Times,* July 1, 1979, p. E21.

[56]See 107 S.Ct. at 1468 (Scalia, J., dissenting).

[57]Paul Brest, "The Supreme Court, 1975 Term—Foreword: In Defense of the Antidiscrimination Principle," *Harv. L. Rev.* 90 (1976), 1, 39–42, 53–54, argues that the claims of those who have suffered because of patterns of discrimination deserve priority over the claims of those who have suffered by the vagaries of fate.

[58]107 S.Ct. at 1475 (Scalia, J., dissenting) (original emphasis).

[59]See id. at 1476: "The irony is that these individuals [the Johnsons of the country]—predominantly unknown, unaffluent, unorganized—suffer this injustice at the hands of a Court fond of thinking itself the champion of the politically impotent."

[60]163 U.S. 537 (1896).

[61]347 U.S. 483 (1954).

chooses to put that construction upon it."[62]

Homer Plessy's attorney had urged the justices to imagine themselves in the shoes of a black person: "Suppose a member of this court, nay, suppose every member of it, by some mysterious dispensation of providence should wake to-morrow with a black skin and curly hair ... and in traveling through that portion of the country where the 'Jim Crow Car' abounds, should be ordered into it by the conductor. It is easy to imagine what would be the result. ... What humiliation, what rage would then fill the judicial mind!"[63] But the justices in the Court's majority in 1896 remained unpersuaded and, indeed, seemed unable to leave the perspective of a dominant group even when they offered their own imagined shift in perspectives. They posed the hypothetical situation of a state legislature dominated by blacks which adopted the same law commanding racial segregation in railway cars that was then before the Court. The justices reasoned that certainly whites "would not acquiesce in [the] assumption" that this law "relegate[d] the white race to an inferior position."[64] Even in their effort to imagine how they would feel if the racial situation were reversed, the justices thereby manifested their viewpoint as members of a dominant and powerful group, which would never feel stigmatized by segregation.

Demonstrating that it was not impossible at that time to imagine a perspective other than that of the majority, however, Justice John Harlan dissented. He declared that the arbitrary separation of the races amounted to "a badge of servitude wholly inconsistent with the civil freedom and the equality before the law." He specifically rebutted the majority's claim about the meaning of segregation: "Everyone knows that the statute in question had its origins in the purpose, not so much to exclude white persons from railroad cars occupied by blacks, as to exclude colored people from coaches occupied by or assigned to white persons."[65]

Justices to this day often fail to acknowledge their own perspective and its influence in the assignment of difference in relation to some unstated norm. Veiling the standpoint of the observer conceals its impact on our perception of the world.[66] Denying that the observer's perspective influences perception leads to the next assumption: that all other perspectives are either presumptively identical to the observer's own or do not matter.

[62]163 U.S. at 551.

[63]Brief for the Plaintiff, Plessy v. Ferguson, reprinted in *Civil Rights and the American Negro: A Documentary History,* ed. Alpert B. Blaustein and Robert L. Zangrando (New York: Washington Square Press, 1968), pp. 298, 303–4.

[64]163 U.S. at 551.

[65]Id. at 537, 562, 557.

[66]Another instance of this assumption in Supreme Court jurisprudence appears in its treatment of the Fourth Amendment, where the perspectives of police officers and victims of crime provide the presumed starting point in assessing alleged violations of the guarantee against unwarranted searches or seizures. See Tracey Maclin, "Constructing Fourth Amendment Principles from the Government Perspective: Whose Amendment Is It, Anyway?" *Amer. Crim. L. Rev.* 25 (1988), 669.

Assumption 4: Other Perspectives Are Irrelevant

In her short story "Meditations on History," Sherley Ann Williams illustrates how people can assume that their perspective is the truth, ignore other perspectives, and thereby miss much of what is going on. In the story a pregnant slave woman waits to be hanged for running away from her master and killing a white man. The owner has confined her in detention until her baby is born; then he will take the baby, to make up for the loss of his grown slave. A white man who is writing a book about managing slaves interviews the slave woman and seems satisfied that he is able to understand her. He concludes that she is basically stupid and confused; he grows especially irritated as she hums and sings during their interview, never considering that she is in this way communicating with other slaves about a rescue plan. When she escapes, with the help of her friends, the writer is baffled; he never comes to understand how incomplete was his understanding of her.[67]

Many people who judge differences in the world reject as irrelevant or relatively unimportant the experience of "different people." William James put it this way: "We have seen the blindness and deadness to each other which are our natural inheritance."[68] People often use stereotypes as though they were real and complete, thereby failing to see the complex humanity of others. Stereotyped thinking is one form of the failure to imagine the perspective of another. Glimpsing contrasting perspectives may alter assumptions about the world, as well as about the meaning of difference.

When judges consider the situation of someone they think is very much unlike themselves, there is a risk that they will not only view that person's plight from their own vantage point but also fail to imagine that there might be another vantage point. When a criminal defendant charged racial discrimination in the administration of the death penalty in Georgia's criminal justice system, the Supreme Court split between those justices who treated alternative perspectives as irrelevant and those who tried to imagine them. The defendant's lawyer submitted a statistical study of over 2,000 murder cases in Georgia during the 1970s, and the Court assumed it to be valid. According to the study, a defendant's likelihood of receiving the death sentence correlated with the victim's race and, to a lesser extent, with the defendant's race: black defendants convicted of killing white victims had the greatest likelihood of receiving the death penalty, and defendants of either race who killed black victims had considerably less chance of being sentenced to death. A majority of the Court concluded that even taking this evidence as true, the defendant had failed to show that the decision-makers in his case had acted with a discriminatory purpose.[69]

---

[67] Sherley Ann Williams, "Meditations on History," in *Midnight Birds: Stories by Contemporary Black Women Writers*, ed. Mary Helen Washington (Garden City, N.Y.: Anchor Books, 1980), p. 200.

[68] James, "What Makes a Life Significant," in *On Some of Life's Ideals*, pp. 49, 81. I want to acknowledge here that "blindness" as a metaphoric concept risks stigmatizing people who are visually impaired.

[69] McCleskey v. Kemp, 107 S.Ct. 1756, 1766 n.7 (1987). The Court noted that it had

Moreover, reasoned Justice Lewis Powell for the majority, recognizing the defendant's claim would open the door "to claims based on unexplained discrepancies that correlate to membership in other minority groups, and even to gender" or physical appearance. This argument, perhaps meant in part to trivialize the charge of race discrimination by linking it with physical appearance,[70] implied that discrepancies in criminal sentences are random and too numerous to control. This formulation took the vantage point of such decision-makers as the reviewing court and the jury but not the perspective of the criminal defendant. Scholars of discrimination law have argued that the effect of discrimination on minorities is the same whether or not the majority group members intended it.[71]

What would happen if the Court in a case like this considered an alternative perspective? Justice William Brennan explored this possibility in his dissent. Perhaps knowing that neither he nor many of his readers could fully grasp the defendant's perspective, he tried to look through the eyes of the defense attorney who is asked by Warren McCleskey, the black defendant in the case, about the chances of a death sentence. Adopting that viewpoint, Justice Brennan concluded that "counsel would feel bound to tell McCleskey, that defendants charged with killing white victims in Georgia are 4.3 times as likely to be sentenced to death as defendants charged with killing blacks . . . [and] there was a significant chance that race would play a prominent role in determining if he lived or died." Moreover, he wrote, "enhanced willingness to impose the death sentence on black defendants, or diminished willingness to render such a sentence when blacks are victims, reflects a devaluation of the lives of black persons." Under these circumstances, he concluded, the judicial system had, in fact, considered race and produced judgments "completely at odds with [the] concern that an individual be evaluated as a unique human being."[72]

To the majority's fear of widespread challenges to all aspects of criminal sentence Justice Brennan responded: "Taken at its face, such a statement seems to suggest a fear of too much justice. . . . The prospect that there may be more widespread abuse than McCleskey documents may be dismaying,

---

permitted statistical evidence of discrimination in the contexts of jury venire selection and Title VII violations because "in those cases, the statistics relate to fewer and fewer entities, and fewer variables are relevant to the challenged decisions" (id. at 1768).

[70]Appearance discrimination may not, in fact, be trivial; for it may disguise racial, ethnic, or gender discrimination, or it may encode other forms of stereotypic and prejudicial thinking. See Note, "Facial Discrimination: Extending Handicap Law to Employment Discrimination on the Basis of Physical Appearance," *Harv. L. Rev.* 100 (1987), 2035, 2051.

[71]See Lawrence, "The Id, the Ego, and Equal Protection," pp. 352–53; and Alan D. Freeman, "Antidiscrimination Law: A Critical Review," in *The Politics of Law: A Progressive Critique,* ed. David Kairys (New York: Pantheon Books, 1982), pp. 96–116.

[72]107 S.Ct. at 1782 (Brennan, J., dissenting); id. at 1790; accord at 1806 (Stevens, J., dissenting). Justice Blackmun argued that overt discrimination is especially pernicious in the criminal justice system because it is "a stimulant to that race prejudice which is an impediment to securing to [black citizens] that equal justice which the law aims to secure to all others" (id. at 1795, Blackmun, J., dissenting) (quoting Strauder v. Western Virginia, 100 U.S. 303, 308 [1880]); id. at 1790.

but it does not justify complete abdication of our judicial role."[73] To the majority of the Court, acknowledging discrimination in this case looked like a management problem for the courts rather than a means of reducing potential injustices suffered by defendants.[74]

Randall Kennedy has emphasized still another perspective deflected by the majority, the perspective of the black communities "whose welfare is slighted by criminal justice systems that respond more forcefully to the killing of whites than the killing of blacks." In this view, black communities are denied equal access to a public good: punishment of those who injure members of that community. Taken seriously, this perspective could lead to the execution of more black defendants who have killed black victims. Kennedy concludes that "race-based devaluations of human life constitute simply one instance of a universal phenomenon: the propensity for persons to sympathize more fully with those with whom they can identify."[75]

It may be impossible to take the perspective of another completely, but the effort to do so can help us recognize that our own perspective is partial. Searching especially for the viewpoint of minorities not only helps those in the majority shake free of their unstated assumptions but also helps them develop a better normative sense in light of the experience of those with less power.[76] Members of minority groups have often had to become conversant with the world view of the majority while also trying to preserve their own. W. E. B. Du Bois's famous statement in his *Souls of Black Folk* describes that effort: "It is a peculiar sensation, this double-consciousness, this sense of always looking at one's self through the eyes of others, of measuring one's soul by the tape of the world that looks on in amused contempt and pity. One ever feels his twoness—an American, a Negro."[77] More recently, Bell Hooks explained her perception of how she and other women of color came to understand the world: "Living as we did—on the edge—we developed a particular way of seeing reality. We looked both from the outside in and from the inside out. We focused our attention on the center as well as on the margin. We understood both."[78] Works of fiction have often powerfully evoked the multiple worlds inhabited by members of minorities and thereby helped to convey the partiality of even a majority world view that presents itself as the one reality.[79]

[73]Id. at 1791.
[74]The courts tended to take the perspective of law enforcement officials rather than defendants in criminal cases. See Maclin, "Constructing Fourth Amendment Principles."
[75]Randall Kennedy, "*McCleskey v. Kemp:* Race, Capital Punishment, and the Supreme Court," *Harv. L. Rev.* 101 (1988), 1388–95.
[76]See Mari Matsuda, "Looking to the Bottom: Critical Legal Studies and Reparations," 22 *Harv. C.R.–C.L. L. Rev.* 323 (1987), urging individuals seeking justice to look to the perspectives of minorities for normative insights.
[77]W. E. B. Du Bois, *The Souls of Black Folk: Essays and Sketches* (New York: Dodd, Mead, 1979), p. 3.
[78]Bell Hooks, *Feminist Theory: From Margin to Center* (Boston: South End Press, 1984), p. ix.
[79]See, e.g., James Baldwin, "Sonny's Blues," in *The Norton Anthology of Short Fiction,* 2d ed., ed. R. V. Cassill (New York: Norton, 1981) (a black ex-convict's middle-class brother comes

Judges have sometimes demonstrated an acute awareness of the perspective of religious persons or groups, contrasted with the view of a secular employer or the government. In Sherbert v. Verner,[80] the Supreme Court considered the claims of a member of the Seventh-Day Adventists who had been discharged by her employer because she would not work on Saturday—the Sabbath observed by her church—and was unable to find other work that allowed her to observe her Sabbath. When she applied for state unemployment compensation, the state commission rejected her claim on the ground that she had refused to accept suitable work. The commission argued that it employed a neutral rule, denying benefits to anyone who failed without good cause to accept suitable work when offered. The Supreme Court reasoned that this rule was not neutral; that from the woman's point of view it burdened her religious beliefs. Indeed, reasoned the Court, the government's failure to accommodate religion, within reasonable limits, amounted to hostility toward religion.[81]

Similarly, in Wisconsin v. Yoder, a majority of the Supreme Court refused enforcement of compulsory school laws against members of an Amish community who claimed that their religious way of life would be burdened if their adolescent children had to attend school beyond the eighth grade. Even though compulsory school laws serve widely supported public purposes, and even though the Amish way of life seemed unfamiliar to the Court, the justices were able to imagine the intrusion represented by compulsory schooling. Yet Justice William O. Douglas, in partial dissent, reminded the Court of another perspective often ignored: the viewpoint of the children, who might have preferred the chance to continue their formal education.[82]

A perspective may go unstated because it is so unknown to those in charge that they do not recognize it as a perspective. Judges in particular often presume that the perspective they adopt is either universal or superior to others. Indeed, a perspective may go unstated because it is so powerful and

---

to understand and appreciate the ex-convict's world of jazz music); Robin Becker, "In the Badlands," in *The Things That Divide Us*, ed. Faith Conlon, Rachel da Silva, and Barbara Wilson (1985) (a disapproving mother learns to accept and appreciate her daughter's lesbian lover); Alice Walker, "Advancing Luna and Ida B. Wells," in Washington, *Midnight Birds* (perspectives shift between a white woman and a black woman on the possible rape of the white woman by a black man). See also Ralph Ellison, *Invisible Man* (New York: Vintage Press, 1972); Richard Wright, *Native Son* (New York: Harper & Row, 1940).

[80]374 U.S. 398 (1963).

[81]Subsequent cases, following the precedent of *Sherbert*, include Thomas v. Review Board, 450 U.S. 707 (1981) (state cannot deny unemployment benefits to a Jehovah's Witness who quit his job for religious reasons when transferred to making military equipment); Hobbie v. Unemployment Appeals Commission, 107 S.Ct. 1046 (1987) (state cannot deny unemployment benefits to individual who was fired when she refused, after religious conversion, to work on Saturdays).

[82]406 U.S. 205 (1972); id. at 205, 241–43 (Douglas, J., concurring in part and dissenting in part). Justice Douglas reasoned: "The Court's analysis assumes that the only interests at stake in this case are those of the Amish parents on the one hand, and those of the State on the other," and "if the parents in this case are allowed a religious exemption, the inevitable effect is to impose the parents' notion of religious duty upon their children." Yet "the views of the child whose parent is the subject of the suit" are crucial.

pervasive that it may be presumed without defense. It has been said that Aristotle could have checked out—and corrected—his faulty assertion that women have fewer teeth than men. He did not do so, however, because he thought he knew.[83] Presumptions about whose perspective ultimately matters arise from the fifth typically unarticulated assumption, that the status quo is the preferred situation.

Assumption 5: The Status Quo Is Natural, Uncoerced, and Good

Connected with many of the other assumptions is the idea that critical features of the status quo—general social and economic arrangements—are natural and desirable. From this assumption follow three propositions. First, the goal of governmental neutrality demands the status quo because existing societal arrangements are assumed to be neutral. Second, governmental actions that change the status quo have a different status from omissions, or failures to act, that maintain the status quo. Third, prevailing societal arrangements are not forced on anyone. Individuals are free to make choices and to assume responsibility for those choices. These propositions are rarely stated, both because they are deeply entrenched and because they treat the status quo as good, natural, and freely chosen—and thus not in need of discussion.

Difference may seem salient, then, not because of a trait intrinsic to the person but because the dominant institutional arrangements were designed without that trait in mind—designed according to an unstated norm reconfirmed by the view that alternative perspectives are irrelevant or have already been taken into account. The difference between buildings built without considering the needs of people in wheelchairs and buildings that are accessible to people in wheelchairs reveals that institutional arrangements define whose reality is to be the norm and what is to seem natural. Sidewalk curbs are not neutral or natural but humanly constructed obstacles. Interestingly, modifying what has been the status quo often brings unexpected benefits as well. Inserting curb cuts for the disabled turns out to help many others, such as bike riders and parents pushing baby strollers. (They can also be positioned to avoid endangering a visually impaired person who uses a cane to determine where the sidewalk ends.)

Yet the weight of the status quo remains great. Existing institutions and language already shape the world and already express and recreate attitudes about what counts as a difference, and who or what is the relevant point of comparison. Assumptions that the status quo is natural, good, and uncoerced make proposed changes seem to violate the commitment to neutrality, predictability, and freedom.

For example, courts have treated school instruction in evolution as neutral

---

[83]"Aristotle maintained that women have fewer teeth than men; although he was twice married, it never occurred to him to verify this statement by examining his wives' mouths" (*Bertrand Russell's Best: Silhouettes in Satire*, ed. Robert E. Egner [New York: Mentor Books, New American Library, 1958], p. 67).

toward religion, even though some groups and some states find that instruction corrosive to particular religious beliefs (as in Edwards v. Aguillard). Similarly, many legal observers have viewed affirmative action as nonneutral, compared with the status quo treatments of race and gender in employment and other distributions of societal resources. Proposals to alter rules about gender roles encounter objections, from both men and women, to what is seen as undesirable disruption in the expectations and predictability of social relationships. Suggestions to integrate schools, private clubs, and other social institutions that have been segregated by race or by gender provoke protests that these changes would interfere with freedom—referring, often explicitly, to the freedom of those who do not wish to associate with certain others.[84]

Yet the status quo is often challenged as burdensome—not neutral, not desirable, and not free—for members of minority religious groups. For example, a seemingly neutral rule, limiting unemployment benefits to those who become unemployed through no fault of their own, offended the constitutional protections of religious freedom—according to the Supreme Court—when the rule burdened an individual who lost her job when she refused to work during her religious Sabbath. In Hobbie v. Unemployment Appeals Commission,[85] the Court concluded that the state's unemployment scheme must accommodate religious adherences. The government's rules cannot be neutral in a world that is not neutral.

Despite judgments such as this one, courts on other occasions have not understood how burdensome apparently neutral governmental rules may be, given other dimensions of differences among people. An ostensibly neutral state policy on unemployment compensation figured also in the case of a woman who had taken a pregnancy leave from her job with no guarantee of reinstatement; upon her return the employer told her there were no positions available.[86] Linda Wimberly applied for unemployment benefits but was denied under a state law disqualifying applicants unless their reasons for leaving a job were directly attributable to the work or to the employer. Wimberly argued that a federal statute forbidding discrimination in unem-

---

[84]See Herbert Wechsler, "Toward Neutral Principles of Constitutional Law," *Harv. L. Rev.* 73 (1959), 1. Judge Skelly Wright's critique of this argument appears in his "Professor Bickel," p. 769. For criticisms of the attempt to use neutral principles, see Mark Tushnet, "Following the Rule Laid Down: A Critique of Interpretive and Neutral Principles," *Harv. L. Rev.* 96 (1983), 781, arguing that neutral principles are incapable of guiding judicial decisions. Also see John Hart Ely, "The Supreme Court's 1977 Term—Foreword: On Discovering Fundamental Values," *Harv. L. Rev.* 92 (1978), p. 5, pointing out that neutral principles tell us nothing about the appropriate *content* of a decision. For a defense of those Supreme Court decisions criticized by Wechsler, see Louis Pollack, "Racial Discrimination and Judicial Integrity: A Reply to Professor Wechsler," *U. Pa. L. Rev.* 108 (1959), 1, arguing that the Supreme Court's decisions not only are correct but also satisfy Wechsler's requirement of following neutral principles. For a thoughtful analysis of the tensions between freedom of association and antidiscrimination, see Deborah Rhode, "Association and Assimilation," *Nw. U. L. Rev.* 81 (1986), 106. This topic has yielded several recent Supreme Court decisions rejecting associational defenses to discriminatory practices. See New York State Club Ass'n v. City of New York, 56 U.S.L.W. 4653 (June 21, 1988); Roberts v. United States Jaycees, 468 U.S. 609 (1984).

[85]107 S.Ct. 1046 (1987).

[86]Wimberly v. Labor & Indus. Relations Comm'n of Missouri, 107 S.Ct. 821 (1987).

ployment compensation "solely on the basis of pregnancy or termination of pregnancy" required accommodation for women who leave work because of pregnancy.[87]

The Supreme Court unanimously rejected Wimberly's claim that this denial of benefits contravened the federal statute. The Court found that the state had not singled out pregnancy as the reason for withholding unemployment benefits; instead, pregnancy fell within a broad class of reasons for unemployment unrelated to work or to the employer. The Court interpreted the federal statute to forbid discrimination but not to mandate preferential treatment.[88] In the eyes of the justices, it was neutral to have a general rule denying unemployment benefits to anyone unemployed for reasons unrelated to the workplace or the employer.[89] A state choosing to define its unemployment eligibility to disqualify not just those who leave work because of pregnancy but also those who leave work for good cause, illness, or compelling personal reasons may thus do so without violating federal law.[90]

Similarly, statistical patterns of racial discrepancies in death-penalty sentencing, as presented in McCleskey v. Kemp, cannot be presumed to establish unconstitutional discrimination, because the status quo is deemed neutral, absent more direct proof of intentional discrimination. The appearance of neutrality in law may thus at times defeat claims that the social and political arrangements are not neutral, unfairly distinguishing some people from others.

This pattern of thought is often connected to the view that rules seen as neutral produce different results for different people only because people make free choices that have different consequences.[91] When women choose to become pregnant and then take leave from their paid employment, they do not deserve unemployment benefits, because they left their jobs voluntarily.[92]

[87]26 U.S.C. sec. 3304(a)(12) (1982).

[88]107 S.Ct. at 825, 826.

[89]The Court explained: "Thus, a State could not decide to deny benefits to pregnant women while at the same time allowing benefits to persons who are in other respects similarly situated: the 'sole basis' for such a decision would be on account of pregnancy. On the other hand, if a state adopts a neutral rule that incidentally disqualifies pregnant or formerly pregnant claimants as part of the larger group, the neutral application of that rule cannot readily be characterized as a decision made 'solely on the basis of pregnancy'" (ibid., p. 825).

[90]Further, under the view that governmental actions changing the status quo raise problems not raised by failures to act, the Court reasoned that if Congress had wanted to require special treatment for pregnancy, it would have said so, and even the federal ban against discrimination on the basis of pregnancy in unemployment compensation schemes lacked sufficient specificity to forbid the denial of benefits to a woman in Wimberly's situation. The Court treated this as a problem of congressional silence: Congress did not mean to authorize preferential treatment because it did not say so. To treat silence as denial of special treatment and to treat accommodation of pregnancy as preferential treatment are both signs of the assumption that the status quo is neutral or good.

[91]Similar assumptions underlie the judicial treatment of differences in wealth as unimportant to constitutional rights and protections. See San Antonio Independent School Dist. v. Rodriguez, 411 U.S. 1 (1973). See generally Laurence Tribe, *American Constitutional Law*, 2d ed. (Mineola, N.Y.: Foundation Press, 1988), pp. 1665–72.

[92]See Finley, "Transcending Equality Theory," pp. 1118, 1136–38.

When a worker chooses to convert to a new religion and then loses a job because of conflict between religious demands and the work schedule, this too may be treated as a personal choice—but the courts have been more solicitous of this kind of choice, given constitutional protections for the free exercise of religion.[93] Courts have traditionally refused to find that a rape occurred, absent proof of force by the defendant and/or resistance by the victim; the victim's silence or lack of sufficient protest has been deemed to constitute consent to sexual relations.[94]

Men and women historically have held different types of jobs. Social attitudes, including attitudes held by women, are the preferred explanation for some who presume that the status quo is natural, good, or chosen. Justice Scalia dissented on this ground when a majority for the Supreme Court approved a voluntary affirmative action plan to improve the positions of white women and minorities in a traditionally segregated workplace. No woman had held the job of road crew dispatcher, but women themselves, explained Justice Scalia, had not sought this job in the past. He acknowledged but rejected the view of some people that "the social attitudes which cause women themselves to avoid certain jobs and to favor others are as nefarious as conscious, exclusionary discrimination."[95] An extensive dispute about the role of women's choices in the gender segregation of the workplace arose in a sex discrimination charge pursued by the federal Equal Employment Opportunity Commission against Sears, Roebuck & Co.[96] Did the absence of women from jobs as commission salespersons result from women's own choices and preferences, or from societal discrimination and employers' refusals to make those jobs available? The legal framework in the case seemed to force the issue into either/or questions: women's work-force participation was due either to their own choices or to forces beyond their control; women's absence from certain jobs was either due to employers' discrimination or not; either women lacked the interest and qualifications for these jobs, or women had the interest and qualifications for the jobs.

Would it be possible to articulate a third view? Consider this one: choices by working women and decisions by their employers were both influenced by larger patterns of economic prosperity and depression and by shifting

[93]In *Hobbie*, the Supreme Court rejected the state's argument that the employee's refusal to work amounted to misconduct related to her work, which rendered her ineligible for unemployment benefits, given a scheme limiting compensation to persons who become "unemployed through no fault of their own." The Court rejected this emphasis on the cause of the conflict because the "salient inquiry" was whether the denial of the unemployment benefits unlawfully burdened Hobbie's free exercise right. The Court also rejected the state's claim that making unemployment benefits available to Hobbie would unconstitutionally establish religion by easing eligibility requirements for religious adherents (107 S.Ct. at 1047–48, 1051 n.11).

[94]Susan Estrich, "Rape," *Yale L. J.* 95 (1986), 1086, 1098–1105, 1130–32.

[95]Johnson v. Transportation Agency, 107 S.Ct. 1442, 1443 (1987).

[96]628 F. Supp. 1264 (N.D. Ill. 1986). See Mary Joe Frug, "On Sears" (New England School of Law, Boston, unpublished manuscript, 1988); Ruth Milkman, "Women's History and the Sears Case," *Feminist Studies* 12 (Summer 1986), 375–400; Nadine Taub, "The Sears Case and Its Relevance for Legal Education," *American Association of Law Schools, Women in Legal Education Newsletter*, Nov. 1986.

social attitudes about appropriate roles for women. These larger patterns became real in people's lives when internalized and experienced as individual choice.[97] Assuming that the way things have been resulted either from people's choices or from nature helps to force legal arguments into these alternatives and to make legal redress of historic differences a treacherous journey through incompatible alternatives.

Sometimes, judges have challenged the assumption that the status quo is natural and good; they have occasionally approved public and private decisions to take difference into account in efforts to alter existing conditions and to remedy their harmful effects.[98] But for the most part, unstated assumptions work in subtle and complex ways. They fill a basic human need to simplify and make our world familiar and unsurprising, yet by their very simplification, assumptions exclude contrasting views. Moreover, they contribute to the dilemma of difference by frustrating legislative and constitutional commitments to change the treatment of differences in race, gender, ethnicity, religion, and handicap.

The Effects of Unstated Assumptions

Unstated assumptions make the difference dilemma seem intractable. If difference is intrinsic, then it will crop up whether noticed or ignored. If difference is knowable by reference to an unstated norm, then the norm itself remains hidden from evaluation. If an observer such as a judge can see differences without a perspective, and already knows whatever is of value in anyone else's perspective, then those who "are different" have no chance to challenge the assignment of difference or its consequences. And if the status quo is natural, good, and chosen, then efforts to alter its differential burdens on people will inevitably seem unnatural, undesirable, and coercive. Noticing difference and ignoring it both recreate difference; both can threaten such goals as neutrality, equality, and freedom.

Moreover, if equality depends on "sameness," then the recurrence of difference undermines chances for equality. The fear of emphasizing difference, whether by acknowledgment or nonacknowledgment, arises as long as difference carries stigma and precludes equality. Jonathan Kozol reported in the 1960s an incident whose dated quality suggests that in some areas, at least, we have learned to disentangle difference from inequality: In an all black urban school one white teacher advised another not to bring up slavery while discussing the cotton gin with her students. The first teacher explained, not with malice but with an expression of intense and honest affection for her class: "I don't want these children to have to think back on this year later on

---

[97]See Kathy E. Ferguson, *The Feminist Case against Bureaucracy* (Philadelphia: Temple University Press, 1984), p. 177.

[98]See, e.g., Swann v. Charlotte-Mecklenburg Board of Educ., 402 U.S. 1 (1971) (approving the use of racial balance goals in a school desegregation plan). See Kathleen M. Sullivan, "Sins of Discrimination: Last Term's Affirmative Action Cases," *Harv. L. Rev.* 100 (1986), 78.

and have to remember that we were the ones who told them they were Negro."[99]

If individuals can be meaningfully categorized in terms that carry negative associations, on the basis of a limited number of traits selected to compare them with others who are presumed the norm, then difference assumes a large and immutable significance. Treating the individual as handicapped or deficient in the English language runs the risk of assigning to that individual, as an internal limit, the category of difference that carries the message of inequality. This is not inevitable, for the categories of handicap and proficiency in English are not the sum total of those individuals, nor are they conclusive indications of those individuals' potential or worth.

Stephen Jay Gould, a gifted observer of biology and zoology, put it this way: "Few tragedies can be more extensive than the stunting of life, few injustices deeper than the denial of opportunity to strive or even to hope, by a limit imposed from without, but falsely identified as lying within. . . . We inhabit a world of human differences and predilections, but the extrapolation of these facts to theories of rigid limits is ideology."[100] Ideology becomes a concern here because expressions of power, approval, and disapproval are at work in the links between categories of sameness and difference and the values of equality and inequality. The assumptions that differences lie *within* people obscures the fact that they represent comparisons drawn *between* people, comparisons that use some traits as the norm and confirm some people's perceptions as the truth while devaluing or disregarding the perspectives of others.

In addition, the assumption that the status quo is good, natural, and uncoerced contributes to a riddle of neutrality, another version of the difference dilemma. If the public schools must remain neutral toward religion, do they do so by balancing the teaching of evolution with the teaching of scientific arguments about divine creation—or does this accommodation of a religious view depart from the requisite neutrality? Governmental neutrality may freeze in place the past consequences of differences. Yet any departure from neutrality in governmental standards uses governmental power to

---

[99]Jonathan Kozol, *Death at an Early Age: The Destruction of the Hearts and Minds of Negro Children in the Boston Public Schools* (Boston: Houghton Mifflin, 1967), p. 68. Kozol continues: "The amount of difficulty involved in telling children they are Negro, of course, is proportional to the degree of ugliness which is attached to that word within a person's mind. . . . What she was afraid of was to be remembered as the one who told them that they were what they *are.* . . . To be taught by a teacher who felt that it would be wrong to let them know it must have left a silent and deeply working scar. The extension to children of the fears and evasions of a teacher is probably not very uncommon, and at times the harm it does is probably trivial. But when it comes to a matter of denying to a class of children the color of their skin and the very word that designates them, then I think that it takes on the proportions of a madness" (pp. 68–69; original emphasis). Yet shielding a minority child from community dislike may disable her from recognizing hostility when it comes her way. See ch. 2 (discussing Audre Lorde).

[100]Stephen Jay Gould, *The Mismeasure of Man* (New York: Norton, 1981), pp. 28–29. Anthony Cohen, *The Symbolic Construction of Community* (London: Tavistock, 1985), p. 110, pushes the point yet another step; he suggests that "the finer the differences between people, the stronger is the commitment people have to them."

make those differences matter and thus symbolically reinforces them. The relationship between means and ends thus becomes so troubled that decision-makers may become paralyzed with inaction. If the goal is to avoid identifying people by a trait of difference, but the institutions and practices make that trait matter, there seems to be no way to remedy the effects of difference without making difference matter yet again.

Debates over affirmative action powerfully depict this dilemma, but the dilemma appears only when the background assumption is that the status quo is neutral and natural rather than part of the discriminating framework that must itself be changed.[101] The dilemma seems especially sharp if the decision-makers assume that the world will continue to make that difference matter.[102] Consider this episode: An instructor in a residential school for blind children points out the mantel of a fireplace to a child who is about to bang his head on it. The child says, "Why don't you put some padding on it? This is a school for the blind; we could hurt ourselves." The instructor replies, "There won't be padding outside the school when you leave here."[103] Deciding not to pad the mantelpiece at the school for the blind may help train the blind students to be wary about such hazards; it may also lead to accidents in the school and contribute to an attitude that the world outside does not need to be renovated to accommodate the needs of people disabled by its current construction.

Finally, the usually unstated assumptions contribute to another form of the difference dilemma. Legal officials often face a choice between using their power to grant broad discretion to others and using their power to articulate formal rules that specify categorical decisions for dispensing public—or private—power. When should courts and legislatures delegate to other public or private decision-makers the discretion to differentiate people, and when should legal institutions instead articulate specific rules restricting such

[101]See, e.g., Van Alstyne, "Rites of Passage," p. 775, arguing that affirmative action itself promotes racism and only neutral rules avoid discrimination. Ruth Colker ("Anti-Subordination above All," pp. 1003, 1013) has responded to similar attacks on affirmative action by noting that "history demonstrates the difficulty of achieving true equality through race- or sex-neutral remedies." She and other defenders of affirmative action argue that the status quo is not neutral, so neutral rules recreate nonneutrality. Derrick Bell, *And We Are Not Saved: The Elusive Quest for Racial Justice* (New York: Basic Books, 1987), has argued that even the goal of "equal opportunity" may entrench an unfair status quo and perpetuate discrimination. The fictional heroine of his eloquent book comments that civil rights reformers found largely illusory the long-sought promise of equal opportunity.

[102]Stephen L. Carter, "When Victims Happen to Be Black," *Yale L.J.* 97 (1988), 420, 435, thoughtfully explores the criticisms of affirmative action which typically deny that all black people are victims in a legal or moral sense while presuming that whites as a group are victimized by racially conscious affirmative action purposes. This insight offers a clue to deep assumptions about what kinds of racial categories are relevant and what social arrangements are the presumed benchmarks.

[103]See James Garfield, *Follow My Leader* (New York: Viking, 1957). See also "Unwanted Help," *New York Times*, Sept. 16, 1984, p. 49: the Association for the Blind opposed an electronic guidance system because it would discourage blind students from developing their own senses.

differentiation? The power to differentiate persists, whether exercised formally or delegated to others.

If legal officials articulate specific rules to cabin the discretion of others
regarding the treatment of difference, this practice can secure adherence to
the goals of equality and neutrality by forbidding consideration of differences except in the manner explicitly specified by the legal rules. Although
likely to promote accountability, this solution of formal rules has drawbacks.
Making and enforcing specific rules engages legal officials in the problem of
reinvesting differences with significance by noticing them. Specifically articulating permissible and impermissible uses of difference may enshrine categorical analysis and move further away from the ideal of treating persons as
individuals rather than as members of groups defined by shared traits.

Alternatively, legal officials can grant or cede discretion to other decision-
makers. Then, any problems from noticing or ignoring difference, any risks
of nonneutrality in means and in results, are no longer problems for courts
but become matters falling within the discretion of other public or private
decision-makers. This solution, of course, merely moves the problem to
another forum, giving the new decision-maker discretion to take difference
into account, perhaps in an impermissible manner.

The choice between discretion and formality vividly occupied the Supreme
Court in its debate over charges of racial discrimination in the administration
of the death penalty in Georgia's criminal justice system. If the criminal
justice system must not take the race of defendants or victims into account, is
this goal achieved by granting discretion to prosecutors and jurors, who can
then make individualized decisions but may also introduce racial concerns?
Or should judges impose formal rules specifying conditions under which
racial concerns must be made explicit in order to guard against them? The
Court's majority emphasized the central importance of jury discretion in the
criminal justice system as a reason for resisting the implication of unconstitutional discrimination from the statistical demonstration of differential risks
of the death penalty, based on the races of both victims and defendants.
Justice Powell reasoned that "it is difficult to imagine guidelines that would
produce the predictability sought by the dissent without sacrificing the discretion essential to a humane and fair system of criminal justice."[104]

Justice Brennan's dissent agreed that individualized assessments are critical to the criminal process, but he argued that "discretion is a means, not an
end" and that under the circumstances of the case the Court must monitor
the discretion of others.[105] The dissenters saw the grant of discretion to prosecutors and juries, though disengaging judges and legislators from directly
endorsing the use of differences in decisions, as allowing *those* decision-
makers to give significance to differences. The majority saw a risk that if
courts and legislatures specify formal rules restricting the discretion of other

[104]107 S.Ct. at 1778 n.37.
[105]Id. at 1790, 1793–94.

decision-makers and directing them not to allow gender, race, or other traits of difference to influence their judgments, this very specificity might make difference newly significant and undermine the goal of justice based on individualized, rather than categorical, consideration.

Articulating the assumptions behind the difference dilemma can expose what hinges on the choice between broad discretion and formal rules. That choice seems a dilemma if difference is intrinsic, for then difference will reappear under either regime. Similarly, if the norm used for defining difference remains unstated and uncontestable, neither grants of discretion nor formal rules can restrain the attribution of difference. Alternative perspectives may be silenced if courts refrain from monitoring decisions by other bodies—but the same result may occur if courts presume to know how to regulate difference without considering the perspectives of others. And if the status quo is taken as a neutral benchmark, neither formal rules nor informal discretion can reach the institutional arrangements that burden some more than others.

If the assumptions behind the difference dilemma are exposed and debated, however, the tension between formal, predictable rules and individualized judgments under discretionary standards becomes simply another terrain for reconsidering the relationships and patterns of power that influence the negative consequences of difference. Stating the assumptions that have gone unstated, I believe, opens room for debate and for new kinds of solutions. Discovering that difference arises in relationships and in contexts that are themselves mutable introduces new angles of vision, new possibilities for change. The next chapter offers glimpses of new approaches to difference and also considers the problems that these approaches themselves may raise.

CHAPTER 3

Ways Out

The point I'm trying to make is that we would prefer to have people laugh with us than at us.

—Burton Minow

The difference dilemma is a symptom of a particular way of looking at the world. The problem arises only in a culture that officially condemns the assigned status of inequalities and yet, in practice, perpetuates them. This ambivalence is itself sustained by a set of usually unstated assumptions. "Different" traits are regarded as intrinsic to the "different" person, and the norm used to identify difference is assumed to be obvious, needing neither statement nor exposure to challenge. Differences are presumed identified through an unsituated perspective that makes other perspectives irrelevant and sees prevailing social arrangements as natural, good, and uncoerced. The chief effect of these assumptions is to deposit the problem of difference on the person identified by others as different. Screened out by these assumptions are the possibilities that difference expresses patterns of relationships, social perceptions, and the design of institutions made by some without others in mind. All such assumptions make it difficult or impossible to fulfill the vision of equality without recreating the differences that were not supposed to matter.

Anthropologist Mary Douglas has explained that "we can never improve our understanding unless we examine and reformulate our assumptions." This statement may seem an innocuous commonplace, but Douglas combines it with an argument that fundamental assumptions are defined not by individuals but by institutions. Institutions establish what count as correct and incorrect patterns of thought. Yet institutions, in Douglas's sense, do their work through what we experience as our own individual judgments. "When the institutions make classifications for us, we seem to lose some independence that we might conceivably have otherwise had. . . . Our social interaction consists very much in telling one another what right thinking is and passing blame on wrong thinking. This is indeed how we build the institutions, squeezing each other's ideas into a common shape so that we can

prove rightness by sheer numbers of independent assent. . . . The high triumph of institutional thinking is to make the institutions completely invisible."[1]

If Mary Douglas is right, then challenging the assumptions that lock the
difference dilemma in place will require more than fresh thinking by individuals. Individual efforts to think differently about difference will be curbed or
stymied by existing institutionalized patterns of thought. Even attempts to
reform treatments of difference risk recreating rather than remaking the
prevailing assumptions.[2] This chapter tackles the assumptions that make
difference a dilemma in two specific contexts and then explores the conun-
drums remaining for those who object to the consequences of difference.

Making a Difference

It is not difficult to state assumptions contrary to those that encase the
dilemma of difference. Difference can be understood not as intrinsic but as a
function of relationships, as a comparison drawn between an individual and
a norm that can be stated and evaluated. Instead of assuming that their own
experiences provide the proper benchmarks for judgment, the people who
assign difference can take into account the alternative perspectives of those
who have been called "different"; their perspectives highlight the process by
which some people's traits are made compatible with social arrangements,
while others are made not to fit in. Existing arrangements that make some
traits stand out as different are neither natural nor necessary; the relationship
between the status quo and the assignment of difference can be renovated.

Making these alternative assumptions concrete is a more difficult matter.
How can we no longer take for granted perceptions, norms, and perspectives
that prevail in the very physical architecture of our buildings and social
architecture of our lives? In the abstract, the question is largely unanswer-
able. But in practice, people often glimpse a gap between prevailing perceptions and their own experiences. People also often experience friction with
prevailing presumptions about what is normal and what is abnormal, either
because they feel that they themselves do not fit in an assigned position as
abnormal or normal, or because someone they know well does not seem to

---

[1]Mary Douglas, *How Institutions Think* (Syracuse, N.Y.: Syracuse University Press, 1986),
pp. 8, 91, 98. Douglas argues that analogies are selected from a variety of possible analogies and
entrenched by social institutions with authority and meaning. Indeed, "for discourse to be
possible at all, the basic categories have to be agreed on. Nothing else but institutions can define
sameness. Similarity is an institution. Elements get assigned to sets where institutions find their
own analogies in nature. On the one hand, the emotional energy for creating a set of analogies
comes from social concerns. On the other hand, there is a tension between the incentives for
individual minds to spend their time and energy on difficult problems and the temptation to sit
back and let founding analogies of the surrounding society take over" (p. 55).

[2]Similarly, exceptional individuals who succeed in escaping the negative meanings of a trait
they manifest make little headway in changing the institutional practices that continue to assign
negative significance to that trait.

fit. Periodically, even what seems given about a situation gives way and opens up possible alternatives. These glimpses arise in specific contexts, such as the ones that follow.

"Appropriate Education" for Handicapped Children

Amy Rowley has profound hearing impairment; she developed this condition before she learned language. Her parents enrolled her in the regular public school kindergarten under state and federal educational laws intended to assure a "free appropriate public education" to all handicapped children. These laws call for identifying any handicapping conditions in enrolled students and developing individual educational plans responsive to the particular child's needs.[3] The individual education plan developed by the school while Amy attended first grade provided that her classroom experience should be supplemented by instruction from a tutor for one hour each day and sessions with a speech therapist for three hours a week. Thus, the individualized plan introduced a few modifications of what was already established as the normal educational experience.

The Rowleys objected that this plan failed to provide the "appropriate" education specified by law.[4] They believed that their daughter should also be provided with a qualified sign-language interpreter in all her classes. The school countered that Amy did not need such an interpreter because she was succeeding academically, and socially, without such assistance. They noted that Amy's achievement levels were above average and that she was easily able to advance from grade to grade along with her classmates. The school even suggested that the interpreter might create a new barrier between Amy and the rest of the students.

The Rowleys challenged the school's plan through the procedure established by statute and ultimately pursued relief in court. They argued that Amy was entitled to complete assistance, including sign language, in order to obtain the same opportunity as other children in the classroom and in life.[5] This dispute became the first case to reach the Supreme Court under the Education for All Handicapped Children Act. Throughout their challenge, the Rowleys maintained that without an interpreter Amy understood a

[3]The federal Education for All Handicapped Children Act, adopted in 1975, provides financial incentives for states that submit plans for complying with the act's requirements (20 U.S.C. sec. 1400–1461 [1982]). See generally Note, "Enforcing the Right to an 'Appropriate' Education: The Education for All Handicapped Children Act of 1975," *Harv. L. Rev.* 92 (1979), 1103.

[4]The Rowleys relied on 20 U.S.C. sec. 1401 (18)(1982): "The term 'free appropriate public education' means special education and related services which (A) have been provided at public expense, under public supervision and direction, and without charge; (B) meet the standards of the state educational agency; (C) include an appropriate preschool, elementary, and secondary school education in the state involved; and (D) are provided in conformity with the individualized education program required under section 1414 (A)(5) of this title."

[5]The Rowleys were committed to a method called "total communication," which involves not only lipreading and speech development but also sign language, fingerspelling, touching, and visual cues.

maximum of 58 to 59 percent of the oral communication in a classroom setting, whereas with an interpreter her comprehension of oral communication tested at 100 percent.[6] Her parents wanted the school to give Amy the same access to instruction as other students, even though it was unlikely that she would have access to a sign-language interpreter for the rest of her life. Obviously, their position would impose greater costs on the school, which claimed that its reasonably priced plan would allow Amy to function and achieve in the classroom setting while developing her own self-sufficiency for a world not likely to accommodate her special needs.

By the time the case reached the Supreme Court, it seemed to present a starkly either/or choice: either the act's guarantee of an "appropriate education" mandated the full-time sign language interpreter for Amy, or else the school's plan satisfied the act. As an inquiry into the proper interpretation of the federal statutory term "free appropriate public education," the Supreme Court explained, the Rowleys' challenge to the school placement should be assessed according to whether (a) the state was complying with the procedures established in the statute and (b) "the individualized educational program developed through the Act's procedures [was] reasonably calculated to enable the child to receive education benefits."[7] The Court concluded that the state had indeed complied with the requisite procedures and that the educational program devised for Amy was "appropriate" in the sense that her success showed the plan reasonably calculated to enable her to receive education benefits.

In many ways, the two sides of the argument agreed more than they differed. Both sides assumed that the problem was Amy's: because she was different from other students, the solution must focus on her. Both sides deployed the unstated norm of the hearing student who receives educational input from a teacher, rather than imagining a different norm around which the entire classroom might be constructed. To some extent the school system and the Rowleys differed in perspective: the school officials understandably assumed the perspective of the school's needs as a whole, while the Rowleys, also understandably, focused on their daughter's special needs. But even this apparent contrast in perspective rested on a shared assumption that the classroom and the school as they already existed set the boundaries for any solution. Only minor modifications, leaving the rest of the school the same, were contemplated by either side.

But there were other possibilities besides those raised by the parties and considered by the Court. One obvious alternative would have been to enroll Amy in a school or class designed entirely for hearing-impaired students. Advocated by some educators and some hearing-impaired adults, specialized schooling may produce better social experiences and more sensitivity to

[6]Rowley v. Board of Educ., 483 F. Supp. 528, 532 (S.D. N.Y. 1980), aff'd, 632 F.2d 945 (2d Cir. 1980); rev'd, 458 U.S. 176 (1982).
[7]Board of Educ. v. Rowley, 458 U.S. 176, 206–7 (1982).

individual student needs.[8] To no small degree, special schools have the opportunity to regard the disabled student as the norm and to design an entire educational and social program taking that student's needs into account. Amy would have been the same as other students in a classroom consisting entirely of hearing-impaired students. There, sign-language instruction could be employed for all of them. Even if the school included students with different handicaps, all the students would need and obtain special assistance responsive to their particular disabilities.

The choice between segregated and integrated education for a deaf child presents the difference dilemma in stark form. In separate schooling the child may feel less different in the classroom but more different in society, while in a mainstream classroom the hearing-impaired child may be treated as different from the other students even while sharing their educational experience.[9] Congress, however, had already selected an alternative: the Education for All Handicapped Children Act directs participating states to mainstream handicapped students, "to the maximum extent appropriate," in regular public school programs.[10] The drafters of the act, in waging a campaign against the legacies of isolation and misunderstanding of disabled people, embraced an overarching legislative commitment to place students in the least restrictive situation that would still meet the individual student's needs. Thus, because the choice between segregated and mainstreamed education had already been curbed by the legislative preference for integrating disabled students, Amy's proven ability to learn in the mainstream classroom would defeat any objection to keeping her there.

Yet there did remain another alternative for Amy, one never discussed in the litigation. To glimpse it, we need first to return to the assumptions behind the choices that were addressed. The lawful choices considered by the Court were to include Amy in regular classroom instruction, supplemented by some separate instruction during part of the week, or else to provide a full-time sign-language interpreter to translate for Amy in the mainstream classroom. Both alternatives assume that the problem of difference is located in the hearing-impaired child. Both conceive of equal treatment as treating this

---

[8]Burton Blatt, "The Integration-Segregation Issue: Some Questions, Assumptions, and Facts," in *An Alternative Textbook in Special Education,* ed. Burton Blatt, Douglas Biklen, and Roger Bogdan (Denver, Colo.: Love, 1977), pp. 128–29, describes the debate over integrated and segregated education for disabled persons and the lack of evidence on either side.

[9]Cost factors would affect each of these alternatives; the state's willingness to reimburse local schools for placements in specialized settings notably affects placement decisions. See Alan Gartner and Dorothy Lipsky, "Beyond Special Education: Toward a Quality System for All Students," *Harv. Ed. Rev.* 57 (1987), 376, 381–84.

[10]To qualify for federal financial assistance, a state should demonstrate that it has established "procedures to assure that, to the maximum extent appropriate, handicapped children, including children in public or private institutions or other care facilities, are educated with children who are not handicapped, and that special classes, separate schooling or other removal of handicapped children from the regular educational environment occurs only when the nature or severity of the handicap is such that education in regular classes with the use of supplementary aids and services cannot be achieved satisfactorily." See 20 U.S.C. sec. 1412 (5)(B)(1982).

child the same as other children, while making unimpaired students—and the classroom designed for them—the norm used in this comparison. The school and the Rowleys simply disagreed about what the "same" treatment would mean under these circumstances: the school reasoned that essentially it meant including Amy in the same educational program as her classmates; her parents argued that the "same" treatment would make available to her the same educational input—100 percent of the oral communication—as her classmates were receiving. Both approaches, in different ways, single her out and assign the difference to Amy.

A difference stance would treat the problem of difference as embedded in the relationships among all the students, making all of them part of the problem. The individual teacher would need to use an approach that would work to the educational benefit of every student in the classroom, resisting the temptation to treat the problem as belonging to the "different" child. Similarly, this different stance would challenge the perspective of any observer who assumed the existing classroom instructional mode to be natural and necessary. Some alternatives to the status quo in the very processes of communication in the classroom would need consideration.

In this light, what if the teacher instructed all the students in sign language and ran the class in both spoken and sign language simultaneously?[11] This approach conceives of the problem as a problem for all the students. After all, if Amy cannot communicate with her classmates, they cannot communicate with her, and all lose the benefit of exchange. Moreover, conducting the class in sign language would engage all the students in the difficult and instructive experience of communicating across traditional lines of difference. All the students could learn to struggle with problems of translation and learn to empathize by experiencing firsthand discomfort with an unfamiliar mode of expression. It would be educational for all of them to discover that all languages are arrangements of signs and to use group action to improve the situation of an individual. Involving classmates in the solution affords a different stance toward the dilemma of difference: it no longer makes the trait of hearing impairment signify stigma or isolation but responds to that trait as an issue for the entire community.[12]

[11]After developing this example I learned of a school in Cambridge, Massachusetts, that had responded to the enrollment of a hearing-impaired child with sign-language instruction for classmates. And recently, Public School No. 1—the "Pluralistic School"—in Santa Monica, California, has experimented with instructing an integrated classroom of hearing-impaired and hearing students in sign language.

[12]Some schools already take an analogous stance toward the problem of an unmanageable child who can disrupt an entire class. Rather than simply placing the child in isolation outside the classroom, one alternative is to pair teachers, either of whom may send the child to the other's classroom. The procedure is introduced to all students through a group discussion so that the defiant child is not singled out, and when that child returns to the original classroom, "the excluding teacher reviews the situation with her class, emphasizing the reasons behind the relevant rules and alternative ways in which the excluded child might have acted. Whenever possible her remarks are channeled into a group discussion that can be used to marshal the support of the class in helping the excluded child. Once children have expressed their expected bitterness toward the defiant child in such discussions, the teacher can elicit more sympathetic

The idea that more people could learn and use sign language, thereby ending the barriers in communication between hearing-impaired and hearing people, has historical support. In her book *Everyone Here Spoke Sign Language,* cultural anthropologist Nora Groce described how an unusually high rate of profound hereditary deafness in Martha's Vineyard from the seventeenth through the early twentieth century created a setting where the cultural meaning of deafness was quite different than it has been elsewhere in the United States. Deaf people were completely integrated into the Martha's Vineyard society, and everyone spoke sign language. Even people who were not hearing impaired sometimes communicated with one another in sign language.[13] The sharp contrast between attitudes toward hearing-impaired people in that community and attitudes elsewhere suggests the considerable contribution of social constructions to the meanings of a "disability" or particular trait of difference among people.[14] Understanding the relationships between people within which differences are constructed and given meaning can offer new alternatives and perhaps some ways out of the difference dilemma.

This solution is not itself the answer for all communities or all classrooms. There is no promise that all non-hearing-impaired students would happily respond to such an approach or that their parents would accept it. Nor does it bear obvious fruit for educational decisions about other kinds of disabled students. And an analogous approach to bilingual education, such as instructing each child in the languages used by classmates at home, could be unwieldy, especially if the class includes students with many different primary languages. But conducting Amy's class in sign language offers a glimpse of what it would mean to relocate the problem in the relationships within which difference arises.[15] This marks a new approach to the dilemma of difference. Taking the students' relationships as the point of departure makes the "problem" one for the whole class, whose members are deprived of

---

interest from them in helping him, especially when she points out that she needs help from the class in teaching the excluded child to follow class rules" (a member of the Yale Psycho-Educational Clinic, quoted in Seymour Sarason, *The Culture of the School and the Problem of Change* [Boston, Mass.: Allyn & Bacon, 1971], p. 138). Here, the issue of discipline becomes an educational process involving all the students in two classrooms. The problem, then, is not located solely in the "different" child but in the demands of the classroom society for managing behavior and following rules.

[13]Nora Groce, *Everyone Here Spoke Sign Language* (Cambridge, Mass.: Harvard University Press, 1985). Perhaps political party affiliation seemed to some a more notable distinction between people than handicaps: one elderly islander answered Groce's question about the disabled in the community with a list of local Democrats (p. 11).

[14]See also Oliver Sacks, "The Revolution of the Deaf," *New York Review of Books,* June 2, 1988, p. 23, describing the success of Gallaudet College students in demanding the appointment of a hearing-impaired president.

[15]See also Mario Fantini and Gerald Weinstein, *The Disadvantaged Child: Challenges to Education* (New York: Harper & Row, 1970); and John Gliedman and William Roth, *The Unexpected Minority: Handicapped Children in America* (New York: Harcourt Brace Jovanovich, 1980), pp. 199–201: a school can develop ethnographic perception of a minority child's learning needs by viewing him as a foreigner in a culture where the educational rules are rigged against him and he needs a map and renovations of that world.

communicating fully with the "different" student just as she is deprived of communicating fully with them. If her classmates learned to communicate with Amy, they could also learn how much of their understanding of disability rests on social practices that they themselves can change. They could discover that differences are features of relationships rather than traits residing in the "different" person. This insight would be helpful as they encountered differences in others and in themselves during the rest of their lives. A relational understanding of difference can replace debates over similar or different treatment with analysis of the ways in which institutions construct and utilize differences to justify and enforce exclusions—and the ways in which such institutional practices can be changed.

A class of students all fluent in sign language would not be an option reached through an individualized special education plan. Planning for an individual, by its very focus on the particular child, tends to ignore the child's relationships with others and the construction of difference in those relationships. At the same time, the individualized plans leave in place the existing classroom methods. Mainstreaming the disabled child means producing expectations that this child will adjust to the existing educational structure, with modifications focused on her through individualized instruction at limited times. It preserves the unstated norm of the nonhandicapped student and continues to make difference seem the handicapped student's problem. As a result the social attitudes about disability which may be the largest obstacle to integrating a disabled person fully would remain barely challenged.[16] Teaching all the students sign language, on the other hand, would involve every member of the class in altering the classroom structure that has disabled one student's participation.

Pregnancy and Parental Leave from Paid Work

Christine Littleton has drawn a similar contrast between two solutions to the problem for women speakers who confront a lecture podium built with the average man in mind.[17] For a woman who can barely be seen over the top of the lectern, one option is to provide a footstool or box to stand on. Another option is to install an adjustable lectern, suitable for men and women of all heights. The first approach leaves in place the physical reminder

---

[16]See "Report of the United Nations Expert Group Meeting on Barrier-Free Design," *International Rehabilitation Review* 26 (1975): 3: "Despite everything we can do, or hope to do, to assist each physically or mentally disabled person to achieve his or her maximum potential in life, our efforts will not succeed until we have found the way to remove the obstacles to this goal directed by human society—the physical barriers we have created in public buildings, housing, transportation, houses of worship, centers of social life and other community facilities—the social barriers we have evolved and accepted against those who vary more than a certain degree from what we have been conditioned to regard as normal. More people are forced into limited lives and made to suffer by these man-made obstacles than by any specific physical or mental disability."

[17]Christine A. Littleton, "Reconstructing Sexual Equality," *Calif. L. Rev.* 75 (1987), 1279, 1314.

that the woman is anomalous and unexpected as a speaker; the second remakes the unstated norm of the average man by acknowledging the range of human conditions. Of course, even the first alternative is better than the status quo—which, after all, is neither natural nor inevitable. The podium was designed and selected by human beings, and if it is used by people whom it does not fit, it seems difficult to dispute that change would benefit both speakers and listeners.

Disputes about change have complicated alternative treatments of difference in many situations. Consider pregnant workers or workers who have recently become parents, given workplaces designed for persons who are neither pregnant nor heavily involved in child-care responsibilities. Here, too, an either/or approach has framed the dilemma of difference: either employers should made no accommodation, or else employers should make pregnancy and maternity leaves available—thus establishing special treatment for these women employees, compared with the workplace norm. If pregnancy and child-care duties interfere with paid work responsibilities outside the home, the first alternative assigns these costs entirely to the mother. The second alternative shifts the costs partially to the employer, who takes on the burden of the leave but may be able to shift these costs to other workers and consumers.[18] Here, the solution assimilates pregnancy to the model of a disability, which should make an employee eligible for job-related benefits. The connotations of such an approach, however, assign negative symbolism to the employee who is "disabled" in relation to the norm presumed in the workplace, and some advocates for women's rights have feared that this solution could revitalize prejudices against women as workers more generally.

The Supreme Court has accepted a third approach: that the employer should ensure both men and women the same opportunities to combine work and family. At minimum, then, the Court allowed state-mandated maternity leaves, despite a federal law prohibiting workplace distinctions on the basis of pregnancy.[19] The Court also suggested that any remaining concerns about unequal treatment could be resolved if employers provided comparable benefits for men, using women's needs as the reference point.

This view begins to break free of the difference conundrum, at least with regard to pregnancy issues in the workplace. The Court's decision allows states to shift costs to the employer, as suggested by the special treatment model, and yet justifies this shift with the rhetoric of equality. How did the

---

[18]We should distinguish between paid and unpaid leave. The latter represents a commitment by the employer to keep the job open for the employee for a specified time period following the birth of the child. The costs and practical difficulties make this option less feasible than it initially may seem.

[19]Cf. California Fed. Sav. & Loan Ass'n v. Guerra, 107 S.Ct. 683 (1987). Note also that "there is no comparable male disability that systematically keeps men as a class out of the workforce and causes them to lose seniority and job tenure benefits in the way that pregnancy does for women" ("The Supreme Court, 1986 Term—Leading Cases," *Harv. L. Rev.* 101 [1987], 326–27).

Court accomplish this result? It continued to rely on the assumption that equality depends on sameness, but it changed the focus on what "similarity" is relevant to the equality inquiry by widening the lens to include both home and job. The similarity that mattered to the Court was the status of each worker as both a public and a private person, a person with workplace duties and family duties. The fact that women have historically had more time-consuming family-related duties than men should be irrelevant to the basic similarity that both women and men may have parental roles and responsibilities. Thus, the "difference" requiring "special treatment" dissolves in the face of a larger similarity between male and female workers, each of whom has the task of juggling work and family obligations. The Court thereby replaced the unstated norm of the male worker without family duties with a new norm of a worker with family duties; the Court also considered the perspective of the women workers rather than presuming that their "difference" emerges inevitably from a naturally constructed workplace.

The Court's solution begins to reject the usual assumptions that frame the difference dilemma by altering conceptions of what persons are the same and what counts as a difference. But it does not completely abandon the traditional assumptions; it still treats the critical question as one of sameness and difference rather than locating the issue of difference within relationships between people and social institutions that make some traits matter and others fit in. For example, the Court's solution draws a new distinction, dividing workers who are "the same" and therefore entitled to similar legal treatment from those who are "different" and can lawfully be treated differently.[20] This new distinction divides workers whose responsibilities outside of employment extend to their children from those with other responsibilities, such as the care of parents or other relatives.

Even in restricting the question to the subject of pregnancy and childbirth, the Court's approach continues to treat these matters as the responsibility of individuals. It neglects the interaction between individuals and social institutions that distributes responsibility for what is, after all, the basic mode of species reproduction, in which all persons—not just the pregnant person—have an interest.[21] Policies that focus solely on women neglect men's role and interest in reproduction.[22] Because 87 percent of the fifty million women earning wages in the United States are likely to become pregnant during their wage-earning years, the treatment of women workers is, in effect, the treatment of mothers.[23] This view, unlike the Court's approach, would make programs like work leaves and adjustable work hours acceptable even in

[20]"To recognize a class of things is to polarize and to exclude. It involves drawing boundaries, a very different activity from grading" (Douglas, *How Institutions Think,* p. 60).

[21]See Lucinda M. Finley, "Transcending Equality Theory: A Way Out of the Maternity and the Workplace Debate," *Colum. L. Rev.* 86 (1986), 1118, discussing notions of responsibility and interconnectedness to justify pregnancy and parenting leaves.

[22]See Wendy Chavkin, Introduction to Part 2 in *Double Exposure: Women's Health Hazards on the Job and at Home,* ed. Wendy Chavkin (New York: Monthly Review Press, 1984), p. 155.

[23]See Zillah Eisenstein, *The Female Body and the Law* (Berkeley: University of California Press, 1988), p. 209, discussing U.S. Census Bureau reports.

light of an antidiscrimination principle, because all workers and employers benefit from pregnancy, childbearing, and child-rearing activities.

Very practically, it is worth noting that several European countries have established parenting-leave policies, day-care programs, and other institutional supports for working families. For the most part child care still remains women's work, but even this is changing.[24] If, compared with men, women cannot secure or keep good jobs because their hours and required uninterrupted service are incompatible with child care or pregnancy, gender difference is the problem. But if employers introduce flexible hours, job sharing, and leaves for family duties, then gender differences are reduced in salience—and men, too, may be able to accommodate both work and family duties. Nancy Dowd, a legal scholar, has argued that gender difference is not the entire issue behind collisions between work and family duties but that gender is "critical to restructuring in order to eliminate its very predominance and prevent its reinstitutionalization at the core of the work-family relationship."[25] Thus, a combination of antidiscrimination strategies and policy initiations to enhance flexibility for all workers offers an alternative that acknowledges pregnancy and child care as a human, not just a woman's, problem.

This alternative contests the ready association of sameness with equality and difference with inferiority or disability. It also abjures a new female norm for use in claiming equality. The point is not merely to analogize women to men in order to secure equal treatment, or even to analogize men to women in order to justify remaking the workplace to suit people for whom it was not originally designed. Replacing the old assumptions with new ones should not simply enshrine a new and better norm against which to judge difference. Instead of assessing difference, or individual traits in relationship to an unstated norm, this alternative inquires about the social arrangements that make those traits seem to matter. It questions why the individual worker must bear responsibility for differing from the norm. The problem is not just a problem for the woman who is pregnant or a new parent but also a problem for men who have family responsibilities; for employers who miss the chance to benefit from the talents of women and men whose family obligations prevent their adjusting to the employer's work schedule; for the wider community, which has interests in reproduction and the rearing of children as well as in production at the workplace. Taking this broader view of the problem challenges the presumed norm dividing work and family duties and also challenges the framework of difference analysis.

What would be the consequences of this broader view? Employers and public officials would need to join workers and family members in acknowledging and protecting these wider relationships and interests. But the costs of

---

[24]See Nancy Dowd, "Work and Family: The Gender Paradox and the Limitations of Discrimination Analysis in Restructuring the Workplace," *Harv. C.R.–C.L. L. Rev.* 24 (1989), 79; and Nancy Dowd, "Work and Family: Restructuring the Workplace" (Suffolk Law School, Boston, unpublished manuscript, 1989).

[25]Dowd, *Work and Family*, p. 82.

adjusting the workplace do not have to shift entirely to employers, because they could pass them on to other workers and consumers. Moreover, this approach would justify more direct public support, financed through general tax revenues, for pregnancy and parental leaves. In some settings, coworkers could help shoulder a shift in workplace duties for a limited time. Like the use of sign language in a classroom that includes a hearing-impaired student, this approach conceives of the treatment of pregnancy and maternity in the workplace as an issue for everyone, not just for the "different" person. The Court's more limited solution secures some protection for "different" persons by abstracting each person from context. Making each person a participant in a legal system of abstract rights which accords each individual the same treatment, the law may be supple enough to conceive of the individual as both a worker and a parent or potential parent, and as someone who deserves the same treatment as anyone else in this same situation. But the Court's solution cabins questions of social relationships implicated in the structures of work and family by emphasizing the rights of distinct individuals.

Reflections

The foregoing examples offer ways out of the difference dilemma because they relate problems to relationships between people and social institutions. Difference then is no longer the problem of the "different person." Instead, we notice and struggle with differences within patterns of relationships between people and in relations between institutional practices that have been designed by people, without other people's needs in mind. The educational program for the hearing-impaired child involves relationships with other students and teachers, and the accommodation for workers who are pregnant or new parents also involves relationships with other workers, employers, and even consumers. If the problem has relational dimensions, then so should the solutions.

Thinking about problems in these terms, however, proves difficult. The difficulties, once examined, reconfirm the power of the usual assumptions about difference—and perhaps illuminate the reasons people hold so strongly to the assumptions that perpetuate the dilemmas of difference.

Difference from Different Perspectives

Many traits that have been labeled "different" by members of a majority or people in positions of authority are sources of pride—even if they may also be sources of stigma. Membership in a minority religion or race, becoming a mother, and for some people even managing a disability may be qualities of identity and experience that lend meaning to existence. Reform movements by women, blacks, Hispanics, and disabled persons have sought to reclaim the strengths in difference. Religious groups in this country celebrate their beliefs and traditions, at times making a virtue of their perceived role as "outsiders."[26] So do many gay and lesbian people.

Still, inequalities drawn on the basis of race, gender, religion, and disability persist in this country. Remedying these inequalities has become an American pastime, yet inequalities remain. The institutional structures and patterns of attitudes by those who define others as different remain resilient, even in the face of renewed policies intended to redress discrimination.

From the vantage point of those who have been labeled different, even the remedies may be problematic. Some intended beneficiaries resist using them. One example is the response to parental leave policies. Not many companies have actually adopted them, but such policies are not universally welcomed where they do exist. Private law firms around the country have announced pregnancy and parenting leave policies; some permit any lawyer in the firm to obtain up to six months of unpaid leave to manage obligations associated with a new baby, without losing the job or its health benefits. But in many firms no men and very few women decide to use the benefit. Why? A few explicit conversations explain: one senior partner tells the associates working for him, "None of you would be sissy enough to take a leave"; women associates say, either candidly or confidentially to friends, "I won't be taken seriously for partnership if I take a leave."[27]

In contrast, many parents seek out special education benefits for children who may simply present difficult behavior or less than above-average achievement.[28] Yet even with the high utilization of special education programs, some parents and some students want to avoid the stigma still associated with special education labels and programs.

These two examples indicate a larger problem: people who fit within a category of "difference" often choose not to avail themselves of programs designed for them because they fear the risk of stigma or other negative social attitudes if they identify themselves by the difference.[29] For individuals who have some latitude of choice but lack the power to remake the social meaning

[26]See R. Laurence Moore, *Religious Outsiders and the Making of Americans* (Oxford: Oxford University Press, 1986), for a nuanced and intriguing argument that religious groups ranging from Mormons to Jews to mainstream Protestants have accepted outsider identity, maintained a sense of separation from the rest of society, and at the same time claimed to be typical Americans; that the status of outsider itself is so familiar in American culture that it provides a familiar and well-received claim to membership.

[27]This response is even more common among those who consider a part-time work schedule to accommodate family responsibilities, even when the firm offers to extend the period for partnership for lawyers exercising this option.

[28]Gartner and Lipsky, "Beyond Special Education," pp. 382, 392. Perhaps parents who push for special education benefits are sufficiently removed from the stigma their children may suffer to avoid letting it dominate their judgment. Yet many people seek out disability benefits for themselves, despite the negative connotations of welfare programs; see Deborah Stone, *The Disabled State* (Philadelphia: Temple University Press, 1984), pp. 141–48.

[29]The long-studied role of stigma in public welfare benefits is a complicated story, because many people support the retention of at least some degree of stigma as an incentive for potential recipients to avoid economic dependency on the state. See Lance Liebman, "The Definition of Disability in Social Security and Supplemental Security Income: Drawing the Bounds of Social Welfare Estates," *Harv. L. Rev.* 89 (1976), 833, 857–60.

of difference, choosing not to identify themselves in terms of the trait of difference may be more attractive than availing themselves of the benefits. Thus, minority applicants often refuse to fill out questions about minority status on college and university admission forms for fear of the negative consequences of being labeled this way; other applicants provide the information but then come to doubt whether the school values any other qualification they present.

Similarly, according to one study, two-thirds of the white women and members of minorities who report that they have experienced discrimination on the job refrain from complaining to any third party, including legal officials, despite their rights under the laws against discrimination. Kristin Bumiller's study of discrimination victims who do not sue concludes that they perceive the high costs of complaining and the real benefits "lumping it," or absorbing the injury without complaint. Her interviews show that complaining through the civil rights laws means accepting the role of victim, which is itself demeaning and also "transforms the conflict into an internal contest to reconcile a positive self-image with the image of oneself as a powerless and defeated victim."[30] In addition, complaining forces the individual into a visible role and, paradoxically, demands the differential treatment of public attention and dispute because of allegations of differential treatment.[31] A new label, "troublemaker," also carries negative consequences for the individual. And besides risking a painful reconstruction of the discrimination event before the agency or court, the potential complainant may fear that the process will be unavailing. Other people may fail to confirm the story, or the legal system will prove unresponsive; meanwhile, the individual loses control over the incident and the process.[32] There are special costs involved in hoping and then losing, costs that may even be more painful than never hoping at all.[33]

Besides avoiding the negative consequences of complaining, people may discover direct benefits from enduring discrimination without complaint. Members of minority groups, especially minority women, come to expect discrimination as inevitable and may find an opportunity to exercise strength and pride in surviving without confrontation.[34] The very act of submission may be an expression of autonomy and dignity precisely because it is a chosen response. Similarly, in her study of a religious Baptist town in Geor-

[30]Kristin Bumiller, *The Civil Rights Society: The Social Construction of Victims* (Baltimore, Md.: Johns Hopkins University Press, 1988), pp. 26, 52.

[31]See Erving Goffman, *Stigma: Notes on the Management of Spoiled Identity* (Englewood Cliffs, N.J.: Prentice-Hall, 1963), p. 24: political action by stigmatized persons risks drawing attention to their situation and consolidating a public image of difference.

[32]Bumiller, *Civil Rights Society*, pp. 91, 104–5. Bumiller also notes that the legal rules demand a focus on the defendant's perspective, which may be a disturbing experience for the discrimination victim (pp. 65, 74).

[33]Richard Weissbourd, "Moral Shock: The Disillusionment of Vietnam Veterans" (Ph.D. diss., Harvard University, 1987), develops the idea of "moral shock" to describe deep disillusionment experienced by individual veterans who had hoped to believe in the American government and in the trustworthiness of their superior officers.

[34]Bumiller, *Civil Rights Society*, pp. 69–70, 84.

gia, anthropologist Carol Greenhouse found women who tended to internalize conflicts within their families, coming to terms with such conflicts by refining their own roles and by focusing on their spiritual identities.[35] Although this solution may work for some, it suggests complex reasons why people refrain from using the avenues of relief that law makes available. Most important, individual decisions to swallow injury fail to alter the sources of hurt or discrimination, leaving those who cause the harm undisturbed.

Individuals who have been identified as "different" by the larger community refuse benefits and avenues for redress designed for them for the same reasons that the assigned "difference" injures them in the first place: remedial programs and complaint processes still locate the source of the difference in the "different" person rather than in social relationships, leaving in place as the unstated norm the person who needs no benefits nor a way to complain.[36] Pregnancy and parenting leaves create a special option for people who need them but maintain the usual workplace patterns and presumptions about what counts as commendable, or even expected, devotion to the job. The perspective of "different" people plays little part in designing benefit programs or complaint processes supposedly intended for them. Nor do these programs challenge larger societal attitudes about women and mothers, who are thought to be vulnerable and distracted; about the minorities who are believed not to "fit in"; or about disabled persons who are presumed dependent and needy. Yet it is these attitudes that infuse the institutional practices that define some people as different, and inferior, in light of the norm.[37]

Solutions to dilemmas of difference cannot work if they redeposit the responsibility for redressing negative meanings of difference on the person who is treated as different. Solutions that emphasize individual responsibility run this danger, perhaps because most social institutions still define "the individual" in light of an unstated norm and degrade those who depart from that norm. Thus, it can be only a partial step out of the dilemma of difference to focus on the individual whose needs have been unmet by the institutional practices that presume a particular norm. Perhaps this is what Mary Douglas meant when she wrote that "justice has nothing to do with isolated cases."[38] The individualized focus of special education legislation does help to identify the needs of a particular student. But many critics note that the individualized focus on the "special student" emphasizes procedures and deemphasizes the development of improved teaching techniques responsive to that

[35]Carol J. Greenhouse, *Praying for Justice: Faith, Order, and Community in an American Town* (Ithaca: Cornell University Press, 1986).
[36]Even efforts to claim a group identity as a basis for challenging prevailing institutional practices risk stigma, but collective action may lodge more effective and symbolic challenges to institutionalized practices that disfavor "different" people. See Renée Anspach, "From Stigma to Identity Politics: Political Activism among the Physically Disabled and Former Mental Patients," *Social Science and Medicine* (Great Britain) 13A (1979), 765–73.
[37]See Harlan Hahn, "Paternalism and Public Policy," *Society*, March/April 1983, 36, 44–45.
[38]Douglas, *How Institutions Think*, p. 124.

student and to that student's relationships with other students.[39] Against the backdrop of the "normal" classroom, specialized programming for the disabled student may accentuate his departure from the norm.

Making All the Difference

Groce noted in her study of Martha's Vineyard: "Perhaps the best description of the status of deaf individuals on the Vineyard was given to me by an island woman in her eighties, when I asked about those who were handicapped by deafness when she was a girl. 'Oh,' she said emphatically, 'those people weren't handicapped. They were just deaf.' "[40] Can we invent other practices that treat difference as just the variety of human experience, rather than the basis for dividing people into the class of the normal and the class of the abnormal? Forging ways out of the difference dilemma requires remaking institutions so that they do not establish one norm that places the burden of difference on those who diverge from it. It means eliminating the attribution of inferiority to people on the basis of their difference from the norm established within traditional social practices. Is this possible?

In the context of schooling, perhaps pushing the individualized approach to encompass all students would eliminate the pattern of attributed deviance, for then all students would be "different." Every student would be addressed as a unique individual, with a unique constellation of needs and abilities that deserve an individualized educational plan. Something approximating this may occur in school systems where 80 percent of the students have already been identified as learning disabled. There, to be "different" is no longer to be in a minority or even to be deviant.[41] The very meaning of difference is remade, and the reference points for comparing people multiply rather than reduce to one trait. Pedagogical innovations such as contract-based learning and other individualized teaching approaches similarly move classroom instruction away from the presumption of a "normal" student and respond to the range of students present.[42] Schools that devise special programs for gifted students as well as for disabled students begin to remake the classroom as a setting for individualized learning. But such programs may also resegregate, or communicate in ever more powerful ways the pecking order used by adults to rank children by traits the adults value.

As this example suggests, conceiving of all people as different remains

---

[39]E.g., Gliedman and Roth, *Unexpected Minority*, pp. 190–95; Joel Handler, *The Conditions of Discretion: Autonomy, Community, Bureaucracy* (New York: Russell Sage Foundation, 1986); Hahn, "Paternalism and Public Policy," p. 42.

[40]Groce, *Everyone Here Spoke Sign Language*, p. 5. For a thoughtful history of persons with hearing impairments, see Harlan Lane, *When the Mind Hears: A History of the Deaf* (New York: Vintage Books, 1984).

[41]See Martha Minow, "Learning to Live with the Dilemma of Difference: Bilingual and Special Education," *Law & Contemp. Probs.* 48 (1985), 157, 179–82.

[42]Gliedman and Roth, *Unexpected Minority*, pp. 196–237, advocates pluralistic teaching and diagnostic strategies.

difficult if not impossible. One reason is an epistemological one. Given our limited ability to hold the complexity of the world in our minds, we summarize and simplify through language. Through these summaries, an individual's uniqueness stems from the particular intersection of group memberships. We cannot know or describe all possible traits that fully distinguish one person from everyone else. We do not know how to describe individuals as unique except by reference to traits that actually draw them into membership in groups of people sharing those traits. There is a very practical, institutional version of this same point. However much the laws governing education for handicapped children embrace the ideal of individualized planning and decisions, educational plans are in practice tailored not only to the child's needs but also to the school system's actual resources. For example, Massachusetts, the state that originally developed what became the model for the federal Education for All Handicapped Children Act, has developed ten "prototype" placements based on the degree to which the mainstream classroom program is modified for a particular student.[43] The availability of these particular options not only influences the placement of a given student but also structures the options themselves by comparing the student to the norm of the regular classroom. In short, the practical limits on resources interfere with treating each child as a unique individual rather than a member of one or another student group. Truly individualized treatment is probably unattainable.

An alternative route to breaking free of the difference dilemma is to take seriously the perspective of those who have not been the norm in the past. From their own perspective, women, members of minority groups, and disabled people may not be abnormal; they may instead introduce more varied and more inclusive definitions of what is normal. The dilemma of difference will recur for them, however, in programs that presume the status quo to be natural, good, or immutable, where the status quo assigns the label of difference and its burdens to some and refuses to make room for a range of human conditions. Reframing social experience to transcend the difference dilemma means challenging the presumption that either one is the same or one is different, either one is normal or one is not.

A related strategy is to expand the definition of who is the same, thus challenging the exclusionary uses of difference. This was the Supreme Court's strategy in regarding pregnancy leaves as a device for treating both male and female workers the same in relation to family duties. Another way to avoid stigma is to broaden the definition of difference. Decision-makers can make

---

[43]The prototypes are (1) regular classroom instruction with some modifications; (2) no more than 25 percent or (3) no more than 60 percent of school time spent in special education classes; (4) special class placement within the regular school setting but mostly separate from the regular program; (5) a special private day school program; (6) teaching or treatment conducted at home or (7) in a hospital; (8) occupational training in a public school; (9) teaching or treatment in a residential school; and (10) combinations of the previous possibilities. See Massachusetts Advocacy Center, *Making School Work: An Education Handbook for Students, Parents and Professionals*, rev. ed. (Boston: Massachusetts Advocacy Center, 1975), p. 48.

more traits relevant to the distribution of a particular benefit, including socially accepted or valued categories alongside devalued ones. Creating special educational programs for a variety of students may reduce the stigma of participation for those who have been singled out as disabled. Similarly, establishing an income support program with wide eligibility can shake public assistance programs free of negative associations.[44] Providing a free school lunch for all students, not just those eligible for public welfare assistance, can eliminate the stigma of participating in the lunch program.

Perhaps the most arresting example of this strategy is a practice developed by hospitals confronting AIDS patients, whose presence warrants special safety precautions by nurses and doctors but who could be injured by public identification of their condition. How are the medical personnel to know, quickly, who has AIDS? The practice of "universal isolation"—treating every patient as though he or she could have AIDS—is a solution that addresses the needs of the medical staff while respecting the privacy of the AIDS patients.[45]

Some may object that these solutions will be too costly, and certainly programs that are deliberately overinclusive do cost more than those that target the group in need. A second objection is that tampering with the lines between normal and abnormal, independent and needy, competent and incompetent risks overwhelming us and undermining a sense of order; opening up and redefining basic patterns of thought is confusing and time consuming. A third objection is that some people simply are abnormal. There is a palpable reality to some differences between people and to the competencies and incompetencies that these differences entail. The differences between an infant and a competent adult are a striking example.

It is possible to respond to each objection in kind. The costs of inclusive solutions can be compared with the long-term costs to society of unremedied inequality and stigma. These are moral as well as economic costs.[46] Disorder, whatever its danger, is defensible precisely where the price of order has been oppression of some people by others. And the teachings of history about erroneous assumptions of incompetence and inferiority, based on gender, race, and disability, should caution against taking even current understandings of these traits for granted.[47]

But no response with these dimensions is likely to persuade someone who raises the objections in good faith. Perhaps this very resistance suggests that

[44]The contrast between Social Security and Aid to Families with Dependent Children (AFDC) is a familiar example of this strategy. See Michael Katz, *In the Shadow of the Poorhouse: A Social History of Welfare in America* (New York: Basic Books, 1986), pp. 266–73.

[45]Given the error rate of the tests for AIDS antibodies, and the lag time in accurate diagnosis, universal isolation has other virtues as well.

[46]See Katz, *In the Shadow of the Poorhouse*, pp. 289–91; and Frank Michelman, "Property, Utility, and Fairness: Comments on the Ethical Foundations of 'Justice Compensation' Law," *Harv. L. Rev.* 80 (1967), 1165, 1214–16, discussing "demoralization costs."

[47]History shows that science may expose errors in assessments of inferiority but has also been used to defend what now would be called prejudice. See Stephen Jay Gould, *The Mismeasure of Man* (New York: Norton, 1981).

the objections are the first line of defense for deeply held, institutionalized beliefs. Institutions such as schools, workplaces, families, and courts establish what counts as a difference and even what counts as a good reason. Rather than respond to objections that may simply be clues to deeper versions of the assumptions that make difference a dilemma, let us consider their roots. How did we come to believe that difference is intrinsic in the "different" person; that the norm used for comparison need not be stated; that an observer can see without a situated perspective; and that competing perspectives of those labeled different are irrelevant? How did we come to believe that the existing institutional arrangements, which treat some people as normal and others as different, are themselves natural, inevitable, and good?

Law provides vivid contexts for studying the assignment of the label of difference, whether by traits of race, gender, disability, or other minority identities. Law uses categories. Judges and administrators identify traits and place people and problems in categories on that basis. Law also backs up words and concepts with power. The names given by law carry real consequences in people's lives. In law, the press of the past has a special weight. Judges deliberately maintain continuity with ideas and practices of the past in order to promote social stability and protect expectations. Even the judicial model of individualized hearings and individualized judgments preserves and reinvents categorical solutions and neglects the relational dimensions of problems of difference.

The next part of the book, therefore, looks for the roots of the legal treatment of difference. It explores the process by which law developed a particular unstated norm, against which difference signaled incompetence. The legacies of the law's history and established modes of legal reasoning about difference can be glimpsed even in contemporary litigation. These legacies offer rich veins to mine in the search for alternatives to the difference dilemma.

HISTORICAL
DIFFERENCE

CHAPTER 4

When Difference Has Its Home

I cannot believe that a rational member of this disadvantaged
class could ever approve of the discriminatory application of the
city's ordinance in this case.
                                                    —Justice John Paul Stevens, 1985

Art restorers use the word *pentimento* to refer to what happens
when one painting has been painted over another: the earlier painting, over
time, may begin to show through.[1] Perhaps it is not surprising that similar
reminders of the past appear in legal arguments: lawyers and judges routinely reuse materials from the past in constructing the new. Yet the reap-
pearance of earlier patterns of thought in legal arguments does not always
reflect deliberate design.

While I was researching historical legal conceptions of the "law of persons" and the "law of abnormal persons," the Supreme Court of the United
States heard arguments in a case concerning one city's treatment of mentally
retarded persons. Although there were no dissenting opinions, the justices
expressed a variety of conceptions of the problem at hand. The opinions at
some points identify and reject earlier legal conceptions of "difference" and
at other moments reiterate or revive earlier conceptions. Thus, the case of
Cleburne Living Center, Inc. v. City of Cleburne[2] affords a window into past
and contemporary legal treatments of difference.

This chapter looks through that window, and the next (Chapter 5) follows
the distinct histories of an early "abnormal-persons" approach to difference
and the more recent approach of rights analysis. The remnants of some
aspects of the "abnormal-persons" approach and other, institutionalized
constraints in the rights method characterize even varieties of contemporary
legal theories that claim to amplify or criticize rights (Chapter 6). An emerging, new view emphasizes social relations, and draws intellectual support
from developments in many other fields of thought (Chapter 7). The earlier

[1]See Lillian Hellman, *Pentimento* (Boston: Little, Brown, 1973).
[2]473 U.S. 432 (1985).

views endure, however, and underlie the institutions that in turn reinforce them.

The Cleburne Story

The city of Cleburne, Texas, refused to grant a building permit for a residential group home for mentally retarded people.[3] A city zoning ordinance required a special permit for the construction of "hospitals for the insane or feeble minded, or alcoholic or drug addicts, or penal or corrections institutions."[4] To receive a permit, an applicant had to obtain "the signatures of the property owners within two hundred feet of the property to be used."[5] When the Cleburne Living Center (CLC) sought such signatures, neighboring property owners objected to the proposed construction and thereby prevented the applicants from building their home.[6]

Because mentally disabled adults often—or usually—cannot live unassisted, and because the factors of cost and psychological well-being require congregate housing, group homes have proved the most effective means of integrating them within residential neighborhoods. Hence, by conditioning the requisite city permit on approval by immediate neighbors, who often fear that such a group home will reduce property values or disrupt their lives, the city's ordinance created a barrier to the assimilation of mentally retarded persons into the community.

The applicants for the permit went to court to challenge the city's action on the grounds that it discriminated against the mentally retarded.[7] As plaintiff in the case, CLC challenged both the denial of the permit and the zoning scheme itself as violations of the Constitution's equal protection clause, which guarantees that no person will be denied the equal protection of the laws. The federal district court rejected these challenges. The judge reasoned that the ordinance, as written and as applied, was rationally related to the city's legitimate interests in "the legal responsibility of CLC and its residents, . . . the safety and fears of residents in the adjoining neighborhood," and the numbers of people to be housed in the residence.[8] The Court of Appeals for the Fifth Circuit disagreed, ruling that "mentally retarded" should be treated as a "quasi-suspect" classification. Under equal protection doctrine, this means that a government action that burdens the interests of individuals within this category deserves more than usual scrutiny and re-

---

[3] Although I prefer to join advocacy groups in replacing the term "mentally retarded" with "developmentally disabled," or "person with a cognitive disability," I retain "mentally retarded" here because the discussion focuses on a Supreme Court decision whose opinions use that term.

[4] 473 U.S. at 436 n.3.

[5] Id. at 455 n.12 (Stevens, J., concurring) (quoting the ordinance).

[6] Id. at 455.

[7] Id. at 437.

[8] Id.; Cleburne Living Center v. City of Cleburne, No. CA3-80-1576-F (N.D. Tex. Oct. 4, 1982) (LEXIS, Genfed Library, Dist File).

quires some justification beyond the typically lax requirement that the government action simply be rational. The most stringent judicial review of government classifications under equal protection law has been applied to distinctions drawn on racial lines because, according to the courts, the history of racial discrimination in this country makes such classifications "suspect."[9]

In the appeal brought by the CLC, the appeals court judges noted that mentally retarded persons have a history of "unfair and often grotesque mistreatment" similar to the treatment of racial minorities. Because mentally disabled people remain vulnerable to deep-seated prejudice and lack power either to change their condition or to influence their treatment through the political process, they deserve the court's special solicitude. Governmental distinctions based on mental retardation are not quite as worrisome as those using race, however, reasoned the judges, because mental retardation remains relevant to many legislative determinations.[10] Applying an intermediate level of scrutiny, then, the court of appeals held that the ordinance was invalid both as written and as applied to the CLC.

The city objected and took the case to the Supreme Court. There, Justice Byron White wrote for the majority, which declined to treat the mentally retarded as a quasi-suspect class. Instead, the majority opinion concluded that under equal protection analysis, legislative categories based on mental retardation need only be rationally related to a legitimate end. The mentally retarded are "different, immutably so, in relevant respect, and the states' interest in dealing with and providing for them is plainly a legitimate one." The efforts by federal, state, and local governments to respond to the needs of the mentally retarded "belies a continuing antipathy or prejudice and a corresponding need for more intrusive oversight by the judiciary."[11]

To support this argument, the Court cited such reforms as section 504 of the Federal Rehabilitation Act of 1973, which forbids discrimination on the basis of handicap in programs receiving federal funds. The Court also noted

[9]For the purposes of equal protection analysis, the Supreme Court has at times applied three levels of scrutiny, depending upon the interests it believed were at stake. The lowest level is applied if the Court sees no issue involving a suspect class or a fundamental right; the test is whether the state action bears a rational relationship to a legitimate state purpose. See United States R.R. Retirement Board v. Fritz, 449 U.S. 166 (1980); San Antonio Indep. School Dist. v. Rodriguez, 411 U.S. 1 (1973). The intermediate level is applied to cases involving gender or illegitimacy; this test asks if the classification is substantially related to the achievement of an important governmental purpose. See Craig v. Boren, 429 U.S. 190 (1976). Finally, the strict-scrutiny level requires the government to prove that a compelling government interest justifies infringement on a fundamental right or a suspect class. Several justices through the years have expressed their dissatisfaction with this tiered mode of analysis and disputed whether the Court actually abides by it. See, e.g., Craig v. Boren, 429 U.S. at 211–12 (Stevens, J., concurring); San Antonio Indep. School Dist. v. Rodriguez, 411 U.S. 1, 99 (1973) (Marshall, J., dissenting).

[10]726 F.2d 191, 197–200 (5th Cir. 1984), reh'g en banc denied 735 F.2d 832 (1984): "We are not prepared to say that they are a full-fledged suspect class. . . . Strict scrutiny has been reserved for classifications, such as race, that 'tend to be irrelevant to any proper legislative goal.' . . . Though mental retardation is irrelevant to many policies it *is* a relevant distinction in some cases" (original emphasis).

[11]473 U.S. at 443.

that Congress included a bill of rights for mentally retarded persons in a federal statute that provided funds for certain state programs.[12] Moreover, reasoned Justice White for the majority, when legislatures act to remedy historic exclusion and maltreatment of a minority, the minority does not deserve additional protection from the judiciary. Elected officials need freedom from judicial scrutiny in developing such remedial efforts, and the burden of satisfying heightened judicial scrutiny could inhibit the government from acting to help mentally retarded persons. Finally, the majority justified its refusal to accord heightened review to a classification based on mental retardation by noting the difficulty of differentiating other groups—the aged, the disabled, the infirm—which, like the mentally retarded, also suffer from immutable disabilities, lack of political power, and vulnerability to public prejudice.[13] Apparently, granting heightened scrutiny to these other groups would invite judicial activity that the Court wished to restrain.

Nonetheless, in a remarkable twist, the majority concluded that the city's ordinance failed to meet the usually minimal requirement of mere rationality in government action. The Court announced that legislative distinctions "between the mentally retarded and others must be rationally related to a legitimate governmental purpose," which can consist neither of a bare desire to harm a politically unpopular group nor of negative attitudes and vague undifferentiated fears about the mentally retarded. The majority reasoned that it would not be rational to treat group homes for the mentally retarded differently from homes for other groups, and that the city had no rational basis to believe that the proposed home posed a special threat to the city's legitimate purposes of protecting safety, controlling population density, and the like.

The Court concluded that although the zoning ordinance itself was lawful, its application to the CLC violated the equal protection clause. Thus, it invalidated the ordinance permit requirement as applied to these applicants yet left in place a regulatory scheme that would require other groups of mentally retarded people to apply for the special permit—without specifying what characteristics made the CLC applicants especially worthy of protection.[14]

As often happens, the Court's views were not unanimous. Justice Thurgood Marshall, joined by Justices William Brennan and Harry Blackmun, thought the majority had not gone far enough to protect mentally retarded individuals. Justice Marshall speculated that the majority appeared "to act out of a belief that the ordinance might be 'rational' as applied to some subgroup of the retarded under some circumstances unspecified by the ma-

---

[12]Id., citing 29 U.S.C. sec. 794, and Developmental Disabilities and Bill of Rights Act, 42 U.S.C. sec. 6010 (1)(2)(1982). But see Pennhurst v. Halderman, 451 U.S. 1, 19 (1981) (stating that sec. 6010 "does no more than express a congressional preference for certain kinds of treatment"). The Court conveniently ignored the fact that the discriminatory ordinance was passed by a city that had nothing to do with those federal funds.

[13]473 U.S. at 445–46.

[14]Id. at 448–50.

jority, even though some nine-tenths of the group covered by the term 'mentally retarded' would fall into the category of 'mildly retarded.' " Justice Marshall further criticized Justice White's majority opinion for failing to identify the interests at stake, for neglecting to demand careful examination of classifications based on mental retardation to assure that they do not rest on impermissible assumptions, and for leaving open the possibility that retarded individuals could be hurt in the future by the prejudicial assumptions preserved in the zoning ordinance permit requirement.[15]

Justice John Paul Stevens also wrote a separate opinion, joined by then Chief Justice Warren Burger, concurring in the majority's rejection of the whole discussion of suspect and quasi-suspect classification and levels of judicial scrutiny. Justice Stevens reasoned that the CLC should win because "the record convinces me that this permit was required because of the irrational fears of neighboring property owners, rather than for the protection of the mentally retarded persons" who sought to live in the group home.[16]

Lawyers and commentators could evaluate these opinions by comparing the justices' views of equal protection analysis. There are many competing views about this realm of constitutional interpretation and contrasting assessments of when "strict," "intermediate," or "minimal" judicial scrutiny is due.[17] Yet, beyond these debates about when to apply what kind of analysis, the very language of legal "tests" and "levels of scrutiny" converts significant social choices into mechanical and conclusory rhetoric.[18] A deeper understanding of the debate is possible only by looking to the clash in world views that occurs behind the justices' arguments over legal doctrine. A traditional view treats classifications on the basis of mental incompetence as natural and immutable. A second view addresses errors in classification and invokes the rights of individuals to be free from such errors by governmental officials. A third emerging view focuses on how classifications reveal relationships of power between those who label and those who are labeled. These views— the "abnormal-persons" approach, the "rights-analysis" approach, and the "social-relations" approach—all appear in the Supreme Court opinions in *Cleburne,* and all three have intriguing historical roots with offshoots in contemporary legal treatment of difference.

The Abnormal-Persons Approach

One version of the debate in the Cleburne case looks back in time to a legal world that divided society into two classes of persons, normal and abnormal;

---

[15]Id. at 474–78 (Marshall, J., concurring in the judgment in part and dissenting in part).
[16]Id. at 454.
[17]See n.9 above.
[18]Cf. Ollman v. Evans, 750 F.2d 970, 994 (D.C. Cir. 1984) (Bork, J., concurring) (criticizing as mechanical the jurisprudence that uses "three-pronged tests, and two-tiered analysis," because cases often cannot be resolved through verbal formulas).

different legal treatments followed from the assignment of individuals to one or the other class. This approach owes its origins in part to feudal notions of fixed-status relations. To this day, some legal rules retain the view that assertions about a person's basic or immutable nature locate him or her in one class or the other. Of special importance are facts about the person's mental competence or capacity. Those with normal competence and capacity enjoy rights; they can be held responsible for their acts because they are able to reason and conform their conduct to reason. Those with abnormal competence and capacity, in contrast, can be subjected to legal restraints on their autonomy and denied rights; they need legal protections to guard themselves and others from the effects of their incapacities. The mentally incompetent, in this view, are typically regarded as "disabled" both because they have "natural" disabilities that limit their mental competence and because they have legal disabilities that remove them from common legal, economic, and political practices.

A further premise is that although there are many variations among abnormal persons, these variations dim in contrast to their similarities in comparison with normal persons. Abnormal persons intrinsically differ from the norm, and anyone can see their difference. Perhaps the legacy of the "Great Chain of Being" idea,[19] which arranged the social hierarchy in line with a conception of divine order, helps to explain why the perceptions of those labeled different were not thought important. The ordering between normal and abnormal reflected deeper distinctions thought to be ordained by divine authority. The status quo embodied a fixed, natural, and eternal order.[20]

Even when liberal legal ideas of freedom and equality appeared on the scene, the distinction between abnormal and normal persons survived. Different legal treatment based on mental competence and incompetence is not only legally permitted; it actually advances the view that "all persons similarly situated should be treated alike"[21] by adopting mental competence as the dividing line between two differently situated groups. That is, it would be wrong for judges to scrutinize governmental distinctions that use mental competence as the dividing line, because constitutional rights do not mean the same thing for mentally incompetent people as they mean for "normal" people. Given the seemingly natural distinctions between the two groups, it would be beside the point for judges to inquire into the relationship between the mentally incompetent and the mentally competent in terms of political power, status, and actual contact with one another.

In *Cleburne*, all the judicial opinions manifest some aspects of this view. Mainly, the opinions treat the mentally retarded as a class of people who share more with each other than with the rest of the community. This, of course, presumes that the characteristic of mental retardation is a more

[19]See Arthur Lovejoy, *The Great Chain of Being* (1936; Cambridge, Mass.: Harvard University Press, 1971).

[20]Thus, the conception of abnormal persons held together the five assumptions that later produced dilemmas of difference.

[21]473 U.S. at 439.

important measure of similarity than, say, religion or age. Justice White's opinion for the Supreme Court majority, in particular, assumes that there is one easily discernible line that divides persons with sufficient mental capacity to be treated as normal from persons who lack such capacity. The opinion emphasizes that although there are variations within the group called mentally retarded, these variations are less important than the fact that "those who are mentally retarded have a reduced ability to cope with and function in the every day world." The majority's mental universe is inhabited by various groups, some with immutable differences that set them apart from the rest of society and thus warrant different legal treatment. The majority opinion expressly embraces the conception that because differences based on mental competence are real, natural, and immutable, governmental action based on this difference is not suspicious but legitimate.[22]

The Rights-Analysis Approach

A contrasting approach applies to mentally incompetent persons arguments about the rights of individuals to be free from unwarranted restraints and discriminations. Drawing primarily from civil rights and civil liberties strategies developed by lawyers and judges during the 1950s, 1960s, and 1970s, advocates for mentally handicapped individuals have developed a rights analysis to challenge mental competence classifications.[23]

Rights analysis begins with the view that legal rights apply to every individual. The facts of personhood and membership in the polity entitle each individual to be free from state interference and to be treated by the state the same as others are treated. In this view, historical denials of such rights to certain groups can no longer be defended. Notions of inferiority based on race, gender, or ethnicity are indefensible, given political and scientific assaults upon many of the old ideas about differences which were used to justify the denial of rights. Even though it still sees some differences as "real" and "natural," rights analysis inspires a skepticism about the accuracy of particular assumptions and classifications of difference, especially where there has been a history of prejudice and cruel treatment. Attributions of difference have so often been faulty, expressions only of prejudice and power, that they must be subjected to intense scrutiny. After that scrutiny, however, some real differences, in implicit comparison with the normal person, may in fact appear—and those differences are inherent. The same legal rights enjoyed by "normal" people then, should be sought for those labeled abnormal and mentally incompetent, unless it can be shown to the satisfaction of a

[22]Id. at 442–43.
[23]See Stanley Herr, "The New Clients: Legal Services for Mentally Retarded Persons," *Stan. L. Rev.* 31 (1979), 553; John Parry, "Rights and Entitlements in the Community," in *The Mentally Disabled and the Law*, ed. Samuel J. Brakel, John Parry, and Barbara Weiner (Chicago: American Bar Foundation, 1985); "Developments in the Law—Civil Commitment of the Mentally Ill," *Harv. L. Rev.* 87 (1974), 1190.

court that the differences between the groups are based on demonstrable evidence rather than prejudice. Invidious, impermissible discriminations are generally assessed from the vantage point of those who are normal, but the perspectives of those labeled "different" may be relevant in exposing error. The status quo must be changed if it denies rights to those who deserve them. This is the position pursued by those who advocate rights for mentally disabled people.

At the same time, and complicating matters, these advocates champion new rights, programs, and protections designed to benefit those labeled mentally incompetent. Special treatment is justified either as a quid pro quo for continued deprivation of such persons' basic rights[24] or as an entitlement founded on their special needs.[25] In these respects, rights analysis contains a central instability. It starts with the idea that everyone enjoys the same rights but proceeds with the possibility that some special rights may be necessary either to remove the effects of past deprivation or to address some special characteristics of certain groups.[26] Special rights, justified by differences, undermine claims of equal treatment predicated on sameness. Thus, not only may the argument for special rights lose for lack of precedent; it may also refuel distinctions and inequality.[27]

The difficulty arises because the rights approach holds on to an assumption from the abnormal-persons view. The rights approach maintains the unstated norm, based on one group of people, and therefore attributes differences to those who diverge from that norm. The analysis takes as a given and as a measure for the future the pattern of rights that developed for those historically included. New rights, responsive to the needs of the historically excluded, both lack foundation and strengthen the divide between those who fit and those who do not fit the norm. The rights approach also retains a general presumption that differences reside in the different person rather than in relation to norms embedded in prevailing institutions. Like the abnormal-persons approach, rights analysis asserts that all persons similarly situated should be treated alike, whereas those differently situated may be treated differently. Both link equal treatment to similarities.

Yet unlike the abnormal-persons approach, rights analysis acknowledges that governments and social groups have at times defined difference er-

---

[24]O'Connor v. Donaldson, 422 U.S. 563 (1975); Rouse v. Cameron, 373 F.2d 451 (D.C. Cir. 1966) (right to treatment as quid pro quo for deprivation of liberty).

[25]See, e.g., Education for All Handicapped Children Act, 20 U.S.C. sec. 1400–1461 (1982).

[26]For a discussion of these issues with respect to blacks, see Randall Kennedy, "Persuasion and Distrust: A Comment on the Affirmative Action Debates," *Harv. L. Rev.* 99 (1986), 1327, examining philosophic and political arguments about affirmative action for blacks; Kathleen M. Sullivan, Comment, "Sins of Discrimination: Last Term's Affirmative Action Cases," *Harv. L. Rev.* 100 (1986), 78, considering alternatives to notions of sin and dependence that have been used to restrict rights and remedies in discrimination contexts.

[27]This has been a problem in articulating women's rights, as well as rights for disabled people, because of legacies of differential treatment of women. For example, the nineteenth-century "cult of true womanhood" excluded women from public life even while claiming to celebrate women's greater virtue. See Barbara Welter, "The Cult of True Womanhood: 1820–1860," *American Queries* 18 (1966), 151, 162–63.

roneously, asserting that some people are different when they really are not, or not in any relevant sense. Therefore, although rights arguments are capable of advocating some change, the rights approach also presumes that the status quo is natural and good, except where it has mistakenly treated people who are really the same as though they were different. To guard against error in the future, rights advocates prescribe legislation and judicial action to protect those who have been labeled mentally incompetent. Rights analysis itself offers no answer to the question it poses: when are historical attributions of difference acceptable, and when are they false? Nor does it specify how to distinguish a violation of rights that can be remedied by treating retarded persons like the nonretarded from a violation that justifies new rights or special treatment. Instead, rights analysis calls for a careful judicial inquiry into these issues; it thus reposes confidence in the perceptions of the judiciary about similarities that transcend as well as differences that endure.

In many ways all three opinions by the justices in the *Cleburne* case subscribe to this form of rights analysis. Yet they also demonstrate divergent views about when rights analysis should reject differential treatment and when it should approve it. This is the problem left unresolved by the rights approach.

Thus, Justice White's opinion for the majority acknowledges that the Court's prior decisions authorize intense judicial scrutiny of classifications affecting groups whose members have experienced "a 'history of purposeful unequal treatment' or have been subjected to unique disabilities on the basis of stereotyped characteristics, not truly indicative of their abilities."[28] Yet the majority concludes that mentally retarded people really are different from others and that this characteristic of difference is relevant to legitimate governmental purposes.[29] The defect in the zoning ordinance's permit requirement, as applied, was that the city failed to provide any reasons that related to mental retardation which did not relate to other potential inhabitants of multiperson dwellings—who would not need such a permit. For this reason, according to the majority, the permit denial was irrational. Mentally retarded persons are wrongly treated differently from others who, like them, seek to live in multiperson dwellings.

For Justice Stevens, the way to distinguish acceptable from unacceptable differential treatment turns on whether the government's purpose behind the disparate treatment transcends the harm to the class disadvantaged by that treatment. In short, different groups may be treated differently if doing so is an acceptable cost of achieving a larger goal. What kinds of larger goals could justify the cost of differential treatment? Granting special benefits to

---

[28] 473 U.S. at 441 (quoting Massachusetts Board of Retirement v. Murgia, 427 U.S. at 313).

[29] There is a risk of tautological thinking here: the majority opinion asks whether the difference is relevant to a legitimate governmental purpose (473 U.S. at 442–43), when the legitimacy of a governmental purpose may well be affected by whether or not the difference is allowed to be relevant. Justice White also treated homosexuality as a "real difference" in refusing a challenge to the enforcement of a sodomy prohibition against a gay man; see Bowers v. Hardwick, 478 U.S. 186 (1986).

the different group certainly would suffice. So would regulation to protect the safety of both mentally retarded persons and others. Justice Stevens does not consider whether the benefit must accrue at least in part to the burdened class and, if so, according to whose estimate. Ultimately, he is left with uncertainty lodged within the rights approach, as to how and when anyone should draw the line between acceptable and unacceptable differential treatment of different people.

Justice Marshall's opinion manifests aspects of rights analysis chiefly in its elaboration of the historical changes in judicial notions about who is the same and who is different. He argues that judicial principles evolve over time in light of shifting patterns that make artificial what was once seen as natural. This is a classic statement of rights analysis both in its explicit reference to earlier reform movements on behalf of racial minorities and women and in its suggestion that while some categories of difference are outmoded, history and prevailing social thought may show that some "real" differences still persist.[30]

At its best, rights analysis adopts a skeptical perspective toward classifications historically used for discriminatory purposes and seeks to expose the hostility and thoughtlessness behind assignments of difference; it calls for intensive examination by judges concerned with equality and liberty. At its worst, rights analysis provides a new layer of conclusory judgments, assigned labels of difference based on widely held views. Some governmental actions imposing differential treatment on the basis of group differences will survive the searching inquiry of rights analysis, yet rights analysis itself does not explain why.

The Social-Relations Approach

A Definition

Undoubtedly the least familiar and most difficult to define of the three approaches to difference is that of social relations. It is the newest and the least embedded in language and practice. Nonetheless, the following elements, drawn from social theories developed since 1920, can be identified. Unlike rights analysis but bearing some resemblance to the concept of abnormal persons, the social-relations approach assumes that there is a basic connectedness between people, instead of assuming that autonomy is the prior and essential dimension of personhood. Yet like rights analysis and unlike the concept of abnormal persons, the social-relations approach is dubious of the method of social organization that constructs human relationships in terms of immutable categories, fixed status, and inherited or ascribed traits.[31]

---

[30]473 U.S. 460–65.
[31]The social relations approach might be understood in a Hegelian dialectical fashion: the feudal, hierarchical qualities of the abnormal-persons thesis yielded its antithesis—a rights

Indeed, even more fundamentally than rights analysis, the social-relations approach challenges the categories and differences used to define and describe people on a group basis. People adopt this approach not only because of an awareness of historical errors in the attribution of difference but also because of a suspicion that the attribution locates the problem in the person who does not fit in rather than in relationships between people and social institutions. The attribution of difference hides the power of those who classify and of the institutional arrangements that enshrine one type of person as the norm, and then treat classifications of difference as inherent and natural while debasing those defined as different. A focus on social relations casts doubt on the notion that difference is located solely in the person who is different. This approach also doubts the very claim to knowledge manifested when public or private actors label any group as different. That claim disguises the power of the namers, who simultaneously assign names and deny their relationships with and power over the named. Naming another as different seems natural and obvious when other professionals, social practices, and communal attitudes reinforce that view—and yet these sources of confirmation may merely show how widespread and deep are the prejudice and mistaken views about the "different" person. The power of institutionalized norms allows the namers to ignore altogether the perspective of the less powerful. The social-relations approach embraces the belief that knowledge is rooted in specific perspectives, and that "prevailing views" or "consensus approaches" express the perspectives of those in positions to enforce their points of view in the structure and governance of society.[32]

Emerging after the rights approach, the social-relations approach must respond to the assumption that people are basically separate, with the legal status of autonomous individuals, unless they fall into an exceptional category. The social-relations view assumes, in contrast, that people live and talk in relationships and never exist outside of them. From this vantage point, assertions of difference may be understood as statements of relationships. "Difference" is meaningful only as a comparison. A comparison draws a relationship: a short person is different only in relation to a taller one. As a relational notion, difference is reciprocal: I am no more different from you than you are from me.

But the statement of difference distributes power. The name of difference is produced by those with the power to name and the power to treat themselves as the norm. Though the difference does not reside in any one person, the comparison is drawn by some to distinguish themselves from others. The taller person calls the other one "short." People live and perceive the world within social relationships, and people use these relationships to construct and express both power and knowledge. Categories for organizing percep-

analysis premised upon autonomous individualism and essential sameness among persons; the social-relations synthesis recaptures the social connectedness of the abnormal-persons view, while also preserving freedom from outwardly imposed categorization and constraint as advanced by rights analysis.

[32]See Steven Lukes, *Power: A Radical View* (London: Macmillan, 1974).

tions assign differences to some but not others and thus perpetuate or increase disparities of power between groups. When public officials organize the world through categories of difference, they select some traits from among many and give them significance in distributing benefits and burdens. And the traits usually selected reflect the experiences and privileges of those making the selection.[33]

As a method of legal analysis, the social-relations approach demands analysis of difference in terms of the relationships that construct it. The approach solicits challenges from the perspective of those labeled different, and it treats existing institutional arrangements as a conceivable source of the problem of difference rather than as an unproblematic background. Besides identifying avenues for inquiry about difference, the social-relations approach points toward a particular, normative evaluation of legal assignments of difference: attributions of difference should be sustained only if they do not express or confirm the distribution of power in ways that harm the less powerful and benefit the more powerful.

Stated this way, the social-relations approach bears some resemblance to philosopher John Rawls's "difference principle." In his *Theory of Justice* Rawls proposes that "assuming the framework of institutions required by equal liberty and fair equality of opportunity, the higher expectations of those better situated are just if and only if they work as part of a scheme which improves the expectations of the least advantaged members of society."[34] Like Rawls's principle, the social-relations approach evaluates social practice with concern for those less well off, but it differs in the following respects: (1) it directs that one who judges assertions of difference should try to assume the perspective of those assigned the label of difference—even though the judge may never fully know or understand that perspective; and (2) it challenges the very positioning of any individual or group as "different" by treating difference as a function of the relationships between those naming the difference and those so named.[35]

---

[33]See Catharine MacKinnon, "Difference and Dominance," in *Feminism Unmodified: Discourses on Life and Law* (Cambridge, Mass.: Harvard University Press, 1987), pp. 32–45; Ruth Colker, "Anti-Subordination above All: Sex, Race, and Equal Protection," *N.Y.U. L. Rev.* 61 (1986), 1003.

[34]John Rawls, *A Theory of Justice* (Cambridge, Mass.: Belknap Press of Harvard University Press, 1971), p. 75. Rawls also provides his own definitions of equal liberty and fair equality of opportunity related to "primary goods" (pp. 62, 92, 178). He states as follows the two principles of justice that he believes would be chosen in the original contractual position: (1) "Each person is to have an equal right to the most extensive basic liberty compatible with a similar liberty for others" (p. 60); (2) "Social and economic inequalities are to be arranged so that they are both (a) to the greatest benefit of the least advantaged [the difference principle] and (b) attached to offices and positions open to all under the conditions of fair equality of opportunity" (p. 83). Rawls defines fair equality of opportunity to mean ideally that everyone has a fair chance to obtain primary goods such as wealth and respect. A fair competition would not be affected by such morally arbitrary factors as economic position or talents at birth. Because life chances are affected by such factors, Rawls concludes that justice requires the difference principle. (His theory concerns political justice, not all of moral life; see his "Justice as Fairness: Political Not Metaphysical," *Philosophy and Public Affairs* 14 [1985], 223, 245.)

[35]In addition, the social relations approach applies not just to the distribution of "primary goods" but also to legal and social practice more generally.

Undertaking such an analysis is a deeply problematic task for a judge who is a state official. That person is obviously in a position of power and helps to maintain existing institutions. The social relations approach exposes the court's own social relation of power vis-à-vis the litigants and other institutions. The very claim to recognize a real difference could be a sign of unacknowledged power over others. As Catharine MacKinnon has observed, when Justice Potter Stewart of the United States Supreme Court declared that he knew obscenity when he saw it, he literally expressed the power of his position to label expression as obscene.[36] Similarly, a judicial assessment that the mentally retarded really are different from others may reiterate rather than challenge the prevailing patterns of social relations, which allow some people to attribute differences that harm the less powerful. Using rights analysis, judges may conclude that some people really are different and thus deserve different legal treatment. But rights analysis treats as unproblematic the perspective of those looking into the bases for a challenged difference, even though the perspective of those doing the looking may itself be critical to the assignment of difference. The social-relations approach, in contrast, calls for the development of new strategies to raise questions about the nature of a court's relationship to the question of difference.

One judicial strategy for the analysis of social relations tries to take the perspective of the group that those in power have defined as different, a strategy that may be quite problematic in two ways. First, it is unclear whether anyone can ever really take the perspective of another. This very difficulty carries with it the invitation to a certain amount of humility and self-doubt in the process of trying to know, and these qualities may allow the judge to glimpse a point of view other than his or her own. But, second, in trying to see the perspective of another the judge may attribute a kind of unitary difference to all members of the "different" group and risk obscuring the range of differences within that very group. A focus by male judges on the perspective of women, for example, could obscure the variety of perspectives among women and thereby reinforce, rather than challenge, the attribution by men of a particular conception of difference to women. Still, the very effort to imagine another perspective could sensitize the court to the possibility of a variety of perspectives. Once judges recognize that they do not possess the only truth, they may be more ready to acknowledge that there are even more than two truths, more than two points of view.

A second judicial strategy adopts the social-relations approach to explore the social meanings that exclusion and isolation carry in a community. This strategy builds on a premise of ongoing relationships and scrutinizes relationships of distance and exclusion. Does the act of naming or labeling cut off or deny relationships of mutual respect?

Some legal scholars and philosophers have pursued social-relations approaches. For example, Judge John Noonan's book *Persons and Masks of the Law* explores the ways in which legal concepts and professional roles can cut

---

[36]Catharine MacKinnon, "Pornography, Civil Rights, and Speech," *Harv. C.R.–C.L. L. Rev.* 20 (1985), 113.

off people's sense of connection with one another and with the consequences of their own official actions.[37] Philosopher Paul Ricoeur has explored Heidegger's notions that naming preserves but also conceals, discloses but also contains. Many other scholars have described as the problem of "reification" the way abstractions, such as names and concepts, transmute experience and distance people's sense of understanding and participation in their own experiences.[38] Social-relations concerns can offer new insights and answers by enabling critiques of the failures of other legal conceptions of naming and human difference. The social-relations approach may be new to law, but it builds on many developments in other fields—and it has made its way into Supreme Court opinions.

Social Relations in *Cleburne*

The majority's opinion in *Cleburne* barely hints at any effort to take the perspective of the mentally retarded people excluded by the denial of the zoning permit; nor does the majority assess the social meanings of exclusion and isolation. In contrast, Justice Stevens's and Justice Marshall's opinions both try to take the perspective of the mentally retarded persons burdened by the denial of the permit and by the zoning ordinance that required a special permit for their group home. Justice Marshall also explores the meaning of social isolation and the relationships between those who are labeled different and those who have sufficient power to adopt and apply the label. Close analysis of judicial language in this case may illuminate an emerging approach to the legal treatment of difference.

Justice Stevens concludes his opinion with this remarkable flourish: "I cannot believe that a rational member of this disadvantaged class could ever approve of the discriminatory application of the city's ordinance in this case."[39] The sentence is remarkable because it treats as significant the views

[37]John T. Noonan, *Persons and Masks of the Law: Cardozo, Holmes, Jefferson, and Wythe as Makers of the Masks* (New York: Farrar, Straus & Giroux, 1976), pp. 14–16. Ursula LeGuin noted a similar phenomenon in her inventive short story "She Unnames Them," in which Eve unnames all that Adam has named in the Garden of Eden—and thereby liberates all the animals (*New Yorker*, Jan. 21, 1985, p. 49).

[38]Paul Ricoeur, *The Conflict of Interpretations: Essays in Hermeneutics* (Evanston, Ill.: Northwestern University Press, 1974), p. 233; Georg Lukács, "Reification and the Consciousness of the Proletariat," in *History and Class Consciousness: Studies in Marxist Dialectics* (Cambridge, Mass.: MIT Press, 1971), pp. 83–222; Karl Marx, "The Fetishism of Commodities and the Secret Thereof," in *Capital: A Critique of Political Economy*, trans. Samuel Moore and Edward Aveling, ed. Frederick Engels (New York: International Publishers, 1967), pp. 81–96; Peter Gabel, "Reification in Legal Reasoning," *Res. in Law and Soc.* 3 (1980), 25.

[39]473 U.S. at 455. This is no stray statement. In the same opinion Justice Stevens similarly notes that "an impartial lawmaker—indeed, even a member of the class of persons defined as mentally retarded—could rationally vote in favor of a law providing funds for special education and special treatment for the mentally retarded. A mentally retarded person could also recognize that he is a member of a class that might need special supervision in some situations, both to protect himself and to protect others" (456). This comment suggests that mentally retarded persons can recognize that they are different from others and need help; Stevens's final sentence affords a more complete shift in perspective by imagining how a mentally retarded person would view the action taken by the government.

of the actual members of the class burdened by the governmental classification. It implies that the Court should consider the perspective of a "different" group, whose views about a governmental classification may differ from the views of others. By imagining the perspective of the mentally retarded individuals, Justice Stevens departs from and implicitly assaults the usual assessment of such persons as incapable of forming reliable judgments about their own interests. Indeed, it is the usual assessment of the abnormality of mentally retarded persons that undergirds the discussion in the majority opinion about why governments may continue to treat the mentally retarded differently from others. Thus, in what may have seemed merely a rhetorical gesture, Justice Stevens opens up a bold new way to consider the legal treatment of mentally retarded persons.

Yet the very sentence making this remarkable call to consider the perspective of the mentally retarded persons blocks out much of the proximity, empathy, and imagination necessary for such consideration. Perhaps instinctively, perhaps deliberately, Justice Stevens tempers his attention to another perspective by adding the lawyerly gloss of the "reasonable person": what would a *rational* mentally retarded person think about the special permit requirement for group homes for mentally retarded people? Whatever the real or subjective perspective of mentally retarded persons, Justice Stevens attends to something else, the perspective of the mentally retarded person filtered through the judicial lens of what he thinks would be reasonable to see or want.

Interestingly, Justice Stevens also omits any specific reference to "mental retardation." Instead, he refers to a "rational member of this disadvantaged class." Perhaps the tension between the usual use of "rational" and the usual image of "mental retardation" explains this omission. Perhaps the author of the sentence could not bring himself to juxtapose the idea of "the rational," with which he himself could identify, and the image of "the mentally retarded," with which he could not fully identify. It is also possible that he meant simply to invoke the general, abstract idea of rational self-interest and to note that no rationally self-interested person would approve of a rule excluding himself from the residential community in which he hoped and planned to reside. If so, the sentence assimilates mentally retarded persons to a standard abstracted from circumstances and leaves open the question of when the judge should abstract a person from circumstances or labels and when not.

Even given these ambiguities, Justice Stevens's sentence manifests a social-relations approach. Considering the perspective of the burdened class exposes the problematic relationship between those enacting the classification and those burdened by it. Looking at the perspective of those in a class subject to a restriction also engages the judge in some effort to relate to and, to some extent, identify with those who seem different from members of the judiciary. This inquiry also suggests that the judge may need to examine critically whether the political process for classification excludes or overshadows the perspective of the burdened group.

Justice Stevens's approach sharply contrasts with the tack taken by the majority, which almost entirely ignores the possibility that the power of the government and the courts over mentally retarded persons might allow them to ignore or even fail to see a contrasting perspective held by the mentally retarded. Power and knowledge are related, suggests Justice Stevens. The majority opinion, in contrast, reasons that the remedial legislation singling out the retarded for special treatment reflects a civilized and decent society, which does not need to provide special judicial attention for these people, and instead needs flexibility and freedom for officials "in shaping and limiting their remedial efforts."[40] In this way, the majority justices fail to acknowledge how their own perspective may differ from the view of the mentally retarded, much less how their power allows them to believe that their perspective about the mentally retarded is the one true perspective.

Justice Marshall, in fact, takes on the majority's conclusion that the presence of remedial legislation benefiting mentally retarded persons eliminates the need for judicial protection on their behalf: "The import of these conclusions, it seems, is that the only discrimination courts may remedy is the discrimination they alone are perspicacious enough to see. Once society begins to recognize certain practices as discriminatory, in part because previously stigmatized groups have mobilized politically to lift this stigma, the Court would refrain from approaching such practices with the added skepticism of heightened scrutiny."[41]

Justice Marshall's own argument focuses on the relationships between powerful and less powerful people, which, he argues, shape the meanings that exclusion and isolation carry. His opinion analyzes the historical experiences of segregation for mentally retarded persons through institutionalization and exclusion from schools, from politics, and from daily community life. This exclusion, reasons Justice Marshall, resulted from decisions by a majority that feared and attributed social problems to a powerless and misunderstood minority. The opinion explicitly discusses the role of social Darwinism in justifying the restrictions placed on mentally retarded persons—restrictions limiting marriage and procreation, even legal sanction of compulsory sterilization. Majority groups continue to attribute differences to mentally retarded people and continue to fear and misunderstand them because of the "prolonged social and cultural isolation of the retarded," and such misunderstandings continue to stymie recognition of the dignity and individuality of retarded people. Justice Marshall analogizes the situation of mentally retarded persons with that of blacks and women, who have been similarly subjected to restrictive legal treatment because of faulty views held by those who make and enforce the rules.[42]

Social isolation is especially a problem, then, given a premise that people require relationships but experience distance and rejection when prevailing relationships enforce inequalities of power. To Justice Marshall, the history of isolation is most important because "lengthy and continuing isolation of the retarded has perpetuated the ignorance, irrational fears, and stereotyping

[40]473 U.S. at 445.
[41]Id. at 466 (Marshall, J., concurring in part and dissenting in part).
[42]Id. 461–71.

that long have plagued them." The root of prejudice is the separation between groups that exaggerates difference.[43]

Under this analysis, the zoning ordinance's special permit requirement must be seen as excluding mentally retarded people from residential communities and prolonging their isolation from other people. Justice Marshall explains the significance of the proposed group home by addressing the meanings of connection and separation in the context of relationships of unequal power. He also attempts to imagine the perspective of the less powerful group. For retarded adults, the right to establish a home "means living together in group homes, for as deinstitutionalization has progressed, group homes have become the primary means by which retarded adults can enter life in the community." He then cites the district court's factual finding—unmentioned in the other opinions—that difficulty in establishing group homes operates to exclude mentally retarded people from the community altogether. Finally, reasons Justice Marshall, denying them group homes "deprives the retarded of much of what makes for human freedom and fulfillment—the ability to form bonds and take part in the life of a community."[44]

Each of these points proceeds from the premises that people depend upon social relationships and that attributions of difference which build obstacles to respectful relationships are suspect. Isolation itself may contribute to false views of difference which impede mutual relationships. When that isolation arises because a majority group chooses to exclude a relatively powerless minority group, the judiciary should inquire with care into the patterns of power which might explain this situation.

Attention to relationships between groups, and the power constructed through those relationships, leads Justice Marshall to emphasize the importance of the context in which a particular trait of difference comes to matter. This emphasis on context is in keeping with Justice Marshall's long-standing effort to establish a sliding scale of equal-protection scrutiny based on the nature of the threatened interest as well as on the nature of the classification.[45] The interest in context is also a feature of the social-relations approach, which stresses actual social experiences and their meanings to the people involved rather than abstract or formal principles. As Justice Marshall points out, although a characteristic may be relevant in some circumstances, it should not be presumed always to be relevant; for example, "a sign that says 'men only' looks very different on a bathroom door than on a courthouse door."[46]

---

[43]Id. at 464 and n. 16, citing Gordon Allport, *The Nature of Prejudice* (Cambridge, Mass.: Addison-Wesley, 1958), which expresses the view that difference is constructed in the relationships between people and that knowledge of difference develops within relationships, including relationships of imposed segregation.

[44]473 U.S. at 461.

[45]See Plyler v. Doe, 457 U.S. 202, 231 (1982) (Marshall, J., concurring); Harris v. McRae, 448 U.S. 297, 341–42 (1980) (Marshall, J., dissenting); Massachusetts Board of Retirement v. Murgia, 427 U.S. 307, 318–21 (1976) (Marshall, J., dissenting).

[46]473 U.S. at 468–69 (Marshall, J., concurring in part and dissenting in part). The next sentence, "But see Bradwell v. Illinois, 16 Wall. 130, 21 L.Ed. 442 (1873)," is a sly reference to an earlier Court that did not perceive the difference in context. In *Bradwell*, the Court rejected a

This sentence is evocative on several levels. On one level, the point is simply that a change in context can make the same thing seem instead quite different: the "men only" sign means something different in the context of the two settings. On another level, the sentence suggests that context can make differences become irrelevant and thus make different people seem the same. We can see the difference in these meanings now because the assumptions about the gender differences have changed; they are no longer so institutionalized as to make unimaginable a challenge to the assignment of men and women to entirely different social and political status. Under present-day views, whatever differences there may be between men and women are irrelevant for the purpose of entrance to the courthouse.[47] It is not just difference in context that matters here; what matters is the relative power represented by the two contexts. The meanings of inclusion and exclusion vary, depending on the significance of those contexts within the particular society.

Justices Stevens and Marshall both adopted the social-relations approach in critical portions of their opinions in *Cleburne,* but neither opinion fully embraces this view. Justice Stevens's analysis ultimately stresses his often advanced single standard for the analysis of equal protection, through which the Court can ask, across varied contexts, what class may be harmed by the legislation, what public purpose animates the law, and how the nature of the class may justify the disparate treatment. By emphasizing this one set of questions for use in all situations, the opinion uses rights analysis. Yet by presuming that real differences exist between groups of people, making some "normal" and some not, the opinion also preserves assumptions stemming from the abnormal-persons approach. Justice Stevens notes that differences between mentally retarded persons and those with greater mental capacity are obviously relevant to certain legislative decisions. He treats as unproblematic the Court's own relationship to knowledge about classifications and harms, thereby failing to recognize the complex relations between knowledge and power.[48] Justice Marshall's opinion also straddles approaches,

woman's claim that she was entitled to become an attorney despite a state ruling refusing women admission to law practice. Since Justice Marshall cites *Bradwell* five paragraphs earlier as an example of an opinion stating as natural and self-evident a social order that it later came to see as "an artificial and invidious constraint on human potential and freedom," this can be seen as a double dig at the majority—which fails in this case to see the importance of shifting contexts, just as court majorities had failed to do in the past.

[47]The significance of bathroom access should not be ignored, however. Restrictions on the basis of race would, given our history of race relations, be a nontrivial issue. Bathroom access can also be quite important where bathrooms are assigned by gender but one gender group has fewer and less accessible bathrooms—perhaps because its members have not traditionally been occupants of the building. See Paula Christ, "Liberation of the Yale Divinity School Library Men's Room," in *Pulling Our Own Strings: Feminist Humor and Satire,* ed. Gloria Kaufman and Mary Kay Blakely (Bloomington: Indiana University Press, 1980), p. 96. University administrators once cited the absence of bathrooms for women as a reason for refusing women admission to various schools. See Kim Baserga, "The Early Years of Co-education at the Yale University School of Medicine," *Yale Journal of Biology and Medicine* 53 (1980), 181, 185: women were admitted after the father of a female applicant donated a women's bathroom.

[48]473 U.S. at 454 (Stevens, J., concurring).

especially in its depiction of rights as evolving when society recognizes past mistakes, and in its discussion of false stereotypes—as if any stereotypes were true.

An opinion fully embracing the social-relations approach would not assign difference to a group and its members but instead locate difference as a comparison drawn—by somebody—between groups. Paying close attention to exactly who names the difference, such an analysis would consider whether a more powerful group assigns meaning to a trait in order to express and consolidate power. Self-assigned difference, names and identities chosen by the group itself, would call for a different analysis. These identities are not the ones embedded in prevailing institutions and assigned to others without their participation. A judicial opinion pursuing the social-relations approach would discuss overtly the relationships between people, including the members of the Court and those affected by the Court's decision. The opinion would avoid the passive voice; its authors would be obliged to disclose their own involvement in and responsibility for their assertions.[49]

The abnormal-persons view makes differential treatment seem natural, unavoidable, and unproblematic. It enacts all the assumptions that make the difference dilemma seem unresolvable: it assumes that difference is intrinsic, compared to an unstated norm; it pretends that there can be an unsituated perspective while ignoring competing perspectives; and it treats existing social arrangements as natural and unproblematic. The social-relations approach contests all these assumptions; in this view, differences can be understood only relationally, and the norms and institutional arrangements that make some seem different must become explicit elements of inquiries about permissible attributions of difference. The relationship between knowledge and the position of the knower becomes significant, and the perspective of those who have been called different becomes an important challenge or corrective to what has passed for an unsituated perspective. Differential treatment becomes a problem of social choice and meaning, a problem for which all onlookers are responsible.

The rights-analysis approach, the dominant framework for contemporary analysis, shares some elements with the two other approaches and yet cannot itself resolve the tension between them. Acknowledging that some differences have been mistakenly attributed, the rights approach offers an opening wedge for challenging the assumptions of the abnormal-persons view. But retaining the premise that equality presumes sameness, rights inquiries look for evidence of difference and often leave such evidence uncontested as though it reflected no particular perspective, no problematic relationships between knowledge and the situation of the knower. While inviting proof that a given assignment of difference reflects prejudice and error, the rights approach presumes that most social arrangements are natural and inevitable. The contemporary predicament of rights analysis, especially its inability to evade

---

[49]Cf. Noonan, *Persons and Masks of the Law*; and Joseph Vining, *The Authoritative and the Authoritarian* (Chicago: University of Chicago Press, 1986).

the dilemma of difference, can be traced to its response to the abnormal-persons view.

A look at the history behind each of these approaches will illuminate their sources and the reasons why they endure in tension with one another.

CHAPTER 5

Different Histories

when we go home
with what we have got
when we climb the stairs reciting ancient deeds
the seas grow deeper
that we rose from

—W. S. Merwin, "Last People"

M any observers have described Western intellectual and legal histories as moving from notions of fixed and assigned status to notions of individual freedom and rights. Sir Henry Maine's famous dictum defined progress as the movement from status to contract.[1] Such broadly gauged summaries risk oversimplification and insensitivity to the variety and contestability of understandings of the past. Nonetheless, the contrast between legal orders premised upon status and those premised upon state-guaranteed rights helps to locate notions of abnormal persons and rights analysis as ways for dealing with differences. And as a historical matter, rights analysis in some ways is a successor to the abnormal-persons view.[2] This chapter pursues both the histories and the persistence of the abnormal-persons and rights approaches to the legal treatment of difference.

From Status to Contract—But Not for All

Someone living in the thirteenth or fourteenth century in Europe probably thought of himself or herself as a member of a people, a family, or a manor—

Epigraph: Reprinted with permission of Atheneum Publishers, an imprint of Macmillan Publishing Company, from *The Carrier of Ladders* by W. S. Merwin. Copyright © 1970 by W. S. Merwin.

[1] For an intriguing critique, see Manfred Rehbinder, "Status, Contract, and the Welfare State," *Stan. L. Rev.* 23 (1971), 941. I have also criticized this view in Martha Minow, " 'Forming underneath Everything That Grows': Toward a History of Family Law," *Wis. L. Rev.* 1985 (1985), 819, 834–39.

[2] Chapter 7 adds to this history the new stage identified as the social-relations approach.

rather than as a unique individual.[3] The medieval legal order reflected and enforced a social, economic, and political system of hierarchical relationships and stations, some of which were hereditary.[4] Estates and orders divided society along several dimensions, including class and social function.[5] Political, social, and religious beliefs converged to justify hierarchical social status.[6] The rules evinced a conception of each individual as occupying a status or office that was situated within a social hierarchy and understood to be part of a natural and divinely inspired order for mutual protection. As an old hymn put it:

> The rich man in his castle,
> The poor man at his gate,
> God made them, high or lowly,
> And order'd their estate.[7]

Status was assigned, not chosen; legal, customary, and religious practices coincided in defining it. Local lords bound their vassals and their serfs into relationships of mutual aid, embedding each person in the hierarchical network of reciprocal obligations.[8] Personal status depended upon relationships with other statuses, and these relationships in turn figured in contrasting obligations and powers in relation to land.[9] The rules of status treated society as a collective, organic whole with a descending line of authority. Obedience to authority and to persons in superior positions was an article of

---

[3]See Jacob Burckhardt, *The Civilization of the Renaissance in Italy*, trans. S. G. C. Middlemore (New York: A. C. Boni, 1935), p. 70. This general description does not pay attention to the variations in feudal and manorial development across Europe and England, which recent scholarship has emphasized.

[4]See generally Marc Bloch, *Feudal Society*, vols. 1 and 2, trans. L. A. Manyon (Chicago: University of Chicago Press, 1961); *Feudalism in History*, ed. Rushton Coulborn (Princeton, N.J.: Princeton University Press, 1956); William Holdsworth, *A History of English Law*, vols. 3 and 9 (Boston: Little, Brown, 1926).

[5]George Duby's classic work *The Three Orders: Feudal Society Imagined*, trans. Arthur Goldhammer (Chicago: University of Chicago Press, 1980), illuminates the conceptual and institutional division of medieval French society into those who prayed, those who fought, and those who labored or farmed—reflecting what was imagined as inevitable inequality. Status could also turn on age (minors held only limited entitlements and limited liabilities) or religion (Jews in many countries were assigned a legal status restricting their ability to hold land and placing them under the direct protection of a king). See R. H. Graveson, *Status in the Common Law* (London: University of London, Atholone Press, 1953). Married women also held a distinct status.

[6]Johan Huizinga, *The Waning of the Middle Ages* (1924; Garden City, N.Y.: Anchor Books, 1954), pp. 57–58.

[7]C. F. Alexander, "All Things Bright and Beautiful" (1848), quoted in *The Oxford Dictionary of Quotations*, 2d rev. ed. (London: Oxford University Press, 1954), p. 3. See Walter Ullmann, *The Individual and Society in the Middle Ages* (Baltimore, Md.: Johns Hopkins University Press, 1966), pp. 5–6, 31–33.

[8]See Graveson, *Status in the Common Law*, p. 14; Hanna Pitkin, *Fortune Is a Woman: Gender and Politics in the Thought of Niccolo Machiavelli* (Berkeley: University of California Press, 1984), pp. 9–10.

[9]Graveson, *Status in the Common Law*, p. 12.

religious faith as well as a subject for legal enforcement.[10] Legal enforcement of personal obligations of loyalty and mutual support took care of both military and economic needs. The law, having both religious and secular sources, established rules about property and duty that would later be seen as constraints on individual freedom.

Knowledge of the actual self-perceptions of individuals living in this medieval world may be ultimately inaccessible to those of us who live by different assumptions. As described by later observers, the absence of individual identity is probably overstated and neglects the gradual transitions toward notions of individual political identity. Such transitions may well have been enabled by the earlier ideas of virtues based on the fulfillment of roles.[11] The transformation of this hierarchical legal order occurred gradually and unevenly in different geographic regions, yet some generalizations can be hazarded. Legal and political transformations, beginning with the Renaissance and continuing into the present, rested on an emerging idea of the individual who has distinct and self-interested desires and who needs freedom of action and protection from the interference of others.[12] Law and politics increasingly addressed the relationship between the individual and the state, replacing attention to feudal obligations.[13] Renaissance political theorists began to define the task of government as protecting the rights and freedoms of each individual. Centralized governments began to overshadow local lords in power and in significance, and eventually national laws became the instrument for effecting sovereign power and preserving individual rights. Extensive trading and marketplace exchanges developed as merchants traveled to buy and sell goods. Contract became the central framework for legal and political relations. Reciprocal—and nonhierarchical—obligations, freely chosen by self-defining beings, became the preferred pattern underlying eco-

---

[10]Ullmann, *Individual and Society*, pp. 12–14, 17–18, 31. See also Arthur Lovejoy, *The Great Chain of Being* (1936; Cambridge, Mass.: Harvard University Press, 1971), pp. 67–98; Steven Seidman, *Liberalism and the Origins of European Social Theory* (Berkeley: University of California Press, 1983), p. 255.

[11]See Hendrick Hartog, "Imposing Constitutional Traditions," *Wm. & Mary L. Rev.* 29 (1987), 75; Alain MacFarlane, *The Origins of English Individualism* (New York: Cambridge University Press, 1979); Linda Kerber, "Making Republicanism Useful," *Yale L.J.* 97 (1988), 1663.

[12]See Robert Cumming, *Human Nature and History* (Chicago: University of Chicago Press, 1969), pp. 2–140; Burckhardt, *Civilization of the Renaissance*, p. 240; Pitkin, *Fortune Is a Woman*, pp. 8–16. For a critical essay proposing that individuals pursued a sense of self-expression and autonomy in the sixteenth century through conscious relation to the groups to which they belonged, see Natalie Zemon Davis, "Boundaries and the Sense of Self in Sixteenth-Century France," in *Reconstructing Individualism: Autonomy, Individuality, and the Self in Western Thought*, ed. Thomas Heller, Morton Sosna, and David E. Wellbery (Stanford, Calif.: Standard University Press, 1986), p. 53.

[13]Ullmann (*Individual and Society*, pp. 64–75, 148–49) argues that many of these changes were latent within the earlier order. For example, the idea of contract as a premise for political relations lies within the personal agreements for mutual aid that structured feudal bonds and obligations. Others argue that the rise of contract notions in political theory marked a return to Roman law. See, e.g., Rushton Coulborn, "The End of Feudalism," in Coulborn, *Feudalism in History*, pp. 288, 312.

nomic transactions and political action. This is the movement from status to contract detailed by Sir Henry Maine and other nineteenth-century observers of the past.[14]

For those who theorized, then and now, this new economic order rested on private property and the market. Legal and political theories used a social contract as a predicate for democracy. These are the ingredients of the world view often known as "liberalism." Liberal theory both assumed and claimed to create the conditions for autonomous, self-determining individuals.[15] The liberal theory of individualism came to fruition in works by John Stuart Mill, who himself built upon Jeremy Bentham, John Locke, and Thomas Hobbes.

Amid these transformations, legal ideas about fixed status and hierarchical relations gave way to newer ideas of individual self-determination and equal justice. But no one claimed that these new ideas would apply to everyone. Certain classes of people and those in certain kinds of relationships would be exceptions: people thought to lack the requisite capacity to reason and others who remained in hierarchical relationships because of their economic or social dependency. Thus, the groups excepted from liberal individualism were infants, married women, slaves, servants, apprentices, the very poor, and the mentally deficient. The legal rules governing these people retained qualities of the status relationships that had been all but eliminated for others. Over the course of the later Middle Ages and the early modern period the range of status categories diminished, but legal incapacities and regulated relationships of dependency still supplied reasons for excepting certain groups from various legal and economic activities.[16] Law continued through the seventeenth, eighteenth, and nineteenth centuries to define the special status of the infant, the married woman, and the imbecile.[17]

---

[14]Henry Maine, *Ancient Law* (New York: Henry Holt, 1864), pp. 180–90, noted that this pattern also characterized developments in the ancient Roman world. When applied to medieval developments, Maine's theory can be criticized for neglecting the contractual bases of feudal relations, for depicting a story of progressive development based on the political ideology of the historian, and for superimposing on another century the pattern Maine detected in Roman history.

[15]C. B. MacPherson, *The Political Theory of Possessive Individualism: Hobbes to Locke* (Oxford: Clarendon Press, 1962); Robert Paul Wolff, *The Poverty of Liberalism* (Boston: Beacon Press, 1968).

[16]Holdsworth (*History of English Law*, 9:3–4) writes that "during this [medieval] period the law of status tended to shrink. Certain of the persons who occupied a peculiar status in the medieval common law disappeared as a result of religious, social and industrial changes. Thus, although from some points of view the clergy still hold a peculiar status, it is not so peculiar as it was in the Middle Ages; and the status of the monk and the nun disappeared during the course of the sixteenth century; and their place was taken by hired servants. The Jews had disappeared when they were expelled by Edward I; and, when they returned, they suffered no disabilities other than those which nonconformity to the established church entailed. . . . On the other hand, the continuity of the development of English law made for the retention of such forms of status as those of the outlaw, the person attainted, and the excommunicate; the status of the married woman, of the lunatic, and of the infant were only just beginning to be modified by the growth of the equitable jurisdiction of the Chancellor; and there was little change in the status of peerage."

[17]The seventeenth century saw the creation of private madhouses, and governments established asylums for pauper lunatics in the eighteenth century; see Michael Macdonald, *Mystical*

Here we have the origins of the abnormal-persons approach to legal status. An explicit discussion of the contrast between special status groups and the norm appears in Thomas Holland's 1880 treatise *The Elements of Jurisprudence*.[18] He observed that "there are some rights in which the status of the person concerned has to be specially taken into consideration, while in others this is not the case." Holland traced to Roman law the distinction between the "law of persons" and the "law of things." This ancient distinction separated the " 'persons' for whose sake all law exists" from the " 'things' about which persons may dispute"; subsequent legal categories divided persons into several classes, while extending "things" to include "incorporeal things" such as obligations. Because Holland believed that these terms remained ambiguous, he recommended using a conception that confined the law of persons to instances involving "abnormal Personality." In all other cases, he proposed making the basis of any right not the status of the person seeking to exercise the right but the object or act with which the right would be concerned.[19] Holland thus articulated a shift in legal ideas about the relationship between personal status and rights—a shift that appeared also in the works of the influential legal theorists William Blackstone, John Austin, and Matthew Hale.[20]

Bedlam (Cambridge: Cambridge University Press, 1981), pp. 1–12. The Introduction in *Order and Disorder in Early Modern England*, ed. Anthony Fletcher and John Stevenson (Cambridge: Cambridge University Press, 1985), p. 13, describes the seventeenth century as a period "when those who were wealthy and who ruled were much preoccupied by human ascendancy over animals and human control of the natural environment"; accordingly, "women and children were regarded by some as nearer to the animal state than men, the former because of childbearing, the latter because they could not control their passions. Those on the margins of human society—the mad, vagrants and negro servants—were seen as the most beastlike of all people and were liable to be treated accordingly. . . . Some men only, it was assumed, should enjoy domination over the brute creation."

[18]Thomas Holland, *The Elements of Jurisprudence* (1880), 12th ed. (Oxford: Clarendon Press, 1916). Roscoe Pound, dean of the Harvard Law School, once described Holland's treatise as the "leading book" of exclusively analytical jurisprudence in the tradition first developed by John Austin (*Jurisprudence* [St. Paul, Minn.: West, 1959], 1:63). On analytical jurisprudence generally, see Joseph William Singer, "The Legal Rights Debate in Analytical Jurisprudence from Bentham to Hohfeld," *Wis. L. Rev.* 1982 (1982), 975.

[19]Holland, *Elements of Jurisprudence*, pp. 135, 136, 140–41: "When the Persons both of inherence and of incidence are human beings who are citizens of full age and sound mind, not under coverture, or convicted of crime, in other words when their personality is 'normal,' the personal dimensions of the right in question is wholly disregarded. It is only when one or both of the Persons concerned are 'abnormal,' i.e., are 'artificial' persons, or infants, or under coverture, or convict, or lunatic, and so forth, that the special effect upon the right in question of this abnormal Personality has to be considered. . . . By abstracting the law of Persons from the rest of the law the description of a right is thus much simplified. The inquiry into the law of Persons is thus supplementary and secondary to that of the residue of the law, commonly called the law of Things."

[20]Duncan Kennedy, "The Structure of Blackstone's Commentaries," *Buffalo L. Rev.* 28 (1979), 205, 280–84, 290–91, has suggested that William Blackstone and James Kent ushered in the shift earlier than Holland by articulating as two systems of law the law of persons and the law of things. This articulation merged the previously distinct fields of "public" and "private" law. Kennedy argues that Blackstone's organizing theory signaled an incomplete transition. For example, Blackstone pulled out the abstract individual, who bears rights, for treatment unlike the legal restrictions maintained for aliens, clergy, and husband and wife; state officials, how-

Thus, to this day, many fields of law divide society into persons who are mentally competent and persons who are not. The competent have responsibilities and rights; the incompetent have disabilities and, perhaps, protections. The competent can advance claims based on principles of autonomy; the incompetent are subject to restraints that enforce relationships of dependence. These "two tracks" of legal treatment reflect the traditional Western idea that responsibility follows only from voluntary, knowing, and intelligent choice. Mental competence signifies the ability to appreciate the consequences of one's actions, to protect oneself from manipulation and coercion, and to understand and engage in transactions of property and commerce. Mental competence serves as the critical indication of the ability to be held responsible or, more precisely, as society's justification for holding a given person responsible.

Despite considerable controversy over where the line is to be drawn, some boundary between competence and incompetence is of fundamental importance in such fields as criminal law, wills, and contracts. Legal defenses, excuses, and exceptions are available to competent persons in many areas because of the concerns that dominate legal treatment of the incompetent: ignorance, mistake, duress, coercion, fraud, and temporary insanity can all be seen as instances where an otherwise competent person may claim the legal treatment that would be accorded an incompetent person. Efforts to distinguish "justifying" and "excusing" conditions in the criminal law reiterate the distinction between the competent and the incompetent: an action is justified when society accepts it as willed and intended for good reasons; an action is excused when society tolerates it because the proper behavior was beyond the individual's capabilities. The emerging idea of an independent identity in early modern England and America relied on contrast with the dependence or incapacity of others, as even independent persons could claim moments or instances of excusable incapacity.

Whenever and however the shift from medieval to liberal legal thought occurred, by the late nineteenth century it had produced one track of legal rules for "normal" people and a residual category of legal statuses where the shift had failed to occur. As presented by legal theorists in the classical period after the Civil War, these two tracks built on the ideology of equal citizenship while justifying exceptions to it. Those accorded special status remained subject to "legal disabilities" and the legal label of incompetence. Cast in this light, doctrines about incompetency reveal areas that a liberal legal order does not reach, areas where an older notion of law continues to operate. The

---

ever, remained within a hierarchy of the law of persons (pp. 291–93). In addition, Kennedy suggests that the attributes of a particular status, attributes such as legal incapacities restricting the ability to enter into contracts, became generalized so that they could be raised as a defense by any individual. See Duncan Kennedy, "The Rise and Fall of Classical Legal Thought, 1850–1940" (unpublished manuscript, 1975), chap. 2. He thus argues that in the past, society attributed some traits—such as vulnerability to more powerful people, and incompetence in knowing one's own interests—only to certain people but has now come to treat these traits as features of any individual's experience.

law grants rights of autonomy and self-determination to most but devises special rules for those whom the legal system deems incapable of exercising these qualities. Law governs relationships between people and justifies protection for those unable to defend themselves from those who could take advantage of them.

The legal distinction between the mentally competent and the incompetent thus has deep roots yet also reflects relatively recent reconstructions of the more distant past. Children, mentally ill persons, mentally retarded persons, and elderly people suffering from what has been called senility all continue to be described as legally incompetent in today's society. These groups represent the remnants of the "law of persons," itself a souvenir of a medieval legal order organized around status relationships. The status categories may well have acquired new meaning as governmental powers grew under the chancellor who executed the king's equity powers. Most notably, the chancellor exercised the *parens patriae* power to control and protect certain individuals and classes, such as wards and married women. Perhaps this strengthening of the separate legal treatment for dependent and "incompetent" persons gave life to the separate track for "abnormal persons." The category of incompetent persons once included married women and sailors and—for some purposes—aliens, persons born out of wedlock, servants, wards, Jews, Quakers, villeins, monks, clergy, excommunicates, lepers, and civil servants.[21] A recent work identifies the old and new status in law of women, children, blacks, illegitimates, tribal Indians, homosexuals, aliens, mental patients, government employees, Asians, military personnel, and prisoners.[22] The development of special statuses that are accorded distinct legal treatment suggests the power of the dichotomy between competent and incompetent persons, even though the particular groups of people assigned to one category or another may change over time.[23]

For example, the same concepts connecting incapacity, dependency, and legitimate restrictions on autonomy appear in the legal rules governing "infants," the "insane, imbecile, etc.," and "married women" in a treatise on contracts written by William Page, a law professor during the early part of this century. Page did draw distinctions between these groups but used the

[21]Holdsworth, *History of English Law*, 9:3–4, 91–99. See also Graveson, *Status in the Common Law*; Aviam Soifer, "The Paradox of Paternalism and Laissez-Faire Constitutionalism: United States Supreme Court, 1888–1921," *Law & Hist. Rev.* 5 (1987), 249.

[22]Michael Phillips, *The Dilemmas of Individualism: Status, Liberty, and American Constitutional Law* (Westport, Conn.: Greenwood Press, 1983), pp. 20–56.

[23]Among works by scholars who emphasize the modernity of the separations of abnormal persons from the community are John Demos, *Entertaining Satan: Witchcraft and the Culture of Early New England* (New York: Oxford University Press, 1981); John Demos, *Past, Present, and Personal: The Family and the Life Course in American History* (New York: Oxford University Press, 1986); Michel Foucault, *Madness and Civilization: A History of Insanity in the Age of Reason*, trans. Richard Howard (London: Tavistock, 1971); David Rothman, *Conscience and Convenience: The Asylum and Its Alternatives in Progressive America* (Boston: Little, Brown, 1980); David Rothman, *The Discovery of the Asylum* (Boston: Little, Brown, 1971).

same basic contrast between capacity and incapacity in describing each of them. His treatise explains that legal limits on the lawful contractual capacity of a child are needed because otherwise the child could injure himself or others. No individualized judicial review of such risks are authorized by the rules; instead, the status of incapacity is assigned an arbitrary age cutoff: the age of majority. At the same time, the rules about infants permitted courts to assess, under the general norms of contract law, whether a particular contract benefited or prejudiced the particular child. The courts could relieve the minor or impose liability on the basis of such an assessment. For the group defined as the "insane, imbecile, etc." Page treated the source of incapacity as the individual's internal mental disturbance rather than a socially assigned status; he authorized individualized judicial inquiry into that mental status but only in relation to the specific contract in question.[24]

Married women, wrote Page, suffered contractual disabilities at common law because marriage assigned to husbands the liability for their wives' obligations and the power over their wives' person and property. The power differential between the marriage partners produced these consequences, according to Page: "It followed that if the primitive notion of his liability for her obligations was to persist, there was a rational basis for denying her capacity to incur new contractual obligations after marriage."[25] Page explained that the treatment of married women as legally incapacitated was a relic of an ancient and vanishing idea that women lost their identities upon marriage. Thus, he acknowledged that the legal incapacity of married women was a mutable, socially assigned position. In fact, however, legal disabilities imposed in this country on married women's right to contract—along with restrictions on women's rights to serve on juries and engage in other activities—persisted in some states until the 1970s.[26]

Reckoning with History

As history, this narrative is not entirely satisfactory. It focuses on ideas rather than human experiences. It relies on statements drawn from legal and political sources, such as treatises written by a select group of professional scholars for an equally select audience of legal practitioners.[27] It is quite

[24]William Page, *The Law of Contract*, 2d ed. (Cincinnati: W. H. Anderson, 1920), 4:2714–33, 2852–2909, 2809–11.

[25]Ibid., 4:2853.

[26]Not until 1975 did the Supreme Court reject as unconstitutional state laws excluding women from juries; see Taylor v. Louisiana, 419 U.S. 22 (1975). An earlier decision had rejected discrimination against women in federal court juries; see Ballard v. United States 329 U.S. 187 (1946).

[27]Duby (*Three Orders*, pp. 148–49) notes that legal sources, such as warrants, richly reveal nuanced social ordering but express the institutionalized image of social relations held by the scribes and lawyers who produced them. This qualification is as important for evaluating a source such as Blackstone's *Commentaries*. Nonetheless, such sources suggest the cultural attitudes held in codes of meaning. See generally Robert Gordon, "Critical Legal Histories," *Stan. L. Rev.* 36 (1984), 57, 117–24.

detached and must be carefully distinguished from the actual experience and practice of daily life in different historical eras.

Moreover, there is considerable controversy over the plausibility of generalizations about such ideas as "individualism" or such systems as "feudalism." For example, although historians support the view that medieval law rested on a culture of fixed status and hierarchical relations, they differ over whether governing law excluded the ideas now known as individualism. It is at least conceivable that a notion of individualism, including a sense of the self as distinct and as capable of free choice, animated the very structure of personal agreements establishing mutual obligations in the feudal and manorial worlds. Perhaps a notion of individual choice operated then as powerfully as notions of free choice do for a person in the late twentieth century who signs an installment sales contract—complete with a heavy interest rate—to purchase a car when his old car, his only means of transportation to his job, has broken down.[28] Moreover, notions of individual freedom developed since the feudal age have emphasized the social nature of the self and the dependence of each individual on society.[29] Claiming that new ideas of individualism displaced the older ideas of social status and hierarchy seems to overstate the case and neglect patterns of continuity.

In addition, the very meaning of "individualism" is unclear when it is used in narratives, such as this one, which try to plot changes from the medieval order to liberal societies. Individualism could mean experiences of subjectivity, related to artistic creativity and free expression; a focus on the separate person as the most important unit in society; a moral theory of personal will and responsibility; or political criticism of centralized, hierarchical authority.[30] Tracing the history of any one of these definitions runs the risk of such abstraction as to deny human agency and grant ideas a life of their own. Perhaps for this reason, many historians reject analysis at this level and limit themselves to local and time-limited studies, while others debate methodologies.

Finally, the history told here covers an extensive period of time—perhaps four or five centuries—during which many changes in legal thought and practices came and went. Of particular importance, but at risk of being overwhelmed by this long stretch of history, was the Golden Age of Contract Law, which prevailed among theorists of law after the Civil War and before World War I. Between 1870 and 1915, authors of legal treatises and leading jurists articulated and defended what became known as "legal formalism"— and was later dubbed, pejoratively, "mechanical jurisprudence."

[28]See Todd Rakoff, "Contracts of Adhesion: An Essay in Reconstruction," *Harv. L. Rev.* 96 (1983), 1173. See also Mary Ann Glendon, *The New Family and the New Property* (Boston: Butterworth, 1981).
[29]See, e.g., Emile Durkheim, *Suicide: A Study in Sociology* (New York: Free Press, 1966), p. 249; Erving Goffman, *The Presentation of Self in Everyday Life* (Garden City, N.Y.: Anchor Books, 1959); R. D. Laing, *Self and Others* (London: Tavistock, 1961); George Herbert Mead, *Mind, Self, and Society: From the Standpoint of a Social Behaviorist*, ed. Charles W. Morris (1934; Chicago: University of Chicago Press, 1967).
[30]See Steven Lukes, *Individualism* (Oxford: Basil Blackwell, 1973).

Legal formalists believed that law could and should be articulated in the form of a few general principles, such as freedom of contract, which entailed more specific rules and determined results of legal contests.[31] By relying on categories to answer disputes, legal formalists sought to infuse law with a sense of rational order, freed from personality or politics. The categorical reasoning of the abnormal-persons approach crystallized during this period and retained the same form even when other areas of legal reason were giving way to more flexible policy analysis after the 1920s. The formalist idea that a few basic principles can be discovered and then relied upon to solve disputes persisted in the identification of some people—whether women, children, or mentally disabled persons—as different from the norm and their assignment to a correspondingly different legal treatment. The history of the abnormal-persons approach probably reflects more of the contribution of the formalist period than of any previous phase of legal thought about difference.[32]

In sum, the history of the abnormal-persons approach recounted here is important not merely as an approximation of what really happened in the medieval period; it also importantly embodies the attitudes and assumptions of historians and lawyers whose work in the nineteenth and early twentieth centuries framed prevailing understandings of the past.[33] Their writings reflect contemporaneous debates about governmental regulation of labor relations and governmental assistance to economically vulnerable people. Their depiction of the Middle Ages as dark, restraining times impinging on personal freedom also helps to sustain as a contrast the image of individual liberty in mass industrial society, despite the complex and subtle incursions on freedom permitted by corporate employment and mass culture.

This look at history thus unearths a striking connection between current conceptions of abnormal persons and remnants or re-creations of a feudal hierarchical order.[34] In recent years some new classes or statuses have been created: persons at risk of serious disease, veterans, former mental patients. Each new status revives some parts of the old notion of status, especially in assigning difference to a person on the basis of some supposedly inherent trait. Like old status assignments, new ones sometimes trigger special protections and sometimes justify exclusions or restrictions. Legal arrangements make it seem legitimate to deploy certain classes or statuses by referring to particular characteristics and designing contrasting rights or obligations on that basis. Have such proclamations of "differences" hidden prejudices against beleaguered minorities? Lawyers and political reformers who suspect an affirmative answer to this question have expanded rights analysis during the past half-century.

[31]See Steven Burton, *An Introduction to Law and Legal Reasoning* (Boston: Little, Brown, 1985), pp. 169–215.

[32]This dimension of the mode of legal reasoning becomes important as a point of contrast to the other two approaches to the legal treatment of difference.

[33]See, e.g., A. V. Dicey, *Law and Public Opinion in England during the Nineteenth Century* (London: Macmillan, 1905); Graveson, *Status in the Common Law;* Burckhardt, *Civilization of the Renaissance.*

[34]See Glendon, *New Family,* pp. 226–36.

From Abnormal Persons to Rights Analysis

The rhetoric of equality appeared in the Declaration of Independence and the Bill of Rights. But the abolition movement and the Civil War gave new form and impetus to equality as a challenge to assigned statuses. By the late nineteenth century new kinds of professionals, ranging from medical doctors to social workers, were taking on the job of defining the needs and the limitations of "abnormal persons." Throughout the early decades of this century women, children, and persons with disabilities and diseases—people who did not fit in—became subjects for professional study and treatment.[35]

Experts talked about differences in ways that made distinctions between types of people ever more rigid, carrying enlarged significance. The eugenics movements adopted scientistic notions as part of a campaign to type people and to alter human reproduction in line with images of approved and disapproved types. Some people draped such notions around racism and disapproval—and fear of new immigrant groups. The collaboration between medical professionals and Nazis in Germany produced the ultimate reinforcement of prejudice in the guise of arguments about racial purity.[36] Even women dedicated to projecting a female ethos of maternal care contributed to the Nazi world view, imagining and enforcing unconditional differences between races and religious groups.[37] The Nazi experience showed that social machinery can label masses of people as different and then, through rules and practices, *make* them different, cursed, and disposable, while neighbors and former friends look on without objection.

Perhaps the shock of Nazism challenged people in the United States to question labels and social practices that degrade persons on the basis of race, disabilities, gender, and assigned social labels. No doubt influenced by social movements, some experts by the 1950s had begun to doubt the use of medical labels that seemed to deny people's humanity. Some specifically focused on the disabled; they rejected diagnostic labels and proposed instead the analysis of people's functional abilities.[38] By the 1950s another movement, the civil rights movement for racial justice, had emerged and was beginning to inspire dramatic reforms on behalf of those historically treated

[35]See Ivan Illich, *Medical Nemesis* (New York: Pantheon Books, 1976); Renée Fox, "The Medicalization and Demedicalization of American Society," *Daedalus* 106, no. 1 (1977), 9; Peter Conrad and Joseph Schneider, *Deviance and Medicalization: From Badness to Sickness* (St. Louis, Mo.: C. V. Mosby, 1980); Foucault, *Madness and Civilization*.

[36]See Robert Jay Lifton, *The Nazi Doctors: Medical Killing and the Psychology of Genocide* (New York: Basic Books, 1986); George Mosse, *Toward the Final Solution: A History of European Racism* (New York: Fertig, 1978); Raul Hilberg, *The Destruction of the European Jews* (Chicago: Quadrangle, 1961).

[37]See Claudia Koonz, *Mothers in the Fatherland: Women, the Family, and Nazi Politics* (New York: St. Martin's Press, 1987), pp. 53–90, 177–219.

[38]In light of a similar challenge to the medical diagnosis of homosexuality as an illness, the American Psychiatric Association removed the classification of homosexuality from its *Diagnostic and Statistical Manual of Mental Disorders* (Washington, D.C.: American Psychiatric Association, 1980), DSM-III. See Ronald Bayer, *Homosexuality and American Psychiatry: The Politics of Diagnosis* (Princeton, N.J.: Princeton University Press, 1987).

as abnormal under law. Working through courts and political action since the turn of the century, the civil rights movement reached national proportions in the 1950s and 1960s when the National Association for the Advancement of Colored People (NAACP) campaigned to desegregate public schools. The Supreme Court's ruling in Brown v. Board of Education[39] demonstrated the power of legal language to transform through rights rhetoric long-standing political struggles over the treatment of differences. In the 1960s the rhetoric of equal rights appeared in declarations for women,[40] for children,[41] and ultimately for persons with disabilities.[42] Articulating harms and desires in the rhetoric of rights gave new power and focus to reform efforts, while directing them toward legal arenas.

Sources of Reform

Motivated in part by humanitarian concerns, advocates for the mentally disabled also wanted to challenge the premises on which institutional treatment had been justified. Changes in medical knowledge about the treatment of both mental illness and mental retardation contributed to this reexamination of public policy. Critics both in and out of the medical community blamed institutionalization itself for at least some of the problems experienced by mentally disabled people.

Long before *One Flew over the Cuckoo's Nest* captured the imagination of novel readers and moviegoers,[43] scholars and professionals were sharply criticizing the medical treatment of people diagnosed as mentally ill. One landmark book blamed the hierarchical structure and the relationships between staff and patients for some of the symptoms of patients in hospitals for the mentally ill.[44] Erving Goffman, the sociologist who later described the workings of stigma and the social scripts people use to make meaning and order in their lives, produced a riveting study of the effects of closed institutions on those who live in them.[45] Perhaps the most radical view was es-

[39]347 U.S. 483 (1954).

[40]Earlier statements of women's rights borrowed phrases and concepts from the Declaration of Independence and the Constitution. See Margaret Forster, *Significant Sisters: The Grassroots of Active Feminism, 1839–1959* (London: Secker & Warburg, 1984). See also Barbara Sinclair Deckard, *The Women's Movement*, 3d ed. (New York: Harper & Row, 1983); and Aileen S. Kraditor, *The Ideas of the Women's Suffrage Movement, 1890–1920* (New York: Norton, 1965).

[41]Starting in the 1950s, social critics attacked the concept of adolescence in particular for stigmatizing and excluding young people from adult worlds and responsibilities. See Richard Farson, *Birthrights* (New York: Macmillan, 1974); Edgar Friedenberg, *The Dignity of Youth and Other Atavisms* (Boston: Beacon Press, 1965); Paul Goodman, *Growing Up Absurd: Problems of Youth in the Organized System* (New York: Random House, 1956).

[42]Harlan Hahn, "Public Policy and Disabled Infants: A Sociopolitical Perspective," *Issues in Law and Medicine* 3, no. 1 (1987), 3.

[43]Ken Kesey, *One Flew over the Cuckoo's Nest* (1973; New York: Penguin Books, 1977), was made into a successful movie starring Jack Nicholson in 1975.

[44]Alfred Stanton and Morris Schwartz, *The Mental Hospital* (New York: Basic Books, 1954).

[45]Erving Goffman, *Asylums: Essays on the Social Situation of Mental Patients and Other Inmates* (Garden City, N.Y.: Anchor Books, 1961). See also Jonathan Borus, "Sounding Board:

poused by Thomas Szasz and R. D. Laing, who in different ways challenged the very definitions of mental illness and argued that the "sane" need the "insane" in order to define themselves.[46]

Some observers criticized institutions for "banishing" the mentally disabled from the rest of the community in ways that disrupted the patient's relationships with family and friends; others cited the harmful and stigmatizing effects of institutionalization itself.[47] Many emphasized that the medical treatment supposedly justifying the institutionalization of mentally ill people was in fact rarely provided. Inadequate staff-patient ratios, the bureaucratic tendency to avoid difficult tasks, and sheer lack of knowledge about how to treat many kinds of mental disabilities produced institutions that warehoused—and at times neglected and abused—those confined there. New drug treatments offered a medical basis for managing certain aspects of some kinds of mental illness outside of institutional settings.[48] For these reasons, professionals and reformers in the 1950s and 1960s began to challenge previously accepted justifications for institutionalizing mentally ill people.[49]

During the same period professionals began to develop new ways of looking at mental retardation. An older view had conceived of people with reduced intellectual function as subhuman and lacking many human sensitivities and abilities.[50] In this respect, the tradition of the abnormal person meant more than a legal category; it captured community fears of difference and combined negative stereotypes that have also, at various times in history, accompanied perceptions of racial, ethnic, and religious minorities, and

Deinstitutionalization of the Chronically Mentally Ill," *New England Journal of Medicine* 305 (1981), 339: long-term hospitalization produces disabilities; David Rosenhan, "On Being Sane in Insane Places," *Science* 179 (1953), 250: expectations play a role in how patients function.

[46]See generally R. D. Laing, *The Divided Self* (New York: Pantheon Books, 1969); R. D. Laing, *The Politics of Experience* (New York: Pantheon Books, 1967); R. D. Laing and Aaron Esterson, *Sanity, Madness, and the Family: Families of Schizophrenics* (New York: Basic Books, 1964); Thomas Szasz, *The Myth of Mental Illness: Foundations of a Theory of Personal Conduct* (New York: Harper & Row, 1961); Thomas Szasz, *The Manufacture of Madness* (New York: Harper & Row, 1970). See also Kai T. Erikson, *Wayward Puritans: A Study in the Sociology of Deviance* (New York: Wiley, 1966): seventeenth-century Puritans constructed definitions of deviance to help maintain social order.

[47]See Milton Greenblatt, Rosina M. Becerra, and F. A. Serafetinides, "Social Networks and Mental Health: An Overview," *American Journal of Psychiatry* 139 (1982), 977; see generally Gerald Klerman, "Better but Not Well: Social and Ethical Issues in the Deinstitutionalization of the Mentally Ill," *Schizophrenia Bulletin* 3 (1977), 617.

[48]Alan Miller, "Deinstitutionalization in Retrospect," *Psychiatric Quarterly* 57 (1985), 160, 167–69, reviews pharmaceutical developments enabling deinstitutionalization. See also Sue Estroff, *Making It Crazy: An Ethnography of Psychiatric Clients in an American Community* (Berkeley: University of California Press, 1981), pp. 68–117: an anthropologist who tried the drug regimen given to deinstitutionalized mental patients experienced many of the side effects that make patients shake and seem foggy even while the drugs enable them to function outside of institutions.

[49]See generally Leona Bachrach, *Deinstitutionalization: An Analytical Review and Sociological Perspective* (San Francisco: Jossey-Bass, 1983).

[50]See Philip Roos, "Basic Facts about Mental Retardation," *Legal Rights of the Mentally Handicapped,* ed. Bruce J. Ennis and Paul Friedman (New York: Practicing Law Institute, 1974), 1:19, 21.

women.[51] Some people pictured mentally retarded persons as threats to society and attributed to them criminal tendencies or wanton proclivities to reproduce and create defective offspring.[52] These attitudes intermingled with discrimination on the basis of race, ethnicity, and class. Couched in scientific language, such sentiments helped to promote legal measures to prevent future generations of retarded—or "substandard"—persons by restricting the marriages of mentally defective persons, segregating them in institutions, and sometimes mandating their sterilization.

In 1927 Justice Oliver Wendell Holmes, Jr., wrote the Supreme Court decision approving compulsory sterilization of mentally handicapped persons even against their will. With the memorable line "Three generations of imbeciles is enough," Justice Holmes justified the measure in part by the particular facts in the case, which he believed established a hereditary problem of mental deficiency.[53] Recent research on the same case by Stephen Jay Gould demonstrates that under any current definitions there were no mentally incompetent persons in the family of Carrie Buck, whose sterilization the Court sanctioned; instead, prejudice against poor, single, pregnant women seems to explain the sterilization practices. Yet in the state involved in Carrie Buck's case and in other places compulsory sterilization continued well into the 1960s.[54]

Indeed, through the middle of this century, legal authorities and public majorities treated the mentally retarded as eternal children, as objects of pity, or as hopelessly diseased. Not until the 1960s and 1970s did professionals begin to see mental retardation instead as an issue of developmental psychology. In this view, mentally retarded people are delayed in their progress along the path of development followed by every human being. Despite their delay, they are capable of growing and learning with appropriate assistance, and the best treatment and education opportunities for the mentally retarded lie in efforts to maximize their participation in the living and working arrangements of "normal" people. Called the "normalization principle," this idea also animates the educational and treatment approach known as "habilitation," which involves training in the skills of daily living.[55] Many advocates have urged changing the label from "mentally retarded" to "developmentally delayed" or "exceptional."

As experts in medicine, psychology, social work, and education changed

[51]See Sander Gilman, *Difference and Pathology: Stereotypes of Sexuality, Race, and Madness* (Ithaca: Cornell University Press, 1985).

[52]See Walter Elmore Fernald, "What Is Practical in the Way of Prevention of Mental Defect," *Proceedings of the National Conference on Charities and Corrections* (New York: Russell Sage, 1915), 192; Stephen Jay Gould, *The Mismeasure of Man* (New York: Norton, 1981), pp. 146–320, examining racism and other prejudices embedded in intelligence testing.

[53]Buck v. Bell, 274 U.S. 200 (1927).

[54]Stephen Jay Gould, "Carrie Buck's Daughter," *Constitutional Commentary* 2 (1985), 331.

[55]See generally Bruce Mason, Frank Menolascino, and Lorin Galvin, "Mental Health: The Right to Treatment for Mentally Retarded Citizens: An Evolving Legal and Scientific Interface," *Creighton L. Rev.* 10 (1976), 124; Wolf Wolfersberger, "The Principle of Normalization and Its Implications to Psychiatric Services," *American Journal of Psychiatry* 127 (1970), 291.

their views of mentally disabled people, their work dovetailed ideologically with and helped to sustain the political and legal activities of advocates for the mentally handicapped. Strategies to extend notions of liberty and equality to previously excluded groups were the stock-in-trade of civil rights and civil liberties reformers during the 1960s and 1970s. Leaders of the rights movement for the mentally handicapped borrowed both rhetoric and strategy from prior civil rights efforts that had attacked racial discrimination and segregation. In the 1960s parents and relatives of mentally handicapped people joined with public interest lawyers and professional associations to focus public attention on the unsanitary, neglectful, and often dangerous conditions prevalent in large public institutions housing mentally disabled people. Congress held hearings and enacted remedial legislation over the course of the next two decades.[56]

In the early 1970s, lawyers working on behalf of clients who had been labeled mentally ill or mentally retarded framed innovative lawsuits challenging the prevailing institutional treatment.[57] One legal argument successfully maintained that when the state deprives people of their liberty on the grounds of mental disability, the state must respect and implement a right to treatment and must do so in the setting least restrictive of individual liberty.[58] Other legal advocates effectively challenged the conditions of confinement—often unsanitary and disrespectful—in institutions that actually provided little more than warehousing for disabled persons.[59] Using the language of legal rights, advocates attacked state policies of failing to pay minimum wages to mentally disabled persons and of restricting the rights of

[56]See Subcommittee on Health of Senate Committee on Labor and Public Welfare, *Mental Illness and Retardation: Hearings on S. 755–756,* 88th Cong., 1st sess. (1963), 16, 46–56. See also Mental Retardation Facilities and Community Mental Health Centers Construction Act of 1963, Pub. L. No. 88–164, 77 Stat. 282 (codified as amended at scattered sections of 42 U.S.C. sec. 1982 [1982]); Rehabilitation Act of 1973, Pub. L. No. 93–112, 87 Stat. 355 (codified as amended at 29 U.S.C. sec. 701–94 [1982]); Rehabilitation, Comprehensive Services, and Developmental Disabilities Amendments of 1978, Pub. L. No. 95–602, 92 Stat. 2955 (codified as amended at scattered sections of 29 & 42 U.S.C. [1982]); Developmental Disabilities Assistance & Bill of Rights Act, Pub. L. No. 95–602, sec. 502, 92 Stat. 3003 (codified at 42 U.S.C. sec. 6000 [1982]); Civil Rights Act, 42 U.S.C. sec. 1983 (1982).

[57]See Stanley Herr, *Rights and Advocacy for Retarded People* (Lexington, Mass.: Lexington Books, 1983), pp. 108–9, 146–47, 230–39. Although legal and political reforms on behalf of mentally ill and mentally retarded persons have at times been coordinated or at least mutually beneficial, the differences between the two populations, and between the political constituencies interested in them, should not be underestimated. See John Parry, "Rights and Entitlements in the Community," in *The Mentally Disabled and the Law,* 3d ed., ed. Samuel Brakel, John Parry, and Barbara Weiner (Chicago: American Bar Foundation, 1985), pp. 607, 614–19.

[58]Rouse v. Cameron, 373 F.2d 451 (D.C., Cir. 1966) (comparing constitutional and statutory theories); Wyatt v. Stickney, 344 F. Supp. 373, 344 F. Supp. 387 (M.D. Ala. 1972). See "The Right to the Least Restrictive Alternative," in *The Mentally Retarded Citizen and the Law,* ed. Patricia M. Wald (New York: Free Press, 1976), comprising essays by David Chambers, Linda Glenn, Alan Abeson, Leonard Lippman, and Dolores Norley. See also Mills v. Board of Education, 348 F. Supp. 866 (D.D.C. 1972) (declaring right to education for disabled); and Pennsylvania Ass'n for Retarded Children (PARC) v. Pennsylvania, 343 F. Supp. 279 (E.D. Pa. 1972) (same).

[59]See New York State Association for Retarded Children v. Rockefeller, 357 F. Supp. 752 (E.D. N.Y. 1973).

mentally handicapped persons to marry, to bear and raise children, to vote, and to live in the community.[60]

One theory underlying these reforms emphasizes that all persons are entitled to rights, regardless of their membership in the class defined by the boundary between mental competence and mental incompetence. To the extent that real differences should matter in the articulation of legal rights, this view suggests, the classifications of mental retardation and mental incompetence are too general and too artificial to identify those differences. As one philosopher has explained, although prevailing social arrangements tend to make a particular minimal level of mental acuity matter, there is nothing "natural" about this chosen level. We could raise the minimum to the level of genius, and then most of us would feel—and be labeled—incompetent. Or we could lower the minimum by revamping basic institutions. We could simplify transportation, banking, and other social structures and thereby enable people currently defined as incompetent to participate more fully in social and economic life.[61]

Even in this argument, however, there remains implicit the idea that an individual must demonstrate some minimal ability to make use of basic social institutions. Not every human being, at each point in the life cycle, can meet even lower competence requirements than the ones currently in operation. While maintaining that the similarities between mentally retarded persons and others overshadow the differences, this view nonetheless suggests that for some purposes, some mentally disabled people can and should be treated differently from other people. Exactly when and where these distinctions should be drawn remains unclear.

A different theory underlying the rights advocacy on behalf of mentally disabled persons holds that these people do, as a group, have special needs but that those needs have been poorly served by the legal model that imposes disability and promises protection. An attempt to modernize conceptions of the needs of the mentally disabled gave rise to the arguments for a right to "habilitation," a form of the right to treatment and a claim committed to enhancing the participation of mentally retarded persons in the larger community.[62] The effort to secure a legal right to habilitation is in tension with the theory that finds suspect any classification on the basis of mental dis-

[60]See generally Samuel Brakel, "Family Laws," in Brakel, Parry, and Weiner, *The Mentally Disabled and the Law,* pp. 307–58; John Parry, "Decision-making Rights over Persons and Property," and John Parry, "Rights and Entitlements," in Brakel, Parry, and Weiner, *The Mentally Disabled and the Law,* pp. 445–46, 607, 619–29, 660–76; Patricia M. Wald, "Basic Personal and Civil Rights," in Wald, *The Mentally Retarded Citizen and the Law,* p. 3.

[61]Wikler, "Paternalism and the Mentally Retarded," in *Paternalism,* ed. Rolf Sartorious (Minneapolis: University of Minnesota Press, 1983), p. 83. This argument expands the definitions of sameness and difference by looking at how all of us are more or less competent in relation to external arrangements that can be changed.

[62]"The word 'habilitation' . . . is commonly used to refer to programs for the mentally retarded because mental retardation is . . . a learning disability and training impairment rather than an illness. [T]he principal focus of habilitation is upon training and development of needed skills"; see Youngberg v. Romeo, 457 U.S. 307, 309 n.1 (1981) (ellipses and brackets in original) (quoting Brief for American Psychiatric Ass'n as Amicus Curiae 4 n.1).

ability. This tension lies at the center of rights analysis as applied to the mentally retarded.

The tension between arguments for similar treatment and arguments for special treatment persisted as advocates drew on analogies to successful civil rights litigation. The civil rights precedents, as translated by the advocates for the mentally disabled, included two elements: (1) arguments, couched in rights rhetoric, expressing the needs, objectives, and hopes of mentally handicapped people as legally enforceable claims; and (2) litigative strategies casting denials of these claims as violations of the constitutional guarantees afforded every person—guarantees of equal protection, due process, and freedom from cruel and unusual punishment.[63]

The legal claims secured victories but expressed dilemmas in visible court decisions. Perhaps the most notable case was Wyatt v. Stickney,[64] in which the plaintiffs' lawyers framed a legal challenge to the involuntary confinement of mental patients in a state hospital and then added a class of mentally retarded residents of state institutions.[65] Invoking the arguments regarding due process, equal protection, and cruel and unusual punishment which advocates had used to challenge the involuntary confinement of mentally ill people held in miserable conditions without treatment, these lawyers also challenged the confinement of mentally retarded people in poor institutional settings. They cited as the basis of the habilitation claim the failure of those institutions to impart the skills necessary to enable the mentally retarded to cope more effectively and efficiently with their own needs and with the larger world.

Analogies with other legal areas helped support the right to habilitation.

---

[63]Some suits rested on a search for due process protections against the stigma arising from institutionalization; see "Developments in the Law—Civil Commitment of the Mentally Ill," *Harv. L. Rev.* 87 (1974), 1190, 1193–1200. Others sought to provide procedural protections to guard against erroneous deprivations of physical liberty and against the substantive grounds for state-ordered confinement; see O'Connor v. Donaldson, 422 U.S. 563 (1975). An important legacy from this litigative effort was the notion of the "least restrictive alternative," based on the due-process idea that state officials pursuing legitimate and important governmental interests should minimize the extent to which they restrict fundamental liberties. See Covington v. Harris, 419 F.2d 617 (D.C. Cir. 1969); Lake v. Cameron, 364 F.2d 657 (D.C. Cir. 1966). States revising their mental health codes following these judicial decisions frequently incorporated a "least restrictive" requirement. See Barbara Weiner, "Rights of Institutionalized Persons," in Brakel, Parry, and Weiner, *The Mentally Disabled and the Law*, pp. 251, 266.

[64]See Wyatt v. Stickney, 325 F. Supp. 781 (M.D. Ala. 1971); 334 F. Supp. 1341 (M.D. Ala. 1971); 344 F. Supp. 373 (M.D. Ala. 1972); and 344 F. Supp. 387 (M.D. Ala. 1972), aff'd sub nom. Wyatt v. Aderholt, 503 F.2d 1305 (5th Cir. 1974).

[65]Involuntary commitment procedures traditionally lumped together mentally ill and mentally retarded people, but in recent years, largely as a result of reform efforts, state statutes have treated the two groups differently. Some states now have distinct legislative regulations for the involuntary commitment of developmentally disabled people; others have abolished involuntary commitment for members of this group as part of deinstitutionalization and community treatment efforts. See Samuel Brakel, "Involuntary Institutionalization," in Brakel, Parry, and Weiner, *The Mentally Disabled and the Law*, pp. 21, 37. Some efforts to devise more due-process protections in the commitment procedures have focused on children, although the Supreme Court has ruled that sufficient due-process safeguards are afforded by the admitting physicians' review. See Parham v. J.R., 442 U.S. 584 (1979).

One analogy pointed to a case, relying on due process, in which the Supreme Court had ruled that the state may not indefinitely confine without treatment a mentally retarded and deaf person found incompetent to stand trial in a criminal action, because there was no reasonable relationship between the nature of the confinement there and its purpose.[66] Another analogy turned to the Eighth Amendment's prohibition of cruel and unusual punishment in a case applying it to the conditions of confinement for mentally impaired people.[67] The district court in *Wyatt* found persuasive these cases and other precedents under the equal protection provision of the Fourteenth Amendment. The court declared constitutional violations and supervised a process of moving people out of the institutions.[68]

With Wyatt v. Stickney the law reformers showed that it was possible to use the courts yet again for social change. Reformers watching that suit pushed for new legislation to implement the same theories. They sought public support to finance changes in medical and educational services—and to promote changes in public attitudes. State legislative reforms also secured important commitments to protect the rights of disabled persons.[69]

The sticking point for the reform movement on behalf of the mentally handicapped was whether the rights framework could be used not only to liberate institutionalized people from abusive and horrible circumstances within the institutions but also to accord them some new entitlements not available to others in the community. The liberty and equality rationales used in litigation and legislation might instead lead to simply treating the de-institutionalized like everyone else—which would mean moving them out of institutions into the streets, with no further services. A rights theory that supported deinstitutionalization specifically appealed to state legislators because it offered substantial cost savings. Less popular was the suggestion that the mentally retarded have a right to supportive services outside of institutional settings.[70]

[66]Jackson v. Indiana, 406 U.S. 715 (1972).

[67]Rozecki v. Gaughan, 459 F.2d 6 (1st Cir. 1972); Cross v. Harris, 418 F.2d 1095 (D.C. Cir. 1969). Cf. Robinson v. California, 370 U.S. 660 (1962) (it is impermissible cruel and unusual punishment to confine a narcotics addict for a condition that is like a disease and beyond the individual's control).

[68]On Jan. 17, 1972, the parties negotiated and produced two Memoranda of Agreement, stipulating standards of minimally adequate treatment at Alabama hospitals. These were submitted to the District Court, which on April 13 issued permanent injunctive relief, including remedial orders in accord with minimum standards of treatment set by the court; see 344 F. Supp. 373, 387 (1972). The first decision applied to two hospitals for the mentally ill, the second to a hospital for the mentally retarded. Both required "minimum Constitutional standards for adequate treatment" that essentially included a "Bill of Rights" for patients to protect basic civil liberties; safe, clean, and humane facilities and food service; adequate staff; and individualized treatment designed to habilitate patients. See id. at 379, 395. In addition, the parties agreed to establish a human rights committee to review all treatment to protect the dignity and human rights of all patients, a monitoring system was established, and costs and attorneys' fees for plaintiffs were assessed against defendants. See id. at 378–79, 394–95.

[69]See, e.g., Ohio Rev. Code Ann. sec. 5122 (Baldwin 1982 & Supp. 1982) (treatment rights and public obligations to monitor patient records); Tex. Rev. Civ. Stat. Ann. sec. 5547–30 (Vernon 1958 & Supp. 1982–83) (same).

[70]Borus, "Sounding Board," p. 339; Steven Sharfstein and Harry W. Clark, "Economics and the Chronic Patient," *Schizophrenia Bulletin* 4 (1978), 339.

A judicial declaration of rights justifying community services is conceptually as well as practically difficult to muster because of the tensions inherent in the rights approach. On the one hand, the rights argument rests on the conviction that the mentally retarded are similar enough to nonretarded people to be entitled to the same rights; on the other hand, the strategy depends on the view that the law should recognize and respond to the special needs of the mentally retarded. If the "sameness" strand of the rights argument is pursued fully, it supports deinstitutionalization and integration in the community—but not special services to help those people who otherwise would have trouble coping with the complex environments of contemporary cities and towns, not to mention the confusing welter of medical insurance, social security, housing subsidies, and other bureaucratic forms. Except under limited programs designed to deal with poverty, nonretarded people have no analogous rights to assistance with housing, financial support, job training, and the like. The complexity of the bureaucratic requirements in the poverty programs has already hampered many from making sense or use of those programs. Subsidized advocates to help mentally retarded persons navigate the welfare system would acknowledge their special needs; so would the development of new, specially tailored assistance programs—but such efforts would also revive arguments for separate institutional treatment, addressing special needs in a completely special environment. As one long-time observer of the problem put it, "How can we protect the rights of persons inside the institutions without legitimating the institutions themselves?"[71]

Focusing on the special needs, or differences, of the mentally disabled could renew the stigma associated with those differences. This problem is not anomalous. It recurs in setting after setting: for women, for members of racial and religious communities, and for others with histories of "difference." Efforts to integrate those historically deemed "different" encounter obstacles both when advocates argue for similar treatment and when they argue for different treatment, as illustrated in the case described below. The obstacles, however, are not rooted in the people with a history of difference. Their roots may lie within rights analysis itself, which remains intertwined with assumptions about individual autonomy and rationality. People who match those assumptions fit comfortably within the framework of rights; those who do not, do not. Renovating rights to fit those who have been considered different could yield new arguments for differential treatment and risk new bases for exclusion and stigma. Extending existing rights to those people who seem different would fail to respond to their very real and often very difficult situations. These problems are raised vividly in litigation over the right to habilitation in cases seeking habilitation rights in an institution in Pennsylvania—cases that have brought the same institution to the Supreme Court three times.[72]

[71]D. Rothman, "Reaction Comment," in Wald, *The Mentally Retarded Citizen and the Law*, 407.
[72]One case alone, Halderman v. Pennhurst State School and Hosp., had this tortured history: 446 F. Supp. 1295 (E.D. Pa. 1977), aff'd in part, re'd and rem'd in part; 612 F.2d 84 (3d Cir.

A Test Case

Terri Lee Halderman, the named plaintiff in this dramatic lawsuit,[73] entered the Pennhurst institution at the age of twelve as a mentally retarded person. Her parents brought Terri Lee to Pennhurst after their marriage nearly broke up under the strain of keeping her at home and after the staff at a private facility reported that the girl was too active and demanding for its caretaking facilities. Terri Lee's mental retardation resulted from brain damage at birth due to Rh incompatibility. A Pennhurst psychologist described her as hyperactive and given to banging her head. A standardized test evaluated her mental age at less than one year.

At Pennhurst, Terri Lee continued to bang her head against the walls, with some injury to herself. She also lost the ability to use the few words she had known before entering the institution. Her mother found these circumstances appalling and contacted David Ferlanger, an attorney who had started a legal advocacy project for mentally disabled persons. On behalf of Terri Lee Halderman and all others in her situation at Pennhurst, he filed a lawsuit in 1974 seeking monetary damages and injunctive relief to improve the conditions at the institution.[74] In 1975 the Pennsylvania Association for Retarded Citizens joined the suit as coplaintiffs, and the United States Department of Justice also intervened on the side of the plaintiffs. In 1976 Ferlanger amended the complaint to request that the court close the institution altogether and order the development of community placements for all the residents. This change in requested relief later became a source of dispute between Ferlanger and Mrs. Halderman and thereby raised the difficult question of who should speak for the interests of a severely mentally retarded person.[75]

The request to shut down the institution, a request joined by the Pennsylvania Association for Retarded Citizens, reflected in part a view that the conditions at Pennhurst were so deplorable as to be beyond remedy; however, it also reflected a view that habilitation would be impossible in any institutional setting so removed from the daily life of the community. The request ultimately exposed the difficulty in using a rights-based theory to obtain services and programs responsive to the special needs of retarded

---

1979), rev'd and remanded; 451 U.S. 1 (1981), on remand, 673 F.2d 647 (1982), rev'd 465 U.S. 89 (1984). For other cases dealing with Pennhurst, see Halderman v. Pennhurst State School and Hosp., 526 F. Supp. 409 (E.D. Pa. 1981) (remedial order not stayed pending appeal); 545 F. Supp. 410 (E.D. Pa. 1982) (phase out of master appointed by court to administer remedy); 555 F. Supp. 1144 (E.D. Pa. 1982) (lack of funds is no defense for state as defendant). See also Youngberg v. Romeo, 457 U.S. 307 (1982) (right to habilitation); Halderman v. Pennhurst, 533 F. Supp. 661 (E.D. Pa. 1982) (transfer decision), rev'd, 707 F.2d 702 (3rd Cir. 1983).

[73]I was serving as a law clerk at the Supreme Court when this case first reached that level of review. I later learned many of the background facts from Robert Burt's fine case study "Pennhurst: A Parable," in *In the Interests of Children: Advocacy, Law Reform, and Public Policy,* ed. Robert Mnookin (New York: W. H. Freeman, 1985), p. 265.

[74]Ferlanger later analogized public treatment of mentally handicapped people to the Nazi treatment of European Jews. See Burt, "Pennhurst," pp. 283–84.

[75]Ibid., pp. 286–87.

individuals while also challenging their segregation in specialized institutional settings.

The district court took evidence and made factual findings attesting to the deplorable conditions at Pennhurst. The court then concluded that those conditions violated the constitutional rights of its residents to liberty, to freedom from harm, and to integration with the community.[76] The court also found that the conditions violated statutory guarantees provided by Pennsylvania state law and by section 504 of the federal Rehabilitation Act of 1973 as amended in 1976. But what remedy could cure these conditions? The judge ordered the closing of Pennhurst and the development of smaller community-based residences, using public funds. The judge was able to cite agreement among all the parties, including the state of Pennsylvania, in support of his conclusion that only community-based care could appropriately serve the needs of the Pennhurst residents. This unanimity disintegrated, however, after the court order. The state began to resist its implementation, and appealed the case.

The court of appeals reached a complicated conclusion. The three appellate judges hearing the case agreed with the trial judge that the conditions at Pennhurst violated some law but restricted this legal conclusion to federal statutory grounds. The appeals judges relied on amended section 504 of the Rehabilitation Act, a new statute adopted after the lawsuit began, which provided federal funds to states that agreed to respect the basic rights of developmentally disabled individuals.[77] And then, when it came to the remedy for the violations of the rights articulated in section 504, the appeals court rejected the trial court's decision to close down Pennhurst. Instead, the reviewing court directed the district court to establish a process for individualized hearings. The district court in turn appointed a master to conduct hearings to determine whether institutional or community care would be appropriate for each resident before admission to or removal from Pennhurst.[78]

The state officials still disagreed with the outcome and took the case to the Supreme Court, which reversed on the ground that the federal statute had not authorized any such relief.[79] The Supreme Court sent the case back to the appeals court, which this time turned to the claims under Pennsylvania law and declared that the federal court had power to interpret and apply state law; further, it found authority for its remedy in state law. Reviewing the case

[76]446 F. Supp. at 1307–12. The district court dismissed a monetary damages claim against the individual employees and found them not personally responsible (id. at 1324).

[77]Although adopted after the initiation of the lawsuit, the new federal statute pertained to activities at issue in the suit, and the appellate court found it applicable. The court specifically relied on the Developmentally Disabled Assistance and Bill of Rights Act, 42 U.S.C. sec. 6001–81 (1976), embodying congressional recognition and endorsement of the litigated victories previously achieved by rights advocates on behalf of mentally disabled people. The act explicitly promoted further advocacy and legal representation for this group.

[78]612 F.2d 84 (3rd Cir. 1979). See also 673 F.2d 628 (3rd Cir. 1982) (affirming order funding the office of the special master).

[79]451 U.S. 1 (1981).

once again, the Supreme Court disallowed this federal court enforcement of state law and again sent the case back to the lower court.[80]

In the meantime the remedy of individualized hearings remained in operation; the Supreme Court had not halted that part of the district court's remedy pending its review. And a separate lawsuit brought on behalf of Nicholas Romeo, an individual resident of Pennhurst, asserted that constitutional violations had occurred when he was beaten, shackled, and denied training of any sort. Unlike the claims on behalf of the class of all people situated like Terri Lee Halderman, this was an individual claim, presenting one person's treatment at Pennhurst—and this claim won success with the Supreme Court. Romeo's lawyer described his client as a thirty-three-year-old profoundly retarded man and alleged that he had been injured at least sixty-three times during his stay at Pennhurst. The legal argument was that this pattern of injuries violated Romeo's liberty interests and rights to freedom and training while institutionalized. The Supreme Court endorsed as plausible the availability of legal recovery under the theory of a federal constitutional violation and sent the case back to the district court for a trial on the facts of that case.[81]

How should this use of law on behalf of "different" people be evaluated? The Pennhurst litigation clearly helped some residents of the institution, who received attention and new placements in the community. Further as conducted by law reform lawyers, the litigation proved an effective tool, in conjunction with other strategies, for increasing the resources devoted to mentally retarded persons in the care of the state of Pennsylvania. The complex and time-consuming process of devising individualized placement reviews and developing plans for improving the institution while also creating alternatives in the community rallied resources and attention to people long neglected by the community at large. The Pennhurst litigation also riveted public attention beyond Pennsylvania and thus added the rhetoric of rights to reform efforts conducted elsewhere.

At the same time, the Pennhurst case produced elaborate technical debates over what source of law (federal or state, statutory or constitutional) could supply the basis for rights for mentally retarded persons, and what court (federal or state) could determine violations of those rights and order redress. This search for clear and sharp distinctions between state and federal, judicial and legislative authority bears a certain similarity to the method of reasoning that emphasizes "real differences" between people as justifications for differential treatment. In each instance there is an effort to find certain boundaries while ignoring the fact that the people doing the finding are themselves implicated in the distinctions: the federal judges demarking the limits of federal authority and the reach of state power are speaking about themselves.

[80]457 U.S. 1131 (1982).
[81]Youngberg v. Romeo, 457 U.S. 307 (1982). Romeo sought monetary damages and training, and freedom from harm and from undue restraint.

Moreover, this method of analysis supports many dodges away from innovation and ultimately narrows the rights available to mentally retarded persons. The court of appeals turned not to constitutional rights for all residents of institutions but to statutory law. Doing so accorded with a general rule preferring a statutory basis for relief if it can address the claims of a plaintiff, yet the preference was somewhat artificial here, where the federal statutes had themselves been adopted to help implement constitutional interpretations reached by prior court decisions. The Supreme Court found even the rights announced in the federal statutes insufficient to support the claims against the institution. The Court treated the Developmentally Disabled Assistance and Bill of Rights Act, named as part of the federal statutory assistance program, as merely hortatory and not binding on the states that received money through that legislation. A small glimmer of hope remained, according to the Court, in a constitutional basis for relief in the limited instance of an individual alleging specific injuries.

Robert Burt attributes some of the intensity and confusion about the Pennhurst litigation to the sense, shared by all the parties and the judges, of the vulnerability and inscrutability of the mentally retarded people involved. Their qualities initially tended to draw all parties close together, partially in an impulse to support the retarded persons but perhaps partially out of mutual self-defense in the face of such overwhelming need. Burt speculates:

> This explanation could also suggest why these other-than-retarded parties would come closer together in their initial encounters than they could sustain over the long haul as the neediness of the vulnerable, inscrutable retarded people seemed to grow endlessly toward insatiability. Mutuality would erode because, as this perception of insatiability grew, the apparent costs to each other-than-retarded party would grow and what had initially seemed sufficient to meet these needs because of the pooling of mutual resources would become transformed into imagined quicksand that threatens to swallow everything remotely in sight.[82]

In a real sense, the needs of the mentally retarded persons highlight the potential insatiability of all human relationships. To respond fully to the needs of any other might be overwhelming. The usual way of handling this problem, under law, is to create a division between public and private obligation. We each have only those private obligations we individually choose or carry on as members of private families. Beyond that, all obligations are managed by the public sphere, which must, by law, treat every person according to the rules established by law. Returning the person with great needs to the "private" sphere of the family home is hardly a solution when the family lacks either resources or support for providing the necessary care. The rhetoric of rights signals the claims each person can make on the community. These are the claims of equality and liberty that the public

---

[82]Burt, "Pennhurst," p. 324.

sphere must assure to every individual—but this rhetoric defines no basis for responding to individual needs or for addressing the special needs of those for whom the general society was not designed. Meeting the goals of special legislation adopted to assist the mentally disabled could require considerable expenditure. Application of the same constitutional rights granted every individual could also support or command expenditures—or the courts could interpret the law to order nothing on the grounds that the mentally retarded person is entitled only to the "same" treatment accorded anyone else.

This is the central confusion about the use of rights analysis for disabled persons. Rights founded on the sameness connecting all people could support deinstitutionalization. The law should liberate people from the segregation and degradation of institutions that provide little care and no training. Yet invoking a right to equal treatment and a right to liberty hardly points to new community services and programs for those who cannot manage life on their own. Moreover, rights founded on their differences—rights justifying community services or improvements within separate institutions—risk merging into the rationale that produced segregation and degradation in the first place. The rationale of fundamental difference has long supported the exclusion of mentally retarded people from the mainstream of society; it implies that the difference is inherent in the "different" people rather than a function of relationships with others and with social arrangements that exclude them. How may advocates demand that law treat mentally retarded persons the same as others for purposes of freedom from constraints and abuse, but differently from others for the purpose of securing the attention, resources, and care that others do not need? Legal innovation may produce the worst of both worlds: a prescription of "same" rights to be free from institutionalization but with no special rights in the community, or of "different" rights to special care without the fundamental rights to freedom from injury due to abuse or negligence by others.

It was not rights analysis, ultimately, which concluded the Pennhurst case. Instead, a complex process of bargaining amid political conflicts continued while the litigation proceeded through the courts—and while the district judge and his appointed master pursued individualized assessments of Pennhurst residents to determine whether each one belonged in community rather than institutional placement. After two Supreme Court decisions rejecting the legal theories for closing the institution, and several appeals court decisions indicating energetic commitment to some form of relief, the state settled the case and agreed to shut Pennhurst down.[83] Nothing within rights analysis could describe, much less orchestrate, the struggles that emerged in this litigation. Nothing in rights analysis could acknowledge the structure of relationships within which mental retardation assumes its meaning. With its assumptions of individual autonomy, self-reliance, and equality founded in people's similarities, rights analysis is an awkward tool for grasping the

[83]Ibid., p. 362.

situations of interdependence among people—and among such institutions as the federal and state courts and legislatures.

These limitations of rights analysis persist even when legal rights are situated within the philosophic traditions that nurture them. Indeed, an examination of contemporary legal theory shows that both the traditional theories justifying rights and the major contending theories replicate the distinction between normal and abnormal persons, thus perpetuating the assumptions that trap us in the difference dilemma.

CHAPTER 6

Rights Theories and Contemporary Legal Debates

Either you will
go through this door
or you will not go through.
——Adrienne Rich, "Prospective Immigrants/Please Note"

As developed by lawyers and theorists during the mid-twentieth century, rights analysis itself cannot remedy the exclusion and degradation of people defined as different by experts and majorities in this society. Despite its liberatory rhetoric of inclusion and fundamental entitlement, the analysis of rights, developed in constitutional and statutory judicial doctrines in this country, runs aground on the shoals of the two-track system of legal treatment. One track offers basic rights to self-determination and participation for those who satisfy the criteria of rational thought and independence; the other offers special treatment and, quite often, social and political exclusion. Those treated as "different" who can demonstrate that they correctly belong with the first track may find considerable help through the rhetoric of rights. Those who fail to satisfy the test of "sameness," however, may find rights analysis a bitter remedy that undermines whatever past acknowledgment of difference there had been without producing social and political inclusion.

The "sameness" between people emphasized by rights analysis challenges special accommodations made for disabled people, women, and others historically treated as different. Under a renewed commitment to provide the same treatment to all, it reconfirms institutional arrangements that deny special accommodations. The result may make those with any kinds of "difference" worse off in light of existing institutions. Thus, efforts to eliminate gender bias in divorce law have removed alimony and child custody provisions that preferred women, and some observers attribute to these reforms the increased impoverishment and worsened bargaining position of women following divorce.[1] Rights analysis offers release from hierarchy and subordination to those who can match the picture of the abstract, autonomous individual presupposed by the theory of rights. For those who do not match that picture, application of rights analysis can be not only unresponsive but also punitive. If an assertion of rights by an individual produces an individualized response, the remedy still leaves in place existing institutions that themselves define and burden difference. One student may be accommodated in a school not designed for her disability, but her experience may leave no mark on the school's usual methods and structure. Responsiveness to an occasional individual suggests that the legal system is fair—and its failures to respond to others seems to demonstrate that their problems reside in themselves. In short, rights analysis preserves rather than alters the dilemma of difference: difference continues to represent deviance in the context of existing social arrangements, and attention to difference can be as inadequate a response as inattention.

Contemporary theories of law include both broad justifications for rights and alternatives to rights-based theories. Among these alternatives are "legal process," which concentrates on the procedures and functions of the branches of government; "law and economics," which bases analysis on comparative utilities; and "critical legal studies," which explores the relationships between language and power.[2] None of these theories addresses the failure of rights analysis to escape the dilemma of difference; indeed, for the most part each one replicates rather than challenges this pattern. Most theories of law developed in this century embody rather than shed light on the premise of the normal, competent individual, and they restrict state power in the name of the liberty of such persons. Presuming an unsituated perspective that coincides with the dominant world view, rights analysis and the alternative theories largely ignore the groups of people historically defined as different and marginal. In its very indifference, legal theory reiterates the marginalization produced by laws themselves.

Let me support these somewhat tendentious assertions by looking first at the justifications for rights analysis both in social contract philosophies and in theories of natural rights, two major forms of rights analysis. I then suggest that two of the contemporary alternatives, "legal process" and "law and economics," preserve the constellation of exclusionary assumptions found in rights analysis and that even though "critical legal studies" criticize the other theories, this school of thought too largely reinforces the assumptions that make difference a dilemma.

---

[1]See Lenore Weitzman, *The Divorce Revolution: The Unexpected Social and Economic Consequences for Women and Children in America* (New York: Free Press, 1985).

[2]Additional contemporary legal theories include "law and society" (which examines the disjunction between law in theory and law in practice while relating contemporary legal developments to the traditions of social theory) and feminist scholarship (discussed in Chapter 7).

Philosophers and Rights Analysis

One source of rights analysis in this country is the philosophy of social contract that influenced the authors and interpreters of our Constitution. Another source, equally influential, is the concept of fundamental or natural rights. Both traditions contribute to liberal political theory, itself a collection of ideas influenced by the works of Niccolo Machiavelli, Thomas Hobbes, John Locke, and John Stuart Mill.[3] The retelling of these traditions has itself become a tradition as scholars justify continued and expanding reliance on the idea of an autonomous individual whose dignity, liberty, and equality demand legal recognition and enforcement of rights.

This painfully brief summary of the story of liberal traditions is merely prelude to a discussion of contemporary legal theories of rights analysis. Oversimplification is an unfortunate yet unavoidable part of this enterprise. As the preceding chapter recounted, the idea of a coherent, hierarchical social order, reflecting the designs of nature and of God, undergirded medieval legal theory, which sought to harmonize law, religion, and social order. Successive challenges to those ideas appeared in the humanism of the Renaissance; the Reformation's emphasis on individual conscience and individual access to divine authority; the American Revolution's calls for independence and autonomy; and the French Revolution's demands for liberty, equality, and fraternity. Rather than accepting the authority of royalty and religious officials as natural or divinely ordained, people began to seek a sense of participation in the governance of their lives.

Political and legal philosophers summarized and symbolized these developments with the idea of the social contract. According to this idea, all members of society band together for common protection against the dangers of a state of nature and reach an agreement that becomes the source of authority for the governance of all. The consent of the governed provides the legitimate basis for governmental authority and thereby replaces the premises of divine authority behind king and church. The ideal of the governed's consent expresses and preserves the idea of individual autonomy, or self-rule, while also providing a basis for a legitimate social order. The social contract tradition points to the processes rather than the substance of legal authority. Rules adopted according to the requisite process are binding. Individuals in this country cannot claim, because the government is not bound by, any set of substantive values beyond those reduced to writing in the founding document of the polity—the U.S. Constitution.

American constitutional practice has provided legal theorists with a histor-

---

[3]See generally Stephen Holmes, *Benjamin Constant and the Making of Modern Liberalism* (New Haven, Conn.: Yale University Press, 1984); Steven Shiffrin, "Liberalism, Radicalism, and Legal Scholarship," *U.C.L.A. L. Rev.* 30 (1983), 1103; Robin West, "Liberalism Rediscovered: A Pragmatic Definition of the Liberal Vision," *U. Pitt. L. Rev.* 46 (1985), 673. Recent critiques of liberalism include Nancy Rosenblum, *Another Liberalism: Romanticism and the Reconstruction of Liberal Thought* (Cambridge, Mass.: Harvard University Press, 1987); and Robert Paul Wolff, *The Poverty of Liberalism* (Boston: Beacon Press, 1968).

ical, if disputed, terrain for philosophic narrative about a social contract and has supplied a rich context for debates over the original intent behind the Constitution and its continuing meanings and applications. Rights analysis, in this light, depends on those rights actually captured in the written document founding the government and susceptible to interpretation by the branches of government established by that document.

Some political and legal theorists have approached the idea of the social contract less as the actual product of a historical process than as a heuristic device. These theorists treat legal rights as the principles and norms that people would agree to if we all engaged in the kind of process signified by the image of the social contract. Asking what rational people would consent to—what the "rational consensus" would be—becomes the touchstone for analysis of this sort, as developed by such theorists as John Rawls, Robert Nozick, Ronald Dworkin, and Bruce Ackerman.[4] Because people are likely to disagree about many important values, the rights established by reference to the hypothetical "rational consensus" will be basic ground rules for ordering society—and for conducting future disagreements. John Rawls expressly used the idea of a social contract by grounding his theory of justice in an imagined situation for fair contractual drafting. In this "original position," all members of society would stand behind a veil of ignorance about our specific roles, abilities, and circumstances in society and then imagine what principles would assure fairness for all. After adopting principles without knowing how they would apply to our own lives, participants in this imagined process would then check the resulting social contract with intuitions and with ideas of rationality. The theorist demands that the terms of the social contract be not only consensual but also consistent with ideas of sound reason.

Both the historical and heuristic versions of social contract theory claim to be inclusive, participatory, and egalitarian, yet both replicate the process of exclusion and subordination that preserves the two tracks of legal treatment. The U.S. Constitution is a document produced through an indisputably exclusionary process. The Constitutional Convention had a limited group of participants: not only were no women, Native Americans, or blacks present, but neither were people without wealth and privilege. The Constitution developed through that process preserved slavery and reserved political participation to free white men. The "social contract" created one track of legal treatment for free and participating citizens and another track for those excluded by the process and the document. The Civil War, followed by dramatic amendments to the Constitution, did produce a more inclusionary document. Yet the battles over inclusion continue in contemporary efforts to secure an Equal Rights Amendment to redress gender-based inequities and in

---

[4]Bruce Ackerman, *Reconstructing American Law* (Cambridge, Mass.: Harvard University Press, 1984); John Rawls, *A Theory of Justice* (Cambridge, Mass.: Harvard University Press, 1971); Ronald Dworkin, *Law's Empire* (Cambridge, Mass.: Belknap Press of Harvard University Press, 1986); Robert Nozick, *Anarchy, State, and Utopia* (New York: Basic Books, 1974). See also David Gauthier, *Morals by Agreement* (Oxford: Clarendon Press, 1986).

antidiscrimination litigation on behalf of minority groups that are still excluded.[5]

Those committed to the social contract idea as a touchstone for rational consensus also preserved a two-track legal system. The very demand of rationality for participants in the process of imagining the social contract excludes those who do not manifest the capabilities for rationality as defined by the theorists. What counts as "rationality" may itself illustrate the unstated norm and pretend an unsituated perspective that calls some people marginal or different. The views of mentally disabled persons, children, and any others deemed to lack capacity for rational thought become relevant only through the imaginations of the "rational" people who ask what they themselves would want if they were in the position of these incompetent persons. This approach may produce normative judgments that are insensitive and even skewed against some people. Rawls's work, for example, stops short of introducing the norms of equality and participation in the family, where the premises of individual autonomy and rationality apparently do not apply.[6] In this respect, Rawls echoes Locke, who presumed the private authority of parents—unless they failed to prepare their children for rational, independent existence.[7] Nothing inherent in the idea of rationality requires such sharp distinctions between those "with reason" and those "without reason," and some scholars have recently proposed ways to reconstruct rationality to facilitate egalitarianism even within families.[8]

In the usual meaning of rationality as adopted by social contract theorists, however, the heuristic device of the social contract presumes to address only autonomous, independent individuals who can separate themselves from others and enter freely, unencumbered, into an agreement about how to conduct private and public affairs. In the exercise for devising a social contract, theorists offer the invitation to imagine the situation of others basically only to those who have the time and ability to reflect on these matters. Any consideration of the situations of people without this time and ability is presented as a task of imagination for that class of people who, like the theorists, fit comfortably within the paradigm of the rational, autonomous individual presumed by social contract theory. A very different design for devising a social contract, or for conceiving of the foundations of a society, would be necessary in order to include directly those who within contemporary society seem disabled and those historically treated as incom-

[5]See generally *The Constitution and American Life,* ed. David Thelen (Ithaca: Cornell University Press, 1988).

[6]See Susan Muller Okin, "Gender and Justice," *Philosophy and Public Affairs* 16, no. 1 (1987), 42: Rawls tacitly follows Kant in excluding women from the generic category of free and rational persons; women are presumed not to be heads of households, and non–heads of households lack direct participation and representation.

[7]Locke's theory etched the two tracks of legal treatment perhaps even more deeply by carving out a division between private and public spheres, removing private roles and their influence on social inequalities from the purview of civil life. See Rogers Smith, " 'One United People': Second-Class Female Citizenship and the American Quest for Community," *Yale J. Law & Humanities* 2 (1989), 229.

[8]The most promising effort along these lines is Susan Muller Okin, *Justice, Gender, and the Family* (New York: Basic Books, 1989).

petent and incapable of participating in the formation of a rational consensus. The idea of a rational consensus and the image of a contracting process afford some degree of equal membership for those ready and able to join such processes. Yet these same ideas erect a boundary distinguishing those who can participate, given the set ground rules, from those who cannot. Abstract ideas about participation then have free reign, immune from the challenge of lived realities.

Abstract ideas provide valuable leverage points for challenging social practices, but they may also be used to hide the distance between theory and practice. The idea of freedom of contract sounds ennobling and promises a basic equality, in contrast to ideas of authority or duties imposed without choice. Freedom-of-contract notions ring resonantly in this culture and especially in the legal culture. During the late nineteenth century freedom of contract became the central paradigm for most of the legal system in the United States.[9] That ideal specifically rejected obligations founded in relationships and roles; it elevated explicit intentional agreements between rational, self-willing individuals as the arrangements deserving legal protection. The commitment to freedom and individual autonomy represented by this ideal, however, also included commitment to judicial power to determine when to bind parties and when to refuse to enforce agreements. The freedom-of-contract ideal also emboldened courts to reject regulatory reforms of employment practices adopted by popular legislation. The sheer abstract statement of ideas in law thus acquires different meaning in the context of the institutional practices of actual law enforcement.

Freedom of contract, both in theory and in practice, simultaneously constructed and marginalized its exceptions. Those arrangements that failed to satisfy the requirements of freedom of contract lost legal enforcement or fell to a different legal treatment, reserved for those who lacked the capacity to engage in the rules of freedom of contract. Just as the ideal of freedom of contract in the nineteenth century created a second track of legal treatment for those arrangements and those persons who failed to fit this ideal, the image of the social contract secured through rational consensus excludes those who do not fit its presuppositions.

Social contract theories do not exclude only those people who lack the requisite mental competence and capacity for reason; any who would identify themselves as members of groups first, rather than as autonomous individuals first, would also find their point of view excluded. Affiliation and identification with others, based on traits not shared by all persons, is precisely what Rawls would have participants leave behind in the process of imagining the social contract.[10] Underlying social contract theory is the idea of the abstract individual. This individual is thought to have wants, desires,

---

[9]See Morton J. Horwitz, *The Transformation of American Law, 1780–1860* (Cambridge, Mass.: Harvard University Press, 1977), pp. 255–64; Elizabeth Mensch, "The History of Mainstream Legal Thought," in *The Politics of Law: A Progressive Critique*, ed. David Kairys (New York: Pantheon Books, 1982), pp. 18, 24–25.

[10]See Michael Sandel, *Liberalism and the Limits of Justice* (Cambridge: Cambridge University Press, 1982).

and needs independent of social context, relationships with others, or historical setting. The individual, in short, is distinguishable from his or her situation and social, political, and religious identities. This idea is a prerequisite for imagining a state of nature, outside of society, from which people enter into a social contract.[11]

An admirable commitment to universality and inclusion accompanies this idea, an idea that all individuals could be self-sufficient and that all individuals, if removed from context, would share a fundamental humanity. The shared human essence, removed from context, once meant that each person was made in the image of God. In a more secular age, the dominant idea replacing religious notions is that each person is a repository of Reason,[12] or the capacity to think.[13] All persons are equal because of this fundamental sameness—yet this sameness seems to be the emptiness left when we are each sheared of all that makes us different. J. R. Pole points out that our Constitution grounds equality in the idea that people could take one another's place in intellectual exchange, in jobs, or in political office if they were disassociated from contexts of family, religion, class, or race and if each one had the same opportunities and experiences.[14] One problem with this approach, for those who worry about the groups who have been labeled "different" in the past, is that the pretense of universal, inclusive norms in the public sphere obscures the power of assigned differences in the private sphere. On the basis of those differences, women, children, and disabled people have historically been denied participation in the governance structure of the public sphere.

Despite the implied aspiration to universal inclusion, the social contract approach has been deeply exclusionary. It is not only that any sign of difference, any shred of situated perspective, threatens the claim to similarity, equality, and identity as an abstract individual—although these problems are serious enough; it is that this conception amounts to a preference for some points of view over others; it takes some types of people as the norm and assigns a position of difference to others (thus adopting the assumptions behind the difference dilemma). The very human being who could be imag-

---

[11]See Steven Lukes, *Individualism* (Oxford: Basil Blackwell, 1973), pp. 73–87.

[12]See Immanuel Kant, *Fundamental Principles of the Metaphysic of Morals*, trans. Thomas Abbott (Chicago: Encyclopaedia Britannica, 1952), p. 282: "Man really finds in himself a faculty by which he distinguishes himself from everything else . . . and that is *reason*." See also Hilary Putnam, *The Many Faces of Realism* (LaSalle, Ill.: Open Court, 1987), pp. 45–50; Roger Scruton, *Kant*, (Oxford: Oxford University Press, 1982), pp. 62–69, describing Kant's view of rational beings, capable of free will and fulfillment of moral duty.

[13]See, e.g., *Powers That Make Us Human: The Foundations of Medical Ethics*, ed. Kenneth Vaux (Urbana: University of Illinois Press, 1985), pp. 75–87. David Lamb, *Death, Brain Death, and Ethics* (Albany: State University of New York Press, 1985), argues for defining human life in terms of capacity for human thought, which would exclude persons in a persistent vegetative state.

[14]J. R. Pole, *The Pursuit of Equality in American History* (Berkeley: University of California Press, 1978), pp. 293–94. But see Charles Larmore, *Patterns of Moral Complexity* (Cambridge: Cambridge University Press, 1987), pp. 121–30, arguing that liberalism acknowledges people's different commitments and identities and devises a distinction between public (where those differences do not matter) and private (where they do).

ined as abstracted from context is a particular sort of person with a specific history and identity. It is a person living sometime after the seventeenth century in western Europe or the United States, a person who avoided feudal bonds and lived away from any religious, ethnic, or family group whose members defined themselves through such a group.[15] The idea of the person who could be abstracted from context was invented by theorists—and challenged by other theorists, who disputed both the possibility and the desirability of such a view of human beings.[16] Recent philosophers have questioned whether the idea of the abstract individual ever did or ever could apply to women.[17] The presentation of a type of human being as though it described all human beings risks excluding any who do not fit or treating such misfits as deviant.[18]

John Rawls offers a generous principle to deal with this problem. He calls upon the participants in the social contract experiment to consider what happens, under any hypothesized social arrangements, to the worst-off person in the society. Since each person stands "behind the veil of ignorance" for the purpose of this experiment, not knowing what traits or preferences he or she would have in fact, this concern helps us focus on the chance that any of us could be the worst off. Such an inquiry also emphasizes the cooperative dimension of the contractual method: all bargainers should think about the effect of the deal on everyone because that effect will influence each person. For Rawls, this line of thought leads to the "difference principle": the benefits of the contract should be distributed so that the worst-off person does as well as possible.[19]

This approach presumes sufficient societal cooperation to permit and make legitimate a redistribution of resources among members of the society. It promotes an idea that talents and abilities are not the belongings of

[15]It is difficult to imagine that such a person would be a woman, a child, or a disabled individual. For a comprehensive effort to locate in its historical context the philosophical effort to imagine human concerns removed from their historical contexts, see Stephen Toulmin, *Cosmopolis: The Hidden Agenda of Modernity* (New York: Free Press, 1990).

[16]See Karl Marx, "Theses on Feuerbach," in *Marx & Engels: Collected Works* (New York: International Publishers, 1976); Sandel, *Liberalism and the Limits of Justice*, pp. 171–74: the self is constituted in part by family and community membership; Michael Walzer, *Spheres of Justice: A Defense of Pluralism and Equality* (New York: Basic Books, 1983), pp. 255–62, 271–80, criticizing Rawls; Jean Bethke Elshtain, *Public Man, Private Woman: Women in Social and Political Thought*, (Princeton, N.J.: Princeton University Press, 1981), pp. 344–45.

[17]See Alison Jaggar, *Feminist Politics and Human Nature* (Totowa, N.J.: Rowman & Allenheld, 1983), pp. 46–47; Susan Muller Okin, *Women in Western Political Thought* (Princeton, N.J.: Princeton University Press, 1979), pp. 197–202; Genevieve Lloyd,*The Man of Reason: "Male" and "Female" in Western Philosophy* (Minneapolis: University of Minnesota Press, 1984). See also John Locke, "An Essay concerning the True, Original Extent and End of Civil Government," in *Social Contract: Locke, Hume & Rousseau*, ed. John Wredhofft Gough (Oxford: Clarendon Press, 1957), pp. 30–56: Locke's discussion of paternal power and political and civil society presumes a male head of household who rules the women and children.

[18]Carol Gilligan, "In a Different Voice: Women's Conceptions of Self and Morality," *Harvard Education Review* 47 (1977), 418, 482; Audre Lorde, "Age, Race, Class, and Sex: Women Redefining Difference," in *Sister Outsider: Essays and Speeches* (Trumansburg, N.Y.: Crossing Press, 1984), pp. 114, 116.

[19]See Rawls, *Theory of Justice*, pp. 75–78.

separate persons, who then deserve their fruits. Instead, talents are to some extent the resources of the society and should be distributed more generally. This dimension of Rawls's argument represents an important challenge to the usual forms of autonomous individualism in liberal political theory and has certainly not escaped attack on this ground.[20] Yet Rawls's difference principle preserves too much of the concept of the abstract individual—a concept that claims but fails to secure universality—to respond fully to issues of difference.

First, many people would not respond to the chance of being the worst-off person by adopting the difference principle. To assume otherwise, as Rawls does, is to posit a particular kind of person in the role of the decision-maker. Many people might instead assess the chances of being the worst-off person and base a calculation of the benefits for that person on such a probability. As one commentator put it, "Since nobody has any reason to suppose that he or she is going to be the worst-off person, it is irrationally cautious to choose rules which are exclusively determined by the aim of making the worst-off person as well off as possible. If we turn out not to be the worst-off person, we may have made unreasonably large sacrifices of our welfare for the sake of the worst off."[21]

Rawls's contrary view depends not on human nature abstracted from context but instead on an idea about human beings that was forged and is maintained by particular historical and cultural attitudes—an idea emphasizing the unique worth of each person, an idea often associated with humanism or with Immanuel Kant or with Judaeo-Christian traditions. This idea contrasts sharply with the assumptions of utilitarianism, to name just one other view. Rawls's individual is specifically *not* a utilitarian—who would care about the worst-off person only to the extent that this person's well-being contributes to the well-being of all others.

An especially telling remnant of particularity within Rawls's failed attempt to posit an individual removed from particular circumstances is that the very form of his questions presumes that the person behind the veil of ignorance is not the worst-off person. It assumes some essence of a self preexisting one's situation, and anyone would approach the possibility of being worst off the same way. Like the assumption of an unsituated perspective that contributes to the dilemma of difference, this approach ignores contrary perspectives while denying that it is partial. Rawls's question is put only to the particular person who is not the worst off, a particular person who is not likely to understand fully the situation of the worst-off.[22]

An example helps here. A young man named Christopher Nolan, who lives

---

[20]See Nozick, *Anarchy, State, and Utopia*, pp. 206–7.

[21]Alan Ryan, "John Rawls," in *The Return of Grand Theory in the Human Sciences*, ed. Quentin Skinner (Cambridge: Cambridge University Press, 1985), pp. 101, 110.

[22]Susan Muller Okin has argued that Rawls must mean for people behind the veil to imagine themselves in all positions, rather than in no position at all (essay forthcoming in *Ethics*). But without conversation with those who are different, even this imaginative process will fail to take their perspective seriously.

in Ireland, recently received considerable attention in the international media because his writing talents won him an award—and because he has been immobilized by cerebral palsy since birth.[23] Except for a small ability to move his neck, Christopher Nolan cannot control his movements; he must painstakingly take twelve hours to type each page while his mother holds his head up before the word processor. A journalist reportedly asked him, "What is the first thing you would do if you could leave your wheelchair?" Nolan replied, "Get right back in."[24] This answer obviously surprised the journalist, who could not imagine choosing the disability. The answer, however, affords a glimpse into the strikingly different experience of this young man and into his perspective, which challenges the assumption that he could still be who he is out of the wheelchair.[25] Moreover, Nolan's response shows the assumption of an autonomous, able-bodied person to be an assumption of a particularly situated person, not an unsituated one.[26]

Like Rawls's principle, the social contract tradition employs a concept of the abstract individual that claims to be universal but actually selects particular views. The alternative tradition of natural rights provides a contrasting source for the rights that ground claims of individual liberty, freedom, and dignity, a source outside of either the actual Constitution or the hypothetical social contract. The natural rights tradition also partakes of the assumptions of the autonomous and abstract individual and excludes or subordinates any who fail to meet those assumptions.[27] From its roots in seventeenth- and eighteenth-century philosophy, the theory has been revived in the twentieth century, with some changes but also considerable continuity. The continuous elements are a belief in human reason as universal and the development of human potential as the principal goal of social and legal order.[28] The notion

[23]See Christopher Nolan, *Under the Eye of the Clock* (New York: St. Martin's Press, 1987).
[24]Confirmed by Kathy Field Stephen, personal communication.
[25]The answer also rejects the view of the disabled as lacking—and wanting—something that those with abilities have. See Harlan Hahn, "Public Policy and Disabled Infants: A Sociopolitical Perspective," *Issues in Law and Medicine* 3, no. 1 (1987), 3–4, 7–8. Surveys of disabled people have indicated that many view their disabilities not as great tragedies but instead as facts of life that are inconvenient but not central to their identities. See Nancy Weinberg and Judy Williams, "How the Physically Disabled Perceive Their Disabilities," *Journal of Rehabilitation* 44 (Aug./Sept. 1978), 31; Robert Ross, Michael Begab, Ernest Dondis, James Giampiccollo, Jr., and C. Edward Meyers, *Lives of the Mentally Retarded: A Forty-Year Follow-Up Study* (Stanford, Calif.: Stanford University Press, 1985). The even more common misunderstanding of disabled persons is that because they differ from others in some respects, they differ in all respects. Jeffrey Lyon, in *Playing God in the Nursery* (New York: Norton, 1985), pp. 330–36, reports quite powerfully how surprised, and self-critical, he became upon discovering that his mentally retarded brother kept a diary, and reported in it a variety of self-reflective emotions.
[26]Some might ask whether Nolan's view shows "false consciousness" rather than self-determination. Surely, people may be mistaken about their preferences. But the very assumption that majority groups know what's best for minorities—contrary to their own espoused views—should give rise to caution in light of the refusal to credit the ability of those with less authority to know their own situation.
[27]Robert Cover, *Justice Accused* (New Haven, Conn.: Yale University Press, 1975), pp. 28–30, 134, explores tensions between positivism and natural rights theory.
[28]See Edgar Bodenheimer, *Jurisprudence: The Philosophy and Method of the Law*, rev. ed. (Cambridge, Mass.: Harvard University Press, 1974), pp. 31–69, 134–68. John Locke launched

of inalienable rights, belonging to every person despite governmental intrusions, helped to animate arguments for both the French and American revolutions. Especially since the Nazi period and World War II, advocates of natural rights have argued that certain absolute postulates define the rights of humans regardless of the particular rules in place under the reigning government. Proponents of natural law have maintained that certain elementary truths about human beings ground universally recognized rights.[29] Yet descriptions of such theories inevitably distinguish between those societies that have recognized these "universally recognized rights" and those that have not and thus remain uncivilized and barbaric.[30] Here, the exclusionary aspect is overt.

Once again, the premise of a basic human nature, found in the abstract individual capable of reason, undergirds the theory and risks excluding any who do not meet it. Theories of natural law locate the justification for universal rights in human reason or cognition. This focus on reason makes problematic any persons who do not manifest to the satisfaction of those in charge the requisite capacities for rational thought. For children, natural rights theorists elaborate the relevance of the potential for developing rational capacities; for mentally disabled persons, they are more at a loss.[31]

Perhaps the defects in the premise of rationality helped to fuel an opposing legal theory, legal positivism. Its adherents, such as Hans Kelsen, argued that the content of justice cannot be determined through reason or through perceptions of social reality because people's immutable differences present value conflicts and subjective preferences.[32] Unamenable to rational analysis, the goals of justice must be excluded from legal theory. Theories of law should be concerned instead with defining and elaborating the processes for adopting and enforcing binding rules. One powerful legal theory in this country, legal process, bears some resemblance to this view, yet it too excludes and subordinates on the basis of difference, without offering a method for altering this process.

---

the continuing debate about how to reconcile the idea of rights with the demands and limits of state authority; see his *Second Treatise of Government* (1690; Oxford: Basil Blackwell, 1976).

[29]See H. L. A. Hart, *The Concept of Law* (Oxford: Oxford University Press, 1961), p. 188.

[30]Bodenheimer, *Jurisprudence*, pp. 216–18. See also John Stuart Mill's discussion of barbarians in *On Liberty;* Günter Frankenberg, "Critical Comparisons: Rethinking Comparative Law," *Harv. Int'l L.J.* 26 (1985), 411, 418–20, 422: feelings of academic marginality can tend toward ethnocentric bias in comparative law.

[31]See Lloyd Weinreb, *Natural Law and Justice* (Cambridge, Mass.: Harvard University Press, 1987), pp. 243–45: an individual's attributes may seem simply present but actually depend on family and societal circumstances; attributes represent a flexible concept that can shift in light of social arrangements.

[32]See Hans Kelsen, *General Theory of Law and State*, trans. A. Wedberg (Cambridge, Mass.: Harvard University Press, 1949); Hans Kelsen, "The Pure Theory of Law and Analytical Jurisprudence," *Harv. L. Rev.* 55 (1941), 44. Kelsen sought to eliminate all value conflicts in law by designating governmental coercion as the essential ingredient of social order, and by treating legal validity as a question to be resolved purely by the presence of a superior legal norm rather than by social or moral values.

The Theory of Legal Process

After World War II legal theorists distrusted grand social visions and ideologies. Many concluded that politics, rather than law, should be the arena for struggles over the values and purposes of the society. In a pluralist and free nation, people will disagree about the ends of the society; individuals have preferences that conflict. Those disagreements belong in the electoral branches of government. Law's special contribution would be to monitor and guide the processes of government. Law can and should articulate proper roles for the branches of government and the proper relationships between them. Each branch should stay within the boundary of its competence; each branch has separate tasks and distinct powers.[33] The judiciary's special competence is to resolve concrete disputes in light of rules of principle, elaborated to connect facts and public purposes.[34] The legislature's special competence is to provide an orderly forum for gathering and summarizing the views of the population about public purposes, and for resolving differences in the views that diverse people bring to politics by compromise or by majority vote. The executive's special competence is to enforce the rules through expertise, using the discretion established for this purpose by the other branches. Law describes these competences and the distinctions between them. Law also constrains any one branch from arrogating power over matters that properly belong within the competence of another.[35]

The treatment of "difference" by the legal-process school is somewhat obscure. By turning to process rather than substantive values as a topic for legal theory, legal process appears to avoid the debates over the meanings of equality, difference, and rights. Some critics might note in just this avoidance an act of exclusion or suppression. A theory that makes certain problems less visible and, indeed, removes them from the agenda could be understood as marginalizing those problems and the people who care about them.[36]

---

[33]The classic work is Henry H. Hart and Albert M. Sacks, "The Legal Process: Basic Problems in the Making and Application of Law" (1958), perhaps the most influential unpublished work in legal scholarship. A good case can be made that Ronald Dworkin is an important heir to this tradition; see Vincent Wellman, "Dworkin and the Legal Process Tradition: The Legacy of Hart and Sacks," *Ariz. L. Rev.* 29 (1987), 413.

[34]Legal-process scholars call upon judges to engage in "reasoned elaboration"; see Hart and Sacks, "The Legal Process," p. 164. See also Karl Llewellyn, Edward Levi, Harry Wellington, and Ronald Dworkin, *Taking Rights Seriously* (Cambridge, Mass.: Harvard University Press, 1978), p. 22. See generally Joseph William Singer, "Legal Realism Now: Review Essay of Laura Kalman, *Legal Realism at Yale, 1927–1960*," *Calif. L. Rev.* 76 (1988), 467: legal-process theorists directed judges to confine their power to the task of connecting specific facts in a given dispute to prior judicial decisions and to the purposes and policies underlying those precedents.

[35]See Hart and Sacks, "The Legal Process." See also Wellman, "Dworkin."

[36]See Steven Lukes, *Power: A Radical View* (New York: Macmillan, 1974). Some scholars, described as the "new legal-process" school, specifically focus on the possibilities for creating new values through politics and law rather than simply justifying existing institutions as "neutral" mechanisms for delivering justice. See, e.g., William Eskridge, "Public Values in Statutory Interpretation," *U. Pa. L. Rev.* 137 (1989), 1007; Daniel Farber and Philip Frickey, "The Jurisprudence of Public Choice," *Tex. L. Rev.* 65 (1987), 873. Yet these new theorists also

Looking at what legal-process theorists do say, however, may be more significant. They have written about the judicial role in assessing the validity of a contract; Lon Fuller, for example, explains that courts are uniquely qualified to evaluate the process of contractual agreement which predicates a legitimate, enforceable transaction. In the very activity of deciding who has the capacity to contract and which contracts deserve judicial recognition, the courts distinguish enforceable and unenforceable contracts, reaching substantive conclusions even through commitments to particular processes.[37]

Legal-process theorists have also discussed the judicial role in school desegregation, remaining preoccupied with articulating the proper allocation of power among the branches of government. Again, this may seem an avoidance of the hot debates over rights and the meaning of equality. Yet there is a curious connection between the concern with separation of powers and the issues of difference, manifested in the use of the word "competence." Of course, the word does not bear precisely the same meaning when applied to branches of government as it does with regard to individual person, yet its use signals a similar pattern of thought: the powers of the branches, like the rights of persons, are determined by reference to their competence, their intrinsic abilities.

A branch of government lacks power to address matters beyond its competence. For example, according to Fuller, courts lack competence to resolve highly political questions or complex disputes affecting multiple interests which require compromise rather than principle.[38] Legal-process theorists would probably argue that a court should stay out of a dispute over a group home for mentally disabled persons if the judge concludes that another branch of the government has greater judicial competence in the matter. Especially where general empirical data must be gathered to formulate a new rule, or where the views of the electorate are germane to the issue, or where the elected branches have not delegated power to the courts, legal-process theorists would advise judges to refrain from resolving the matter. The notion of competence creates a boundary between legitimate activities and unauthorized activities, just as competence labels the distinction between the legitimate actions of competent people and the sphere of incompetents, who are removed from the standard rules of legal rights and legal liabilities.

---

neglect complex issues presented by a heterogeneous society for the processes of creating public values through the practical reason and statutory interpretation that they advocate. For a cogent evaluation of these and other shortcomings, see Daniel B. Rodriguez, "Review Essay: The Substance of the New Legal Process," *Calif. L. Rev.* 77 (1989), 919.

[37]Lon Fuller, "The Forms and Limits of Adjudication," *Harv. L. Rev.* 92 (1978), 353, 398.

[38]Fuller, "Forms and Limits of Adjudication." For a contrasting view, see Abram Chayes, "The Role of the Judge in Public Law Litigation," *Harv. L. Rev.* 89 (1976), 1281. See also Wellman, "Dworkin," pp. 413, 429–50. Not all people identified with legal process would reach the same conclusions on these matters. Albert Sacks, for example, emphasizes the dynamic quality of judicial reasoning in light of statutory and constitutional purposes; for him the initial school desegregation case was correct and unproblematic even though it put the Supreme Court in the midst of political controversy (author's interview with Albert Sacks, Jan. 23, 1990).

On a different level, the concern with establishing the proper boundaries between the branches of government mirrors the concern in rights theory with the autonomous individual. Legal-process scholars search for certain boundaries prescribing spheres of independence and authority for governmental institutions, much as those interested in rights analysis search for boundaries prescribing spheres of independence and authority for individuals.[39] While addressing different issues, legal process inhabits the same conceptual world as rights analysis. It is a world concerned more with distinctions than with connections, a world using bounded spheres as the components of conceptual order, whether their boundaries define individual persons or branches of government or conceptual categories. It is a world that treats differences as intrinsic to the person or institution, as functions of internal competencies and abilities. And it is a world that view as relatively unimportant issues of marginality, degradation, and exclusion on the basis of group membership.

Similar indifference to issues of exclusion characterize a burgeoning literature in legal theory that borrows concepts from microeconomics. The methods and assumptions of law and economics reconfirm the two-track approach to difference.

The Theory of Law and Economics

Many areas of legal activity, such as antitrust law, have provided obvious targets for analysis by economists. Many legal problems involve business and market evaluations. In 1972, however, a new and wider focus on economics became apparent among legal scholars with the creation of a journal devoted to "the application of scientific methods to the study of the legal system."[40] That journal and soon other journals gathered articles applying microeconomics, the theory of social choice, cost-benefit analysis, econometrics, and other related tools to legal problems. Standard texts for use by lawyers and law students on the economic analysis of law have since been published.

Economic analysts address some legal problems that explicitly present monetary or distribution questions, such as the allocation of damages in tort cases. But the law-and-economics school, led by Richard Posner—formerly a law professor at the University of Chicago and now a federal court judge—has turned also to problems less obviously suited to economic analysis.

[39]Somewhat similar to the idea of the abstract individual is the idea of reasoning by analogy in legal process, which urges removing decisions from one context and applying them to an entirely different context. Some legal theorists challenge the persuasiveness and value of a precedent removed from context; others urge exploration of multiple lines of precedent for each new context.

[40]Richard Posner, "An Afterword," *J. Legal Stud.* 1 (1972), 437. See also *An Introduction to Law and Economics,* ed. A. Mitchell Polinsky (Boston: Little, Brown, 1983, 1987); *Economic Analysis of Law,* 3d ed., ed. Richard Posner (Boston: Little, Brown, 1986).

Criminal law and administration, family law, privacy, and freedom of speech have each received treatment by law-and-economics scholars.[41] Perhaps most controversial is Elisabeth Landes and Richard Posner's defense of baby selling in articles on the regulation of adoption.[42]

Refusing to be misled by sentiment or tradition, law-and-economics scholars have used economic analysis to describe what is at stake in legal rules and to articulate criteria for reaching otherwise problematic decisions. They try to explain law's development by exposing an economic logic implicit within legal rules and practices. They maintain that judges, consciously or not, fashion legal rules to achieve economic efficiency. The logic of efficiency also provides a criterion for criticizing judicial decisions that fail to secure it. The goal of efficiency, or wealth maximization, uses the concept of utility, measured by each person's willingness to purchase a given entitlement; that willingness establishes the value of that entitlement in market terms.

The theory of law and economics also seeks to identify the rules that would promote the results it defines as desirable by mimicking what people would choose if they could freely bargain for exchanges, by arranging incentives so that private actors will achieve such bargains, or by inducing individuals to reveal information needed for legal authorities to approximate freely bargained exchanges. Society should arrange institutions and transactions to maximize benefits and minimize costs overall. Toward this end the scholars have articulated economic definitions of efficiency, selecting one or another form of optimal distribution of costs, benefits, and incentives to evaluate particular legal rules or to predict the effects of proposed legal decisions.[43] They use efficiency to identify rules that would promote the results they define as desirable by mimicking what bargained-for exchanges would yield, or by placing incentives and disincentives so that private actors would choose such bargains or reveal information needed by legal authorities to mimic them.

[41]E.g., Harold Votey, "Detention of Heroin Addicts, Jobs, Opportunities, and Deterrence," *J. Legal Stud.* 8 (1979), 585; Ronald Coase, "Advertising and Free Speech," *J. Legal Stud.* 6 (1977), 1; Gary Becker, *A Treatise on the Family* (Cambridge, Mass.: Harvard University Press, 1981).

[42]Elisabeth M. Landes and Richard Posner, "The Economics of the Baby Shortage," *J. Legal Stud.* 7 (1978), 323; Richard A. Posner, "The Regulation of the Market in Adoptions," *B.U.L. Rev.* 67 (1987), 59.

[43]Efficiency is defined by the "Kaldor-Hicks" concept as that allocation of resources by voluntary transactions in which subjective value is maximized after compensating any adversely affected third parties; see Richard A. Posner, *Economic Analysis of Law,* 3d ed. (Boston, Mass.: Little, Brown, 1983), pp. 12–13. Polinsky uses Pareto optimality to define efficiency; allocation of resources satisfies this test so that no further exchange will make any person better off. This differs from Posner's definition because it measures value objectively, not subjectively, and it does not limit transactions; some forced redistribution may be efficient. See Mark Kelman, "A Guide to Critical Legal Studies," in Polinsky, *Introduction to Law and Economics,* p. 120: "Law should promote all alterations in social arrangements that are Pareto efficient (that is, those in which at least one party's position is improved while no one's is worsened) and those that are *potentially* (or Kaldor-Hicks) efficient (that is, those in which the party whose lot is improved doesn't actually compensate the harmed party but *could* do so to the point where the initially harmed party would be indifferent between the new and old regime) while remaining better off himself."

An advocate of law and economics would approach the dispute over locating a group home for mentally retarded persons by asking first whether the benefits of placing the group home in the residential neighborhood outweigh the costs. Whether and how to calculate nonmonetary benefits would pose a problem and an issue for debate. But if the benefits will outweigh the costs, however calculated, the analysis would turn to why people do not naturally produce housing for mentally retarded persons. The problem might lie in transaction costs—barriers based on the difficulty of obtaining information or of banding together to create the group that would present a demand for collective, supervised housing. Another problem might be the allocation of externalities: developers and owners of housing may dominate the market in ways that protect them from experiencing the negative consequences to others of their own exchanges. The law-and-economics analysis then asks what incentives could be created to make a rational community inclined to accept the group home. The developer or, as a last resort, the relevant governmental entity could devise a package that includes something like a park or public recreational facility, as well as the group home, for the community that accepts the zoning variance. Linking the variance with some payoff to the neighbors or the town sweetens the deal.

To make the exchange competitive, some theorists would advocate an auction or contract bidding procedure: the private or public developer would solicit bids from various neighborhoods or towns for the package linking the zoning variance and the payoff. The community making the lowest bid would win the package. This procedure injects a competitive dimension and elicits a voluntary exchange.[44] Absent this bidding process, the law-and-economics approach demonstrates no interest in changing community attitudes about mentally retarded people; instead, it gives local residents incentives to predict the massive injuries they would sustain should the group home enter their neighborhood. The bidding process at least rewards the community that shows a sufficient degree of acceptance (or places high enough value on the dollar) to lead them to accept the home with a less valuable linkage package. Even with the bidding process, however, communities that are more well off and less in need of the payoff offered would have no incentive or need to alter their negative attitudes about the mentally retarded persons. In any case, the rights of mentally retarded persons are irrelevant.

It is conceivable that for distributional purposes a state could articulate rights for mentally retarded persons through economic entitlements such as housing vouchers; this would create a market in which they have purchasing power and would thereby overcome transaction costs that prevent the ex-

[44]See Michael O'Hare, "Not on *My* Block You Don't: Facility Siting and the Strategic Importance of Compensation," *Public Policy* 25 (Fall 1977), 407; Michael O'Hare, Lawrence Bacow, and Debra Sanderson, *Facility Siting and Public Opposition* (New York: Van Nostrand Reinhold, 1983), which discusses compensation and auction analysis to deal with opposition to the siting of public utility and hazardous waste facilities. See also Mancur Olsen, *The Logic of Collective Action* (Cambridge, Mass.: Harvard University Press, 1965).

changes enabling them to live in the community. But such a program would depend on a distributional judgment quite aside from a public utility assessment of what is good for the entire community and would therefore require normative judgments outside the standard economic analysis. Under a utilitarian calculus, the decision-maker should propose rules to elicit desired behavior by private persons who seek to maximize their own welfare.

Behind the approach of law and economics are assumptions—familiar to any student of economics—about the nature of human choice and the proper role of the state in light of that nature. Much like those behind rights theories, these assumptions identify each individual as a distinct being having unique wants and a capacity for self-reliance, at least upon reaching adulthood. Those wants and preferences are subjective and taken as givens—free from second-guessing by society. Society and the polity must both be restrained from interfering with each unique self—except for those individuals who so differ from the norm that they need help and do not deserve protection from interference with their own preferences. Most people's preferences must be taken at face value; society and the scholars assume that individual preferences can indeed be discerned.[45]

By constructing a picture of a world in which only exceptional people cannot be trusted to know their preferences, and in which society's task is to promote private bargaining free from interference in rational exchange, the law-and-economics theorists adopt a standpoint that treats a particular kind of person as the norm and alternative traits as deviant. This approach rejects the apparent concerns of rights analysis for fundamental entitlements, guaranteed beyond private exchanges, yet the law-and-economics scholars share rights theorists' basic assumptions that the individual is the important locus of choice-making in society and that individual preferences are located within the self. Moreover, by isolating as odd those people who cannot be presumed to know or express their true preferences—by creating an exceptional status for children and mentally incompetent persons[46]—the law-and-economics scholars deny the possibility that at times even "normal" people may not know their own desires. There is little room in this analysis for the possibility that people's prejudices against the mentally retarded are simple errors, nor does the analysis allow consideration of whether such prejudices should be allowed to influence preferences in voting for zoning laws or in accepting a variance. There is clearly no possibility in this analysis that the community might be better off through the inclusion of the mentally retarded

[45]Kelman ("Guide to Critical Legal Studies," p. 126) emphasizes that "the basic Pareto efficiency criterion can operate only where we are sure that we can discern meaningful content to individual will" and where we can discern when a party's position has improved. He notes a flaw in economic analyses that presume people's preferences from the way they act, since we "need to know what people really want, not just their behavior."

[46]See, e.g., Gary Becker and Kevin Murphy, "The Family and the State," *J. Law & Econ.* 31 (1988), 1, 6: because children cannot be party to the contracts that would rationalize investment decisions by parents, the state or social norms are necessary to regulate parental conduct.

persons—or that the community's well-being depends, at least in part, on the perspective of the mentally retarded persons themselves. Law and economics denies that "normal" people have unstable preferences or irrational desires that would not promote maximization of their own welfare. For both normal and abnormal people, social context and social arrangements are taken for granted. These arrangements may importantly affect what people want and what they oppose, but the theory treats such condition of preference as beyond the reach of analysis. If the prevailing arrangements burden some more than others, that poses a distributional question, beyond the bounds of microeconomic analysis.

Critics have identified the complexity of human interaction and motivation obscured by law and economics.[47] Robin West, for example, argues that people often form choices out of masochistic motives or out of a desire to surrender self-control.[48] Mark Kelman maintains that people often experience regret and ambivalence about their choices and often face constraint and duress in forming or expressing their desires.[49] Critics have pointed out that economics presumes preferences to be stable and unchanging, yet, as Tom Schelling points out, the person who set the alarm clock last night and the person whose sleep is disturbed by it in the morning do not entirely share preferences, even if they share a body.[50] For theorists of law and economics, such concerns apply only to that exceptional group of people whom law should not permit to contract. One is either competent or incompetent, capable of forming reliable preferences or not. However much rights theorists and law-and-economics scholars may disagree on some matters, they all reinforce rather than challenge the tradition of two-track legal treatment based on assumptions about competence. They treat the existing social institutions as given and identify people who seem different in their light. Law and economics thus shares deep assumptions with rights analysis and provides no challenge to a legacy of separate, exceptional treatment for people who do not fit the model of the rational, independent individual.

[47]Duncan Kennedy and Frank Michelman, "Are Property and Contract Efficient?" *Hofstra L. Rev.* 8 (1980), 1, 711; Arthur Leff, "Economic Analysis of Law: Some Realism about Nominalism," *Va. L. Rev.* 60 (1974), 451; Edwin Baker, "The Ideology of the Economic Analysis of Law," *Philosophy and Public Affairs* 5 (1975), 3; Edwin Baker, "Starting Points in Economic Analysis of Law," *Hofstra L. Rev.* 8 (1980), 939.

[48]Robin West, "Authority, Autonomy, and Choice: The Role of Consent in the Moral and Political Visions of Franz Kafka and Richard Posner," *Harv. L. Rev.* 99 (1985), 384. See also Richard Posner, "The Ethical Significance of Free Choice: A Reply to Professor West," *Harv. L. Rev.* 99 (1986), 1431; and Robin West, "Submission, Choice, and Ethics: A Rejoinder to Judge Posner," *Harv. L. Rev.* 99 (1986), 1499.

[49]Kelman, "Guide to Critical Legal Studies," p. 129. See Jon Elster, *Sour Grapes* (Cambridge: Cambridge University Press, 1983).

[50]Thomas Schelling, "Tanner Lecture on Human Values," *Ethics, Law, and Self-Command* 4 (1983), 55–57. See also Jon Elster, *Ulysses and the Sirens: Studies in Rationality and Irrationality* (Cambridge: Cambridge University Press, 1979): like Ulysses, people may make commitments knowing that they later will change their minds, thus intending to bind themselves despite later protests.

Critical Legal Studies and the Critique of Rights

A forceful and emphatic critique of rights theories, legal process, and law and economics emerged in the 1980s among scholars identified with the movement called critical legal studies. The self-conscious group of scholars who founded the Conference on Critical Legal Studies in 1977 proposed to gather together people interested in critical approaches to studies of law and society.[51] They indicated interest in exposing the gap between law on the books and law in actual practice. The organizers described law as an ideology that helps to justify social, economic, and political domination of some groups in society by others. Scholars associated with critical legal studies have written widely in law reviews and held annual conferences addressing legal scholarship, law teaching, and social issues. Although often expressing conflicting points of view, affiliates of this school share a commitment to demonstrating that legal principles and doctrines do not contain determinant answers but depend on historically contingent assumptions and values rather than eternal or objective truths.[52] Critical legal scholars often seek to demonstrate that legal doctrine is indeterminate;[53] that particular entrenched economic interests and privileged social groups benefit from the overall course of legal developments;[54] that legal analysis and culture mystify outsiders and legitimate their own results;[55] and that new or previously disfavored social

[51]See Kelman, "Guide to Critical Legal Studies," p. 287 n.1, for the original outreach letter; and Robert Gordon, "New Developments in Legal Theory," in Kairys, *The Politics of Law,* p. 281.

[52]See Mark Tushnet, "Critical Legal Studies: An Introduction to Its Origins and Underpinnings," *J. Legal Educ.* 36 (1986), 505; Duncan Kennedy, "Critical Theory, Structuralism, and Contemporary Legal Scholarship," *New Eng. L. Rev.* 21 (1986), 1669; Gary Pellar, "The Metaphysics of American Law," *Calif. L. Rev.* 73 (1985), 1152.

[53]I.e., any given set of legal principles can be used to produce and justify competing or contradictory results. This indeterminacy does not merely result from the vagueness of language but emerges from deep contradictions in the social values embedded in the legal system and animating legal actors. See Joseph William Singer, "The Player and the Cards: Nihilism and Legal Theory," *Yale L.J.* 94 (1984), 1; Joseph William Singer, "The Reliance Interest in Property," *Stan. L. Rev.* 40 (1988), 611, 624 n.40.

[54]See Horwitz, *Transformation of American Law;* Clare Dalton, *Losing History* (New York: Oxford University Press, forthcoming); Mary Joe Frug, "Securing Job Equality for Women: Labor Market Hostility to Working Mothers," *B.U.L. Rev.* 59 (1979), 55; Fran Olsen, "Statutory Rape: A Feminist Critique of Rights Analysis," *Tex. L. Rev.* 63 (1984), 387; Karl Klare, "Judicial Deradicalization of the Wagner Act and the Origins of Modern Legal Consciousness, 1937–1941," *Minn. L. Rev.* 62 (1978), 265.

[55]Here, the question addressed is something like this: if legal doctrine itself is indeterminate and open-textured, and legal decisions and practices yield predictable results in patterns favoring some groups and some social visions over others, how do the legal system and legal scholarship maintain the image of fairness, neutrality, and continuing possibilities for successful initiatives on the part of losing groups? This inquiry takes the scholars back to legal materials instead of social and historical ones. They ask how the legal community constructs a system of shared meanings that are made to look natural rather than chosen. See Gordon, "New Developments in Legal Theory," p. 288; Duncan Kennedy, "Toward an Historical Understanding of Legal Consciousness: The Case of Classical Legal Thought in America, 1850–1940," in *Research in Law and Sociology,* vol. 2, ed. Steven Spitzer (Greenwich, Conn.: JJAI Press, 1980), p. 3. A related question would ask how legal roles and legal discourse distance legal officials and

visions can be advocated through legal and political practice.[56] These scholars have charged law and economics with imposing formalist ideas that rest on simplistic and faulty assumptions about human beings. They have also cited legal process for pretending but failing to secure neutrality toward purposes and values.[57]

One large target of their criticism has been the notion of rights in legal theory. For Duncan Kennedy, for example, rights represent a "liberal" response to an unavoidable contradiction in human experience: people need one another in order to develop and to attain freedom, and yet the world of others threatens each individual's identity and freedom through coercion and pressures to conform. Kennedy describes the "fundamental contradiction" that "coercion of the individual by the group appears to be inextricably bound up with the liberation of the same individual," and that "relations with others are both necessary to and incompatible with our freedom."[58] Each of us incorporates others through language and psychological development. Thus, we have the chance for a sense of fusion, but we also develop a sense of collective control. Altering the circumstances of collective control seems, however, to require more collective control.[59]

Rights provide a way to pretend to resolve this problem, but the problem remains. As Mark Kelman has restated the argument of critical legal studies, the liberal rights solution implies that "I will interact with others as long as they respect my rights. If no boundary has been crossed we can pretend that the interaction has been painless. Because state officials might, in the ostensible course of policing private boundary crossing, themselves become a source of painful oppression, we limit them both by insisting that they enforce only clear rules and by establishing some separate rights that are relevant only vis-à-vis the state."[60] Yet the process of articulating and applying these rights actually amounts to pacifying and reassuring people that they are safe—

---

citizens from their own experiences and moral judgments. See Peter Gabel, "Reification in Legal Reasoning," in Spitzer, *Research in Law and Sociology*, p. 25; William Simon, "Homo Psychologicus: Notes on a New Legal Formalism," *Stan. L. Rev.* 32 (1980), 487. Although they would not appropriately be identified as critical legal scholars, Cover in *Justice Accused* and John T. Noonan in *Persons and Masks of the Law: Cardozo, Holmes, Jefferson, and Wythe as Makers of the Masks* (New York: Farrar, Straus & Giroux, 1976) similarly probe these themes.

[56]See Singer, "The Player and the Cards"; Singer, "The Reliance Interest in Property"; Roberto Unger, "The Critical Legal Studies Movement," *Harv. L. Rev.* 96 (1983), 562, 576–601, 618–48.

[57]Singer, "Legal Realism Now."

[58]Duncan Kennedy, "The Structure of Blackstone's Commentaries," *Buffalo L. Rev.* 28 (1979), 205, 211–13, discusses the "fundamental contradiction."

[59]Although intriguing, these critiques of rights seem to rest on the view that society consists entirely of individuals plus a collective represented by the state. Missing is a notion of the relationships between individuals—in pairs and in groups—and between groups. Relationships of solidarity and love, competition and coordination may be the contexts through which individuals define themselves and come to know one another quite apart from a tendency to merge into the collective of the entire society. Perhaps the critical scholars mean to evoke these complex patterns of relationships, but their arguments deploy abstract terms that do not clarify how connection can respect individuality rather than simply produce a collective entity.

[60]Kelman, "Guide to Critical Legal Studies," p. 63.

while subjecting everyone to the incessant and unpredictable power of the state. The content and application of rights remain indeterminate and subject to the shifting views of officials, and the problem of needing others and fearing others recurs in any intellectual effort to articulate the scope of a right in a given circumstance. A rule that enforces contracts bargained for by autonomous, self-determining people leaves to the judge the question of when the individual's need for freedom to bargain should bind and limit the freedom of another, who seeks to avoid the contract.[61]

Mark Tushnet has elaborated the critique of rights as four related critiques: "(1) Once one identifies what counts as a right in a specific setting, it invariably turns out that the right is unstable; significant but relatively small changes in the social setting can make it difficult to sustain the claim that a right remains implicated. (2) The claim that a right is implicated in some setting produces no determinant consequences. (3) The concept of rights falsely converts into an empty abstraction (reifies) real experiences that we ought to value for their own sake. (4) The use of rights in contemporary discourse impedes advances by progressive social forces." Tushnet argues that the language of rights is meaningful only within a complex social and legal context, and yet we lack general criteria for evaluating particular uses of rights analysis. Rather than use abstract language that makes rights seem outside of human choice, we should acknowledge the political choices and test them against the specific goals of benefiting progressive social forces.[62]

Peter Gabel, another critical legal scholar, uses what he has called a phenomenological method to explore the ways in which legal consciousness and the language of rights interfere with a direct sense of interpersonal connection. The sense of personal isolation, he argues, is not inevitable, but instead represents interference with natural human desires to be connected with others. The interference arises when children learn to distrust their own desires for connection and instead develop a false sense of self expressed through the roles they learn in social settings. Legal language and legal structures distance people from their immediate desires and experiences while providing explanations that make the very sensation of distance seem natural and necessary.[63]

[61]See Clare Dalton, "An Essay in the Deconstruction of Contract Law," *Yale L.J.* 94 (1985), 997.

[62]Mark Tushnet, "An Essay on Rights," *Tex. L. Rev.* 62 (1984), 1363–64 (this article appears in a symposium on the critique of rights from varied perspectives).

[63]Peter Gabel, "The Phenomenology of Rights-Consciousness and the Pact of the Withdrawn Selves," *Tex. L. Rev.* 62 (1984), 1563, 1566, 1568–73, 1576. Gabel's work suggests that the personal traits we commonly use to describe ourselves—such as gender, occupation, and race—express illusory ideas that interfere with our capacity to feel connected to one another except through these very labels. Finding a sense of connection and commonality with others often depends on these assigned roles, which are made meaningful by the community rather than by the individual. Therefore, the very experience of connection depends on affirming "a contingent and culturally produced particularity that is a badge of alienation itself" (p. 1587). The powerful idea that identities are culturally constructed rather than intrinsic is related to notions about the social construction of identity developed in the next chapter, but Gabel's pessimism about making assigned identities newly authentic, combined with the romantic idea that there is an authentic self behind the assigned identity, limits the usefulness of his theory from my perspective.

Gabel ultimately criticizes social movements that seek to use law for social change. The short-term practical gains that may be achieved and the op-portunities for mobilizing people cannot overcome the drawbacks of legal rights, which maintain an illusion that distances people from their own experiences and capacities. Gable urges instead a critique of rights and of authority that can inspire us all "to be ourselves, make contact, have a good time, 'take control of the means of production,' and generally come out from behind the fabric of appearance through which we make each other hostage to the illusion that is it distance rather than a good heart turned outward that the law in us required."[64] Gabel thus strings together colloquial calls to informality and fun, a slogan from Marxist theory, an existential call for authenticity, and a belief that in essence we have the capacity for empathetic connections, despite the interference of alienating language and culture.[65] This theory oddly flattens all human experiences to fundamental similarities; interestingly, though, Gabel reverses the claim of liberal individualists that we are similar in our fundamental separateness; he argues instead that our fundamental similarity lies in our desire to merge with one another.

Besides their critique of rights, most critical legal scholars provide little suggestion for dealing with the problems of people made marginal through social and legal systems. This is not an explicit topic in much of their scholarship, and little of this scholarship on any subject suggests avenues for resolving problems within the system of currently existing courts and bu-reaucracies. Yet there are illuminating moments of insight about the ways in which marginal legal status depends on prevailing ideas that could be re-placed. In the examples that follow, critical theorists explore relationships between thought about and experience of marginality. Here and elsewhere in critical legal studies there are also suggestions of new methods of argument that could help shift the framework of rights analysis, which has not rem-edied the problems of marginality.

The first example appears in work by the critical legal scholar who most directly addresses issues of discrimination. Alan Freeman develops an argu-ment that racial discrimination law has adopted the perspective of the "per-petrators" of discrimination rather than the perspective of the "victims."[66] The critique of rights afforded by this argument introduces the possibility that reality is not unified but multiple and is based on the situation of the particular people perceiving it. Freeman suggests that there is an important relationship between knowledge and power, between what is known and who does the knowing. This idea, which can be traced to Marxist notions of class consciousness, also opens up questions about how relationships be-tween people influence their knowledge about one another, and about how

---

[64]Ibid., pp. 1596, 1599.

[65]There is an odd notion here that somehow we could all dig out from under illusions created by language and social practice and find authentic selves underneath. What, then, does "reality" mean, once language and social structures are removed?

[66]Alan Freeman, "Antidiscrimination Law: A Critical Review," in Kairys, *The Politics of Law*; Alan Freeman, "Race and Class: The Dilemma of Liberal Reform," *Yale L.J.* 90 (1981), 1880.

legal rules make some perspectives seem simply true rather than selected over others.

A second theorist, Duncan Kennedy, offers some important insights about the relationships between knowledge and power in an article defending "paternalist motives" by judges. Despite the traditional commitment to preserving free choice, the basic goal behind legal rights, Kennedy defends paternalist motives, which he illustrates by the desire of a judge to change a rule "in order to improve someone's welfare by getting them to behave in their 'own real interests,' rather than in the fashion they would have adopted under the previous regime." Because of historical patterns of domination and subordination, some people have inferior knowledge and remain subject to the power of others; some people are incapacitated because of their circumstances. Thus, Kennedy notes, the law of incapacity prevented children and insane persons and, in earlier times, women, blacks, and seamen from the onerous enforcement of contracts against their interests.[67]

Kennedy maintains that similar rationales can and should be applied to other people, including adult white males at risk of making bad investment decisions, people entering marriage or consumer contracts, and people thinking of purchasing, selling, or possessing illicit drugs. He claims that "there is no such 'thing' as capacity, and there can be no such thing as its 'absence' either." Rather than two classes of people—those with capacity and those without—he asserts the "capacity-to-make-this-decision." This idea engages an observer in assessing whether another is occupied by "false consciousness" while estimating the consequences of a given choice. Kennedy also directs the observer to consider the possibility that he or she wants to render the other dependent through paternalism.[68]

On the basis of such considerations, Kennedy justifies paternalist decisions to overrule the choice of another, given such identification and intimate knowledge as to produce intersubjective unity between the two people. Kennedy acknowledges that this circumstance may be unusual in a social setting that segregates groups from one another and produces fear and misunderstanding across the cultural divides between many judges and litigants. Indeed, he says, there are strong reasons not to act paternalistically: because the intuition that the other suffers from false consciousness may be wrong; because it may be better for that person to make a mistake, suffer the consequences, and learn rather than grow more dependent and incompetent; and because paternalism is unavoidably an aggressive interference with another person. Yet refraining from paternalist action, Kennedy argues, may also deny the "knowledge of the relative incapacity of groups, of their characteristic mistakes."[69] Mere respect for individual rights and self-determination is

[67]Duncan Kennedy, "Distributive and Paternalist Motives in Contract and Tort Law, with Special Reference to Compulsory Terms and Unequal Bargaining Power," *Md. L. Rev.* 41 (1982), 563, 570, 588–90, 631–33.
[68]Ibid., pp. 572, 631–32 (quoting Robert Clark), 644.
[69]Ibid., pp. 638–40, 647, 648–49. Kennedy criticizes a judge who neglects the specific incapacities of tenants and poor workers. Elsewhere (pp. 588–89), he identifies legacies of

not enough. Instead, decision-makers should investigate the consciousness of others, break down the barriers of segregation that interfere with such knowledge, and help to mobilize those groups so that they can tell the decision-maker what they want.

Kennedy's work on paternalism offers important criticism of the legacy of the abnormal-persons approach and the failure of the rights approach to redress those legacies. For Kennedy, the study of treatment of people at the margins and studies of exceptions to normal legal rules highlight alternatives to dominant legal discourse, alternatives already present yet marginalized within it. He offers a promising suggestion that traits of dependence may stem from historical and social circumstances rather than qualities intrinsic to the person—and that those qualities of dependence which law has usually associated with certain categories of people actually pertain to all people some of the time. Kennedy thus challenges the belief that humankind can be divided between those who are competent and those who are not and that different legal rules should be assigned to each group.

Yet his argument in many ways creates a new group of incapacitated people: people who are poor or relatively powerless, people who are likely to be subject to "false consciousness" because of their economic position and distance from those in power. Even his notion of the "capacity-to-make-this-decision" still treats the matter as a problem in a person—in a given situation—to be judged by another person. Kennedy acknowledges that the observer may be motivated to dominate the other person but fails to elaborate the fact that the very assessment of capacity, false consciousness, and consequences to the other person depend on the relationship between these two people and that their relationship in turn depends on other relationships embedded in the social, economic, and political structures of society.

Perhaps most troubling is that Kennedy's justification for paternalism in the name of intersubjective identification or a sense of "unity" with the other is the closest he comes to describing a good relationship, but it depends on eliminating the sense of the other as a distinct person. Kennedy is left with the contrast between paternalist interventions that "seem like naked aggression against the human dignity of the supposed beneficiary" and interventions that seem like moral duties to protect another.[70] Rather than pursuing the insight about relationships between knowledge and power, Kennedy too is caught by the assumption of individual autonomy. The idea of individual autonomy remains unexplored—as does the possibility that it may be itself a product of a particular historical context, and a goal embraced by some people for some purposes, rather than a basis for respecting all kinds of persons. Kennedy's own arguments are snagged by the apparent dilemma between preserving individual autonomy and invading it—a dilemma that

---

racial, gender, and class differences that make group identities continue to be meaningful, though he notes that acknowledging them would bother members of the elite who believe in individuality.

[70] Ibid., p. 638.

arises at least in part from the very assumption of individual autonomy that is at work in his argument. He makes available only two models for human relationships: oppressive ones, and those where two people merge or fuse. In emphasizing the dilemma that individuals simultaneously need and fear one another, he still uses individuals as the primary unit for analysis. Granted, these are individuals who are continually and conflictually involved with one another, but individuals, rather than relationships between them, remain the focus.

Kennedy's alternative to the existing ways of understanding and organizing human social life seems to be more collective action to challenge the power of the collective embedded within each of us. For Peter Gabel, the chief alternative seems to be more authentic individualism. Both alternatives preserve the separate individual, juxtaposed to the collective whole, as the focus for analysis, rather than shifting to consider the relationships between distinct and yet connected people as a subject for study. Missing is the idea that some instances of individual dependence might change with the renovation of particular social institutions; missing is the possibility of locating the sources of problems of "difference" in part in patterns of work, school, architecture, and other social arrangements that do not take into account the variety of human needs and experiences.

Critical legal scholars have often turned also to concrete problems with a goal of resolving them, though only the feminist scholars influenced by critical legal studies have given sustained attention to issues of gender discrimination and marginalization.[71] How would critical legal scholars respond to the problem of housing mentally retarded persons in communities rather than in institutions that isolate and degrade them? Those who critique rights would expose the instability and potentially mystifying consequences of asserting a right for mentally retarded persons to live in the community. Those who emphasize the indeterminacy of legal doctrine would show that the equal protection analysis used in the Cleburne case could have produced judgments either way, and therefore principle provides no basis for criticizing the compromise reached by the Court—rejecting the exclusion of that particular group home but leaving in place both the zoning ordinance and the framework that accords only minimal scrutiny to restrictions based on the classification of mental retardation.

Alan Freeman's work provides a model for imagining the perspective of the "victims" and for considering the relationship between knowledge and perspective but little hint that these themes might apply to contexts beyond race. Duncan Kennedy's work on paternalism usefully calls for self-analysis by those who would "help" the mentally retarded persons and offers the argument that many traits of dependence stem from social circumstances rather than from intrinsic personal qualities. Yet his tendency to identify

---

[71]The intersections and divergencies between feminist work and critical legal scholarship are examined in Carrie Menkel-Meadow, "Feminist Legal Theory, Critical Legal Studies, and Legal Education or 'The Fem-Crits Go to Law School,'"*J. Legal Educ.* 38 (1988), 61.

groups of dependent people with whom others may seek to merge denies the possibility, or probability, of more complicated relationships between them. Merger is another form of domination, or a refusal to accept the fundamental difference and resilience of another. Neither Kennedy nor Gabel offers a vocabulary for examining and evaluating the quality of relationships within which differences may be constructed or remade.

Despite these limitations, there are promising avenues of inquiry within critical legal scholarship. Its practitioners employ tools of analysis from linguistics, anthropology, history, and literary studies, and this interdisciplinary activity itself challenges and remakes customary academic boundaries. The scholars' efforts to unearth categories or tensions at work behind the surface layer of legal talk offer models for breaking out of the assumptions that marginalize some people.[72] In addition, critical legal scholars often seek to explore ideas and practices that have been officially disfavored and yet remain within the legal system—practices such as paternalism. These exceptions, claim the critical scholars, bear important relationships to the general rules. Exceptions preserve the image that the rules govern, while making available to judges and to parties competing arguments that draw as much on powerfully held motives and values as do the general rules. Thus, critical scholars explore the relationship between the marginal ideas and the core norms and also suggest elaborating visions for the whole from the exceptions at the margin.

Strategies from critical legal studies thus include exploring the relationships between knowledge and power, considering the historically contingent assignment of legal status, and salvaging for general use values that have been explicit only in legal exceptions. Each of these strategies emphasizes relationships instead of presuming separations between such categories as knowledge and power, legal status and social context, exceptions and rules. When brought to bear on the problems of people made marginal through legal doctrine, these strategies can help expose the limitations of rights analysis even more directly than the critical scholars have suggested. Aside from whatever alienating or mystifying consequences rights analysis may have for people, rights analysis relies on claims about knowledge, legal status, and rules that obscure how rights analysis itself helps judges and legal officials assign people to categories that carry negative consequences. Rights analysis depends on claims to know what counts as a real difference between two people that justifies treating them differently. If those claims about knowledge are assessed in light of the power relationships between those assigning the labels and those receiving them, the meaning of the differences may become a subject of debate rather than an observable "fact."

Rights analysis also relies on ideas about legal status. People of dependent status—children, mentally disabled people, and (historically) married

---

[72]E.g., competing desires for freedom and for security become expressed and masked in a doctrine like freedom of contract, which justifies the use of state power to bind people to agreements they entered into in the past. See Dalton, "Deconstruction of Contract Law," p. 997; Kennedy, "Distributive and Paternalist Motives," p. 563.

women, sailors, and slaves—have not been able to claim the same rights as others. Yet when legal status is located within social contexts and historical struggles, its meanings and consequences for rights are also subjects for debate rather than referring to clearly bounded categories that match up to the world. And when we observe how rules and exceptions define each other, and how exceptions to rules express values that are also germane to cases falling within the general rule, we see that the ready assignment of a particular problem to the rule or to the exception deserves reexamination.

These themes, I suggest, contribute to the emerging social-relations approach to the legal treatment of difference. The history of this approach traces it to sources originating long before critical legal studies; indeed, critical legal scholarship is an offshoot of some of the same seeds. It is to these roots that I turn next, and to the question of what would happen if we focused on the relationships in which individuals forge their identities. Would we gain better leverage on the issues of stigma associated with assigned roles of difference and incompetence? Knowing that how we talk influences what we see, can we now define problems differently to engender new, if temporary, solutions?

CHAPTER 7

The Emergence of the
Social-Relations Approach

The struggle to disentangle self from other is itself a source of insight—potentially into the nature of both self and other. It is a principal means of divining what Poincaré calls "hidden harmonies and relations." To this end, the scientist employs a form of attention to the natural world that is like one's idea of attention to the human world: it is a form of love.
—Evelyn Fox Keller, *Reflections on Gender and Science*

The limitations of rights analysis were not unknown to the reformers who challenged the institutional treatment of mentally retarded people. They worked within a rights framework but also looked to other disciplines to reimagine the legal entitlements of marginalized people. Litigators developed an argument that the label of mental retardation is a stigma that deprives individuals of their liberty; therefore, the right to due process applies before the label can be assigned.[1] To build this argument, the critics of labeling drew on a theory developed by sociologists and shifted the focus from the deviant person to the process by which an individual is labeled deviant.[2] The critique of labeling, and the debate it engendered, contained several ideas that underlie the emerging social-relations approach to difference, and thus its history affords an entry to the social-relations movement in

Epigraph: Reprinted from Evelyn Fox Keller, *Reflections on Gender and Science*, by permission of Yale University Press. Copyright © 1985 by Yale University.

[1] This argument drew analogies with the school desegregation claim about the stigma experienced by black children in racially segregated schools.

[2] The earliest scholar espousing this approach in sociology was Frank Tannenbaum. His *Crime and the Community* (1938) is commonly cited as the forerunner of the labeling theory, a school of thought that became popular among sociologists and social psychologists in the 1960s and 1970s. See generally, Walter Gove, *The Labeling of Deviance: Evaluating a Perspective*, 2d ed. (Beverly Hills, Calif.: Sage, 1980); Edwin Schur, *Labeling Deviant Behavior: Its Sociological Implications* (New York: Harper & Row, 1971), pp. 8–13; Alex Thio, *Deviant Behavior*, 2d ed. (Boston: Houghton Mifflin, 1983), pp. 56–65.

other fields.[3] Traces of these ideas appear in several areas of legal debate, and these developments resonate with other intellectual debates in philosophy, literary interpretation, psychology, anthropology, feminist theory, and even mathematics and science. In each field, scholars have argued for attention to relationships—relationships between people, between concepts, and between the observer and the observed. The relational approaches enable critiques of the ways issues about difference have been framed and thereby open up avenues to new strategies.

The Controversy over Labeling Theory

As developed in the 1960s and 1970s by researchers in sociology and social psychology, labeling theory studies the process by which an audience or community identifies some people as deviants. That very pattern of identification has consequences for the labeled person which are difficult to escape. Those consequences include recurring patterns of exclusion and deviant behavior.[4] Labeling theory thus treats difference as an idea developed by some people to describe others and to attribute meaning to others' behavior. Difference or deviance is not something that resides in given individuals or in their own acts or characteristics.[5] Howard Becker, a founder of the labeling approach who worked in the field of criminal justice, put it this way: "Social groups create deviance by making the rules whose infraction constitutes deviance, and by applying those rules to particular people and labeling them as outsiders. From this point of view, deviance is not a quality of the act the person commits, but rather a consequence of the application by others of rules and sanctions to an 'offender.' The deviant is one to whom that label has successfully been applied; deviant behavior is behavior that people so label."[6]

Labeling theory, then, deliberately rejects some of the assumptions behind the difference dilemma: that difference resides in the different person and that there are an unproblematic, unstated norm and an unsituated perspective from which to see differences in people.

---

[3]This history focuses more on contests over ideas fought within academic circles than on political and legal doctrines and strategies. This is not to imply that changes in general occur through intellectual changes that then filter into legal circles—though such intellectual changes are not unimportant. Nor do I advance here any casual theory about which ideas are causes and which are effects. I do mean to suggest that thinking about how we think opens one avenue for change, and this avenue seems the road traveled by advocates of the social-relations approach. Moreover, the ideas and debates among theorists constitute an important field of politics, alongside the legislative and judicial arenas.

[4]See generally Erich Goode, *Deviant Behavior,* 2d ed. (Englewood Cliffs, N.J.: Prentice-Hall, 1984), pp. 32–35.

[5]See Kai T. Erikson, "Notes on the Sociology of Deviance," *Social Problems* 9 (1962), 307–8: "Deviance is not a property *inherent in* certain forms of behavior; it is a property *conferred upon* these forms by the audiences which directly or indirectly witness them."

[6]Howard Becker, *Outsiders: Studies in the Sociology of Deviance* (London: Free Press of Glencoe, 1963), p. 9.

Most advocates of the theory also accept "symbolic interactionism,"[7] a theory asserting that one can best understand human behavior by examining the interrelationships between people, especially as expressed through language and other symbolic systems.[8] This perspective presumes that people act in relationship to meanings and that meanings grow out of people's efforts to make sense of their interactions with others. Simply put, the concept is that "we view ourselves in part through the eyes of others, and when others see us in a certain way, at least for long enough or sufficiently powerfully, their views are sure to have some effect."[9] The effect of others' views when those views assign the label of deviance may well cause the individual to internalize that label and to feel degraded.

As used in the past by advocates for reform of the treatment of mentally disabled people, labeling theory focused attention on the majority that both assigned the label of mental incompetence and used the label to justify exclusion. Theorists contended that some of the characteristics used to support the label were either figments of the imagination of those assigning it or responses of the labeled person to its effects. The advocates of labeling theory did not assert that mental disability is itself fictional.[10] Instead, they targeted the consequences of the label's application: that is, the social meanings of mental disabilities rather than the fact of mental disability.

Some theorists focused on the ways that labeling created as reality the premise behind the label: a person labeled schizophrenic, for example, could do nothing to overcome the tag, because the label colored everyone's perceptions even of that person's objections to the label.[11] Others showed that once a person was labeled mentally incompetent and placed in an institution as a result, the institution itself created circumstances of powerlessness and dehumanization that fulfilled the label. The sheer fact of institutionalization stigmatized the person and, in many institutions, defined the individual as less than a person. Reformers in the 1960s and 1970s usually employed labeling theory to call for better procedures *before* labels could be imposed or

[7]Goode, *Deviant Behavior*, p. 32; Erdwin Pfuhl, *The Deviance Process* (New York: Van Nostrand, 1980), pp. 202–4; Thio, *Deviant Behavior*, pp. 56–61. Other general perspectives such as functionalism could also underlie some uses of the labeling theory, but symbolic interactionism poses a general inquiry into the social construction of meaning, which is closely linked to the study of labeling. See Ken Plummer, "Misunderstanding Labeling Perspectives," in *Deviant Interpretations*, ed. David Downes and Paul Rock (New York: Barnes & Noble, 1979), pp. 92–93.

[8]Francis Cullen and John Cullen, *Toward a Paradigm of Labeling Theory* (Lincoln: University of Nebraska Press, 1978), pp. 29–37.

[9]Barry Glassner, "Labeling Theory," in Michael Rosenberg, *The Sociology of Deviance*, ed. Robert Stebbins and Allan Turowetz (New York: St. Martin's Press, 1982), p. 71.

[10]See Schur, *Labeling Deviant Behavior*, pp. 15–16. But see Thomas Szasz, *The Myth of Mental Illness: Foundations of a Theory of Personal Conduct*, rev. ed. (New York: Harper & Row, 1974): mental illness is a label conferred by professionals who intervene in and damage other people's lives; and Thomas Szasz, *Ideology and Insanity: Essays on the Psychiatric Dehumanization of Man* (Garden City, N.Y.: Anchor Books, 1970): mentally ill persons are simply people who have difficulties or who make other people uncomfortable; coercive psychiatric institutionalization is an oppressive use of power.

[11]See David Rosenhan, "On Being Sane in Insane Places," *Science*, Jan. 19, 1973, p. 250.

to challenge the particular implications of the various labels of mental disability. This approach left in place the idea that it is only the handicapped person who has the problem; it remained for later challengers to introduce the idea that the problem includes the whole community, its social practices, and the design of all of its institutions.[12]

Yet implicit in labeling theory and in social interactionism is a more fundamental challenge to the notion that difference resides solely in the person who is labeled different. Labeling theory emphasizes the community's responsibility in assigning the label and in attributing particular meanings of exclusion to it. Labeling theory also identifies the possibility that the rules about such labeling may be politically controversial. "In addition to recognizing that deviance is created by the responses of people to particular kinds of behavior, by the labeling of that behavior as deviant, we must also keep in mind that the rules created and maintained by such labeling are not universally agreed to. Instead, they are the object of conflict and disagreement, part of the political process of society."[13] While lawyers primarily used labeling theory to bolster rights analysis, the premises and consequences of the theory resemble the emerging approach in legal discourse that takes social relations as the starting point.

Criticism of labeling theory has become a lively business in the academic community. Some critics further advance thinking about relationships as central to difference or deviance; others part company with advocates of the relational aspects of the theory. For example, some attack labeling theory for failing to distinguish adequately between deviance and nondeviance. In particular, these critics note, labeling theorists claim that deviance is only that behavior so labeled—and not the same behavior if it goes unlabeled or even undiscovered.[14] This looks rather like a criticism from the abnormal-persons approach: there really are different people, and once they are identified, they belong in a category that can be sharply distinguished from the category of normal people. A common and predictable response to this criticism cites the culturally relative nature of the norms each society uses to define deviance.[15] Precisely this emphasis on relativism and the social construction of reality disturbs the opponents.[16]

From quite the other direction, some criticize labeling theory for failing

---

[12]See generally Comment, "We Have Met the Imbeciles and They Are Us: The Courts and Citizens with Mental Retardation," *Neb. L. Rev.* 65 (1986), 768, 797, 804–7, criticizing reforms that leave in place stereotypes of mentally retarded persons and second class citizens.

[13]Becker, *Outsiders*, p. 18.

[14]Jack P. Gibbs, "Conceptions of Deviant Behavior: The Old and the New," *Pacific Sociology Review* 9 (1966), 9. See also Glassner, "Labeling Theory," pp. 79–81.

[15]Schur, *Labeling Deviant Behavior*, pp. 14–16.

[16]Empirical studies showing that people can overcome the negative effects of labeling also challenge labeling theory. One elaborate study, tracing forty years in the lives of individuals who had been officially labeled mentally retarded, found that all had had difficulties in interpersonal adjustment and in social and intellectual skills, yet they reported reasonable satisfaction in their lives. Moreover, while some had felt shame and inferiority when placed in special education classrooms, others thought that school had been helpful and that the assignment to special education had had no detrimental effect on their lives. See Robert Ross, Michael Begab, Ernest Doudis, James Giampiccolo, and C. Edward Meyers, *Lives of the Mentally Retarded: A Forty-*

fully to embrace a focus on the interaction between ways of knowing and kinds of knowledge. In particular, labeling theory has been criticized for attending simply to the effect of a label on the conduct of the labeled person, rather than to the meaning of the label to those doing the assigning, those receiving the label, and those acting in some way as an audience to this process.[17] Similarly, some criticize labeling theory for treating persons labeled deviant as passive victims instead of attending to their activities, motivations, and self-understandings. Such critics warn against a perspective that legitimates either the labelers or those labeled rather than focusing on their interaction and the meanings the two groups exchange and reshape. Implicit in this criticism as well is a view that the relational approach encompasses also the social scientist who is construing the meanings others make of the labeling process.[18]

Devised in part for instrumental and political purposes, labeling theory also reflects shifts in the assumptions guiding social science, physical science, and social thought during the twentieth century. The shifts remain incomplete and contested; even those theorists who embrace any one new theme may still dispute another. Nonetheless, throughout this century scholars in varied fields have explored the relationships and interactions between subjects under study and have also examined the impact of their own observations on what they observe. They pay attention to the possibility of multiple norms and perspectives and to the mutability of the researchers' own assumptions. In these ways, twentieth-century scholars challenge deeply held assumptions, assumptions about how to observe the differences in the world that have contributed to difficulties in escaping the negative meanings of differences between people. An exploration of the range of theorists engaged in these challenges precedes a more detailed examination of some of their work.

Twentieth-Century Studies of Interactions and Relations

Initiatives bearing strong resemblances to labeling theory have triggered debates in the social sciences and in social thought more generally. While diverse and divergent, these lines of inquiry share a suspicion that knowledge

---

Year Follow-Up Study (Stanford, Calif.: Stanford University Press, 1985), pp. 144–45. Perhaps most telling is the suggestion that the factors producing the label "mentally retarded" were most salient in the school context; once outside of school, these individuals (all in the "upper range of retarded performance") responded as much to demands and expectations in the environment as to any measures of individual limitation (pp. 145–46). Of course, this study supports a basic thesis of labeling theory: that the meaning of a disability can shift depending on social context and relationships between people.

[17]See Glassner, "Labeling Theory," pp. 71, 75–83; Goode, *Deviant Behavior*, pp. 35–37.

[18]George Becker, *The Mad Genius Controversy: A Study in the Sociology of Deviance* (Beverly Hills, Calif.: Sage, 1978), pp. 127, 129–31. See also Craig Little, *Understanding Deviance and Control: Theory, Research, and Social Policy* (Itasca, Ill.: F. E. Peacock, 1983), pp. 259–74; and Edwin Schur, *Labeling Women Deviant: Gender, Stigma, and Social Control* (New York: Random House, 1984). Some critics stress that labeling theory itself can serve a political purpose in supplying meanings that either legitimate or challenge the status quo.

is deeply influenced by who makes the knowledge claims and from what vantage point, what material circumstances, and what degree of power. Innovative theorists working at the turn of the twentieth century and at midcentury also shared an emphasis on context and particularity and a skepticism about the validity or utility of abstract rules. They rejected analysis that divided problems into disassociated components and found particularly inadequate the traditions of "formalism," resting upon deductive or a priori reasoning. They criticized the world view that drew sharp distinctions between fact and value, self and other. They stressed instead the significance of relationships, calling attention to interconnections between knowledge and the contexts in which people claim to know, between parts and the whole, between problems and the settings in which they arise, and between individuals and their social contexts.[19]

At an even more fundamental level, theorists in many fields began to reject the standard assumption that objects are isolated and individuals are separate. Instead, they argued that connections between objects, between concepts, and between people should be central to study and to prescription.[20] This is an obvious focus in fields such as ecology, which address the mutual dependence of living things, but many theorists also emphasize less obvious interconnections. Scientists have recommended studying the relationships among genes on a chromosome rather than assuming that isolated genes control certain traits within an organism. Some psychologists maintain that we should see people as fundamentally connected rather than as separate or autonomous. Even seeming contradictions or opposing forces—whether in biology, physics, philosophy, or literature—should be understood through their connections and mutual definitions.

Perhaps the most significant assertion of the new theorists is that the relationships between the world and what people think about it must be part of any claims to understand the world. The ways people think about the world influence even what seems to be natural or given. Self-reflection about the thinking process reveals that what seems given actually comes from a humanly constructed conceptual scheme: People do not discover a transparent universe but instead project, as natural, categories that are human inventions. Scholars in history, psychology, anthropology, sociology, literature, philosophy, science, and mathematics have focused on relationships between thought and perception as the means of opening up possibilities for new kinds of choices, new perceptions, and better worlds. Doubting that knowledge claims may be made from an unsituated perspective, they seek out alternatives to the perspectives that have been taken for granted.

Many recent theorists hope to show that what seems natural in the world

[19]Richard Levins and Richard Lewontin, *The Dialectical Biologist* (Cambridge, Mass.: Harvard University Press, 1985), pp. 54–55; *Culture Theory: Essays on Mind, Self, and Emotion,* ed. Richard Shweder and Robert LeVine (Cambridge: Cambridge University Press, 1984).

[20]See, e.g., Levins and Lewontin, *Dialectical Biologist,* p. 287, for biology; and Carol Gilligan, *In a Different Voice: Psychological Theory and Women's Development* (Cambridge, Mass.: Harvard University Press, 1982), for human development.

is instead often the construction of human imagination and cultural meanings. Patterns of thought through which people perceive and judge are themselves mutable. For those concerned with the treatment of "different people," these claims are especially intriguing, for they offer the possibility that difference and its meanings are not fixed but socially constructed. If so, then stigma, exclusion, and other negative aspects of the treatment of difference can be challenged in new ways.

Part of the challenge involves reflecting on why we have devised the particular conceptions and perspectives that dominate. What interests and needs do they serve? In a book on the ideology of stereotyping Sander Gilman describes our use of stereotypes to structure the world and shows that the order we impose reduces anxiety and lends an appearance of legitimacy and self-evident truth to what we have invented:

> Our internal, mental representations of the world become the world. We act as if this world were real, external to ourselves; as Albert Einstein observed, "To the discoverer . . . the constructions of his imagination appear so necessary and so natural that he is apt to treat them not as the creations of his thought but as given realities." The flux of reality is made static, and the static that we produce further hardens our sense that our world view is "real." The stereotypical categories that we use are rarely without some point of tangency with reality (biological, social, medical), but their interpretation is colored by the ideology that motivates us.[21]

As the reference to Albert Einstein suggests, arguments of this sort partly grow out of the twentieth-century changes in scientific thought and in the philosophy of science. The scientist interacts with what he or she observes.[22] Categories of knowledge are limited; contradictions in descriptions of the world indicate constraints in the ways we know. Einstein demonstrated that observers in different systems moving in relation to one another would perceive the world differently. He used mathematical calculations to demonstrate that Euclidean geometry does not adequately describe the physical universe, and he showed how an alternative set of mathematical notions not only meet the tests of internal coherence but also better predict phenomena in the physical world.[23] His work thus supported the demand for empirical tests of systems generated a priori and also underscored the impact of the observer on what is observed. Similarly, Werner Heisenberg and other founders of quantum mechanics showed how the very act of observing can influ-

---

[21]Sander Gilman, *Difference and Pathology: Stereotypes of Sexuality, Race, and Madness* (Ithaca: Cornell University Press, 1985), p. 240, citing Albert Einstein, "On the Method of Theoretical Physics," *Philosophy of Science* 1 (1934), 162.

[22]See Max Jammer, *The Philosophy of Quantum Mechanics* (New York: Wiley, 1974), pp. 55–84; and Michael Polanyi, *Personal Knowledge: Toward a Post-Critical Philosophy* (Chicago: Chicago University Press, 1958). For an intriguing effort to relate these developments in science to law, see Laurence Tribe, "The Curvature of Constitutional Space: What Lawyers Can Learn from Modern Physics," *Harv. L. Rev.* 103 (1989), 1.

[23]Edward Purcell, *The Crisis of Democratic Theory: Scientific Naturalism and the Problem of Value* (Lexington: University Press of Kentucky, 1973), pp. 50–52.

ence what is observed, how the very act of measurement indeed can alter what is being measured.

Efforts to generalize about the empirical world usually assume that the particular observer's own situation is representative of any other observer's perspective, whereas in fact the limitations of the observer's perspective must also be made part of the effort to investigate, describe, and theorize about the world. Indeed, the search for new understandings may require not merely the creation of new categories to replace old ones but the rejection of the idea that only one set of stable categories naturally matches up with the world. For example, Jerome Bruner reports that Niels Bohr reached the idea of complementarity in quantum theory, when "he thought of the impossibility of considering his son simultaneously in the light of love and in the light of justice, the son just having voluntarily confessed that he had stolen a pipe from a local shop. His brooding set him to thinking about the vases and the faces in the trick figure-ground pictures: you can see only one at a time. And then the impossibility of thinking simultaneously about the position and the velocity of a particle occurred to him."[24]

Work by people like Einstein, Bohr, and Heisenberg prompted others to challenge the remnants of a Cartesian world view in science: a picture of the world as a clock composed of small bits, each with its own properties and all adding up to the whole. Instead, they inquired how systems acquire properties different from those of any of their parts, how force and patterns depend on relationships among parts or units, and how causes and effects interact.[25] Instead of certainties, some scientists pursued probabilities.[26] Instead of linear relationships between cause and effect, they explored the idea of mutuality, the idea that effects cause causes as well as the other way around.[27]

Going a step further, some investigators observed how the very categories of inquiry shaped what could be known—and at times produced paradoxes, the price of the inevitable limits of a humanly constructed scheme. Kurt Gödel demonstrated that mathematical systems need not be complete, in the

[24]Jerome Bruner, *Actual Minds, Possible Worlds* (Cambridge, Mass.: Harvard University Press, 1986), p. 51.

[25]See Levins and Lewontin, *Dialectical Biologist;* and Rita Lévi-Montalcini, *In Praise of Imperfection: My Life and Work* (New York: Basic Books, 1988), p. 129, exploring theories of the brain that emphasize global rather than local activity.

[26]Research using statistics flourished. Prediction and sampling and other tools to describe probabilities changed science and social science. Law, too, began to consider probabilities even in establishing liability for injuring people. See Richard Hoffman, "The Use of Epidemiology in the Courts," *American Journal of Epidemiology* 120 (1984), 190; David Rosenberg, "The Causal Connection in Mass Exposure Cases: A 'Public Law' Vision of the Tort System," *Harv. L. Rev.* 97 (1984), 849. Not all scientists were fully pleased with the results of these new ways of reasoning; for example, Einstein said that God does not play dice with the universe; he was not satisfied with a physics relying on probabilistic explanations. See Stephen Toulmin, *The Philosophy of Science: An Introduction* (New York: Hutchinson's University Library, 1953), p. 123.

[27]See Rupert Riedl, "The Consequences of Causal Thinking," in Erfundene Watzlawick, *The Invented Reality: How Do We Know What We Believe We Know?*, ed. Paul Watzlawick (New York: Norton, 1984), p. 69; Tribe, "The Curvature of Constitutional Space."

sense that the postulates behind the system cannot by themselves alone prove or disprove all well-formed formulas in the system.[28] Some theorists wrote to some degree as heirs of Immanual Kant, who long ago maintained that the mind is an active organ of understanding which shapes sensations and changes the chaotic multiplicity of experience in the very effort to know it; they argued that we think we find what we know but in fact invent it in our interaction with the world, and then we forget that we have invented our understanding and treat it as the world.[29] Work in this tradition also implies that knowledge must include self-reflective attention to the relationship between the knower and the known.

As scientists and mathematicians rejected certain uses of a priori and deductive reasoning—and at the same time rejected simple empiricism with renewed attention to the influence of the knower on what can be known— they encouraged others to challenge formal systems of reasoning and legacies of simple empiricism in economics, political theory, and law. Philosophers and political theorists around the turn of the twentieth century started to criticize prevailing thought for its inattention to relationships and to the social construction of knowledge. They doubted the transparency of the world and instead emphasized the arbitrary imposition of human conceptions on the world in the course of efforts to know it. These theorists made direct references to science, and scientific experimentation, as a model for exposing the human construction of ideas and for challenging them with the test of experience. This was not the science of positivism but the science of experimentalism, which recognized that the growth of knowledge depends on intersubjectivity within a community of people confronting a world to be shaped rather than simply discovered.[30] And some philosophers explicitly rejected the idea that the world could be understood by breaking it into component parts instead of exploring relationships.[31] A brief summary of leading advocates of these views demonstrates the nuances and the commonalities in their work.

[28]In particular, formal systems contain propositions that cannot be shown to be right or wrong: e.g., "This sentence has no proof" cannot be proved either true or false. See Francesco Varela, "The Creative Circle," in Watzlawick, *The Invented Reality*, pp. 309, 315.

[29]Nelson Goodman, *Ways of Worldmaking* (Indianapolis, Ind.: Hackett, 1978); Gregory Bateson, *Mind and Nature: A Necessary Unity* (Toronto: Bantam, 1979). See also Jean Piaget, "Structuralism: Introduction and Location of Problems," in *The Essential Piaget*, ed. Howard E. Gruber and J. Jacques Voneche (New York: Basic Books, 1977), pp. 767–74.

[30]See Walter Lippmann, *Drift and Mastery: An Attempt to Diagnose the Current Unrest* (Englewood Cliffs, N.J.: Prentice-Hall, 1961), pp. 295, 329. As historian James Kloppenberg has recently summarized in *Uncertain Victory: Social Democracy and Progressivism in European and American Thought, 1870–1920* (New York: Oxford University Press, 1986), p. 113, some political theorists around the turn of the century developed a theory that "erased the distinction between subject and object and isolated immediate experience, the intersection of knower and known, as the locus of knowledge. According to this analysis, the subject is embedded in an external world from which he cannot be abstracted. He becomes, in a word, historical, wrapped in a bundle of socioeconomic and political contexts."

[31]See Kloppenberg, *Uncertain Victory*, pp. 49–52, 58, 97, 135.

Pragmatism in Philosophy

The first distinctively American school of philosophy emerged early in the twentieth century with the name of pragmatism. Its proponents articulated conceptions of knowledge and human experience that rejected prior views framed by Plato, Aristotle, and Kant. For example, Charles Sanders Peirce, a philosopher well regarded by his peers even though he lacked an academic post, maintained that people cannot try to know the world without prior understandings that are themselves not apparent or palpable yet prevent infallible inspection by the individual. Inquiry by an individual alone cannot decisively test the truth. Instead, knowledge depends upon collaborative efforts within a community of inquirers who reach provisional agreement, subject to subsequent challenge.[32]

William James, working at Harvard in both philosophy and psychology, focused less on the relationship between the individual observer and the community than on the relationship between the observer's situation and what that observer can know. Each person unconsciously selects what to know from an array of stimuli; other individuals receiving the same stimulation perceive a different world.[33] According to James, experience is shaped by habit, and habit is shaped by social custom. The differences in individual perspectives are due not merely to the uniqueness of each individual but to the situation and experiences of that individual in the society. James argued that his ideas bore consequences for moral decisions. Rather than relying on abstract and preexisting rules, a decision-maker should confront the uniqueness of each situation. Truth itself is not the inherent property of an idea, James argued but what happens to an idea in relation to events in the world.[34] Truth appears in the usefulness of an idea. Understanding truth requires bridging the gap between theory and practice.

Another thinker from this period was Wilhelm Dilthey, who worked in Germany. Agreeing with James, he argued that understanding human experience requires a process of examining parts in relation to the whole, and even oneself in relation to others. Dilthey revived and enlarged the practice of hermeneutics—textual interpretation developed originally in the context of

[32]See *Critical Essays on Charles Sanders Peirce*, ed. Charles Hartshorne and Paul Weiss (Cambridge, Mass.: Belknap Press of Harvard University Press, 1960); *Perspectives on Peirce*, ed. Richard Bernstein (New Haven, Conn.: Yale University Press, 1965); Israel Scheffler, *Four Pragmatists: An Introduction to Peirce, James, Mead, and Dewey* (London: Routledge & Kegan Paul, 1974), pp. 51–54; Drucilla Cornell, "Institutionalization of Meaning, Recollective Imagination, and the Potential for Transformative Legal Interpretation," *Pa. L. Rev.* 136 (1988), 1135, 1198–1206, 1212–28.

[33]"The world of each of us, howsoever different our several views of it may be, all lay embedded in the primordial chaos of sensations, which gave the mere matter to the thought of all of us indifferently. . . . My world is but one in a million alike embedded, alike real to those who may abstract them. How different must be the worlds in the consciousness of ant, cuttlefish, or crab!" (William James, *Principles of Psychology* [1890; New York: Dover, 1950], pp. 288–89).

[34]William James, *Pragmatism*, ed. Frederick Burkhardt (1907; Cambridge, Mass.: Harvard University Press, 1975), pp. 44, 97, 106.

theology—as a method for interpreting parts in relation to the whole and as a method for pursuing knowledge through the interpretation of meanings within contexts.[35]

In the United States social theorist George Herbert Mead drew on the new theory of relativity in science and on studies of human consciousness in his focus on the importance of perspective to human knowledge.[36] The theory of relativity in physics exposed the contingency of the perceived physical world on the position of the perceiving person. Similarly, any human experience is embedded in the situated perspective of the observer. To understand the implication of his or her own conduct, Mead claimed, each person must try to see from the perspective of others.[37] Mead argued that selfhood depends on the ability to assume the attitudes and roles of others. He asserted that the individual becomes an individual only in relation to others. Exploring child development and language acquisition, he concluded that each individual develops by internalizing the shared language and culture of the society—by interacting with the social world. Indeed, Mead's work is widely understood to be the inspiration for social interactionism, the framework behind labeling theory.

Perhaps the most broad-gauged and influential thinker in this vein was John Dewey, who contributed to philosophy and education with his emphasis upon the analogy between a scientific method that tests ideas against experience and a political philosophy that rejects fixed norms and looks to the relationship between ideas and practice. He opposed the traditional idea that explanation consists in classifying things or events, and argued that there are no ultimate categories.[38] Knowledge is inevitably plural because human experience is plural, and so are human ways of knowing. And knowledge depends on the individual's action in and interaction with the world, with deliberate reflection on that experience. Dewey argued for efforts to understand the connections between self and other, mind and body. He maintained that each individual is formed in social interactions, that the notion of autonomous individualism fails to match up with social experience or the political good.[39] Ideas ultimately must be tested in light of social experience

[35]See Wilhelm Dilthey, *Selected Writings*, ed. and trans. H. P. Rickman (Cambridge: Cambridge University Press, 1976).

[36]See generally George Herbert Mead, *Selected Writings*, ed. Andrew Reck (Indianapolis, Ind.: Bobbs-Merrill, 1964); George Herbert Mead, *The Philosophy of the Present*, ed. Arthur Murphy (1932; Chicago: Chicago University Press, 1980).

[37]Mead proposed trying to take the perspective of the generalized other, however, and in this respect may have lapsed into a conception of the reasonable person—which implicitly creates the contrast of the deviant person. See George Herbert Mead, "The Genesis of the Self and Social Control," in *The Philosophy of the Present*. See also Seyla Benhabib, "The Generalized and the Concrete Other: The Kohlberg-Gilligan Controversy and Feminist Theory," in *Feminism as Critique*, ed. Drucilla Cornell and Seyla Benhabib (Minneapolis: University of Minnesota Press, 1987), p. 77.

[38]See John Dewey, *The Quest for Certainty: A Study of the Relation of Knowledge and Action* (1929; New York: Minton, Balch, 1960).

[39]See John Dewey, *Liberalism and Social Action* (New York: Putnam, 1935); John Dewey, "The Future of Liberalism," in *John Dewey: The Essential Writings*, ed. David Sikorsky (New York: Harper & Row, 1977), p. 197.

and by asking who is helped or hurt by them. Perhaps for this reason, Dewey worked to implement his ideas in practice by setting up innovative school programs. Continuing his philosophic work, he developed the notion that social or political exclusion injures not only the individuals excluded but also the whole social body, which is deprived of their contributions.[40]

These philosophers drew on developments in science; soon the social sciences too were rocked by these twentieth-century ideas about the relationship between the observed and the observer and the related challenges to "formalism" as the dominant method for organizing knowledge.[41]

The Social Sciences

Even as scholars defined separate disciplines within social science and thereby drew tighter boundaries distinguishing one from another, some social scientists pursued relational insights across these divisions.

Anthropology is an intriguing case. Early in this century Franz Boas led a challenge to the prevailing ideas of universal laws in physical and cultural evolution. He and his students rejected the idea that social science could reveal one true human experience; they believed that a scientific method deploying detailed factual inquiry would demonstrate the variety rather than uniformity of human cultures, human natures. Although Boas and his followers in anthropology endorsed the goal of value-free investigations, they also affirmed that no one's evaluation of a culture can be free from cultural preconceptions; no universal categories can apply to all cultures, because every set of categories has a specific cultural origin.[42] The imposition of frames of thought on the world, they said, affected not just evaluations but even basic perceptions. Similarly, the linguist Benjamin Whorf summarized the view that there is no ideal pattern of relative likeness and difference frozen into reality and waiting to be discovered.[43] Indeed, followers of Boas and Whorf throughout the twentieth century found that all concepts used to describe the world are culturebound. A basic term such as "the person" expresses assumptions from one culture that may misdescribe the self-understandings of people in another culture.[44] Even stating the insight in

---

[40]John Dewey, "Democracy and Educational Administration," in *The Middle Works, 1899–1924,* 15 vols., ed. Jo Ann Boydston (Carbondale: Southern Illinois University Press, 1976–1983), 1:16.

[41]See generally Morton White, *Social Thought in America: The Revolt against Formalism* 3d ed. (New York: Oxford University Press, 1976).

[42]"There is no more reason to infer cultural or psychological universals from Trobriand culture than from our own. That is the first and by now quite elementary lesson of anthropology" (A. L. Kroeber, "History and Science in Anthropology," *American Anthropologist* 37 [Oct.–Dec. 1935], 562).

[43]Benjamin Whorf, *Language, Thought, and Reality* (Cambridge, Mass.: MIT Press, 1956), pp. 214–15, 252.

[44]See Michael Mauss, *A Category of the Human Mind: The Notion of Person; The Notion of Self,* trans. W. D. Halls; orig. published 1938, reprinted in *The Category of the Person: Anthropology, Philosophy, History,* ed. Michael Carrithers, Steven Collins, and Steven Lukes (Cambridge: Cambridge University Press, 1985), p. 1. See also Clifford Geertz, " 'From the

this way deploys aspects of individualist thought, typical of modern Western culture, which take the separate individual as the unit of analysis.[45] Perhaps because of a new self-consciousness about the unavoidable impact of one's own categories on perception and judgment, many contemporary anthropologists are studying culture itself as a system of shared meaning.

A major focus for study among these anthropologists, then, is not habit and behavior but how individuals and the groups within which they live mutually participate in the creation and use of language, symbols, and collective representational schemes. These anthropologists called for an interpretive method of study: the scholar should move back and forth between local detail and global structure. One influential theorist, Clifford Geertz, has explained that the scholar should move between "the whole conceived through the parts that actualize it and the parts conceived through the whole that motivates them" so that the anthropologist can try to craft explanations from within the culture under study. Out of sensitivity to the relationship between the observer and the observed, interpretive anthropologists emphasize contextual studies of the relationship between the parts and the whole of meanings within a given culture.[46] Some criticize this work for sponsoring cultural relativism: since the observer tries to suspend his or her own perspective by becoming immersed in the texts of the culture, interpretive social science seems to lose moral moorings—a charge which, interestingly, accompanies many scholarly endeavors that make the interpretive turn.[47]

A contrasting tradition in anthropology, launched by Claude Lévi-Strauss, has become known as structuralism. Rather than studying cultural phenomena themselves, structuralists propose to examine the relations between phenomena and the systems formed through those relations. Lévi-Strauss looked at kinship patterns, for example, and described basic units of relationships within families that become the building blocks for kinship. He also examined myths to discover underlying patterns that relate the ideas beneath the surface stories. Unlike the interpretivist anthropologists, who emphasize particular contextual studies, the structuralists favor abstract models that generalize from particulars. Through such abstract categories as his opposition between "raw" and "cooked," Lévi-Strauss organized the themes of seemingly disparate myths to disclose unities. He explained his own analysis as a rejection of "the Cartesian principle of breaking down the difficulty into as many parts as may be necessary for finding the solution." Instead, he saw the task as trying to discern something analogous to a grammar or syntax of a given language, worked out from observing individual sentences.[48] This

---

Native's Point of View': On the Nature of Anthropological Understanding," in Shweder and LeVine, *Culture Theory*, p. 123.

[45]Steven Lukes, Conclusion in *The Category of the Person*, pp. 282, 298.

[46]Geertz, " 'From the Native's Point of View,' " p. 134. See generally Clifford Geertz, *Local Knowledge: Further Essays in Interpretive Anthropology* (New York: Basic Books, 1983).

[47]For one response to this charge, see Clifford Geertz, "Anti-Anti-Relativism," *American Anthropologist* 86, no. 2 (1984), 263–78.

[48]Lévi-Strauss was influenced by a particular school of linguistics, also called structuralism.

requires developing methodological rules to translate from the observer's own experience to the patterns from the divergent culture. The structuralist uses concepts about relationships, such as "symmetry," "inversion," "equivalence," "homology," and "isopomorphism." Key analytic inquiries involve comparing opposites and exploring kinds of similarities, whether between people, ideas, images, or emotions.[49]

Structuralist anthropologists, following Lévi-Strauss, have viewed relationships embedded within cultural artifacts, such as myths, as clues to deeper structural models that the researcher may sketch, even though these models may be unknown at a conscious level to the members of the observed culture. This approach suggests that the existing structures do satisfy human needs, that they are functional. The match between structures and human needs, argue the structuralists, reveals a pattern of basic and universal laws. Perhaps because of these claims, the approach has been criticized for failing to account for social change. If structures exist because they are functional, what would cause or produce change? The functionalism of structuralist anthropology also disables criticism of any particular cultural patterns, since whatever is, is presumed to work. The structuralists' interest in relationships thus differs from that of the interpretivists, especially because of the structuralists' search for abstract, general rules of social organization and their manifest interest in contexts only insofar as contexts supply the empirical data for analyzing the structures behind relationships. Yet the similarities between the two groups are intriguing: structuralist anthropology, like interpretive anthropology, is preoccupied with the relationships between parts and wholes, and it acknowledges to some degree the impact of the observer on the observed.

Relational thought of several varieties characterizes work in psychology, too. Again, relational approaches have persisted even as scholars in the twentieth century divide into camps. Feuding factions respond to and build theories far away from Sigmund Freud's foundational work. A structuralist tradition, notably advocated by Jean Piaget, has emphasized individual psychological development through "systems of transformation." Known for articulating universal stages of cognitive development, Piaget believed that interactions between the child and the world are essential for an individual's progress through these stages of development. Under the right circumstances, the child's encounters with a demonstration of physical causality, for example, trigger an intellectual understanding of causality. Piaget described and endorsed what he called "a relational perspective, according to which it is neither the elements nor a whole that comes about in a manner one knows not how, but the relations among elements that count."[50]

With a focus on the process by which the whole develops—the process by which a child grows—structuralist developmental psychology addresses the

[49]Claude Lévi-Strauss, *The Raw and the Cooked*, trans. John and Doreen Weightman (New York: Harper & Row, 1969), pp. 5, 7–8, 11, 31.
[50]Piaget, "Structuralism," pp. 767, 768, 770.

interaction between the child, who has inborn capacities, and the environ-ment. For Piaget, knowledge is a process of constructing views of the world; it requires an individual to interact with the world. Structuralist developmen-tal psychology risks a kind of abstraction and claims a kind of universal application that ignores other forms of relational thought, yet it provides a powerful framework for understanding the relationships between a growing child's cognitive abilities and the world that the child encounters.

An entirely different tack has been taken by the "object relations" scholars in psychoanalytic theory, who became dissatisfied with Freud's conception of internal drives that motivate individuals and their development—though their theories do bear some resemblance to Piaget's structuralist development at particular points.[51] For object-relation theorists, more central to individ-ual development than the relations between the child and the general en-vironment are those between the child and adult caretakers. Starting with the assumption that people need other people and that infants especially need other people, these theorists study relationships between individuals and the people to whom they are attached. The child's development critically in-volves crafting a sense of self in relationship to another. A "self" is a symbolic construct that depends on and emerges through relationships with others.[52] Rather than locating an original core self inside the child, object-relations theory stresses that the normal course of human development includes the gradual growth of a sense of self alongside a growing recognition that there are others outside the self. The boundaries of the self are defined in relation to those other people; the boundaries are where we are in touch with others.[53] Our knowledge of others is mediated through interactions with them.[54]

Some object-relations theorists emphasize the fantasy and imagination involved in developing an internal sense of others; some stress the motivation to seek other people as an alternative to Freudian conceptions of internal drives.[55] D. W. Winnicott's work eloquently describes the mother's function in enabling the infant's sense of self to emerge. She acts as a mirror reflecting the infant's experience and gestures, confirming the infant's emerging sense of existence and then sense of separate existence. By seeing the mother seeing him, the child starts to develop a sense of self.[56] Heinz Kohut has maintained similarly that the child needs to display her developing capabilities and be admired for them, and she needs to form an ideal image of at least one adult and merge with it.[57]

[51]Jay Greenberg and Stephen Mitchell, *Object Relations in Psychoanalytic Theory* (Cam-bridge, Mass.: Harvard University Press, 1983), pp. 228, 293.
[52]See Michael Franz Basch, "The Concept of Self: An Operational Definition," in *Develop-mental Approaches to the Self,* ed. Benjamin Lee and Gil Noam (New York: Plenum Press, 1983), pp. 7, 53.
[53]See Josephine Klein, *Our Need for Others and Its Roots in Infancy* (New York: Tavistock, 1987), p. 253.
[54]Greenberg and Mitchell, *Object Relations,* p. 90 (discussing Henry Stack Sullivan).
[55]Ibid., pp. 130–36, 149–50 (discussing Melanie Klein); 154–60 (discussing W. R. D. Fairbairn).
[56]D. W. Winnicott, *Playing and Reality* (New York: Basic Books, 1971), p. 134.
[57]Greenberg and Mitchell, *Object Relations,* p. 354.

Each of the object-relations theorists analyzes the relational matrix between individuals, rather than the separate person.[58] The very development
of a sense of oneself as an autonomous person, according to these theorists,
depends on the child's continuing relationship with others. The child starts as
a person-in-relationship-to-others and internalizes a sense of boundaries
between self and others. The focus on the child's own active contribution and
the contribution of others to the process of development represents one
dimension of the relational turn. An emphasis on the social, cultural, historical, and economic context in which the child develops represents another
relational dimension. And self-consciousness about how the very discipline
of psychology is shaped by and in turn shapes the political and cultural
milieu in which its adherents operate is still another dimension, expressing
particular concern about the relationship between knowledge and political
context.[59] Conceptions of childhood and development are cultural inventions, as is developmental psychology itself, and all are embedded in and
shaped by larger cultural forces.

Recently, developmental psychology has taken such concerns one step
further. Criticizing the focus on the parent-child connection as artificially
abstracted from social context, theorists have called for attention also to how
the parents' relationships with one another affect the child and how the
parents' gender, racial, and class identities influence the child's development
of a sense of self. These theorists argue that social context is not a background for but a critical constituent of experience.[60] Cultural conditions
partially determine whether a child develops a sense of self as a self-reflecting
agent.[61] The social construction of reality and the varieties of socially constructed realities have thus come to form a critical framework for understanding child development.

Scholars pursuing work of this sort expressly acknowledge their debt to
the earlier work of Mead, James, and Dewey.[62] Some do criticize Mead,
however, for neglecting the conflicts and struggles that occur between infant
and adult in the child's process of seeking and gaining approval and confirmation.[63] Others criticize the early theorists of social relations for treating
both the social realm and the individual as unitary items interacting with one

[58]Ibid., p. 220.

[59]Urie Bronfenbrenner, Frank Kessel, William Kessen, and Sheldon White, "Toward a Critical
Social History of Developmental Psychology: A Propaedeutic Discussion," *American Psychologist* 41 (Nov. 1986), 1220–21, 1224–25, 1227.

[60]Paul Light, "Context, Conservation and Conversation," in *Children of Social Worlds:
Development in a Social Context,* ed. Martin Richards and Paul Light (Cambridge, Mass.:
Harvard University Press, 1986), pp. 170, 185.

[61]W. Peter Robinson, "Children's Understanding of the Distinction between Messages and
Meanings: Emergence and Implications," in Richards and Light, *Children of Social Worlds,*
pp. 213, 225.

[62]See ibid., p. 225; and Martin Richards, Introduction, in Richards and Light, *Children of
Social Worlds,* pp. 1, 2–3. In Bronfenbrenner et al., "Critical Social History of Developmental
Psychology," pp. 1218, 1223, 1228, Kessen cites John Dewey as precursor to the current view
that psychological development is neither progressive nor predictable.

[63]Cathy Urwin, "Power Relations and the Emergence of Language," in *Changing the Subject:
Psychology, Social Regulation, and Subjectivity,* ed. Julian Henriques et al. (London: Methuen,
1984), pp. 269, 319.

another, and for reducing the social world to what the individual absorbs cognitively from it rather than dealing with the actual, palpable dimensions of money, power, and social institutions.[64] If the relationships between individuals and social factors are deeply pursued, then the individual is inevitably implicated in the social world through language and culture, and the social world is known only by individuals. Some theorists conclude that scholars must examine meanings as expressed through language, which is inherently embedded in social practices and is thus intersubjective.[65]

Concerned with language, social scripts, and codes of meaning, the new psychologists read and refer to theories of linguistics, philosophy, and interpretation. Indeed, in this respect, study of the socially constructed self converges with a general flourishing of theory in academic circles—especially theories about meaning, hermeneutics, and phenomenology (the philosophy of experience). As one observer notes, all these theoretical movements, "despite their apparent diversity, have a common origin in the philosophical and political reaction against Enlightenment notions" and reject in particular the conception of the individual as "a conscious, rational agent whose existence was logically prior to that of the social world." Seeing consciousness as embedded in language and language as unavoidably collective, these theories at the same time reject forms of structuralism that make people mere "bearers of categories" rather than persons initiating and contributing to their own development.[66]

Some theorists find support in work by "poststructuralists," including Michel Foucault, who have explored relationships between knowledge and power. Foucault's detailed expositions of the historical treatment of madness, criminal behavior, and sexuality regard knowledge as a codification of social practices and see experts as socializers who construct environments that in turn manage the activities and even the emotions of people. His study of madness, for example, explores the rules and procedures developed in society to define what would be treated as normal or rational and asserts that experts who guide society in these matters exercise the power to control or silence those they name as irrational or mad. The expert discourse is both cause and effect in this process.[67]

Literary Theory

By turning toward theory and interdisciplinary research, social scientists also converge with work in literary theory. There, a structuralist school has

[64]Introduction to Section One: "From the Individual to the Social—A Bridge Too Far," in Henriques et al., *Changing the Subject*, pp. 11, 23–25.

[65]David Ingleby, "Development in Social Context," in Richards and Light, *Children of Social Worlds*, pp. 297, 305. Ingleby (pp. 309–10) and others find support in Ludwig Wittgenstein, *Philosophical Investigations*, 2d ed., trans. G. E. M. Anscombe (London: Oxford University Press, 1958).

[66]Ingleby, "Development in Social Context," pp. 297, 306, 310–11.

[67]See, e.g., Michel Foucault, *Discipline and Punish: The Birth of the Prison*, trans. Alan Sheridan (New York: Pantheon Books, 1977); Michel Foucault, *Madness and Civilization: A History of Insanity in the Age of Reason*, trans. Richard Howard (London: Tavistock, 1971); Michel Foucault, *Power/Knowledge: Selected Interviews and Other Writings, 1972–1977*, trans. and ed. Colin Gordon (Brighton, Eng.: Harvester Press, 1980).

examined literature as a system of signs or internal rules about how to operate within language.[68] Structuralists talk of literature as a mode sent by a writer to a receiver through a medium. Using work in linguistics and borrowing from Lévi-Strauss, literary structuralists have suggested that there is a set of relationships between core notions that recur in all individual narratives as paired opposites: these include self/other, love/hate, life/death, and concepts more closely attached to literature itself, such as speech/writing. Structured patterns tend to prefer or give a place of privilege to one term over another in such paired ideas as speech versus writing, subject versus object, or sender versus receiver. The relationships between these notions provide the context for meaning in any particular literary work.

Relationships are if anything even more critical to literary theorists who engage in poststructuralist work and use strategies of interpretation which seek to explore the varieties and pluralities of meanings within texts rather than to elaborate a universal code behind all texts. Building from the structuralist idea that ordered, hierarchical pairs of notions lie behind the surface of literary texts, some poststructuralists argue that an item stated in a text, such as the conscious hero, depends on its opposite—the unconscious. Jacques Derrida is particularly known for emphasizing that any sign emerges from a system of differences.[69] Taking apart a text by exploring the hidden differences behind an explicit sign in a text has been called "deconstruction."

One deconstructionist strategy is to study the relationships between what is present and what is absent in a text—and to emphasize what is absent as necessary to meaning. Some poststructuralists draw from Foucault's work to explore the language of literature as an expression of the power and interests of those who speak. Here, too, the relationship between what is said and what is unsaid becomes critical, for in examining this relationship the critic can articulate unspoken rules or constraints about what may be said. Alternatively, poststructuralist literary theorists examine texts for tensions, exploring the contradictory meanings within a given work and observing how the relationships between these meanings explode the idea of a unitary author or intent.

Structuralist and poststructuralist literary strategies focus on relationships between ideas, while reader-oriented literary theories focus on the relationships between the literary text and the reader—between the observed and the observer. Some reader-response theorists lay claim to phenomenology and hermeneutics, stressing the role of the reader as central to determining meaning through the experience of reading a text. Grasping the whole of the text in context, the reader also supplies a standpoint and a realm of consciousness to organize multiple possible meanings and even to fill in gaps in

[68]See generally *Structuralism: A Reader,* ed. Michael Lane (London: Jonathan Cape, 1970); Terrance Hawkes, *Structuralism and Semiotics* (London: Methuen, 1977); Robert Scholes, *Structuralism in Literature: An Introduction* (New Haven, Conn.: Yale University Press, 1974).

[69]Derrida's idea of *différance* refers to how signs both differ and defer, postponing presence; see *Of Grammatology,* trans. G. Spivak (Baltimore, Md.: Johns Hopkins University Press, 1974).

the text through the process of internalizing and reformulating what the author produced.[70] The process of knowing, in this account, depends on the relationship between the knower and the object and between the knower's past and the object's present.

Some theorists concerned with the reader's role try to articulate the conventions of reading which a text implies. Stanley Fish, in particular, has stressed the role of interpretive communities of people who would read the text in certain predictable ways.[71] Others criticize this notion for producing closure once again rather than opening up the meanings of texts to the varieties of interpretations that different readers could reach.[72] Nevertheless, advocates on both sides of this debate share a commitment to the relationships between texts and readers as central to the process of making meaning.

Political and Constitutional Theory

Community in a different sense has figured prominently in recent political and constitutional theory. American historians have often pointed to the themes of classical, civil republicanism, which persisted alongside liberal individualism.[73] Classic republicanism contemplated a civic community in which public participation in the process of self-governance would elicit from political equals a sense of common good beyond the aggregation or swapping of private interests. Political theorists have articulated similar themes,[74] both in recommendations for the future and in canvassing the past.[75] Although its traditional form rested on an exclusive community, restricting the process of governance to landowning white men who would be independent enough to grasp the shared public interest, civic republicanism has found contemporary supporters among many who would modify its legacy with an egalitarian commitment to broad-based participation.[76]

---

[70]See Umberto Eco, *The Role of the Reader: Explorations in the Semiotics of Texts* (Bloomington: Indiana University Press, 1979).

[71]Stanley Fish, *Is There a Text in This Class?* (Cambridge, Mass.: Harvard University Press, 1980).

[72]See, e.g., Jonathan Culler, *On Deconstruction: Theory and Criticism after Structuralism* (Ithaca: Cornell University Press, 1982), pp. 39–41, 65–75.

[73]Joyce Appelby, "The American Heritage: The Heirs and the Disinherited," in *The Constitution and American Life*, ed. David Thelen (Ithaca: Cornell University Press, 1988), p. 138; Gordon S. Wood, *The Creation of the American Republic, 1776–1787* (New York: Norton, 1972). See also Max Lerner, "The Constitution and Court as Symbols," *Yale L.J.* 46 (1937), 32.

[74]See, e.g., Benjamin Barber, "The Compromised Republic, Public Purposelessness in America," in *The Moral Foundations of the American Republic*, ed. Robert Horwitz (Charlottesville: University Press of Virginia, 1977), p. 19.

[75]J. G. A. Pocock, *The Machiavellian Moment* (Princeton, N.J.: Princeton University Press, 1975); Hanna Pitkin, *Fortune Is a Woman: Gender and Politics in the Thought of Niccolo Machiavelli* (Berkeley: University of California Press, 1984).

[76]See Frank Michelman, "The Supreme Court, 1985 Term—Foreword: Traces of Self-Government," *Harv. L. Rev.* 100 (1986), 4; Frank Michelman, "Law's Republic," *Yale L.J.* 97 (1988), 1493; Cass Sunstein, "Interest Groups in American Public Law," *Stan. L. Rev.* 38 (1985), 29; Cass Sunstein, "Beyond the Republican Revival," *Yale L.J.* 97 (1988), 1339. But see Kathleen Sullivan, "Rainbow Republicanism," *Yale L.J.* 97 (1988), 1713.

Some political theorists have attempted to articulate new versions of communitarianism, focusing less on the state than on the construction of identity through participation and membership in groups sharing commitments.[77] Both communitarian and republican theorists search for an alternative to replace or modify the conception of the polity founded on separate, distinct individuals, each pursuing self-interest. Communitarians and republicans both discuss visions of substantive community commitments beyond mere tolerance and respect for individual freedom. They articulate the importance of group membership, public values, and moral duties, thereby suggesting a departure from the assumptions that the individual is the focus for political theory and that the self has meaning apart from context and commitments.

Critics of republicanism and communitarianism, and critics within these camps, dispute whether there can ever be one public good or whether there are instead multiple perspectives on the good, given individual and group differences. Others warn against the risk of suppressing differences in the name of community. These debates are characterized by a sense that the whole of political life could be more than the sum of its parts, and that the experience of political participation provides a means of transforming the self through interaction with others.

Relational Thought in Perspective

The internal debates are fascinating, but the larger connective patterns across all the foregoing disciplines are even more striking. In field after field of scholarship, twentieth-century theorists have explored the significance of relationships and challenged modes of thought that rest upon autonomous and discrete items or persons. To the extent that legal ideas about the world and about persons depend on such notions of separate items—distinctions between knower and known and between autonomous individuals—these intellectual challenges from other fields afford provocative sources of criticism and alternative strategies. There are ready connections between the relational turn in so many fields of scholarship and the search for new legal treatments of "different" people: attention to the social construction of meaning, challenges to the hierarchical pairing of concepts about difference, and study of the relation of power embedded in asserted knowledge about difference.

Yet there is a serious risk that this quick summary of vast ranges of intellectual activities not only mistreats their ideas but also dazes the reader with sheer abstraction. Indeed, abstraction often remains a problem even after close and immersed engagement with a given theorist. Merely borrow-

[77]Michael Sandel, "Democrats and Community," in *New Republic*, Feb. 22, 1988, p. 21; Philip Selznick, "The Idea of a Communitarian Morality," *Calif. L. Rev.* 75 (1987), 445. For a nuanced consideration of community and political membership, see Kenneth L. Karst, *Belonging to America: Equal Citizenship and the Constitution* (New Haven, Conn.: Yale University Press, 1989).

ing theories and applying them to law may result in an exchange of abstractions rather than a grounded reconsideration of law's treatment of difference.

For this reason, among others, I find the feminist movements in each of these theoretical fields most accessible and congenial. Building from both the women's movement of the 1960s and the increasing presence of women in the academy, women—and men—have addressed anthropology, psychology, sociology, philosophy, history, literature, and even science with questions about women's experiences and perspectives. Feminist work is varied and complex, but across many fields it shares an immediate concern with the omission of women from bodies of knowledge. The connections between knowledge and power and between what is known and who does the knowing are palpable to feminist critics.

Feminists have also actively reconsidered the theory of an autonomous self and examined the interpersonal and social relationships within which people develop a sense of self. And feminist work has discovered how patterns of connections and similarities—relations between ideas, relations between theories and context—may prove more illuminating than refined analysis of the separate elements or ideas under study. By grounding concern for relationships in the social and historical experience of women, feminist studies in many fields avoid floating abstractions and help to articulate and sustain value judgments amid the challenges of relativism. Advocating plural perspectives, and sensitive to the partiality of any one point of view, feminists also engage in interdisciplinary work and advocate plural strategies that cannot be reduced to one set of principles or methods. After exploring feminist works, this chapter returns, with new perspective, to the conflict over a group home for mentally retarded persons in Cleburne, Texas.

Feminist Scholarship

Feminist scholarship flourished during the 1970s and 1980s and invigorated many fields with new questions, new methodologies, and new perspectives. Influenced no doubt by the women's movement in political and legal arenas, feminist scholars have also made the academy an arena for change. Across academic disciplines, they have challenged the exclusion of women from the canon of established works and from the subjects for study. Strikingly, feminist work also pursues relational insights on several levels.[78]

[78]Theorists in feminist scholarship often draw analogies between their work and "paradigm shifts" in modern physics and other fields, where again the focus is on relationships. Robin Morgan noted that the classical theory of physics presumed a universe divided into building blocks, the ultimate one being the atom. Similarly, political theory presumed building blocks of family, class, race, and gender, the ultimate unit being the individual. The special theory of relativity, in contrast, introduced the ideas that mass and energy are one, space and time are one, and relative; feminist theory introduced the idea that females share the same condition of humanity as men, relative to male experience. She also pursued analogies to quantum mechanics, the uncertainty principle, and the theory of complementarity. See "A Quantum Leap in Feminist Theory," *Ms.,* Dec. 1982, pp. 101–2 (excerpted from Robin Morgan, *The Anatomy of Freedom: Feminism, Physics, and Global Politics* [New York: Doubleday, 1982]).

Many feminists find relational insights critical to any effort to recover women's experiences, because the exclusion, degradation, or devaluation of women by political theorists, historians, social scientists, and literary theorists implies and imposes a reference point based on male experience. Feminists have contributed incisive critiques of the unstated assumptions behind political theory, law, bureaucracy, natural science, and social science which presuppose the universality of a particular reference point. Dominant conceptions of human nature have taken men as the reference point and treat women as "other," "different," "deviant," or "exceptional." Besides criticizing as artificial this denigration of women, feminists argue that the experience of relative powerlessness has helped women to shape alternative ways of thinking about the world which accentuate an awareness of human interdependence. Women's traditional roles as wives and mothers have cultivated the ability to provide daily care and a responsiveness to the experiences and needs of others.[79]

The very idea of "gender" as a subject for study brings to light the relationships between the categories of male and female and between the society and the individual, which work together to name and internalize a given gender identity.[80] The historical meaning of gender has signaled particular relationships of power. Men with power have tended to see themselves as free of "gender" while defining women as having a gender—as having a difference. Scholars interested in women's experiences cannot help attending to the relationships between men and women that have organized knowledge identities.

Even more specific relational insights emerge from feminist scholarship. First, feminist work explores and expresses the relationship between the knower and the known: how does the material historical perspective of the investigator influence or shape what is seen or understood? Second, feminist methods look for wholes and relationships rather than simply separate parts, and they emphasize experience and intuition, not just analysis of distinct and separate units. Third, feminist work specifically reflects upon relationships between people rather than treating people as autonomous, with identities existing prior to their social relationships. Feminists criticize the assumption of autonomous individualism behind American economic and political theory and legal and bureaucratic practice, for this assumption rests on a picture of public and independent man rather than private and often dependent, or interconnected, woman. And fourth, feminist work expresses a suspicion of general rules abstracted from context and instead considers the significance of contexts and particularities. That very tendency makes this abstract summary seem jarring and inapt, a situation that the following examples seek to remedy.

[79]See, e.g., Sara Ruddick, *Maternal Thinking* (Boston: Beacon Press, 1989).
[80]See Simone de Beauvoir, *The Second Sex*, trans. H. M. Parshley (1953; New York: Vintage Books, 1974); Jane Flax, "Postmodernism and Gender Relations in Feminist Theory," *Signs* 12 (1987), 621, 628; Gayle Rubin, "The Traffic in Women: Notes on the 'Political Economy' of Sex," in *Toward an Anthropology of Women*, ed. Rayna Rapp Reiter (New York: Monthly Review Press, 1975), pp. 157–210.

Carol Gilligan's "Different Voice"

Carol Gilligan's work in psychology and moral development exemplifies all four of these concerns with relationships. Her work on moral development notably exposes the distortion of knowledge resulting from the exclusion of female subjects. She observes that studies by Piaget and Lawrence Kohlberg completely exclude female participants and yet claim to summarize human development. Gilligan shows how a "different voice" can be heard not only in female subjects but also in male subjects, once the researcher starts to recognize through the inclusion of women subjects some alternative modes of perception and reasoning. She discusses the "masculinist bias" in the influential traditions in psychology which were established by Freud and Piaget and continued by contemporary scholars such as Kohlberg.[81]

Kohlberg asked people to comment on situations that present moral dilemmas. He and his associates then rated the participants' responses in hierarchically ordered stages of development in moral reasoning, moving from egocentric concerns for concrete reward and punishment through a stage of attention to approval within social relationships and conventions, then progressing to a later stage of adherence to abstract and general rules and, finally, to respect for universal principles against which even rules can be judged. Gilligan notes that people who respond chiefly with care and sensitivity to the needs of others—people who exhibit the traits traditionally identified with and rewarded as feminine—are marked by this scale as deficient in moral development.[82] Kohlberg's scheme devalues an alternative voice of moral development through which individuals come to value caretaking, interdependence, and contextual solutions. Looking at the relationships between the assumptions of the investigators and the results of their studies, Gilligan exposes this serious omission and bias in work built upon Kohlberg's theories.

In addition, Gilligan's work stands as an example of research that looks at wholes rather than parts.[83] She thinks about large patterns in the kinds of responses people gave to questions about moral dilemmas and detects a mode of thinking that seems undervalued by the scheme advocated by established scholars in her field. Only by looking at the larger patterns of styles of reasoning and gender relations, rather than at individual scores on tests, did Gilligan develop her insight. She drew on her intuition, based on her own experiences in listening to people and to herself. Relationships between experience and theory inform her work.

Relationships assume importance in a third way in Gilligan's research.

[81]Gilligan, *In a Different Voice,* pp. 18, 7–11. See also Lawrence Kohlberg, *The Philosophy of Moral Development* (San Francisco: Harper & Row, 1981).
[82]Gilligan, *In a Different Voice,* pp. 7–11.
[83]This is true of *In a Different Voice* and also of a later work, Carol Gilligan, Lyn Mickel Brown, and Annie Rogers, "Psyche Embedded: A Place for Body, Relationships, and Culture in Personality Theory," in *Studying Persons and Lives,* ed. A. Rabin et al. (New York: Springer, 1989), which articulates a process for interpreting the moral concerns of interviewed adolescents by reading and rereading their statements to listen for multiple types of moral frameworks.

The "different voice," an alternative conception of moral problems and responses, vividly expresses a conception of the significance of interconnections between people. Gilligan found that instead of viewing moral conflicts as the results of clashes between autonomous persons, who exist prior to their relationships, some people respond to statements of moral dilemma with concern for the failure of connection, or failure of care.[84]

Gilligan's depiction of the contrasting views of "Jake" and "Amy" has become a classic articulation of the contrast between assumptions of human separation and assumptions of human connection in moral development. Two eleven-year-olds, Jake and Amy, responded to a question devised by Kohlberg about a man named Heinz, who wondered whether to steal a drug he could not afford to purchase in order to save his wife's life. Should Heinz steal the drug? The two children offered strikingly different answers. Jake described the situation as "sort of like a math problem with humans." He then articulated an abstract principle to resolve the problem: life is worth more than money. Jake also distinguished between law, which would punish stealing in this case, and morality, which would express higher obligations. Amy, in contrast, seemed at first to evade the problem: she did not want Heinz to steal the drug, but neither did she want his wife to die. She saw the consequences of the problem in terms of the ongoing relationships between husband and wife. She worried that if Heinz stole the drug, he might land in jail and be unavailable when his wife needed him. Moreover, Amy argued that the druggist should also be drawn into the problem, that his failure to offer the drug was itself a moral failure to respond to the need of another. From this vantage point, the problem was not an abstract conflict of principles or realms of justification but a failure of communication and responsiveness. Heinz should talk with the druggist, or with other people who could help pay for the drug.[85]

Gilligan concludes that Amy saw a world "of relationships rather than of people standing alone, a world that coheres through human connection rather than through a system of rules." On Kohlberg's evaluative scale Amy would seem less mature than Jake, less capable of reasoning abstractly and beyond social conventions. But Gilligan argues that the scale itself, rather than anything in Amy's answer, is defective; indeed, Amy and Jake simply construed the question differently. Their relationships to the interview questions contributed to their understandings and influenced their answers: Jake perceived "a conflict between life and property that can be resolved by logical deduction," while Amy perceived "a fracture of human relationship that must be mended with its own thread."[86] And if Amy failed to see what Jake

[84]This response was characteristic of many but not all female participants, and some males also voiced dominant concerns for relationships. Gilligan's study thus does not assert inherent or even descriptive differences between males and females so much as it posits an alternative perspective that is enabled when the researcher includes women in studies and builds frameworks of analysis from their statements rather than judging them in relation to frameworks constructed with men in mind.

[85]Gilligan, *In A Different Voice*, pp. 26, 28.

[86]Ibid., pp. 29, 31.

perceived, Jake equally failed to see what Amy understood. One presumed human identities forged in connection and imagined an ethic of care; the other presumed an identity of separation and imagined an ethic of rights. In a follow-up interview four years later, Gilligan found Jake willing to express concern about the feelings in the situation, about the relationships between the druggist and the dying woman and between the dying woman and her husband. She noted, however, that Kohlberg's scale would credit no moral growth to Jake's increased sensitivity to these dimensions of the problem.[87]

Gilligan explores the themes of connection and concern for relationships also in interviews with individuals facing choices about whether to abort a pregnancy and in others about what career to pursue. By highlighting concerns for relationships to others, her studies contrast sharply with traditional theories, based on the model of male development, which depict individual autonomy and self-development as the usual destination of a mature person. Women interviewed during their deliberations about abortion expressed conflict and moral struggles chiefly by contrasting what they considered selfish concerns and what they considered to be obligations or responsibilities to others. Some construed the problem as one of personal survival versus social acceptance; others turned to discuss responsibilities to the self as well as to others. Rather than focusing on fulfillment of personal goals, however, the women tended to discuss how to avoid hurting others and how to take on responsibilities to care for others. More mature women also addressed the question of how to find connections with others through a recognition of interdependence that does not deny the self. Once the themes of connection and relationship were named and identified, Gilligan found that these themes also appeared, though with less frequency, in the responses of some males to dilemmas in their lives.[88]

Already implicit in this description of Gilligan's work is a fourth dimension of relational concerns: attention to the relationships between a problem and its context and particularities, rather than preoccupation with abstracting a problem away from its context. This distinction characterized the different responses of Amy and Jake to the Heinz dilemma. It also characterizes Gilligan's own style of reasoning and argumentation. She presents narratives and dialogues developed through the interviewing process; she does not articulate rules or principles of development. She describes the situations of the people interviewed—not only their gender and ages but also their aspirations and self-conceptions—rather than treating their answers as distinct from who they are. When Gilligan considered the meaning of her work for the development of mature moral reasoning, she found that the morality of care and the morality of rights or autonomy converged as the understanding of complexity and context became more sophisticated. In studies of how

[87]"Feminist Discourse, Moral Values, and the Law—A Conversation: The 1984 James McCormick Mitchell Lecture," *Buffalo L. Rev.* 34 (1985), 11, 41–42 (Isabel Marcus and Paul J. Spiegelman, moderators; Ellen C. DuBois, Mary C. Dunlap, Carol J. Gilligan, Catharine A. MacKinnon, and Carrie J. Menkel-Meadow, conversants).

[88]Gilligan, *In a Different Voice*, pp. 64–127.

college graduates change during the first five years after graduation, she found that men and women both move away from commitments to absolutes, whether the absolute is conceived in terms of obligations to care for others or in terms of the rights of autonomy. Both men and women become increasingly aware of the power of both frameworks and the centrality of context to moral decisions: "For both sexes the existence of two contexts for moral decision makes judgment by definition contextually relative and leads to a new understanding of responsibility and choice."[89]

Gilligan's more recent writing has shown how the traditional denial of gender differences in theories of psychological development demanded a radical separation of psyche from body, and how an integration of the self and the body and a study of their interrelations would require remaking conceptions of knowledge, language, and truth, given the reverberations of a relational approach.[90]

Carol Gilligan's work illuminates the persistence and convergence of relational themes in the work of a feminist researcher. Other feminists also display (1) attention to relations between what we know and who we are and where we stand; (2) concern for relationships and wholes rather than parts; (3) interest in human connections rather than posited individual autonomy; and (4) consideration of contexts and particularities rather than of abstractions and generalities. Further, unlike relational thought uninformed by feminist perspectives, feminist work tends to focus also on conflict, power, domination, and oppression as features especially of past relationships between men and women. The relational turn thus represents not a denial of or lack of interest in conflict and disunity but a focus on the interpersonal and social contexts in which these and all other human relations occur. Indeed, feminist work increasingly demonstrates acute sensitivity to the plurality— and divisions—among feminists.[91]

Feminist Histories

In studying the relationship between the knower and the known, feminist historians criticize depictions of the past that exclude women and perpetuate images of the power structures that denied women access to levers of authority. In efforts to recover the untold stories of women's experiences, feminists, like scholars of black history, have discovered leaders, inventors, and other contributors to public life whom traditional historians simply neglected

---

[89]Ibid., p. 166. And "in women's development, the absolute of care, defined initially as not hurting others, becomes complicated through a recognition of the need for personal integrity. This recognition gives rise to the claim for equality embodied in the concept of rights, which changes the understanding of relationships and transforms the definition of care. For men, the absolutes of truth and fairness, defined by the concepts of equality and reciprocity, are called into question by experiences that demonstrate the existence of differences between other and self. Then the awareness of multiple truths leads to a relativising of equality in the direction of equity and gives rise to an ethic of generosity and care."

[90]Gilligan, "Psyche Embedded."

[91]E.g., "Feminist Discourse, Moral Values, and the Law" reveals deep disagreements.

because of their own assumptions about gender and race. This work illuminates the contributions of such people as Jane Addams, whose creation of a settlement house in Chicago at the opening of the twentieth century helped to launch a movement of progressive social reform.[92] Addams is a particularly interesting figure because she shared many of John Dewey's views and worked with him in experimental, innovative education programs. Moreover, in her role as a pioneering woman leader, popular public speaker, and author, Addams herself articulated a basis for women's participation in public life which drew on women's traditional roles as wives and mothers. She elaborated the idea that women could be housekeepers for the world, and that women's campaigns for world peace could build on their traditional understandings of the needs of children.[93]

Feminist historians have not only pursued the histories of the exceptional women neglected by other historians but discovered to have been contributors to society on the same terms as their male counterparts; they have also studied the experiences of all women and thereby helped to change the definition of what matters for historical inquiry. They participate with other social historians in challenges to the dominance of political history—defined in terms of who ruled, who fought wars, and who won.[94] By examining family practices and structures, circles of friends, informal reform networks, education, immigrant laborers, and small-scale commercial activities, feminist historians have recovered what previous histories submerged from view and have introduced new questions about the meanings of power, the relations between public and private life, and the historical construction of gender, social roles, and other dimensions of identity.[95]

Such work unsettles the periods used in the past to organize history. No longer are wars or shifts in electoral politics or other indicators of public power the primary markers of historical experience. Instead, reflecting the interests of the researchers, history becomes a terrain for studies of relations between public and private power, along with studies of intimacy, friendship, identity, courtship and marriage, romantic love, child rearing and education, reproduction and contraception, violence and resistance. Historians engaged

---

[92]See Ann Firor Scott, *Making the Invisible Woman Visible* (Urbana: University of Illinois Press, 1984); Katharine Kish Sklar, *Doing the Nation's Work: Florence Kelley and Women's Political Culture, 1880–1930* (New Haven, Conn.: Yale University Press, forthcoming).

[93]Chapter 8 below discusses this movement and also the darker side of Progressive era women's motives to control the conduct of others.

[94]See Gerda Lerner, *The Majority Finds Its Past* (New York: Oxford University Press, 1979); Linda Gordon, Persis Hunt, Elizabeth Pleck, Rochelle Goldberg Ruthchild, and Maria Scott, "Historical Phallacies: Sexism in American Historical Writing," in *Liberating Women's History: Theoretical and Critical Essays*, ed. Berenice A. Carroll (Urbana: University of Illinois Press, 1976), pp. 55, 64.

[95]See, e.g., Nancy Cott, *The Bonds of Womanhood: 'Women's Sphere' in New England, 1780–1835* (New Haven, Conn.: Yale University Press, 1977); Carroll Smith-Rosenberg, "Beauty, the Beast, and the Militant Woman," in *A Heritage of Her Own: Toward a New Social History of American Women*, ed. Nancy F. Cott and Elizabeth H. Pleck (New York: Simon & Schuster, 1979); Laurel Uhlrich, *Good Wives: Image and Reality in the Lives of Women in Northern New England, 1650–1750* (New York: Knopf, 1982), p. 197.

in this work also devise new scales to measure previously hidden achievements by women and new conceptions of power and authority representing women's experiences. In addition, because many have acted with careful self-consciousness about the impact of their own interests on what they study, they have addressed history itself as an area struggle over whose perspective on reality can be acknowledged by others.[96] Rather than accepting the traditional aspiration of "objective" history, feminist historians—while debating among themselves—have self-consciously discussed the relationship between who they are and their historical studies.[97]

By attending to their own perspectives and by researching and writing about both women leaders and "anonymous" women neglected in traditional accounts, feminist historians have exposed and altered the relationships between historians and historical narratives. They have examined relationships between the knower and the known even more profoundly, however, by studying gender as a socially constructed category for defining experience. Rather than taking gender or women's experience for granted, feminist historians have inquired into the many meanings of gender across time, place, class, ethnicity, religion—across all the circumstances in which women have found themselves. Depicting gender itself as variable, and as both an idea with shifting content and a process for producing social and personal meaning, feminist historians pursue the social construction of a fundamental category of human experience and suggest how experiences even at this level change through human action. Moreover, because they do not accept as immutable women's traditional roles and devalued status, they challenge explanations for women's circumstances that treat women as passive victims—and also contest narratives that assign sole responsibility to the women themselves on the basis of their biology or their psychology.[98] Feminist historians have investigated historical relationships between social structures and the development of individual identity, and between material circumstances and ideologies.

Efforts to recover the experiences of women neglected by traditional histories also have illuminated feminist concerns for relationships in fields where women have worked with little previous public acclaim. For example, sensitivity to relationships between a knower and the known is coupled with attention to wholes and relations among parts in Evelyn Fox Keller's study of

[96]Feminists thus alter the usual categories of analysis and the sources gleaned for evidence; see Lerner, *The Majority Finds Its Past.*

[97]See, e.g., Margaret Forster, *Significant Sisters: The Grassroots of Active Feminism* (London: Secker & Warburg, 1984), p. 9: "A history ought to be objective and not prejudiced by the historian intruding. But in this particular case it seems to me not only justifiable but also relevant that I should state where I stand. (Researching the material for this book has in fact radically altered where I *do* stand.)"

[98]Gordon et al., "Historical Phallacies," pp. 55, 70. See Linda Gordon, *Heroes of Their Own Lives: The Politics and History of Family Violence, Boston, 1880–1960* (New York: Viking, 1988); and Elizabeth Pleck, *Domestic Tyranny: The Making of Social Policy against Family Violence from Colonial Times to the Present* (New York: Oxford University Press, 1987).

the corn geneticist Barbara McClintock.[99] A member of the first generation of women to attend college, McClintock further distinguished herself by studying genetics in the 1920s. Keller recounts a familiar story of the established academy's refusal to open for a woman the usual channels to success. The scientific community denied her the career path open to her male counterparts, resisted her discoveries, and marginalized her work.

Besides reclaiming an important place for McClintock's accomplishments, Keller probed her reasoning processes and found evidence there of a strikingly relational mind. McClintock's central insights, resisted for generations but now receiving renewed admiration, rejected the method of scientific analysis that concentrates on the properties and behaviors of particular genes, removed from the organism as a whole and distinct from its process of growth. Studying generations of corn and looking to each detail as a clue to the whole, McClintock developed an idea, which she called "transposition," about how chromosomes could rearrange their parts or activate parts of their genetic materials at different times. Her method depended on developing and maintaining a direct recognition of the relationship between chromosomal structure and a plant's actual characteristics, and attending to the plants' continuing process of growth, change, and replication.[100]

In the 1940s McClintock observed a particular pattern of variegation that mutated differently from the rest of the plant, and she discovered behind this pattern a process of cell division that gave one cell what the other one lost. She traced this process to a system within the plant that signaled controls to different parts of the chromosomal structure. These discoveries emerged because of McClintock's focus on the relationships between cells and between patterns in parts of the plant and the nature of the plant as a whole. She detected a feedback system that could better explain mutations than reigning theories, which emphasized the separateness of each part of the plant and each part of its genetic makeup. James Watson and Francis Crick subsequently won the Nobel prize for determining that DNA carries and communicates genetic information not in the variety of its bases but in their sequences, in their relationships to one another. But McClintock's work remained neglected and discounted for many more decades.

McClintock's own account of her methods, as quoted in Keller's book, offers fascinating statements of her sense of her own relationship to what she studied, as well as elaborations of her focus on the relationships between parts and wholes. She described a critical moment when she discovered that she had to "reorient herself" in order to integrate what she saw and, indeed, had to see the things she looked at as close to her, like friends or even like part of herself. She, and any observer of living things, needed to develop a "feeling for the organism": if the observer would remain open to what the organisms

[99]Evelyn Fox Keller, *A Feeling for the Organism: The Life and Work of Barbara McClintock* (San Francisco: W. H. Freeman, 1983).

[100]See ibid., pp. 92–97, 123.

have to say, she claimed, scientists could develop a new way to understand how cell processes integrate and at the same time yield variety and complexity. She opposed any reasoning that distanced objects from their contexts and called for conceptions of relationships and understandings of whole. Through these new ways of thinking, she said, "we're going to have a completely new realization of the relationship of things to each other."[101]

Evelyn Fox Keller, herself a physicist and molecular biologist, explains that what McClintock came to see depended upon her own perspective and her own private vision. Other scientists, as members of a close scientific community sharing tacit assumptions that imposed "unconscious boundaries between what is thinking and what is not," resisted her work. McClintock blamed their faulty assumption that there would be one central explanation for the genetic workings of an organism on their failure to see clues to the interactive and interrelated parts of the organisms they observed. Keller compared McClintock's conception of the wholeness of what she studied with the thinking of such atomic physicists as Einstein and Bohr, who called upon Eastern philosophy for images of harmony and human understanding.[102] Attention to relationships between parts and wholes and between the observer and the observed can provide important correctives to the limitations of scientific methods that subdivide the parts and lose sight of the wholes.

Feminist Literary Theory

Feminist strategies for analyzing literature through deconstructive methods also exemplify attention to the relationships between parts and wholes— relationships that further implicate the observer and the observed, abstraction and particularity, theory and practice, self and other. Barbara Johnson's work is emblematic. A professor of French and comparative literature, Johnson explains that her goal is to "recontextualize a certain way of reading." She defends and employs the strategies of deconstructive literary interpretation associated with Jacques Derrida and Paul de Man, but she locates the interpretation of texts within the context of political power relationships in her society.[103] She asks, "How can the study of suppressed, disseminated, or marginalized messages within texts equip us to intervene against oppression and injustice in the world?" The literary text and the process of interpreting it are part of a larger whole, a cultural world. Johnson has argued for a method of reading that does not seek answers but instead pursues "new questions and new ways in which the literary and nonliterary texts alike can be made to read and rework each other." The search for openness and the effort to

---

[101]Ibid., pp. 117, 101, 207.

[102]Ibid., pp. 150, 178, 204.

[103]Barbara Johnson, *A World of Difference* (Baltimore, Md.: Johns Hopkins University Press, 1987), p. 6. Johnson also considers French society, as when she analyzes both the text and the French editors' notes to Molière's *School for Wives*, which is used, she explains, in French high schools to help inculcate prevailing attitudes toward gender, sexuality, and education.

unsettle meanings is for Johnson a political practice and must include the economic and social relations and the institutional underpinnings of those people doing the interpreting.[104]

Even given this challenge to traditional literary analysis, Johnson warns, readers may reach such a level of comfort and ease that they fail to encounter what is "other" in any text: what can surprise or what can remind the reader that there are other persons, other ways of knowing, other experiences that the reader does not control. From the fact that the knower influences the known, readers should draw an obligation to encounter their ignorance rather than to usurp a text with their own meanings. The strategies of reading must become surprising all over again. Johnson concludes that "if I perceive my ignorance as a gap in knowledge instead of an imperative that changes the very nature of what I think I know, then I do not truly experience my ignorance."[105] That is, the gaps in the reader's knowledge are parts of a whole—but the reader may mistakenly think the whole is his or her knowledge, albeit with missing information to be filled in, whereas instead, the whole is the process of encountering what is outside the reader's experience directly enough to challenge his or her prior knowledge and frameworks for understanding. Rather than thinking we comprehend an allegory, for example, we should consider that we are already comprehended by it.[106]

Johnson and other deconstructive critics dispute the very idea of "woman" and any claim to know women's experience. Such claims amount to another form of reduction, simplification, and domination, denying the multiplicity and variety of experience. Just as dominant modes of interpretation have tended to exclude women, new assertions of feminist interpretation risk fitting variety into a new and misleading unity. Johnson thus rejects unification—the idea that disparate parts can fit into and be subsumed in some whole—as unacceptable simplification and as a fantasy of domination, not understanding. She identifies the task of the writer rather as narrating both the appeal and the injustice of universalization, through an endless process of relating the whole to particulars or the general to the individual.[107] As an example, she looks at the opening paragraphs of Zora Neale Hurston's novel *Their Eyes Were Watching God*, which move subtly from seemingly universal language describing man's experience to particularizing language describing, first, women in general, then the novel's protagonist, and finally, the group in the community ready to gossip about her.[108] Rejecting universals and cele-

---

[104]Johnson, *World of Difference*, pp. 7, 14–15.

[105]Ibid., p. 16.

[106]I cannot begin to describe the layers of nuance in Johnson's discussion of this insight in connection with two of Baudelaire's prose poems that are allegories of figure and yet focus on disfigurement (ibid., pp. 100–115). Similarly multileveled and shimmering with suggestion is her analysis of the relationships between psychological experience and images of the inside of a house in a work by Zora Neale Hurston (pp. 162–71).

[107]Ibid., p. 46.

[108]"Ships at a distance have every man's wish on board. For some they come in with the tide. For others they sail forever on the horizon, never out of sight, never landing until the Watcher turns his eyes away in resignation, his dreams mocked to death by time. That is the life of men.

brating particularity, Johnson alerts the reader to the risk of asserting differences between people without paying attention to the social relationships within which difference is declared.[109]

For Johnson and other feminist theorists, knowledge cannot be secured simply by adding up information to fill in gaps. Instead, knowledge emerges when individual people challenge frameworks of understanding. A sense of other persons cannot be obtained simply by comparing them with oneself; one must also reconsider oneself in relation to the other. Johnson's attention to how parts and wholes depend on each other includes, then, sensitivity to the relations between knower and known and between abstractions and particularities. Moreover, her method of inquiry helps to explore the ways in which individual identities implicate and are implicated in networks of relationships with others. Studying the relationship between addresser and addressee—between writer and reader—in women's poetry about abortion, Johnson notes the use of apostrophe, the rhetorical ploy through which a first-person speaker addresses an absent, dead, or inanimate being. By making the absent fetuses present, the poems imply their humanness and yet also imply that the poet's creative product can exist only because of their absence. The very mode of address implies relationships, and "rhetorical, psychoanalytical, and political structures are profoundly implicated in one another."[110]

These concerns are mirrored in Johnson's attention to the connection between literary interpretation and political life. She addresses the charge from left-wing critics that because deconstructive strategies make language seem "undecidable," these strategies are "politically suspect as an oppositional strategy."[111] She offers in response an allegory by Charles Baudelaire in which the poet "pictures himself as a philosopher testing out a theory of human dignity by beating up a beggar until the latter begins to defend

---

"Now, women forget all those things they don't want to remember, and remember everything they don't want to forget. The dream is the truth. Then they act and do things accordingly.

"So the beginning of this was a woman, and she had come back from burying the dead. Not the dead of sick and ailing with friends at the pillow and the feet. She had come back from the sodden and the bloated; the sudden dead, their eyes flung wide open in judgment.

"The people all saw her come because it was sundown" (Zora Neale Hurston, *Their Eyes Were Watching God* [1937; Urbana: University of Illinois Press, 1978], p. 9). Johnson explains this passage as "a brilliant and subtle transition from the seduction of a universal language through a progressive de-universalization that ends in the exclusion of the very protagonist herself" (*World of Difference*, p. 170).

[109] Johnson also interprets Zora Neale Hurston's essay "What White Publishers Won't Print," finding in the work of this often neglected black female author of the Harlem Renaissance the argument that white publishers do not want to publish writings that portray the Negro as just like anyone else, given "the public's indifference to finding out that there is no difference. Difference is a misreading of sameness, but it must be represented in order to be erased. The resistance to finding out that the other is the same springs out of the reluctance to admit that the same is other. If the average man could recognize that the Negro was 'just like him,' he would have to recognize that he was just like the Negro" (*World of Difference*, p. 178). Unfortunately, Johnson uses "average man" to signify white man, presuming therefore the norm that would make a black man not average.

[110] Ibid., pp. 184–99.

[111] Ibid., p. 25. Johnson points out the commonalities between her approach and those of John Dewey and Charles Peirce (pp. 25–26).

himself, then signaling to him that the discussion is over, since the two combatants are now equal. The unexamined authority of theory—of language—is here acted out as the power to turn violence into a declaration of equality."[112]

Through examples like this one, Johnson advances the idea that examining the ambiguities within texts is not apolitical; in fact, it permits a greater challenge to the established order than would a theory assigning everything a clear meaning.[113] Here, Johnson draws a direct connection with feminist politics, which redefines what is deemed political by moving from abstract argument to the texture of daily, historical social relations. Searching for the multiple meanings within literary texts and the meanings suppressed or hidden by them, then, parallels political struggles to validate in daily life the perceptions of the relatively powerless. The task of feminist literary criticism, informed by deconstructive strategies, is not to unearth the attitudes about women, gender, and sexuality buried in texts but to explore the hiding and the silences as parts of the whole. Rather than seeking a oneness of knowledge, a mastery of the text, feminist postmodern theories challenge knowledge claims that actually close off contradictory or contrasting experiences and viewpoints.[114] Unlike the deconstructive and poststructuralist criticism practiced by some nonfeminists, Johnson's work has insisted on connecting literary interpretation with its social and political consequences and effects; it defends the attention to textual multiplicity explicitly in these terms.[115]

---

[112]Ibid., p. 27.

[113]Ibid., pp. 30–31.

[114]See ibid., p. 85. See also Toril Moi, *Sexual/Textual Politics: Feminist Literary Theory* (London: Methuen, 1985), p. 62: "For if we are truly to reject the model of the author as God the Father of the text, it is surely not enough to reject the patriarchal ideology implied in the paternal metaphor. It is equally necessary to reject the *critical practice* it leads to, a critical practice that relies on the author as the transcendental significance of his or her text."

[115]Contemporary French feminist scholars have similarly attended to the ways that psychoanalytic, political, and literary structures mutually constitute and reconfirm one another; see generally Moi, *Sexual/Textual Politics*. Hélène Cixous, in "The Laugh of the Medusa," trans. Keith Cohen and Paula Cohen, *Signs* 1 (1976), 875–99, has argued against the persistence of such binary contrasts as activity and passivity, male and female, culture and nature, claiming that these conceptual dichotomies reinforce social patterns of male domination; literary critics should instead pursue in texts their open-endedness and multiplicity. Julia Kristeva has rejected the dichotomy between masculine and feminine as anything but a metaphysical relationship. Each of us is the subject of others' language and is thus subject to a shared discourse; at the same time, each is irreducibly different from others. See Julia Kristeva, *Desire in Language: A Semiotic Approach to Literature and Art*, ed. Leon Roudiez, trans. Thomas Gora, Alice Jardine, and Leon Roudiez (New York: Columbia University Press, 1980), pp. ix–x. She advocates explorations of multiple, heterogeneous forms and patterns of identity. Scholars should look to what has been made marginal in relation to a center; women have been made marginal in relation to men, and avant-garde artists are marginal in relationship to the art establishment. Kristeva uses the term "intertextuality" to indicate relationships among systems of signs or meanings in human psychology, in social practices, and in texts studied by scholars. See Tzvetan Todorov and Mikhail Bakhtin, *The Dialogical Principle*, trans. Wlad Godzich (Minneapolis: University of Minnesota, 1984), pp. 60–61. Relationships connect the self and the community through the shared medium of language. Each individual's identity is embedded in patterns of language and social relationships. Each relationship—between people, or between domains of language and society—must be understood as not merely the sum of two distinct parts but the process of mutual

Feminist Psychological and Moral Theories

Feminist psychologists and students of psychoanalysis have worked to articulate theories of the human psyche that emphasize relationships in ways disallowed by orthodox theories. Jane Flax has argued that Freud's theory of internal drives in part reflected his own unconscious motive to deny and repress aspects of children's experiences that are relational because of dependence on the primary caretaker, who is usually a woman.[116] Feminist interpretations of human development in terms of object relations have sometimes, but not often enough, challenged that very phrase, for the "object" typically signifies the parent or other person with whom the child develops a primary bond, and in the course of that relationship the child develops a sense of separateness. I refrain from using the term "object" here and substitute "mother," as this is the person typically implied. Interestingly, women figured prominently in the articulation of relational theories of human development long before Carol Gilligan's work on moral development.[117]

Some of the first women involved in psychoanalysis and interested in child development departed from Freud's teachings. Melanie Klein, for example, studied children directly, whereas Freud's theories of child development derived from reconstructions based on adults' recollections.[118] Where Freud described the power of parents' voices in the child's struggle to develop a superego and resolve the Oedipal crisis, pivotal in Klein's theory is the child's ability to internalize a conception of the mother as a whole person, rather than as partial aspects of the mother that the child likes and does not like. The mother becomes, gradually, no longer simply a vehicle for satisfying the child's needs but an "other" with whom the child develops and maintains intimate personal connection. For Klein, human motivations after this early development in the first year of a child's life pertain more to concerns about this other person (whether real or fantasized) than to innate drives without an "object." The child learns to inhibit aggression and destructive impulses out of care and love for the mother.[119] Klein emphatically maintained chil-

---

construction by the parts in relation to the whole. Strategies of interpretation should pursue multiplicity and disruption rather than mystery and order. There is a considerable risk that this work allows texts and signs to take on lives of their own and downplay or ignore material circumstances. In addition, it is curious that many of the French feminists were not originally French—and yet they subordinate marginality based on ethnicity to the exclusive focus on gender difference. Since many of them expressly propose to make their writing inaccessible and thereby to problematize the process of communication, I hesitate to pursue my criticisms further.

[116]Jane Flax, "Psychoanalysis as Deconstruction and Myth: On Gender, Narcissism, and Modernity's Discontents," in *The Crisis of Modernity: Recent Theories of Culture in the United States and West Germany*, ed. Kurt Shell (Boulder, Colo.: Westview Press, 1966).

[117]Men who played critical roles in founding object-relations theories include W. R. D. Fairbairn, D. W. Winnicott, Heinz Hartmann, Otto Kernberg, and Heinz Kohut. John Bowlby and Michael Balint provided significant original work on the infant need for attachment and for self-experience in connection with others.

[118]Anna Freud also developed studies of children but remained closer to her father's teachings.

[119]Melanie Klein, "A Contribution to the Psychogenesis of Manic-Depressive States," in *Contributions to Psychoanalysis, 1921–1945* (New York: McGraw-Hill, 1964).

dren's abilities to care about and sympathize with others, although her work has been criticized for holding on to a Freudian notion of internal drives originating inside the child and apart from any actual relationships.[120]

Margaret Mahler introduced the achievement of a stable personal identity with realistic perceptions of others as a measure of successful personal development; she thereby shifted concern from the usual psychoanalytic preoccupation with genital issues after resolution of the Oedipus complex. Mahler described the process of development in terms of separation and individuation by the child in relation to a specific other person, the mother: an infant starts with a sense of fusion with the mother but grows by constructing a sense of separate self, in relation to others. The mother, too, must change her stance, from an initial availability to buffer the child from the rest of the world to a more distant relationship with an increasingly autonomous individual. Commentators have observed that Mahler accommodated and renovated earlier Freudian ideas about internal drives as a bridge to later theorists who focused on interpersonal relationships.[121] Mahler's work introduces themes of tenderness, love, and adult human relationships markedly differing from conceptions of the adult as an entirely separate person.

More explicitly feminist versions of object-relations theory, fashioned by Dorothy Dinnerstein and Nancy Chodorow, start with the recognition that the "object" is not only a person but a person with a gender. In a deliberately unsystematic and unscientific book, Dinnerstein assesses the effect of mothering by women on the development of gender identity in both boys and girls.[122] Her work is rich in imagery, references to anthropology, history, literature, and other cultural sources about gender relations. She examines the development of gender identity in preverbal infants and the difficulty of thinking anew about gender relations, given the distinction between male and female that is a critical building block to every aspect of our thinking processes. For Dinnerstein, girls' ability to identify with their mothers as powerful figures while simultaneously retaining a childish dependency contrasts with boys' fears of never being as large or powerful as their fathers and boys' association of separate identity with strength and independence. Dinnerstein locates destructive human relations with nature and between nation states in the historical psychic development of gender identity embedded in fixed gender roles. She advocates male involvement in child rearing to alter the gendered meanings of identity and separation.

[120]Jay Greenberg and Stephen Mitchell, *Object Relations in Psychoanalytic Theory* (Cambridge, Mass.: Harvard University Press, 1983), pp. 147–49.

[121]Ibid., pp. 272, 301. Thus, Mahler herself developed her theory of continuity and change in relation to her predecessors. For her, "One could regard the entire life cycle as constituting a more or less successful process of distancing from and interjection of the lost symbiotic mother, an internal longing for the actual or fantasied 'ideal state of self,' with the latter standing for a symbiotic fusion with the 'all good' symbiotic mother, who was at one time part of the self in a blissful state of well-being" (p. 303, quoting Margaret Mahler, "On the First Three Subphases of the Separation-Individuation Process," *International Journal of Psychoanalysis* 53 [1972], 333, 338).

[122]Dorothy Dinnerstein, *The Mermaid and the Minotaur: Sexual Arrangements and Human Malaise* (New York: Harper & Row, 1976), p. 247.

Because the primary caretaker in most children's lives, historically and at present, has been female, Dinnerstein asks what difference this makes in the development of a sense of separate self for a child who happens to be female and for a child who happens to be male. How does the fact that women mother influence the reproduction of gender identity? Nancy Chodorow, addressing these questions within the more traditional methods of psychology as a discipline, answers that girls develop a sense of themselves as similar to their mothers and forge an identity through attachment, while boys define themselves in opposition or contrast to their mothers and embark upon a "more emphatic individuation and a more defensive firming of experienced ego boundaries."[123] The very sense of self differs, then, for boys and girls, as does their stance toward others. The girl is more likely to emerge with a capacity to experience another's needs and feelings as her own—that is, to empathize; the boy is more likely to assume a stance of distance and even to experience relationships as threatening to the sense of self. Moreover, given the historical division of labor and status on the basis of gender, the boy's separation from the mother includes an identification with the father and the superior male position in economic and political spheres. Thus, his separate identity includes a sense of superiority even in relation to the mother. Like Dinnerstein, Chodorow argues for more involvement by men in the daily care of children as the only way to alter these deep patterns of gender identity formation.

For feminists turning to object-relations psychology, study of the origins of gender identity also carry important consequences for understanding each self as fundamentally forged in connection with others. The sense of oneself as autonomous depends on the development of a trusting relationship with a stable caretaker, as well as internalization of cultural messages about exactly what kind of person one is, with resemblances and differences in relation to specific others.

The feminist turn in moral theory, building on the idea of the self as foundationally connected with others,[124] also illuminates a fourth dimension of relational thought in feminism: the commitment to context and particularity rather than abstraction. Seyla Benhabib, a philosopher trained in critical theory, draws on Gilligan's work to provide an alternative to the argument advanced by George Herbert Mead and Jürgen Habermas that an ethical stance assumes the standpoint of the "generalized other." Benhabib argues that this standpoint "requires us to view each and every individual as a rational being entitled to the same rights and duties we would want to ascribe to ourselves. In assuming this perspective, we abstract from the individuality and concrete identity of the other." Only what is the same among persons, each assumed to be a rational agent, can provide the founda-

---

[123]Nancy Chodorow, *The Reproduction of Mothering: Psychoanalysis and the Sociology of Gender* (Berkeley: University of California Press, 1978), pp. 150, 166. See also Nancy Chodorow, *Feminism and Psychoanalytic Theory* (New Haven, Conn.: Yale University Press, 1989).

[124]Carol Gilligan expressly relies on Chodorow in her studies of moral development; see *In a Different Voice*, pp. 7–9.

tion for ethical treatment: "Our relation to the other is governed by the norm of *formal reciprocity*" and accompanied by the moral categories of right, obligation, and entitlement.[125]

This approach, Benhabib claims, cannot secure the vision of universal equality and reciprocal ethical relations that it supposedly advances. The notion of the generalized other surreptitiously identifies the experiences of a subgroup, usually white adult males, with the experiences of all and thus tends to deny the differences among people while removing from moral concern questions of each individual's most significant relationships to others. Moral reasoning premised upon "learning to recognize the claims of the other who is just like oneself" proves disabling in the face of claims by others unlike oneself. Moreover, the idea that each person stands alone before acquiring goals or desires is incoherent, since the development of a sense of self, limits, and choices occurs only in relation to others.[126]

Benhabib proposes instead assuming the standpoint of the "concrete other," which "requires us to view each and every rational being as an individual with a concrete history, identity, and affective-emotional constitution." Then the distinctiveness of the other, rather than the sameness across all people, becomes a central focus. The important question is what are the needs, motivations, desires of that particular person. This remedies the exclusion of "our affective nature" from moral theory and the corresponding inability to treat human needs and desires through anything except abstraction and silence. Agreeing with Gilligan and Chodorow, Benhabib identifies this relational perspective with the experiences of women as currently socialized. But Benhabib would not restrict the argument to women or to the private sphere.[127] She advocates that one should formulate moral reasoning for making decisions only after trying to take the standpoint of the concrete other. Attention to the concrete other would enable each person to expect from and give to the other treatment that makes each one feel recognized and confirmed as a specific individual with specific needs, talents, and capacities. From this idea of the particularity of each person should grow the moral feelings of solidarity, friendship, love, and care. The focus on the concrete other would also allow moral reasoning to include rather than ignore concern for differences between people. Because such differences mean that we cannot know another simply by reflecting on our own experiences, concern for the concrete other requires actual dialogue rather than hypothetical thought processes carried out singly by the moral agent.[128]

---

[125]Seyla Benhabib, *Critique, Norm, and Utopia: A Study of the Foundations of Critical Theory* (New York: Columbia University Press, 1986), p. 340.

[126]Benhabib, "The Generalized and the Concrete Other," pp. 77, 85. Benhabib asserts: "If all that belongs to [people] as embodied, affective, suffering creatures, their memory and history, their ties and relations to others, are to be subsumed under the phenomenal realm, then what we are left with is an empty mask that is everyone and no one" (p. 89).

[127]Benhabib, *Critique, Norm, and Utopia*, pp. 341, 409 n.124.

[128]Benhabib, "The Generalized and the Concrete Other," p. 93. This marks a rejection of Kantian moral theory, which Benhabib describes as treating moral agents "like geometricians in different rooms who, reasoning alone for themselves, all arrive at the same solution to a

Advocates of feminist ethics integrate conceptions of interpersonal relations into notions of moral concern about concrete persons. Two noted
feminist theorists of morality and ethics are Beverly Harrison and Nel Noddings. Harrison's work has relied on Christian traditions, though it challenges their historical emphasis on gender difference and their historical
separation of mind and body. Harrison argues that ethics must reflect on real
women's real experiences before articulating even what may be a moral
problem and what should be a moral response. She has rejected the approach
that starts with abstract principles as wrongly obscuring the variety of
human realities. Christian moral theology must be "answerable to what
women have learned by struggling to lay hold of the gift of life, to receive it,
to live deeply into it, to pass it on," because what is authentic in faith arises
only out of actual human struggles and experiences in the world.[129]

Concern for concrete reality challenges a separation between mind and
body: Harrison has argued that people should view bodies as sources of
moral power and human relationships as primary sources for experiences of
"the divine." Disembodied rationality cannot be the foundation of morality.
Instead, we should understand all knowledge as mediated by bodies, all
reasoning as rooted in feelings, and all meanings as transmitted through a
socially constructed language. Rather than serving as a transparent conveyer
of thought, language expresses and shapes power relationships growing out
of concrete, material conditions. For Harrison, moral reasoning must start
with a recognition that people's lives are interconnected, rather than a presumption that people live disconnected from one another. Moreover, she has
argued for analyzing social problems from the point of view of those on the
underside: women, older people, poor people, lesbians, gay men.[130] Concrete social experience, rather than abstract principle, must be the starting
point for moral reasoning.

Nel Noddings's writing about philosophy and education has similarly
criticized approaches to ethics which establish principles and have a "mathematical appearance"; she recommends a "feminine approach" of caring and
acting with "the memory of being cared for." Ethics should use not detach-
ment but relatedness and responsiveness. The subject of ethics should be not
hypothetical but complex and detailed moral situations. Rules cannot be
counted upon as guides, and treating another as a type instead of as a unique
individual is already to endanger an ethical response. Indeed, we must guard
against switching prematurely from the experience of seeing and feeling to
the more distant process of rational, objective thinking if we want to act on
an ethic of caring. This requires a process of "concretization that is the
inverse of abstraction": instead of deducing answers from principles super-

problem" (p. 91). See also Michelman, "Traces of Self Government," *Harv. L. Rev.* 100 (1986),
1, criticizing Ronald Dworkin, *Law's Empire* (Cambridge, Mass.: Belknap Press of Harvard
University Press, 1986).

[129]See Beverly Wildung Harrison, *Making the Connections: Essays in Feminist Social Ethics*,
ed. Carol Robb (Boston: Beacon Press, 1985), pp. 1–2, 8.

[130]Ibid., pp. 16, 81.

imposed on a situation, moral reasoning should fill out situations with ever more concrete details.[131]

Noddings has claimed that this process is more characteristic of women's reasoning than of men's, and in this sense her work echoes Gilligan's empirical analysis. Central to Noddings's approach is the effort to articulate the stance of a person who cares for another and the stance of the one receiving that care. The caring relationship and the contribution of both people to it represent an experience everyone can recognize and aspire to in a situation of ethical choice. Noddings considers the consequences of this idea for schooling and describes the needs of both students and teachers for dialogue and mutual confirmation.

In sum, feminist theories range from critiques of traditional science to social science, literary theory, philosophy, history, and ethics. Feminist work tends to emphasize the partiality and perversity of social understandings produced from the unstated standpoint of the observer. Some feminist theorists join with other scholars interested in the relational dimensions of knowledge in challenging the pretense of any universal claims about reality or nature, or about the self and others.[132]

Feminism, Relational Thought, and Law

Inspired by the movement for women's rights and by feminist scholarship in other fields, feminist legal scholarship began in the 1970s to challenge the overt exclusion or subordination of women.[133] Legal scholars argued that gender distinctions in law lacked justification for denying equal treatment, given basic similarities between men's and women's abilities and interests. By the late 1970s feminist legal scholarship was specifically criticizing the pretense of neutrality in legal standards that use male experience as the benchmark for universal human experience and, in effect, marginalize women or treat as deviant any difference drawn in relation to men.[134] Some feminist

[131]Nel Noddings, *Caring: A Feminist Approach to Ethics and Moral Education* (Berkeley: University of California Press, 1984), pp. 1, 2–3, 55, 66, 26–27, 36.

[132]See Sandra Harding, *The Science Question in Feminism* (Ithaca: Cornell University Press, 1986), pp. 26–29; Evelyn Fox Keller, *Reflections on Gender and Science* (New Haven, Conn.: Yale University Press, 1985); Jane Flax, "Political Philosophy and the Patriarchal Unconscious: A Psychoanalytic Perspective on Epistemology and Metaphysics," in *Discovering Reality: Feminist Perspectives on Epistemology, Metaphysics, Methodology and Philosophy of Science,* ed. Sandra Harding and Merrill Hintikka (Boston: Reidel, 1983), p. 216.

[133]See Barbara Babcock, Ann Freedman, Eleanor Holmes Norton, and Susan Ross, *Sex Discrimination* (Boston: Little, Brown, 1975). Elizabeth Schneider, "Task Force Reports on Women in the Courts: The Challenge for Legal Education," *J. Legal Educ.* 38 (1988), 87, 89–90, describes the 1972 Symposium on the Law School Curriculum and the Legal Rights of Women.

[134]Lucinda Finley, "Transcending Equality Theory: A Way Out of the Maternity and the Workplace Debate," *Colum. L. Rev.* 86 (1986), 1118; Ann Freedman, "Sex Equality, Sex Differences, and the Supreme Court," *Yale L.J.* 92 (1983), 913; Mary Joe Frug, "Securing Job Equality for Women: Labor Market Hostility to Working Mothers," *B.U.L. Rev.* 50 (1979), 55; Nancy Gertner, "Bakke on Affirmative Action for Women: Pedestal or Cage?" *Harv. C.R.–C.L. L. Rev.* 14 (1979), 173; Sylvia Law, "Rethinking Sex and the Constitution," *Pa. L. Rev.* 132

legal scholars have sought to validate women's experiences and differences as
new starting points for equality analysis;[135] others emphasize the systematic,
gender-based oppression and subordination embedded in both social structures and the legal rules available to challenge them.[136] Some have urged
reflection on women's experiences as the grounding for legal norms and legal
strategies;[137] others have explored images of women in legal texts as powerful, unstated messages and frameworks affecting decisions.[138] In both kinds
of work, feminists challenge the presupposition that there is a neutral norm
against which to judge experience, and the accompanying assumption that
male experience and perceptions conform to that neutral norm.

Little of the feminist work in law has yet reached beyond the legal treatment of women to deal with other issues.[139] Yet relational ideas of the self

(1984), 955; Christine Littleton, "Reconstructing Sexual Equality," *Calif. L. Rev.* 75 (1987),
1267; Frances Olsen, "Statutory Rape: A Feminist Critique of Rights Analysis," *Tex. L. Rev.* 63
(1984), 387; Catharine MacKinnon, "Feminism, Marxism, Method, and the State: Toward
Feminist Jurisprudence," *Signs* 8 (1983), 635; Ann Scales, "The Emergence of Feminist Jurisprudence: An Essay," *Yale L.J.* 95 (1986), 1373.

[135] Carrie Menkel-Meadow, "Portion in a Different Voice: Speculations on a Women's Lawyering Process," *Berkeley Women's L.J.* 1 (1985), 39; Kenneth Karst, "Women's Constitution,"
Duke L.J. 1984 (1984), 447; Herma Hill Kay, "Equality and Difference: The Case of Pregnancy," *Berkeley Women's L.J.* 1 (1985), 1; Paul Spiegelman, "Court-Ordered Hiring Quotas
after Stotts: A Narrative on the Role of the Moralities of the Web and the Ladder in Employment
Discrimination Doctrine," *Harv. C.R.–C.L. L. Rev.* 20 (1985), 339; Robin West, "Women's
Hedonic Lives," *Wis. Women's L.J.* 3 (1987), 81.

[136] Ruth Colker, "Anti-Subordination above All: Sex, Race, and Equal Protection," *N.Y.U. L.
Rev.* 61 (1986), 1003; MacKinnon, "Feminism, Marxism, Method, and the State"; Janet Rifkin,
"Toward a Theory of Law and Patriarchy," *Harv. Women's L.J.* 3 (1980), 83; Diane Polan,
"Toward a Theory of Law and Patriarchy," in *The Politics of Law: A Progressive Critique,* ed.
David Kairys (New York: Pantheon Books, 1982), p. 294.

[137] Elizabeth Schneider, "The Dialectic of Rights and Politics," *N.Y.U. L. Rev.* 61 (1986), 589;
Catharine MacKinnon, *Sexual Harassment of Working Women: A Case of Sex Discrimination*
(New Haven, Conn.: Yale University Press, 1979), pp. 233–35.

[138] Leslie Bender, "A Lawyer's Primer on Feminist Theory and Tort," *J. Legal Educ.* 38 (1988),
3; Mary Joe Frug, "Re-Reading Contracts: A Feminist Analysis of a Contracts Casebook," *Am.
U.L. Rev.* 34 (1985), 1065; Clare Dalton, "An Essay in the Deconstruction of Contract Doctrine," *Yale L.J.* 94 (1985), 997.

[139] Recent scholarship has addressed gender and law teaching; see, e.g., Patricia Cain, "Teach-
ing Feminist Legal Theory at Texas: Listening to Difference and Exploring Connections," *J.
Legal Educ.* 38 (1988), 165; Catharine W. Hantzis, "Kingsfield and Kennedy: Reappraising the
Male Models of Law School Teaching," *J. Legal Educ.* 38 (1988), 155; Sallyanne Payton,
"Releasing Excellence: Erasing Gender Zoning from the Legal Mind," *Ind. L. Rev.* 18 (1985),
629; Toni Pickard, "Experience as Teacher: Discovering the Politics of Law Teaching," *U.
Toronto L.J.* 33 (1983), 279; Jennifer Jaff, "Frame-Shifting: An Empowering Methodology for
Teaching and Learning Legal Reasoning," *J. Legal Educ.* 36 (1986), 249. Ann Scales has recently
turned to issues of pacifism; see her "Feminism and Peace" (University of New Mexico School of
Law, unpublished manuscript, 1988). Mari Matsuda's work importantly combines feminist
methods with attention to minority race experiences; see "Looking to the Bottom: Critical Legal
Studies and Reparations," *Harv. C.R.–C.L. L. Rev.* 22 (1987), 323. Interestingly, work that
began as a critique of the treatment of women in a given legal area has also turned to more
broadly gauged analyses of those fields. See, e.g., Bender, "Lawyer's Primer," p. 3; Lucinda
Finley, "A Break in the Silence: Including Women's Issues in a Torts Course," *Yale J. Law &
Feminism* 1 (1989), 41. Margaret June Radin, "Market-Inalienability," *Harv. L. Rev.* 100
(1987), 1849, a critique of commodification, includes distinctively feminist concerns. And
Robin West has powerfully employed feminist strategies to critique patterns of arguments

and relational theories of knowledge and reasoning offer much to legal thought and to the legal treatment of "differences" that include but are not limited to gender differences. Explicit relational strategies may contribute to the legal treatment of disabled persons and of members of racial and religious minorities—or even to legal theories of rights and of the relationships between branches of government (see Part III).

For legal analysis, relational approaches may best be articulated as imperatives to engage an observer—a judge, a legislator, or a citizen—in the problems of difference: *Notice* the mutual dependence of people. *Investigate* the construction of difference in light of the norms and patterns of interpersonal and institutional relationships which make some traits matter. *Question* the relationship between the observer and the observed in order to situate judgments in the perspective of the actual judge. *Seek out* and *consider* competing perspectives, especially those of people defined as the problem. *Locate* theory within context; *criticize* practice in light of theoretical commitments; and *challenge* abstract theories in light of their practical effects. *Connect* the parts and the whole of a situation; *see* how the frame of analysis influences what is assumed to be given.

Some lawyers and judges have already drawn on relational insights, especially in legal challenges to socially assigned statuses that yield isolation and stigma. I have called hints of this development the social-relations approach in several Supreme Court opinions in the Cleburne case. There, Justice Stevens and Justice Marshall, in different ways, questioned the assignment of difference that the community had treated as obvious. They sought out the perspective of the mentally retarded persons involved and considered the isolation and stigma those persons had experienced because of zoning restrictions. They looked at the social practices that had isolated mentally retarded people and allowed fears about them to grow. They questioned the motives, self-interest, and misconceptions behind the zoning ordinance. They asked why members of the residential community did not want a group of mentally retarded people living in their midst and what the objections indicated about relationships in this community.

Some may doubt the utility of a judicial review of such questions. What can or should a court do with the perception that neighborhood residents are frightened and uncomfortable about living close to people who seem different? What good will talking about this do? The hope of relational approaches is that if we talk about these things, the people behind the labels will become more vivid to those who would exclude them. The community's negative attitude toward those they call different will be itself conceived as part of the problem, rather than as an immutable given.[140] Notions of difference will no longer be the end but rather the beginning of an inquiry about how all people, with all their differences, should live.

---

between feminist theorists and between feminist and other legal theorists; see "Jurisprudence and Gender," *Chi. L. Rev.* 55 (1987), 1.

[140]Cf. the law-and-economics approach, Chapter 6 above.

One month after the Supreme Court ruled that the city of Cleburne could not deny the permit, Community Living Concepts, Inc. (formerly Cleburne Living Center, Inc.) did open a group home, and the resistant neighbors began to turn around. Some even started to call the residents of the home "good neighbors."[141] The dentist with an office across the street, who had initially spearheaded the drive against the group home, now contracted to provide dental work for the residents. He subsequently retired and sold his practice to a younger dentist, who provides services not only to the residents across the street but to residents of all the group homes run by Community Living Concepts. Similarly, a pharmacist who signed the petition in opposition to the original home obtained the business of the residents who need prescription medication. The residents, who are all mentally disabled, walk around the neighborhood, visit the parks and the shops, and have had no problems with the neighbors—or vice versa. Community Living Concepts has since opened three additional group homes, and the residents of these, too, have integrated well in their neighborhoods. Because of their new community relationships, they already have self-identities different from those they had before. And so do the people who would have excluded them.[142]

Looking Ahead

Part II of this book has introduced three approaches to the legal treatment of difference and located each one in distinct histories of ideas and social practices. Another way to describe them is to explain how each deals with solutions to problems.

The abnormal-persons approach converts the problem of legal treatment of persons into an either/or construction: a given individual should be treated like a normal person or else like an abnormal person. There are two, and only two, solutions, each defined in reference to the other.

The rights approach enables advocates to challenge initial answers that otherwise would take this either/or form: asserting the rights of a disabled person, for example, can challenge the exclusion of that person from the community inhabited by "normal" people. Yet the rights approach still permits different treatment for those who are "really different" or who, in the minds of decision-makers, have traits that continue to distinguish them from the majority. In a sense, the rights approach also preserves the either/or construction of the problem: it allows people to move the line between the

[141]On February 10, 1988, the parties to the suit reached an out-of-court settlement; the city paid damages amounting to the cost of attorneys' fees and lost profits from the time of the denial of the permit in 1980 until the opening of the residence. Information here is based on a conversation with Jan Hannah, president of Community Living Concepts, on February 22, 1988. Thanks to Jim Rasband for this research assistance.

[142]In many communities, people who plan to open group homes for mentally disabled persons, juveniles, or others otherwise subject to institutionalization have found ways to build relationships within the community in advance, thus avoiding legal or less formal hostilities.

norm and the abnormal but maintains the idea of the distinction and its legal consequences.

The social-relations approach, in contrast, questions the construction of the problem in either/or terms. A concern with relationships should alert a decision-maker to the power expressed in the process of categorizing people, or problems. Relational concerns also illuminate the dependence of the alternative solutions on one another: the exceptional treatment depends upon a norm that can itself be questioned. Further, the relational approach invites a focus on context and particularity; it resists solution by category.

Each of these approaches persists in contemporary legal debates about the treatment of people who have been or could be identified as "different." Why do all three endure, and what are their strengths and weaknesses? The abnormal-persons approach endures through the power of labels and categories to simplify what otherwise might seem overwhelming confusion and disorder. Assigning difference to the "different" person and keeping undisclosed the norm used for comparison, the abnormal-persons approach also treats as unproblematic the perspective from which difference is perceived. By deeming some people abnormal, it makes sources of knowledge about differences among people unproblematic and makes assignments of difference seem obvious and natural. Reinforced by social institutions built on these same assumptions, the abnormal-persons approach offers no vantage point from which to criticize current practices and enables inquiry only into whether the legal treatment of people fits or departs from historic schemes of differential status. The perspective of those who have been named "different" is thought to be inconceivable—and irrelevant. Compared with rights analysis, the abnormal-persons view appears to deny rights and to obscure that denial in the name of care or protection for dependent people. It shares with a relational approach a concern for human relations rather than presumptive autonomy, but it imposes a static, hierarchical set of relations that reinforce existing distributions of power. At the same time, it seems to provide certainty by reinforcing people's prejudices about those who differ from themselves.

Rights analysis offers the possibility of individualized solutions. For example, sites for group homes for deinstitutionalized persons have often been sought in neighborhoods of middle-class blacks or other minority groups, who in turn may protest that their property values will decline just as they are beginning to "make it" in America. The objecting minorities see continuing prejudice against them contributing to decisions about the location of homes for still others against whom there is widespread prejudice. In the face of such disputes, the rights approach is appealing. It offers a way to criticize any prejudices that interfere with treating "different" people like anyone else. But as this example suggests, rights analysis leaves in place the larger patterns that define the mentally retarded as inferior and devalue property where they live. The property in middle-class white neighborhoods is already too expensive to be acquired for the group homes, and the political battles are perhaps too difficult. Thus, rights analysis provides incremental reforms but leaves the larger sources of the problem in place.

Rights can also be asserted on conflicting sides of a dispute: advocates for deinstitutionalized persons can advance their right to move into a neighborhood; the minority homeowners can claim a right to be no more valuable to an "undesirable" development than members of any other neighborhood. Rights analysis enables people to assert their similarities to others and thus permits different groups to express competing claims of similarity in reference to preferred legal treatments.

Most fundamentally, rights analysts face the dilemma of attempting to justify both equal and special treatment. Rights help those who can analogize themselves to independent persons but provide little assistance to those who remain dependent and to those who can achieve independence only through the aid of others. Unlike the abnormal-persons approach, rights analysis treats each individual as a separate unit, related only to the state rather than to a group or to social bonds. With rights arguments, reformers can criticize a social order that imposes hierarchical and fixed statuses or permits the assertion of immutable differences while distributing benefits and burdens on this basis. Yet rights analysis still presumes that real differences can be discerned—or dissolved—under scrutiny. It offers little insight into how an observer constructs what is "real" and poses a special dilemma for those whose differences seem "real" against the backdrop of social institutions and practices that make that difference matter. Rights analysis is also problematic for those who want to preserve their differences yet also claim the power of rights to challenge stigma or exclusion. What kind of sameness must they assert to attain the freedom to be different?

A relational approach, like the abnormal-persons approach, assumes that people live within networks of relationships; but unlike the abnormal-persons view, it challenges fixed status and attributed difference. And unlike rights analysis, the relational approach inquires into the institutional practices that determine a norm against which some people seem different, or deviant. Also unlike rights analysis, relational ideas raise questions about how anyone knows and how the observers' relationship to the observed influences what they think they know. By stressing the unavoidability of perspective, the relational approach makes all claims of knowledge vulnerable to the same charge: "But that's just your view." It encourages more debate and highlights as human choices—rather than acts of discovery—the ways we treat people, the traits we call "different," and the social institutions that embody and reinforce those assumptions. To address relationships is to resist abstraction and to demand context.

Nevertheless, relational approaches too confront objections and potential misunderstandings.

A Misunderstanding and a Restatement

One misunderstanding arises when scholars try to accommodate the feminist notions of care, borrowed particularly from Gilligan's work. Doing so risks a kind of simplistic and wooden reasoning, and it is especially disappointing if the tactic simply injects compassion or sympathy into an otherwise resilient structure of legal analysis and institutions. Simply transporting an ethic of care into the legal system can leave in place the system's established rules about what counts as a conflict, its adversary method, and its assumptions about human personality. Moreover, conceptions of care may ignore the significance of power differentials which the legal framework of rights more explicitly acknowledges.[143] Simply adding an emphasis on caretaking responsibility and compassion neglects the profound challenge to conventional legal understandings introduced by the relational methods of feminist theories.

Thus, the challenge presented by feminist strategies is not just to deepen an interest in "responsibility" or "care," contrasted with "fairness" or "rights." The challenge is to maintain a steady inquiry into the interpersonal and political relationships between the known and the knower; a concern for the relations between wholes and parts; a suspicion of abstractions, which are likely to hide under claims of universality what is in fact the particular point of view and experience of those in power; and a respect for particularity, concreteness, reflection on experience, and dialogue. Through these relational themes, feminist methodologies frame the issues in ways that avoid the constraining assumptions behind the dilemma of difference.[144] Both historical and sociological strategies identify "difference" as a function of contingent patterns of relationships; literary and psychological strategies help to articulate the naming of difference in relationships of disparate power.[145] Many feminists urge recasting issues of "difference" as problems of dominance or subordination in order to disclose the social relationships of power within which difference is named and enforced.[146] In sum, feminist strategies question the assignment of difference to the "different person" by locating difference within relationships of differential power.

Further, by questioning the choice of the norm, theory, or context within which difference has been named and assigned, feminist theorists force the

[143]See Schneider, "Dialectic of Rights and Politics"; Lisa Lerman, "Mediation in Wife Abuse Cases: The Adverse Impact of Informal Dispute Resolution on Women," *Harv. Women's L.J.* 7 (1984), 57; and Janet Rifkin, "Mediation from a Feminist Perspective: Promise and Problems," *Law & Inequality* 2 (1984), 21. Carol Gilligan, "Do Changes in Women's Rights Change Women's Moral Judgment?" in *The Challenge of Change: Perspectives on Family, Work and Education,* ed. Matina Horner, Carol Nadelson, and Malka Notman (New York: Plenum Press, 1983), p. 39, shows how women incorporate conceptions of legal rights into conceptions of caretaking and responsibility.

[144]Feminists emphasize the need for multiple accounts and methodologies, given the partiality of any one approach or point of view. See Flax, "Postmodernism and Gender Relations," p. 621; Nancy Fraser and Linda Nicholson, "Social Criticism without Philosophy: An Encounter between Feminism and Postmodernism," in *The Institution of Philosophy: A Discipline in Crisis?* ed. Avner Cohen and Marcelo Descal (La Salle, Ill.: Open Court, 1988); Sandra Harding, "The Instability of the Analytic Categories of Feminist Theory," *Signs* 11 (1986), 645; Deborah Rhode, "Gender and Jurisprudence: An Agenda for Research," *U. Cin. L. Rev.* 56 (1987), 521.

[145]See Dale Spender, *Man Made Language,* 2d ed. (London: Routledge & Kegan Paul, 1985), pp. 163–90.

[146]See Colker, "Anti-Subordination above All"; MacKinnon, "Feminism, Marxism, Method, and the State."

statement of those norms that have remained implicit. What has been taken for granted must be stated. And once stated, norms based on the male experience become a subject for contest; alternative norms can be articulated and defended. For example, "maternal thinking" can be freed from the "private sphere" of family and transposed to the "public sphere" of politics as a basis for critique and reform.[147] Similarly, rather than assuming that women must adjust to a workplace designed for men, one can advocate designing a workplace for both men and women.[148] The idea of an un-situated perspective on issues of difference fails amid repeated demonstrations of the influence of the observer on the observed. Feminist critics note that the legal definitions of rape, for example, adopt a male perspective and ignore female perceptions: thus, the observer's situation influences what is observed.[149] Similarly, previously ignored perspectives become plausible contestants for illuminating and debating the legal treatment of divorce, child custody, domestic violence, and pregnancy and the workplace.[150]

When those who have been considered "different" become the source of information about a critical but previously suppressed perspective on the legal issues affecting them, the social and institutional patterns that ignore this perspective themselves become questionable. The status quo no longer seems natural and inevitable but is revealed instead as a reflection of choices made and choices that can be remade. Individualized solutions that leave the status quo in place—by accommodating one person, or making an exception—no longer appear unproblematic. By challenging the classifications drawn on gender lines that have been taken for granted in legal rules because they mirror social practices, feminist legal theorists open the way for more creative alternatives to the exclusion of or impositions on women based on legal rules that either ignore or acknowledge "their" difference. New strategies include acknowledging more fundamental similarities between people,

[147]See Lynn Henderson, "Legality and Empathy," *Mich. L. Rev.* 85 (1987), 1574; Ruddick, *Maternal Thinking;* and the discussion of Jane Addams in Chapter 8 below.

[148]Doing so would accommodate not only pregnancy and child-care duties but also health and safety features. E.g., employers in industrial settings that have proved hazardous to women's reproductive conditions have refused to hire any woman who would not "voluntarily" agree to sterilization. An alternative to this draconian solution would be to make the workplace safe for women. The additional cost might be warranted not only to avoid charges of discrimination but also because there is some possibility that those settings have been unsafe for men too. See Judith Areen, *Family Law,* 2d ed. (Mineola, N.Y.: Foundation Press, 1985), p. 876.

[149]See Susan Estrich, "Rape," *Yale L..J.* 95 (1986), 1087. Susan Brownmiller has argued that "penetration" is the name for the male experience that a woman might instead call "enclosure" (*Against Our Will: Men, Women, and Rape* [New York: Simon & Schuster, 1977], p. 334). See also Olsen, "Statutory Rape," pp. 387, 424, arguing that pervasive male sexual aggression, rather than women's vulnerability to it, is the problem to be addressed by rape laws.

[150]See Frug, "Securing Job Equality for Women," p. 55; Kathleen Lahey, ". . . Until Women Themselves Have Told All That They Have to Tell . . . ," *Osgoode Hall L.J.* 23 (1985), 519; Nancy Polikoff, "Why Mothers Are Losing: A Brief Analysis of Criteria Used in Child Custody Determinations," *Women's Rights L. Rep.* 7 (1982), 235; Elizabeth Schneider, "Equal Rights to Trial for Women: Sex Bias in the Law of Self Defense," *Harv. C.R.–C.L. L. Rev.* 15 (1980), 623. Women's perceptions may be complicated and may engage women in debates among themselves about equality and victimization. See Martha Fineman, "Implementing Equality: Ideology, Contradiction, and Social Change," *Wis. L. Rev.* 1983 (1983), 789.

such as the interests shared by men and women in combining work and family duties. Another strategy explores the pervasive differences distinguishing each individual and the possibilities of responding to a variety of traits rather than simply classifying people as "normal" or "abnormal."[151] Still another is to devise inclusive solutions: to include within the basic design of social institutions the facilities and treatments that respond to those who have been marginalized in the past.[152]

These strategies are not simply expressions of empathy, altruism, or an ethos of care toward the "different" person. Those impulses may be helpful, but they fundamentally preserve the pattern of relationships in which some people enjoy the power and position from which to consider—as a gift or act of benevolence—the needs of others without having to encounter their own implication in the social patterns that assign the problems to those others.

Feminist psychology highlights each person's dependence on others for a sense of self; feminist literary theory illuminates the reliance of any apparently dominating category on a relationship with what it excludes or devalues. These relational insights show a mutual dependence between "normal" and "abnormal" people, and between male norms and women who do not fit them. Hierarchical pairings that deny the mutual dependence of both elements provide clues to deeper motives that make oppression and degradation seem natural and inevitable. Such patterns deposit on some people the fears of all of us about vulnerability and danger. The relational turn in feminist work asks us instead to examine the connections between what seems disconnected, the larger patterns that conjoin what has seemed different. The conception of each self as fundamentally relational carries implications for the enterprise of judging as well as for the content of norms for judgment.[153] For no longer can the act of judgment—whether done with dispassion or compassion—seem possible from an unsituated perspective or from a person with no relationship to the one being judged. The act of judgment depends on and simultaneously forges a relationship. What qualities that relationship should attain becomes the important question for law, informed by feminist theory.

An Example and New Questions

A short story first published by Susan Keating Glaspell in 1917, "A Jury of Her Peers," illuminates promising and troubling dimensions of relational

---

[151]Attention to language and the hidden assumptions in the prevailing terms of debate also characterize feminist work. See, e.g., Marie Ashe, "Law-Language of Maternity: Discovered Holding Nature in Contempt," *New Eng. L. Rev.* 22 (1988), 521.

[152]Making sidewalks and other facilities accessible to wheelchairs and treating all patients with the precautions suited to someone with the AIDS virus are the examples here. See also Finley, "Transcending Equality Theory"; Christine Littleton, "Equality across Difference: A Place for Rights Discourse?" *Wis. Women's L.J.* 3 (1987), 189.

[153]See Judith Resnik, "On the Bias: Feminist Reconsiderations of the Aspirations for Our Judges," *S. Calif. L. Rev.* 61 (1988), 1877; Robin West, "The Authoritarian Impulse in Constitutional Law," *Miami L. Rev.* 2 (1988), 531.

thought in conjunction with problems of legal rights, legal duties, and legal judgments.[154] In the story, the district attorney and the sheriff go to a farmhouse to investigate a farmer's murder. The sheriff's wife and a friend come along to gather some belongings for the farmer's widow, who is being held in jail as a suspect in the case. While the sheriff and district attorney tramp through the house and barn looking for clues, the two women in the kitchen find themselves imagining the movements of the farmer's wife and reviewing her entire life experience. Through keen observation and efforts to place themselves in her shoes, they locate clues the men would never have discovered: a half-spilled sugar pot; pieces of a quilt with one stretch of poor stitches amid the otherwise careful sewing; an empty birdcage; and a dead pet bird with a broken neck, wrapped in a piece of silk and hidden in a sewing box. From these curious and unobtrusive items—and through their own efforts to identify with the farmer's wife—the two women construct a story of her harsh and lonely life. They imagine how she was badgered by an unsympathetic and cold husband, how she delighted in her pet bird, how her husband strangled the bird, and how she responded with anger, desperation, and finally murder. They blame themselves for never visiting her and thus contributing to her isolation. One of them almost absentmindedly fixes the stitches in the quilt piece, picking up where the farmer's wife left off.

The two women do not always see eye to eye. Indeed, they seem awkward and uncomfortable in exchanging their thoughts. The process of empathizing and identifying with the absent woman, then, is presented as something that obviously takes work, not as the natural result of something that all women always feel toward one another.

The women decide to share neither their clues nor their conclusions with the men. They hide the dead canary and wait quietly while the men belittle as "trifles" their conversation about the quilt pieces. Besides trying to view the world from the perspective of the absent woman and besides discerning facts missed by the men, the two women form a judgment that implicitly distinguishes them from the men. But what is this judgment? Have the women tried the farmer's wife and either excused or exonerated her? I think not. Instead, they conclude that they themselves are implicated in her act, and in her life, by their failures to attend to her needs earlier. Believing that the formal legal system—the men's justice—would not understand what they now understand, they decline to share their knowledge or otherwise assist the men's search for a clinching motive. This does not seem an easy decision for them; especially for the sheriff's wife, someone "married to the law," resistance to the system takes courage.

[154]Susan Glaspell, "A Jury of Her Peers," *Every Week*, Mar. 5, 1917, reprinted in *The Best Short Stories of 1917*, ed. Edward O'Brien (Boston: Small, Maynard, 1918), p. 256. Glaspell, a member of the Provincetown Players, also cast the story as a play called *Trifles*. For analysis by contemporary literary critics, see, e.g., Annette Kolodny, "A Map for Rereading: Gender and the Interpretation of Literary Texts," in *The New Feminist Criticism: Essays on Women, Literature, and Theory*, ed. Elaine Showalter (New York: Pantheon Books, 1985), pp. 46, 55–58. The story has been used as a teaching vehicle for college students, law students, law professors, and judges. See Carol Weisbrod, "Images of the Woman Juror," *Harv. Women's L.J.* 9 (1986), 59.

The women finally decide to deceive even the widow herself through a comforting lie. She had worried about the jam she had just jarred before she was arrested, and the two women find that it has burst and spilled from most of the jars, as sometimes happens. But there is one unbroken jar, and they decide to take it to the widow to assure her that all has gone well.

Glaspell wrote "A Jury of Her Peers" as an argument for allowing women to serve on juries. It may seem a curious argument, however. The story seems to say that women see facts, events, and emotions differently from men, and that women act on values that differ from—that are indeed at odds with— the prevailing justice system run by men. In a sense, the argument underlying the story echoes the ideology of separate spheres: the historical idea that men belong in the public and women in the private sphere and that members of each gender are experts and sovereigns in their separate domains. Until women are allowed to judge women, suggests the story, women should not be judged; a formal legal order that excludes some points of view cannot comprehend those points of view when they do appear. Excluded people should not be judged by the rules of the game but should instead resist the risk of being misunderstood by refusing to participate altogether. Implicit in this conception is the claim that women should be included as jurors because they are different from men, not because they are the same. The story depicts women as profoundly different from men, whether the difference is due to biology or social experience. The women's outlook on the world, their methods of knowing, and their bases for judgment differ from those of the men. Thus, the story explores relationships between knowledge and power, between who does the judging and what that person can and cannot understand. Suppressed points of view may look deviant from the perspective of the dominant system, but the dominant norms may look wrong or insensitive from the perspective of those marginalized by it.

On yet another level, the story suggests that the task of judgment should be not the application of general principles to a problem but instead a process of taking the perspective of another. Those who would judge should reflect on their own relationships to the one they would judge, not just the actions and motives of that other person. Moreover, the story implies that people's actions and motives are formed not autonomously but in relationship to others and may even result from the failure of others to attend to a person who lands in trouble. The desperation of the farmer's wife had something, although not everything, to do with the other women's failure to visit her. The two women use their own positions of relative powerlessness in the formal legal system and in their society to keep silent about what they have discovered and even tell a comforting lie to the widow. They operate according to a moral code different from the prevailing social rules and affirm their own connections to each other in the process.

Some may worry that the story—and many versions of relational thought—condone a kind of relativism, a suspension of judgment about right and wrong. The women seem to excuse or forgive the murder of a man apparently committed by his wife after he killed her pet bird. Even if it does not condone any act, the story does demonstrate the power of contrasting points of view and the power of interpersonal relationships on the qualities of people's lives and on human moral judgments. Like current relational frames in scholarship, the story declares that knowledge and identities are forged in relationship and that meaning is social rather than natural, mutable rather than fixed. Scholars pursuing these themes invite charges of indifference to truth. Once one participant in the debate says, "All claims of knowledge carry a perspective: none is based in an unchanging reality," then anyone else who claims to know an unchanging reality at least becomes vulnerable to the challenge, "What is the perspective that so entitles you or so blinds you to make such a claim?" Once there is more than one point of view, no point of view can be treated as not a point of view. Such relational concerns prompt worries about relativism and worries about obligations without limits.[155] Relational approaches even invite the charge that the relational view itself is simply a point of view. There is no end to a process of continual debate among competing points of view. Relational concerns do not "tell us what to do" in times of conflict and difficulty. The admonition to care and to connect does not dictate whether to lie to the widow or to tell her the truth, whether to hold her responsible for her act or excuse her in some formal or informal way. Indeed, relational approaches reject the whole idea that principles, norms, or abstractions can or should "tell us" anything.

The response defending relational views will not satisfy objectors, because it calls for shifting the frame of reference, the very criterion for judging normative judgments. The response starts by challenging the pretense that abstract norms ever "tell us" what to do. Norms seem clear only when they have subtracted all that makes a given context unique. Norms seem unproblematic only when they implicitly embody, or else ignore, the features of a given context that they leave unstated. The contrasting approach, an emphatic attention to contextual details, does not reject normative considerations or alter them on a premise that any value is as good as another. As the women in "Jury of Her Peers" demonstrate, there can be normative dimensions in a commitment to paying closer attention to the relationship between particular contexts and particular values.[156] Denying the multiplicity of moral perspectives and demands does not make them go away; instead, it marks a rigid either/or thinking that constrains moral understanding.[157]

The editors of a recent volume of essays on this subject put it this way: "But what justifies the relativist in taking the line that there are many truths rather than joining the skeptic in denying the possibility of knowing truth?

[155]Widespread debates about the attractions and risks of relativism have accompanied the recognition of plural sources of knowledge and values in many fields. See, e.g., *Rationality and Relativism*, ed. Martin Hollis and Steven Lukes (Cambridge, Mass.: MIT Press, 1984).

[156]See Jeffrey Stout, *Ethics after Babel: The Languages of Morals and Their Discontents* (Boston: Beacon Press, 1988), pp. 82–105; Charles Larmore, *Patterns of Moral Complexity* (Cambridge: Cambridge University Press, 1987), pp. 1–21.

[157]See Martha Nussbaum, *The Fragility of Goodness: Luck and Ethics in Greek Tragedy and Philosophy* (Cambridge: Cambridge University Press, 1986); Geertz, "Anti-Anti Relativism."

The relativist observes that the absence of criteria for ascertaining a single objective truth does not mean that there are no criteria of truth at all. Instead, societies, methodologies, and individuals have their own criteria of truth. . . . People still do distinguish between what is right and what is wrong, between what is true and what is false."158 Truth becomes relative to a society or an individual.

Besides relativism, relational concerns threaten limitless responsibility for others. If we take seriously the impact we each have on the lives of others, and if we treat any failure to care as morally culpable, there may seem no limits, no way to say no to others.159 Maybe, because people do have the capacity to identify with others and to understand their pain, society devised moral and legal theories in order to limit obligations to care and respond. Relational approaches undermine such limits; they challenge traditional limits by exposing the status quo as humanly constructed and mutable. Relational approaches also disturb the limits of obligation established by legal analysis that takes the competent, adult, white male as the norm and treats others as different and as reasonably treated differently. Equating sameness with equality, rights analysis offers a kind of certainty and a set of limits: equal treatment, yes, but limited to a comparison with the other group. This method provides a minimal check against crudely assigned and degrading categories represented by the abnormal-persons approach. Rights analysis seems to provide a way to set limits on responsibilities without losing a basis for challenging gross unfairness.

But the relational challenge suggests that these limits reflect a particular perspective not because it is correct but because it expresses the world view of those who have had sufficient power to shape prevailing social institutions. Limits on a sense of obligation may work all too well. When social policies turn to a politics of selfishness, denying public responsibility for social problems, those who have the weakest toeholds in the dominant social structure become most vulnerable to poverty and degradation. For people who are members of groups traditionally labeled as "different," these risks are compounded by new forms of paternalism asserted on their behalf. Claims to act on behalf of another have often been used to justify exclusion,

158Introduction to *Relativism: Cognitive and Moral,* ed. Michael Krausz and Jack Meiland (Notre Dame, Ind.: Notre Dame University Press, 1982), p. 3. See also the discussion of William James, Charles Peirce, and John Dewey, above.

159See Nussbaum, *The Fragility of Goodness,* p. 81: "If, for example, we could ever see clearly and be moved by the value of each unique person in the world, we could never without intolerable pain and guilt be able to act so as to benefit any one of them rather than any other—as love, or justice, might in some cases require." Nussbaum elaborates her own statement of the problem with a response that seems comforting because it fits existing social arrangements for parenting children: "If I saw and valued other people's children as I do my own, my own could never receive from me the love, time, and care she ought to have, that is just and right for her to have." The very conventionality of this line may deserve skeptical probing. See generally James Fishkin, *The Limits of Obligation* (New Haven, Conn.: Yale University Press, 1982): obligation seems overwhelming when applied to public and social problems, yet traditional techniques for limiting obligation rest on limited conceptions of individual boundaries.

deprivation, and attributions of difference that stigmatize and hinder acceptance. People may even act in the name of care—in the name of relational
concerns—to specify what others need and to control their behavior and
participation. This kind of charge has been levied against some of the social
reformers at the turn of this century who, under the banner of Progressivism,
implemented ideas spawned by John Dewey, Jane Addams, and other early
advocates of relational thought. And limits on obligation that work through
the rhetoric of rights may obscure the actual patterns of relationships that
rights enforce. When reformers seek to apply the language of rights, taking
the rhetoric of equality and freedom literally, they encounter the dilemma
that rights crafted for the norm reiterate the differences of those at the
margin, and special rights crafted for those at the margin risk perpetuating
the negative effects of difference.

To find a way out of the dilemma of difference, law reformers are borrowing from relational insights developed in many disciplines. It is a new enterprise and one fraught with uncertainty and risk. Pursuing relational themes
in law may threaten the very idea of law as authoritative and commanding; it
may invite new challenges to established justifications for both the exercise
and limitations of coercive state power. Yet compared with prior approaches
toward the legal treatment of difference, the relational turn holds some
promise.

The certainty and limited obligations that in the past accompanied the
abnormal-persons view treated differences as "out there," in a reality that
could be discovered. This view justified exclusion and denigration of people
on the basis of their gender, race, or mental ability. The rights-analysis
approach cast suspicion on attributions of difference if they landed upon
minority groups historically disfavored by majorities, yet the rights approach
retained and confirmed differential treatment if people with the power to
judge believed those differences to be not only real but justification for
distinguishing those with the difference from others. A relational stance
instead challenges the usually unstated point of view of the one who "sees"
differences. Issues about the "reality" of difference fade in light of new
concerns over the meanings and uses of those differences. Differences that
yield social distance and exclusion are likely to be condemned as the self-
serving expressions of the more powerful. The framework for analysis, the
framework that makes some differences salient and others unimportant,
becomes itself a subject for debate, because knowledge itself depends on the
conceptual scheme or point of view employed. Contextual judgments and
acknowledgment of the mutual dependence of people in their construction of
identities and in their fulfillment of daily needs might remedy the defects of
both the abnormal-persons approach and rights analysis. Using relational
insights, reformers may forge tools for renovating the social practices and
institutions that have assigned to some the burdens of all human variety, vulnerability, and need, thereby denying the mutual dependence of humanity.

PART III

RIGHTS IN RELATIONSHIP

CHAPTER 8

Problems in Relationship: Today's Feminism and Yesterday's Progressivism

And though one says that one is part of everything,
There is a conflict, there is a resistance involved;
and being part is an exertion that declines:
One feels the life of that which gives life as it is.
            —Wallace Stevens, "The Course of a Particular"

There is a Chinese fable about two men who were walking along the river. One said to the other, "Look how happy the fish are as they swim in the river!" The other said, "You are not a fish. How do you know whether the fish are happy?" The first one said, "You are not me. How do you know whether I know what the fish think?"

Thinking we are close enough to another to understand poses a risk of presumption. We may wrongly think we know another, yet we may also wrongly doubt anyone's ability to know, or care knowingly, for another. We may object, on this ground, to any efforts at connection and consign ourselves to the impoverished state of disconnection from all except our most intimate companions.

This part of the book considers the risks of presumption in relational approaches and, in light of those risks, reconsiders rights. One theme of this book is that the relational turn can offer law a new model for dealing with problems of difference. It is a relational solution to invite the classmates of a hearing impaired student to learn sign language and thus learn to communicate with her, for this approach remakes the relationships within which she otherwise experiences isolation. It is also a relational approach to reimagine

Epigraph: Copyright 1950 by Wallace Stevens. Reprinted by permission of Alfred A. Knopf, Inc., from "The Course of a Particular," by Wallace Stevens, in *The Harvard Book of Contemporary American Poetry*, edited by Helen Vendler (Cambridge, Mass.: Harvard University Press, 1985).

pregnancy and early child rearing as a normal human activity around which workplace duties should be arranged, rather than to treat the workplace designed with only men in mind as the immutable norm. And it is a relational approach that rejects a community's resistance to a group home for mentally retarded individuals and invites community acceptance once neighbors get to know one another.

These examples all draw upon an assumption that people are fundamentally connected rather than autonomous, that differences between people are to a significant degree socially constructed and changeable, and that theories of difference reiterate assumptions built into societal institutions that also may be reconstructed. Relational approaches are complicated and cannot be reduced to a simple norm or list of principles. Relational concerns cannot be reduced either to an idea of maximizing the utility of the entire group or to an idea of the rights of any individual to participate in school, work, or community on the terms available to other individuals. Nor does a social-relations model for law reject rights; instead, this is a way of remaking rights so that they do not recreate the differences etched by prejudice and misunderstanding into the structures and crevices of inherited institutions.

Stemming from these complications is another of the themes I develop in this part of the book. Relational approaches are risky. Inquiring about interpersonal relationships and about the impact of the observer's situation on what the observer claims to know seems to undermine premises of autonomy and objectivity that have been important in challenges to hierarchical authority. What happens to individualism? What happens to confident claims of right and wrong, to knowing assertions of distinctions and differences? Moreover, relational ideas seem complicated and diffuse. And finally, relational ideas seem to require too many changes, changes in basic vocabulary as well as world view, changes in social structure and architecture. For all these reasons, relational ideas trigger resistance.

This chapter explores three problems presented by such ideas, developed as the social-relations approach. The first problem is that it is difficult to enact. Categorical thought and stereotypes have resilience. They resist renovation. Even people who declare that categories are socially constructed and claim to reject the idea that a person's traits represent an essential nature unwittingly revive formalist thought and stereotypes. For example, feminist scholars have done much to reveal the persistence of faulty assumptions, particularly the assumption that the needs and experiences of men are the standard for individual rights. Yet some feminist analyses have recreated the problems they sought to address, elaborating the idea of "woman's experience" while leaving unstated the race, ethnicity, religion, and bodily condition presumed in identifying "woman's" point of view.

The second problem is that relational concerns are easily misunderstood. Given the enduring reign of a nineteenth-century conception that pitted individualism against organicism—or socialism—we remain today plagued by an either/or construction of the problems of social, political, and economic life: one favors either freedom for each individual or submerging the individual in the whole. This construction, of course, neglects precisely the insights of relational work in many fields. The challenge of relational thought is to pursue a commitment to the mutual interactions between individuals, and between parts and wholes. Absent this concern for interaction, the risks of mistaking the interests of some for the interests of all remain large. A new unstated norm against which some seem different may be created by the very people who set out to expose the power of an unstated norm.

This risk is linked to the third problem: even when pursued fully, relational ideas carry risks for vulnerable people if the underlying patterns of power remain unchanged. Defining procedures and policies that acknowledge people's mutual needs for one another may exacerbate the dependence of those who have historically been more dependent without remaking the underlying social arrangements that produced that pattern. Acts of care may unwittingly express the self-interests or biases of the actor who claims to know what is good for the recipient. Moreover, reforms premised on relational conceptions may actually advance the perspective and needs of those with greater privilege and authority. Developing a method of attending to relationships without losing sight of larger patterns of power will be critical to those who want to redress the legal treatment of difference.

This chapter, therefore, provides a prelude to the book's final chapters, which attempt to integrate the insights of both relational and rights-based analyses. The first part of the chapter looks at feminist theories both as efforts to challenge categorical thought and as evidence of the grave difficulties in doing so. The second part focuses on reforms advocated by leaders in the Progressive era in the United States, from about 1890 to 1930. Many Progressives espoused views that resemble the relational approaches advocated in this book, and they established institutions that seemed to pursue a commitment to community responsibility for problems of poverty, pregnancy, and delinquency. Yet by failing to alter the dominant ideology of individualism the Progressives limited their own capacity to protect even the changes they won. Moreover, many remained wedded to preserving social patterns that contributed to injustices they claimed to want to redress. The examples explored here illuminate the differences between Progressive reforms and the approaches advocated in this book.

Why Relational Insights Slip Away

Theorists and reformers have asserted that members of many groups have been wrongly labeled as different, that their perspectives have been ignored, and that the status quo can and should be changed. Yet the critics often repeat in new contexts a version of the old assumptions they set out to contest. This problem has appeared even in the work of feminists who have contributed to contemporary critiques of assigned differences.

Indeed, feminist scholars have developed incisive critiques of the unstated assumptions behind political theory, law, bureaucracy, science, and social science. In field after field their work exposes the dominance of conceptions of human nature which take men as the reference point and treat women as "other," "different," "deviant," "exceptional" or "baffling."[1] Feminist work has thus named the power of naming and has challenged both the use of male measures and the assumption that women fail by them. For example, feminists have challenged the stereotypes of women as dependent, weak, passive, and incapable of engaging in public governance, analytic scholarship, or physical labor. They have also disputed the assumption that traditionally "female" traits such as nurturing ability, emotional expression, and empathy are less worthy than such traditional "male" traits as aggression, stoicism, and individual autonomy; in fact, feminists have criticized autonomous individualism as a male construct and have argued that the development of interpersonal and social relations is critical to personal development.[2]

If, at times, feminists appear contradictory in this sense—if they argue that women have both the right to be regarded and treated like men and the right to special treatment or valorization of women's differences[3]—they offer an explanation: the inconsistencies lie in a world and set of symbolic constructions that have simultaneously used men as the norm and demeaned any departure from the norm; hence, feminism demands a dual strategy. First, feminists challenge the assumption of female inferiority: the belief that women fall too short of the unstated male norm to enjoy male privileges and that women's own traits make male privileges inappropriate for them. Second, feminists protest the assumption of separate but equal spheres that has characterized social and political thought since the mid-nineteenth century. Women's experiences and perspectives offer distinctive resources for constructing more empathic, more creative, and better theories of law and social practices—but the recognition of gender differences should not spell exclusion or degradation along that divide.

There is a more profound problem with these feminist arguments, however, than their internal tension. By urging the corrective of a woman's

---

[1]See, e.g., Simone de Beauvoir, *The Second Sex*, trans. H. M. Parshley (1953; New York: Vintage Books, 1974), p. 161; Carol Gilligan, *In a Different Voice: Psychological Theory and Women's Development* (Cambridge, Mass.: Harvard University Press, 1982); Nancy Hartsock, *Money, Sex, and Power: Toward a Feminist Historical Materialism* (New York: Longman, 1983); Alison Jaggar, *Feminist Politics and Human Nature* (Totowa, N.J.: Rowman & Allenheld, 1983); Evelyn Fox Keller, *Reflections on Gender and Science* (New Haven, Conn.: Yale University Press, 1985); Jean Baker Miller, *Toward a New Psychology of Women* (Boston: Beacon Press, 1986); *The New Feminist Criticism: Essays on Women, Literature, and Theory*, ed. Elaine Showalter (New York: Pantheon Books, 1985); Susan Okin, *Women in Western Political Thought* (Princeton, N.J.: Princeton University Press, 1979); Anne Firor Scott, *Making the Invisible Woman Visible* (Urbana: Illinois University Press, 1984); *Woman, Culture and Society*, ed. Michelle Rosaldo and Louise Lamphere (Stanford, Calif.: Stanford University Press, 1974); Catharine MacKinnon, "Feminism, Marxism, Method, and the State: An Agenda for Theory," *Signs* 7 (1982), 515; Catharine MacKinnon, "Feminism, Marxism, Method, and the State: Toward Feminist Jurisprudence," *Signs* 8 (1983), 635.

[2]See generally Gilligan, *In a Different Voice*.

[3]See Fran Olsen, "The Sex of Law" (unpublished manuscript, 1985); Wishick, "To Question Everything: The Inquiries of Feminist Jurisprudence," *Berkeley Women's L.J.* 1 (1985), 63.

perspective or even a feminist standpoint, feminists jeopardize their own challenge to simplification, essentialism, and stereotyping. Women fall into every category of race, religion, class, and ethnicity, and they vary in sexual orientation, handicapping conditions, and other sources of assigned difference. There are sharp differences among women in political viewpoint.[4] Even exclusively female traits, such as pregnancy, signal women's variety. Not all women, at all times, are pregnant; indeed, some women will never become pregnant, and some who already have been never will be again. The medical, social, and psychological meanings of pregnancy vary by culture and by individual, as do needs for medical and other assistance. Some women may argue that health benefits for pregnancy are far less relevant to their needs than are benefits assisting their duties toward a dependent parent or non-spousal household members.

Claims to speak from the women's point of view, or to use women as a reference point, threaten to suppress this multiplicity and to install a particular view to stand for the views of all.[5] Assertions of a unified "women's experience" deny the history of conflicts between women. White women, for example, have often found a source of power in supervising women of color.[6] Any claim that "women's experience" is more unifying than racial, religious, or other bonds fails to take account not only of domination beyond sexism but also of women's own varied experiences. Philosopher Elizabeth Spelman argues effectively that any account of gender relations that "obscure[s] the workings of race and class is likely to involve—whether intentionally or not—obscuring the workings of racism and classism."[7]

In a thoughtful paper on this danger, Nancy Fraser and Linda Nicholson

---

[4]E.g., Kristin Luker, *Abortion and the Politics of Motherhood* (Berkeley: University of California Press, 1984), pp. 186–91, describes the sharp divisions between pro-choice and pro-life activists.

[5]See Sandra G. Harding, *The Science Question in Feminism* (Ithaca: Cornell University Press, 1986), p. 195: "The [feminist] standpoint epistemologies appear committed to trying to tell the 'one true story' about ourselves and the world around us that the postmodernist epistemologies regard as a dangerous fiction." Bell Hooks, *Ain't I a Woman: Black Women and Feminism* (Boston: South End Press, 1981), pp. 194–95, argues that white females bring racism to feminism. See also Audre Lorde, *Sister Outsider: Essays and Speeches* (Trumansburg, N.Y.: Crossing Press, 1984), p. 116: "There is a pretense to a homogeneity of experience covered by the word *sisterhood* that does not in fact exist"; Omolade, "Black Women and Feminism," in *The Future of Difference*, ed. Hester Eisenstein and Alice Jardine (Boston: G. K. Hall, 1980), pp. 247, 255–56: black experience is needed in feminism for black women to pursue dialogue with white feminists; *With Wings: An Anthology of Literature by and about Women with Disabilities*, ed. Marsha Saxton and Florence Howe (New York: Feminist Press, City University of New York, 1987): women's experiences with disabilities deserve attention; Deborah L. Rhode, "The Woman's Point of View," *J. Legal Educ.* 38 (1988), 39, 46: there is a danger of attributing to women any undervalued dimension.

[6]See, e.g., Elizabeth Clark-Lewis, " 'This Work Had a' End': African-American Domestic Workers in Washington, D.C., 1910–1940," in *"To Toil the Livelong Day": America's Women at Work, 1780–1980*, ed. Carol Groneman and Mary Beth Norton (Ithaca: Cornell University Press, 1987), pp. 196, 202–3, 207.

[7]Elizabeth Spelman, *Inessential Woman: Problems of Exclusion in Feminist Thought* (Boston: Beacon Press, 1988), p. 112.

conclude that "since women's oppression is not homogeneous in content, and since it is not determined by one root, underlying cause, there is no one 'feminist method,' no 'feminist epistemology.'"[8] Audre Lorde puts it powerfully: "Some problems we share as women, some we do not. You fear your children will grow up to join the patriarchy and testify against you, we fear our children will be dragged from a car and shot down in the street, and you will turn your backs upon the reasons they are dying."[9]

These critiques are internal: these are feminists admonishing feminists. In a sense, the method of consciousness-raising—personal reporting of experience in communal settings in order to explore what has not been said—enables self-criticism among feminists even about feminism itself. Yet why, when it comes to our own arguments and activities, do some feminists forget the very insights we advance about the power of unstated reference points and points of view, the privileged position of the status quo, and the pretense that a particular is the universal? I suggest that our own insights elude us because feminists—along with everyone else—are attracted to simplifying categories, maintaining unconscious attachments to stereotypes, and thinking within contested versions of reality that tend to treat some realities as more valid than others.

Philosophers and psychologists have studied the human need to simplify experience through categories.[10] Distinctions such as same and different, good and bad offer a certainty that otherwise eludes us in this world. Language figures prominently in the activity of classifying: we use language to relate something new to something we have already known.[11] Through language, we label and name experience; with the catalogue that results, we feel at home.[12] Philosophers and psychologists have joined literary critics in an interest in metaphor and analogy, modes of expression that draw sim-

[8]Nancy Fraser and Linda Nicholson, "Social Criticism without Philosophy: An Encounter between Feminism and Postmodernism," in *The Institution of Philosophy: A Discipline in Crisis?* ed. Avner Cohen and Marcelo Descal (La Salle, Ill.: Open Court, 1988), p. 35. Fraser and Nicholson nonetheless agree that feminism can continue to mean something: a commitment to actual diversity and a complex, multilayered feminist solidarity.

[9]Lorde, *Sister Outsider*, p. 119.

[10]See William James, *The Principles of Psychology* (1890; New York: Dover, 1950); Howard Gardner, *The Mind's New Science: A History of the Cognitive Revolution* (New York: Basic Books, 1985), pp. 304–5 (discussing others).

[11]For young children, selecting, labeling, and mediating experience with symbols are critical tasks, accomplished as the child learns to use language. See Lev Vygotsky, *Mind in Society: The Development of Higher Psychological Processes*, ed. Michael Cole, Vern John-Steiner, Sylvia Scribner, and Ellen Souberman (Cambridge, Mass.: Harvard University Press, 1978), pp. 32, 34, 123; A. R. Luria, *Cognitive Development: Its Cultural and Social Foundations* (Cambridge, Mass.: Harvard University Press, 1976), p. 11.

[12]See Giles Gunn, *The Culture of Criticism and the Criticism of Culture* (New York: Oxford University Press, 1987), p. 44: "Our conceptions of the thing called reality, no less than the statements we make in an effort to define it, are cultural constructs whose veracity or validity is wholly restricted to what our linguistic equipment permits us to know and say about it." Cf. George Kateb, *Hannah Arendt, Politics, Conscience, Evil* (Totowa, N.J.: Rowman & Allenheld, 1987), p. 194: "Philosophers persist by pretending to know what cannot be known, and they cover up their pretense by deliberately or helplessly converting reality into patterns that repeat those of mental activities."

ilarities between things or ideas. No longer conceived as the luxury of poets, metaphor and analogy are increasingly studied as basic to the way the human mind works.[13] These modes of expression depend upon and manifest a person's ability to draw similarities—to conceive of relations—and to substitute one thing for another in an implicit or explicit comparison. From an early age, children use language to describe one thing in terms of another, in that way extending their ability to describe and know the world beyond the limited vocabulary they have already mastered.[14] Recent theoretical work suggests that adults similarly project from images and experiences they have already understood in order to grasp new experiences and make them meaningful.[15] We use categories to sort perceptions and experiences by traits that are familiar.

Unfortunately, however, we have tended to treat the categories we use as dictated by the essence of things rather than established by our decision to focus on one trait rather than another. We conceive of our placement of an item in one category instead of another as obvious or self-evident instead of recognizing our decision to reshape a category to accept or reject a new item. We select the particular features to focus upon in building categories for the world, and then we attribute to the whole the consequences related to those selected features.[16] Mundane examples appear in common speech patterns. We talk about the "third baseman" as though this person's only identity pertained to his position in a baseball game. Less benign, perhaps, are the locutions that equate a person's race or gender with desirable or undesirable conduct, as though that particular trait explained the behavior. Whatever causal pattern we may devise to connect the trait and the behavior, the locution that equates them obscures other factors.

Most pernicious may be our tendency to label a particular individual by selecting a given trait and then to assume that the consequences we connect to that trait naturally attach to the individual. Harold Herzog, the animal behaviorist, has observed that the labels we use can skew our moral responses: we may define a mouse, for example, as a pest or as a pet—and produce an entirely different moral status accordingly.[17] Other recent em-

[13]See *Metaphor and Thought*, ed. Andrew Ortony (Cambridge: Cambridge University Press, 1979); Ellen Winner, *The Point of Words: Children's Understanding of Metaphor and Irony* (Cambridge, Mass.: Harvard University Press, 1988).

[14]Winner, *The Point of Words*, pp. 90–109.

[15]Mark Johnson, *The Body in the Mind: The Bodily Basis of Meaning, Imagination, and Reason* (Chicago: University of Chicago Press, 1987), pp. 65–100. See also Stephen Jay Gould, *Wonderful Life: The Burgess Shale and the Nature of History* (New York: Norton, 1989). Gould explores the ways scientists may misinterpret data because they are intent on using concepts that they already believe.

[16]James, *Principles of Psychology*, pp. 670–71; George Lakoff, *Women, Fire, and Dangerous Things: What Categories Reveal about the Mind* (Chicago: University of Chicago Press, 1980), pp. 67–84, discussing Rosch and others on the use of prototypes in language and conceptual categories. See also Hilary Putnam, "Is Semantics Possible?" in *Mind, Language, and Reality* (Cambridge: Cambridge University Press, 1975), pp. 140–42.

[17]See David Gelman, "Of Mice and Men—and Morality: Something in a Name," *Newsweek*, July 18, 1988, p. 65, reporting on an article by Harold A. Herzog, Jr., "The Moral Status of Mice," in *American Psychologist*, June 1988.

pirical and analytic studies have challenged an earlier view that categories simply match the world, while existing outside of the world, and that knowledge progresses toward an increasingly more accurate description of reality.[18] In the process of knowing, language itself shapes experience, just as people use experience to remake language.

These lessons from psychology and philosophy apply to feminists as much as to anyone else. Full acknowledgment of all people's differences threatens to overwhelm us. If women are really different from one another, then we risk losing the leverage of a critique of the world from "women's" point of view. Cognitively, we need simplifying categories, and the unifying category of "woman" helps to organize experience, even at the price of denying some of it. Ideas that defy neat categories are difficult to hold on to, even if the idea itself is about the tyranny of categories. We especially attach ourselves to such categories as male and female because our own psychological development occurred in a culture that made gender matter.[19] Moreover, cultural practices deploy and exchange stereotyped images that organize people's perceptions and judgments.

Stereotypes are a notable example of the categories that people use as though they matched rather than simplified the world we perceive. A stereotype describes a group of people on the basis of a trait they share, and it assigns either positive or, usually, negative consequences to people who happen to have that particular trait.[20] Stereotypes persist because they help to fill the psychological need to simplify the world. If learned during childhood, stereotypes become sturdy enough to revive under stress even after people have consciously rejected them. Social psychologists have contributed to the understanding of stereotypes the insight that assigning labels of difference helps people confirm their own identities and also displace their own

[18]See Gardner, *The Mind's New Science*, pp. 128–37; Johnson, *The Body in the Mind*, pp. xi–xii. Hilary Putnam, *The Many Faces of Realism* (La Salle, Ill.: Open Court, 1987), has led an analytic inquiry into the unavoidable influence of conceptual schemes on what humans know. George Lakoff, Mark Johnson, and others working at the intersection of philosophy, psychology, and cognitive science have synthesized a comprehensive challenge to the view that language and concepts exist independently and yet provide a transparent avenue toward reality. Instead, they have noted that concepts and basic metaphors depend upon bodily experiences, that language embodies and expresses contestable assumptions about what is a paradigmatic or typical instance from an array of diverse instances; and how imagination and creativity are critical to using language and knowing about the world. See Johnson, *The Body in the Mind;* George Lakoff and Mark Johnson, *Metaphors We Live By* (Chicago: Chicago University Press, 1980); and Lakoff, *Women, Fire, and Dangerous Things.* For similar work in feminist theory, see *Discovering Reality: Feminist Perspectives on Epistemology, Metaphysics, Methodology, and Philosophy of Science,* ed. Sandra Harding and Merrill Hintikka (Boston: Reidel, 1983); Harding, *The Science Question in Feminism.*

[19]See Nancy Chodorow, *The Reproduction of Mothering: Psychoanalysis and the Sociology of Gender* (Berkeley: University of California Press, 1978). But children's racial, religious, and other identities are also formed in relation to their parents, and Chodorow's theory neglects this complexity. See Spelman, *Inessential Woman,* pp. 80–113.

[20]Sander Gilman, *Difference and Pathology: Stereotypes of Sexuality, Race, and Madness* (Ithaca: Cornell University Press, 1985), pp. 11–35.

doubts and anxieties onto those now called "different."[21] By looking at the social contexts in which people use labels to describe one another, social psychologists have observed that basic cognitive processes simplify an overwhelming world by interlacing sharply drawn distinctions between us and them—same and different—with pronouncements about better and worse, normal and deviant.[22] Stereotypes help people manage enormous fears by depositing them on the category described as "other" in comparison with the self.[23]

Some social theorists have suggested that labels and categories carrying negative associations reach into webs of further negative associations. When some people assign others to a group, such as a racial minority, this assignment may trigger in the observers mental associations with other traits of "difference," perhaps low intelligence and immorality.[24] When individuals who have been labeled try to resist the demeaning consequences of those labels, they encounter complex layers of meanings that they cannot control.[25] One strategy of resistance is to separate oneself from the group given the negative label and to demand treatment as an individual. Yet this response leaves in place the negative meaning of the label.[26] People assigned to

[21]See ibid., pp. 12, 18–23; Gordon Allport, *The Nature of Prejudice* (Garden City, N.Y.: Doubleday, 1958); *The Labelling of Deviance: Evaluating a Perspective*, 2d ed., ed. Walter Gove (Beverly Hills, Calif.: Sage, 1980); Jack Levin, *The Functions of Prejudice* (New York: Harper & Row, 1975); *In the Eye of the Beholder: Contemporary Issues in Stereotyping*, ed. Arthur Miller (New York: Tavistock, 1982). See also Anthony Cohen, *The Symbolic Construction of Community* (New York: Tavistock, 1985): community boundaries are essential to community identity; Kai T. Erikson, *Wayward Puritans: A Study in the Sociology of Deviance* (New York: Wiley, 1966), pp. 4–15, 69–81, 196–99: Puritans used attributions of deviance to sustain community identity and boundaries; David Reiss, *The Family's Construction of Reality* (Cambridge, Mass.: Harvard University Press, 1981), pp. 230–31: a family may scapegoat one member as a ritual to displace other fears.

[22]Social psychologists also point to the power of interactions on both people who label others and those who receive the label: if people act in response to meanings that grow from interactions with one another, then encounters with people who assign you a negative label will affect your self-conception. See Erving Goffman, *Stigma: Notes on the Management of Spoiled Identity* (Englewood Cliffs, N.J.: Prentice-Hall, 1963); Robert Page, *Stigma* (Boston: Routledge & Kegan Paul, 1984).

[23]See Gilman, *Difference and Pathology.* Audre Lorde "The Master's Tools Will Never Dismantle the Master's House," in *This Bridge Called My Back: Writings by Radical Women of Color,* ed. Cherríe Moraga and Gloria Anzaludúa (Watertown, Mass.: Persephone Press, 1981), p. 101, has pointed out that we must explore our own attitudes before expecting to bring about changes: "I urge each one of us here to reach down into that deep place of knowledge inside herself and touch that terror and loathing of any difference that lives there. See whose face it wears. Then the personal as the political can begin to illuminate all our choices" (italics omitted).

[24]See Gilman, *Difference and Pathology,* pp. 12, 25–35, 131–62. Charles Lawrence, "The Id, The Ego, and Equal Protection: Reckoning with Unconscious Racism," *Stanford L. Rev.* 39 (1987), 317, 337, discusses the correlation of race with intelligence and a propensity for violence.

[25]For this reason, some decide to resist by absorbing and internalizing the pain, rather than by objecting.

[26]See Castenda v. Partida, 430 U.S. 482, 503 (1977) (Marshall, J., concurring): "Members of minority groups frequently respond to discrimination and prejudice by attempting to dissociate themselves from the group, even to the point of adopting the majority's negative attitudes

groups with negative associations have struggled in recent years to invest with positive meaning the words used to assign negative status. Historical arguments over whether to use the term "Negro," "colored," "black," or "a person of color" suggest the difficulties that members of minorities have had in reclaiming words to describe the self when those words have become infused with negative meanings. Mary Daly has deliberately chosen highly disapproving words about women as reclamation projects, and she has used the shock value of taking on words like "revolting" and "hag" to challenge settled attitudes.[27] Who it is that does the naming partially determines the meaning of the word, but not entirely. There may well be remnants of self-hate or internalized negative labels assigned by others when, for example, a Jewish college student describes herself as a "JAP"—short for "Jewish American Princess."[28]

Alongside individual and group efforts to resist the negative meanings of particular labels or categories, the theoretical insights from psychology, social psychology, and philosophy can provide analytic tools to challenge the seeming inevitability of prevailing ways of thinking about people.[29] Strategies developed by literary theorists to "interrogate" a text may also be useful, especially in exposing the rigidity and limitations of patterns of thought that force perceptions into dualities: good/bad, same/different, white/black, male/female. Becoming adept at recognizing how each half of a given duality depends upon the other half in self-definition, and how crudely each duality divides varieties and ranges of perceptions and experience, can help people challenge the seeming inevitability of dualisms in social practice.

Yet, feminists are not free from the stereotypes that occupy thought throughout the culture.[30] White feminists may well carry stereotypes about people of color, and similar stereotypes may divide women who differ in religion, political persuasion, abilities and disabilities, and sexual prefer-

---

toward the minority"; Richard Sennett and Johnathan Cobb, *The Hidden Injuries of Class* (New York: Knopf, 1972).

[27]Mary Daly, *Beyond God the Father: Toward a Philosophy of Women's Liberation* (Boston: Beacon Press, 1973).

[28]See Sandy Tobuk and Debbie Lukatsky, *Jewish American Princess Handbook* (Chicago: Contemporary Books, 1982).

[29]See also Paulo Freire, *Pedagogy of the Oppressed* (New York: Continuum, 1986), pp. 29–34, which notes that the true focus of revolutionary change is never merely an oppressive situation but instead that piece of the oppressor planted deep within each of us.

[30]See Elizabeth Spelman, "Theories of Race and Gender: The Erasure of Black Women," *Quest* 5, no. 4 (1982), 36; Michael Omni and Howard Winant, "By the Rivers of Babylon: Race in the United States, Part One," *Socialist Review*, Sept.–Oct. 1983, pp. 31, 53: "Every individual is subjected to the particular racial order that obtains during the historical period in which he or she lives." The racial prejudices of white women who advocated rights for women in the nineteenth century are well documented. See Elisabeth Griffith, *In Her Own Right: The Life of Elizabeth Cady Stanton* (New York: Oxford University Press, 1984), pp. 124–26. Sojourner Truth's now famous line "Ain't I a woman" reminded her audience of white reformers that black women are women as well as black (See Hooks, *Ain't I a Woman*).

[31]In "The Id, The Ego, and Equal Protection," Lawrence explores insights from both Freudian and cognitive psychology that help to explain unconscious racism. Cognitive psychologists

ence.[31] Majority and minority women stereotype each other, but the majority's stereotypes of minorities carry more power to implement the exclusion and control that stereotypes imply. Stereotypes remaining within feminist theory and practice provide clues to who has the power to define agendas and priorities within feminist communities. Ignoring differences among women may permit relatively privileged women to claim identification with all discrimination against women, while also claiming special authority to speak for women unlike themselves.

Feminists thus adopt categories that others have used and at times reinforce particular prejudices and general modes of argument that assign difference to others and ignore the social meaning of the act of assignment. Simplifying constructions of the world are not made either by individuals or by a unanimous society. Rather, simplifying constructions reflect political, economic, and social structures that are usually taken for granted. Sometimes, however, they can become subjects for debate. Such debates produce competing pictures of reality. The winners secure their picture of reality as authoritative; their views about what differences matter, and why, acquire the earmarks of factuality.[32] When a conception of reality triumphs, it comes to convince even those injured by it.[33] Political and cultural success itself submerges the fact that any conception of reality represents the perspective of certain groups, not a picture of reality free from any perspective.[34] Power may be at its peak, then, when it is least visible: when it shapes preferences, arranges agendas, and excludes serious challenges from either discussion or

locate attitudes about race in the processes of categorization through which people sort experience to provide order and meaning, as well as in each individual's assimilation of attitudes shared by the community of origin (pp. 336–37). He suggests that stereotypes of racial minorities are deeply ingrained in American culture and transmitted tacitly, even as people learn consciously to reject racism. Because of the conflict between racist images and a public ethic condemning them, people tend to exclude from consciousness racist images that nonetheless continue to influence their perceptions and actions (pp. 322–23). See Lillian Smith, *The Winner Names the Age: A Collection of Writings* (New York: Norton, 1978), p. 26: "White southerners are rigorously trained in childhood to believe in their whiteness. They are trained in distinctions, segregations, special privileges, as they are trained in toilet habits." Describing her own generation, raised before the civil rights movement, Smith explains that even if racial distinctions are consciously unlearned later in life, earlier attitudes are so basic to the individual's sense of self that they reemerge in times of stress.

[32]Christopher Hill, *The World Turned Upside Down* (New York: Viking Press, 1972), offers unusual narratives from the perspective of reformers who lost. Gertrude Himmelfarb, *The New History and the Old* (Cambridge, Mass.: Belknap Press of Harvard University Press, 1987), contrasts histories told from the vantage point of the powerful with new social histories of common people.

[33]E. P. Thompson, *The Making of the English Working Class* (New York: Pantheon Books, 1964); and Eugene Genovese, *Roll, Jordan, Roll: The World the Slaves Made* (New York: Pantheon Books, 1974), both develop the resistance theme. See generally Albert Memmi, *The Colonizer and the Colonized* (New York: Orion Press, 1965); and Raymond Williams, *Culture and Society, 1780–1950* (New York: Columbia University Press, 1958), p. 289, exploring the role of culture in coordinating beliefs about society.

[34]See Michel Foucault, *The History of Sexuality*, trans. Robert Hurley (New York: Vintage Books, 1980), p. 86: "Power is tolerable only on condition that it mask a substantial part of itself. Its success is proportional to its ability to hide its own mechanisms."

imagination.[35] Thus, it becomes difficult to hold on to glimpses of the contestability of prevailing understandings of social differences, since to prevail is to make the conceptions seem real or natural.[36]

As a result, feminists fall into patterns of argument that are well established, even though these patterns may be part of the world view that feminists seek to undo. We all internalize scripts about how to argue and, indeed, how to know. Schools, books, public and private authorities establish certain criteria for what counts as a persuasive claim in academic circles, in legal institutions, and in scientific communities. And the dominant forms of authoritative discourse in these arenas have, thus far, favored arguments that draw distinctions, deploy categories, and advance claims to a definitive, encompassing truth. Some existing modes of argument offer points of entry to new claims while limiting the scope of those claims, once made. For example, legal rules couched in the language of universal applicability invite claims that they apply to women. Yet if the doctrines use white middle-class men as their reference point—as rules about the legitimate expectations of privacy are likely to do—experiences that do not fit those preexisting terms may be resoundly excluded and sealed off from criticism in the guise of neutral application of the law. A judicial decision that a person has no legitimate expectation of privacy in a paper bag, for example, neglects groups of people who may treat a paper bag the way others treat a suitcase.[37]

The rules in established academic institutions about what counts as theory offer another example. The criteria of coherence, value neutrality, and abstraction may embody the false universalism that feminists criticize. Yet to be counted by establishment institutions as theory, feminist approaches must resemble the objects of their attack.[38] This may be why feminist Jane Flax notes that "we cannot revision the world with the tools we have been given."[39] We risk becoming embroiled in what we critique, entranced by what we would demystify. This is a problem of much criticism: preoccupation with the subject of criticism.[40]

[35]See Steven Lukes, *Power: A Radical View* (New York: Macmillan, 1974), pp. 22–25. There are two strands in this argument: generic views that see society as oppressing every individual while enlisting the individual in its service through socialization; and particularized views that conceive of some winning groups oppressing particular losing groups.

[36]The very prevalence of visual metaphors—such as "glimpses"—may reinvoke the idea of an unmediated reality.

[37]Cf. Cardwell v. Lewis, 417 U.S. 583 (1974) (plurality opinion) (search of an automobile is less intrusive than search of a building because a person's expectation of privacy in the car is less), and United States v. Ross, 456 U.S. 798 (1982) (police may search closed or concealed containers found during a legitimate search of an automobile), and United States v. Chadwick, 433 U.S. 1 (1977) (luggage contents not open to public view cannot be inspected by police because of legitimate expectations of privacy).

[38]See Jaggar, *Feminist Politics,* pp. 355–57.

[39]Jane Flax, "Mother-Daughter Relationships: Psychodynamics, Politics, and Philosophy," in Eisenstein and Jardine, *The Future of Difference,* pp. 20, 38. See also Lorde, "The Master's Tools."

[40]Insights criticizing dominant views are necessarily parasitic on what they criticize, and in that sense they reestablish the terms and preoccupations of the very frameworks they seek to undermine. See Paul Rabinow and William M. Sullivan, "The Interpretive Turn: Emergence of

The prevailing forms of argument and knowledge provide some sense of certainty even to those who challenge arguments that have prevailed in the past. Feminists, no less than anyone else and perhaps more than people who have felt at home with the prevailing conceptions of reality, want something to hang on to, some sense of the validity of their own perceptions and experiences, some certainty—not more doubt. Yet each form of certainty hazards a new arrogance: the projection of oneself, one's experience, or one's kind as the model for all.

The reasons feminists lose sight of their insights are clearly interrelated. Simplifying constructions of reality are not made by individuals or by a society in unanimity; instead, they are shaped by political, economic, and social struggles over competing pictures of reality. Those who win a given struggle for control may have better access to the means of producing knowledge, such as mass media and schools. Such control may even shape the terms of access so that exclusions of other points of view appear neutral, based on merit or on other standards endorsed even by those who remain excluded. Thus, those who set out to reform or challenge social and legal practices may become enthralled by those very practices or may mistake their own perspective for a new, total truth. This describes, in part, what happened around the turn of this century, for example, when a new middle class justified industrialism and the control of immigrants by spreading its members' understanding of science, technology, and bureaucracy as neutral and progressive.[41] Because some of the relational ideas I develop here resonate with—and have roots in—theories invented at that time, the lessons from that era are especially worthy of note.

A History of Progressivism

Claiming to narrate history is always problematic. No one has direct access to the past. Even if we did, we could not avoid bringing to it our own concerns, assumptions, and perspectives.[42] Shifting historical understand-

an Approach," in *Interpretive Social Science: A Reader,* ed. Paul Rabinow and William M. Sullivan (Berkeley: University of California Press, 1979), p. 1. See also Alexander Nehamas, *Nietzsche: Life as Literature* (Cambridge, Mass.: Harvard University Press, 1985), pp. 45–46, 137: "Nietzsche's problem is that he wants to attack the tradition to which he belongs and also escape it. An explicit attack . . . would perpetuate that tradition. A complete escape from it directly into art (something he did at times consider) would simply change the subject but leave the tradition intact."

[41]See Robert Wiebe, *The Search for Order, 1877–1920* (New York: Hill & Wang, 1967), pp. 111–13.

[42]Historians have long understood the interaction between observer and observed which has come to occupy the attention of scholars in other fields. See Marc Bloch, *The Historian's Craft,* trans. Peter Putnam (New York: Knopf, 1953), pp. 48–78; Bendetto Croce, *History as the Story of Liberty* (London: George Allen & Unwin, 1941), p. 19; Edward Hellett Carr, *What Is History?* (New York: Vintage Books, 1961), pp. 4–35; Peter Novick, *That Noble Dream: The "Objectivity Question" and the American Historical Profession* (Cambridge: Cambridge University Press, 1988); Hayden White, *Metahistory: The Historical Imagination in Nineteenth-*

ings of a given event or epoch provide clues to the preoccupations of the observers as much as new insights about what indeed happened, or how people in the period under study understood what happened. Historians revise past accounts in light of present concerns.

Such revisionism is pronounced in histories of Progressivism (typically dated 1890–1920), the movement for social and political reform in the United States following the Civil War and continuing through World War I. Within historians' debates over Progressivism arise contests over the proper or desirable role of the state in regulating social and economic activities, and shifting but continuous conflicts about dividing people by class, ethnicity, religion, race, and gender.[43] Even describing the fights among historians about Progressivism risks an unwitting declaration of alignments on political issues that carry into contemporary society. I could characterize the historiographic shifts in terms of changing attitudes about paternalism, for example, but this already gives a pejorative treatment to the idea that privileged groups can and should use the state to help those less fortunate.[44]

Events receding in time become elusive in part because later observers simply do not share the assumptions of those they try to study. David Rothman explores this difficulty in examining the Progressives: "The optimism and confidence that progressives shared, both about the wisdom and potential effectiveness of their social polities, their firm sense of having diagnosed the problem of dependency and formulated the right programs to eliminate it, their belief in the superiority of their values and all that meant to

Century Europe (Baltimore, Md.: Johns Hopkins University Press, 1973). But women's and blacks' historians have criticized standard histories for imposing a point of view that neglects other perspectives. See Berenice Carroll, *Liberating Women's History: Theoretical and Critical Essays* (Urbana: University of Illinois Press, 1976); W. E. B. Du Bois, *Black Reconstruction in America* (New York: Russell & Russell, 1962). See also Genovese, *Roll, Jordan, Roll.*

[43]Richard McCormick, *The Party Period and Public Policy: American Politics from the Age of Jackson to the Progressive Era* (New York: Oxford University Press, 1986), pp. 263–65, discusses the historiography of Progressivism.

[44]"Paternalism" has acquired negative connotations in late twentieth-century parlance. See David Rothman, Introduction to *Doing Good: The Limits of Benevolence*, ed. Willard Gaylin, Ira Glasser, Steven Marcus, and David Rothman (New York: Pantheon Books, 1978), pp. x, xiii; *Paternalism*, ed. Rolf Sartorius (Minneapolis: University of Minnesota Press, 1983). Rothman explains that by the 1960s the claim to be acting benevolently—through paternalist interventions—had become suspect as power in disguise. Ellen Ryerson, *The Best-Laid Plans: America's Juvenile Court Experiment* (New York: Hill & Wang, 1978), pp. 4–5, described the historiography of the Progressive era as a thicket: "One question is whether the movement for which it is named was peopled by an older middle class acting out status frustrations, or by a new middle class acting out professional ambitions, or by a business elite seeking a predictable environment in which to pursue its own interests"; another question is whether humanitarian reform failed or a movement of capitalist conservatism succeeded. See also Susan Lehrer, *Origins of Protective Labor Legislation for Women, 1905–1925* (Albany: State University of New York Press, 1987), pp. 14–15: Progressive era protective labor legislation for women could be understood as sex discrimination inspired by capitalism or by men, or as one of Progressivism's few beneficial reforms, or as part of a reform movement responsive to interest groups, or as the conscious creation of leaders of giant corporations, or as an unstable equilibrium of compromises between the nondominant and the dominated.

their ability to define and to attempt to implement the proper life-styles in all citizens and classes, have disappeared and can hardly be resurrected."[45]

One influential historian has argued that "the heart of progressivism was the ambition of the new middle class to fulfill its destiny through bureaucratic means": that is, attacking political bosses in the name of democracy and then proposing management by a class of new experts, who would secure power to reorder society to benefit themselves.[46] Others have argued that Progressivism actually served corporate interests.[47] Still others find in Progressive reforms the thread of humanitarian political action that can be traced back to earlier periods, ahead through the New Deal, and even into the reform movements of the 1960s.[48] Whatever the motives of Progressive reformers, the policies they pursued may well have benefited chiefly middle- and upper-middle-class people, despite their avowed purpose of improving the quality of life for and expanding democracy to include the excluded.[49]

I make no claim to resolve the historians' debates; instead, I try to learn from them, particularly in exploring Progressivism's partial efforts to implement relational approaches—and the danger that people may unknowingly misuse their own power when claiming to act in the interests of others.

The Roots of Progressivism

This much is not in dispute: between 1880 and 1920 the number of people living in American cities trebled—from 15 million to 45 million, even though the total population less than doubled.[50] The country shifted from one-third to one-half city dwellers; massive immigration brought to the cities largely Catholic and Jewish newcomers from southern and eastern Europe. In the face of burgeoning ethnic and religious variety, many people already long

[45]David Rothman, "The State as Parent: Social Policy in the Progressive Era," in Gaylin et al., *Doing Good*, pp. 67, 94–95.

[46]Wiebe, *The Search for Order*, pp. 166–68. See also Samuel P. Hays, *The Response to Industrialism, 1885–1914* (Chicago: University of Chicago Press, 1957).

[47]See Gabriel Kolko, *The Triumph of Conservatism: A Reinterpretation of American History, 1900–1916* (New York: Free Press, 1963); James Weinstein, *The Corporate Ideal in the Liberal State, 1900–1918* (Boston: Beacon Press, 1968).

[48]Depending upon one's stance and one's questions, the period may be seen as the "Indian summer of an outmoded order," or as the seedtime for reforms that blossomed in the New Deal, or as a precursor to modern bureaucratic capitalism. See Ellis Hawley, *The Great War and the Search for a Modern Order: A History of the American People and Their Institutions, 1917–1977* (New York: St. Martin's Press, 1979), p. vi. See also McCormick, *The Party Period*, pp. 263–65: debates over Progressivism mirror debates over liberalism.

[49]See William Graebner, *The Engineering of Consent and Authority in Twentieth Century America* (Madison: University of Wisconsin Press, 1987), pp. 188–90: "Invariably, democratic social engineering was employed in an environment laced with inequalities in status, knowledge, influence, agency, and interactive skills. As a result, the objects of this form of authority remained unaware of the intent of the subject to exert influence, or, more commonly, of the methods being employed" between buyers and sellers, workers and employers, children and parents.

[50]Ryerson, *The Best-Laid Plans*, pp. 5–8.

settled in America grew alarmed at the rate of immigration and sought both to restrain it and to train the new arrivals for citizenship. Statutory racial segregation became the rule rather than the exception in southern states, and race-related violence, especially lynching, mounted and spread to the North.

Throughout the country, the economy became increasingly industrialized. Factory work conditions, mass-produced food, and urban transportation raised unprecedented health and safety questions. Existing systems of government, public services, and law enforcement became strained under extraordinary demands.[51] For those who wanted change, such as improvements in public health, the magnitude of the problems seemed to demand new solutions—and new solutions did indeed emerge. A complex amalgam of social experiments took the form of both public policy and private beneficence. Philosophers and political activists, volunteer benevolent associations (many of them women's organizations), and middle-class groups interested in preserving social order and efficiency all contributed to the reforms.[52]

In retrospect, nineteenth-century political thought seems to have offered two options for conceiving of political and economic life. Laissez-faire government would rely on the acts of self-interested individuals to produce results benefiting the entire society. Socialism—inspired by Saint-Simon, François Fourier, Robert Owen, and perhaps Marx and Engels; pursued by British Fabians and, soon, by the Bolsheviks in Russia—represented an uncertain but bold commitment to collective solutions. Its opponents condemned socialism as a severe threat to individual liberty.

During the late nineteenth and early twentieth centuries a group of philosophers and political activists in the United States, and selected individuals in other countries, tried to articulate a route beyond either laissez-faire or socialism.[53] For these theorists of pragmatism and social progress, there had to be something besides leaving individuals to fend for themselves or submerging all people in a grand collective scheme of shared economic and social duties. They emphasized the social nature of every individual and tried to articulate a role for the state as a catalyst for social integration. They believed that through commitment to democracy and rationality they could forge some alternative to either public paternalism or public neglect for those in need. They also sought a theory that would steer away from both the

[51]See Wiebe, *The Search for Order*, p. 133.

[52]The variety and diversity of reform groups known as Progressive have been examined by historians. See Daniel Rodgers, "In Search of Progressivism," *Reviews in American History* 10 (1982), 113–32; and Peter Filene, "An Obituary for the Progressive Movement," *American Quarterly* 22 (1970), 20–34.

[53]See James Kloppenberg, *Uncertain Victory: Social Democracy and Progressivism in European and American Thought, 1870–1920* (New York: Oxford University Press, 1986), p. 6. Kloppenberg's study focuses on William James, John Dewey, Wilhelm Dilthey, Thomas Hill Green, Henry Sidgwick, Alfred Fouillée, Beatrice and Sidney Webb, Eduard Bernstein, Jean Jaurès, Richard Ely, and Walter Rauschenbush. Kloppenberg maintains that these individuals shared a commitment to extending equality to all spheres of society and to using gradual reform rather than revolution.

dangers of idealism and the limits of amoral empiricism. John Dewey, for example, urged schools to design programs in which students would learn from their own experiences—and so would educators. Connecting theory and practice, the philosophers whose work inspired or infused Progressive reforms championed commitment to mutual understanding and respect. John Dewey and others sought to build a new theory of knowledge as well as a theory of political action.[54]

Meanwhile, the actual range of political beliefs during the period defies the neat categories of laissez-faire individualism and socialism. Varied forms of mutual aid and anarchist organizations cropped up. Many Americans around the country built on long-standing traditions of local, volunteer reform activities. Alexis de Tocqueville had noted in the 1840s the American penchant for organizing clubs and associations with specialized social purposes. Such groups often began with the goal of promoting the personal spiritual uplift of their members, then turned to social service and even political reform. Reflecting both older evangelical traditions seeking to purge the world of sin and newer faiths in science and social science, voluntary associations studied social problems and proposed collective solutions, often demanding new government responsibilities. One of the untold stories in American history, brought to light by recent scholarship in women's history, concerns the vast numbers of middle- and upper-middle-class nineteenth-century women who filled their time with such philanthropic and reform activities. Women's groups usually coalesced initially around problems confronting children and women in the community, such as the destitution of orphans and widows. Other marginal people—the disabled, the destitute, and even immigrants—often became the focus for reform campaigns.

As women's reform work reached beyond immediate domestic matters, spokespersons drew upon the rhetorical power of women's traditional domestic roles to justify the activities of these women; such rhetoric helped the women situate their qualifications for public service and advocacy within the traditional wifely and maternal caretaking functions. Moreover, according to the rhetoricians of the movement, even to fulfill the traditional responsibilities of wives and mothers to their own families in complex industrial urban society, women had to become involved in public and industrial settings. Only policies regulating the production of meat, milk, and the like could protect families against the dangers of impure and unhealthful food. Jane Addams, whose settlement-house work in Chicago made her world

---

[54]Legal realism paralleled pragmatism in its challenge to formalist reasoning, but lawyers and judges persisted in using formalist reasoning throughout this period. See Edward Purcell, Jr., *The Crisis of Democratic Theory: Scientific Naturalism and the Problem of Value* (Lexington: University Press of Kentucky, 1973), pp. 74–94; Morton Keller, *The Revolt against Formalism;* Joseph William Singer, "Legal Realism Now: Review Essay of Laura Kalman, *Legal Realism at Yale, 1927–1960,*" *Calif. L. Rev.* 76 (1988), 467. See also the discussion of wage/hour regulations below.

famous,[55] put it this way: "If woman would keep on with her old business of caring for her home and rearing her children she will have to have some conscience in regard to public affairs lying outside of her immediate household."[56] From this stance, women organized benevolent associations to help needy and worthy poor people, to organize schools and libraries, to aid soldiers, to promote cultural improvement, and to address public issues such as sanitation and child labor.[57] Women's right to vote and to obtain legal equality also occupied the attention of some reformers, but for many of the "social feminists" public social reform took precedence as women tried to make the world more homelike.[58] Prohibition, protective labor laws for women and children, sanitation codes, and other social welfare programs—as well as women's suffrage—can be traced directly or indirectly to the work of women in voluntary associations and Progressive reform activities.

Advancing an ethos of mutuality and a recognition of interdependence, these associations supported and were supported by reformers who thought of themselves as forging relationships with those they sought to help.[59] In these activities women challenged the role determined by the social ideology of separate spheres, which assigned women to the home; they also helped to manage a kind of shadow government, establishing institutions and programs to implement the values—moral uplift, communal responsibility for dependents, restraints on the excesses of industrialization—which they felt were lacking in the official government. Feminists even promoted the claim—perhaps the fiction—that women shared something by virtue of their wom-

[55]By the time Addams was asked to second Theodore Roosevelt's presidential nomination at the 1912 Progressive Party Convention, she was described in the press as one of the foremost citizens in the country. See Allen F. Davis, *American Heroine: The Life and Legend of Jane Addams* (London: Oxford University Press, 1973), p. 191.

[56]Jane Addams, "Why Women Should Vote," *Ladies Home Journal* 27 (Jan. 1910), 210. Other Progressive era women reformers often justified women's participation in politics in terms of women's traditional family roles. See, e.g., Rheta Childe Dorr, *What Eight Million Women Want* (Boston: Small, Maynard, 1910), 327: "Woman's place is in the home. But home is not contained within the four walls of an individual home. Home is the community. The city full of people is the Family. The public school is the real Nursery. And badly do the Home and the Family and the Nursery need their mother." See also Maureen Karen Fastenau, "Maternal Government: The Social Settlement Houses and the Politicization of Women's Sphere, 1889–1920" (Ph.D. diss., Duke University, 1982); Nancy Weiss Pottishman, "Save the Children: A History of the Children's Bureau, 1903–1919" (Ph.D. diss., University of California, 1974), pp. 34, 170 n.101.

[57]See Barbara Berg, *The Remembered Gate: Origins of American Feminism, The Woman and the City, 1800–1860* (New York: Oxford University Press, 1978), pp. 160–61, 178; Scott, *Making the Invisible Woman Visible*, p. 329.

[58]J. Stanley Lemons, *The Woman Citizen: Social Feminism in the 1920's* (Urbana: University of Illinois Press, 1973).

[59]Jane Addams wrote that the middle-class residents of Hull House "must be content to live quietly side by side with their neighbors, until they grow into a sense of relationship and mutual interests" (*Twenty Years at Hull-House* [1910; New York: New American Library, 1960], p. 98). See also Martha Minow, " 'Forming underneath Everything That Grows': Toward a History of Family Law," *Wis. L. Rev.* 1985 (1985), 819; Ruth Smith and Deborah Valenze, "Mutuality and Marginality: Liberal Moral Theory and Working-Class Women in Nineteenth-Century England," *Signs* 13 (1988), 277, 278, 287.

anhood which could fuel associations to better conditions for all women.[60] It is possible that women found it easy to identify with victims because of personal experiences. Clearly, women reformers found reasons to blame men and male society for the misfortunes of the poor, of prostitutes, and of others in need.[61] Yet men, too, acted as social reformers; founded and supported settlement houses; promoted housing reform, food and drug regulation, and civic improvement. Some individual reformers, and the reform movement as a whole, combined a pursuit of economic justice, an expanded democracy, and opportunities for individual development with a search for new modes of social control, techniques to assimilate new immigrants to an "American" norm, and managerial efficiency to replace the politics of big city bosses. They combined commitments to social justice and social control; they urged a new understanding of the interdependence of all people, requiring collective solutions to problems.[62]

Thus, Progressive reformers advocated benevolence and responsiveness to individual need but also pursued a faith in bureaucratic forms, expertise, and a rational social consensus that could be articulated by the reformers rather than by popular democratic process.[63] Although some individuals voiced concerns about bureaucracy,[64] many Progressives had a profound faith in experts and on that basis supported legal grants of discretion to professionals, thereby converting political questions into managerial ones.[65] Some supported city managers to replace politicians. Others advocated civil service reform to curb patronage, political graft, and corruption. Reformers believed that discovering social facts could yield answers to what had been conceived as moral problems. They invented and supported new fields of social science and new professions and teams of experts, including social workers, public health nurses, labor statisticians, and probation officers.

Settlement houses epitomized all three strands of Progressivism: the philosophy of pragmatism, volunteer activities pursued in the name of benevolence, and the promotion of fact-gathering investigations and bureaucratic and professional initiatives for efficient and rational government. In 1889 Jane Addams and Ellen Starr developed a plan to move into a poor section of Chicago and create a neighborhood setting for educational, cultural, and social service programs; the result was Hull House. Addams quite consciously conceived of this plan as a way for privileged young people, especially the first generation of female college graduates, to find a sense of

---

[60]See Nancy Cott, *The Grounding of Modern Feminism* (New Haven, Conn.: Yale University Press, 1987), p. 6.

[61]See Berg, *The Remembered Gate*, pp. 172–75, 179–84.

[62]See McCormick, *The Party Period*, pp. 280–83.

[63]These are themes developed notably in Wiebe, *The Search for Order*, pp. 150, 160–62, 176. See also Ryerson, *The Best-Laid Plans*, pp. 8–14.

[64]According to Ellen Starr, Jane Addams did not want Hull House to be an organization or institution because "the world is overstocked with institutions and organizations; & after all, a personality is the only thing that ever touches anybody" (letter quoted in Scott, *Making the Invisible Woman Visible*, p. 115).

[65]Lemons, *The Woman Citizen*, pp. 125–40; McCormick, *The Party Period*, pp. 276–86.

purpose and usefulness. According to Starr, "Jane's idea which she puts very much to the front and on no account will give up is that it is more for the benefit of the people who do it than for the other class."[66] Addams was only too aware of the need of the privileged to be needed; she herself had suffered bouts of depression and lethargy before finding her place in settlement-house work. Inspired by the writings of Tolstoy and by the model of Toynbee Hall in England, Addams and Starr joined other reformers to launch the settlement-house movement, which by 1900 had produced more than a hundred similar establishments. Groups of reformers, some as residents and some as periodic visitors, built a core group at Hull House and at similar settlement houses in other cities.

Addams expressed initial ideas about uplifting impoverished people by setting an example of a middle-class home. Yet she and Starr remained open to what they could learn from their new neighbors as part of their effort to tear down the "half imaginary walls between classes."[67] By opening Hull House as a center for community activities, its women residents soon learned from their new neighbors about the real conditions of poverty, sweatshops, and urban danger. In response, the Hull House residents and their friends mounted crusades to reform work conditions, improve sanitation, and fight political corruption; they created the model for the first public playground in the city and experimented with educational programs for students and adults; they pushed for the creation of the nation's first juvenile court and developed consumer protection activities.

Their reform activities often led to legal and political work. Hull House resident Julia Lathrop became a member of the Illinois State Board of Charities and then the first head of the federal Children's Bureau, a legal innovation launched in part through the lobbying of settlement-house workers. Florence Kelley, another Hull House resident, became a factory inspector through a gubernatorial appointment; she helped draft the state's first factory safety law before moving to New York, where she created an influential lobbying group called the Consumers League. Alice Hamilton, who founded the field of industrial medicine, was so devoted a member of the Hull House community that when Harvard Medical School offered her a faculty job— she was the first woman so honored—she negotiated a half-year contract that permitted her to continue her work at Hull House. Grace Abbott, Edith Abbott, and Sophinisba Breckenridge each taught at the University of Chicago School of Civics and Philanthropy while living and working at Hull House.[68] Workers at other settlement houses similarly connected direct service, institutional and political reform, and philosophic debate. Lillian Wald,

[66]Quoted in Davis, *American Heroine,* p. 56.
[67]Ellen Starr, quoted in Scott, *Making the Invisible Woman Visible,* p. 115. The Hull House residents also forged a community of women, a community supporting reform activities while providing emotional bonds. See Kathryn Kish Sklar, "Hull House in the 1890s: A Community of Women Reformers," *Signs* 10 (Summer 1985), 658–77. A similar experiment emerged in New York under the leadership of Lillian Wald. See *Lillian D. Wald: Progressive Activist,* ed. Clare Loss (New York: Feminist Press, 1989).
[68]Grace Abbott later succeeded Julia Lathrop as head of the U.S. Children's Bureau. See Scott, *Making the Invisible Woman Visible,* pp. 116–17.

of the Henry Street Settlement in New York, invented a public health nursing program and persuaded the New York City Board of Public Health to adopt and expand it.

The cross-fertilization between Addams and progressive theorists was direct. John Dewey decided to join the faculty of the newly founded University of Chicago after visiting Hull House, and he became a regular participant in the social and educational world of the settlement house. William James became a devoted reader of Jane Addams's writings and declared her first book, *Democracy and Social Ethics*, "one of the great books of our time."[69] Addams argued in that book that democracy should be understood as a commitment to equality in all human relationships, not simply as a process of electoral politics. The charity agent and the client should see each other as equals because the causes of poverty lie in the environment, not in the moral character of the one in need. Problems stemmed from people's relationship to the workplace, to the city, and to one another, not from traits intrinsic to individuals. Along with other Progressive women, Addams helped to articulate reform goals that distinctively built upon domestic virtues while modeling what later became a well-established link between social science and public policy.[70]

Settlement houses drew together women—and men—who wanted to bridge the distance between wealthy and poor, between citizens and immigrants. They also provided settings where academic scholars could test their ideas about philosophy and social theory. And they established a model of group civic participation by documenting urban abuses, lobbying and pressuring politicians for change, and crafting laws and new legal institutions to implement ideas about a better government. Three particular Progressive era reforms illustrate these dimensions, as well as the problems that the reformers soon encountered.

Three Attempted Reforms

One major reform effort involved members of Hull House and other settlement houses in lobbying Congress for the creation of a Children's Bureau, and one of their most persuasive claims concerned high levels of infant mortality.[71] The Children's Bureau, once established in 1912, set about gathering information on infant mortality and helped to create a research base for legislation to prevent infant deaths. Studies demonstrated that the mortality rate stemmed from low standards of prenatal and infant care, themselves largely due to the ignorance and poverty of families and the medical community's indifference to preventive care.[72]

[69]Davis, *American Heroine*, pp. 97, 128. Jane Addams reported Dewey's lectures on social psychology at Hull House; see Addams, *Twenty Years at Hull-House*, p. 299.
[70]See Harold Faulkner, *The Quest for Social Justice, 1898–1914* (New York: Macmillan, 1931).
[71]Susan Tifflin, *In Whose Best Interest? Child Welfare Reform in the Progressive Era* (Westport, Conn.: Greenwood Press, 1982), pp. 229–47.
[72]See Lela Costin, *Two Sisters for Social Justice* (Urbana: University of Illinois Press, 1983), pp. 130–33. Costin provides a comprehensive and rich account of the act's history. See also *The*

Julia Lathrop, Grace Abbott, and Florence Kelley—all Hull House alumnae—joined Lillian Wald, director of the New York Henry Street Settlement, and Grace Meigs, a physician, to design federal legislation addressing maternal and infant health. Their plan was to avoid the images of charity and poor relief which traditionally stigmatized recipients. Instead, they chose a voluntary education model. They successfully proposed a federal program granting states money to design local public programs that would educate women about pregnancy and infant care. Participating states would develop plans for educational conferences, collect health and childbirth data, and promote more accessible health facilities and a visiting-nurse program. The Children's Bureau itself would continue to gather data, train nurses, develop educational materials about child nutrition and hygiene, and provide technical advice to the state programs.

The conception of the plan reflected its origins in the settlement-house movement. Rather than assigning the problems to those individuals most directly affected, the infant and maternal health program framed the issues as communal. The reformers also took the perspective of those they hoped to help by devising an educational model, seeking to enlarge and enhance the participation of the mothers in their own health care and in the project of improving conditions for their offspring. The program thus rejected the stigma and degradation that could be associated either with ignoring the problems or with devising programs that subordinated the recipients to the ministrations of expert caretakers.

As the first grant of federal funds for welfare purposes, the Sheppard-Towner Act drew strong support and was widely understood to be the first fruit of women's suffrage. Yet the legislation also prompted opposition: two lawsuits challenged its constitutionality on the grounds that it arrogated to federal control a field assigned to state authority. Ultimately reaching the Supreme Court, these cases were dismissed for want of jurisdiction. The Court reasoned that the question was a political matter and pointed out that the legislation merely proposed federal partnership with states, leaving the choice of participation to each state.[73]

Nevertheless, this judicial skirmish encouraged political opponents of the act to assert states' rights, to argue against women's suffrage and government spending, and to warn of the dangers of left-wing ideology. By 1927, opposition was such that renewal of the act had become a question. The Daughters of the American Revolution (DAR), which had joined many other women's organizations in initial support of Sheppard-Towner, denounced its proposed renewal as Bolshevism.[74] Many groups called the infant and maternal health legislation Communist or socialist and associated it with other social welfare legislation that interfered, they claimed, with the free market econ-

---

Autobiography of Florence Kelley: Notes of Sixty Years, ed. Kathryn Kish Sklar (1926–27; Chicago: Charles H. Kerr, 1986); and Josephine Goldmark, *Impatient Crusader: Florence Kelley's Life Story* (New York: Augustus M. Kelley, 1966).
[73]Frothingham v. Mellon, 43 S.Ct. 597 (1923).
[74]Lemons, *The Woman Citizen*, pp. 124, 159–60.

omy. One senator sponsored thirty-five pages in the *Congressional Record* supporting charges that the program was part of a conspiracy for nationalizing American children.[75] Other critics feared that women would reject their traditional roles, given the act's encouragement of women to seek information about their own bodies and health. Historian Lela Costin has noted that critics who voiced this claim as a defense of individualism could not have meant female individualism, for that seemed to threaten the social order premised on male political power. If individualism was the defense, it was individualism pertaining to men.[76]

Officials in the Public Health Service and leaders of the American Medical Association (AMA) opposed the Sheppard-Towner renewal and also attacked the Children's Bureau's commitment to viewing health matters in conjunction with economic and social welfare. The AMA opposed anything that smacked of state medicine; moreover, it specifically rejected the infant and maternal health programs because they contravened the prevailing medical model by considering the child's health in relation to the rest of the child's life. AMA leaders also opposed sharing what they perceived as medical tasks with anyone else.[77] Yet defenders of the Children's Bureau maintained then and later that under the act, women were just doing on a larger platform what women had always been supposed to do—care for women in childbirth and nurture infants and children.[78] Senators opposed to the legislation attacked the women running the Children's Bureau as celibates and old maids,[79] and as individuals associated with such questionable causes as pacifism, child labor regulation, and help for immigrants.

In 1927, animated by a variety of these oppositional arguments, four senators conducted an eight-day filibuster, which ended only with the compromise that the act would be repealed after a two-year extension. Supporters were unable to muster sufficient votes for a new statute following this mandated expiration date of 1929. A White House Conference on Child Health and Protection in 1929 essentially served as an occasion for a political power play. Officials in the Public Health Service effectively sought to strip the Children's Bureau of its responsibilities for child and maternal health.

Elements of the infant and maternal health programs reappeared during the New Deal in social welfare legislation, and the Children's Bureau properly deserves credit for pioneer work in this area. But as a political matter, as a contribution to remaking public philosophy, and as an initiative seeking to alter actual health results in its own time, the Sheppard-Towner Act did not succeed.[80] The organized medical profession outmaneuvered the women's

[75]Kelley, *Autobiography,* p. 32, describes Senator Thomas Bayard.

[76]Costin, *Two Sisters,* p. 141.

[77]Ibid., pp. 147, 175.

[78]See Kelley, *Autobiography,* pp. 31–32; and Addams, "Why Women Should Vote," p. 22.

[79]Costin, *Two Sisters,* p. 142.

[80]See Dorothy E. Bradbury, *Five Decades of Action: A Short History of the Children's Bureau,* U.S. Children's Bureau Publication (Washington, D.C.: Government Printing Office, 1964), pp. 6–11, 13–14.

movement, which was losing political power during the 1920s. Even beyond the political loss leading to the extinction of the program, the demise of Sheppard-Towner reveals the reformers' inability to reshape the terms of the political debate. The reformers were in part misunderstood. At a rhetorical level the defenders of the act confronted the labels of socialism and Communism against an ideological backdrop offering no other category for state-financed social programs. Opponents could voice the rhetorics of states' rights and of individualism, even though the Sheppard-Towner Act reserved choice to the states and promoted individual autonomy for women.[81] There was a philosophic clash, as well as professional jealousy, behind the assault on the Children's Bureau's comprehensive approach to children's health, which encompassed the child's relations to parents, social and economic circumstances, and local conditions.[82]

A similar limitation in the reformers' abilities to remake the terms of the political debate is revealed in my second example: the juvenile court, which became an emblem of the Progressive era. It too traces its origins to the Hull House community. Julia Lathrop, before she left to head the Children's Bureau, had joined with local lawyers, judges, and other reformers to organize the nation's first juvenile court in 1899. Another Hull House resident, Alzina Stevens, became its first probation officer.[83] Conceived as a separate judicial institution for protecting and guiding dependent, neglected, and delinquent children, the juvenile court rested on the conviction that children needed care rather than rights—that children should not be held to adult standards of individual responsibility, because their troubles could be traced to the dangers and temptations of the city and bad companions. All children were at risk in the new industrial environment, so the distinctions between delinquent and dependent children should be unimportant to the business of the juvenile court.

The founders of the juvenile court believed that delinquency and neglect arose out of the poverty and pressures of the urban environment.[84] Thus, the relationship between the community and those at risk warranted the establishment of a special institution with a distinct set of rules. The designers of the court believed that judges should be trusted to pursue each child's best interests. Normal legal rules and restrictions should not apply; instead, as one contemporaneous authority wrote, "the juvenile judge has simply the parental and human problem of trying to do just what the child needs to have

[81]Gender conflicts appeared at many levels. Political opposition reflected a backlash against the initial success of women's suffrage; the program's emphasis on educating women to understand and control their own bodies in relation to pregnancy and childbirth contributed to public anxiety about changes in women's roles; male physicians and public officials resented the new and dramatic power exercised by women in the Children's Bureau and in the network of women reformers that had launched the act.

[82]This, too, may have had a gendered component, since the relational, comprehensive approach devised by the Children's Bureau reflected innovations espoused by its director, Julia Lathrop, and such prominent social feminists as Jane Addams and Florence Kelley.

[83]Davis, *American Heroine*, pp. 76, 80.

[84]See Tifflin, *In Whose Best Interest?* pp. 8–10.

done for him."[85] The reformers envisioned participation by doctors, social workers, psychologists, and probation officers in the assessment of each child's needs and their provision of programs to guide the individual away from dangerous distractions in the environment. The juvenile court thus fused humanitarianism with the new faith in social science and professional expertise to create an optimism about the uses of discretionary governmental power to promote the well-being of individuals and the community at large.[86] Unlike the Sheppard-Towner Act, which sought to increase private control—by mothers—over the problem it addressed, the juvenile court reform placed hope in public experts and new public institutions.[87]

Nearly every state followed Illinois's lead; by 1905, state legislatures had created juvenile courts across the nation, engendering the first wave of what became a continuous stream of criticism. By the end of the decade the critics were attacking juvenile courts for failing to live up to their promises and for being misguided in the first instance. The courts were criticized as too lenient with juvenile offenders—and also criticized as too intrusive in the lives of young people who were not criminals.[88] Few courts actually fulfilled the vision of interdisciplinary teams of social workers, psychologists, and other professionals working together to promote each child's interests. To the extent that professionals did join the programs, over time they pursued ever more individualized assessments and departed from the emphasis on each child's relationships to families, communities, and larger environments. It was too difficult for social workers and psychologists to tackle the forces producing crime and dependency; moreover, the growing dominance of Freudian ideas focused mental health professionals on the psychic world of each individual. The investigations actually conducted by juvenile courts were superficial, and the placement facilities for juveniles found by the courts to be in need of help or supervision were overcrowded, punitive, and lacking in any demonstrated effectiveness.[89]

By the 1940s new theories of delinquency as the activity of a deviant subculture had made the premises of the juvenile court seem naive and faulty. Moreover, the therapeutic model did not seem to be reducing youth crime and dependency. Critics started to charge the juvenile court with contributing to the irresponsibility of young people toward social obligations and rules by explicitly exempting minors from the norm of individual responsibility and legislated punishment. Some postwar scholars argued that the

[85]Henry Thurston, "The Relation of the Juvenile Court to Public Schools and other Social Agencies," in *Proceedings of the 14th Illinois Conference of Charities and Correction* (Springfield: Illinois Conference of Charities and Correction, 1909), p. 657.

[86]See generally *The Child, the Clinic, and the Court*, ed. Jane Addams (New York: New Republic, 1925); *Children's Courts in the United States: Their Origin, Development, and Results*, 58th Cong., 2d sess., 1904, H. Doc. 701 (reports from the states on the juvenile court experiments).

[87]Even when the juvenile court made the family the unit for intervention, the dominant emphasis was on expert guidance or regulation of private conduct.

[88]See Ryerson, *The Best-Laid Plans*, pp. 78–97.

[89]Tifflin, *In Whose Best Interest?* p. 226.

juvenile court's individualized, discretionary approach contributed to juveniles' disrespect for law and their conceptions of courts as hypocritical and
whimsical.[90] Some critics asserted that juvenile court judges were pushing
their jurisdiction to encompass any child arguably in need of help, that these
judges commanded sprawling empires of social service agencies, corrections
facilities, and probation officers without subscribing to articulated rules.[91]
Others claimed that the juvenile court labeled and stigmatized youth who
had committed no crimes—and punished those who had with time in refor-
matories that exceeded the period of punishment prescribed for adults who
committed similar offenses.[92]

In this climate of scholarly and political criticism, a new generation of
reformers pursued constitutional challenges to juvenile court practices and
secured a series of Supreme Court victories mandating legal restrictions on
the discretion of juvenile court judges. Most notably, in 1967 the Court's
decision in *In re Gault* reasoned that the juvenile court had become so
marked by abuses that it no longer justified the suspension of procedural
rights available to adults: rights to a hearing, to cross-examination, and to
access to legal counsel.[93] Children deserve and need rights, declared the
Court, because state power, even clothed in paternalist language, represents
coercion.[94] Subsequently, many states have directed that some minors, for
some offenses, be tried as if they were adults; other states have imposed
specific sentences for certain offenses, regardless of the age of the offender;[95]
and most states have devised methods to remove from court altogether those
youngsters who have committed no crimes.[96] Recent assessments of juvenile
court practices, even as regulated by constitutional rights, document continuing abuses, irregularities, and even scandals.[97]

Thus, though Progressive reformers introduced for children an alternative
to the dominant legal conception of individual autonomy and responsibility—an alternative emphasizing human dependence and certain individuals'
lack of autonomy, given the effects of environmental and group pressures—
their conception was seldom if ever fulfilled in practice. Reforms since the

[90]See Stanton Wheeler and Leonard Contrell, *Juvenile Delinquency: Its Prevention and Control* (New York: Russell Sage Foundation, 1966).

[91]See generally Anthony Platt, *The Child Savers: The Invention of Delinquency* (Chicago: University of Chicago Press, 1969).

[92]Rothman, "The State as Parent," p. 80; Tifflin, *In Whose Best Interest?* p. 226.

[93]387 U.S. 1 (1967). Justice Abe Fortas concluded that "the condition of being a boy does not justify a kangaroo court" (id. at 28).

[94]See Walter Trattner, *From Poor Law to Welfare State: A History of Social Welfare in America,* 3d ed. (New York: Free Press, 1984).

[95]See "Killing Young Killers," *New York Times,* Jan. 9, 1986, p. A22; and "South Carolina Executes Killer: Age Stirs Protest," *New York Times,* Jan. 11, 1986, sec. 1, p. 6.

[96]The juvenile court over time did not pursue in practice the vision of addressing children's relationships to families and communities in order to assure each child the supports needed to succeed in the world. See Minow, "Rights for the Next Generation: Feminist Approach to Children's Rights," *Harv. Women's L.J.* 9 (1986), 1.

[97]See Patrick Murphy, *Our Kindly Parent . . . the State: The Juvenile Justice System and How It Works* (New York: Viking Press, 1974); Peter Prescott, *The Child Savers: Juvenile Justice Observed* (New York: Viking Press, 1982).

1960s have prescribed even for minors the familiar liberal formulas of individual rights and responsibilities.

What happened? One scholar concludes that the juvenile courts had too much power and too little knowledge.[98] Others emphasize that the creators of the juvenile court concept underestimated the effects of self-interest and overestimated the competencies of experts and bureaucracies.[99] Moreover, optimistic faith in the juvenile court led judges and officials to expand its reach into the lives of any children whom they believed to be in need of help.

This seems a dramatic instance of underestimating the abuse of power that can be unleashed when reformers build new institutions. Given the structure of the institutions and the myth of expertise, the problems faced by children were soon redeposited on the children who were supposedly in need of protection against the hazards of their environments. Of course, it could also be that urban youth crime and adult abuse and neglect of children reflected deeper patterns of conflict and disturbance, which remained unaddressed by the juvenile court apparatus. In any case, individualized judicial determinations based on discretionary judgments about each child's interests could not yield fair results or even an appearance of consistency.[100] The corrective of legally enforceable individual rights against state deprivations of liberty seemed the most reliable method for curbing this otherwise almost limitless assertion of governmental authority. The Progressives themselves failed to provide an effective framework for understanding the problems of persistent crime patterns, changing family and urban experiences, and the rigidities of bureaucratization; critics were able to deploy the dominant ideology of individual rights and responsibilities.

My third example of Progressive reform is protective labor legislation. The reformers were initially successful in regulating hours and working conditions but encountered opposition to their proposed expansions of such regulation—and to the minimum wage that they thought crucial to overcome risks that restrictions on hours and conditions would serve to impoverish workers further, especially women workers. The opposition reflected the continuing power of employers, divisions among workers, and the inability of the reformers to transform the terms of debate. Despite legislative success in securing state laws regulating work conditions and in some circumstances assuring minimum wages, the reform movement met significant judicial obstacles. Employers argued in courts around the country that protective legislation interfered with constitutional guarantees of freedom of contract. The wage relationship, they argued, must remain unregulated in a laissez-faire system committed to property rights and individual freedom. Regulation of employment conditions and terms would be socialist or Communist.

In memorable decisions such as Lochner v. New York, the judiciary agreed

[98]See Ryerson, *The Best-Laid Plans*, p. 158.

[99]See Paul Boyer, *Urban Masses and Moral Order in America, 1820–1920* (Cambridge, Mass.: Harvard University Press, 1982).

[100]Robert H. Mnookin, "Foster Care—In Whose Best Interest?" *Harvard Education Review* 13 (1973), 599, 602.

with the employers and enunciated as absolute principles the requisites of due-process protections against public regulation of employment contracts.[101] Justice Rufus Peckham's opinion for the Supreme Court majority in *Lochner* has been widely described as consummately "formalist" in its effort to justify the result as compelled by the Constitution and in its refusal to examine the moral, political, and economic consequences of the decision. As one commentator has put it, "The formalistic judge, committed to strict adherence to a prescribed model, arrives at a particular judgment through a mechanical process of deductive logic."[102] The power of formalist reasoning seemed undeterred by practical objections: the courts rejected protective labor legislation by declaring that the Constitution protects the employee's freedom to enter into any kind of contract, as well as the employer's freedom to do the same. This reasoning ignored the social and economic inequalities that had led the reformers to pursue regulation.

Different views were quite imaginable. Justice Oliver Wendell Holmes, Jr., for example, dissented in *Lochner,* objecting that the majority had simply used a natural-rights rationale to treat one economic theory—laissez-faire— as constitutionally protected. He argued, in contrast, that the Constitution "is not intended to embody a particular economic theory, whether of paternalism and the organic relation of the citizen to the State or of *laissez-faire.* It is made for people of fundamentally different views."[103] For Justice Holmes, then, the popularly elected branches of government should be free to experiment with different regulations, so long as the experiments were reasonable. Taking their cue from Holmes, some lawyers thenceforth defended protective legislation as reasonable. Others followed the route suggested by Justice John Harlan's dissent, which emphasized the factual context that had led the legislature to adopt the statute limiting bakery employees to ten hours of work per day. Justice Harlan offered an empirical analysis to refute the majority's denial of the regulation's reasonableness.[104]

Despite judicial defeats, reformers decided to renew their efforts by concentrating on the needs of women and children in the industrial labor force. Exploiting prevailing stereotypes of women and children as especially vulnerable in both physical and political terms, they asserted that women were the most exploited and least well-treated workers.[105] The reformers also turned

[101]198 U.S. 45 (1905). The majority reasoned that the due-process clause prevented unreasonable legislative intrusion upon the rights of property and liberty of contract; therefore, the Constitution forbade the state statute setting a maximum ten-hour day for bakery workers.

[102]Gary J. Jacobsohn, *Pragmatism, Statesmanship, and the Supreme Court* (Ithaca: Cornell University Press, 1977), for definitions of formalism and comments about Peckham in *Lochner;* to the past, derives absolute principles grounded in Nature, and reasons that human inequality in civil society can be deduced from these principles rooted in the past (p. 27). Cf. Morton Horwitz, *The Transformation of American Law, 1780–1860* (Cambridge, Mass.: Harvard University Press, 1977), for definitions of formalism and comments about Peckham in *Lochner*); and Morton White, *Social Thought in America: The Revolt against Formalism,* 3d ed. (New York: Oxford University Press, 1976).

[103]198 U.S. at 45.

[104]Id. at 65–74.

[105]See Lehrer, *Origins of Protective Labor Legislation,* p. 3. Restrictions on child labor also met with initial legislative victory and persistent judicial failure, culminating in the introduction

to the facts of social science to challenge the syllogisms of formalist legal reasoning. With this dual strategy—concentrating on women and marshaling empirical data about the effect of work conditions on women's physical vulnerabilities—they achieved greater though uneven success in defending protective legislation in the courts.[106]

The landmark and still most famous effort advancing this dual strategy joined Louis D. Brandeis, a prominent Boston lawyer later appointed to the Supreme Court, and Josephine Goldmark, a colleague of Florence Kelley at the National Consumer League in New York. Together, to defend an Oregon statute limiting women's employment to ten-hour working days, they produced a brief that assembled sociological data demonstrating the link between women's poor health and long hours. This "Brandeis Brief" convinced the Supreme Court in Muller v. Oregon to uphold the legislation against constitutional challenge.[107] Breaking out of the usual mode of constitutional litigation, the brief emphasized the factual predicate for the statute—and the consequences of the judicial choices—in order to persuade the Court to depart from formalist and precedential reasoning. The brief included evidence not only of special risks to women from long hours and hazardous employment but also of risks to the health of male workers.[108] Many supporters of protective labor laws for women conceived of such legislation as only the first step toward general, sex-neutral reforms establishing an eight- or ten-hour day, safer working conditions, and minimum wages.[109]

After *Muller,* reformers successfully deployed sociological evidence to defend laws setting a minimum wage for women and even laws limiting working hours for both men and women.[110] By organizing facts, the reformers convinced reviewing courts that protective legislation was a reasonable means of assisting the weaker parties to contractual bargains and that such legislation thus deserved a presumption of constitutionality. Nevertheless, judicial contests over protective legislation continued throughout the first three decades of the twentieth century. Opponents continued to cite constitutional protection of freedom of contract and the dangers of Bolshevism as arguments against protective legislation. These arguments helped persuade the Supreme Court to reject a minimum wage law in 1923.[111] Efforts to secure a ban against child labor succeeded in Congress, but the

---

of an unsuccessful constitutional amendment to override federal judicial rejection of federal legislation.

[106]Actually, this is a complicated story. See Frances Olsen, "From Paternalism to False Equality: Judicial Assaults on Feminist Community, Illinois, 1869–1895," *Mich. L. Rev.* 84 (1986), 1518. In 1895 an Illinois state court struck down an eight-hour law for women and in 1910 upheld a ten-hour law. Ritchie v. People, 155 Ill. 98, 40 N.E. 454 (1895). Other courts rejected some protective laws while still others upheld them. See Lehrer, *Origins of Protective Labor Legislation.*

[107]208 U.S. 412 (1908).

[108]See Mary Becker, "From Muller v. Oregon to Fetal Vulnerability Policies," *U. Chi. L. Rev.* 53 (1986), 1219, 1223 n.25.

[109]See Ronald K. Collins and Jennifer Friesen, "Looking Back on Muller v. Oregon," *A. B. A. J.* 69 (1983), 294, 298.

[110]See Bunting v. Oregon, 243 U.S. 426 (1917).

[111]Adkins v. Children's Hospital, 261 U.S. 525 (1923).

Supreme Court quickly struck it down.[112] Victories in court depended in part upon a tactical use of Victorian sentimentality, bolstered by an empirical demonstration of women's needs; hence, the tactics of reform contained an internal limit that could not extend protective legislation to all workers.[113] As historian Alice Kessler-Harris has argued, the reformers broke free from the freedom-of-contract idea only by emphasizing women's weaknesses and helplessness—and thereby exacerbated the dilemma for women who sought equality as well as transformation of the workplace.[114]

This internal limit contributed to a major conflict among women reformers and their supporters during the 1920s. After women finally secured the vote in 1919, the National Women's Party advocated an Equal Rights Amendment (ERA) to the federal Constitution, to forbid any discrimination on the basis of gender. To feminists working for protective labor legislation, the ERA represented a serious threat: its commitment to gender neutrality could be used by the courts to undo the incremental achievements in regulating the terms of employment. At a public meeting in 1921, Florence Kelley asked Alice Paul, a leader of the National Women's Party and proponent of the ERA, to tailor the amendment so that it would focus exclusively on political disabilities and thus preserve protective labor legislation. As Kelley explained elsewhere, "So long as men cannot be mothers, so long as legislation adequate for them can never be adequate for wage-earning women; then the cry Equality, Equality, where Nature has created Inequality, is as stupid and as deadly as the cry Peace, Peace, where there is no peace."[115] Paul refused to narrow the ERA. She sought advice from Felix Frankfurter, a Progressive Harvard Law School professor and later a Supreme Court justice. Frankfurter himself was soon pursuing the defense of minimum wage laws for women, based on gender differences, in a brief coauthored with Molly Dewson, another researcher from the National Consumer's League.[116]

[112]See Hammer v. Dagenhart, 247 U.S. 251 (1918); Bailey v. Drexel, 259 U.S. 20 (1922). State reforms had raised the minimum working age and tightened compulsory school attendance, which was mandatory in every state by 1918. See Lawrence A. Cremin, *American Education: The Metropolitan Experience, 1876–1980* (New York: Harper & Row, 1988), p. 297.

[113]See Lemons, *The Woman Citizen*, p. 142; Sybil Lipshultz, "Workers, Wives, and Mothers: The Problem of Minimum Wage Laws for Women in Early Twentieth Century America" (Ph.D. diss., University of Pennsylvania, 1986). Lipshultz notes that courts upheld protective legislation for men on gender-specific bases (p. 11): Bunting v. Oregon approved restrictions on men's work hours given their duties of citizenship.

[114]Alice Kessler-Harris, "Law and a Living: The Gendered Content of 'Frei Lubine,'" in *Differing Realities: Gender, Race, and Class in the Progressive Era*, ed. Nancy Schrom Dye and Noralee Frankel (Lexington: University Press of Kentucky, forthcoming); Alice Kessler-Harris, *Out to Work: A History of Wage-Earning Women in the U.S.* (New York: Oxford University Press, 1982), pp. 180–214.

[115]Florence Kelley, *Shall Women be Equal* (N.p.: National League of Women Voters, 1922), p. 41, quoted in Cott, *The Grounding of Modern Feminism*, p. 138. Jane Addams defended protective legislation as a means to achieve equality—by overcoming nature's handicaps (see Cott, p. 140).

[116]Dewson went on to become perhaps the most influential woman politician during the New Deal. See Susan Ware, *Partner and I: Molly Dewson, Feminism, and New Deal Politics* (New Haven, Conn.: Yale University Press, 1987).

The conflicts between advocates of the ERA and defenders of protective legislation splintered the coalition that had helped to secure suffrage. Even though both sides ultimately wanted protective labor legislation for both men and women, the social reformers favored defending legislation for women's wages, hours, and safety as a first step,[117] while the ERA advocates feared that the use of gender-based distinctions would revitalize gender stereotypes and hinder women's abilities to compete in the workforce. Opponents of the ERA maintained that abstract equality would hurt women by ignoring their differences, while proponents warned that retaining legal distinctions based on gender would render gender distinctions irradicable. Historian Nancy Cott has recently noted the paradox in the position taken by the proponents of the ERA: these members of the National Women's Party tried to mobilize women as a class to defeat discrimination against them as a class.[118] Cott observed that this dilemma—a version of the difference dilemma—remained a paradox for women in the 1920s, because ignoring sex differences would undermine any effort to mobilize women against them, yet highlighting women's differences in relation to men would deny women's differences from one another and confine them to a gender stereotype.[119] Given the drawbacks both for women who sought treatment as individuals and for those who sought treatment as members of a group, no one made headway in articulating an alternative that would enable both protection and equality.

With protective labor regulation, as with the infant and maternal health legislation and the juvenile court reforms, the grip of prevailing ideologies about individualism, freedom of contract, and gender differences limited the arguments Progressives could make—and limited their imagination as well.

The Constraints on What Could Be Imagined

In some ways, these three Progressive era initiatives can all be described as endorsements of relational concerns. For at least three reasons, however, their fate does not represent a fair test of relational ideas. First, actual political power and social conditions had more to do with the duration and shape of the programs than did any particular innovative idea they represented. Second, although these reforms manifested some relational ideas, the reformers themselves were never able to change the terms of the debate sufficiently to counter the prevailing notions of individual freedom and limited government. Finally, either the reformers lacked self-consciousness about the conflict between their own self-interests and the goals they pur-

---

[117]See *Alice Hamilton: A Life in Letters,* ed. Barbara Sicherman (Cambridge, Mass.: Harvard University Press, 1984).

[118]Cott, *The Grounding of Modern Feminism,* p. 142. Cott also explores a similar tension for women professionals during the 1920s: should they pursue a professional identity, ignoring their gender, or would this defeat their ability to organize as a group against the continued male domination of professional life? (pp. 233–39).

[119]Ibid., p. 276.

sued, or their goals involved more modest help to those in need than the kinds of social reconstruction suggested by some of their ideas.

Nonetheless, the Progressive reforms reveal intriguing relational dimensions. Each of the initiatives sprang from a recognition that people are connected to one another and that people in need or in trouble deserve some response from others in the community. The infant and maternal health legislation depended upon the view that high levels of infant mortality were a problem not simply for the families involved but for the country, and that state governmental responsibilities could be fulfilled through a partnership with the federal government. In addition, the architects of the original legislation specifically sought to break away from the mold of demeaning welfare or relief programs. They designed instead educational programs that would enable women to know more about their needs during pregnancy and child care. Conceiving of children's health-care issues as inextricably connected to their parents' health, knowledge, and sense of mastery, the administrators of the Children's Bureau introduced interdisciplinary approaches that departed from the traditional medical model's isolation of physical needs from other needs. Finally, the Children's Bureau administrators pursued a faith in the power of facts to reshape theory and the power of theory to shape facts as they gathered data about infant and maternal health and then revised their plans and programs in light of those data.

The juvenile court emerged in part from a conception of children as people fundamentally in relationship to others, rather than as autonomous individuals who could be held solely responsible for their acts or could be solely burdened by the neglect of their parents or guardians. Supporters of the juvenile court manifested a faith in interdisciplinary approaches, and especially in the helping relationship between a probation officer and a child under supervision. Reformers also drew an analogy to the parent-child relationship as the model for the judge's relationship to the juvenile.

Defenders of protective labor legislation fundamentally believed that the power relationship behind contractual agreements must be examined rather than ignored, and that abstract concepts such as freedom of contract must not trump the factual dimensions of social experience. Legal rules should change in light of sociological evidence, and the workplace should be remade so that vulnerabilities based on gender or age would not make a difference in people's lives. Abstract ideals such as equality should not obscure or deflect social practices that make people differ. A mix of moral vision and empirical study, they thought, should shape legal arguments and public policies.

Yet in each instance the reformers could not alter the power of a prevailing ideology of individualism. Adherents to this ideology labeled any state-initiated change as a dreaded left-wing conspiracy and also, in effect, reserved a separate, second track for people who could not function effectively in the mainstream designed for autonomous individuals. It was largely the needs of persons in this second track—women, children, impoverished people—that motivated many Progressive reforms and highlighted the Progressive critique of urban industrial society. But the reformers had no effective rejoinder to the charge of Bolshevism or socialism when they advocated infant and maternal health legislation and protective labor laws. Probably because they shared the pervasive belief in individualism, they were unable to rebut the charge that individuals are compromised by collective or joint activities. Some intellectuals tried to renovate ideology by arguing that each individual depends upon collective systems, such as courts and legal rules, to protect his or her freedom and that pervasive public schemes already assisted some—such as corporate owners—against others.[120] But none of these academic efforts to challenge prevailing assumptions succeeded in transforming public debate. Reformers found themselves battling one another about tactics and goals framed by the traditional world view, especially when it came to regulating labor.

I suggest that the dilemma that divided women over protective legislation could have been revised, on a purely intellectual level, by positing as the norm not the worst employment conditions created by new industrialists but the maximum hours and minimum wages legislation. This would have required challenging the baseline used for an assessment of equal treatment— and a more deliberate immersion in the relational, comparative nature of the equality inquiry itself.[121] An Equal Rights Amendment would be no threat to protective legislation if protection for all workers were the norm used for comparison. Instead, in the 1920s the women's movement emphasized individualism and individual achievement to eradicate gender differences.[122] Advocates of the ERA simply made more explicit the individualist turn in the movement. Individualism, suited to a laissez-faire economy, could hardly provide a sufficient point of leverage to enable an alternative vision or to reject the workplace designed with disparate workers in mind.

Further, when reformers emphasized empirical study as a way to dispute formalist justifications for judgment of contract, that focus risked turning social and political questions into technical questions. The statistics marshalled in the "Brandeis Brief" narrowed the question to whether women were different enough from men to justify treating them differently, rather than addressing what kinds of workplaces the legislature should be allowed to promote and prohibit.[123] By either accepting the distinction between men

---

[120]See Morris Cohen, "Property and Sovereignty," *Cornell L. Q.* 13 (1927), 8; John Dawson, "Economic Duress—An Essay in Perspective," *Mich. L. Rev.* 45 (1947), 253; Robert Hale, "Coercion and Distribution in a Supposedly Non-coercive State," *Political Science Quarterly* 38 (1923), 470; Robert Hale, "Law Making by Unofficial Minorities," *Colo. L. Rev.* 20 (1920), 451. See also Hawley, *The Great War,* p. 11, describing Progressives who saw a role for the state midway between collectivism and individualism; Kloppenberg, *Uncertain Victory,* p. 278: the idea of liberty as freedom from oppression worked in the eighteenth century but not in the nineteenth and twentieth, when private economic power could be oppressive, and "individual property rights lost their progressive significance and became barriers to the further expansion of freedom."

[121]This method was not unknown to Progressives. Sophinisba Breckenridge, who taught at the School of Civics and Philanthropy (later the School of Social Administration) at the University of Chicago and participated in Hull House affairs, said in 1923, "If there is inequality on the basis of sex, let it be admitted as part of a predatory scheme that has neither reason nor justice, only habit and power, back of it" (quoted in Lipshultz, "Workers, Wives, and Mothers," p. 29).

[122]See Cott, *The Grounding of Modern Feminism.*

[123]See Lehrer, *Origins of Protective Labor Legislation.*

and women or else lapsing into abstract individualism, the Progressive reformers missed the relationship between men and women in an economy that
had made gender matter. They failed to see that regulation of only women's
hours and wages would not only reiterate gender stereotypes but also succeed only under the presumption of a traditional family structure, allowing
underpayment of women for their labor because they were presumed not to
provide the sole financial support for a family.[124] Thus, gender-based protective legislation launched on a collision course with the ideology of individualism that itself obscured the traditional roles of women. Perhaps, then, it is not
surprising that the Progressive reformers battled the advocates for women's
equality who laid claim to individualism themselves.

The confines of individualist ideology also hampered the defense—and
fulfillment—of the juvenile court vision. Implicit in the creation of the court
was a polarized view: either children should be treated like adults and held
responsible for their transgressions, or they should be given care and supervision; either children are independent, or they are dependent. The ideology of
individualism carries with it a second track for those who do not fit, those
defined in opposition to competent and self-determining individuals. The
juvenile court increasingly seemed founded on an unworkable premise, especially if the goal was to help children within the court's jurisdiction grow into
responsible, autonomous persons. The rhetoric of need and dependence had
no limits. Upon examination, all children have "best interests" that are not
fully served by the adults who attend them. The expanding catchment area
defined by judges' conceptions of those who needed help could only over-
burden social workers, probation officers, and the judges themselves, who
were surfeited with problems they could not solve. Juvenile courts, suffering
from basic inefficiencies, failed to end or even notably curb juvenile crime
and neglect. Critics articulated more rigid forms of the individualist ideology.
By the 1940s, delinquents had come to represent a deviant subclass that
deserved heightened, not relaxed, efforts of social control; by the 1960s, the
Supreme Court was reflecting national sentiment in directing that the norms
of individual rights and duties should structure the juvenile court and thus
conform it to the model it had been intended to replace.

The Progressives sought to remedy the costs of urbanization, especially the
costs borne by women, children, and impoverished people. They encountered and failed to surmount the ideology of individualism, which resisted
collective responses to reform even as it divided the community into two
classes: autonomous, self-reliant citizens, and others. Sometimes the category of "others" was filled by women, sometimes by children, sometimes by
immigrants, sometimes by socialists. Sometimes the Progressives reinvigorated the distinctions between themselves and "others" in the very gesture of
becoming advocates for those in need.

Perhaps the impulse toward differentiation and separation is especially

[124]See ibid., p. 227. See also Alice Kessler-Harris, "Regulating Gender and Wages" (paper
presented to the Women and Progressivism Conference, sponsored by The American Historical
Association and the Smithsonian, May 1988).

American.[125] A conception of "we" and "they" was difficult for the reformers themselves to escape, even for Progressives who struggled to deny differences between themselves and those they wanted to help. Jane Addams urged full democracy, under which social workers and clients would acknowledge one another as equals, but putting this ideal into practice proved difficult if not impossible. Most people remained unselfconscious about their tendencies to divide the world into different groups, and most privileged white people remained unaware of their presumption in believing that they could know what was best for everyone else. The Progressive reformers were mainly middle-class, native-born, urban-based professionals. They wanted a stable and humane society, but they imagined ways to accomplish it that were compatible with and helpful to their own professional aspirations. They did not want much to change that would alter their positions, and they did not develop methods to discover whether their plans for health and safety reforms, juvenile courts, and other innovations would be favored by those people they claimed to be saving.[126]

A vivid example appeared across the Atlantic in Beatrice Webb, a Fabian socialist and participant in settlement-house work in England. She dissented from social insurance programs developed by the Royal Commission on the Poor Law in 1909, calling them regressive and superficial, yet she inserted in her minority report a call for compulsory labor exchanges to organize, train, and create jobs for able-bodied unemployed people, regardless of their own desires.[127] Criticized for favoring social control over social reform, Webb retained patrician sensibilities along with her commitment to humanitarian activities.

At least some reformers were acutely aware that they had no credible or legitimate claim to know the interests of those they proposed to help. They responded with protests of commonality and shared experience. Women reformers, for example, tended to claim commonalities with other women, based on shared experiences as wives, mothers, and daughters. Yet these claims papered over the differences among women—differences that nonetheless surfaced even as people denied them.

At a conference in 1923, for example, social reformers, manufacturers, government officials, and notably women labor leaders assembled to discuss women and industry. After formal presentations, black women protested the exclusion of black concerns in the debates over protection legislation; they noted the irony that white female reformers often were free to pursue their activities only because they hired women of color to perform their domestic work. Later in the discussions the question arose of class conflict between middle-class reformers and the working-class women they sought to help.

---

[125]See Hawley, *The Great War*, p. 169; and R. Laurence Moore, *Religious Outsiders and the Making of Americans* (New York: Oxford University Press, 1986), a powerful account of how each religious group helped create a sense of belonging in America by cultivating the status of the outsider.

[126]Tifflin, *In Whose Best Interest?* p. 285.

[127]See Kloppenberg, *Uncertain Victory*, p. 273.

Tension between professional women and middle-class women deepened as members of each group claimed solidarity with working-class women. When one woman called upon "all actual wage earners to stand up," nearly every woman in the audience promptly stood, in an act of identification with working-class women. This very moment unleashed dissension among the conference participants over whether women who volunteered their time could count themselves as workers, rejecting their domestic identities in order to claim the label. But the unpaid volunteers claimed additional identification with working-class women as wives and mothers—which the professional women tended not to be. In their contest over who had solidarity with the working-class, the professionals and volunteers enacted differences among women without learning much about actual working-class women.[128]

In another setting a group of San Francisco women, lobbying for reforms after securing the vote in 1912, sought particularly to vindicate what they considered to be women's values: they opposed urban and political corruption and the double standard for illicit sex. As part of their campaign they attempted to shut down the dance halls, which the reformers saw as dens of vice. These middle-class women did not blame the dance hall girls and offered to find them other employment, but most of the girls rejected such offers. They declared either that they could not earn enough to support their families in other lines of work or that they enjoyed their independence and financial success in the dance halls. The reformers were surprised that the girls did not welcome their help. They had wrongly assumed that, as women, they knew what the girls wanted and what was good for them.[129]

Historians have charged such reformers with the self-interested desire to protect their own status and enlarge their own power to regulate the conduct of others. Even assuming more altruistic motives, there was a gap between the reformers' desire to help others and their understanding of what others would perceive as help. Their effort to treat those in need as persons like themselves mistook common humanity for shared values and interests. In this context, then, even the Golden Rule would not be enough, despite its historical place as a central ethic or tenet across cultural and religious groups. The injunction to do unto others as you would have them do unto you is subject to two risks: first, we may assume that we know the perspective of the other, when we do not; and second, we may assume that the other person is too different for us to know his or her perspective. The first risk creates a false unity or universalism, treating others as though they were just like us, replicas with no different qualities. The second risk creates a false dichotomy, treating others as though they were sharply and essentially different from us. Nothing in the Golden Rule challenges the notion that difference resides in

---

[128]Lipshultz, "Workers, Wives, and Mothers," pp. 23, 35–36, 45–46.

[129]See Gayle Gullett, "City Mothers, City Daughters, and the Dance Hall Girls: The Limits of Female Political Power in San Francisco, 1913," in *Women and the Structure of Society*, ed. Barbara Harris and JoAnn McNamara (Durham, N.C.: Duke University Press, 1984), pp. 149, 158. See also Judith Walkowitz, *Prostitution and Victorian Society: Women, Class, and the State* (New York: Cambridge University Press, 1980), pp. 6–8, 131–46.

those who are different. If anything, the rule reinforces the use of the individual actor's own experience as the reference point for treating a different person: Do not do unto others as *you* would not have them do unto you. The unstated reference point for treating the other is the self, and it is from the self's point of view, not the other's, that treatment is to be evaluated. Competing perspectives are invisible, and difference may continue to seem intrinsic to the other. The status quo can well remain unchallenged, even if it produces harms to the other, who is the supposed object of help. Treating me as you would want to be treated could be translated, in your mind, into treating me as you would want to be treated *if you were someone in my position*. Assume a world of sharply hierarchical social classes, such as the world of the Progressives, in which you are a member of the elite class, like a Progressive reformer. I am your employee or a target for your help. If you treat me as you would wish to be treated if you were in my position, you may rest unperturbed in the view that someone in my position—lower than yours—does not expect or would even be embarrassed by being accorded an unfamiliar kind of equal respect.[130] If the task of imagining what the other wants opens no chance of changing your own understanding, there is little hope of learning about the other and the other's needs and wants.

The real chance to learn about the other is by talking with that person. Social reformers seeking to improve the lot of others would improve their chances if they would communicate with those they hope to help and share with them the process of deciding what to do. Some observers argue that reformers succeed best when they take on the goal of empowering others to define and pursue their own interests and needs.[131] As Jane Addams knew, reformers need those they seek to help, and they work chiefly to fulfill those needs unless they become open to change themselves.[132] The Progressive

---

[130]Bernard Williams, *Ethics and the Limits of Philosophy* (Cambridge, Mass.: Harvard University Press, 1985), p. 90, claims that the idea of reversing roles with the other necessarily includes a prediction of the probabilities that the imagined situation of the other would ever happen to you. Since the probability is zero—given that you will never be anyone else—your perceptions about the other person's preferences will accordingly be weighted in the direction of insensitivity. See also Michael Theunissen, *The Other: Studies in the Social Ontology of Husserl, Heidegger, Sartre, and Buber* (Cambridge, Mass.: MIT Press, 1986), pp. 323–36, describing the discontinuity in time and space between oneself and anyone else.

[131]See Freire, *Pedagogy of the Oppressed;* and Lucie White, "To Learn and to Teach: Lessons from Drie Fontein on Lawyering and Power," *Wis. L. Rev.* 1988 (1988), 699.

[132]Addams, *Twenty Years at Hull-House*, p. 76: "Hull-House was soberly opened on the theory that the dependence of classes on each other is reciprocal; and that as the social relation is essentially a reciprocal relation, it gives a form of expression that has peculiar value." Addams also maintained that "the one thing to be dreaded in the Settlement is that it lose its flexibility, its power of quick adaptation, its readiness to change its methods as its environment may demand" (p. 98). A more critical evaluation suggests that the reformers had to learn how to recognize the interests of the immigrants who actively resisted the pressure to assimilate; see Rivka Shpak Lissak, *Pluralism and Progress: Hull House and the New Immigrants, 1890–1919* (Chicago: University of Chicago Press, 1989). A first-person account by an immigrant aided by Hull House shows enormous gratitude, and little evidence of knowledge that the reformers needed those they claimed to help. See Hilda Satt Polacheck, *I Came a Stranger: The Story of a Hull-House Girl*, ed. Dena J. Polacheck Epstein (Urbana: University of Illinois Press, 1989).

reformers, for the most part, lost this opportunity by failing to include at the planning stage those who were supposed to benefit from their plans. This idea was present to some extent in settlement houses where the reformers lived alongside those they hoped to help and learned as a result to change their presuppositions and priorities. But the more engaged the reformers became with affecting public policies, changing laws, and establishing new institutions, the more remote was their contact with those who would be helped. Missing altogether were settings of genuine democracy, through which people would share decisions about their collective future.[133]

Absent opportunities to challenge the inequality of the helper and the one to be helped, the act of helping may unleash attitudes of domination, superiority, and denigration of the other. Lionel Trilling, in a 1946 essay, powerfully summarized this risk: "Some paradox in our nature leads us, once we have made our fellow men the objects of our enlightened interest, to go on to make them the objects of our pity, then of our wisdom, and ultimately of our coercion."[134] Progressive reformers were so convinced of their lofty purposes and secure in their optimism that they missed the self-interest and coercion implicit in some of their own programs—notably, the juvenile court. Moreover, the Progressives failed to observe that their initiatives were perhaps being administered in the best interests of the administrators rather than of the clients.

Reformers have self-interests, and so do members of bureaucracies—facts that the Progressives neglected in their enthusiasm for experts and managerial solutions. Progressives had faith in expert discretion and seldom perceived expert self-interest and fascination with power. The members of the Children's Bureau became caught up in a bureaucratic struggle with the Public Health Service over control of infant and maternal health programs.[135] Advocates of protective labor legislation were swept up in the constant competition between courts and legislatures for power and control. Juvenile court judges and officials aggrandized their authority and for some fifty years resisted the criticism that began shortly after the court was invented. Here, the Progressive reformers' faith in bureaucracy and expertise undermined their commitment to democracy and to the belief that empirical and analytic knowledge could dislodge settled and privileged views.[136] De-

---

[133]Graebner, *The Engineering of Consent*, p. 191. Achieving understanding of those they wanted to help and devising procedures for genuine participation represented goals in the writings of some Progressives, including Jane Addams. But these purposes were countered by institutional practices and people's actual treatment of one another.

[134]Lionel Trilling, "Manners, Morals, and the Novel," in *The Liberal Imagination: Essays on Literature and Society* (1950; New York: Scribner, 1976), p. 205.

[135]Interestingly, Lemons (*The Woman Citizen*, pp. 159–60) noted that opponents of the Sheppard-Towner Act attacked members of the Children's Bureau not only as feminists and Bolsheviks but also as self-interested bureaucrats seeking to enlarge their own power.

[136]See Kloppenberg, *Uncertain Victory*, pp. 386–87: "One of the larger ironies of this period, as the difference between Weber and the American progressive theorists illustrates, concerns the contrast between the liberating effect of the radical theory of knowledge which frees man from dogma and emphasizes experience and volition, and the process of bureaucratization, which, by using the techniques of science, tends to usurp power from the individuals whose liberation, both intellectual and political, these theorists sought to secure. In a sense, then, their ideas about

spite the Progressives' hopes, bureaucracy would not resolve the conflict between collective forms of power that risked individual oppression and collective forms of neglect that did the same, even if bureaucracy did seem to produce social order and cohesion.[137]

Perhaps behind the Progressives' faith in bureaucracy and their neglect of truly participatory processes were large anxieties and fears about changes they could not control. Sometimes their assertions of commonality were really demands for conformity. Failures to conform could produce massive public disapproval. Jane Addams, once perhaps the most celebrated woman in America, herself became an outcast when she opposed United States involvement in World War I.[138] She was castigated as disloyal, Communist, impertinent, meddling, anti-American—as different. Similarly, most Americans hoped that new immigrants would assimilate—which meant losing any distinguishing traits. Progressive reformers advocated Americanization programs for this purpose.[139] Yet the turn of the century was a period of nonassimilation for many groups. Subcultures emerged, including the black culture of the Harlem Renaissance[140] and distinct identities for Irish Catholics, Polish Catholics, and Italian Catholics.[141] Many Progressives, wittingly or not, participated in the widespread nativist response, demanding restrictions on immigration, loyalty tests for immigrants, and other measures of social control for those who were different from themselves.

Robert Wiebe's classic historical study of the Progressives, *The Search for Order,* offers an explanation for these practices which may be too simplistic: it emphasizes one factor, status anxiety, as the reason reformers searched for order in a shifting, industrial society. Yet even if it was only one factor among many, this notion of status anxiety provides an interesting interpretation of the reformers' failure to remake the individualist framework for understanding the social problems they sought to address. Wiebe argues that followers of bureaucratic thought needed a solution to the problem of social dissension and incoherence and that some searched for tighter social cohesion either by promoting assimilation of those who were different or by exploring deep human commonalities in theories of psychology or of human nature. Alternatively, Wiebe suggests the power of fear and prejudice in bureaucrats' responses to immigrants.

A time-honored device was exclusion: draw a line around the good society and dismiss the remainder. Just as the defenders of the community and the men of power late in the nineteenth century each had denied their enemies a place in the

knowledge and action both entailed, and were challenged by, their ideas about reform. They focused on individual experience, validated socially by the pragmatic methods, as the source of power, but the generalized form of that knowledge, bureaucratic administration operating on scientific principles, undercut the people's ability to govern themselves."

[137]See Wiebe, *The Search for Order,* p. 159.
[138]Davis, *American Heroine,* pp. 232–81.
[139]See Wiebe, *The Search for Order,* p. 210.
[140]See, e.g., Arnold Rampersad, *The Life of Langston Hughes,* vol. 1, *1902–1941: I, Too, Sing America* (New York: Oxford University Press, 1986).
[141]See Moore, *Religious Outsiders,* pp. 63–64.

true America, so worried people in the twentieth also separated the legitimate from the illegitimate. The most elaborate method—a compound of biology, pseudo-science, and hyperactive imaginations—divided the people of the world by race and located each group along a value scale according to its distinctive, inherent characteristics. Those alternatively called Anglo-Saxon or Teutonic or Nordic always rested on the top. Bristling with the language of the laboratory, such doctrines impressed an era so respectful of science. At the same time, they remained loose enough to cover almost any choice of outcasts: one could discard all new immigration as "refuse of the murder breed of Southern Europe," all slum dwellers as "degenerate," all Jews as congenitally treacherous, all people of yellow, brown, or black skin as innately inferior. Even in the more moderate guise of eugenics, or selective breeding, racism was used to shut out those who did not belong, not to improve those who did.[142]

Progressive reformers could not replace the dominant individualist ideology. They avoided participatory processes that could have challenged their biases, imposed their interests on those they claimed to help, and perpetuated a world distinguishing "us" from "them" while expanding bureaucratic power. Yet they also articulated visions of mutual support and public policies to care for the dependent and protect the vulnerable.[143] The Progressives sharpened the dilemmas they sought to resolve: they demonstrated that benevolence can be a form of neglect of the interests of others, just as neglect can be a form of oppression. Thus, one legacy of the Progressive era is another version of the dilemma of difference: collective neglect of individual need denies relationships and oppresses individuals, but so may efforts to acknowledge need and responsibility toward others.[144]

[142]Wiebe, *The Search for Order*, pp. 156–57.

[143]Perhaps they were expressing a fear of real and unavoidable dependence. See the discussion of infancy in Gaylin et al., *Doing Good*.

[144]Ira Glasser, "Prisoners of Benevolence: Power versus Liberty in the Welfare State," in Gaylin et al., *Doing Good*, p. 97, poses the questions of how society may respect rights and yet not ignore needs, and how social rules can allow for and protect individual autonomy and yet fulfill social obligations. I suggest that our vocabulary for framing and addressing such questions already deploys assumptions that lock us into the dilemma. We need to reconceive of the relationships already presumed and reinforced by rights to individual autonomy, and the social dimension of both needs and rights.

CHAPTER 9

Rights and Relations:
Families and Children

> And so I appeal to a voice, to something shadowy,
> a remote important region in all who talk:
> though we could fool each other, we should consider—
> lest the parade of our mutual life get lost in the dark.
> —William Stafford, "A Ritual to Read to Each Other"

Progressive reformers and sympathetic theorists at the turn of the century criticized liberal rights for permitting an abusive capitalism and for rendering poor and working-class people vulnerable to urban, industrial hazards and onerous working conditions. Contemporary critics cite the impoverished vision of human community implicit in liberal rights.[1] Something was lost through the triumph of liberal rights, some sense of community and mutual obligation.

But Progressivism had problems, too. Its reformers and their spiritual progeny—New Dealers, Great Society staffers, and advocates of social welfare and judicial programs throughout the twentieth century—defined their objective as caring for those in need. Yet these public assistance and social work interventions too often in effect controlled and restricted those people and subjected them to governmental regulation without protection against power imbalances. Chapter 8 considered the example of the discretionary process of the juvenile court, described as a "kangaroo court," by a disapproving Supreme Court. Another example is the expansion of welfare state controls, using social workers to regulate the private conduct of aid recip-

---

Epigraph: Excerpt from "A Ritual to Read to Each Other" from *Stories That Could Be True* by William Stafford. Copyright © 1966, 1977 by William Stafford. Reprinted by permission of Harper & Row, Publishers, Inc.

[1] See Robert Bellah, Richard Madsen, William Sullivan, Ann Swidler, and Steven M. Tipton, *Habits of the Heart: Individualism and Commitment in American Life* (Berkeley: University of California Press, 1985), arguing that because of the dominance of individualist rhetoric, Americans lack a language to describe the affiliations that matter to them.

267

ients.[2] "Reforms" like these have helped to fuel powerful critiques of state intervention in the lives of dependent people.[3]

Moreover, these and similar programs provoke persistent political objections. To many observers, state-supported social welfare jeopardizes individual autonomy, independence, and freedom. Ideas about these psychological and political needs animate liberalism and distinguish a modern polity from feudalism. The American Revolution enacted the search for independence on a national scale. Earlier struggles to secure legal restraints on power, dating back to the Magna Carta, imbued rights with the symbolic and practical function of protecting individuals against the power of the sovereign. Throughout much of Western history, liberal rights have looked like the solution to the risks of paternalism and tyranny.

Is there no way to rescue what seemed valuable in a world of mutual obligation while still pursuing the protection of rights against coercive power? Especially from the vantage point of "different" people—disabled persons, children, women, and members of historically disfavored minorities—danger comes from either a system of hierarchical status relations or a system of autonomous individualism that leaves each person "free" to protect himself or herself in an indifferent or hostile world. The history of family law demonstrates both dangers. For families, the rights revolution was partial: power relations unchecked by legal restraints endure. Women and children have historically lacked the kinds of individual rights both inside and outside the family that the male head of household (himself historically white and monied) has enjoyed. Yet, simply extending to them the preexisting set of individual rights fails to acknowledge the special situations and needs of women and children—and neglects the significance of relationships within the family.

In short, to family members who have lacked power and privilege there are dangers both from rights-based approaches that ignore their historical differences and from relational approaches that deny them the basic rights accorded to others. This conundrum returns us to the dilemma of difference. The family context offers an especially vivid demonstration of the limits of both rights-based and relational approaches.

When rights have been introduced to the family, they have failed to remake patterns of relationships both within and outside it; instead, they have subtly imposed on the most vulnerable members the previous patterns of power. New rights have presumed that men and women are the same for purposes of

[2]See Michelle Meldon, "Sexual Abuse and Confidentiality Rules" (unpublished paper, 1988, in author's possession): social workers are drawn into testifying against their clients; and Abraham Blumberg, "The Practice of Law as a Confidence Game: The Organizational Cooptation of a Profession," *Law & Soc'y Rev.* 1 (June 1967), 15–39: defense lawyers serve as double agents because they will repeat their roles and need working relationships with other court personnel. See also Ira C. Lupu, "Welfare and Federalism: AFDC Eligibility Policies and the Scope of State Discretion," *B.U.L. Rev.* 57 (1977), 1–38: states express varied negative attitudes in welfare regulations.

[3]This is one impetus for the warning that we should be most wary of government when it acts benignly, for then comes the greatest danger of tyranny.

child custody battles, postdivorce finances, and other family matters. These rights ignore the differences historically drawn on gender lines and the reinforcement of those differences in institutions surrounding the family. But this need not be the only course for rights. After examining historical developments in family law, this chapter considers how locating rights within actual relationships can help us construct rights that attend to differences.

Legal theorists writing during the early part of this century reevaluated public and private power by examining the relationships contemplated by the patterns of rights that prevailed at that time. These "legal realists" exposed the limits of liberal rights that presumed and reinforced existing distinctions between the public and private spheres. The work of these scholars focused on the distinction between government and private property.[4]

Another historical distinction in this country's law, rather than drawing the boundary between the public and the private marketplace, divides private families from all other institutions, including market and state.[5] Law has long regulated relationships not only between public and private realms but between children and state officials, parents and children, husbands and wives. Applying insights from the realists helps to reveal the connections between public and private realms which define and regulate family relationships. Similarly, an examination of the legal treatment of children during this country's history helps to expose the public uses and public neglect of children. With this analysis, we can reimagine rights as instruments for illuminating these relationships. Rights can redress assigned differences without succumbing to historical patterns of family relationships; rights can be responsive to relationships without destroying them. This chapter, then, seeks to exemplify one form of relational analysis that seeks to recover rights.

Family Law: Divorce and Domestic Violence

Traditional family law, forged in the eighteenth and nineteenth centuries, treated the while male head of household as a family's representative to the state. Rights in this context attached to the man, who exercised suffrage, held the family property, and entered into contracts. His wife and minor children were generally excluded from the right to sue or be sued, to enter into contracts, or to hold property or earnings. The head of household secured, under law, powers over the property and services of his wife and children, including the power to discipline them.[6] The traditional allocation of power

[4]Their work, in many ways, laid the foundation for the New Deal. See Cass R. Sunstein, "Constitutionalism after the New Deal," *Harv. L. Rev.* 101 (1987), 421–510.

[5]See Frances Olsen, "The Family and the Market: A Study of Ideology and Legal Reform," *Harv. L. Rev.* 96 (1983), 1497–1579.

[6]See Sir William Blackstone, *Commentaries on the Laws of England* (New York: Collins & Hannay, 1930), 1:433–36; Helen I. Clarke, *Social Legislation: American Laws Dealing with Family, Child, and Dependents* (New York: Appleton-Century, 1940), pp. 63–66; Joan M. Krauskopf, "Partnership Marriage: Legal Reforms Needed," in *Women into Wives: The Legal and Economic Impact of Marriage*, ed. Jane Roberts Chapman and Margaret Gates (Beverly

in the family permeated legal rules about marriage, giving the husband legal power to select the marital domicile and to serve as head of the household, as well as the legal obligation to support the family financially. In return, the wife under the traditional marriage agreement was to provide domestic services as housewife, mother, sexual partner, and companion.[7]

Besides enforcing gender-based roles, traditional family law embraced a particular notion of family autonomy which barred the legal system from invading the private enclave of the family and the sphere of power reserved to the head of the family.[8] Influenced largely by religious teachings and by the conception of the family as the stable reserve for child rearing, the law treated marriage as a permanent and indissoluble union. Well past the middle of the nineteenth century, marriage represented a permanent bond that the state should protect. The state would not make its courts available for resolving disputes between husband and wife or among other family members. This was to be a realm where affection and mutual commitment would resolve disagreements.

The family was constructed, by law, as a group largely removed from liberal rights and autonomous individualism. In the view of judges during the nineteenth century, fathers had dominion over mothers and over children.[9] Divorce—a judicial decree ending a marriage and allowing its members to remarry during the lifetime of the other party—was essentially unheard of before the mid-nineteenth century. English law did not make divorce available until 1857.[10] At about the same time a few midwestern and southern

Hills, Calif.: Sage, 1977), pp. 93–101; Wendy McElroy, "The Roots of Individualist Feminism in 19th-Century America," in *Freedom, Feminism, and the State,* 2d ed., ed. Wendy McElroy (New York: Homes & Meier, 1989), pp. 3–26.

[7]Lenore J. Weitzman, "Legal Regulation of Marriage: Tradition and Change," *Calif. L. Rev.* 62 (1974), 1169–83, 1187–97. Her dower interest in her husband's property was a mere expectancy, not a right. As common law developed in this country, in a majority of states the widow obtained a right to inherit a fixed share of her husband's estate. Actual social practices in many respects diverged from the formal legal rules. See Martha Minow, " 'Forming underneath Everything That Grows': Toward a History of Family Law," *Wis. L. Rev.* 1985 (1985), 819–98.

[8]As described by Stephen J. Morse, "Family Law in Transition: From Traditional Families to Individual Liberty," in *Changing Images of the Family,* ed. Virginia Tufte and Barbara Myerhoff (New Haven, Conn.: Yale University Press, 1979), pp. 319, 321, one traditional formulation treated marriage as the merger of husband and wife into one legal personality—"and the husband was 'the one.' " For Roman law, see Edgar Bodhenheimer, *Jurisprudence: The Philosophy and Method of the Law,* rev. ed. (Cambridge, Mass.: Harvard University Press, 1974), pp. 332–33. Historians debate what kind of private enclave was represented by families in colonial and revolutionary America, and to what extent such families were nuclear or extended. Cf. John Demos, *A Little Commonwealth: Family Life in Plymouth Colony* (New York: Oxford University Press, 1970), pp. 62–81; Edward Shorter, *The Making of the Modern Family* (New York: Basic Books, 1975), p. 242; and Ralph J. Crandell, "Family Types, Social Structure, and Mobility in Early America: Charlestown, Massachusetts, a Case Study," in Tufte and Myerhoff, *Changing Images of the Family,* pp. 61, 67–74.

[9]The nineteenth century was a period of legal change for the family, with an increasing role for judges as ostensible protectors of women and children. See Michael Grossberg, *Governing the Hearth: Law and the Family in Nineteenth-Century America* (Chapel Hill: University of North Carolina Press, 1985).

[10]A rare exception: in the late seventeenth century, adultery could justify a special act of Parliament to end a marriage. See Lenore J. Weitzman, *The Divorce Revolution: The Unexpected Social and Economic Consequences for Women and Children in America* (New York: Free Press, 1985), p. 6.

jurisdictions in the United States, with the experimental tone of the frontier, began to permit divorce upon demonstration of cruelty. Massachusetts, for example, did not permit divorce even for this reason until 1870, after which, the typical divorce was granted on grounds of desertion or drunkenness. New York permitted only legal separation upon proof of desertion or cruelty; it reserved divorce for proof of adultery until the 1950s.[11] And beyond divorce proceedings, for most of the nineteenth century, state courts provided few avenues for relief from domestic violence or for settling other disputes within a family.[12] Where rights appeared for individual family members, they were constrained by the larger conception of the family sphere as removed from the realm of liberal values.[13]

Public concern about violence against children led to the establishment of private protective associations in the 1870s, which in turn lobbied for legislation and helped to justify government initiatives for removing children from the homes of drunken or neglecting parents. But a persistent reluctance to allow governmental authorities to invade the family shielded especially middle- and upper-class families from the enforcement of neglect and abuse laws; class prejudice may explain the more constant state intrusion in the lives of poorer families.[14] Beyond the protection of children against serious physical or psychological harm, there has been public neglect of children, justified by the theory that only parents are responsible for them.[15]

[11]See Elizabeth Hafkin Pleck, *Domestic Tyranny: The Making of Social Policy against Family Violence from Colonial Times to the Present* (New York: Oxford University Press, 1987), pp. 56–66.

[12]Puritan church courts had enforced moral codes, but this activity had declined by the mid-eighteenth century (ibid., pp. 32–33), and a few states criminalized wife beating in the nineteenth century (p. 63). Traditional rules denied families access to court for enforcement of contracts or recovery for torts among their immediate members. See Judith Areen, *Cases and Materials on Family Law*, 2d ed. (Mineola, N.Y.: Foundation Press, 1985).

[13]Hendrik Hartog, "Mrs. Packard on Dependency," *Yale J. Law & Humanities* 1 (1988), 79.

[14]See Michael Wald, "State Intervention on Behalf of 'Neglected' Children: A Search for Realistic Standards," *Stan. L. Rev.* 27 (1975), 985–1040; Barbara Nelson, *Making an Issue out of Child Abuse: Political Agenda Setting for Social Problems* (Chicago: University of Chicago Press, 1984); David Gil, *Violence against Children: Physical Child Abuse in the United States* (Cambridge, Mass.: Harvard University Press, 1970). An especially rich and nuanced work is Linda Gordon, *Heroes of Their Own Lives: The Politics and History of Family Violence, Boston, 1880–1960* (New York: Viking Press, 1988).

[15]It may seem odd to speak of public neglect of children in what has been called a child-centered society. There certainly are periodic public outcries about the treatment of children. See, e.g., "Recent Development, the Insurance Crisis: Who's Looking after Day Care?" *Harv. Women's L.J.* 9 (1986), 199–214, discussing the magnitude of response to child abuse in day-care centers; and Nelson, *Making an Issue*. But simply in terms of the physical well-being of children in this country, the case can be made that ours is a relatively neglectful society. Despite our wealth, twelve countries do better in keeping their infants alive; see Children's Defense Fund, *A Children's Defense Fund Budget: An Analysis of the President's FY 1986 Budget and Children* (Washington, D.C.: Children's Defense Fund, 1985), p. 4. Over 20 percent of all children in this country live in families whose incomes fall below the poverty line (p. 18). To put the same point another way, nearly 40 percent of people in poverty in this country are children (p. 33). Only 35 percent of mothers raising children alone receive any child support from fathers; see Sar A. Levitan, Richard S. Belous, and Frank Gallo, *What's Happening to the American Family? Tensions, Hopes, Realities*, rev. ed. (Baltimore: Johns Hopkins University Press, 1988), pp. 71–72. Nearly one million children under the age of five have no adult supervision during the day; see U.S. Commission on Civil Rights, *A Growing Crisis: Disadvantaged Women and*

Violence against wives remained for the most part a hidden issue; not until advocates for women's rights campaigned for reforms in the 1970s and 1980s did courts and legislatures alter the premise that interactions between husbands and wives deserved privacy and were off limits for the state. As late as 1980, opponents of statutes to fund shelters and services for battered women warned against the risks to the nuclear family of such state intervention.[16]

Since courts became available for divorces, the divorce rate has grown so steadily that most people's only significant contact with the law is through the divorce process.[17] Until the late 1970s, divorce law tended to reiterate the gender-based division of marriage roles, presuming that the wife would continue to provide child care and the husband to provide financial support, unless the wife was the guilty party in the grounds justifying the divorce. Thus even legally divorced couples remained bound in roles that presumed the traditional family structure. Under that presumption, combined with their continuing disadvantage in the paid labor force,[18] women remained financially more dependent following divorce and typically more burdened with family responsibilities.

Or so it seemed, before the "divorce revolution." California adopted the first "no fault" divorce law in 1970, and since then nearly every state has

---

Their Children (Washington, D.C.: U.S. Commission on Civil Rights, 1983), p. 13. Between 1950 and 1977, adolescent suicide for minors aged eighteen to nineteen increased from 3 in 100,000 to 10 in 100,000; see *Better Health for Children: Action for the Eighties*, ed. Stephen L. Buka, Magda G. Peck, and Jane D. Gardner (Boston: Harvard School of Public Health, 1982), p. 75. About 15 percent of all white children and one-third of all black children suffer some nutritional deficit (p. 76). Such developments have something to do with a public/private distinction that treats children's welfare primarily as a private, familial duty and exonerates anyone but the child's parents from responsibility. See Martha Minow, "Rights for the Next Generation: A Feminist Approach to Children's Rights," *Harv. Women's L.J.* 9 (1986), 1–24.

[16]Pleck, *Domestic Tyranny*, pp. 182–200; Franklin E. Zimring, "Legal Perspectives on Family Violence," *Calif. L. Rev.* 75 (1987), 521–39. Pleck concludes that both resources and ideology pose obstacles to those who would combat family violence: "Most Americans support such abstractions as parents' rights, family autonomy, and domestic privacy, especially when these values are presented in opposition to the power of the state. In an era when almost every politician holds aloft the banner of 'family values,' an attack on the Family Ideal is unlikely to be popular. Yet it is precisely the family values that contemporary politicians so much affirm that permit, encourage, and serve to maintain domestic violence." See also Kathleen J. Tierney, "The Battered Women Movement and the Creation of the Wife Beating Problem," *Social Problems* 29, no. 3 (1982), 211.

[17]See Weitzman, *The Divorce Revolution*, p. xvii. Divorce rates have increased as the ideal of the companionate marriage replaced notions of marriage for economic security, raising both expectations and the risk of marital dissatisfaction. See Robert L. Griswold, *Family and Divorce in California, 1850–1890: Victorian Illusions and Everyday Realities* (Albany: State University of New York Press, 1982), pp. 174–86; Elaine Tyler May, *Great Expectations: Marriage and Divorce in Post-Victorian America* (Chicago: University of Chicago Press, 1980). As of 1985, the "total number of children affected by divorce has more than tripled since 1960. . . . it is now projected that more than half of all the children in the United States will experience a parental divorce or dissolution before they reach age eighteen" (Weitzman, *The Divorce Revolution*, p. 215).

[18]See Mary Joe Frug, "Securing Job Equality for Women: Labor Market Hostility to Working Mothers," *B.U.L. Rev.* 59 (1979), 55–103.

followed suit. Enabling grants of divorce without demonstration of such grounds as adultery or cruelty, this wave of legislative reform also spawned innovations aimed at equalizing the positions of men and women in relationship to divorce. California and other states have directed that marital property be divided equally upon divorce, that courts prefer joint custody of children, and that financial support following divorce be designed only for a transition period, until both former spouses can become financially self-sufficient.[19] Finally, since 1970, family law has embraced the premise of autonomous individualism and equality, freed from gender roles. Yet critics have charged that this introduction of liberal values into the sphere long shielded from liberal rights has merely applied abstract, formal rules on top of social and economic patterns that preserve traditional family roles.

Sociologist Lenore Weitzman studied the California experience and concluded that the reforms have effectively made women far worse off by depriving them of recognition of the value of their distinct contributions to family life. Specifically, she found that (1) on the average, divorced women and the minor children in their households experience a large decline in their standard of living in the first year after divorce; (2) their former husbands, in contrast, experience a considerable rise in their standard of living; (3) courts typically have excluded from division, and therefore from the principle of equally dividing marital property, the most valuable assets, such as the major wage earner's salary, pension, medical insurance, education, and professional practice; (4) by including the family house in the pool of assets for division, courts have commonly forced its sale, thus dislocating women and children from neighborhoods, schools, and friends; and (5) despite the legal preference for joint custody, most men and most women prefer not to share postdivorce parenting, and most women continue to perform the major parenting role.[20]

What explains these "unexpected" consequences of introducing formal equality into divorce laws? Perhaps the chief explanation is that the reformers failed to foresee how enacting formal equality in the narrow realm of divorce and custody reform would make matters more difficult for women, given existing social and economic conditions that treat men and women differently. In short, these were reforms that took the male norm and simply extended it to women, ignoring the array of social institutions and practices that have made women different and subjecting women to the burdens of that difference.

First, women continue, for the most part, to serve as primary parents. Dividing assets equally between two households yields inequality, if one of

---

[19]Thus, we see the development of "rehabilitative alimony," or short-term payments, to help the dependent party (typically, the wife) "retool" to become self-supporting.

[20]See Weitzman, *The Divorce Revolution*, pp. xii–xiii, 358–59, 251. The harms to women and children from divorce are probably more notable for middle- and upper-class families, since poor families typically had less property and fewer resources to divide even before the reforms. See Janine Hecker, "An Examination of No-Fault Divorce: Has It Affected Minority Women to the Same Degree It Has Affected White Women?" (unpublished paper, 1987).

the households has the children.[21] And if women, as well as men, prefer maternal custody, eliminating a legal rule guaranteeing this result may mean that a divorcing woman has to bargain away something else—such as adequate financial support—in order to negotiate this arrangement.[22]

Second, financial arrangements contemplating that both spouses will be able to earn reasonable incomes disadvantage a woman who did not work outside the home during marriage. If she seeks paid work after the divorce, she may be further disadvantaged not only by a lack of workplace skills but by the various forms of sex discrimination in the labor market. Rules adopting formal equality fail to acknowledge that she may be situated differently from her former husband. People who marry with full knowledge of the egalitarian rules may conduct their married lives differently, giving greater attention to developing and preserving individual financial self-reliance. But aside from the time lag before people's expectations catch up to divorce law, there remains the normative question: should law reform presume and push for a world in which both spouses must be financially independent?[23] And

[21] A different view of equality would replace the idea of equal division of all assets (and debts) attributable to the marriage partners with a division producing similar results in standard of living (Weitzman, *The Divorce Revolution*, p. 105). Since the man and woman may be situated differently in relation to the job market and competing demands (such as child rearing) on their time, divorcing couples that use an equality-of-results standard would not be likely to divide the assets and liabilities equally (pp. 72–73). See also William K. Frankena, "The Concept of Social Justice," in *Social Justice*, ed. Richard Brandt (Englewood Cliffs, N.J.: Prentice-Hall, 1962), p. 20: "Equal concern for the good lives of its members . . . requires society to treat them differently." The special problems for divorcing spouses who remarry or take on other important relationships and obligations obviously complicate the questions of equality and fairness in the distribution of financial assets and obligations after divorce.

[22] The introduction of "mediation"—negotiation supervised by a third party to produce an agreement, rather than a court-imposed solution—also appears to be an advance (see Robert Coulson, *Fighting Fair: Family Mediation Will Work for You* [New York: Free Press, 1983]), yet mediation risks reiterating the power imbalance within a marriage. See generally Lisa Lerhman, "Mediation in Wife Abuse Cases: The Adverse Impact of Informal Dispute Resolution on Women," *Harv. Women's L.J.* 7 (1984), 57; Janet Rifkin, "Mediation from a Feminist Perspective: Promise and Problems," *Law & Inequality* 2 (1984), 21. See also Richard E. Crouch, "The Dark Side of Mediation: Still Unexplored," in *Alternative Means of Family Dispute Resolution* (Washington, D.C.: American Bar Association, 1982), p. 339. Richard Delgado, Chris Dunn, Pamela Brown, Helena Lee, and David Hubbert, "Fairness and Formality: Minimizing the Risk of Prejudice in Alternative Dispute Resolution," *Wis. L. Rev.* 1985 (1985), 1359–1404, explores the danger that arbitration and mediation may foster racial and ethnic prejudice by abandoning the formalities of traditional adjudication. Mediation looks like a "relational" approach in its rejection of adversarial, either/or solutions; it discourages a focus on legal rights and aims at restructuring the relationships after divorce. In practice, however, mediation risks undermining the legal entitlements of the party more inclined to compromise and protect the remnants of a personal relationship; and it may actually produce more involvement by court personnel or social workers. See Martha Fineman, "Dominant Discourse: Professional Language and Legal Change in Child Custody Decision-Making," *Harv. L. Rev.* 101 (1988), 789–886. Some courts have also introduced mediation to handle cases of wife battery. There is a sharp distinction to be made here: mediating the details of implementing a court order against physical abuse may help enforce the law; but negotiating, in the absence of a court order, about actual danger to physical safety seems indefensible.

[23] And in the meantime, are all women to be treated the same, including the twenty-five-year-old with a professional degree and no children, and the fifty-five-year-old with three children and no labor market experience? Or should men and women of comparable age and work experience be treated the same? Those deciding on equal treatment, here as always, should first ask which people, according to which characteristics, are to be compared and treated comparably.

should dependence lead to reliance on the state, rather than reliance on family members?[24] Reforms achieving formal equality for men and women in the sphere of family roles and family financial interests can leave in place— or worsen—inequalities in the spheres of employment and public life.[25] In addition to imposing an unstated male norm and ignoring the competing perspective of women, divorce reforms—and their unexpected consequences— reveal the difficulties of superimposing the liberal conception of the autonomous, self-determining individual on people in interdependent relationships. The family, perhaps not surprisingly, has remained an alternative to the workplace and the polity, a possible "haven in a heartless land,"[26] characterized by duties and responsibilities, embedded in intimate relationships. The reality of family life obviously has often fallen short of the ideal of domestic harmony, and the case for extending individual freedom to the family is compelling: women and men should be able to free themselves from hellish marriages.[27] Yet when people have organized their lives around the social and economic presumptions of ongoing relationships, introducing individual rights to liberty can be quite harmful to others—such as the other spouse and the children. No-fault divorce means that unilateral action by one spouse can end a marriage. Privileging individual freedom in this way in essence harms the weaker party in the union.[28] In short, one person's freedom can be another person's disaster.

The family context simply sharpens the paradox of liberty: there are social preconditions for individual freedom. Only if groups agree to respect individual freedoms—and to enforce such respect even at the cost of interfering with other individuals' freedoms—can anyone be free. I can be free only if you are disciplined, and you can be free only if I am disciplined enough to protect your freedom.[29] When it comes to family relationships, the irony only deepens. For only if people choose to turn their freedom to some mutual goals can they form relationships. The freedom to form relationships would mean little without a willingness to pursue something besides freedom to

[24]Mary Ann Glendon, *The New Family and the New Property* (Boston: Butterworth, 1981), suggests that in both legal and social practice in five industrial countries, employment and government benefits eclipse the family as the means of creating and protecting individuals' economic security.

[25]See Martha Fineman, "Implementing Equality: Ideology, Contradiction, and Social Change: A Study of Rhetoric and Results in the Regulation of the Consequences of Divorce," *Wis. L. Rev.* 1983 (1983), 789–886; Frug, "Securing Job Equality."

[26]See Christopher Lasch, *Haven in a Heartless World: The Family Besieged* (New York: Basic Books, 1977).

[27]It may be hard to conjure up the world view that condemned two unhappy people to the private misery of a mutually disagreeable marriage, but that view is not long gone. See Rankin v. Rankin, 181 Pa. Super. 414, 424 (1956); 124 A.2d 639, 644 (1956): "Testimony which proves merely an unhappy union, the parties being high strung temperamentally and unsuited to each other and neither being wholly innocent of the causes which resulted in the failure of their marriage, is insufficient to sustain the decree. If both are equally at fault, neither can clearly be said to be the innocent and injured spouse, and the law will leave them where they put themselves."

[28]Weitzman, *The Divorce Revolution*, pp. 19, 26.

[29]It is said that the dancer Edward Villella once pushed the paradox even further by noting that only through discipline can the dancer himself be free.

leave them. Even this understates the irony. For only by preserving the possibility of leaving—the possibility of individuality—can anyone survive the connection in a relationship.[30]

From one angle, then, individual freedom demands submission to societal ground rules; from another, freedom demands the submersion of individual whim in binding attachments; from still another, freedom requires limits even upon the limits on freedom. Such contrasting meanings of freedom have been bound up in our culture with views about dependence and independence, and with views about gender roles. The very freedom of the traditional male role—to participate in public life and move in and out of the private family realm—depended upon the traditional female role, which maintained continuity in the family realm and provided someone—a wife—to be subject to the husband's freely exercised power. Men's power has obscured their own dependence upon women. Introducing legal rights of formal equality and freedom, with each party having a direct relationship with the state, does not provide actual equality; it exposes the perplexities of freedom in a world of relationships.[31]

The introduction of legal rights to family members highlights the injustice of treating people the same if they are situated differently; the history of domestic violence and brutality demonstrates the dangers of carving a separate family sphere in which some members are subjected to the unrestrained authority of others. The problem seems in part that liberal rights were never extended fully to the family, and formal legal statements to that effect now simply obscure continued patterns of inequality and vulnerability unchecked by legal restraints.[32]

Yet that last phrase is misleading if it implies that the family was ever free from law. Rather than marking a boundary limiting state intervention in the family, laws governing the family define the kinds of families the state approves. The state once authorized the male head of household to discipline his wife and children; later practices that refused police protection for family members victimized by the husband established the kind of behavior the law tolerated.[33] Given background social practices, a policy of "nonintervention" by the state bolstered the authority of the man.[34] State-created rules

[30]This may be especially true for parents. Albert Memmi, *Dependence: A Sketch for a Portrait of the Dependent*, trans. Phillip A. Facey (Boston: Beacon Press, 1984), p. 68, put it this way: "Parents want to give the maximum to their children and, at the same time, keep a little for themselves; otherwise, as they see it, they would be swallowed up. In one of his works, Henry Moore, the great sculptor, has depicted a mother gathering her children to her and, at the same time, pushing them away. It is easy to see from the way her progeny are behaving that if she didn't push them away, they would devour her. A provider has to defend herself from her dependent. . . . If she doesn't defend herself, she perishes in her role as provider."

[31]See Bellah et al., *Habits of the Heart*, p. 111.

[32]See also Susan Okin, *Justice, Gender, and the Family* (New York: Basic Books, 1989).

[33]See Pleck, *Domestic Tyranny*, pp. 187–92. See also Bruno v. Codd, 90 *Misc.* 2d 1047 (1977); 396 *N.Y.S.* 2d 974 (1977) (ordering change in conduct by law enforcement officials to respond to domestic violence).

[34]See Frances Olsen, "The Myth of State Intervention in the Family," *U. Mich. J.L. Ref.* 18 (1985), 835, 848–55. Olsen concludes that "the state cannot be neutral, nor can it be a neutral arbiter of rights" (p. 864 n.78). And see Frances Olsen, "Statutory Rape: A Feminist Critique of Rights Analysis," *Tex. L. Rev.* 63 (1984), 387.

about what counts as a criminal assault regulate the family, determining, for example, whether the state recognizes or refuses to recognize marital rape as "real rape," which can trigger the criminal justice enforcement apparatus.[35] Similarly, the laws governing who may marry, as well as who may divorce, put the power of the state behind some agreements and not others.[36] More recently, adult and minor women have secured the legal right to obtain an abortion free from the interference of other family members.[37]

Tracing the presence of state power in the family sphere, historically described as removed from the state, suggests something powerful about boundaries: both sides of a boundary are regulated, even if the line was supposed to distinguish the regulated from the unregulated. Indeed, this analysis of family law's history, itself a "marginal" tale compared with the "center" of law's concerns, provides an angle of inquiry about the failure of traditional liberal rights to acknowledge the threats of private power to liberty and equality—and to acknowledge the government's involvement in structures of private power. This inquiry affords a basis for revitalizing rights, once they are located within relationships.

Public and Private Power: The Limits of Liberal Rights

Locating rights within relationships initially seems simply a matter of logic. Any system of law demands a collective, communal structure for recognizing and enforcing norms. When the system assigns rights to individuals, it actually sets in place patterns of relationships, for legal rights are interdependent and mutually defining. They arise in the context of relationships among people who are themselves interdependent and mutually defining. In this sense, every right and every freedom is no more than a claim limited by the possible claims of others.[38] Rights thus are simply the articu-

[35]Susan Estrich, *Real Rape* (Cambridge, Mass.: Harvard University Press, 1987).

[36]See generally Carol Smart, *The Ties That Bind: Law, Marriage, and the Reproduction of Patriarchal Relations* (Boston: Routledge & Kegan Paul, 1984); Michèle Barrett and Mary McIntosh, *The Anti-Social Family* (London: NLB, 1982). See also Loving v. Virginia, 388 U.S. 1 (1967) (acknowledging that anti-miscegenation laws regulated families through the prism of white racism).

[37]Bellotti v. Baird, 443 U.S. 662 (1979) (minors); Roe v. Wade, 410 U.S. 113 (1973) (adult women). But this innovation did not create law where previously there was none; see below.

[38]Wesley Hohfeld, a legal author during the Progressive era and a participant in the "legal realist" movement, provided an elaborate articulation of the relational contexts in which rights assertions arise. See Hohfeld, "Some Fundamental Legal Conceptions as Applied in Judicial Reasoning," *Yale L.J.* 23 (1913), 16. Hohfeld reasoned that each legal right relies on a structure of correlatives and opposites (p. 30):

Jural Opposites			
right	privilege	power	immunity
no right	duty	disability	liability

Jural Correlatives			
right	privilege	power	immunity
duty	no right	liability	disability

Thus, for any right, one must have one, but not both, of each member of the jural opposite pairs; and having any one of those dimensions of a right confers a correlative on someone else. Legal

lated legal consequences of particular patterns of human and institutional relationships. For example, rather than expressing some intrinsic autonomy, property rights announce the complex and often overlapping relationships of individuals and the larger community to limited resources.[39] Contract rights specifically govern the formation and dissolution of commercial relationships and detail the specific consequences to differing parties of agreeing and not agreeing.[40] Constitutional rights—such as freedom of expression, freedom of association, freedom of religion, and the fundamental rights to marry, procreate, and protect family ties—expressly describe legal claims to relationships.[41] Perhaps less obvious, but no less powerful, are legal rights regarding tort liability, which give legal significance to relationships between strangers.[42] The rights of the tort victim cannot be defined without reference to those who caused the injury or who should pay for it. Most notably involved is the tort-feasor, but also implicated are those to whom costs may be shifted, through insurance or pricing mechanisms.[43]

---

rights in this sense are relations, and different legal relations have different features. If I have a right that you stay off my land, you have a duty to stay off: "When a right is invaded, a duty is violated" (p. 32). If you have no duty to stay off the land, you may have a privilege to enter; Hohfeld discusses the common use of the phrase " 'That is your privilege,'—meaning, of course, 'You are under no duty to do otherwise' " (p. 39). Finally, if you have an immunity with regard to some action, you are not liable to me for the commission of that action: "An immunity is one's freedom from the legal power or 'control' of another as regards some legal relation" and "the opposite, or negation of liability" (p. 55). See generally Joseph William Singer, "The Legal Rights Debate in Analytical Jurisprudence from Bentham to Hohfeld," *Wis. L. Rev.* 1982 (1982), 975.

[39]See Joseph William Singer, "The Reliance Interest in Property," *Stan. L. Rev.* 40 (1988), 611.

[40]Ian R. MacNeil, *The New Social Contract: An Inquiry into Modern Contractual Relations* (New Haven, Conn.: Yale University Press, 1980), urges recognition of long-term relationships rather than single transactions as theory for contract law; Stewart Macaulay, "Non-Contractual Relations in Business: A Preliminary Study," *American Sociological Review* 28 (1963), 55, discusses contractual planning as used in renegotiating long-term relationships; Zipporah Wiseman, "The Limits of Vision: Karl Llewellyn and the Uniform Commercial Code," *Harv. L. Rev.* 100 (1987), 465, 504–9, explains Llewellyn's notion of merchant transactions, in which relationships within a community of repeat players should influence the nature of the rules so that merchant regulations apply only to merchants, rather than to all buyers and sellers. See generally Gidon Gottlieb, "Relationalism: Legal Theory for a Relational Society," *U. Chi. L. Rev.* 50 (1983), 567, which advocates a perspective on the relational nature of legal arrangements among institutions, groups, and others; and Leon Green, "Relational Interests," *Ill. L. Rev.* 30 (1935), 314, which explores the significance to law of political, group, familial, professional, and commercial relations.

[41]See Carol Weisbrod, "Family, Church and State," Legal History Program Working Paper 2, University of Wisconsin, Madison Legal History Program (Madison: Institute for Legal Studies). See also Note, "Too Close for Comfort: Protesting outside Medical Facilities," *Harv. L. Rev.* 101 (1988), 1856, exploring restrictions on speech by antiabortionists based on regulating the space between speaker and listener.

[42]See Guido Calebresi, *The Costs of Accidents: A Legal and Economic Analysis* (New Haven, Conn.: Yale University Press, 1970); Martha Minow, "Many Silent Worlds," *W. New Eng. L. Rev.* 9 (1987), 197.

[43] Product liability rules transcend the boundaries between producers and victims, even where separated by merchants; as a result, the law reminds producers that potential victims are on the other side of their decisions. See generally Calebresi, *The Costs of Accidents;* Henry Steiner, *The Transformation of Tort Law* (Madison: University of Wisconsin Press, 1988).

Rights, according to a traditional conception, carve out spheres of authorized individual action, beyond which an individual becomes liable for action. Accordingly, rights spell out relationships as logical consequences—but these consequences are not self-enforcing; they involve the government. Rights thus critically articulate relationships between individuals and the state; they represent the rules governing when the state will affirm an individual's liberty to act or fail to act, and when the state will listen to a person's objections about another's conduct.

It is this last dimension of the state's relationship to individuals that is central to family law. Within a sphere cordoned off as "private," removed from state intervention, family members remain individuals who have or who lack rights to appeal to the state. Within the "private" realm of the family, the law has always articulated rules about relationships, and rules about when individuals may object to the government about those relationships; historically, legal theories excluded family relations, along with rules governing those with decreased competence, from the reach of legal rights.[44] The law thus helped to shield from view the governmental refusal to see some kinds of power or abuse as warranting public restraint. It would be false to say that family relations were unregulated: they *were* regulated by the government's grant of financial, physical, and social privileges to the male head of household and refusal to hear any objections of other family members.

During the early part of this century the legal scholars known as legal realists explored a similar pattern of governmental regulation hidden behind the veil of privacy in relation to the marketplace. They pursued many of the insights and political purposes of the contemporaneous Progressive movement. John Dewey was among them, and Oliver Wendell Holmes, Jr., was a forerunner; other renowned realists included Roscoe Pound, Karl Llewellyn, Robert Hale, Jerome Frank, Morris Cohen, and Felix Cohen.[45] They called themselves realists because they sought to make law a pragmatic tool for advancing social purposes rather than a self-contained, abstract, conceptual system for generating uncontestable answers. They argued that judges are simply human beings, struggling with competing goals and personal pre-

[44]See Joseph William Singer, "Legal Realism Now: Review Essay of Laura Kalman, *Legal Realism at Yale: 1927–1960*," *Calif. L. Rev.* 76 (1988), 467.
[45]See John Dewey, "Logical Method and Law," *Cornell L.Q.* 10 (1924), 17; Oliver Wendell Holmes, Jr., "Privilege, Malice, and Intent," *Harv. L. Rev.* 8 (1894), 1; Roscoe Pound, "Liberty of Contract," *Yale L.J.* 18 (1909), 454; Roscoe Pound, "The Call for Realist Jurisprudence," *Harv. L. Rev.* 44 (1931), 697; Karl Llewellyn, "A Realistic Jurisprudence—The Next Step," *Colum. L. Rev.* 30 (1930), 431; Karl Llewellyn, "Some Realism about Realism—Responding to Dean Pound," *Harv. L. Rev.* 44 (1931), 1222; Robert Hale, "Law Making by Unofficial Minorities," *Colum. L. Rev.* 20 (1920), 451; Robert Hale, "Coercion and Distribution in a Supposedly Non-coercive State," *Political Science Quarterly* 38 (1923), 470; Jerome Frank, *Courts on Trial: Myth and Reality in American Justice* (1949; Princeton, N.J.: Princeton University Press, 1973); Jerome Frank, *Law and the Modern Mind* (New York: Tudor, 1936); Jerome Frank, "Mr. Justice Holmes and Non-Euclidean Legal Thinking," *Cornell L.Q.* 17 (1932), 568. Morris Cohen, "Property and Sovereignty," *Cornell L.Q.* 13 (1927), 8 (property rights depend on state enforcement); Felix Cohen, "Transcendental Nonsense and the Functional Approach," *Colum. L. Rev.* 35 (1935), 809.

dilections, rather than oracles capable of discerning the one true path; they sought to expose the ways in which particular legal rules and conceptions unfairly privilege certain economic and social interests. This last goal drew the realist scholars into an analysis of the role of legal rules in marketplace relationships, and into a challenge to the conception of the marketplace as either natural or private, removed from humanly constructed regulations.

The realists criticized the then prevailing view of property and contract rights, which portrayed the market as an area of free, private action.[46] In that arena, classical views of law assured people freedom to act according to their own desires, without duties toward others and thus outside government control. Contract rights protected the will of the parties and warranted state enforcement as long as the contract resulted from no physical coercion—no gun to the head. Thus, employment contracts were deemed voluntary and enforceable, even if the worker accepted pitiful wages and conditions because of economic duress. Property rights treated existing distributions of resources as natural and worthy of governmental protection; any interference represented a violation deserving legal restraint. A company's economic relationships with workers, captured in existing employment contracts, was protected property in this sense, and therefore anyone who interfered with the company's employment practices—by seeking to unionize the employees, for example—transgressed legally guaranteed property rights and fell subject to judicial restraints.

The realists criticized these views as conceptual sleight of hand. They argued that contract rights did not merely enforce the private will of the parties but instead represented governmental grants that allowed some people, at some times, to invoke state power to enforce their agreements.[47] The governmental rules about enforceable contracts implemented public, not private, values about what kinds of agreements should be enforced, even when events transpired that neither party had anticipated. And the realists argued that all contracts involved some degree of mutual coercion, rather than freedom, because each party remained free to withhold what the other needed.[48] By defining which power imbalances amounted to unlawful coercion, contract law implemented public values about the acceptable distribution of power in the marketplace. Employment contracts between poor workers and large companies were acceptable not because the parties on both sides were free but because the law defined their relationship as meeting the prerequisites of legal enforcement. When it came to property rights, realist scholars maintained that the state was unavoidably involved in the creation and recognition of economic power and wealth. Legal rules governed property and market relationships. Legal rules determined whether unionizing activity was unlawful interference with employers' property rights—or whether, instead, restraints against unions unlawfully interfered with workers' property rights in their own labor. Similarly, governmental decisions

[46]See generally Singer, "Legal Realism Now."
[47]See Morris Cohen, "The Basis of Contract," *Harv. L. Rev.* 46 (1933), 553; Morris Cohen, "Property and Sovereignty," *Cornell L.Q.* 13 (1927), 8.
[48]Singer, "Legal Realism Now," pp. 482–87.

monitored the scope of economic competition, whether by allowing or by disallowing competition that interfered with the property rights of others.[49]

The legal realists were motivated in part to demonstrate how private as well as public power threatened liberty. The private power of employers and wealthy property owners could effectively coerce those with less power. Was the legal system dedicated to the principles of freedom? If so, the realists asked, freedom for whom? They exposed how courts and legislatures systematically preferred some people's freedom over that of others and thereby unmasked a pretense of neutrality in the rules of law. They also showed how not just governmental action but also inaction could jeopardize freedom. Refusing a hearing or a remedy to someone who claimed interference with freedom meant effective approval of that interference. The realists took one more step and located government involvement in what had been known as the private sphere of the marketplace. It was the government that defined what constituted an enforceable bargain and a legitimate property claim and, indeed, it was the government that defined tortious and criminal invasions of economic and personal interests; therefore, it was public power that set up and enforced the ground rules for the exchange of goods and services and for the distribution of economic resources. The government was thus inextricably implicated in patterns of private power. Seemingly divided compartments were actually connected; the parts of society constituted a whole obscured only by the theories differentiating the public and private spheres.[50] If the purpose of government was to restrain power and protect liberty, the realists argued, then the less powerful workers had rights to claims that the state should recognize.[51]

Like the realists, feminist scholars during the 1970s and 1980s explored private power's threats to liberty and the government's implication in the private spheres of both family and private employment.[52] Advocates for the

[49]Ibid., pp. 492–95, discussing Hitchman Coal & Coke v. Mitchell, and Vegelahn v. Gunter.

[50]It may be fair to say that the legal realists understood not only the need to connect parts and wholes but also the important relationship between observer and observed in judicial reasoning; judges, they argued, were not neutral but situated and influenced by their training and by their positions in society; see Frank, "Mr. Justice Holmes." Their interest in relativity and other developments in theoretical physics appeared in the analogies they drew exposing the indeterminacy of legal rules that depended on the position of the decision-maker. The realists tended not to carry this insight over into social science, believing instead in the possibility of finding social facts and revising law to match them; see Llewellyn, "Some Realism about Realism." They indicated little awareness that individual autonomy is constructed through relationships, although Jerome Frank showed a deep interest in Freudian psychology; see Frank, *Courts on Trial*. Yet many of them strongly emphasized the importance of contextual analysis; their marked aversion to abstract concepts and "formalist reasoning" may be the realists' most noted contribution to legal theory.

[51]The realists did not, for the most part, think that their analysis produced a new, self-contained system of rights and remedies, only reversing who would win and who would lose; instead, they understood their analysis as identifying conflicting rights and interests and exposing the political choices embedded in law. Critical legal theorists—and, to some extent, law-and-economics scholars—claim to be heirs to these realist traditions and, in different ways, pursue the realists' conception of law as unavoidably embroiled in policy choices.

[52]Feminist scholars, most notably Frances Olsen ("The Family and the Market," p. 1497), have identified the use of two different public/private splits in legal ideology: one divides government and the marketplace, and another divides the family from the rest of society.

rights of children (see below) have pursued a similar line of analysis.[53] This approach reaches people the law defines as "different"by exposing the uses of power, both private and public, to construct the social meaning of a trait of difference and to erect and maintain structures of exclusion and discrimination on the basis of that difference.[54] Legal struggles against racial discrimination have frequently battled the ostensible line between public and private power and challenged the role of the state in enforcing racial restrictions in the private sale of homes, in private employment, and in other contractual and property exchanges.[55] Religious groups as well have successfully challenged the public/private line. The Supreme Court ruled in one case that a privately owned "company town" could not invoke state trespass laws to exclude Jehovah's Witnesses from proselytizing on its streets.[56] Religious groups have also secured rights against discrimination by private employers.[57]

These developments could be understood as an application of the realists' insights to the social construction of difference: private power threatens liberty to the extent that it implements structures of domination and discrim-

[53]For rights of the sick, see Chapter 10; for rights of older persons as a subject for law reform and even constitutional analysis, see Laurence Tribe, *American Constitutional Law,* 2d ed. (Mineola, N.Y.: Foundation Press, 1988).

[54]Compare Plessy v. Ferguson, 163 U.S. 537, 551 (1896) (court rejects a racial discrimination challenge to segregated railway cars and notes that any stigma experienced by blacks is due to their own attribution of meaning to the segregation), with Loving v. Virginia, 388 U.S. 1, 11 (1967) (Court notes that the social meaning of an antimiscegenation statute announces and reinforces white supremacy).

[55]After the Civil War, the Supreme Court struck down many Reconstruction era reforms on the theory that they regulated private conduct that was off-limits from governmental control. See Civil Rights Cases, 109 U.S. 3 (1883). Yet starting in the 1960s, and spurred by the civil rights movement, courts began to challenge the distinction between public and private and to permit regulation of private conduct that discriminated on the basis of race. See United States v. Guest, 383 U.S. 745 (1966); and District of Columbia v. Carter, 409 U.S. 418, 423–24 n.8 (1973) (the Court noted in dictum that the Fourteenth Amendment does not shield merely private conduct from congressional regulation). See also Runyon v. McCrary, 427 U.S. 160 (1976); Jones v. Alfred H. Mayer Co., 392 U.S. 409 (1968). In 1989 the Supreme Court affirmed the constitutionality of statutes forbidding racial discrimination by private employers while restricting the statutory coverage to actions creating and dissolving the work relationship, thereby removing harassment during employment from the scope of regulation; see Patterson v. McClean Credit Union, 109 S.Ct. 2363 (1989). Yet still in place as lawful authority is Shelley v. Kraemer, 334 U.S. 1 (1948), where the Supreme Court ruled that state action would be involved were a court to enforce a private, racially restrictive covenant, and therefore such enforcement itself was barred by the Constitution. The potential scope of this ruling reaches any invocation of judicial power, and the courts have been unwilling to reinforce, much less extend, the ruling in *Shelley.* See, e.g., Moose Lodge No. 107 v. Irvis, 407 U.S. 163 (1972) (no state action in a racially discriminatory private club, even where government agency grants liquor license). See generally Tribe, *American Constitutional Law;* Neil Gotanda, "Towards a Critique of Colorblind: Abstract and Concrete Race in American Law" (S.J.D. diss., Harvard Law School, 1987); Derrick Bell, "The Legacy of Racial Discrimination: Who Pays the Cost?" (Harvard Law School, unpublished draft, 1988).

[56]Marsh v. Alabama, 326 U.S. 501 (1946).

[57]See Title VII. Judicial interpretations of Title VII and similar measures have also required some accommodation of the religious practices of minority religious groups. See Hobbie v. Unemployment Appeals Comm'n, 480 U.S. 136 (1987).

ination, based on social and historical meanings of particular traits of difference such as gender, age, race, and religion. After the realists, legal theorists can readily ask what relationships existing rights establish between the rights-bearing individual, the government, and other people? If a right protects liberty, whose liberty does it protect and at what cost to whom? Neither privately entrenched patterns of social hierarchy nor publicly maintained arrangements remain immune from this inquiry about the relationships fostered by particular rights. Criticized and refashioned from this vantage point, legal rights indeed may reach those still embedded in social hierarchies and respond to those who understand that social life demands more than autonomy.

The realists, for the most part, offered searing critiques of law. When it came time to construct something new, some realists manifested a faith in facts or in social science which is no longer shared; contemporary theorists are too sensitive to the relationship between facts and the assumption used by those who "find" them to trust that difficult legal choices can be made on the basis of data.[58] Other realists joined the New Deal and showed by their actions, rather than further theoretical work, where they thought constructive efforts should go. The task of reconstructing rights, given a recognition of their inevitable relational dimensions and given sensitivity to the threat to liberty of both private and public power, remains undeveloped. The next section is an effort in that direction.

A Look at Children

Children are the paradigmatic group excluded from traditional liberal rights. Long considered "different," children for the most part still stand in official relationships to their parents under law, rather than assuming the position of autonomous individuals. Thus, children are a striking group whose "difference" has excluded them from rights but whose relationships may offer a point of entry to a new conception of rights in relationship. A look at their legal treatment underscores the limitations of traditional conceptions of rights but also offers a glimpse of rights reconstructed as features of important, communal relationships.

Children and Legal History

Our society has historically distinguished children from adults, but the meaning of this distinction and the criteria for drawing it have shifted over time. The idea that adolescents should be separated from the daily work of adults developed only with the industrialization of the economy, and then it applied to all young people only after middle- and upper-class reformers

[58]See John Henry Schlegal, "American Legal Realism and Empirical Social Science: From the Yale Experience," *Buffalo L. Rev.* 28 (1979), 459.

pushed for laws restricting child labor and making schooling compulsory.[59] Over the past several centuries members of Western societies, including parents, have valued children less for their economic contributions than as objects of love and affection. Adolescence has become a period of preparation for adulthood through study and activities removed from adult society.

Meanwhile, laws governing minors have developed into a complex welter of rules. The definition of a minor at times turns on age, but different ages matter for different purposes. Sometimes age plus economic dependency on a parent signals minority status. Minority status in turn justifies withholding both rights and obligations from the child[60] and creating a legal relationship of dependence on adults, who have legally enforceable obligations to care for and protect the child. Federal, state, and local laws have drawn a complex and inconsistent pattern of lines between childhood and adulthood. The law in most states permits a girl under eighteen to consent to her own abortion, without telling her parents, but the truancy laws and school regulations may well require her to obtain parental permission to miss school for a doctor's appointment. Someone who is sixteen may be charged, tried, convicted, and punished as an adult for committing a violent crime; he may even be subject to the death penalty. But the same person would be treated as a child for purposes of employment and other contractual relations, including marriage. A seventeen-year-old may be allowed to operate an automobile but not to purchase liquor or cigarettes. A six-year-old may not consent to her own medical care, but she may be asked to testify in court and be treated as a credible witness. The law may compel payment of child support for an individual who is past the age of eighteen if he is still attending school but recognize that same person as an independent adult if school attendance ceases. A person may thus be treated as dependent and incompetent but also as autonomous and rights-bearing, depending upon the context. What accounts for these seemingly inconsistent legal treatments of young people?

An initial explanation would proceed from the assumption that the law draws rational lines between children and adults, based on assessments of varied kinds of competencies. Children need custody and care when they are incompetent, rights and autonomy when they are competent. Legal rules

---

[59]See Philippe Ariès, *Centuries of Childhood: A Social History of Family Life,* trans. Robert Baldick (New York: Vintage Books, 1962); Demos, *A Little Commonwealth;* John Demos, *Past, Present, and Personal: The Family and the Life Course in American History* (New York: Oxford University Press, 1986); Joseph Kett, *Rites of Passage: Adolescence in America, 1790 to the Present* (New York: Basic Books, 1977); Bernard Wishy, *The Child and the Republic* (Philadelphia: University of Pennsylvania Press, 1968); Viviana Zelizer, *Pricing the Priceless Child: The Changing Social Value of Children* (New York: Basic Books, 1985); Arlene Skolnick, "The Limits of Childhood: Conceptions of Child Development and Social Context," *Law & Contemp. Probs.* 39 (Summer 1975), 38. Some of these works may have overstated the view that childhood was only recently invented. Linda A. Pollock, *Forgotten Children: Parent-Child Relations from 1500 to 1900* (New York: Cambridge University Press, 1983), offers evidence of tender attitudes toward children and a distinct concept of childhood in the sixteenth century.

[60]Historically using the term "disabilities," the legal rules prevented—that is, "disabled"— minors from entering into enforceable contracts or otherwise binding themselves or their property.

may treat differently a given person who has developed some but not all of the competencies society deems relevant to a range of tasks or responsibilities. At any given time in a child's development, he or she may be competent for some purposes and not for others.

However appealing this view may be as a normative theory,[61] it fails to describe the contemporary legal universe. It is bizarre to justify the variable treatment of young people currently manifested in the patchwork of legal regulations as though it expressed careful judgments about their competencies for various tasks and responsibilities. Why would a sixteen-year-old be competent to consent to her own abortion but not to miss school for her doctor's appointment without parental permission? Why would the sixteen-year-old be competent to be treated as an adult in criminal court but not competent to purchase alcohol? A theory of variable competence may make theoretical sense, but it does not supply the rationale for legal choices up to this point. Moreover, competence itself is hardly an uncontroversial idea. Competence to act with "independence" as a political or moral matter represents a societal choice about who may be included as a full, participatory member. This is quite distinct from social scientific measures of cognitive or emotional development. One philosopher has said: "To regard people *as equals* is to take a stand on how they are to be treated, not to make a remark about their capacities. It is to recognize that they have something about them which justifies their being accorded the same status as others irrespective of their ability to achieve that status for themselves."[62] Children's needs for protection concern their capacities, not their political status. Moreover, legal rules granting rights only to adults do not distinguish between those having and those lacking a certain defined level of cognitive and emotional development. Some adults lack many cognitive and emotional abilities; some lose them; and all adults remain dependent in many ways.

The lines drawn between childhood and adulthood actually reflect social choices about many issues. At stake are ideas not only about children's competence but also about what adults think children need and about how to control risks to the community. Rules applying to children respond to all these issues. The rules express public decisions about children's relationships—to parents, to the community, and to the state.[63] Until recently, these relationships were not described as "rights" for children.[64] Public reform

[61]See Willard Gaylin, "Competence: No Longer All or None," in *Who Speaks for the Child: The Problems of Proxy Consent,* ed. Willard Gaylin and Ruth Macklin (New York: Plenum Press, 1982). Four members of the Supreme Court recently reasoned that minors are too immature and irresponsible to be capable of acting with the degree of culpability that justifies the death penalty. See Thompson v. Oklahoma, 108 S.Ct. 2687 (1988). The dissenters queried the significance of a difference between age fifteen and age sixteen on these issues.

[62]John Harris, "The Political Status of Children," in *Contemporary Political Philosophy: Radical Studies,* ed. Keith Graham (New York: Cambridge University Press, 1982), p. 35.

[63]See Andrew J. Kleinfeld, "The Balance of Power among Infants, Their Parents, and the State," *Fam. L.Q.* 4 (1970), 319, 409, and 5 (1971), 63. See also Hilary Rodham, "Children under the Law," *Harvard Education Review* 43 (1973), 487.

[64]The preference for the language of welfare and need was deliberate. The first juvenile courts were constructed as courts of equity, able to act outside the framework of individual rights. See

movements on behalf of children have often swept through this country, producing legislative and judicial alterations in children's legal relationships with parents and the state. The common school movement of the 1820s and 1830s and the child labor and juvenile court initiatives of the Progressives combined arguments that children need protection with assertions about the needs of a democratic society.[65] Reformers justified distinct legal rules on the grounds of children's differences from adults—but those differences ranged, in the reformers' rhetoric, from the child's innocence and impressionability to the child's dangerous and uncontrolled impulses.[66] Laws adopted over the course of the twentieth century have implemented varied conceptions of children's differences from and dependence on adults. Compulsory schooling laws punished parents of absent children and also mandated vaccination. Child labor laws and curfew laws provided sanctions for parents as well as for children. Juvenile court, child abuse and neglect laws, and rules obliging professionals to report any suspected instances of child abuse or neglect all conceived of children as dependent and in need of state protection, even to the extent of imposing duties on a variety of adults.

By the 1960s, however, new reformers concerned with children were advocating "rights" rather than protection.[67] The successful litigation demanding constitutional protections for minors in juvenile court was simply one of many legal initiatives seeking to extend adult rights to children.[68] Another addressed the freedom of minors to express themselves and culminated in a Supreme Court declaration that children do not "shed their constitutional rights to freedom of speech . . . at the schoolhouse gate."[69]

The judicial treatment of children's rights under the First Amendment

Julia Lathrop, "The Background of the Juvenile Court in Illinois," in *The Child, the Clinic, and the Court* (New York: New Republic, 1925), pp. 290–97; Harvey Baker, "Procedure of the Boston Juvenile Court," *Survey*, Feb. 5, 1910, pp. 643–52; Julian Mack, "The Juvenile Court," *Harv. L. Rev.* 23 (1909), 104–22.

[65]See Florence Kelly, "On Some Changes in the Legal Status of the Child since Blackstone," *International Review* 13 (Aug. 1882), 83–98; Herbert Croly, *The Promise of American Life* (1914; New York: Da Capo Press, 1985), pp. 400–407. See also Richard Pratte, *The Public School Movement* (New York: David McKay, 1985), pp. 38–74; Zelizer, *Pricing the Priceless Child*, pp. 56–72. The reform movements also represented conflicts between older and newer immigrant groups and different social classes.

[66]See Skolnick, "The Limits of Childhood."

[67]Academic and polemical tracts advocated children's "liberation," clearly echoing themes in the women's and civil rights movements. See Richard Farson, *Birthrights* (New York: Macmillan, 1974); Edgar Friedenberg, *The Dignity of Youth and Other Atavisms* (Boston: Beacon Press, 1965); *The Children's Rights Movement: Overcoming the Oppression of Young People*, ed. Beatrice Gross and Ronald Gross (Garden City, N.Y.: Anchor Books, 1977); Henry J. Foster, Jr., and Doris Jonas Freed, "A Bill of Rights for Children," *Fam. L.Q.* 6 (1972), 343.

[68]See In re Gault, 387 U.S. 1 (1967). Reformers did not succeed entirely in grafting adult rights onto the juvenile court. See McKeiver v. Pennsylvania 403 U.S. 528 (1971) (denying minors the same jury trial right as adults); Schall v. Martin, 467 U.S. 253, 265 (1984) (authorizing preventive detention for juveniles, with the explanation that "juveniles, unlike adults, are always in some form of custody"). Some legal reform movements simply turned to children as one important group implicated in other social reforms. See, e.g., Brown v. Board of Educ. 347 U.S. 483 (1954) (racial desegregation of public schools, following twenty years of cases desegregating higher education); Planned Parenthood of Central Missouri v. Danforth, 428 U.S. 52 (1976) (rejecting statutory requirement of parental consent before a minor obtains an abortion).

[69]Tinker v. Des Moines Indep. Community School Dist., 393 U.S. 503, 506 (1969).

demonstrates the confusion that persists over whether to treat children the same as adults or whether to adjust their legal rights on the grounds of their differences and their relationships to others. In 1969 the Supreme Court ruled that students' First Amendment rights protected them against suspension from school for wearing black armbands to protest the Vietnam War—but also recognized that the school's functions, clientele, and need for order might be incompatible with a wide-ranging exchange of views and full expression rights; therefore, reasonable fear of substantial disruption of the school's activities would permit school officials to limit student speech.[70] In subsequent cases the Court has reaffirmed and extended this ruling, permitting teachers and administrators to restrict student expression as part of the educational and social mission of the schools.[71]

Interestingly, legal arguments can be made both to restrict and to extend students' First Amendment rights in light of the school's mission to socialize young people, to prepare them for adulthood, and to inculcate habits of good citizenship. The Court's majority wrote in an earlier case, upholding a student's right to refuse to salute the flag, that "educating the young for citizenship is reason for scrupulous protection of Constitutional freedoms of the individual, if we are not to strangle the free mind at its source and teach youth to discount important principles of our government as mere platitudes."[72] Precisely because minors, unlike adults, are forced to attend school, students may not be treated as "closed-circuit recipients of only that which the state chooses to communicate." At the same time, courts have cited their solicitude for the "special characteristics of the school environment" in justifying restrictions on students' expression rights.[73]

Freedom of expression is thus treated differently in the school setting than it is in the larger community. Speech may be restricted to accomplish the task of socialization or to guard against disorder within the school. When confronted by a school board that removed books from the school library over the objection of students and parents who cited First Amendment protections, the Supreme Court divided precisely on the question of whether the special features of the school community and its mission to inculcate values justified restrictions on speech or instead demanded a full exchange of ideas.[74]

Such debates reveal the ambivalence about whether children are more like or more unlike adults while demonstrating—intentionally or not—the sig-

[70]Ibid.
[71]Hazelwood School District v. Kuhlmeier, 108 S.Ct. 562 (1988); Bethel School District v. Fraser, 106 S.Ct. 3159 (1986).
[72]West Virginia State Board of Educ. v. Barnette, 319 U.S. 624, 637 (1943).
[73]393 U.S. at 511, 503, 506, 509.
[74]Compare the opinion of Justice Brennan, joined by Justices Marshall and Stevens, in Board of Educ. v. Pico, 457 U.S. 853 (1982), and the opinion of Justice Blackmun (id. at 879–80), with the dissenting opinion of Chief Justice Burger, joined by Justices Powell, Rehnquist, and O'Connor, and the dissenting opinion of Justice Powell (id. at 894–95), and the dissenting opinion of Justice Rehnquist, joined by Chief Justice Burger and Justice Powell (id. at 908–10). All the opinions refer to both the students' First Amendment rights and the school board's legitimate socialization function. Justice Brennan's opinion—which secured merely a plurality of the Court—identified the students' right to receive information; rejection by the other opinions

nificance of children's relationships to the adults who instruct and guide them. Because children are considered different from adults, they need and spend time in the special environment of the school.[75] But because they are also not to be excluded ultimately from the world of adults, they need some experience in the world awaiting them. Conceiving of children as potential adults does not resolve the ambivalence, because this could justify either denying children the free expression rights of adults until they become adults or granting children those rights in deference to what they will become.[76] In the school setting children are different from adults because their attendance is compulsory and they are treated as dependent on the instruction and guidance of the school officials. Similarly, within families, children are different from adults because they are dependent, legally and practically, on the adults entrusted with their care. Children are thus doubly dependent: their dependence is constructed by legal rules and also by their financial, emotional, and physical needs.

To complicate matters, both children's dependence and their emerging independence may be invoked to justify rights. "Rights" may be claimed to underscore children's similarity to adults, but rights may also be invoked to call attention to children's differences. The notion of "children's rights" has been seized by advocates of both separate, protective treatment for children and identical, equal treatment for children and adults. This confusion bears a striking parallel to the special- versus equal-treatment debate—the dilemma of difference—in the contexts of women's rights and rights for mentally disabled persons.[77] Rights for children, thus far, have expressed rather than resolved adult ambivalence about them.[78] Children's rights include many of the rights enjoyed by adults—but to a lesser degree. Courts have announced for children a somewhat foreshortened right to freedom of expression;[79] to freedom from unwarranted searches and seizures, which can be curbed with

---

marks a contrasting view of the school as a more protected enclave. See generally Stephen Arons, *Compelling Belief: The Culture of American Schooling* (New York: McGraw-Hill, 1983), pp. 65–74; Tyll van Geel, "The Search for Constitutional Limits on Governmental Authority to Inculcate Youth," *Tex. L. Rev.* 62 (1983), 197. See also Tribe, *American Constitutional Law*, p. 1318: "Since schools are expressly permitted, indeed even created, to promote the very same lessons in the classroom which they are prohibited from dispensing by shibboleth and coerced ceremony, the allocation of power and control in the educational system has been the object of frequent struggles among groups and individuals within the community" who fight over their competing meanings of liberty.

[75]Note that because disabled and language-minority students are considered different from others, schools devise special environments for them.

[76]This, of course, is another version of the difference dilemma: does treating the different one as though he or she were not different promote sameness or confirm difference?

[77]See Wendy Williams, "Equality's Riddle: Pregnancy and the Equal Treatment/Special Treatment Debate," *N.Y.U. Rev. L. & Soc. Change* 13 (1984–85), 325.

[78]The ambivalence sometimes takes the form of jokes: a newspaper cartoon tyke, introducing a stranger to his parents, says, "Mom and Dad, I'd like you to meet my lawyer." We select out oddities for humorous jibes not simply at random but because they make us uncomfortable. Jokes about children's rights often express, through the art of trivializing, the positions of power adults generally have over children. A best-selling humor book does so in rhyme: see Shel Silverstein, *A Light in the Attic* (New York: Harper & Row, 1981), pp. 128–29.

[79]Besides the limitations on speech in the school setting, noted above, see Ginsberg v. New

less justification than the similar adult right;[80] and to freedom of choice about whether to terminate a pregnancy, which may be limited by an obligation to notify a parent.[81] Children's rights may take the form of claims to independence and freedom from constraint, but they may also represent claims to care and protection or claims to relationships with others.[82] Some children's rights are uniquely tailored for them, such as a right to an education designed for the individual's special needs,[83] a right to decent foster care when in state custody, and a right to a hearing before being suspended from public school.

Children's Rights, Community, and Language

The Supreme Court's dispute about a student's right to a hearing prior to suspension from school articulates the ambivalence about children's rights in terms of concern about their relationships with others. This dispute also demonstrates the predominance of the conception of rights as claims by autonomous, self-determining, and self-interested individuals, in contrast to an alternative conception of rights as features of interpersonal connection.

Indeed, couched as an argument over children's rights, the divisions between litigants and between justices in Goss v. Lopez[84] involved competing views of human relationships. The plaintiffs demanded due process hearings before a student could be suspended from school. This demand invoked the autonomy and entitlement of each student: each student has dignity as an independent person and therefore deserves an opportunity to be heard, to give reasons and to be given reasons, before facing the punishment of suspension. Because school officials have the power to suspend students, each child needs a judicial grant of the individual right to restrain the actions of school authorities and prevent them from so disciplining the student without a prior hearing.

In contrast, the defendants presented a conception of the school as a community, or family. In such a setting, the interests of different individuals are shared. Continuing relationships among people with shared interests

---

York, 390 U.S. 629 (1968) (approving conviction of adult for sale of magazines to minor, although the magazine would not be obscene if sold to an adult).

[80]New Jersey v. T.L.O., 469 U.S. 325 (1985) (ruling that children do enjoy Fourth Amendment protections but to a lesser degree than adults; search may be justified by suspected violation of a school rule).

[81]See H.L. v. Matheson, 450 U.S. 398 (1981) (states may require parental notification before an unemancipated minor dependent upon her parents may obtain an abortion).

[82]See Howard Cohen, *Equal Rights for Children* (Totowa, N.J.: Littlefield, Adams, 1980); Michael D. A. Freeman, *The Rights and Wrongs of Children* (Dover, N.H.; F. Pinter, 1983); Laurence D. Houlgate, *The Child and the State: A Normative Theory of Juvenile Rights* (Baltimore, Md.: Johns Hopkins University Press, 1980); *Whose Child?: Children's Rights, Parental Authority, and State Power,* ed. William Aiken and Hugh LaFallotte (Totowa, N.J.: Rowman & Littlefield, 1980). See also "An Interview with Marian Wright Edelman," *Harvard Education Review* 44 (1974), 53, 66–67, criticizing "liberation" for children, who instead need "special protections"; Bruce C. Hafen, "Children's Liberation and the New Egalitarianism: Some Reservations about Abandoning Youth to Their 'Rights,'" *B.Y.U. L. Rev.* 1976 (1976), 605, warning that rights for children neglect their needs.

[83]See Education for All Handicapped Children's Act, 20 U.S.C. sec. 1400 (1982).

[84]419 U.S. 565 (1975).

would be frustrated by the formality and distance imposed by legal procedures—that is, by rights. Justice Lewis Powell felt so strongly about the case
that he read aloud from the bench his dissenting opinion in *Goss:*

> in assessing in constitutional terms the need to protect pupils from unfair minor
> discipline by school authorities, the Court ignores the commonality of interest of
> the State and pupils in the public school system. . . . In mandating due process
> procedures the Court misapprehends the reality of the normal teacher-pupil
> relationship. There is an ongoing relationship, one in which the teacher must
> occupy many roles—educator, adviser, friend, and, at times, parent-substitute.
> It is rarely adversary in nature except with respect to the chronically disruptive
> or insubordinate pupil whom the teacher must be free to discipline without
> frustrating formalities.[85]

Justice Powell treated a recognition of rights as defining and accentuating the
distances between people, seeming to pin students in adversarial relationships to teachers and school administrators.

The debate over the proper rules governing relationships are especially
intense when they involve children and public schooling. Choices about the
next generation require society to make decisions for the future about fundamental values. The rules that govern life within the school also convey a message to students about the world beyond the school. The significance of the
choice of rules was not lost on the plaintiffs in the *Goss* litigation. Lawyers
for the students sought to weave into their arguments the idea that "freedom
and democracy are necessary in the schools to teach the young democracy."[86]
Justice Powell adopted an equally emphatic argument on the other side:
"Education in any meaningful sense includes the inculcation of an understanding in each pupil of the necessity of rules and obedience thereto. . . .
When an immature student merits censure for his conduct, he is rendered a
disservice if appropriate sanctions are not applied or if procedures for their
application are so formalized as to invite a challenge to the teacher's authority—an invitation which rebellious or even merely spirited teenagers are
likely to accept."[87]

Implicit in Justice Powell's position are two objections to the assertion and
grant of rights for children. The first is that rights, when claimed and when
recognized, create conflict and adversarial relations between children and
adults where there otherwise would be community and shared interests.[88]
The second is that children lack the kind of autonomy and competence
presumed by the idea of a right and therefore require protection from adults.

[85]Id. at 593–94 (Powell, J., dissenting); see also Parham v. J.R., 442 U.S. 584 (1979)
(presuming nonadversarial relationship between children and parents who seek to commit
children to mental hospitals, and treating medical professionals as capable of providing independent review of parents' decisions).

[86]Letter from Eric Van Loon to Denis Murphy and Ken Curtin, quoted in Frank Zimring and
Raymond Solomon, "Goss v. Lopez: The Principle of the Thing," in *In the Interest of Children:
Advocacy, Law Reform, and Public Policy,* ed. Robert H. Mnookin (New York: W. H. Freeman,
1985), pp. 450, 476.

[87]419 U.S. at 593 (Powell, J., dissenting).

[88]See also Joel Handler, *The Conditions of Discretion: Autonomy, Community, Bureaucracy*
(New York: Russell Sage Foundation, 1986), pp. 72–76, 121–58; Jerry Mashaw, *Bureaucratic*

Children's rights would undermine this critical relationship between children and adults.[89] Yet a choice between rights (premised upon independence and adversarial relations) and dependence (premised on shared interests among children and adults) is too simplistic to capture the interconnections between children, parents, school officials, and the state. Thinking seriously about these relationships[90] and drawing on relational modes of interpretation[91] can suggest ways to reconstruct rights for children in response to these objections.

To believe that rights, when claimed and recognized, create conflict and adversarial relations between children and adults is to presume that there would otherwise be community and shared interests. I suggest instead that legal language translates but does not initiate conflict.[92] The fear that judicial

Justice: Managing Social Security Claims (New Haven, Conn.: Yale University Press, 1983), discussing detriments and benefits of mass delivery of adversarial process in the context of government benefits programs; William H. Simon, "Rights and Redistribution in the Welfare System," *Stan. L. Rev.* 38 (1986), 1431, 1499–1504, arguing that welfare jurisprudence is distorted by rights rhetoric and analogies to private law. The claim of rights, however, need not predetermine the forms of requisite process; people can use rights discourse to develop new procedures and remedies as well as new claims. Handler, in *The Conditions of Discretion*, pp. 141–53, separates adversariness from liberal legalism and calls for cooperative dimension in reconstructing rights. Arguments against unions in the university setting also presuppose only one model of labor relations, rather than acknowledging that in a new setting, collective bargaining may take a new shape.

[89]Although child-rearing notions are themselves deeply imbued with political attitudes dominant in a particular culture, many theorists have emphasized that the relationship between parent and child demands parental authority to restrict children's personal freedom; see, e.g., Jerome Kagan, *The Nature of the Child* (New York: Basic Books, 1984), pp. 257–64. Some theorists have maintained that the child must internalize a sense of parental authority and that external intervention undermines the development of internalized limits; see, e.g., Joseph Goldstein, Albert J. Solnit, and Anna Freud, *Beyond the Best Interests of the Child* (New York: Free Press, 1973), pp. 174–78. The child will grow up feeling weak and will want to find others to scapegoat. See Lasch, *Haven in a Heartless World*, pp. 174–78: "Delegation of discipline to other agencies" outside the family promotes the projection of "forbidden impulses" onto outcast groups; Else Frenkel-Brunswick, "Parents and Childhood as Seen through the Interviews," in *The Authoritarian Personality*, ed. T. W. Adorno, Else Frenkel-Brunswick, Daniel Levinson, and R. Nevitt Sanford (New York: Harper, 1950), pp. 358–59: "The existing identification with the parents is often accompanied by a more basic identification with mankind and society in general." One legal observer suggests that "in a paradoxical but important sense, a child has a basic right to be protected against freedom" precisely because learning about the consequences of bad judgments is an important part of childhood; see Bruce C. Hafen, "Exploring Test Cases in Child Advocacy," *Harv. L. Rev.* 100 (1986), pp. 435, 446 (reviewing Mnookin, *In the Interest of Children*). Thus, Hafen and others have warned against "abandoning children to their rights" (pp. 445–46).

[90]I am helped here by Sara Lawrence Lightfoot, *Worlds Apart: Relationships between Families and Schools* (New York: Basic Books, 1978).

[91]Many scholars have recently developed a literary or interpretive turn in law. See generally James Boyd White, *When Words Lose Their Meaning: Constitutions and Reconstitutions of Language, Character, and Community* (Chicago: University of Chicago Press, 1984); "Symposium: Law and Literature," *Tex. L. Rev.* 60 (1982), 373; Milner Ball, *Lying Down Together: Law, Metaphor, and Theology* (Madison: University of Wisconsin Press, 1985); Robert Cover, "The Supreme Court, 1982 Term—Foreword: Nomos and Narrative," *Harv. L. Rev.* 97 (1983), 47; Patricia Williams, "Alchemical Notes: Reconstructing Ideals from Deconstructed Rights," *Harv. C.R.–C.L. L. Rev.* 22 (1987), 401, 424.

[92]As with so many translations, something may be lost in the process. See George Steiner, *After Babel: Aspects of Language and Translation* (New York: Oxford University Press, 1975).

recognition of rights for children would inject conflict and invite rebellious-
ness is mistaken in the very context of the Goss v. Lopez litigation because
conflict was present long before anyone asserted in court that students had
rights. For example, minority students were suspended without hearings
after racial conflicts erupted in the Columbus, Ohio, schools in 1971.[93] The
school administration had canceled an assembly program organized by black
students for Black History Week. Shortly thereafter, two black students were
shot by white students. These events precipitated further disturbances, and
subsequently the local chapter of the NAACP met with parents and students
to discuss racism in the school's disciplinary practices.

In such a context it is difficult to believe that the introduction of legal rights
would disrupt a community of shared, nonadversarial interests uniting students and teachers. Similarly, where a pregnant minor seeks an abortion
without parental consent because of her parents' religious or philosophical
opposition, warm family consultation might be preferable to litigation but is
probably impracticable. Denying the minor her independent legal rights in
such a situation hardly prevents conflict.[94] Assertion of rights in these contexts does not initiate conflict but rather gives existing conflict public expression and invites public resolution.[95] The language of rights may give voice to
what would have been silence, but not consensus.[96]

Using language that is not one's own can limit, distort, and even silence. See generally Lisa
Redfield Peattie and Martin Rein, *Women's Claims: A Study in Political Economy* (New York:
Oxford University Press, 1983), pp. 102–26: how the prevailing system shaped the claims of the
U.S. women's movement, which in turn raised new categories of claims; Katherine O'Donovan,
"Family Law and Legal Theory," in *Legal Theory and Common Law*, ed. William Twining
(New York: B. Blackwell, 1986), pp. 184, 191. Yet the law itself can be reshaped by the conflicts
brought to it. See, e.g., California Fed. Savings & Loan Ass'n v. Guerra, 107 S.Ct. 683 (1987),
interpreting Title VII's antidiscrimination commitment to be consistent with California's pregnancy disability leave statute; Catharine MacKinnon, *Sexual Harassment of Working Women:
A Case of Sex Discrimination* (New Haven, Conn.: Yale University Press, 1979), offering a new
theory of sex discrimination.
[93]Zimring and Solomon, "Goss v. Lopez," pp. 459–72.
[94]See "Planned Parenthood v. Danforth," 428 U.S. 52, 75 (1976): "It is difficult, however, to
conclude that providing a parent with absolute power to overrule a determination, made by the
physician and his minor patient, to terminate the patient's pregnancy will serve to strengthen the
family unit. Neither is it likely that such veto power will enhance parental authority or control
where the minor and the nonconsenting parent are so fundamentally in conflict and the very
existence of the pregnancy already has fractured the family structure." See also H.L. v. Matheson, 450 U.S. 398, 425 (1981) (Marshall, J., dissenting).
[95]The use of rights rhetoric, and the aggressive nature of litigation, can make covert conflict
overt and may therefore appear disruptive. See Francis Fitzgerald, "A Reporter at Large: A
Disagreement in Baileyville," *New Yorker*, Jan. 16, 1984, p. 47. Litigation may enlarge disputes
that would otherwise smolder, but it may also narrow disputes that would otherwise expand.
See David M. Trubek, "The Construction and Deconstruction of a Disputes-Focused Approach:
An Afterword," *Law & Soc'y Rev.* 15 (1980–81), 727, 732–33. Some may claim that the two
problems suggested by *Goss* and *Danforth* represent extreme cases of conflict in settings usually
characterized by harmony and that we should not devise rules for the extreme situation.
Frank H. Easterbrook, "The Supreme Court 1983 Term—Foreword: The Court and the Economic System," *Harv. L. Rev.* 98 (1984), 4, 10–14, urges judicial attention to future consequences of principles laid down today rather than merely retrospective responses to particular
fact situations. I suggest that the rules we devise help create the exceptions. The important
challenge for the legal community is to build frameworks illuminated by what we have made
marginal in the past.
[96]As Adrienne Rich has written about silence, "Do not confuse it/with any kind of absence"

In other contexts, the charges that rights introduce conflict and an adversarial stance have been levied by people who do not want to change existing patterns of domination and hierarchy. Such objections have been raised to criminalizing rape committed within a marriage,[97] and to giving employees rights.[98] Rights, as both initial efforts to demand public debate about existing patterns of private power and as official rules enforcing changes in those patterns, create conflict only by giving public voice and force to people previously ignored. Although such expression may amplify conflict and focus attention on it, it also may transform physical conflict into verbal dispute.

Moreover, rather than insinuating conflict, the introduction of rights to the school disciplinary process can reconfirm community.[99] The particular right ultimately announced in *Goss* amounted to no more than minimal notice and an opportunity for the student to have a conversation with a social official, much as any sensitive school official or parent would talk to a child before punishing her.[100] This right to a conversation is a good example of the way in which asserting rights may actually affirm, rather than disturb, community. By invoking rights, an individual or group claims the attention of the larger community and its authorities. At the same time, this claim acknowledges the claimant's membership in the larger group, participation in its traditions, and observation of its forms.

James Boyd White puts it this way: "The law establishes roles and relations and voices, positions from which and audiences to which one may speak, and it gives us as speakers the materials and methods of a discourse. . . . It is this discourse, working in the social context of its own creation, this language in the fullest sense of the term, that is the law. It makes us members of a common world."[101] Similarly, political philosopher Hanna

---

(*The Fact of a Door Frame: Poems Selected and New, 1950–1984* [New York: Norton, 1984], pp. 232–33). See also Susan Griffin, *Pornography and Silence: Culture's Revenge against Nature* (New York: Harper & Row, 1982); Aviam Soifer, "Listening and the Voiceless," *Miss. C. L. Rev.* 4 (1984), 319.

[97]The traditional marital exception to rape laws was defended on these grounds. See Michael Gary Hilf, "Marital Privacy and Spousal Rape," *New Eng. L. Rev.* 16 (1980), 31, 32–34; Comment, "Rape and Battery between Husband and Wife," *Stan. L. Rev.* 6 (1954), 719; Note, "Litigation between Husband and Wife," *Harv. L. Rev.* 79 (1966), 1650. The current trend, however, expresses the contrary view that rape within marriage is blameworthy and typically expresses unequal power, and wife abuse. See "Note, To Have and To Hold: The Marital Rape Exemption and the Fourteenth Amendment," *Harv. L. Rev.* 99 (1986), 1255.

[98]See Paul Weiler, "Striking a New Balance: Freedom of Contract and the Prospects for Union Representation," *Harv. L. Rev.* 98 (1984), 351, 357–63 (discussing institutional and conceptual obstacles to realizing employee rights).

[99]What constitutes a community is a perplexing issue. Many communities may be present within one geographic area, or no community may exist at all: that is, the people do not experience themselves as members of a collective enterprise of mutual interdependence. Yet the adoption and use of the same language provides a basis for some sense of community, and a given legal language signifies some assent to the use of collective processes to resolve disagreements and problems of governance.

[100]*Goss v. Lopez*, 419 U.S. 594–96 (1975) (Powell, J., dissenting). At a school superintendents' seminar (Harvard Graduate School of Education, June 17, 1986), some school officials suggested that *Goss* actually promotes educational opportunities by framing discussions of discipline and fairness; others, that *Goss* procedures adopted within the school promote the settlement of issues that might otherwise go to court.

[101]White, *When Words Lose Their Meaning*, p. 266. Milner Ball (*Lying Down Together,*

Pitkin explains: "Drawn into public life by personal need, fear, ambition or interest, we are there forced to acknowledge the power of others and appeal to their standards. . . . We are forced to find or create a common language of purposes or aspirations, not merely to clothe our private outlook in public disguise, but to become aware of its public meaning. We are forced, as Joseph Tussman has put it, to transform 'I want' into 'I am entitled to,' a claim that becomes negotiable by public standards."[102]

Although the language of rights, on its surface, says little of community or convention, those who exercise rights signal and strengthen their relation to a community. Those who claim rights implicitly agree to abide by the community's response and to accord similar regard to the claims of others.[103] In a deeper sense, those claiming rights implicitly invest themselves in a larger community, even in the act of seeking to change it. When Martin Luther King justified "direct action" as a way to assert the rights of blacks, he intertwined the demands for change with notions of communal connection:

> Just as Socrates felt that it was necessary to create a tension in the mind so that individuals could rise from the bondage of myths and half-truths to the unfettered realm of creative analysis and objective appraisal, so must we see the need for nonviolent gadflies to create the kind of tension in society that will help men rise from the dark depths of prejudice and racism to the majestic heights of understanding and brotherhood. The purpose of our direct-action program is to create a situation so crisis-packed that it will inevitably open the door to negotiation. . . . Too long has our beloved Southland been bogged down in a tragic effort to live in monologue rather than dialogue.[104]

Community means not total agreement but, instead, commitment to share a "communicative framework."[105] Stating a claim in a form devised by those who are powerful in the community expresses a willingness to take part in

p. 122) similarly proposed "law as medium—law as connecting rather than disconnecting, enhancing a flow of dialogue, containing the dynamics of life in common." See also Michael Walzer, _Interpretation and Social Criticism_ (Cambridge, Mass.: Harvard University Press, 1987): membership in the community is a precondition for effective social criticism.

[102]Hanna Pitkin, "Justice on Relating Private and Public," _Political Theory_ 9 (1981), 327, 347, citing Joseph Tussman, _Obligation and the Body Politic_ (New York: Oxford University Press, 1960), pp. 78–81, 108, 116–17. See also Frank Michelman, "Justification (and Justifiability) of Law in a Contradictory World," _Nomos_ 28 (1986), 71, 92: "A right, however much it may be a claim to respect as a distinct person, is, equally fundamentally, a claim grounded in human association."

[103]Beverly Wildung Harrison put this essentially Kantian insight this way: "If any of us is prepared to invoke anything as a human moral right on our own behalf, that very act implies the existence of a similar claim for every other member of our species" (_Making the Connections: Essays in Feminist Social Ethics_, ed. Carol Robb [Boston: Beacon Press, 1985], p. 168).

[104]Martin Luther King, Jr., "Letter from a Birmingham Jail," quoted in Juan Williams, _Eyes on the Prize: America's Civil Rights Years, 1954–1965_ (New York: Viking Press, 1987), p. 187. Similarly, King's notion of civil disobedience involved a willingness to accept the penalty, to arouse the conscience of the community—and to manifest membership in the community respecting the law.

[105]The phrase is Lief Carter's, in _Contemporary Constitutional Lawmaking: The Supreme Court and the Art of Politics_ (New York: Pergamon Press, 1985), p. 15.

the community, as well as a tactical decision to play by the rules of the only game recognized by those in charge.

The skeletal due process mandated by *Goss* exposes how dependent individual rights are upon the established community order, and how those rights forge connections between individuals by requiring people to respond to one another.[106] Can the student persuade the vice-principal not to suspend her? Maybe not. For the student, having the right to try depends upon the willingness of the vice-principal to take that right seriously. Similarly, the *Goss* ruling announcing that right depended upon the willingness of the justices to engage in a serious conversation about students' needs and, indeed, a willingness to include students as members of the community, bound together through rights.[107]

The right to due process is special, among other rights, in its specific call for communication and attention to the individual's dignity. Thus, both in its initial assertion and in its ultimate form in *Goss,* the right to a hearing before suspension from school engages students and school administrators in a process of discussion that can build a community of respect. Yet even beyond the particular right granted by the Supreme Court, the claim of any right initiates a form of communal dialogue. A claimant asserts a right and thereby secures the attention of the community through the procedures the community has designated for hearing such claims. Milner Ball explains that "a person arguing with you is giving you her time in a joint effort at mutual understanding. That way, argument is a form of cooperation. . . . And the outcome is something other than victory for one party and defeat for the other"; rather, argument is like a joint enterprise whose purpose is "a performance that works."[108] The conclusion, reached by a legal authority figure, represents a response, a response that is temporary and limited in scope, one that provides the occasion for the next claim. Legal rights, then, should be understood as the language of a continuing process rather than as fixed rules. Rights discourse reaches temporary resting points from which new claims can be made.

This conception rejects the tinge of legal positivism or objectivity often associated with rights—the implication of an authoritative basis and content beyond historically contingent human choices. Insofar as a given set of rights embodies the results of past struggles, it expresses a particular substantive commitment. The civil rights movement, for example, created a legacy of meanings for the Fourteenth Amendment. That legacy reflects the commitments of the civil rights activities and the officials persuaded by them to

[106]The results of some rights claims may be a ruling that some people do not have to deal with others; esp. successful privacy claims and restraining orders in domestic abuse cases have this effect. Yet even these rulings result from an institutionally framed discussion, forcing people to recognize one another's boundaries.

[107]See Honora O'Neill, "The Public Use of Reason," *Political Theory* 14 (1986), 523, 527, 548: toleration is necessary for the "plurality of potentially reasoning beings"; Laurence Tribe, "Structural Due Process," *Harv. C.R.–C.L. L. Rev.* 10 (1975), 269, 305–6: a commitment to the real dialogue includes an agreement to avoid the privileged place of some views over others.

[108]Ball, *Lying Down Together,* p. 133.

incorporate elements of the movement into the formal legal system. Invocation of those commitments and that history can add to the persuasive force generated in rights discourse even when that discourse depends on nothing beyond current and future human choices.

Rights in this sense are not "trumps" but the language we use to try to persuade others to let us win this round.[109] Particular rights may assert a power to "trump," but their origins and their future viability depend upon a continuing, communal process of communication.[110] No rights are self-enforcing. Enforcement remains contingent upon the willingness of the community's officials to signal their meaning to the community through force or threatened violence. When advocates for children ask a court to recognize children's rights to privacy, due process, or other protections, they seek judicial statements that will articulate new boundaries and connections between children and adults. They seek the chance to use these judicial articulations to negotiate new relationships between children and adults in the arrangements of daily life.

This notion of a continuing process of setting and resetting boundaries through communal debate over rights claims resembles the conception of continual redefinition of the self's boundaries which is powerfully present in the work of many psychologists.[111] Patricia Williams offers this analogy: "Rights are to law what conscious commitments are to the psyche."[112] Rights provide a language that depends upon and expresses human interconnection at the very moment when individuals ask others to recognize their separate interests. Giving children the right to testify in court about suspected child abuse—and even the right to testify on videotape, away from the defendant—tips the balance of power toward children, temporarily, without throwing them off the seesaw with adults.

The language of rights thus draws each claimant into the community and grants each a basic opportunity to participate in the process of communal debate.[113] The discourse of rights registers commitment to a basic equality

[109]But see Ronald Dworkin, "Rights as Trumps," in *Theories of Rights*, ed. Jeremy Waldron (Oxford: Oxford University Press, 1984), p. 153.

[110]Whether rights are "determinate"—whether their stated content determines their specific meaning in particular contexts beyond the choices made by particular decision-makers—has been a subject of considerable dispute, esp. pursued by critical legal scholars. Cf. Mark G. Kelman, "Trashing," *Stan. L. Rev.* 36 (1984), 293 (suggesting the indeterminacy of rights and legal categories), with James Boyle, "The Politics of Reason, Critical Legal Theory and Local Social Thought," *U. Pa. L. Rev.* 133 (1985), 685 (urging resolution of debates by reference to local, situated analysis), and Owen M. Fiss, "Objectivity and Interpretation," *Stan. L. Rev.* 34 (1982), 739 (taking issue with indeterminacy thesis). This dispute seems beside the point once we conceive of rights as part of legal language, used to express claims whose meanings depend upon particular choices in specific contexts.

[111]See, e.g., Robert Kegan, *The Evolving Self: Problem and Process in Human Development* (Cambridge, Mass.: Harvard University Press, 1982); Jessica Benjamin, "The Bonds of Love: Rational Violence and Erotic Domination," in *The Future of Difference*, ed. Hester Eisenstein and Alice Jardine (Boston: G. K. Hall, 1980), pp. 41, 47–51.

[112]Williams, "Alchemical Notes," pp. 401, 424.

[113]"The [legal] case establishes an essential equality between people . . . and it proceeds by a method of argument and conversation that both recognizes the individual's view of his own

among the participants as participants, even when the participants are children. It is important, however, to distinguish between the ways in which this
basic form of equality creates a kind of community and the ways in which
inequality of power and status may well remain within the community.
Children provide important examples on both counts. Including children as
participants alters their stance in the community, from things or outsiders to
members.[114] Yet children are usually less powerful than others economically
and politically and more vulnerable physically, emotionally, and cognitively.
The assertion of membership accomplishes something important but does
not itself disturb or challenge unequal arrangements of political or economic
power.[115] It is, of course, no news to either the powerful or the powerless that
those with power have power. As Carol Gilligan has noted, "If you have
power, you can opt not to listen. And you do so with impunity."[116]

What, then, is the equality signaled by rights discourse? The equality
embodied by rights claims is an equality of *attention*. The rights tradition in
this country sustains the call that makes those in power at least listen.
Rights—as words and as forms—structure attention even for the claimant
who is much less powerful than the authorities, and even for individuals and
groups treated throughout the community as less than equal. Unstated here
are assumptions about the presumed standard for comparison: equal to
whom? An adult, white, competent male citizen is the likely reference. But by
including any who can speak the language of rights and by signaling deserved
attention, rights enable a challenge to unstated norms, to exclusion, and to

situation and complicates that view by forcing him to recognize the claims of another" (White,
When Words Lose Their Meaning, p. 274).

[114]In Smith v. Org. of Foster Families for Equality and Reform, 431 U.S. 816 (1977), a group
of foster parents challenged state decisions to remove foster children from their placements;
their attorney, drawing from an older view that adults have rights to children, as if children were
property, claimed to represent both the foster parents and the foster children in their shared
interest in maintaining relationships. The district court, however, holding that a potential
conflict of interest required separate representation, appointed an attorney to speak for the
foster children. Although the case yielded no answer to the constitutional question of whether
due-process rights required more protection for the foster parents, the case does represent a
judicial commitment to conceive of children as distinct persons deserving independent consideration. Moreover, Justice Stewart, joined by Chief Justice Burger and Justice Rehnquist, emphasized that the state law at issue definitively rejected the idea that long-term custody creates some
sort of "squatters' rights" to the children (id. at 857, quoting Bennett v. Jeffreys, 40 N.Y.2d 543,
552 n.2 [1976]; 356 N.E.2d 277, 285 n.2 [1976]).

[115]There is a risk that claims made in established legal forms can never adequately challenge
oppressive practices at the heart of the legal or political system. Audre Lorde analyzed this
problem in her powerful essay "The Master's Tools Will Never Dismantle the Master's House,"
in *Sister Outsider: Essays and Speeches* (Trumansburg, N.Y.: Crossing Press, 1984), p. 110. Yet,
just as her own prose transformed inherited language and ideas, and claimed difference as "that
raw and powerful connection from which our personal power is forged" (p. 112), an emphatic
claiming of differences through rights language could help transform existing legal and social
structures. To continue the metaphor of the Master's House, the tools may be used to make new
tools, which then can help renovate the house for others.

[116]"Feminist Discourse, Moral Values, and the Law—A Conversation: The 1984 James
McCormick Mitchell Lecture," *Buffalo L. Rev.* 34 (1985), 11, 62 (Isabel Marcus and Paul J.
Spiegelman, moderators; Ellen C. DuBois, Marx C. Dunlap, Carol J. Gilligan, Catharine A.
MacKinnon, and Carrie Menkel-Meadow, conversants).

exclusive perspectives. Rights discourse implicates its users in a form of life, a pattern of social and political commitment.[117]

Claims of rights have a special resonance in our culture,[118] but they are still vulnerable to rebuff. The rhetoric of rights draws those who use it inside the community and urges the community to pay attention to the individual claimants, but it underscores the power of the established order to respond or withhold response to the individual's claims. In addition, the rhetoric of rights remains available for yet another individual or group to participate and to claim attention which, by inviting a different community response, may complicate or even jeopardize the claims already made.

Which claims will persuade, and how, and with what consequences for prior and subsequent claims and for past and future relationships? Which claims, indeed, will be recognized as even deserving communal attention? These are difficult and persistent questions in a community committed to rights discourse. There is a risk that those points of view which have been silenced in the past will continue to go unheard and will be least adaptable to the vocabulary of preexisting claims. These are issues for struggle, and some struggles may well take place beyond rights discourse, beyond language. Some people may feel so shut out that the appeal to a communal commitment to rights makes no sense to them. Others may find the very act of claiming too risky to their limited control over their own lives and dignity.[119] Nonetheless, this interpretive conception of rights as a medium for expressing and strengthening communal relationships is a way to take the aspirational language of the society seriously. It is a way to promote change by reliance on inherited traditions. And it is a way to challenge those who want to close the doors, now that some of the previously excluded have fought and found their way in.

Comparing rights to language and conversation enables a conception of community forged through an exchange of words in a struggle for meaning. In an eloquent novel about contemporary South Africa, Nadine Gordimer's Rosa Burger responds to a critic of liberalism: "I'm not offering a theory. I'm talking about people who need to have rights—*there*—in a statute book, so that they can move about in their own country, decide what work they'll do and what their children will learn at school. . . . People must be able to create institutions—institutions *must evolve* that will make it possible in practice. That utopia, it's inside . . . without it, how can you . . . act?"[120]

---

[117]Ludwig Wittgenstein, *Philosophical Investigations,* 3d ed., trans. G. E. M. Anscombe (New York: Macmillan, 1973), secs. 46c–92c, explores the relation between language games and forms of life.

[118]See Hendrik Hartog, "The Constitution of Aspiration and 'The Rights That Belong to Us All,'" in *The Constitution and American Life,* ed. David Thelen (Ithaca: Cornell University Press, 1988), pp. 353–74.

[119]See Kristin Bumiller, *The Civil Rights Society: The Social Construction of Victims* (Baltimore, Md.: Johns Hopkins University Press, 1988).

[120]Nadine Gordimer, *Burger's Daughter* (New York: Viking Press, 1979), p. 3. The contrast between South Africa and the United States is telling. A South African visitor who watched the televised special *Eyes on the Prize,* chronicling the American civil rights movement of the 1950s,

The use of rights discourse affirms community, but it affirms a particular kind of community: a community dedicated to invigorating words with power to restrain, so that even the powerless can appeal to those words. It is a community that acknowledges and admits the historical uses of power to exclude, deny, and silence—and commits itself to enabling suppressed points of view to be heard, to making covert conflict overt. Committed to making available a rhetoric of rights where it has not been heard before, this community uses rights language to make conflict audible and unavoidable, even if it is limited to words, and certain other forms of expression.[121] If the very introduction of rights rhetoric to a new area triggers conflict, it is over this issue: should the normative commitment to restrain power with communal dedication reach this new area? The power in question may be public or private. With children's rights, large disagreements persist over whether and how communal limits should constrain the exercise of private, especially parental, power. Children's rights may enlarge state power over both children and adults, rather than simply recognizing children's preexisting autonomy. But it is the meaning of autonomy, and its relation to rights, that claims attention next.

Children's Rights and Autonomy

A persistent argument against rights for children is that children lack the autonomy necessary to engage in adversarial exchange, to protect their own interests, and, indeed, even to know their own interests.[122] Another challenge stresses indeterminacy and the seeming limitlessness of children's needs.[123] These objections grow out of the widely accepted conception of rights which relies on the idea that the rights-bearing person is an autonomous individual capable of exercising choice for personal ends and of pro-

---

told me that he was most amazed that Martin Luther King and others invoked the symbols of the United States as banners for their struggles, that the constitution and the Supreme Court represented ideals which could be claimed by the excluded. See also John Dugard, "The Jurisprudential Foundation of the Apartheid Legal Order," *Philosophical Forum* 18 (1986–87), 115, 122: the black majority lost confidence in South African law, given its role in apartheid; David Goldberg, "Reading the Signs: The Force of Language," *Philosophical Forum* 18 (1986–87), 71, 89–90: the language of racial difference reinforces historical race relations, acting as "a brake upon the rate of social transformation."

[121]For successes and failures in the translation of claims brought to the legal system, see Richard Harris, *Freedom Spent* (Boston: Little, Brown, 1976); Richard Kluger, *Simple Justice: The History of Brown v. Board of Education and Black America's Struggle for Equality* (New York: Knopf, 1976); John Thomas Noonan, *Persons and Masks of the Law: Cardozo, Holmes, Jefferson, and Wythe as Makers of the Masks* (New York: Farrar, Strauss, & Giroux, 1976).

[122]See, e.g., Hafen, "Exploring Test Cases," pp. 644–56; Robert Mnookin, "The Enigma of Children's Interests," in Mnookin, *In the Interest of Children*, p. 16. But see Victor Worsford, "A Philosophical Justification for Children's Rights," *Harvard Educational Review* 44 (Feb. 1974), 142.

[123]Similarly, Robert Burt, "Pennhurst: A Parable," in Mnookin, *In the Interest of Children*, p. 324, points out that all potential parties are moved by the needs of mentally retarded people—until the needs seem "insatiable" and overwhelming.

tecting personal freedom from the pressure and power of others.[124] Yet this notion of the autonomous rights-bearing individual presupposes a community—a community willing to recognize and enforce individual rights; hence, even this usual conception of rights, premised on autonomy, relies on a social and communal construction of boundaries between people. Autonomy, even as an aspiration, is the invention of a cultural and linguistic community. Boundaries, whether social, psychological, or legal, do not exist naturally; they are invented and reinvented by people in formal and informal ways.[125] As a psychological matter, the very experience of a bounded personal identity requires not just one individual but many, who help constitute the boundaries.[126] In the words of one theorist, autonomy is a process of "parts that mutually specify themselves," like M. C. Escher's drawing of two hands, each drawing the other.[127]

These insights about relationships as the precondition for autonomy undergird current work in psychology, anthropology, and philosophy. Recent theories of human development emphasize how aspects of the self develop from experiences with others, notably the mothers, such that "the core of the self, or self-feeling is also constructed relationally."[128] The child needs to see

[124]Gerald Dworkin, "Paternalism: Some Second Thoughts," in *Paternalism,* ed. Rolf Sartorious (Minneapolis: University of Minnesota Press, 1983), p. 105; Joseph Raz, "Right-Based Moralities," in Waldron, *Theories of Rights,* pp. 186–95. For alternative notions of rights, see Staughton Lynd, "Communal Rights," *Tex. L. Rev.* 62 (1984), 1417; Elizabeth Schneider, "The Dialectic of Rights and Politics: Perspectives from the Women's Movement," *N.Y.U. L. Rev.* 61 (1986), 589; William Simon, "Rights and Redistribution in the Welfare System," *Stan. L. Rev.* 38 (1986), 1433. See also Takeo Doi, *The Anatomy of Dependence,* trans. John Bester (New York: Kodansha International, 1973), contrasting the Japanese conception of human interdependence with the Western emphasis on autonomy.

[125]See generally Anthony Cohen, *The Symbolic Construction of Community* (New York: Tavistock, 1985), which explores the social construction of membership and exclusion as elements of community; and Kai T. Erikson, *Wayward Puritans: A Study in the Sociology of Deviance* (New York: Wiley, 1966), which argues that the Puritans assigned people to deviant positions as a way of conceiving boundaries for their cultural universe.

[126]See Nancy Chodorow, *The Reproduction of Mothering: Psychoanalysis and the Sociology of Gender* (Berkeley: University of California Press, 1978), pp. 57–73, 99–110, 191–205: the psychological development of an individual depends on having a relationship with a parent through which individual boundaries are established.

[127]Francisco Varela, "The Creative Circle," in *The Invented Reality,* ed. Paul Watzlawick (New York: Norton, 1984), pp. 309–11.

[128]Nancy Chodorow, "Toward a Relational Individualism: The Mediation of Self through Psychoanalysis," in *Reconstructing Individualism: Autonomy, Individuality, and the Self in Western Thought,* ed. Thomas Heller, Morton Sosna, and David E. Wellbery (Stanford, Calif.: Stanford University Press, 1986). See also Dorothy Dinnerstein, *The Mermaid and the Minotaur: Sexual Arrangements and Human Malaise* (New York: Harper & Row, 1976): the mother-child relationship affects the child's development of boundaries. Chodorow relies in part on the work of object-relations theorists; she quotes Joan Riviere (pp. 402–3), who wrote: "There is no such thing as a single human being, pure and simple, unmixed with other human beings. Each personality is a world in himself, a company of many. . . . These other persons are in fact therefore parts of ourselves, not indeed the whole of them but such parts or aspects of them as we had our relation with, and as have thus become parts of us. And we ourselves similarly have and have had effects and influences, intended or not, on all others who have an emotional relation to us, have loved or hated us. We are members one of another" ("The Unconscious Phantasy of an Inner World Reflected in Examples from Literature," in *New Directions in Psychoanalysis,* ed. Melanie Klein, Paula Heiman, and R. E. Money-Kyrle [New York: Basic Books, 1955], pp. 358–59).

the mother; the mother needs to see the child. But most important to the process of individuation, the child needs to see the mother seeing her.[129] Even beyond theories of child development, psychologists have begun to identify the capacity to form commitments and connections to others, rather than autonomy, as the destination for the maturing person.[130] Philosophers have developed similar insights. Drucilla Cornell interprets Hegel's views to suggest that "one becomes a self-identified ego only through interaction in which one experiences oneself as a self by being mirrored in the eyes of others."[131] The metaphor of conversation, used by legal theorists who make an interpretive or literary turn, adopts a similar view of the interdependence of individuals and the aspiration of connection.[132]

Autonomy, if defined as the condition of an unencumbered and independent self, is not a precondition for any individual's exercise of rights.[133] The only precondition is that the community be willing for the individual to make claims and to participate in the defining and redefining of personal and social boundaries. When a court acts, it defines boundaries between people by accepting or rejecting particular claims of entitlement or obligation. Even these acts of judicial power connect words to relationships and individuals to other individuals in complex ways. Judicial acts enable subsequent claims to be made, allowing formal and informal resistance to the very boundaries enunciated by the court.[134]

The invocation of community implied by rights claims does not force

[129]Donald W. Winnicott, *The Family and Individual Development* (San Diego: Tavistock, 1965); Margaret Mahler, "Symbiosis and Individuation: The Psychological Birth of the Human Infant," in *The Selected Papers* (New York: Jason Aronson, 1979), p. 149; Donald W. Winnicott, "The Theory of the Parent-Infant Relationship," in *The Maturational Processes and the Facilitating Environment: Studies in the Theory of Emotional Development* (New York: International Universities Press, 1965), p. 37; Margaret Mahler, "Thoughts about Development and Individuation," *Psychoanalytic Study of the Child* 18 (1963), 307.

[130]See Carol Gilligan, *In a Different Voice: Psychological Theory and Women's Development* (Cambridge, Mass.: Harvard University Press, 1982), pp. 151–74.

[131]Drucilla Cornell, "Toward a Modern/Postmodern Reconstruction of Ethics," *U. Pa. L. Rev.* 133 (1985), 291, 361, discussing Hegel's Jena manuscripts. See also Michael Sandel, *Liberalism and the Limits of Justice* (Cambridge: Cambridge University Press, 1982), criticizing protection of "unencumbered self" as the goal of social arrangements.

[132]See, e.g., Ball, *Lying Down Together,* p. 138; White, *When Words Lose Their Meaning,* p. 18. And legal rights themselves are interdependent and mutually defining.

[133]The dichotomous definitions of autonomy and connection or dependence deserve to be rejected. The important questions about any given person's autonomy are these: with whom is this person connected, to what degree, for what purposes, and in relation to what other connections? How much latitude is there for self-assertion, and how much self-control over the boundaries forged in connection with others?

[134]For discussion of rights consciousness and people's resistance to law, see, e.g., E. P. Thompson, *Whigs and Hunters: The Origin of the Black Act* (New York: Pantheon Books, 1975); and William Forbath, Martha Minow, and Hendrik Hartog, "Introduction: Legal Histories from Below," *Wis. L. Rev.* 1985 (1985), 759. Even paternalist, rather than rights-based, ideologies of social order can have the effect of inspiring new interpretations; see Eugene Genovese, *Roll, Jordan, Roll: The World the Slaves Made* (New York: Vintage Books, 1976), p. 6: "Slaves, by accepting a paternalistic ethos and legitimating class rule, developed their most powerful defense against the dehumanization implicit in slavery. Southern paternalism . . . unwittingly invited its victims to fashion their own interpretation of the social order it was intended to justify."

individuals or subcommunities to lose their own boundaries or to merge into the larger community. Some rights, as defined in their specific content, articulate boundaries protecting individuals or groups against certain kinds of connections with others. Rights against assault, for example, such as a child's right not to be subject to physical abuse, are not exceptions to the notion of rights as tools of communal dialogue; historically, they are products of precisely the kind of communal inquiry I am suggesting. Through litigation and legislation, such rights have been articulated and enforced. The particular content of the enforceable right summons members of the community to respect boundaries within the community as a commitment to implement the decisions reached through community discussion.[135] Rights that recognize boundaries underscore communal ties, for it is through reference to one another that we establish and articulate our boundaries. When I experience a sense of constraint because another claims a right, whether I accept or reject the particular boundary he or she seeks to draw, I also experience connection to that person through the process of mutual recognition.

Obvious examples of interdependence arise for adults in the family context. Even in matters never likely to go to court, adults in a family reveal interdependence and potential conflict in discussing everyday questions: Who will run which errands? Who will take care of the children this afternoon? Who will have time to be alone? Converting these questions into conflicting claims of autonomy misses the point that each question implies how lives are shared. When the rights claims reach official attention, the interdependence of the claimants is no less palpable. An adult woman's right to choose to terminate a pregnancy without spousal consultation or consent clearly implicates and modifies the claims of the father and of the potential child. A contrary right of the father to consult or consent would similarly implicate and modify the rights of the mother and of the potential new life. Whatever the rules, whether they criminalize abortion or immunize it from police and prosecutorial action, the law articulates a pattern of rights that speaks to relationships among individuals, whichever particular individual's right is declared the winning claim. A woman's right to control her own procreative choice, once announced and enforced by legal authorities, remakes a woman's relationships and alters her power—but not because law has suddenly "intervened" where it previously was absent. The law always prescribes consequences for particular relationships—even by its inaction, as the legal realists knew.

Similarly, the rights of shareholders implicate their relationships to management and workers.[136] The rights of trust beneficiaries implicate their relationships with trustees and donors. Each statement of an individual's rights implicitly or explicitly draws reference to others and thus expresses interconnection at the very moment that the individual asserts his or her autonomy. In this respect, children's rights are no more problematic than

[135]Drucilla Cornell, "Should a Marxist Believe in Rights?" *Praxis International* 4 (1984), 45 (discussing Habermas).
[136]Work settings foster relationships that can create mutual reliance. See Singer, "The Reliance Interest in Property," pp. 611, 618–22, 652–99.

adults' rights, because all rights claims imply relationships among mutually dependent members of a community.

Does locating the interdependence of any human being with others obscure the differences between children and adults? No. Instead, it rejects the notion that our society should answer questions about children's legal status simply by asking how children differ from adults. That inquiry wrongly suggests that such differences are real and discoverable rather than contingent upon social interpretations and choices. And the inquiry into differences risks creating and then submerging a norm for inquiring about sameness and difference, rather than raising for debate the substantive questions about how we should live together. To assert that children differ from adults by their relative powerlessness, for example, obscures the range of power held and exercised by different adults and also neglects the fact that power itself is a quality of relationships, not a quantum or a possession of an isolated person. Children, no less than adults, are implicated in these relationships, which the rhetoric of rights can articulate and hold to account. Looked at this way, rights rhetoric can connect parts and wholes.

Articulating children's interests in terms of rights arguably risks undermining the relationships through which their needs are usually met. This objection assumes that because of their dependence on others, children would be better off if families and schools were removed from the purview of public scrutiny permitted by rights claims. Public review itself may damage some children or disturb the adults who care for them.[137] This is also an argument that state power is a serious threat and must be restrained.

Yet there are more serious dangers to children if the adults who care for them are free from public review, under a policy promoting state inaction. Children are, all too often, the unnamed victims. Parents, teachers, neighbors, and strangers exercise physical and emotional control over children and sometimes do great violence to them. The rates of child abuse are difficult to estimate, but observers agree that the problem is widespread and that the child's relatives and friends—not strangers—are by far the most common perpetrators.[138] Judicial inaction in this context, or in the context

---

[137]See Mary Avery, "The Child Abuse Witness: Potential for Secondary Victimization," *Criminal Justice Journal* 7 (Fall 1983), 1, discussing potential harms to child from participation in prosecution; John Myers, "The Legal Response to Child Abuse: In the Best Interests of Children?" *J. Fam. L.* 24 (1985–86), 151: the "goal of protecting children" is often disserved by litigation. Estrich, *Real Rape;* and Charles Nemeth, "Legal Emancipation for the Victim of Rape," *Human Rights* 11 (Winter 1984), 30, discuss the harm done to adult rape victims by the criminal justice system. Bumiller, *The Civil Rights Society,* argues that the system imposes costs on a complainant who assumes the role of the discrimination victim.

[138]Jon Conte, "The Justice System and Sexual Abuse of Children," *Social Service Review* 58 (Dec. 1984), 556, 557–58, reports one study in which 38 percent of adult women respondents said they had been sexually abused as minors, and another indicating that 47 percent of perpetrators are members of child's own family and 42 percent more are known to the child. Sally Fuller, "Child Abuse Rises," *A.B.A. J.* 72 (Feb. 1, 1986), 34, reports a study estimating 1.793 million abused and neglected children in 1985. Robert ten Bensel, "The Scope of the Problem," *Juvenile & Family Court Journal* 35 (Winter 1984–85), 1–2, estimates that under a broad definition, four to five million children per year are neglected or abused and notes the dramatic increase in reporting of sexual abuse.

of a system that neglects to provide care when parents fail, exposes dependent children to physical and emotional harm.[139] Child pornography subjects individual children to actual violence and also uses their images to damage and devalue all children.[140] Labels assigned by medical professionals can consign individuals to the scorn and abuse of others. Invoking law may shift the balance of power in an already oppressive situation. By speaking of all these things, we may challenge and demand prevention of public and private injuries to children, and by speaking, we enlarge a human capacity to be what we could be.[141] The language of rights may assist efforts to rectify larger social patterns that damage people, especially when that language is reclaimed by those who have in the past been excluded.[142] The image of rights as damaging and weighty instruments that should be reserved for adults must be challenged in light of the damage suffered by children who have been denied them.

The ready objection that children's knowledge and competence levels ill equip them to represent their own views or to instruct another to do so is a serious problem. There are immediate grounds to distrust an adult representative for a child, whether the representative claims to serve as a mouthpiece for a child capable of knowing her own view or as a guardian who supplies his view of the child's interest.[143] The adult who offers the child's view, unmediated, may advance an irrational or misguided position;[144] the adult

[139]See Kenneth Wooden, *Weeping in the Playtime of Others: America's Incarcerated Children* (New York: McGraw-Hill, 1976), pp. 47–57, describing Charles Manson's harrowing journey through temporary custody arrangements and institutions during his childhood.

[140]See New York v. Ferber, 458 U.S. 747, 758 (1981) (rejecting First Amendment challenge to legislation against child pornography and citing studies of harm to children). See also Shirley O'Brien, *Child Pornography* (Dubuque, Iowa: Kendall/Hunt, 1983); and Victor Cline, Roger Croft, and Steven Courrier, "The Desensitization of Children to TV Violence," in *Where Do You Draw the Line?* ed. Victor Cline (Provo, Utah: Brigham Young University Press, 1974), p. 147.

[141]See Hannah Arendt, *The Human Condition* (Chicago: University of Chicago Press, 1958), pp. 175–81.

[142]The significance to excluded groups of the effort to reclaim language is a topic of wide discussion. See, e.g., Bell Hooks, *Feminist Theory: From Margin to Center* (Boston: South End Press, 1984); *The (M)Other Tongue: Essays in Feminist Psychoanalytic Interpretation,* ed. Shirley Garner, Claire Kahane, and Madelon Sprengnether (Ithaca: Cornell University Press, 1985). A significant power of language is to name oneself and one's own experience. See Paulo Freire, *Pedagogy of the Oppressed,* trans. Myra Bergman Ramos (New York: Continuum, 1970), pp. 11, 88, 119; William Felstiner, Richard Abel, and Austin Sarat, "The Emergence and Transformation of Disputes: Naming, Blaming, Claiming . . . ," *Law & Soc'y Rev.* 15 (1980–81), 631. See also Marilyn Frye, "On Being White: A Feminist Understanding of Race and Race Supremacy," in *The Politics of Reality: Essays in Feminist Theory* (Trumansburg, N.Y.: Crossing Press, 1983), pp. 110–27.

[143]See Kim Landsman and Martha Minow, Note, "Lawyering for the Child: Principles of Representation in Custody and Visitation Disputes Arising from Divorce," *Yale L.J.* 87 (1978), 1126, 1138–53. The problems of defining lawyers' proper roles are rivaled only by the ethical dilemmas presented when lawyers retreat behind their "roles" to justify their conduct. See Gerald Postema, "Moral Responsibility in Professional Ethics," *N.Y.U. L. Rev.* 55 (1980), 63; Deborah Rhode, "Ethical Perspectives on Legal Practice," *Stan. L. Rev.* 37 (1985), 589.

[144]It is not obvious, however, that children generally lack understanding of their own needs or an ability to express them in language that adults understand. In our culture even children often find rights rhetoric familiar and appropriate. See "Statement of Alvin Puissant, Assoc. Prof. of Psychiatry, Harvard Medical School," in *Television, Children, and the Constitutional Bicenten-*

who supplies a preference other than the child's has no obvious tether and lands in the thicket of general uncertainty about what is good for the child. These problems apply to lawyers representing adult clients as well: the lawyer who does only what the adult client wants may be criticized for failing to advise a different strategy;[145] the lawyer who acts solely on her or his own view also provokes criticism.[146] The issue becomes particularly apparent when the lawyer works for a large organization such as a law firm, which has its own interests, distinct from those of the clients.[147] As Robert Mnookin explains:

> The problem of assuring that advocates work towards the best interests of the client is inherent in any system which uses counsel to represent clients. Where one party is given the authority to put forward another's interests, there is always the danger that the agent will not be faithful to the interests of his client. The agent may have misperceived what the client wanted. The agent may believe something to be in the client's interests when it actually is not. Finally, wherever power is delegated, there is always the potential and incentive for the agent to put his own interests ahead of those of his client. The problems infect almost every human relationship.[148]

---

nial: A Report, ed. Peggy Charren and Carol Hulsizer (Cambridge, Mass.: Action for Childrens' Television, 1986), pp. 34–35: "I think children do understand the idea of equality and individual rights, but I think a direct connection between their lives and the Constitution has been missing in the way we educate them." See also Kagan, *The Nature of the Child*, pp. 112–53, describing the development of standards for judging as part of children's growth.

[145]Richard Crouch, "Divorce Mediation and Legal Ethics," *Fam. L.Q.* 16 (Fall 1982), 219, 224–34, assesses risks to a client left without independent legal advice; Richard Wasserstrom, "Lawyers as Professionals: Some Moral Issues," *Human Rights* 5 (1975), 1, finds that the lawyer's role enables an alternative moral point of view. The failure of lawyers to restrain and challenge clients' actions may be a detriment to their clients and to society as well. See generally Robert Nelson, "Ideology, Practice, and Professional Autonomy: Social Values and Client Relationships in the Large Law Firm," *Stan. L. Rev.* 37 (1985), 503; Reiner Kraakman, "Corporate Liability Strategies and the Costs of Legal Controls," *Yale L.J.* 93 (1984), 857.

[146]The most elaborate criticism has appeared in discussions of class actions, where the clients have less control than in individual party suits. See Derrick Bell, "Serving Two Masters: Integration Ideals and Client Interests in School Desegregation Litigation," *Yale L.J.* 85 (1976), 470; Deborah Rhode, "Class Conflicts in Class Actions," *Stan. L. Rev.* 34 (1982), 1183. Charges have been levied against lawyers representing individual adult clients as well. See, e.g., Robert Burt, "Conflict and Trust between Attorney and Client," *Georgetown L.J.* 69 (1981), 1015; David Luban, "Paternalism and the Legal Profession," *Wis. L. Rev.* 1981 (1981), 454. A response of sorts to charges that the lawyer's role as advocate is incompatible with moral values appears in Charles Fried, "The Lawyer as Friend: The Moral Foundations of the Lawyer-Client Relation," *Yale L.J.* 85 (1976), 1060.

[147]"Food for Thought," in *The Social Responsibilities of Lawyers: Case Studies*, ed. Philip B. Heymann and Lance Liebman (Westbury, Conn.: Foundation Press, 1988), explores lawyers' conflicting concerns with firms' reputation in Food and Drug work and with the needs of particular clients. See also Douglas Rosenthal, *Lawyer and Client: Who's in Charge?* (New Brunswick, N.J.: Transaction Books, 1977), pp. 96–105, discussing the conflict between a lawyer's financial interests and the client's interests; Abraham Blumberg, "The Practice of Law as a Confidence Game," *Law & Soc'y Rev.* 1 (June 1967), 15, discussing conflicts between criminal defense lawyers' ongoing commitment to the organization of the criminal process and their obligations to a particular client.

[148]Robert Mnookin, "The Paradox of Child Advocacy," in Mnookin, *In the Interest of Children*, p. 54.

Children are often less articulate and less self-knowing than most adults, but these qualities need not render them peculiarly vulnerable within a legal system. If there are reasons to distrust legal representatives of children, there are reasons to distrust legal representatives of adults, and confronting both kinds of distrust may demand more, not less, legal conversation. Courts could appoint multiple representatives to offer contrasting views of children's interests and rights,[149] or else demand fuller exploration by the initial representatives of the range of interests potentially raised by the litigation. Courts have long been assigned the special task of guarding the interests of children in litigation;[150] what seems needed are practical steps to prepare and equip the courts to fulfill this responsibility.

Why Rescue Rights?

Why advance this conception of rights, including children's rights, as a vocabulary used by community members to interpret and reinterpret their relationships with one another? It is a clumsy vocabulary; it can never fully express individual experience. Its very claim to communal meanings, its dependence directly and indirectly on official sanctions, and its created past preclude that possibility. Michael Ignatieff advocates a language of needs instead, finding rights language too limited: "Rights language offers a rich vernacular for the claims an individual may make on or against the collectivity, but it is relatively impoverished as a means of expressing individuals' needs for the collectivity. . . . It is because money cannot buy the human gestures which confer respect, nor rights guarantee them as entitlements, that any decent society requires a public discourse about the needs of the human person."[151]

I, too, have criticized rights rhetoric for its impoverished view of human relationships and its repeated assignment of labels that hide the power of those doing the assigning. And I find something terribly lacking in rights for children that speak only of autonomy rather than need, especially the central need for relationships with adults who are themselves enabled to create settings where children can thrive. Rights rhetoric can and should be exposed for its tendency to hide the exercise of state authority, even authority exercised in the name of private freedoms. Rights discourse, like any language, may mislead, seduce, falsely console, or wrongly inflame.

I have the luxury, as a scholar, to step back and criticize a basic tool of legal practice for preserving assumptions about human autonomy that I believe are contrary to social experience and likely to limit social change. Yet when I

---

[149]David L. Chambers and Michael S. Wald, "Smith v. OFFER," in Mnookin, *In the Interest of Children*, p. 144, recommends appointing additional counsel to offer contrasting perspectives in test case litigation involving children.

[150]Ellen Ryerson, *The Best-Laid Plans: America's Juvenile Court Experiment* (New York: Hill & Wang, 1978), pp. 63–72, discusses *parens patriae* power.

[151]Michael Ignatieff, *The Needs of Strangers* (London: Chatto & Windus, 1984), p. 13.

write a brief, supervise students in their clinical work, or talk to professionals in the trenches, I wonder sometimes whom I am helping and whom I am hurting by criticizing rights. It turns out to be helpful, useful, and maybe even essential to be able to couch a request as a claim of right—and not just for winning a given case or persuading a particular official to do a good thing but for working to constitute the kind of world where struggles for change can in fact bring about change, and where struggles for meaning and communality can nurture both.

There is something too valuable in the aspiration of rights, and something too neglectful of the power embedded in assertions of another's need, to abandon the rhetoric of rights. That is why I join in the effort to reclaim and reinvent rights. Whether and how to use words to constrain power are questions that should be answered by those with less of it. For this task, rights rhetoric is remarkably well suited. It enables a devastating, if rhetorical, exposure of and challenge to hierarchies of power. In Patricia Williams's words, people using the language of rights "imply a respect which places one in the referential range of self and others, which elevates one's status from human body to social being."[152] Law professor Elizabeth Schneider has explained how lawyers and their clients, drawing upon their own experiences, can bring new meaning to legal rules, how they can appeal to legal officials to give force to those meanings, and how they can reflect on the results and develop new visions.[153] Legal vocabulary, including that of rights, can be invested with meanings that challenge power and recover submerged or suppressed experiences.[154] Once constructed and officially embraced, normative language can become loosened from its past uses and turned around to limit its authors, if only through their own shame or courageous self-restraint.[155] For the individual speaker, as Fred Dallmayr puts it, an inherited language is less a collection of preordained meanings than "a means of transgressing factual constellations in the direction of an uncharted future."[156] As a bridge between the world-that-is and alternative worlds-that-might-be, rights claims cannot belong exclusively to any state or set of officials. Those without official roles are equally important to the task of bridging present and future.

This conception responds both to those who criticize newly articulated rights for lacking objective foundations and to those who criticize rights for their analytic indeterminacy. By analogizing rights to language and treating

---

[152]Williams, "Equality's Riddle," p. 416.

[153]Schneider, "The Dialectic of Rights and Politics," pp. 589, 604–10. Gerald López has developed a conception of "lay lawyering," in which nonlawyers too persuade by crafting compelling stories, mediating between personal experience and "stock stories" that have cultural meaning ("Lay Lawyering," *U.C.L.A. L. Rev.* 32 [Oct. 1984], 2).

[154]Mari Matsuda, "Looking to the Bottom: Critical Legal Studies and Reparations," *Harv. C.R.–C.L. L. Rev.* 22 (1987), 323.

[155]This was Mahatma Gandhi's and Martin Luther King's strategy.

[156]Fred Dallmayr, *Language and Politics: Why Does Language Matter to Political Philosophy?* (Notre Dame, Ind.: University of Notre Dame Press, 1984), p. 97, discussing Jean Paul Sartre's *Being and Nothingness*.

rights rhetoric as a particular vocabulary implying roles and relationships within communities and institutions, this approach suggests how rights can be real—without being fixed; and can change—without losing their legitimacy.[157]

The language of rights helps people to articulate standards for judging conduct without pretending to have found the ultimate and unalterable truth. Rights as a language for expressing meaning persist even beyond their use within legal institutions. Jean-Paul Sartre's conception of language not as a set of rulebound meanings but as a mode of human action and creative self-expression is helpful here.[158] Similarly, Ludwig Wittgenstein, in his later work, emphasized that the meanings of words are determined by their use and that their use depends on context, situated in forms of life.[159] Language in these senses is necessarily intersubjective and communal.[160] People use rights and claims to particular freedoms or entitlements to refer to what they perceive as their due, even when the formal legal apparatus has not acknowledged or approved of those perceptions. People often speak spontaneously of rights, far from legal institutions. For example, they may make assertions of entitlement, need, and interest when they collide at the bus stop or on the playground. Children no less than adults can participate in the legal conversation that uses rights to gain the community's attention.

Rights are hardly neutral. With them, we pick from among a variety of possible legal consequences for human relationships and thereby influence the pattern of existing and future relationships. Claims of rights that call for negotiation, consultation, and discussion in handling disputes demand recognition of each disputant by the other. When the juvenile court sends to the Children's Hearings Project in Cambridge, Massachusetts, parental complaints about "unruly" children, the project staff create settings in which parents and children can negotiate contractual agreements to resolve their disputes and establish procedures for addressing future disputes. This de-

[157]Ball (*Lying Down Together*, p. 18) quotes Thomas Reed Powell, who in turn quoted one James Beck: "The constitution is neither, on the one hand, a Gibralter rock, which wholly resists the ceaseless washing of time and circumstance, nor is it, on the other hand, a sandy beach, which is slowly destroyed by the erosion of the waves. It is rather to be likened to a floating dock, which, while firmly attached to its moorings, and not therefore at the caprice of the waves, yet rises and falls with the tide of time and circumstance" (Powell, "Constitutional Metaphors," book review, *New Republic*, Feb. 11, 1925, p. 314).

[158]Jean Paul Sartre, *Being and Nothingness: An Essay on Phenomenological Antology*, trans. Hazel Barnes (New York: Washington Square Press, 1956), pp. 559–707.

[159]Wittgenstein, *Philosophical Investigations*.

[160]Robert Cover, *Justice Accused: Antislavery and the Judicial Process* (New Haven, Conn.: Yale University Press, 1975), pp. 126–30, develops an analogy between law and language, and contrasts those who "speak law-language poorly" with those who "speak according to the rules" and are masters in the law, providing new statements that articulate what people now know they need or need to consider: "When there is a departure from the rules, however, that which determines whether the rules have been changed is not so much another rule determining changes in rules as it is the acceptance of the change by others over time. In this respect the language analogy is far better than the extended game analogy" as a way to understand law. See also Dallmayr, *Language and Politics*, pp. 174–92, on the ways in which language and politics interact and mutually construct each other.

mands that the parents take their children's complaints as seriously as their own.[161]

Interpreting rights as features of relationships, contingent upon renegotiations within a community committed to this mode of solving problems, pins law not on some force beyond human control but on human responsibility for the patterns of relationships promoted or hindered by this process. In this way the notion of rights as tools in continuing, communal discourse helps to locate responsibility in human beings for legal action and inaction. John Noonan, now a judge in the U.S. Court of Appeals for the Ninth Circuit, once wrote: "Those who suppose that the legal system is a self-subsistent set of rules existing outside of its participants and constraining lawyers and judges to act against their consciences will always be prevalent among lawyers, judges and legal historians. . . . But every so often in a human heart the ice will crack, and a human person will acknowledge his responsibility for other human persons he has touched."[162] Seeing rights as features of relationships may help us reinvest legal activity with a believable aspiration to create communal meanings in a world scarred by justifiable skepticism.

It would be wrong, however, to ignore the fact that what judges do with law involves power and violence. Robert Cover has reminded us that law embeds interpretations of political texts in institutions that exercise the state's monopoly over legitimate violence.[163] People lose money, their children, and even their lives on the basis of judicial judgments. The hope of law is to discipline these decisions within collective processes,[164] but the government too must remain subject to challenge and check when it claims to act— or refrains from acting—in the name of the community.

The very act of summoning "community" through a language of rights may expose the divisions within the community—and even beyond it. Rights then can be understood as a kind of language that reconfirms the difficult commitment to live together even as it enables the expression of conflicts and struggles. The struggle to make meaning of human existence may well de-

---

[161]See Sally Engle Merry and Ann Marie Rocheleau, *Mediation in Families: A Study of the Children's Hearings Project* (Cambridge, Mass.: Children's Hearings Project of Cambridge Family and Children's Service, 1985), pp. 91–101. This setting may transform the power imbalance rather than replicating it, as sometimes happens with divorce mediation. See Lerhman, "Mediation in Wife Abuse Cases"; and Rifkin, "Mediation from a Feminist Perspective." The use of mediation between parents and children may inject greater equality by demanding mutual respect, while it may undermine equality between a husband and wife by removing formal procedures that constrain the interpersonal dynamic.

[162]John Thomas Noonan, *The Antelope: The Ordeal of the Recaptured Africans, in the Administrations of James Monroe and John Quincy Adams* (Berkeley: University of California Press, 1977), p. 159. A similar theme animates *Persons and Masks*, in which Noonan took three cases and probed beneath the labels of legal analysis and roles to find the persons and lines of responsibility routinely suppressed. See also Cover's exploration (in *Justice Accused*) of jurisprudential and psychological reasons why judges who opposed slavery nonetheless enforced the Fugitive Slave Laws.

[163]Robert Cover, "Violence and the Word," *Yale L.J.* 95 (1986), 1601–2; Robert Cover, "The Bonds of Constitutional Interpretation: Of the Word, the Deed, and the Role," *Ga. L. Rev.* 20 (1986), 815, 817–31.

[164]Cover, "Violence and the Word," p. 1628.

mand our separation into groups away from, even antagonistic to, the larger community. If this is the case, then the discourse of rights may be all the more important as a medium for speaking, across conflicting affiliations, about the separations and connections between individuals, groups, and the state. What rights and patterns of rights can protect groups when their norms conflict with those countenanced or enforced by the official system?[165]

At such moments, legal interpretation happens not just in official acts by official actors but also through resistance, compliance, and investment of old forms with new meanings. Legal interpretation happens when nonofficials seek to hold officials to account, either in terms the officials themselves have offered as rationales or in new terms embodying normative commitments that have not before made their way into the official canon of meaning. Legal language is never transparent to experience; it constrains and limits what individuals mean even as it conveys a communal meaning. And the communal meaning may well occlude the conflict it resists. Legal meanings pronounced by officials cannot be severed from the violence and power they seek to rationalize; nor can they be reduced to those acts of violence and power. Because private violence can be as bad as official violence, both public and private efforts to craft legal meanings and normative commitments are critical to freedom and to struggles against oppression.

What happens after the law, after official legal pronouncements good or bad, to rights? Rights pronounced by courts become possessions of the dispossessed.[166] We can listen to rights as a language that contains meaning but does not engender it, as sounds that demonstrate our sociability even while exposing the uniqueness of the speaker. Legal language, like a song, can be hummed by someone who did not write it and changed by those for whom it was not intended.[167]

Language is nuanced enough to express, "No, that's not what I meant," or even, "There are no words to say what I mean." The language of rights is, or could be, nuanced enough to express, "I am connected to you in my very willingness to observe your boundaries," or, "I do not belong to your community, but I lay claim to some shared terms in demanding that you respect

---

[165]This problem is acute for members of minority groups. The conflict with the majority may be simply over acquiring sufficient space to pursue the minority group's beliefs and practices; or the conflict may concern deep division about what norms should govern everyone. See Weisbrod, "Family, Church, and State." See also Robert Cover, "*Nomos* and Narrative," *Harv. L. Rev.* 97 (1983), 60–68; Sanford Levinson, "Constituting Communities through Words That Bind Reflections on Loyalty Oaths," *Mich. L. Rev.* 1986 (1986), 1440, 1447–48, 1454–56.

[166]Joyce Appelby, "The American Heritage: The Heirs and the Disinherited," in Thelen, *The Constitution and American Life,* p. 138, notes that others describe constitutional interpretation as a battle among the heirs of the Founding Fathers, and offers instead the conception of a battle among the disinherited.

[167]See Sanford Levinson, "Professing Law: Commitment of Faith or Detached Analysis?" *St. Louis U. L.J.* 31 (1986), 3; Gerald López, "The Idea of a Constitution in the Chicano Tradition," *J. Legal Educ.* 37 (1987), 162. See also Carol Rose's argument for rights for the environment in "Environmental Faust Succumbs to Temptations of Economic Mephistopheles; or, Value by Any Other Name Is Reference: Review of *The Economy of the Earth* [Cambridge: Cambridge University Press, 1988] by Mark Sagoff," *Mich. L. Rev.* 87 (1989), 1631.

my separateness." Perhaps people can work through legal interpretation to communicate disjunction, misunderstanding, even the right to avoid conversation. Such work requires context as well as theory, actual settings and ongoing relationships in which discourse is part of a way of life. Beyond our talk of rights we have each other, and the steady burden of learning to live together and apart.

Dying and Living

We feel deflated too. We too are nettled.
To see the curtain down and nothing settled.
How could a better ending be arranged?
Could one change people? Can the world be changed?
Would new gods do the trick? Will atheism?
Moral rearmament? Materialism?
It is for you to find a way, my friends,
To help good men arrive at happy ends.
—Bertolt Brecht, *The Good Woman of Setzuan*

Because of changes in medical technology, the birth of a baby born with severe defects now signals a moment of decision.[1] It is a decision about medical treatment; it is also a decision about what meanings the family and society want to give to the life of the infant. It is a decision that cannot be answered by reference to rights—or without them. Finally, it is a decision about patterns and qualities of relationships beyond that one family.[2]

Epigraph: Excerpted from: "Good Woman of Setzuan," by Bertolt Brecht, © by Eric Bentley 1947, 1956, 1961. *Parables for the Theatre: Two Plays by Bertolt Brecht,* Eric Bentley, editor, © 1948 by Eric Bentley. Reproduced courtesy of the University of Minnesota Press.

[1] See generally President's Commission for the Study of Ethical Problems in Medicine and Biomedical and Behavioral Research, *Deciding to Forgo Life-Sustaining Treatment: A Report on the Ethical, Medical, and Legal Issues in Treatment Decisions* (Washington D.C.: U.S. Government Printing Office, 1983), pp. 197–223. For a review of "representative birth defects," see Nancy Rhoden, "Treatment Dilemmas for Imperiled Newborns: Why Quality of Life Counts," *S. Cal. L. Rev.* 58 (1985), 1283, 1287–94. According to some definitions, severe disabilities include chronic disease, severe spinal deformities, uncontrolled hydrocephalus (accumulation of fluids in the brain, causing swelling and brain damage), and mental disabilities measured by an IQ lower than 60; see John Lorber, "Ethical Problems in the Management of Myelomeningocele and Hydrocephalus," *Journal of the Royal College of Physicians* 10 (1975), 54. Scholars and professionals call such infants "defective newborns," "handicapped newborns," "imperiled newborns," or "severely disabled infants." The first label is especially offensive, although none is attractive, and all are ambiguous. I use the latter two terms interchangeably.

[2] Changes in medical technologies also pose choices about how to define death, whether to allow the transplanting or sale of tissues and organs, and how to organize human reproduction;

Babies who in earlier times would have died may now be rescued through surgery and other medical intervention, but the intervention often will not correct the physical and mental disabilities the child may face. Take as an example a child born with spina bifida—a defective spinal cord from which a sac protrudes, filled with spinal and cerebral fluid. Medical measures now may guard this child against infection, enclosing the sac and repeatedly draining the fluid to prevent damaging pressure on the brain. But depending on where the opening in the spinal cord occurs, the child's legs may be paralyzed, and this cannot be medically altered; kidney problems and complications arising from repeated efforts to drain the fluids may also occur, despite medical precautions. Many of these infants will be moderately or severely mentally disabled, though some will develop normal cognitive and affective capacities.[3] As another example, children born with Down's syndrome often also present a physical problem, such as a heart defect or intestinal blockage. The physical problem can be readily corrected by surgery, but the mental retardation accompanying the syndrome cannot.[4]

Either pursuing or not pursuing medical treatment for these seriously disabled infants offers both dangers and opportunities. Some observers advocate analyzing these issues in risk and benefit terms, calling for attention to the financial costs of short-term medical treatment and long-term care and to the actual benefits of continued life under compromised conditions.[5] Others argue for recognition of the sanctity of life—any life—and an obligation to save life whenever possible. Lawyers, as experts in conflict resolution, are drawn into these sharp disagreements about how treatment decisions should be made. Lawyers are also increasingly involved because the issue can be framed as one of discrimination: how should society treat those who are "different?" In the context of medical treatment decisions for severely disabled newborns, this issue implicates relationships, hidden and not so hidden, between apparently contending principles, between infants and parents, and between families and society. Abstract principles cannot resolve the issue. Contemporary contexts for decisions create contentious dramas of

these, too, are choices that implicate social meanings and patterns of relationships. See, e.g., John A. Robertson, "Relaxing the Death Standard for Organ Donations in Pediatric Situations," in *Organ Substitution Technology: Ethical, Legal, and Public Policy Issues,* ed. Deborah Mathieu (Boulder, Colo.: Westview Press, 1987), pp. 69–76; Joan Hollinger, "From Coitus to Commerce: Legal and Social Consequences of Non-Coital Reproduction," *U. Mich. J.L. Rev.* 18 (1985), 865–932; Martha Field, *Surrogate Motherhood* (Cambridge, Mass.: Harvard University Press, 1988).

[3]See generally Ruth Macklin, *Mortal Choices: Bioethics in Today's World* (New York: Pantheon Books, 1987); and Helga Kuhse and Peter Singer, *Should the Baby Live? The Problem of Handicapped Infants* (Oxford: Oxford Press, 1985), pp. 48–73.

[4]The meaning of the mental retardation, however, may shift, depending upon the expectations of those surrounding the child and the educational opportunities offered to him or her. See Kuhse and Singer, *Should the Baby Live?* and the discussion of Phillip Becker below.

[5]Phillip Heymann and Sara Holtz, "The Severely Defective Newborn: The Dilemma and the Decision Process," *Public Policy* 23 (1975), 381, advocates utilitarian principles in treatment decisions. See also Willard Gaylin, "No Longer All or None," in *Who Speaks for the Child: The Problems of Proxy Consent,* ed. Willard Gaylin and Ruth Macklin (New York: Plenum Press, 1982), pp. 40–50.

doubt and blame. Public scrutiny is riven by deep ambivalence, while private families bear the consequences. Attention to connections between theory and context, between disability and social meanings, and between the people caught in these situations offers a way to embed rights in relationships.

Competing Principles

When technology converts tragedy into choice, what principles should guide that choice? Typical state statutes regarding child abuse and neglect oblige parents to provide medical care for their children but establish only minimum standards; they do not resolve the question where medical advice includes a range of options.[6] Public opinion and medical experts themselves have been divided about the kinds of treatment severely disabled newborns deserve.[7] As a result, legal analysis has turned to two noted ethical principles, pointing toward different degrees of medical intervention.

A decision to pursue all possible measures to prolong and sustain the infant's life may be informed by a "right-to-life" or "sanctity of life" principle. This principle represents a basic commitment to the fundamental equality of all persons, regardless of their condition, and to their basic entitlement to whatever society has to offer. Without such commitments, its proponents maintain, no person's life stands secure against devaluation by others.[8]

An alternative principle emphasizes the infant's "quality of life." In general, it postulates that medical personnel should undertake life-prolonging measures only if the infant will be able to know love, form relationships, or experience other aspects of human society which give human life a quality worth living.[9] The quality-of-life position may support only limited treat-

[6]See generally Angela Holder, *Legal Issues in Pediatrics and Adolescent Medicine* (New York: Wiley, 1977), p. 11. See also American Academy of Pediatrics et al. v. Margaret Heckler, 561 F. Supp. 395, 400 (D.D.C. 1983) (district court concluding, after testimony, that "there is no customary standard of care for the treatment of severely defective infants").

[7]See "Survey Shows Split on Issue of Treating Deformed Infants," *New York Times*, June 3, 1983, p. A14: a Gallup poll showed the public evenly divided on whether a severely handicapped newborn should be allowed to die. See also Committee on Bioethics, "Treatment of Critically Ill Newborns," *Pediatrics* 72 (1983), p. 565, finding no consensus on treatment; and President's Commission, *Deciding to Forego Life-Sustaining Treatment*, pp. 198–220, acknowledging medical profession's lack of certainty and knowledge about premature congenitally handicapped infants.

[8]See C. Everett Koop, "The Slide to Auschwitz," *Human Life Review* 3 (1977), 103, 107. Commenting on a particular case of federal intervention, Koop noted, "If we do not intrude into the life of a child such as this, whose civil rights may be abrogated? The next person may be you." See "Baby Jane's Defender," *New York Times*, Nov. 11, 1983, p. A30. See also Nat Hentoff, "The Awful Privacy of Baby Doe," in *Atlantic*, Jan. 1985, pp. 54, 58; and Helga Kuhse, *The Sanctity-of-Life Doctrine in Medicine: A Critique* (Oxford: Clarendon Press, 1987).

[9]See Kuhse and Singer, *Should the Baby Live?* pp. 33–36, 60–67; John Lorber, "Ethical Concepts in the Treatment of Myelomeningocele," in *Decision Making and the Defective Newborn: Proceedings of a Conference on Spina Bifida and Ethics*, ed. Chester A. Swinyard (Springfield, Ill.: C. C. Thomas, 1978), p. 66; Rhoden, "Treatment Dilemmas." See also William K. Frankena, "The Ethics of Respect for Life," in *Ethical Principles for Social Policy*, ed. John Howie (Carbondale: Southern Illinois University Press, 1983), p. 34: "Mere life, whether that of a vegetable, animal, or human organism, has no moral sanctity as such, though it may

ment to alleviate pain, withdrawal of life-sustaining treatment, or even active acts of euthanasia. It diverges from the right-to-life principle by rejecting life itself as the most important human value; it calls instead for an assessment of the potential quality of the individual's life before life-extending or life-sustaining medical treatment is applied.[10]

Both principles are more than idealized arguments. They are used by real people, in real situations, and it is important to consider how they function in practice. Both principles can be couched in terms of rights, although they draw upon different kinds of rights theories. The quality-of-life principle reflects utilitarian notions and directs an assessment of risks and benefits for the individual involved; the rights at issue include the right of the infant to the medical treatment that would assure either an acceptable quality of life or a right to die with dignity.[11] This position gains support from the adults' right to refuse treatment.[12] Moreover, the quality-of-life principle appears in the legal doctrines of wrongful life and wrongful birth. Under those doctrines, parents have argued successfully that incorrect medical advice about genetic risks or other predictable sources of an infant's disability warrant tort damages based on the diminished quality of the child's life and the burdens to the attending family.[13] The right-to-life principle, with roots in the deon-

---

have esthetic and other kinds of nonmoral value, and may be a necessary condition of consciousness, rationality, or morality"; but life acquires moral sanctity when "it is a condition of something more," such as consciousness.

[10]See Kuhse and Singer, *Should the Baby Live?* pp. 118–39, arguing that morally relevant traits are not membership in the human species, but the capacity to develop self-awareness, self-control, a sense of past and future, rationality, language, and the ability to relate to others. Often mentioned in this context is the venerable medical ethic of "do no harm," which can be cited to support both the right-to-life and quality-of-life positions. Some would claim that neglecting any possible measures to prolong life is to do harm; others would argue that prolonging life may itself, in some circumstances, cause harm. See Robert F. Weir, *Selective Nontreatment of Handicapped Newborns: Moral Dilemmas in Neonatal Medicine* (New York: Oxford University Press, 1984), p. 86. One expert, made uncomfortable by a decision to withhold treatment if the result could be a slow and lingering death, finds himself at times "in the schizophrenic position of advocating either active euthanasia or vigorous treatment." See *Practical Management of Meningomyelocele*, ed. John M. Freeman (Baltimore, Md.: University Park Press, 1974), p. 24. See also Kuhse and Singer, *Should the Baby Live?* pp. 87–97. Another principle often invoked is "antidiscrimination," which means in this context that an infant's handicap should play no role in a medical treatment decision about a life-threatening condition independent of that handicap. Another version suggests that treatment should proceed as long as the child "unquestionably can experience and enjoy life" (Rhoden, "Treatment Dilemmas," p. 1229), but this test preserves the line-drawing—or discriminating—process between those who deserve treatment and those who do not, simply drawing the line differently than some might. And, the meaning of this principle is precisely what is in doubt.

[11]Analytically distinct are the utilitarian inquiry into the greatest good for the greatest number and the comparison of risks and benefits for the particular individual. The latter focus on the individual is a better statement of the quality-of-life position. Yet in practice, it may be difficult to distinguish the infant's right to quality of life from societal rights to reasoned choices in allocating limited resources.

[12]See John A. Robertson, *The Rights of the Critically Ill* (New York: Bantam Books, 1983), pp. 28–48; Fay A. Rozovsky, *Consent to Treatment: A Practical Guide* (Boston: Little, Brown, 1984), pp. 424–30.

[13]In a wrongful life suit, the infant claims injury and seeks recompense; in a wrongful birth action, the parents sue for the injury to them posed by the economic and emotional costs of raising a handicapped child. See Note, "The Trend toward Judicial Recognition of Wrongful

tological theory of Immanuel Kant, places as primary a respect for persons, quite aside from consequences for others. The right-to-life principle also draws legal support from general criminal statutes against murder, specific statutes punishing infanticide, and statutes requiring medical care regardless of an infant's disabilities.[14]

Despite their apparent differences, the two principles do converge, especially in their need for contextual applications if they are to become meaningful. The right-to-life principle, as actually advocated, is not nearly so absolute as it would seem. If pursued in its pure form, it could produce, at the extreme, the absurd result of requiring heroic efforts to keep everyone alive forever by the use of technological life supports.[15] Moreover, medical experts disagree about what constitutes "standard medical practice" in the care of newborns with serious handicaps.[16] Given the variety of treatments, each with risks and benefits, which medical professionals can recommend with the aim of preserving the life of a given infant, the right-to-life principle alone provides no selection criteria. Parents may be presented with a choice of surgery or no surgery; a choice from among surgical techniques; a choice in the timing of the surgery or the selection of the surgical team; even a choice about the use of experimental or nonconventional treatments.[17] Efforts to

---

Life: A Dissenting View," *U.C.L.A. L. Rev.* 31 (1983), 473, 495–96. Cf. Curlender v. Bio-Science Laboratories, 106 Cal. App. 3d 811 (1980); 165 Cal. Rptr. 477 (1980) (allowing infant plaintiff with Tay-Sachs disease to recover damages), and Turbin v. Sortini, 31 Cal. 3d 220 (1982); 643 P.2d 954 (1982); 182 Cal. Rptr. 337 (1982) (allowing infant with hereditary deafness to recover damages under wrongful life) with Park v. Chessin, 60 A.D.2d 80 (1977); 400 N.Y.S.2d 110 (1977) (recognizing causes of action for both parents and their child who died of kidney disease), and Becker v. Schwartz, 46 N.Y.2d 401 (1978); 386 N.E.2d 807 (1978); 413 N.Y.S.2d 895 (1978) (permitting cause of action for parents but not for child, overruling *Park* in part). A big issue remaining concerns the measure of damages in such cases.

[14]See T. S. Ellis, "Letting Defective Babies Die: Who Decides?" *American Journal of Law and Medicine* 7 (1982), 393, 401–10; John A. Robertson and Norman Fost, "Passive Euthanasia of Defective Newborn Infants: Legal Considerations," *Journal of Pediatrics* 88 (1976), 883–89; John M. Scheb, "Termination of Life Support Systems for Minor Children: Evolving Legal Responses," *Tenn. L. Rev.* 54 (1986), 1.

[15]See Norman Fost, "Proxy Consent for Seriously Ill Newborns," in *No Rush to Judgment: Essays on Medical Ethics,* ed. David Smith (Bloomington, Ind.: Poynter Center, 1978), p. 16.

[16]Weir, *Selective Nontreatment,* pp. 59–61; Steven R. Smith, "Life and Death Decisions in the Nursery: Standards and Procedures for Withholding Lifesaving Treatment from Infants," *N.Y.L. Sch. L. Rev.* 27 (1982), 1125, 1153–59.

[17]Commentators disagree about whether anyone should be allowed to consent to experimental treatment for a child. Cf. Paul Ramsey, *The Patient as Person: Explorations in Medical Ethics* (New Haven, Conn.: Yale University Press, 1970), p. 15 (opposing proxy consent for experimental treatment because no one can consent to making someone else an adventurer), with Charles Fried, "Children as Subjects for Medical Experimentation," in *Research on Children,* ed. Jan van Eys (Baltimore, Md.: University Park Press, 1978), pp. 107, 111–15 (arguing that even infants should have opportunities to help do a good thing, such as advance medical knowledge), and Richard A. McCormick, "Proxy Consent in the Experimentation Situation," *Perspectives in Biology and Medicine* 18 (1974), 2, 13–14 (presuming that the child would want promise of benefit from experiment). Comments of the Department of Health and Human Services indicate that the federal child abuse amendments do not demand use of experimental treatment, and that the standard is always "reasonable medical judgment." See 50 Fed. Reg. 14,886 (April 15, 1985), codified at 45 C.F.R. pt. 1340. See also 52 Fed. Reg. 3995 (Feb. 6, 1987), codified at 45 C.F.R. pt. 1340 (App.).

distinguish ordinary or conventional care, which would be required, from extraordinary and nonrequired treatment have failed conceptually and legally.[18] To avoid absurd results and to acknowledge the actual areas of ambiguity and discretion created by medical treatment choices, the right-to-life principle has come to involve judgments about when to seek and when not to seek aggressive medical treatment—just as the quality-of-life principle does.

But the right to life principle has not yielded a clear definition of when it condemns a failure to provide medical care. Implementing the principle is relatively straightforward in rules against killing, but societies have historically assigned different consequences to an act of direct killing and more passive conduct that in some sense produces the death of a child.[19] An omission becomes culpable where it represents a failure to fulfill a well-understood duty, but whether such a duty exists is the unanswered question concerning medical treatment decisions for a severely disabled infant. The availability of certain medical options is a precondition for finding their non-use culpable. A complex, tertiary-care hospital capable of administering the most advanced organ transplants and experimental treatments can provide treatment to some infants who cannot be helped elsewhere. Failure to provide such treatment will mean something different at a hospital with less sophisticated options. Therefore the right-to-life principle would seem to vary on the basis of the medical facilities accessible. Even beyond this distinction, defining which omissions are culpable runs into tangled scholarly debates about which one of multiple causes should be treated as the moral cause of an individual's death.[20]

On omissions and on definitions of extraordinary care, then, the right-to-life principle demands contextual judgments rather than an absolute commitment. The principle requires contextual judgments also about what constitutes "futile" or "inhumane" medical treatment, and whether treatment would "merely prolong dying." Amendments to the federal child abuse statute have redefined child abuse and neglect (for states accepting federal funds under the act) to include "the withholding of medically indicated treatment" from disabled infants with life-threatening conditions—unless the baby is "chronically and irreversibly comatose"; or unless "the provision of such treatment would (i) merely prolong dying, (ii) not be effective in ameliorating or correcting all of the infant's life-threatening conditions, or (iii) otherwise be futile in terms of the survival of the infant"; or unless "the

[18]See Kuhse and Singer, *Should the Baby Live?* pp. 26–47.
[19]See Weir, *Selective Nontreatment*, p. 25: ancient Romans and Renaissance Italian societies permitted passive child destruction; Kuhse and Singer, *Should the Baby Live?* pp. 76–80: most British and American doctors indicate a willingness sometimes to allow an infant to die, but far fewer are willing to kill it. See Smith, "Life and Death Decisions," pp. 1166–68 (comparing active and passive euthanasia as artificial distinctions). Smith also discusses medical and public debates about when treatment should be required.
[20]See H. L. A. Hart and A. M. Honoré, *Causation and the Law* (London: Oxford University Press, 1959).

provision of such treatment would be virtually futile in terms of the survival of the infant and the treatment itself under such circumstances would be inhumane."[21] This congressional initiative was prompted by concerns for the right to life of disabled infants.[22] Congress ultimately acknowledged, however, a need to draw lines between infants for whom medical treatment is worthwhile and those for whom it is not.[23] It remains unclear exactly when medical treatment is futile, or when it makes sense to characterize a severely ill infant as dying. A premature infant with a low birth weight who cannot breathe or pump her own blood without assistance may be helped temporarily by pulmonary and circulatory devices, but her undeveloped organs may also rupture with the exertion.[24]

Advocates of the right-to-life principle strongly endorse antidiscrimination policies, opposing denial of medical treatment on the ground that the patient has a disability. Yet even this position requires distinctions based on the severity of the disability. As one physician-ethicist has noted, "We withhold dialysis from an anencephalic infant girl precisely because she is so handicapped that she cannot experience any benefit from the treatment."[25] Because the right-to-life principle does not direct the automatic use of all medical devices in all circumstances, it raises line-drawing problems. And because it requires drawing lines between those who should be treated medically and those who should not, the right-to-life principle converges with the quality-of-life principle in a need for contextual, factually drenched decisions.

The quality-of-life position also requires contextual applications because it affords no internal guide to what constitutes a life worth preserving. Indeed, although it may initially seem to presume that the "difference" of the disabled child is inherent, this difference can be understood only relationally. Quality-of-life assessments involve critical evaluation of the child's relationships with other people and the social meaning as well as medical meaning of the infant's disabilities.[26]

[21]Pub. L. No. 98–457, sec. 121 (3), 98 Stat. 1749, 1752 (1984), codified at 42 U. S. C. sec. 5102 (3)(1988). See also 45 C.F.R. sec. 1340.15 (1987); and President's Commission, *Deciding to Forgo Life-Sustaining Treatment,* pp. 199–227.

[22]See Kuhse and Singer, *Should the Baby Live?* p. 46.

[23]The Department of Health and Human Services issued regulations under the amendments which balance "the need for an effective program and the need to prevent unreasonable governmental intervention." See 50 Fed. Reg. 14,880 (1985); 45 C.F.R. pt. 1340 (App.)(4). The department explained that it interprets the futility or "merely prolong dying" exception to the child abuse amendments as inapplicable to instances "where treatment will not totally correct a medical condition but will give a patient many years of life."

[24]See Weir, *Selective Nontreatment,* p. 52, for a case study; Custody of a Minor, 385 Mass. 697 (1982): Nancy Rhoden, "Treatment Dilemmas for Imperiled Newborns: Why Quality of Life Counts," *S. Calif. L. Rev.* 58 (1985), 1283; 434 N.E.2d 601, 610 (1982) (considering when prolonging life increases suffering).

[25]Norman Fost, "Putting Hospitals on Notice," *Hastings Center Report* 12 (Aug. 1982), 7.

[26]When dealing with medical treatment decisions about adults who are incompetent to choose, courts have tried to rule out quality-of-life considerations in the sense of the relative worth of that person's life to others, but preserved assessments of the individual's quality of life as judges imagine that person himself or herself would value it. See Allen Buchanan and Dan W.

The quality-of-life principle ostensibly refers to the individual's quality of life rather than to financial and emotional burdens that may affect the quality of others' lives. Yet the quality of a family's life may directly or indirectly enter into the calculus of the child's rights under the circumstances.[27] Allowing a child's medical treatment to turn on the willingness of his own parents to provide ongoing care and love burdens that child with the accidental circumstances of birth. In this light, parents, medical professionals, and ethicists have begun to consider the potential availability of foster or adoptive parents willing to care for the disabled child. These options deeply alter a quality-of-life assessment.[28] Similarly, if an infant's likely destination is a poorly financed or poorly managed state institution, the potential quality of that infant's life is lowered. The available option has less to do with the child than with the society's decisions about resources and priorities. To some degree, any patient's relationships and home situation are important factors in any medical prognosis.[29] This interdependence is only more obvious in the situation of an infant and more dramatic in the situation of a disabled infant. Thus, even if every effort is made to consider only the child's perspective rather than the needs or wants of the adults involved, the child's life potential may largely turn upon the degree of care and love that parents or custodians will grant.[30]

The quality-of-life principle also requires contextual examination of the social meaning of disability, which is embedded in networks of societal relationships. The quality of a person's life, especially a disabled person's life, is deeply influenced by the actual context of the individual's interpersonal and social relationships. Changes in community attitudes markedly affect the quality of life for the disabled person. The quality of life for a wheelchair-

---

Brock, "Deciding for Others," *Milbank Quarterly* 64 (Supp. 2, 1986), 17, 74–75 (discussing Superintendent of Belchertown State School v. Saikewicz, 370 N.E.2d 417 [1977]). Yet even an analysis of the individual's interests turns partially on the actual options available to that person, which in turn depends on the preferences of others (p. 80).

[27]Preston H. Longino, Jr., "Withholding Treatment from Defective Newborns: Who Decides, and on What Criteria?" *U. Kan. L. Rev.* 31 (1983), 377, 389, notes that the family's interests are seldom discussed expressly, but courts may tacitly rely on them. Weir, *Selective Nontreatment,* p. 78, discusses the position of Raymond Duff, pediatrics educator, who claims that "families need to be spared the chronic sorrow of caring for infants with little or no possibility for meaningful lives," and (pp. 81–82) of Everett Koop, who "thinks that physicians who engage in selective nontreatment of infants often do so primarily to prevent parents from having burdens they do not want to bear."

[28]The contrast between the judicial assessments of Phillip Becker's quality of life in the dependency hearing and then the guardianship hearing (see below) provides vivid evidence of this phenomenon.

[29]See Mark Pilisuk and Susan Parks, *The Healing Web: Social Networks and Human Survival* (Hanover, N.H.: University Press of New England, 1986), pp. 33, 56, discussing the impact of family ties on health and on success and failure rates of medical treatments.

[30]See Anthony Shaw, "Conditions in Newborns That Pose Special Problems," *Contemporary Surgery* 11 (Oct. 1977), 51, arguing that the potential quality of life of an infant with Down's syndrome depends on home and parents as well as on the child's mental and physical abilities. This is actually a specific instance of the wider truth: we are all deeply affected by the company we keep. See Wayne Booth, *The Company We Keep: An Ethics of Fiction* (Berkeley: University of California Press, 1988), pp. 169–82.

bound person, for example, depends greatly on how disabling is the social and physical environment. Norman Fost has written, "If buildings had ramps, if colleges would not exclude [wheelchair-bound persons] from dormitories . . . and if airlines would not require them to be accompanied by adult companions, many such individuals would not see themselves as significantly handicapped."[31] How handicapped individuals see themselves is interdependent with how others see them and how others construct their shared environment. If changes in the physical environment can bring about significant changes in the social meaning of a handicap, the handicap itself resides not solely in the handicapped person but also in the relationships between that person and the community. These relationships can change and thus alter to some extent the effect of a handicap on the handicapped person's daily life.

This mutability of the social meaning of handicaps applies to mental disabilities as well. Historical shifts in attitudes about particular disabilities have expanded the actual opportunities made available to mentally disabled people and improved the quality of the lives open to them.[32] Down's syndrome, for example, once spelled institutionalization because of very low estimates of the individuals' mental ability and competence to care for themselves. More recent assessments urge community care and predict varying degrees of self-sufficiency. Many individuals with Down's syndrome can experience and generate considerable love and joy. Transformation in the public understanding of this disability and others have remade the life experiences of many disabled persons, reflecting both medical advances and advocacy activities designed to change public attitudes.[33]

At the same time, the changeable meaning of particular handicaps offers reason to doubt that disabled people inevitably suffer greater unhappiness and a lesser quality of life than others.[34] It is hardly an adequate response to confine handicapped persons to a stigmatized status and to deprive them of opportunities to become more than others expected. Some parents and doctors initially assume that an infant with spina bifida and predicted to spend her life in a wheelchair would lack sufficient quality of life to justify a medical rescue. These advocates of the quality-of-life principle run a serious risk of preserving old assumptions about the meaning of various disabilities. Information from advocates for the handicapped and from parents of chil-

[31]Norman Fost, "How Decisions Are Made: A Physician's View," in Swinyard, *Decision Making and the Defective Newborn*, p. 224.
[32]See Michael MacDonald, *Mystical Bedlam: Madness, Anxiety and Healing in Seventeenth-Century England* (Cambridge: Cambridge University Press, 1981), examining shifting conceptions of mental illness; David J. Rothman and Sheila M. Rothman, *The Willowbrook Wars: A Decade of Struggle for Social Justice* (New York: Harper & Row, 1984), describing the historical treatment of mentally disabled persons and the legal and political challenges to dismal and substandard institutional care.
[33]See *An Alternative Textbook in Special Education,* ed. Burton Blatt, Douglas Biklen, and Roger Bogdan (Denver, Colo.: Love, 1977).
[34]See R. B. Zachary, "The Neonatal Surgeon," *British Medical Journal* 2 (1976), 869: "Extreme disability is not synonymous with unhappiness, and we are only at the beginning of finding ways of developing the capabilities of these patients to the maximum."

dren in similar situations could well alter negative assessments.[35] Such information, together with the possibility of future medical advances, pushes quality-of-life assessments higher and supports greater efforts to preserve a severely disabled infant's life.

The results converge with those of the right-to-life principle. Like right-to-life advocates, quality-of-life proponents must consider when treatment is futile or would only prolong dying, and the inquiries begin to look quite similar in specific contexts.[36] Preserving life in a doubtful case may be the only way to guard against underestimations of the potential life experience of the disabled person. Once we recognize the extent to which social attitudes construct the meaning of disabilities—that disabilities are critically relational in their social meanings and their actual impact on people's lives—we may work for changes in institutional arrangements to benefit those who have been labeled handicapped. The prospect of enlarging the potential for the most severely handicapped may seem quite small, but the historical record cautions against underestimating and stigmatizing those whose prospects may well change with medical advances and changes in social attitudes. Hence, the fact of life alone—and the possibilities for change that it implies—may supply the core meaning to its quality.

Still, contextual judgments made on a case-by-case basis are required in medical treatment decisions premised on the quality of life, and measures to guard against mistakes, however defined, will never entirely succeed. Because the infant cannot make the decision, other people's assessments will always control the outcome.[37] Other people may crudely misjudge the effect of the handicaps and grossly undervalue the life of a handicapped person.[38] Or they

[35]It is undoubtedly with this in mind that former Surgeon General Koop called for making available to parents of handicapped newborns (1) information about competent diagnostic services; (2) a list of governmental and private agencies able to help parent and child; and (3) names of parents "with similar situations who have managed the problem successfully"; see C. Everett Koop, "The Handicapped Child and His Family," *Linacre Quarterly* 48 (Feb. 1981), 23, 29, quoted in Weir, *Selective Nontreatment*, p. 83. Given his commitment to the right-to-life position, however, Koop did not recommend access to parents who have chosen not to authorize aggressive medical treatment, or who have not been pleased with the results of such treatment.

[36]See Macklin, *Mortal Choices*, p. 224: contextual assessments merge Kantian and utilitarian perspectives.

[37]The notion of self-determination, used in arguments for patient autonomy in the context of euthanasia, can have no application to severely disabled newborns. Some people advocate euthanasia because they anticipate wishing to die when they conclude that their own lives are no longer worth living. For them, autonomy and dignity are preserved through self-determination; the patient's own desires guide the medical treatment decisions. See *The Dilemmas of Euthanasia*, ed. John A. Behnke and Sissela Bok (Garden City, N.Y.: Anchor Books, 1975); *Euthanasia and the Right to Death: The Case for Voluntary Euthanasia*, ed. A. B. Downing (London: Peter Owen, 1969); Philippa Foot, "Euthanasia," *Philosophy and Public Affairs* 6, no. 2 (1977), 85, 109–12. See also Natural Death Act, Cal. Health & Safety Code, sec. 7185–95 (West Supp. 1989) (authorizing adults to sign statement permitting withdrawal of life-sustaining treatment and freeing medical personnel from liability). See generally Brian Clark, "Whose Life Is It Anyway?" in *Best Plays of the Seventies*, ed. Stanley Richards (Garden City, N.Y.: Doubleday, 1980), a drama exploring voluntary euthanasia in dramatic form.

[38]Sondra Diamond, who has cerebral palsy, attended college despite the doctors' prediction that there was little or no hope that she would achieve meaningful humanhood. When she suffered burns in her twenties, she had to fight for medical treatment, because doctors believed it

may romanticize life and underestimate the deprivations or suffering presented by the infant's condition. Even if some agreement could be reached regarding what quality of life should mean—what measure of consciousness it involves, what ability to communicate and to experience joy or relatedness—such definitions involve the internal world of the infant and of the person that the infant will become, an internal world that others cannot know.

Both the right-to-life and quality-of-life positions, then, depend on established legal doctrines, yet both give rise to conceptual and practical problems that are resolvable only in specific contexts. The apparent certainty of the right-to-life principle gives way under scrutiny to a more difficult set of assessments about the exact duties of parents and doctors in particular circumstances and about the meanings of futility, dying, and life for actual infants born with particular disabilities. The quality-of-life position turns into a question about the actual interdependent relationships between a particular infant and the adults in his or her life.[39] Yet the two principles share the tendency of legal and philosophical reasoning to approach difficult problems through abstract standards and to pitch debates as conflicts of rights. The right-to-life position translates highly complicated, emotionally charged medical determinations into a conflict between the infant's right to life and other rights, such as parental rights. The quality-of-life position similarly relies on abstractions, converting the complicated factual situation into an ideal or a set of ideal minimum capacities.

Approaching problems in the world with abstract principles has real drawbacks. Abstractions tend to obscure the ambiguity of the problems and the complex human relationships implicated in both the problems and any solutions to them. There is a risk of separating the medical treatment decision from the whole of the person's life. Who will care for the infant and for the person he or she will become? Before bold slogans are framed, whether for or against treatment, this larger context must also be addressed. Abstract principles distract attention from contexts and carry an illusion of uncontroverted answers. Abstract principles may empower their advocates to regard opponents as wrong, even though the contrasting positions converge. Competing principles, removed from the facts of a particular case, also allow their

---

was not worthwhile for someone who could not lead a normal life. She herself concluded, "I do not believe that any human being does not deserve the opportunity to live." See " 'I Am Not What You See': A Film Dialogue between Sondra Diamond and Roy Bonisteel," reprinted in *Law, Science, and Medicine,* University Casebook Series, ed. Judith Areen, Patricia A. King, Steven Goldberg, and Alexander Morgan Capron (Mineola, N.Y.: Foundation Press, 1984), pp. 1199, 1202. See also John A. Robertson, "Involuntary Euthanasia of Defective Newborns: A Legal Analysis," *Stan. L. Rev.* 27 (1975), 213, 254: "Life, and life alone, whatever its limitations, might be of sufficient worth" to a disabled child. Robert Burt, *Taking Care of Strangers: The Rule of Law in Doctor-Patient Relations* (New York: Free Press, 1979), recounts the case of a burn victim who, treated over his own opposition, went on to become a successful law student. Burt also observes that all persons involved in the treatment of the seriously ill risk an impulse to delegate authority for the decision to someone else in an effort to avoid acknowledging the interdependent relations of all the parties.

[39]Both principles also significantly implicate, without resolving, the question of who is to make the medical treatment decision for the infant; see below.

adherents to assume poses of self-righteousness that may hamper real communication or persuasion.

Such poses already characterize the debate over abortion, in which the principles of right to life and quality of life structure debate. But there, the either/or quality of the dispute is even more stark, making rapprochement seem impossible.[40] Each side stereotypes the other and forces disagreement into crude opposition.[41] Yet each principle actually reflects complex judgments about the contexts in which people face the abortion question, involving divergent pictures of the world.[42]

In context, the general principles converge: both actually stand for the infant's right to individualized attention in the difficult process of decisions about medical treatment. Both the right-to-life and the quality-of-life principles require attention by special people, who then must make a decision. Neither principle resolves, though, the critical question: Who decides? This can be understood as a procedural rather than a substantive question, for it concedes irresolution on the merits of the medical treatment debate in general and turns instead to structuring the processes for contextual decision-making.[43] Perhaps, as the convention goes, when substance confounds, pro-

---

[40]There is one large difference in the two debates: the argument for the woman's right to choose whether to abort a pregnancy depends on the fact of her own bodily involvement and on women's historical lack of power over important decisions in their own lives. In the medical treatment context, arguments for parental autonomy lack both the bodily connection and the claim of historical powerlessness, especially since parents have had power over their children and have been known to abuse that power. The two debates may begin to converge as new technologies alter the timing and meaning of fetal viability, established by the Supreme Court as the cut-off period for the constitutionally protected privacy rights of the pregnant woman and her doctor to decide upon abortion. See *Test-Tube Women: What Future for Motherhood?* ed. Rita Arditti, Renate Duelli Klein, and Shelley Minden (London: Pandora Press, 1984), estimating the effects of new reproductive technologies on women's choices; and Patricia A. King, "The Juridical Status of the Fetus: A Proposal for Legal Protection of the Unborn," *Mich. L. Rev.* 77 (1979), 1647. Debates over handicapped newborns draw in different participants, however, such as advocates for the rights of the handicapped.

[41]See Clifford Geertz, "Anti-Anti-Relativism," *American Anthropologist* 86, no. 2 (1984), 263–64, criticizing view that anti-anti-abortion means pro-abortion rather than pro-choice). See also Carol Gilligan, *In a Different Voice: Psychological Theory and Women's Development* (Cambridge, Mass.: Harvard University Press, 1982), pp. 70–104, noting that women tend to characterize the abortion decision as a conflict between *responsibilities* (to care for the child and to care for the self or other children) rather than a conflict of *rights*.

[42]Kristin Luker, *Abortion and the Politics of Motherhood* (Berkeley: University of California Press, 1984), pp. 158–91, contrasts the world view of right-to-life advocates, who think one must accept what life deals out, and that of right-to-choose advocates, who think one should learn to choose one's life options. Kathryn Pyne Addelson, "Baby-Killers and Fetus Fetishists: Review of *Abortion and the Politics of Motherhood*," *Women's Review of Books* 2, no. 2 (1984), 14, 15, argues that Luker fails to uncover the complexity of coalitions on each side of the abortion debate; "each side includes some supporters who are closer to the other side's supporters on nearly every issue but that of abortion." Many right-to-life activists advocate state intervention to overturn parental rejection of medical care for a severely disabled newborn. A. Lawrence Washburn, the lawyer who initiated a lawsuit against the parents in one such case, had previously initiated legal action on behalf of fetuses in an effort to halt abortions; see Marcia Chambers, "Advocates for the Right to Life," *New York Times Magazine*, Dec. 16, 1984, pp. 94, 97, 100.

[43]The allocation of choice, rather than the substance of the choice itself, became under the rubric of privacy the central constitutional question in the United States treatment of abortion. See Roe v. Wade, 410 U.S. 113 (1973).

cedure beckons. Here, too, contextual relationships matter much more than abstract principles.

Who Decides?

When we cannot agree about what to do, we want to know who will have the final say. Deciding who should have the final say about medical treatment for a severely disabled newborn raises difficult questions about the relationship between parents and the state, between parents and medical professionals, and between parents and the infant. The Western liberal commitment to individual autonomy and self-determination make problematic any choice of a decision-maker other than the patient. This commitment relies on a view that only the self can have the self's interests at heart.[44] Any other possible actor could misunderstand the patient's needs and interests or implement a contrasting self-interest instead.

The problem is difficult enough when the patient is someone who once was capable of expressing preferences but has become unable to grant or withhold consent for medical treatment. For adults who are comatose or otherwise incapacitated, courts have devised notions of "proxy" decision-making. The term "proxy" implies someone who knows the affected person's interests and indeed has received decisional power directly from that person, as with proxy voting for corporate shareholders. Yet even in the corporate context there are reasons to doubt that a shareholder always knowingly assigns his voting interest or that a proxy assignment advances his interest. In the medical care context, proxy decision-making introduces several more complications. Should the decision-maker inquire into what the affected person would have chosen if he or she could choose? Evidence about the person's prior wants, expressed or implied, become the basis for proxy decisions made under the legal doctrine of "substituted judgment."[45] But this effort is

[44]See, e.g., John Rawls, *A Theory of Justice* (Cambridge: Belknap Press, 1971), pp. 136, 142. Philosophers also debate the certainty with which anyone may know his or her own interests and note that a person's preferences may be molded by others; see Joel Feinberg, "The Child's Right to an Open Future," in Howie, *Ethical Principles,* pp. 97, 117–19. Others cast doubt on whether anyone may know even his or her own experiences and perceptions. See Saul A. Kripke, *Wittgenstein on Rules and Private Language: An Elementary Exposition* (Oxford: Basil Blackwell, 1982), pp. 60–83; and Hilary Putnam, *Reason, Truth, and History* (Cambridge: Cambridge University Press, 1981), pp. 71–72. These two forms of skepticism produce some irony: while some philosophers maintain that no one can understand what goes on in another's mind, others maintain that no one can understand what goes on in his or her own mind without reference to communal enterprises such as language. These positions are not inconsistent, however, given a relational perspective that locates all human knowledge in the society and culture in which it forms. E.g., W. V. Quine, "Epistemology Naturalized," in *Ontological Relativity and Other Essays* (New York: Columbia University Press, 1969), pp. 69, 89–90, argues that the building blocks of perception may be culturally variable.

[45]See Barbara Bolsen, "MDs, Lawyers, Probe Ethical Legal Issues in Ending Treatment," *American Medical News,* April 6, 1984, p. 11; Charles H. Baron, "Medicine and Human Rights: Emerging Substantive Standards and Procedural Protections for Medical Decision-Making within the American Family," in *The Resolution of Family Conflict: Comparative Legal Perspectives,* ed. John M. Eekelaar and Sanford N. Katz (Toronto: Butterworth, 1984), p. 575.

fraught with guesswork. It relies on the imaginative effort of the decision-maker to construct what the patient would want, given what the surrogate knows—about the patient and, perhaps, about himself.[46] But whatever success family members or friends may achieve in imagining the past wants of a comatose eighty-year-old, substituted judgment makes little sense for a newborn, who has no history or prior expression of wants.[47] In this context the very term "proxy decision-making" simply preserves the image of self-determination where it is actually impossible.[48]

An alternative form of proxy decision-making known as best-interests analysis addresses the interests rather than the desires of the patient.[49] The decision-maker determines needs, risks, and benefits from an external stance. The pretense of attributing any portion of the choice to the patient is nearly gone, although some may defend best-interests analysis as the inquiry the rational patient would undertake if she could. Because there is obviously no way for another to know fully what assessment a particular "rational" infant would reach, however, such analysis cannot help being a judgment, made by someone else, about the infant's interests. To speak of "best interests" also veils the very present risk that the decision will fall short of its name. For this reason, some scholars have advocated replacing the term, in many areas of legal doctrine governing children, with the phrase "least detrimental alternative."[50] This phrase may at least humble the decision-maker with the recognition that any child in need of such a determination is already far from his or her best interests. It also reminds the decision-maker to try to minimize the harms and risks that remain.

Perhaps prime among the risks that remain is the danger that the decision-maker's interests actually conflict with the interests of the patient. Professor Alexander Capron has surveyed legal treatment of decisional authority in many areas to derive lessons for medical treatment decisions about children. From his review of the rules governing witness testimonial capacity, criminal culpability, trustee powers over an estate, attorney-client relationships, and class action representation, Capron elicited the principle that substitute decision-makers should have no conflict of interest with the incompetent person about whom they will decide.[51] But what are the interests of the

[46]See, e.g., Kripke, *Wittgenstein*, p. 140, discussing Wittgenstein's notion that one individual can conclude that another has pain by reference to his or her own experience with pain.

[47]See In re L.H.R., 253 Ga. 439, 440–41 (1983); 321 S.E.2d 716, 719 (1984) (discussing difficulties of applying substituted judgment to a child).

[48]See Gerald Dworkin, "Consent, Representation, and Proxy Consent," in Gaylin and Macklin, *Who Speaks for the Child*, p. 196; Nancy K. Rhoden, "Litigating Life and Death," *Harvard L. Rev.* 102 (1988), 375.

[49]In use, the term "interests" tends to combine the individual's own wants or needs with society's views about what the individual should want or need, therefore combining what could be called subjective and objective concerns.

[50]See Joseph Goldstein, Albert J. Solnit, and Anna Freud, *Beyond the Best Interests of the Child* (New York: Free Press, 1973).

[51]Alexander Morgan Capron, "The Authority of Others to Decide about Biomedical Interventions with the Incompetent," in Gaylin and Macklin, *Who Speaks for the Child*, pp. 123, 133. Yet if the decision-maker is a family member, then potentially, conflicts among self-interest,

patient, and how are either those interests or the interests of the substitute decision-maker to be assessed? If we knew the answer, we would be well out of the thicket created by these thorny medical treatment problems. In practice, however, the ideal of a decision-maker with no conflict of interest may break down when juxtaposed with the actual, contending decision-makers in a given case. The choice, in context, presents various persons with different kinds and degrees of conflicting interests.

Consider the infant's parents. Since the child's birth and certainly during the months of waiting for the birth, parents may have grown attached and committed to the child. The parents appear to have the advantage of closeness, commitment to the child, love and attachment through the parent-child relationship. From these sources the parents may bring persistence and hope to the medical treatment decision. Ideally, they will work to preserve the child's life, or to end it if they perceive that the child's suffering is too great. From this vantage point, any decision-maker other than the parents sits too far removed from both the emotional fabric and actual responsibility in the situation to be entrusted with the medical treatment decision.[52]

Yet many observers cite parents' closeness as a disadvantage, a conflict of interests, because their life-style and opportunities are intertwined with the child's future. When parents worry about the economic and emotional costs of raising a handicapped child, their very closeness to the child may disadvantage them in determining the child's own interests. Alternatively, closeness to the child may interfere with parents' judgment because they care for and love the child too much: their love may lead them, on the one hand, to choose life-prolonging treatment despite the pain or futility of such measures, or, on the other, to refuse extended medical treatment that continues the infant's pain. Problems of bias, subjectivity, or overinvolvement persist in each alternative. Rather than enforcing the parents' choice in the name of constitutionally protected privacy interests, then, the state may need to second-guess or supplant the parents' decisions, through child neglect or abuse proceedings or some similar action.

Compared with the conflicting interests of parents, the interests of other decision-makers may seem helpfully distant and in that sense "objective." Medical personnel can make a judgment based on the medical prognosis, acknowledging familial concerns only insofar as they affect the patient's health potential. A hospital ethics review committee—assembled from members of the community and persons trained in ethics, as well as medical experts—could similarly reach a decision without the competing tugs of self-interest.[53] Detached from self-interest also are state officials, such as a judge or a court-appointed guardian.

---

concern for the patient, and concern for others in the family will abound. Even if the decision-maker is a stranger, conflicting interests are likely.

[52]Arguments such as these have supported decisions recognizing the right of parents or guardians to refuse treatment for another. See Superintendent of Belchertown State School et al. v. Joseph Saikewicz, 373 Mass. 728 (1977); 370 N.E.2d 417 (1977); and In re Karen Quinlan, 70 N.J. 10; 355 A.2d 647, cert. denied; 429 U.S. 922 (1976).

[53]Before the Supreme Court decision that rejected the regulatory effort premised on section 504 of the Rehabilitation Act of 1973—Bowen v. American Hosp. Ass'n, 54 U.S.L.W. 4579

Or are they? The idea that each of these persons would be free from conflicting interests equates conflict-free interests with distance and with freedom from continuing responsibility for the child's well-being. This is actually a dubious equation. Medical personnel certainly have interests: interests in preserving life, trying out new medical technologies, advancing their careers, and filling hospital beds. Members of the ethics review committee each have individual interests, and as a group they have interests in achieving a certain reputation, resolving conflicts, developing guidelines to facilitate the resolution of future conflicts, and avoiding subsequent litigation by disgruntled private or public parties. State officials similarly have personal career and reputational interests, as well as explicit and implicit institutional concerns and values.[54] State officials, in particular, risk conflicting interests because the state may become responsible financially for the child if the parents default on their duty.

Moreover, even an absence of implication in the child's future does not make these potential decision-makers neutral or objective. That very distance represents a position, in relation to the child, which influences their judgment. They lack the sense of attachment and commitment that could allow them to care enough to push for the child's survival—or to make an achingly difficult decision to forgo further treatment in light of the pain or futility the infant seems to face. If the closeness of the parents signifies greater responsibility and care, then distance disqualifies a decision-maker.

In short, though there are different reasons to trust and distrust parents and other actors, no decision-maker is entirely free from interests that could be at odds with those of the child. The situation of the observer affects what is observed. State officials, doctors, and treatment committees share with parents the limitation that no one can fully know the interests of anyone else or fully promote self-determination for those who cannot speak for themselves. To the extent that parents' roles in the child's life disqualify them as decision-makers, other possible decision-makers suffer from comparable or even identical disqualifications. The state especially risks conflicting interests because it may become the caretaker or financial provider for the infant. Each possible decision-maker has self-interests that may conflict with the infant's

---

(June 10, 1986); 585 F. Supp. 541; 106 S.Ct. 2101 (1986)—federal regulations stimulated the use of hospital ethics committees. See Bolsen, "MDs, Lawyers, Probe Ethical Legal Issues," p. 19; 50 Fed. Reg. 14,880, 14,896 (1985) (encouraging committees that would combine information, resources, and referral services with mechanisms to report cases to court or state child protective services). Deciding who should sit on such committees represents judgments about whose values should prevail. Robert M. Veatch, *Case Studies in Medical Ethics* (Cambridge, Mass.: Harvard University Press, 1977), pp. 40–41, notes that clergymen, judges, utilitarians, and formalists each have special expertise and values. Hospital use of ethics advisory committees increased during the 1980s, but such committees cannot themselves authorize treatment over parental objection without a court order. See generally Robyn S. Shapiro and Richard Barthel, "Infant Care Review Committees: An Effective Approach to the Baby Doe Dilemma?" *Hastings L.J.* 37 (1986), 827.

[54] See generally Mary Douglas, *How Institutions Think* (Syracuse: Syracuse University Press, 1986). See also David L. Bazelon, "The Experiment: 1954–1972," in *Questioning Authority: Justice and Criminal Law* (New York: Knopf, 1988), pp. 49–70, examining how self-interests of judges and mental health experts affected a judicial experiment to consider mental health testimony in criminal cases.

interests, and each bears a frame of reference that is unalterably different from the child's.

Ultimately, the state unavoidably selects a decision-maker.[55] By allowing the parents to choose or refuse the medical treatment, the state enforces their authority, shields them from competing decision-makers, and assigns them continuing responsibility for the child. If a case never goes to court, and parents make the treatment decision, they are allowed to do so under the state's rules. Similarly, by subjecting parental decisions to the threat of review by hospital committees or a child abuse agency, the state influences the parental choices and to some extent induces the parents to internalize the choices that public bodies would approve.[56] When the state authorizes intervention by other parties—a hospital review committee, a judge, a private advocate for the rights of handicapped persons—or permits such parties to supplant the parents' judgments, the state decides who decides the medical treatment issue.[57] A richer, more detailed picture of the contexts in which such decisions have occurred in the recent past helps to demonstrate why the state's choice of decision-makers cannot be generalized or resolved in the abstract—and why particular contexts may be worse than others for attending to the infant.

Problems in Context

In recent years, controversies over medical treatment for severely disabled newborns have filled newspapers and other popular media. When a given infant's condition becomes a public *cause célèbre*, daily reports create a sense of crisis and prolong community preoccupation with the case. In a sense, the readers of the unfolding news story are like the audience watching tragic drama, which demands its viewers' attention but immobilizes them, since they can do nothing but witness.[58] Yet because the matter has become public,

[55]Theoretically, the state could (1) order medical treatment (or forbid it), regardless of what parents or doctors want; (2) approve or disapprove medical treatment (or nontreatment) as decided by others; or (3) assign to others unreviewable decision-making power over the medical decisions. In fact, contemporary legal debates all occur within (2), although some advocates make statements sounding like (1) and (3). Thus, the allocation of initial decision-making power, the criteria for public review, and the presumptions or deference accorded to the initial decision-maker remain central concerns.

[56]For a discussion of alternative ways to organize review committees, see Shapiro and Barthel, "Infant Care Review Committees," p. 827.

[57]Self-appointed "friends of the child"—family members or representatives of interest groups—may seek judicial intervention, and it is a state choice whether to recognize their claims. Although the legal doctrine of "standing" provides courts with a method for determining which people should be allowed to complain about an issue, and who should be allowed to assert the rights of another (Charles A. Wright, *The Law of Federal Courts*, 4th ed., Hornbook series [St. Paul, Minn.: West, 1983], pp. 59–74), courts are often willing to entertain unusual procedures when the rights of an infant or child are at stake. The courts' own *parens patriae* responsibility represents a residual duty, beyond any affirmative grant of legislative authority, to protect dependents within the jurisdiction. See, e.g., Ellen Ryerson, *The Best-Laid Plans: America's Juvenile Court Experiment* (New York: Hill & Wang, 1978).

[58]Stanley Cavell, "The Avoidance of Love: A Reading of *King Lear*," in *Must We Mean What*

the question of who decides what should happen itself becomes a matter for debate and, at times, a competition among claimants for the role of decision-maker.

One such case involved a child named, for the public, Baby Jane Doe. Newspapers and broadcasters gave major billing to the story. Headlines announced "The Life-or-Death Question of Baby Jane Doe," and "Baby Doe's Parents Call U.S. Action Intimidating."[59] The infant—born with spina bifida and other severe disabilities—attracted the attention of state and federal courts, legislative debates, executive action, and continued media coverage.[60]

Her parents, who probably had never heard of these medical conditions before, listened to their doctors, and heard a range of treatment options. They declined to authorize surgery to close the spinal opening; they approved measures to guard against infection and to keep the infant well fed and comfortable. Then a private citizen, who had previously initiated or intervened in lawsuits involving abortion, brought suit to challenge the decision made by Baby Jane Doe's parents.[61] The state trial court in Suffolk County, New York, agreed to hear his challenge and authorized a guardian *ad litem* to consent to surgical procedures on the infant's behalf.[62]

When Baby Doe's parents appealed the trial court's decision, the appellate division endorsed the notion that courts have *parens patriae* power to review parents' choices about medical care for their children but nonetheless rejected the exercise of state power to supersede the parents' decisions in this case. The appeals court concluded that the parents' refusal of surgery did not

---

We Say? A Book of Essays (Cambridge: Cambridge University Press, 1976), pp. 314, 322, 329–30.

[59]Michael Betzold, "The Life-or-Death Question of Baby Doe," *Detroit Free Press*, Nov. 11, 1983, p. B1; Marcia Chambers, "Parents of 'Baby Doe' Criticize 'Intrusion' by U.S.," *New York Times*, Nov. 6, 1983, p. L45.

[60]Initial reports cited not only the opening of the spinal cord known as spina bifida but microcephaly (an abnormally small head) and hydrocephalus (an accumulation of fluid in the cranial regions); doctors apparently told the parents that the baby "probably had brain malfunction" and that "the part of the brain that controls much of our awareness was either missing or not entirely formed" (Chambers, "Parents of 'Baby Doe' "). Later observers criticized the initial press coverage for overly pessimistic estimates of the infant's prognosis. See Steven Baer, "The Half-Told Story of Baby Jane Doe," *Columbia Journalism Review*, Nov.–Dec. 1984, p. 35; Nat Hentoff, "A Case of Deformed Journalism at 60 Minutes," *Village Voice*, April 3, 1984, p. 6. Another way to look at this skirmish about press coverage is to note that the dispute extended even into the meaning of the medical diagnosis.

[61]Weber v. Stony Brook Hospital, 60 N.Y.2d 208, 211 (1983); 456 N.E.2d 1186, 1187 (1983); 469 N.Y.S.2d 63, 64 (1983), cert. denied, 464 U.S. 1026 (1983). It is unusual for a stranger to obtain judicial review in such a case, and some may argue that parents should have a right to stop such intervention. See Michael Vitiello, "Baby Jane Doe: Stating a Cause of Action against the Officious Intermeddler," *Hastings L.J.* 37 (1986), 863.

[62]Weber v. Stony Brook Hospital. The *New York Times*, June 18, 1985, reported that Baby Jane Doe's "spinal abnormality closed naturally, accomplishing what the surgery was intended to achieve, and the parents permitted treatment to reduce the hydrocephalus, but she remains a severely handicapped baby." Without surgery, Baby Jane Doe was not supposed to live past the age of two. However, the last mention of her in the *New York Times*—on June 10, 1986—said she was still alive.

constitute a decision to bring about the child's death, because their treatment decision was an acceptable, if debatable, one and the decision to forgo surgery created no imminent risk of death. The court stated that it found "no basis for judicial intervention" even as it was interposing its own judgment, independently reviewing the record, and finding the parents' determination "to be in the best interest of the infant."[63] The court also reasoned that the individual who initiated the lawsuit had no direct relationship to the infant and therefore no direct interest in her medical treatment; the trial court had erroneously allowed his suit in the first place. According to the appeals court, the state's Department of Social Services could have invoked review of the parents' decision; since this agency had not done so, the courts lacked authority over the case.[64]

Meanwhile, the federal government had entered the fray. The Department of Health and Human Services (HHS), under the administration of Ronald Reagan, had often pursued an antiabortion agenda and sometimes linked it with demands for medical treatment for handicapped newborns. Here, HHS filed suit in federal district court against the hospital treating Baby Jane Doe, citing the federal statute prohibiting discrimination against the handicapped, section 504 of the Rehabilitation Act of 1973.[65]

The district court accepted the suit as a proper invocation of federal authority under the statute, but it rejected the agency's claim because the government failed to establish that the hospital had violated the statute and discriminated unlawfully against a handicapped person. The court reasoned that the hospital declined to perform surgery on the infant because her parents refused to consent to surgery—not because of the hospital's view about her handicap—and the court concluded that the parents' refusal was reasonable.[66] And it is the parents' decision, not the hospital's or health care providers', which determines whether medical treatment is pursued or forgone.[67] The court also concluded that section 504 did not authorize the federal government to force the hospital to release its records to the agency or

[63]Weber v. Stony Brook Hospital, 95 A.D.2d 587, 589 (1983); 467 N.Y.S.2d 685, 686–87 aff'd (1983); 60 N.Y.2d 208 (1983); 456 N.E.2d 1186 (1983); 469 N.Y.S.2d 63, cert. denied (1983); 464 U.S. 1026 (1983); 95 A.D.2d 589; 467 N.Y.S.2d 686–87.

[64]The court did not specify whether a family member or other person asserting a direct interest in the child might be allowed to initiate suit in comparable circumstances but indicated that any such persons would need explicit court approval to file a petition for a hearing. See 60 N.Y.2d 208, 212; 456 N.E.2d 1186–87; 469 N.Y.S.2d, 63, 64. The state agency did conduct an inquiry into the case but concluded that it had no basis for intervention. See United States v. University Hosp., 729 F.2d 144, 147 (2d Cir. 1984).

[65]United States v. University Hosp., 575 F. Supp. 607 (1983); E.D. N.Y. (1983), aff'd 729 F.2d 144 (2d Cir. 1984).

[66]Id. at 613–14. This amounts to a straightforward interpretation that sec. 504 has no application to parental decisions, since the act prohibits discrimination "under any program or activity receiving federal financial assistance"; see 29 U.S.C. sec. 794 (1982). The government itself has conceded that parents are not covered by the act; see 49 Fed. Reg. 1631 (1984).

[67]This was the central rationale in the Supreme Court's decision in the subsequent related case, Bowen v. American Hosp. Ass'n, 476 U.S. 610 (1986), which affirmed a district court's decision, relying on United States v. University Hosp. 729 F.2d 144 (2d Cir.), and rejected the department's regulations as unauthorized by sec. 504 of the Rehabilitation Act.

the court; further, it agreed that the individual who had initiated the state court suit and sought appointment of a guardian for Baby Jane Doe lacked sufficient interest to bring suit.[68]

HHS already had regulatory action in the works, initiated after an earlier publicly visible case: a Down's syndrome infant had died in Indiana in 1982 after the parents declined to consent to surgery to remedy a malformed esophagus.[69] Responding to public criticism from handicapped rights and right-to-life groups, President Reagan instructed the secretary of HHS to notify health care providers that section 504 governed the treatment of handicapped patients.[70] HHS so notified 7,000 hospitals and later issued regulations that required health care providers receiving federal funds to post large signs in public view, warning that discriminatory treatment of disabled newborns violated section 504 and that any observer should report suspected violations to a telephone hotline maintained by HHS.[71] Such calls triggered federal investigations, and presumably, if an investigation produced a finding of a violation of section 504, the department could move to terminate federal funds to the offending facility.

Many hospital personnel found these guidelines an unacceptable intrusion on their relationships with patients. The American Academy of Pediatrics, the National Association of Children's Hospitals, and the Children's Hospital National Medical Center decided to contest the regulations in court. At an initial judicial hearing, these plaintiffs submitted affidavits describing medical conditions of certain infants that could not, in the medical groups' view, be treated and yet might be forcibly treated under the HHS regulation.[72] Surgeon General Everett Koop, testifying for HHS, actually agreed that these kinds of infants could not be treated but explained that the regulations were never meant to prolong their lives.

After the initial hearing, the federal district court judge rejected the interim rules on procedural grounds: HHS had failed to follow the federally prescribed steps for soliciting public comments on proposed regulations. In response HHS resubmitted the rules, with few changes, but also indicated that they were not intended to require futile therapies that would merely prolong life.[73] The revision acknowledged that medical judgments could differ; it prescribed government regulation only where nonmedical factors—

[68]United States v. University Hosp., 575 F. Supp. 613–14, 616.

[69]Those parents also declined nutritional support for the infant, who was called in the press "Baby Doe." See Abigail Lawlis Kuzma, "The Legislative Response to Infant Doe," *Ind. L.J.* 59 (1984), 377, 378–79. See also Jeff Lyon, *Playing God in the Nursery* (New York: Norton, 1985).

[70]49 Fed. Reg. 1622–23 (1984) (detailing history); David Bird, "U.S. Role in 'Baby Doe' Case Defended by Surgeon General," *New York Times*, Nov. 7, 1983, p. B4.

[71]48 Fed. Reg. 9630 (1983) (interim final rule).

[72]The affidavits described anencephaly, intracranial hemorrhage, and lack of a substantial part of the digestive tract as situations that could not be remedied medically. See Kuhse and Singer, *Should the Baby Live?* pp. 24, 25.

[73]45 C.F.R. sec. 84.55 (1984). The revised rules also reduced the size of the signs indicating the applicability of sec. 504 and directed that they be posted where authorized medical personnel, rather than members of the public, could see them.

such as subjective judgments that an "unrelated handicap" makes a person's life not worth living—infect the decision-making process.[74] Many groups submitted comments on the new regulations; HHS received nearly 17,000 submissions.[75]

The agency then issued a final rule that softened the requirements to some extent but reiterated the application of section 504 to medical treatment decisions in facilities receiving federal funds. It also encouraged the use of infant care review committees within the health care facilities, as proposed by such organizations as the American Academy of Pediatrics, but still imposed the federal presence through the hotline and investigations.[76] Several medical groups, finding even the final rule an intolerable governmental interference with medical practice, initiated a new suit and successfully argued that medical treatment decisions about disabled newborns belong with parents and their own physicians and medical teams. The district court struck down the regulation as beyond the scope of section 504 and relied expressly on the appellate decision a few months earlier in the Baby Jane Doe case.[77] The Supreme Court reached the same conclusion in rejecting the final rule as unauthorized by section 504 of the Rehabilitation Act.[78]

Because the courts had closed off section 504 as a possible statutory basis for federal supervision of these medical treatment decisions, the government next pursued new legislation. Congress adopted an amendment to an appropriations program intended to combat child abuse and neglect, requiring that all states accepting federal grants under the program must develop procedures to prevent the withholding of "medically indicated treatment from disabled infants with life-threatening conditions."[79] Thus, the federal gov-

[74]49 Fed. Reg. 1623, 1630 (Jan. 9, 1984). See 45 C.F.R. sec. 1340.15 (1987) (the regulations "do not sanction decisions based on subjective opinions about the future 'quality of life' of a retarded or disabled person"). The meaning of an "unrelated handicap" remained ambiguous and probably inadequate to fulfill the agency's purpose; presumably, denial of medical treatment due to a related handicap would offend the antidiscrimination principle in some circumstances.

[75]Marcia Chambers, "Broad Effects Expected from Case of Baby Doe," *New York Times,* Nov. 30, 1983, p. B2. Although 97 percent of the comments supported the rule, many of these were identical and seemed orchestrated by such groups as the "Christian Action Council"; 72 percent of the pediatricians and neonatal specialists who wrote comments opposed the rule. See Kuhse and Singer, *Should the Baby Live?* p. 43.

[76]See Gerald M. Boyd, "U.S. Is Easing Rules on Birth-Defect Infants," *New York Times,* Jan. 7, 1984, p. 24.

[77]American Hosp. Ass'n v. Heckler, 585 F. Supp. 541, 542 (S.D. N.Y.) (1984).

[78]Bowen v. American Hosp. 476 U.S. 610 (1986). This was the case affirming the grant of declaratory and injunctive relief, prohibiting the HHS requirements that health care recipients post notices and that state child protective agencies report and intervene to protect handicapped infants from known or suspected discrimination in treatment decisions. The Supreme Court concluded that sec. 504 of the Rehabilitation Act of 1973 does not authorize governmental intervention when the nontreatment decision is made by parents, rather than by the health care provider that receives federal funds. The Court also reasoned that the regulations exceeded their statutory authority in requiring absolute benefits rather than merely nondiscrimination in the treatment of infants.

[79]Child Abuse Amendments of 1984, Pub. L. No. 98–457, 98 Stat. 1749 (1984), codified at 42 U.S.C. sec. 5101–06, 5111–13, 5115 (West Supp. 1985). See James Bopp and Thomas J. Balch, "The Child Abuse Amendments of 1984 and Their Implementing Regulations: A Sum-

ernment used the carrot of federal monies to solicit state enforcement of federally established standards to monitor the medical treatment decisions made by parents and physicians.

Although these standards were more flexible than those the government had initially sought, some observers have criticized even this approach for forcing physicians to act contrary to their own medical judgments, for limiting parental discretion, and for forcing an allocation of medical resources without evaluating alternative instances of need—such as the needs of elderly patients or the need for parental care to reduce the risks of disability at birth.[80] Others, however, suggest that the regulations leave considerable discretion to physicians, while reminding the public of the uncertainty in medical judgments about disabled newborns.[81]

The Risks of Adversarial Responses

The regulatory collisions surrounding the case of Baby Jane Doe may not be typical, but they illustrate the contemporary contexts for medical treatment decisions concerning severely disabled newborns. Competing principles—right to life and quality of life—quickly recede into the background, though they summarize and perhaps stiffen the motivations of adversaries in public debate. The irresolution over who decides these problems may permit recurring initiatives by different actors and governmental bodies. By reestablishing the framework of state child abuse laws as the dominant legal response to this problem, the federal government to some extent has reconfirmed the presumption of respect for parental decisions, unless those decisions breach prevailing public standards. Yet because the child abuse framework permits private persons and public officials to report a given case for state investigation, it may also preserve and exacerbate a community's adversarial responses to a family facing a terribly difficult decision.

An adversarial response to a family in such circumstances rests on a faulty

---

mary," *Issues in Law & Med.* 1 (1985), 91. Congress defined "withholding of medically indicated treatment" as "the failure to respond to the infant's life-threatening conditions by providing treatment (including appropriate nutrition, hydration, and medication) which, in the treating physician's or physicians' reasonable medical judgment, will be most likely to be effective in ameliorating or correcting all such conditions, except that the term does not include the failure to provide treatment (other than appropriate nutrition, hydration, or medication) to an infant when, in the treating physician's or physicians' reasonable medical judgment, (A) the infant is chronically and irreversibly comatose; (B) the provision of such treatment would (i) merely prolong dying; (ii) not be effective in ameliorating or correcting all of the infant's life-threatening conditions, or (iii) otherwise be futile in terms of the survival of the infant; or (C) the provision of such treatment would be virtually futile in terms of the survival of the infant and the treatment itself under such circumstances would be inhumane"; see sec. 121 (3), codified at 42 U.S.C. sec. 5012 (3).

[80]See John C. Moskop and Rita L. Saldanha, "The Baby Doe Rule: Still a Threat," *Hastings Center Report*, April 1986, pp. 8–14.

[81]William Weil, Jr., "The Baby Doe Regulations: Another View of Change," *Hastings Center Report*, April 1986, pp. 12–13.

conception of the family as the repository of untrustworthy motives. It is more likely that everyone involved in the situation of a severely disabled infant has conflicting and complex responses.[82] An adversarial response fails to address the relationship of the larger society to the problem—a relationship characterized mainly by neglect. Society places the emotional and financial burden of caring for a severely disabled person on the nuclear family, even though giving birth to a disabled person is a predictable social risk. When seriously handicapped infants survive and go home from the hospital, some grow up to lead normal or relatively normal lives, but many spend years connected to breathing and feeding tubes.[83] They require constant care. Most families do not have the resources to hire others to care for the child, and public and private medical insurance covers only a small portion of the severely handicapped individual's needs.[84] When parents consider whether to authorize life-extending medical treatment, they do so within the context of a society that assigns to them the ultimate burden of caring for the individual and then blames them if they do not want to or cannot do it. The problems of the infant's difference are assigned to the family, and family members risk self-doubt and public disapproval with any choice they make.

The tendency to blame rather than assist the family is especially pronounced because assigning blame helps people to manage their own ambivalence about what should happen. It may be especially satisfying to sort out ambivalent feelings toward the severely handicapped person by directing toward the parents the bad feelings of rejection and reserving for ourselves the more righteous feelings of love and sympathy. Ambivalence toward the disabled newborn reflects the simultaneous connection and separation that we feel about a "different" person. People tend both to distance themselves from the situation and also to identify with one or more of the principal figures in cases such as Baby Jane Doe's.[85]

People identify with the vulnerable infant despite a sense that she is "other" and radically different. Everyone has been an infant and in that capacity has dealt from a position of vulnerability with powerful adults who

[82]See Burt, *Taking Care of Strangers*, pp. 1–21; and Sander L. Gilman, *Difference and Pathology: Stereotypes of Sexuality, Race, and Madness* (Ithaca: Cornell University Press, 1985), pp. 11–35, discussing stereotypes that express and project fears.

[83]Cathy Trost, "Medical Puzzle: Handicapped Infants Pose Tough Question: Who Provides Care?" *Wall Street Journal*, June 13, 1988, p. 1: the Office of Technological Assessment estimates that up to 17,000 children rely on breathing and feeding tubes.

[84]Moreover, public funds often link reimbursement to institutional treatment and force families to send the individual to a hospital because they cannot afford to provide care at home (ibid.). Home limitations generally mean that one or more family members, usually women, devote their lives to the physical care of a very dependent person.

[85]For the psychological concept of identification, see Jay R. Greenberg and Stephen A. Mitchell, *Object Relations in Psychoanalytic Theory* (Cambridge, Mass.: Harvard University Press, 1983), pp. 70–72, 160–61, 171, 331, discussing internalization of aspects of others as developmental dimension; Jerome Kagan, *The Nature of the Child* (New York: Basic Books, 1984), pp. 139–43, discussing the process by which a child develops identification with distinctive qualities of others and on this basis constructs standards of behavior. Adults, as well as children, recognize themselves in the roles and attitudes of others; we develop conceptions of ourselves in part by internalizing a sense of others.

make decisions for the child. Identification with the infant may exist unconsciously and subtly, or it may be intense and disturbing. Childhood vulnerability may undergird adult memory and identity.[86] Identification with
the vulnerable infant may stir up memories of one's own vulnerability and
make the medical treatment decision seem terribly important—but still difficult to resolve.

Identification does not mean knowing the other's best interests. Identification with the infant may lead some to support aggressive medical care and
elaborate methods to preserve or prolong life, but it may also encourage
more conservative treatment. One adult may imagine a desire on the part of
the child to live, to receive all possible care, and to gain assurances of
attention and comfort. Another adult may as easily imagine preferring refusal of treatment, or even suicide, as an alternative to extensive medical
treatment that cannot ameliorate the underlying handicapping conditions.
Still another may imagine wanting to relieve family members of the burden of
caring for a severely disabled child, or imagine living inert and unloved in an
institution. Any of these adults may develop a sense of distrust about anyone
else's ability to know and understand what the infant needs.[87] Remembering
that no one knew perfectly their needs as children, they all have reasons to
distrust others to care for this child.

At the same time, an adult may identify with the parents of a handicapped
infant and may find this identification horrifying, for it can involve feeling
both revulsion at having given birth to a handicapped newborn and revulsion
at this revulsion. An adult identifying with the parents of Baby Jane Doe may
discover both an inclination to abandon the child and disgust with that
inclination. He or she may also feel drawn by a moral view of duty to resolve
this emotional turmoil by renouncing instinct in favor of conscience.[88] Yet
any duty constructed from identification with the infant's parents may support contrary courses of action. A duty of care, extrapolated from the role of
parent, may command consent to all measures to preserve or prolong the

[86]Many theorists assert that the child's early life may be characterized by vulnerability and
helplessness; see Joseph Goldstein, Anna Freud, and Albert J. Solnit, *Before the Best Interests of
the Child* (New York: Free Press, 1979), pp. 7–10. These experiences remain in the individual's
psychic world even during adulthood. See Herbert Fingarette, *The Self in Transformation:
Psychoanalysis, Philosophy, and the Life of the Spirit* (New York: Harper & Row, 1963), p. 59;
Martin E. Seligman, *Helplessness: On Depression, Development, and Death* (San Francisco:
W. H. Freeman, 1975), pp. 104–5, 150.

[87]Burt, *Taking Care of Strangers*, intricately develops the argument that patients and doctors
may distrust one another because of their mutual impact and because of the deeper psychological construction of self and others. See also Alice Miller, *The Drama of the Gifted Child and the
Search for the True Self*, trans. Ruth Ward (Boston: Faber & Faber, 1983): some children
develop a sense of self by trying to please their parents but then must submerge their real self
behind a false, pleasing self; and Alice Miller, *Thou Shalt Not Be Aware: Society's Betrayal of
the Child*, trans. Hildegarde and Hunter Hannum, (New York: Farrar, Straus & Giroux, 1984),
pp. 7–8, 31–36: adults and psychoanalysts deny the abuse of children by parents and ignore the
children's signals.

[88]Sigmund Freud, *Civilization and Its Discontents*, pt. 7 (in *The Major Works of Sigmund
Freud*, trans. Joan Riviere [Chicago: Encyclopedia Brittanica, 1952], pp. 793–96), describes
conscience as emerging from a renunciation of instinct.

child's life, yet that same duty may also direct attention to the dignity of that child, including the dignity of death without elaborate technological intrusion. Identification with the parents' emotional ambivalence and obligations provides a basis for distrusting those parents, because the identifying adult discovers through that identification a basis for self-distrust.

Finally, some people may identify with the medical personnel drawn into a case, and this too may produce ambivalence. They may feel drawn by the medical team's commitment to preserve life, but they may also resent the medical professionals' focus on technology, anxiety about malpractice, and indifference to the human dimension of the problem.

A public media event surrounding the medical treatment of a severely disabled newborn may thus expose people's fears about their own vulnerability to the power of others. Public fascination with these cases is linked to people's conflicting experiences of being moved and repelled by the plight of the infant. They may fear betraying a sense of duty with emotional responses and also fear cutting off emotional responses with a sense of duty. The media coverage gives the stories of disputed treatment a sense of crisis while offering little room to resolve or accommodate these fears. News coverage recounts the treatment of the vulnerable infant but does not discuss the feelings this treatment may arouse. Nor do the media draw attention to the societal dimensions of the case. The family's private responsibility stems from a societal policy; the future meaning of the life of the handicapped person depends in part on the meaning the watching society gives to the handicap. The media's tendency to cast villains and heroes, combined with the adversarial posture of legal and administrative decision-making, conveys the players as opponents and strangers, submerging the ways in which they—and we—are connected to one another.

Public debates about such medical treatment decisions take on an adversarial cast in part because of the dominance of the conception of each individual as separate and each family as private. Despite empirical and theoretical work exploring the critical interdependence of each person with others and the deep involvement, rather than separation, represented by the contact between families and the state, it remains easier to treat another as radically separate and as a source of distrust. Thinking about problems in either/or terms fits neatly into the psychological construct that treats the self as separate from others. Yet the either/or terms may hide the very bases of relationships between people and between alternatives. An adversarial structure overemphasizes antagonism and separation while obscuring communality and mutual need. The public drama, enacted in courtrooms and government agencies and depicted by the media, may exaggerate the separation of the audience from the anguish of the actors. Conceptions of the problem as belonging to the infant may underestimate the vulnerability of the adults to the infant and the interdependence of human interests. The struggle over who will make the medical treatment decision may overstate a need for separation and undervalue a need for consultation. The carving of problems into rigid dichotomies between self and others, right to life and quality of life, intervention and nonintervention, may emerge from psychic preoccupations only partially understood.

Debates over medical treatment for severely disabled newborns are not just about rights. They are critically about relationships. Relationships between the medical treatment issue and the rest of the infant's life, between the newborn and the family, between the family and society (observed and observers), and between abstract ideals and contextual applications all shape and are shaped by these debates and decisions. What would happen if we took these relationships seriously as important features of the legal treatment of these issues?

Relational Responses: Conditions for Trust

New medical knowledge and changes in the social meaning of various handicapping conditions may partially address the current uncertainty about medical treatment for severely disabled newborns. Over time, new rules may well secure public confidence and recede into the background of settled expectations. Such developments seem distant now, however, because the controversy is increasing, not abating. Some experiments in extended care have been rejected.[89] The growing numbers of infants born with AIDS, and the costs accompanying their treatment, will provide new occasions for debate.

In a related context, Jay Katz—himself a doctor—has argued that doctors and their patients can remedy their mutual distrust through conversation and the sharing of information and decisional authority. He suggests that physicians must first face the limits of their own professional knowledge and admit their distrust of themselves in order to learn to trust their patients and share authority with them. Similarly, not only medical professionals but legal authorities, media commentators, and parents need to acknowledge their distrust of themselves in order to resist projecting that distrust onto others when difficult decisions arise. As Katz concludes, such a climate of trusted decision-making "cannot be implemented by judicial, legislative, or administrative orders. At best, such outside interventions can prod doctors; at worst, they only substitute bureaucratic authority for professional authority."[90] Similarly, neither external authorities nor public enactments of private ambivalence can attend to the sources of distrust that fuel public debate and fascination with medical treatment decisions for severely disabled infants. Continued public debate is in store, but there are better ways to conduct it than we have done in the past.

How can public debate be structured to address the needs of the infant and

[89]See Kuhse and Singer, *Should the Baby Live?* pp. 49–59: doctors in Sheffield, England, concluded that efforts to treat spina bifida infants yielded so many with severe disabilities, resulting in high medical and schooling costs, that they turned to selective treatment methods.

[90]Jay Katz, *The Silent World of Doctor and Patient* (New York: Free Press, 1984), pp. 102–3, 228–29.

the families, removed from a public drama of blame and controversy? Gathering information can challenge presuppositions about disabilities and also expose the financial burdens of rules placing the responsibility for the infant's difference on the parents. More hospital review committees could assume duties other than second-guessing parental decisions. Instead, they could foster local and public debate about prospective guidelines, developed outside a crisis situation, to take account of shifting medical and social understandings of particular disabilities and treatment options.[91] This alternative would address the confusion, inconsistency, and secrecy of treatment decisions by making the development of guidelines a task shared by medical and nonmedical people, without exacerbating the difficult decisional process at the very moment when they must decide for a particular infant.

Thus, hospital review committees could shift their focus from reviewing particular parental decisions and instead encourage more general exchanges of information. Parents, doctors, and representatives of the government would then have greater opportunities to learn from one another in nonadversarial settings.[92] Conflicting estimates of a child's medical condition become entrenched by the time parents, doctors, and state decision-makers assume formal roles in a hearing or in litigation; people tend to have become locked into their positions at that point. Hospital committees could serve as clearinghouses to organize and channel information from medical associations, organizations for the rights of handicapped persons, and other parents with experiences to share. Doctors, hospitals, and parent support groups could encourage a pregnant woman and her partner to think in advance about the issues involved in a medical treatment decision for a severely disabled newborn, a decision they might otherwise confront in an emergency situation. By developing their views removed from that context, with full exposure to the positions advanced by advocates of right-to-life and quality-of-life positions, parents would not only become better prepared to make decisions themselves if necessary but would also be more informed participants in public debates and policy initiatives.

In considering a particular patient, hospital ethics committees could provide a method for bringing people together for emotional support and for enhancing attention to the uniqueness of one patient and situation. Rather than becoming an abstract debate over principles of ethics, medicine, and law, such conversations could create a sense of community in the room to assist the family facing the decision. People could help one another focus on the patient while attending to the interpersonal relationships implicated in any decision.

Specific decisions and more general discussion of medical treatment for disabled newborns would also be improved if we connected the treatment

---

[91]See Weir, *Selective Nontreatment,* pp. 210–11.

[92]When the HHS proposed an information-gathering and exchange function for infant care review committees, it combined this function with reporting cases to protective agencies for legal action; see 50 Fed. Reg. 14,893–94. A committee given this monitoring and enforcement function would be unlikely to provide a nonadversarial setting.

decision with the ultimate questions about the infant's care, whether or not treatment is authorized. The usual framework of analysis distinguishes the medical treatment decision, and who should have the authority to make it, from the question of who will care for the infant and with what support from others. The usual analysis fails to address the matter of care even when the state itself may become the caretaker. Parents, the medical professionals, and the state all have potential interests in the child's future care, and the press could respond to public interest by pursuing this question.[93] Rather than argument about whether parents' interests conflict with those of the child, one option would be to alleviate their conflicting interests. As part of any process in which the state rejects a parental decision to forgo medical treatment for the infant, the state should provide a different choice for the parents: you may decline to care for the child, but in that case the state will find someone else to do so.[94] Then, it would be obliged to develop in advance plans for actual placement with adoptive or foster parents who agree to care for a severely disabled child.

In a similar vein, Joseph Goldstein has proposed that the state should not conclude a medical care decision for a child while refusing to assume responsibility for the subsequent costs of the child's medical care;[95] treatment decisions made by actors other than the parents would then carry with them the financial obligation to pay for that treatment and to assist the parents or others who end up providing that care. This, too, would alleviate to some extent the conflicting interests parents may have in making the decision. There are drawbacks to the proposal: it might convert the medical treatment decision into a cost-benefit calculus in simple economic terms, or it might encourage parents to refuse treatment deliberately in the belief that the state will displace their judgment and then pay the costs. Public and private reimbursement programs would employ criteria, and establishing those criteria would reopen the question of who deserves treatment. The problems of reimbursement, perverse incentives, and partnerships between families and public and private insurers represent the underlying relationships of care and mutual obligation invoked by the medical treatment decision. These problems must be addressed, however, whether or not Goldstein's proposal becomes part of a serious political agenda.

The goal should be to solve the large public problem shared by parents, state officials, the public, and the disabled infant: how can the patterns of relationships and care among all these actors acknowledge the infant's needs both to live and to die with dignity? This problem reaches beyond the medical treatment decision to the larger social treatment of disabled persons;

---

[93]See, e.g., Trost, "Medical Puzzle," p. 1.

[94]This is the general rule governing the relinquishment of children for adoption.

[95]Joseph Goldstein, "Medical Care for the Child at Risk," in *Who Speaks For the Child*, p. 169: "If society insists through law that such children, indeed any children, receive medical treatment rejected by the parents, the state should provide the special financial, physical, and psychological resources essential to making real for the child it 'saves' the value it prefers. The state should become fully responsible for making 'unwanted' children 'wanted' ones."

addressing it will reveal that the family and the state share responsibility for the child, whether or not medical treatment is authorized. Child-care and job arrangements as shaped by present public policies make caring for a severely handicapped child a difficult task for parents. Existing state and private institutions at best usually offer less to the child than a home with an attentive family; institutions at worst offer neglect and shameful circumstances. Parents, and others who claim a right to participate in the medical treatment decision, need to know what help may be available in caring for the child: help in the form of homemaker support for the parents, state-facilitated adoption, guidance through the maze of public and private reimbursement programs. Developing such options would engage state and private actors in a process of comprehensive planning—and in struggles to reallocate funds to address this large problem. Within the institutional structures currently in place, no single set of decision-makers can plan or reallocate resources. Greater humility in the face of the issues left unresolved after the medical treatment decision is made would alleviate the blaming and defensiveness surrounding parents' decisions and would help redirect attention to the larger, practical, and less symbolic meanings of both a right to life and the quality of life.

Some describe the birth of a disabled infant as a tragedy; others call this description itself a debasement of the sanctity of that infant's life. The real tragedy is pretending that the question is simple.[96] Simplifying a problem into either/or solutions fails to capture the complexity of the human relationships involved. Pretending that there can be an unsituated perspective from which to judge the situation also neglects the complex relationships at work. The vantage point afforded by our relationships with one another offers an important corrective to the assumption of individual autonomy which usually predominates. Most important, however, are efforts to retain both angles of vision. Our ambivalence—wanting to feel connected and also wanting to feel separate—is especially pronounced in relation to a severely handicapped person, who can inspire a sense of recognition and connection but also feelings of unfamiliarity and separation. A relationship with a severely disabled infant may include, at times, wanting him or her to disappear. Yet the relationship also invites care, connection, and a sense of shared human dignity.

Bringing ambivalence to the surface will not eliminate it, but neither will ignoring it. Talking about the ambivalence that lurks behind either/or solutions is at least a way to gain freedom from our ignorance about what may propel debate. Acknowledging ambivalence about the severely disabled child could help us understand why we may oscillate between feeling that "this could be my child" and that "this has nothing to do with me." Efforts along

[96]See Martha C. Nussbaum, *The Fragility of Goodness: Luck and Ethics in Greek Tragedy and Philosophy* (Cambridge: Cambridge University Press, 1986), pp. 25–82: Greek tragedies depict people who oversimplified a problem and ignored the competing tug from another direction.

these lines might help us understand that we are all on the same side here, all of us caught by difficulties in the human condition. We all could be related to this child. And as advocates for the handicapped have reminded us, we able-bodied persons are only *temporarily* able-bodied; we could all at some time return to the position of dependence on others.

Meanwhile, we have the chance to struggle, in context, with these issues. Martha Nussbaum, in her eloquent meditation on Greek tragedy and ethics, writes: "we reflect on an incident not by subsuming it under a general rule, not by assimilating its features to the terms of an elegant scientific procedure, but by burrowing down into the depths of the particular, finding images and connections that will permit us to see it more truly, describe it more richly."[97] Just as our usual ways of talking tend to obscure this critical reflection on the relationships between the particulars, our usual way of thinking about law underplays the significance of relationships between people. An unusual case, with an unusual ending, provides an example of a struggle to recognize the relationships involved in a medical treatment decision for a disabled person.

"In a Case Like Ours*": The Story of Phillip Becker*

Shortly after his birth, Phillip Becker's parents learned that he had Down's syndrome.[98] On the advice of doctors, they institutionalized him. Because Phillip was also born with a heart defect, his institutional caretakers and doctors repeatedly sought consent from his parents for medical procedures to assess and repair the defect.[99] The Beckers repeatedly refused consent, and the delay made the surgery increasingly risky. The Beckers visited Phillip only infrequently and moved him to a better facility only after someone else alerted them that the first one did not provide adequate care.

Volunteers who worked at the second facility found Phillip a lively, likable child. One couple, the Heaths, befriended and worked with him through the volunteer program over the course of several years. Starting when Phillip was five years old, they brought him to their own home for overnight visits and on holidays. The Heaths became attached to Phillip, and he to them. His parents, the Beckers, gave permission for his stays away from the institution but still refused consent for the medical treatment, although the Heaths pushed for some solution.

What legal options existed for Phillip? As a child, he was dependent on

[97]Ibid., p. 69.

[98]Down's syndrome, also called trisomy 21 and formerly called mongolism, is a permanent condition associated with an extra chromosome. It is characterized by a small skull flattened in front and back; a short, flat-bridged nose; short fingers; and moderate to severe mental retardation. See Richard Sloane, *The Sloane-Dorland Annotated Medical-Legal Dictionary* (St. Paul, Minn.: West, 1987).

[99]A centricular septal defect, a hole between the right and left ventricles, produces greater strain on the health and ultimately leads to death but is correctable by surgery.

decisions made by his parents or legal guardians; except in emergency circumstances, any doctor performing surgery on a child without parental
consent can be liable for a tort, for nonconsensual invasion of the child's
body.[100] Until the age of majority or, for some medical procedures, the age of
maturity, the child could not provide his own consent.[101] That Phillip had a
mental disability further undermined any argument that he could manifest
the requisite competence to authorize his own medical treatment. Mentally
disabled adults are also usually considered incompetent to consent to their
own medical care; they require the approval of a legal guardian to supply the
missing competence.[102] Thus, the usual rules prescribe legal action concerning the medical needs of a child, still in the legal custody of his parents, only if
a public entity—an agency or a court—determines that the parents have
violated statutory standards of care and placed the child at serious, life-
threatening risk. Similarly, a legal guardian is entitled to make medical
treatment decisions for the mentally disabled person entrusted to his or her
care, unless a decision violates the applicable legal standard of care and
triggers review by a state agency.

Intervention by state agencies in a family requires overcoming the usual
presumptions that child care is the private responsibility of parents and that
parents in general know what is best for their own children[103]—or that the
care of any dependent person is the responsibility of the legal guardian. And
because of historical abuses by states in their operation of facilities for
mentally disabled persons and their intervention in the lives of poor and
minority families in order to regulate conduct, most states have developed
safeguards against unwarranted state intrusion.[104] The parents' rights to

[100]See Guardianship of Phillip Becker, Superior Court of Santa Clara, California, No. 101981
(1981), hereinafter cited as Trial Court Opinion. A physician is liable for the tort of battery upon
treatment of a child without parental consent, no matter how beneficial the result or slight the
treatment. Most states, however, have limited physicians' liability in such cases to negligent or
intentional wrongdoing, and many states allow physicians a "good faith" reliance on their
reasonable belief that the minor has the capacity to consent. All fifty states immunize physicians
from liability for venereal disease treatment for a minor who has reached a specified minimum
age. In general, many states allow "mature" minors to consent to their own medical treatment,
and also create exceptions to physicians' liability for life-threatening emergencies. See Rhonda
Cohn, "Minor's Right to Consent to Medical Care," *Medical Trial Technique Quarterly* 31
(1985), 286, 304; Macklin, *Mortal Choices*, p. 109.

[101]See Cohn, "Minor's Right," pp. 286, 384. About two-thirds of the states allow minors to
consent to drug abuse treatment; half allow such treatment even without parental notification.
Generally, minors may not be denied access to birth control services by parental consent
requirements. No state may entirely obstruct a minor's access to abortion through a parental
consent requirement but must instead offer some possibility for securing approval through a
judicial or other process. Bellotti v. Baird, 428 U.S. 132 (1979); Planned Parenthood of Central
Missouri v. Danforth, 428 U.S. 52 (1979).

[102]Comment, "The Role of the Family in Medical Decision-Making for Incompetent Adults,"
U. Pitt. L. Rev. 48 (1987), 539.

[103]See Trial Court Opinion: "Our courts take the view that the government through the
Superior Court should not run family life. We feel that the law has limited ability to supervise
interpersonal relationships" (citing Goldstein, Solnit, and Freud, *Beyond the Best Interests of
the Child*). See also Parham v. J.R., 442 U.S. 584, 602–3 (1979).

[104]See Goldstein, Solnit, and Freud, *Beyond the Best Interests of the Child;* and Goldstein,
Freud, and Solnit, *Before the Best Interests of the Child.*

familial privacy thus are countered only by a special state duty to protect children through civil or criminal actions against the parents. Such actions can lead to limited court orders authorizing medical treatment,[105] or to more considerable supervention of parental authority: removing the child from the parents' physical custody, or even terminating the parental rights and finding the child a foster home or an adoptive family.

In Phillip's case, after the Beckers refused to consent to heart surgery, the state initiated a hearing about the boy's needs in the form of a dependency proceeding. The court asked whether Phillip was a "dependent" person under state law and in need of state intervention to assure him the necessities of life. It concluded that surgery to correct the heart defect could be more risky for a person with Down's syndrome than for a "normal" person.[106] Perhaps that court was influenced by the argument that the threat to Phillip's health and life was real but that death was not imminent; no emergency situation justified state supervision of the child and his medical care. The court clearly indicated that it deemed the surgery less necessary for Phillip because his disability gave him a presumptively lesser quality of life.[107]

In an unusual legal move, the Heaths then initiated legal proceedings themselves. They sought to be declared Phillip's guardians; they also sought court authorization to provide the necessary consent for the surgery. Their lawyer, Jay Spears, in consultation with Stanford law professor Robert Mnookin, thus transformed the medical treatment decision into a custody battle. The argument they crafted was that from Phillip's perspective the Heaths *were* his parents, and interference with their relationship with him would cause him detriment.[108] Without seeking to terminate the Beckers' parental rights, the Heaths most unusually requested guardianship status to enable them to have custody of and to care for Phillip.[109] Normally, a custody claim under the guardianship device is made by an adult with whom the child has actually been living, such as foster parents or a stepparent after the death of the child's custodial parent. In this case, Phillip lived neither with the Heaths nor with his own parents, yet the Heaths framed the lawsuit as an assertion that they really provided the psychological and emotional support that Phillip needed.

[105]This often happens where parents object to medical treatment on grounds of religious beliefs that the courts conclude wrongly jeopardize the health and safety of their children. See, e.g., In re Sampson, 65 Misc. 2d 657; 317 N.Y.S.2d 641 (Fam. Ct. 1970), aff'd 37 A.D.2d 668; 323 N.Y.S.2d, 253 (1971), aff'd 29 N.Y.2d 900; 278 N.E.2d, 918; 328 N.Y.S.2d 686 (1972).

[106]See In re Phillip B., 92 Cal. App. 3d 796; 156 Cal. Rptr. 48 (1979), cert. denied 445 U.S. 949 (1980) (affirming trial court's denial of dependency petition, under Cal. Welf. & Inst. Code sec. 300b). After prevailing, the Beckers then initiated a defamation suit against the media, the institution's staff, the Heaths, Phillip's doctor, and various state agencies, ultimately suing some forty-five defendants. See Mnookin, "The Guardianship of Phillip B.: Jay Spears' Achievement," *Stan. L. Rev.* 40 (1988), 841, 844, 847.

[107]George J. Annas, "Denying the Rights of the Retarded: The Phillip Becker Case," *Hastings Center Report,* Dec. 1979, pp. 18, 19.

[108]Mnookin, "Guardianship," includes a tribute to Spears upon his early death.

[109]Trial Court Opinion, p. 2. See also Guardianship of Phillip Becker, 139 Cal. App. 3d 407; 188 Cal. Rptr. 781 (1983) (affirming trial court decision on totality of the circumstances); In re Phillip B., 92 Cal. App. 796, 156 Cal. Rptr. 48, cert. denied, 445 U.S. 949 (1980).

Thus, the Heaths, through their lawyer, converted the early legal question—whether the Beckers had fallen so low in their conduct as parents as to justify state intrusion in the private family—into a contested custody case between two plausible sets of parents or guardians. Not only did this reworking of the case suggest an easier standard to justify intervention; it also helped to overcome a major judicial reluctance to intervene. The suit seemed more like a private contest between two competing sets of custodians than an occasion for reconsidering the difficult question of when the state should intervene in the private choices made by a family. Moreover, the new litigation concretely offered the Heaths as caretakers and decision-makers who would be a plausible alternative to both the biological parents and state officials, should any risk to Phillip be assessed by the judge.

The case produced an extended twelve-day trial, remarkable for any but the most protracted family law cases. A full crowd filled the courtroom, including friends of the Beckers, reporters, and advocates for the rights of mentally retarded persons. The trial court concluded that the Heaths had become Phillip's psychological parents; he seemed to treat them as the people he trusted and loved.[110] The court further awarded guardianship to the Heaths and permitted them to authorize medical treatment; the court itself authorized a medical procedure to determine the feasibility of surgery on the heart defect.[111] Moreover, the judge crafted an innovative arrangement that designated the Heaths as guardians and physical custodians but preserved the Beckers' role and rights as parents.[112]

The trial judge, William Fernandez, wrote an extensive and unusually emotional opinion. He began by asking, "Who speaks for the child?" Is it his parents, his friends, or his institutional caretakers? Quickly, the judge recast the question to contrast the quality of care offered by Phillip's parents and by the Heaths and to compare the conceptions each couple held of Phillip and his quality of life. According to the court, the Beckers regarded Phillip as an unskilled and devalued person, incapable of loving others; this was the conception they had acquired when Phillip was born, based on the assessment offered by doctors at that time. The Heaths, in contrast, pictured Phillip as an educable and valuable person, capable of love. The court treated these comparative assessments as central evidence concerning both who should make the medical treatment decision and whether the heart surgery should

[110]The concept of "psychological parent" was developed by Goldstein, Solnit, and Freud, in their classic work on the legal and psychological needs of children, *Beyond the Best Interests of the Child*, pp. 17–20.

[111]Trial Court Opinion. The Beckers challenged this result and lost; see 139 Cal. App. 3d 407; 188 Cal. Rptr. 781.

[112]See 139 Cal. App. 3d 407, 412; 188 Cal. Rptr. 781, 783–94. Recent scholarship has challenged the assumption that a child may have only one set of legal parents. See Katherine T. Bartlett, "Rethinking Parenthood as an Exclusive Status: The Need for Legal Alternatives When the Premise of the Nuclear Family Has Failed," *Va. L. Rev.* 70 (1984), 879, 886–89, 944–61; Marsha Garrison, "Why Terminate Parental Rights?" *Stan. L. Rev.* 35 (1983), 423, 439–48, 474–89.

go forward.[113] The Heaths' conception was more persuasive, reasoned the judge, and offered the least detrimental alternative for Phillip: a life worth living.[114]

Yet before reaching a finding of detriment to the child, as required by law prior to granting a guardianship petition, the judge decided that he had to consider "Phillip's rights" and in fact appointed an attorney to represent the boy. Although nothing in the law governing guardianship specified rights for the child or incompetent person, the judge noted without citing any particular authority: "It is said that those who are [mentally retarded and gravely disabled] are possessed of an inviolable constitutional right to habilitation," a right to acquire and maintain skills to cope with their own needs in the world, and a right to lead more useful and meaningful lives in society. The judge also observed that California had been developing laws to protect the rights of mentally retarded and gravely disabled minors, including each person's entitlement to "be free of any injury to his reputation and an interest in not being improperly or unfairly stigmatized as mentally ill or disordered."

From these legal principles, and from the fact that Phillip had reached the age of fourteen and would someday be an adult, the judge inferred a right for Phillip to state a preference regarding his placement. Acknowledging that the state provided no method for a mentally retarded child to state preferences about medical treatment or custody, he adapted the idea of "substituted judgment," developed in other jurisdictions, which obliges a court to discern "as nearly as possible the incompetent persons 'actual interests and preferences.'"[115]

The judge then applied an unusual method to accomplish this substituted judgment, a "platonic dialogue with the court posing the choices to Phillip and Phillip's preferences being ascertained from the more logical choice."[116] This imagined dialogue turned the question of who should decide Phillip's future back to the choices between alternative futures and the competing pictures of his quality of life presented by the Beckers and the Heaths. For Judge Fernandez, Phillip's own views could no more be ignored than they could themselves be determinative. The constructed dialogue enabled the

---

[113]The judge actually assembled in table form (Trial Court Opinion, n.41) his comparison between the two views.

Becker Thesis: Phillip cant' [*sic*] talk Phillip can't communicate Phillip is a low Downs. Phillip can't write his name Phillip can't draw. Phillip can't cook. Phillip is not Educable. Phillip can't form loving attachments. Phillip has few basic skills.

Friends of Phillip Becker Anti-Thesis: Phillip can talk. Phillip can communicate. Phillip is a high Downs. Phillip can write his name. Phillip can draw. Phillip can cook. Phillip is educable. Phillip can form loving permanent attachments. Phillip has many basic skills.

[114]See Goldstein, Freud, and Solnit, *Before the Best Interests of the Child.*

[115]Trial Court Opinion, pp. 15–16.

[116]Ibid., pp. 16–17. Philosophers have analogously constructed imagined dialogues to explore, e.g., parental decisions over whether to abort a severely handicapped fetus. See Richard Hare, "Survival of the Weakest," in *Moral Problems in Medicine*, ed. Samuel Gorovitz et al. (Englewood Cliffs, N.J.: Prentice-Hall, 1976), pp. 364–75, a dialogue between the fetus and an as yet unconceived possible brother.

judge to combine what he had learned about the child with his best effort to imagine what the child would want—and with the judge's own perceptions of the situation.[117]

The judge acknowledged that he had no precedent for consulting the preference of the mentally retarded child. But after casting this perspective in dialogue form, he concluded that Phillip suffered detriment through the parenting methods of the Beckers. In this context, the judge in essence chastised the Beckers for clinging to the assessment they had formed of Phillip at birth, rather than changing their view on the basis of the changing opinions of experts and on Phillip's own conduct and personality. They had stigmatized him as permanently disordered and provided no benefits because they held no expectations for him.[118] The court also credited the psychological closeness between Phillip and the Heaths and the better opportunities they afforded the child.[119] Judge Fernandez concluded that this proceeding could authorize the preliminary medical procedure but not the surgery itself; that would be a parental decision. "This is a hearing for the purpose of giving Phillip Becker another parenting choice. It is a hearing responsive to Phillip's need for habilitation, and responsive to his desire for a chance to secure a life worth living. *I will give him that chance.*" The trial judge granted guardianship to the Heaths, and his decision was affirmed a year and a half later by the appellate court.[120]

The opinion registered considerable sensitivity to the multiple relationships in the child's life, relationships in which neither closeness nor distance could direct who should decide the medical treatment. By imagining the opportunities promised by the two sets of parents, the court concluded that Phillip would prefer to have custody and decision-making authority vested in the Heaths. For the judge, the substance of the medical treatment decision

[117]It is an odd sort of dialogue: the judge asking and answering questions, and describing two choices for Phillip that would affect the rest of his life—to stay in the institution and receive basic care but no opportunity to become attached to any person; or to live in a private home and be "bathed in the love and affection of your psychological parents" who would also provide training and medical treatment. After stating these choices, the judge concluded: "In my view, the dialogue would end with Phillip choosing to live with the Heaths" (Trial Court Opinion, p. 17).

[118]Judge Fernandez also found it irrational for the Beckers to spend so much time and money battling in court rather than trying to improve Phillip's life or allowing the Heaths to do so. The Beckers may have felt a need to defend the position they had taken from their first impression at the time of Phillip's birth; as a result, they may have been unable to think of the child any differently. In addition, the adversarial nature of the litigation may have locked them into this defensive stance. After losing the case and the appeal, they defended their position and objected to state involvement in a national news magazine; see Warren Becker and Patricia Becker, "Mourning the Loss of a Son," *Newsweek*, May 30, 1983, p. 17.

[119]The Heaths' lawyers proffered evidence that Phillip regressed when the Beckers restricted his contact with the Heaths in reaction to the litigation; see 188 Cal. Rptr. 788.

[120]Trial Court Opinion, p. 200. Mnookin ("Guardianship," p. 852) notes the inexplicable and reckless decision by the California Supreme Court to stay (hold off) the heart catheterization pending the appellate decision, despite the Heaths' argument that exploration of Phillip's surgical needs required the utmost timeliness. Phillip did ultimately undergo successful heart surgery (pp. 841, 853).

could not be separated from who should decide; questions about the kind of life Phillip would face could not be separated from the people who had contrasting conceptions of who he was. The kind of life open to the child seemed to depend on which relationships he could maintain.[121]

The judge's self-awareness that he too had a relationship to the child demonstrated a degree of honesty usually avoided by judges, who may hide behind presumptions, precedent, and professional role.[122] Indeed, the judge expressed an extraordinary self-consciousness about his own relationship to Phillip and to the issues in the litigation. He explained that the cause haunted him outside the courtroom, that it brought to mind the treatment of disabled people he had known in his own neighborhood and the treatment of disabled people in literature and in other cultures. At the same time, the judge indicated how concerned he was that his opinion and decision be considered objective. With some awkwardness, he moved back and forth between first person and third ("the court"), finally asserting that while the court tried to remain objective,

> judges are human and not machines. From my point of view I believe that we prefer to be judged by a real person with emotions and common sense, and all those other important characteristics of a Homo sapiens. . . . As I read his file and I could see that this little boy was beginning on his trip towards death, and that he realized it, I was stricken with anguish and parental grief. . . . It may be argued that I used the footnotes too much to philosophize and state some personal views, experiences, and anecdotes. My defense is that in a case like *ours* which is so fundamental and basic for life, people should know how some of their "governors" think and have their opportunity to judge the judgment of the judge.[123]

Judge Fernandez placed himself within the case by calling it "a case like ours."

It is a moving opinion, and one that pierces the usual gray prose of official state documents. It gives both an encouraging sense of a real human being, struggling with his relationship to others in the face of moral issues, and a disturbing sense of how thin is the veneer of laws on a justice system of men.[124] Judge Fernandez revealed his relationship to Phillip by breaking through the usual conventions of distance and anonymity to share with the

---

[121]The impact of relationships on the quality of life may be especially notable for disabled persons. See generally Pilisuk and Parks, *The Healing Web*, which explores the significance of human relationships to the individual health and well-being of any person.

[122]Cf., e.g., Parham v. J.R., 442 U.S. 584, 602–3 (1979) (contrasting assumptions about effect of professional and parental proximity to child in making a civil commitment decision), with In re Sampson, cited in n. 105 above (holding that religious belief of parent cannot support refusal of medical care; state must protect the child).

[123]Trial Court Opinion, pp. 18–19 nn.68, 68a, 70; p. 23 n.70 (emphasis added).

[124]Most literature conveys the opposite image of the remote judge, capable of grasping a truth beyond human experience. But see Bertolt Brecht, *The Caucasion Chalk Circle*, rev. Eng. version, ed. Eric Bentley (New York: Grove Press, 1965), which presents a judge who abandons commitment to laws in favor of revealing a personal dimension of justice.

public his personal moral struggle between respecting and rejecting the parents' choice. He exposed the decisional process as he experienced it: he implicated his own relationships to the child, to the two sets of parents, and to the general public as well.

It was an unusual opinion in an unusual case. The result broke out of the usual either/or framework for such situations: either the parents win or the state wins; either the Beckers remain the parents or the Heaths become the parents; either the child can give competent testimony about his own interests and needs or he cannot; either the judge is objective or he is subjective and biased. The Heaths' generosity and compassion and their lawyer's creativity constructed a third alternative, and the judge crafted an arrangement to preserve the Beckers' ties to the child while enabling the Heaths to take over daily care and decision-making.[125]

It was also judicial opinion infused with relational concerns. The decision depended upon particular relationships between facts and between people. The court and the parties probed beneath abstract rules about parental rights and standards of care; they departed from prevailing rules in terms of specific facts. The decision's most significant precedential value is its encouragement of other context-specific analyses in future cases. Another relational dimension appears in the judge's effort to consider the case by imagining Phillip's point of view. In this respect, it is also an important opinion about rights. Out of concern for Phillip's rights, not merely his interests, the judge paid attention to Phillip's own expressions of desire, if only those shown through his conduct. Citing the general rights of someone who has been assigned the label of mental disability by others, the judge crafted a way to learn about Phillip's preferences and needs from his behavior and from a comparison of the pictures of Phillip held by the competing sets of parents.

Because the judge also brought unusual self-reflection to the standard difficulty in balancing the desired objectivity and desired humanity of the judicial observer, the relationship between the knower and the known became central: Fernandez realized that Phillip's quality of life depended largely on the expectations and hopes of those who knew him. Nor did Phillip's own lack of autonomy disqualify him from entering into relationships or from being taken seriously, in part through the constructed judicial dialogue. Further, the court recast the medical treatment decision as a larger question of Phillip's life options and thereby addressed the relationship between parts and the whole, unlike the prior initial dependency hearing, which had focused narrowly on the medical risks and benefits from the proposed heart

---

[125]After appeals, and after the successful heart surgery, the Heaths and the Beckers reached a settlement: the Heaths agreed to assume responsibility for Phillip's care and related costs and to permit the Beckers to visit at least two days a year; the Beckers agreed to dismiss with prejudice the state court actions against the Heaths and refrain from any further challenge to their custody of Phillip, absent a substantial and material change. After Phillip turned eighteen, the Heaths converted their guardianship into a conservatorship and then successfully petitioned for adoption. As of the fall of 1987, Phillip was living with the Heaths, attending school, working part-time bussing tables at the school cafeteria, playing sports, performing chores around the house, and learning to read. See Mnookin, "Guardianship," pp. 853–54, 841.

procedures. As handled by Judge Fernandez, the case of Phillip Becker notably attended to the meanings and potential meanings of interpersonal relationships: Phillip's relationships to the Heaths and to the Beckers, potential relationships between the Heaths and the Beckers themselves, and the judge's relationship to Phillip.

Let us tell the story of Phillip Becker when asked about medical treatment decisions for disabled persons—and the chance of deepening our relationships to judging and living in this polity.

CHAPTER *I I*

Knowing and Judging

We make just dreams
out of our unjust lives.
          —Lisel Mueller, "Reading the Brothers Grimm to Jenny"

The case of Phillip Becker is special. It brought together a remarkable judge who felt unusually connected to the people in the litigation, a developmentally disabled youngster, and two volunteers who offered him a better life. What's more, the unfolding of the case can be described, retrospectively, as a series of challenges to the unstated assumptions common to other cases about mentally retarded persons and about the role of the courts. For example, Judge Fernandez compared the Beckers' assumption that Phillip's differences were intrinsic and immutable with the Heaths' view that Phillip is more like than unlike "normal" people and that the meaning of his condition could shift with a shift in who was observing him. However awkward or contrived his method, the judge sought out Phillip's own point of view and thereby tried to gain perspective on the perceptions of Phillip and on his interests as described by everyone else. With the ingenuity of the Heaths' lawyer, the judge recast what seemed to be the natural course of affairs—that either Phillip's parents would determine his medical treatment, or else the court would find them defective as parents. Rather than accepting either of these alternatives, the litigation reshaped the question as a custody contest, which was settled by allowing the Heaths to assume responsibility for Phillip without at the same time entirely cutting off the Beckers from involvement with their son.[1]

This transformation of the case represented good lawyering by the Heaths'

Epigraph: Reprinted by permission of Louisiana State University Press from "Reading the Brothers Grimm to Jenny" by Lisel Mueller in *The Private Life*. Copyright © 1976 by Lisel Mueller.

[1]Thus, the judge (1) rejected the idea that differences are intrinsic; (2) saw that the differences in Phillip's life depended upon norms that could be reexamined; (3) considered the impact of different observers on the assessment of Phillip's quality of life; (4) sought out hidden points of view; and (5) challenged the idea that the status quo was immutable and natural.

350

counsel, compassionate understanding by Judge Fernandez, and commitment by the Heaths to take responsibility for Phillip and offer him a different
kind of life. The judge, the lawyers, and the parties in effect showed how an
individual like Phillip has an identity only in relation to others and how the
description of his situation depends upon who is offering the observations.
As a result, the case required a choice among points of view. The judge
resolved this choice not by deciding which was more accurate but by addressing the purposes served by the contrasting points of view, the effects on
Phillip's future health and well-being. The judge reexamined labels (such as
Down's syndrome) and roles (such as parent and judge), rather than taking
them for granted, and evaluated them in light of larger purposes. The outcome was a new theory about the medical treatment decision and about child
custody, a new doctrine about guardianship growing from the context of this
case.[2]

The resolution did not follow from a new abstract principle about medical
treatment care or parenthood, nor did it emerge from a step-by-step formula
for solving problems. Instead, the decision reflected a stance, a willingness to
look behind names and given definitions, to break out of dilemmas by
considering the relationships between people and between problems and the
names people give them.

This chapter explores two more examples of problems that initially seem
to pose dilemmas of difference and constraints of labeling. Possible ways out
of the dilemmas emerge after we examine unstated assumptions that interfere with the recognition of relationships and pursue possible relationships
within which differences are constructed. The alternatives are not new, neat
solutions but options that can be debated. In the course of such debates we
can change our world by making it a place where the status quo is debatable
and where the meanings of difference arise from our conscious choices.
Living in such a world may be less comfortable for some—but hopeful,
interesting, and likely to promote more mindful ways of life.[3]

The Mashpee Indian Land Dispute

On August 26, 1976, Indians from Mashpee, Massachusetts, filed a lawsuit in federal district court claiming that they possessed about 16,000 acres
of land in the area called Mashpee on Cape Cod.[4] The suit proceeded, like

---

[2]Thus, the resolution drew on relations between self and other, observer and observed, theory
and context, and parts and wholes. Similarly, the example of sign language offered to a class that
included one hearing-impaired student represents an understanding that the hearing disability is
relational, that multiple perspectives on a "problem" in the classroom can be obtained, and that
the status quo can be changed to remake the range of solutions.

[3]See Ellen Langer, *Mindfulness* (Reading, Mass.: Addison Wesley, 1989).

[4]Mashpee Tribe v. New Seabury, et al. 447 F. Supp. 940 (D. Mass. 1978) off'd 592 F.2d 575
(1st Cir. 1979). See Paul Brodeur, *Restitution: The Land Claims of the Mashpee, Passamaquoddy, and Penobscot Indians of New England* (Boston: Northeastern University Press, 1985);
James Clifford, *The Predicament of Culture* (Cambridge, Mass.: Harvard University Press,

other recent suits by Indians claiming lands, with the claim that the Non-Intercourse Act of 1790 protected tribal groups from exploitation by whites who sought to purchase tribal lands without paying full compensation. The act required congressional permission before Indian lands could be alienated, and in the 1970s federal courts began to apply this act to the benefit of Indians who challenged land transfers stretching back through the prior two centuries. As the result of a suit by the Passamaquoddy and Penobscot in Maine, the tribes received in an out-of-court settlement over $80 million and authority as tribes to acquire a mass of land.[5]

As the Mashpee case unfolded, a crucial, threshold issue emerged even before the court would examine the land claim: were the plaintiffs in fact a "tribe" entitled to assert a claim under the Non-Intercourse Act? The defendants, who included a large land development company, more than a hundred individual landowners, insurance companies, and businesses, did not doubt that the plaintiffs had Indian ancestry; no one disputed that Mashpee historically had been known as the Indian town on the Cape. But the defendants built an argument that unlike the Passamaquoddy and Penobscot in Maine, and other tribes that had secured relief under the Non-Intercourse Act, the Mashpee plaintiffs represented the descendants of Indians who had intermarried with whites and blacks and had lost their identity as a distinctive tribe if, in fact, they had ever had it. Real estate developers and others interested in changing the area to a tourist resort wanted to persuade the court that the dispute involved competing views about the future of the town rather than violations of the rights of a distinctive Indian tribe.

A jury listened to forty-one days of testimony on the matter of whether or not the plaintiffs indeed were an Indian tribe for the purposes of the act. As framed, it was a classic legal categorization question: did these people fit within the defined term? Their opportunity to seek protection under the act depended upon an affirmative answer to that question.[6] What is relevant to the tribal status of the Mashpee Indians? Cultural characteristics of language, religion, dress, diet, and traditions? The political and ethnic self-consciousness of the group's members? Treatment as a distinctive group by others? The witnesses testifying in court offered evidence on all these grounds; the result was a complex picture that could yield entirely different conclusions, depending upon what the observer tried to see. In fact, both the plaintiffs and the defendants engaged academics as expert witnesses to assemble supporting interpretations of Mashpee history. James Clifford, an

---

1988), p. 278; Francis Hutchins, *Mashpee: The Story of Cape Cod's Indian Towns* (West Franklin, N.H.: Amarta Press, 1979). Other, more successful land claim litigation brought by Native Americans established rights to bona fide tribes that lacked federal recognition. See Oneida Indian Nation v. County of Oneida, 464 F.2d 916 (2d Cir. 1972). See also Jack Campisi, "The Trade and Intercourse Acts: Land Claims on the Eastern Seaboard," in *Irredeemable America: The Indians' Estate and Land Claims*, ed. Imre Sutton (Albuquerque: University of New Mexico Press, 1985).

[5]Clifford, *The Predicament of Culture*, p. 278.

[6]Indian tribes have a special status in American law; in 1789 they were proclaimed distinct from the states, although still subject to the power of the federal government.

anthropologist who sat through the trial and then wrote about it, recounted two versions of the histories that emerged from the trial.

In the first version there never was an Indian tribe in Mashpee. People from varied Indian tribes and other minority groups settled in the area and inter-married with whites; they sought full citizenship in Massachusetts and in the United States and assimilation into American culture. During the course of the eighteenth century, most of the residents had converted to Christianity. During the early nineteenth century property was held in a collective planta-tion form that was used also in other parts of Cape Cod and thus was not special. Mashpee became a town in 1834. Restraints on land sales persisted, but most of the common lands were divided in 1840–41 among individual proprietors, who could buy and sell within the existing group. A political dispute over whether to remove all barriers to alienation of property and all remnants of the communal form continued for several decades, and in 1868 the town considered a petition in favor of such reforms as a means to assure full citizenship and to encourage individual initiative. Those who opposed the change spoke of fears that the people would lose their land and their homes, that they lacked adequate preparation for the removal of the land restrictions. These opponents prevailed, although the recorded discussions "clearly showed a consensus in favor of ultimately ending Mashpee's special status, with disagreements only on the timing."[7]

The Massachusetts General Court (the legislature) responded by formally abolishing the status of "Mashpee proprietor" in 1870. From then on all the lands were held without restrictions on sales, and transfers of land to out-siders have taken place ever since. Thus, at the time of the land suit in 1977 the plaintiffs were all American citizens who looked, worked, and lived like other Americans. Like other Americans, the Mashpee citizens showed an attachment to their ethnic heritage but lacked a distinctive claim to an identity that could be called tribal membership in the sense the law would require. Even if the critical dimensions of a "tribe" for these purposes in-volved "continuity of tribal organization and not the relative degree of retention of pre-white-contact cultural characteristics,"[8] the Mashpee plain-tiffs failed to demonstrate not only continuity of tribal organization but its existence at any time.

The alternative history, however, emphasized that the idea of a "tribe" as defined in terms of organizational forms stemmed from white Americans' regulation of Indians during the nineteenth century. Ad hoc meetings and informal structures could be as much a preservation of continuous political form as could a hierarchical or more formal organization comporting with white American notions of politics. Indian traditions themselves would not use the categories used by whites to distinguish political organization, kin-ship, or religion. Even conversion to Christianity would not mean abandon-ment of Indian identity to Indians who viewed religion more inclusively and

[7]Clifford, *The Predicament of Culture*, pp. 294–302.
[8]Hutchins, *Mashpee*, p. 179.

pragmatically than did white Christians. Moreover, most of the Christian ministers in Mashpee had for centuries been self-identified Indians, and the churches in Mashpee had long served as institutions for preserving community and identity.

The early plantation form was imposed by the English but was consistent with the collective ownership of land practiced by the Indians. The retention of this form until 1870, long after it was abandoned elsewhere in Cape Cod, reflected outsiders' perspectives that the Mashpee were different; it perhaps implied racist notions as well but in any case helped to maintain the community's distinctiveness. The majority of the Mashpee sought to preserve the plantation land system; it was changed not by them but by the Massachusetts legislature. The majority continued to prefer to preserve the restrictions against sales of land to outsiders. That most people talked about the end of these restrictions as ultimately inevitable reflected not preference so much as practical political understanding.

The intermarriage between Indians and non-Indians did not terminate the presence of an Indian community but demonstrated the capacity of that community to absorb outsiders. Census reports during the nineteenth century indicated 371 "natives" of the "Mashpee tribe" and 32 foreigners. During the twentieth century, members of the Mashpee joined with other Indians in revival movements that revitalized cultural practices. Most important, the group continuously saw itself as a group apart, maintained a continuous presence on the same land, and claimed identity as Indians even when that did not help or in fact hurt their relations with the larger majority community.

As shaped by the trial, the choice between interpretations of the Mashpee experience was cabined by the court's demand for a yes-or-no answer. The experts themselves were constrained by questions seeking yes-or-no answers rather than the nuanced versions they might have preferred: "The anthropologists on the stand were clearly more comfortable with a polymorphous notion of culture than with the political category of tribe."[9] Moreover, the question presented to the jury—are the Mashpee plaintiffs a tribe?—implied that some traits intrinsic to the Mashpee would be critical to the answer, rather than their relationships with others. The question also implied that it had a single answer, one that would not be affected by who answered it or whose perceptions counted.

The jurors, interestingly, seemed to resist these constraints, as if to say they had been asked the wrong question. Unanimously, they rejected the plaintiffs' claim that a tribe, under federal law, had existed continuously from the precolonial period through the present—but they also rejected the defendants' claim that there had been no tribe in existence at all, at least since 1670. The jury concluded that a tribe did exist in Mashpee in 1834 and 1842 but found insufficient evidence to conclude that a tribe existed either before or after that time.[10] After surveying this ambiguous result, the judge inter-

---

[9]Clifford, *The Predicament of Culture*, p. 323.

[10]The judge had asked the jury to answer whether a federal tribe existed in Mashpee in 1790, 1834, 1842, 1869, 1870, and 1976, these being the critical dates pertinent to the land claim.

preted their finding as a conclusion that tribal status had been abandoned and therefore could not be resumed for the purposes of the lawsuit.

The jury's resistance to the question posed may reflect problems with the notion of "tribe," especially as a concept defined by whites to describe and regulate nonwhites. Or the jury's result may express discomfort with the pretense of a singular history, given the complex and competing narratives offered by the witnesses. An alternative account offered by the anthropologist watching the trial suggests that the idea of any cultural group as distinctive is no longer meaningful—if, indeed, it ever was—given the varieties of contacts and mutual interactions among groups. The American understanding of Indian tribes includes nineteenth-century photographs of individual Native Americans—but, as Clifford notes, the clothing and even the poses in the photographs were contrived by the white photographer.[11] The Mashpee plaintiffs saw themselves as members of a tribe; how should that count in the assessment of difference?[12]

I suggest that the question about the identity of a group as a tribe will forever be befuddling if it is detached from the purposes for which the question is being asked. Once the purposes are disclosed, the perspective of the inquirer and the perspective of the evaluator become critical. For some purposes, self-proclaimed identity will be most significant; for others, external community responses and understandings. But the perceptions of outsiders are not "objective" or removed from the interests of the outsiders themselves. There is elaborate documentation of the historical disregard by whites of the interests of Native Americans, disregard sometimes taking the form of paternalistic rules and sometimes involving the suspension of those rules when it served the interests of whites. In this light, the Massachusetts legislature's decision to remove restrictions on the Mashpee lands in 1870 is hardly an unproblematic fact in interpreting the status of the Mashpee as a tribe.

Paying attention to the mutual construction of identity by self and other, insider and outsider, complicates our understanding. So does noting the impact of theory on context and context on theory, as the expert witnesses indicated in their struggle over application of abstract terms to the experiences of the Mashpee. And acknowledging the impact of perspective—who is doing the observing—on what is observed may make it seem impossible to answer the question for the jury in the Mashpee case.

But maybe it *is* the wrong question. If the purpose for asking the question is to determine whether the plaintiffs should obtain protection against land sales or compensation for past land sales, given their history, that purpose is itself cut off or foreclosed from consideration by the intervening question, are the Mashpee a federal tribe? Allocation of land and compensation are obviously difficult and contested questions too, but if those were the matters at stake, shouldn't the law permit them to be addressed and debated directly?

[11]Clifford, *The Predicament of Culture*, pp. 336, 323.
[12]For a view of the Mashpee constructed by a member, see Russell M. Peters, *The Wampanoags of Mashpee* (Somerville, Mass.: Media Action, 1987).

Otherwise, the law reduces important social questions to the *Sesame Street* game of "Which one of these things is not like the others?"

The legitimate role for courts is at issue in either case: the courts may seem to some observers to be acting beyond their proper role if they permit debate over allocation of resources aside from clearly defined legal categories of past entitlement. But the courts may seem to other observers to lack legitimacy if they foreclose claims that can carry moral weight through definitional games of analogy and distinction. These legitimacy questions deserve further examination as a prelude to the final case study.

Judicial Legitimacy

Lawyers, scholars, and political figures often argue that the very legitimacy of law may be threatened if any branch violates the limits of its role.[13] Charges of illegitimate action notably arise over initiatives taken on behalf of "different" people.[14] Courts acting on behalf of minority and powerless groups embark on tasks that seem unusual for that branch of government. School desegregation stands as the first and perhaps most memorable example of dramatic judicial action that altered established institutions on behalf of a group long considered different by others in society, and school desegregation triggered charges that courts had violated the boundaries of judicial power.[15] The recalcitrance of local school boards and communities to comply with the desegregation mandate drew courts into ever more detailed and elaborate regulation and monitoring of the compliance with their orders.[16]

[13]See, e.g., David L. Shapiro, "Courts, Legislatures, and Paternalism," *Va. L. Rev.* 74 (1988), 519, 521, reviewing and defending this idea. But see Joseph William Singer, "The Reliance Interest in Property," *Stan. L. Rev.* 40 (1988), pp. 611, 744–48, rejecting this idea as incoherent and impracticable. Some expressly distinguish innovative judicial remedies in statutory contexts, which may be corrected by Congress and therefore are acceptable, from innovative judicial action in constitutional contexts, where the courts have the last word and therefore should be more cautious. See, e.g., Daniel Meltzer, "Deterring Constitutional Violations by Law Enforcement Officials: Plaintiffs and Defendants as Private Attorneys General," *Colum. L. Rev.* 88 (1988), 247, 293; Richard Stewart, "The Reformulation of American Administrative Law," *Harv. L. Rev.* 88 (1975), pp. 1667, 1740–42.

[14]See *In the Interests of Children: Advocacy, Law Reform, and Public Policy,* ed. Robert H. Mnookin (New York: W. H. Freeman, 1985), pp. 25–42. See, e.g., Gerald Gunther, "Some Reflections on the Judicial Role: Distinctions, Roots, and Prospects," *Wash. U. L.Q.* 1979 (1979), 817, 818: "The problem of legitimacy is most closely associated with the establishment of new rights, not with the development of new remedies. By contrast, the problem of judicial competence—of institutional expertise and effectiveness—is characteristically associated with remedies, not rights."

[15]E.g., Herbert Wechsler, "Toward Neutral Principles of Constitutional Law," *Harv. L. Rev.* 73 (1959), 1, demanded that courts adhere to "neutral principles" of law in order to avoid naked exercises of power.

[16]See Reed Sarratt, *The Ordeal of Desegregation: The First Decade* (New York: Harper & Row, 1966); Owen M. Fiss, *The Civil Rights Injunction* (Bloomington: Indiana University Press, 1978); Note, "Implementation Problems in Institutional Reform Litigation," *Harv. L. Rev.* 91 (1977), 428. See also Paul Gewirtz, "Choice in the Transition: School Desegregation and the Corrective Ideal," *Colum. L. Rev.* 86 (1986), 728. See also Cooper v. Aaron, 358 U.S. 1 (1958) (Supreme Court asserts the full reach of its power in enforcing school desegregation in Arkansas over the objection of the governor).

As courts prescribed prospective relief and, in some cases, appointed judicial officers to supervise the implementation of judicial decrees, critics charged that judges had gone beyond their spheres of competence and authority.

Scholars cite first the courts' limited abilities to handle complex problems. When a case concerns multiple parties and interconnected issues, it requires experimentation and persuasion—not the standard modes for a court.[17] Because judges must await the initiative of parties to set the business of the courts, to frame the issues, and to gather facts, critics maintain that courts are not competent to devise social reforms on the scale represented by citywide school desegregation.[18] Courts that manage schools become engaged in political negotiations and bargaining, departing sharply from their traditional roles in enunciating and enforcing rights.[19] These activities strain both the abilities of judges and the appearance of legitimacy necessary to the fulfillment of their tasks. Moreover, since courts are supposed to look only retrospectively to ascertain guilt or violations of rights, and then pronounce remedies tethered by underlying rules and precedents, the business of planning and managing the reform of complex institutions is beyond judicial abilities and legitimate action.[20] Courts particularly lack the power to redistribute resources—except through the indirect, and extreme, measure of holding particular government officials in contempt—unless they are able to secure additional funding from the executive or legislature.

Defenders of the judiciary identify traditional rules that authorize judicial initiatives in institutional reform cases and the flexible, innovative uses of information-gathering and monitoring devices that judges have adopted in those cases.[21] They further argue that the courts are performing their usual role of enforcing rights and providing essential protection for groups otherwise powerless in society. Some defenders argue that courts are flexible enough to adopt adjustments to deal with the limits of their competence and any appearances of impropriety. Thus, courts may make a greater use of

[17]See Lon L. Fuller, "The Forms and Limits of Adjudication," *Harv. L. Rev.* 82 (1978), 353 (written in 1957); William A. Fletcher, "The Discretionary Constitution: Institutional Remedies and Judicial Legitimacy," *Yale L.J.* 91 (1982), 635–37.

[18]See generally Donald L. Horowitz, *The Courts and Social Policy* (Washington, D.C.: Brookings Institution, 1977); Robert F. Nagel, "Separation of Powers and the Scope of Federal Equitable Remedies," *Stan. L. Rev.* 30 (1978), 706–12.

[19]Colin Diver, "The Judge as Political Powerbroker: Superintending Structural Change in Public Institutions," *Va. L. Rev.* 65 (1979), 43. The increasingly managerial dimension of judicial action in many fields is explored in Judith Resnik, "Managerial Judges," *Harv. L. Rev.* 96 (1982), 374. The argument that judges in these cases actually engage in legislation action is developed in Henry J. Friendly, "The Courts and Social Policy: Substance and Procedure," *Miami L. Rev.* 33 (1978), 21. Another approach criticizes the courts' lack of candor when they modify remedies in light of actual or predicted resistance. See Paul Gewirtz, "Remedies and Resistance," *Yale L.J.* 92 (1983), 585, 665–74.

[20]Horowitz, *The Courts and Social Policy.* See also Shapiro, "Courts, Legislatures, and Paternalism."

[21]The most influential defenses are Abram Chayes, "The Role of the Judge in Public Law Litigation," *Harv. L. Rev.* 89 (1976), 1281; Fiss, *The Civil Rights Injunction;* Owen Fiss, "The Supreme Court, 1978 Term—Foreword: The Forms of Justice," *Harv. L. Rev.* 93 (1979), 1; and Theodore Eisenberg and Stephen C. Yeazell, "The Ordinary and the Extraordinary in Institutional Litigation," *Harv. L. Rev.* 93 (1980), 465. See also Abram Chayes, "Public Law Litigation and the Burger Court," *Harv. L. Rev.* 96 (1982), 4.

notice to and solicitation of participation by third parties in the negotiations over proposed settlements in institutional reform cases.[22] Or judges may use experts and special masters to gather information and to monitor the implementation of decrees. Finally, courts may modify decrees over time in light of their relative effectiveness and any continuing opposition.[23]

The debate over judicial competence and legitimacy intensified when courts began to reform institutions for mentally retarded persons and for prisoners and to declare new rights for women and children.[24] Litigants initiated test cases for the express purpose of harnessing judicial power to achieve not only results for themselves but massive social change. Following the model of the NAACP in its campaign for racial justice, public interest lawyers during the 1960s and 1970s initiated test case litigation on behalf of women, children, and mentally disabled persons. These cases urged judges to declare that the plaintiff had rights that were violated by a particular governmental program or practice and that the violation warranted judicial action. Thus, these test cases often embroiled bureaucracies and states in contests with the federal government and placed federal courts in the position of demanding improvements in state services which in effect required new legislative appropriations.

Scholarly studies abound with tales of the public controversies such cases provoked. In his introduction to a collection of five case studies, Robert Mnookin summarized the objection that children's rights litigation, in particular, threatens the legitimacy of courts because it engages courts beyond their capacities and authority and treads on turf assigned to the elected branches of government.[25] A judge who orders a state to spend money to remake schools, housing, or public institutions entrenches on the territory of the legislature and the executive. Moreover, courts in such cases encounter charges of incompetence because no one can be certain of children's interests. The same kinds of objections have been leveled against litigation pursued on behalf of mentally disabled persons (as in the Pennhurst case; see Chapter 5) and even on behalf of groups of women, since women themselves disagree about what is in "women's" interests.[26]

There are several possible rejoinders to these charges. First, children, women, disabled persons, and members of racial minorities have been either unable to vote and lobby or otherwise ineffective in dealing with the elected branches of government; therefore, they deserve judicial protection. Second, even in the test cases the courts do not depart from their usual adherence to formal rules, evidentiary restrictions, and constraints requiring a link be-

---

[22]See Maimon Schwarzschild, "Public Law by Private Bargain: Title VII Consent Decrees and the Fairness of Negotiated Institutional Reform," *Duke L.J.* 1984 (1984), 887, 929–34.

[23]See Note, "The Modification of Consent Decrees in Institutional Reform Litigation," *Harv. L. Rev.* 99 (1986), 1020.

[24]Court activities managing other public institutions, such as housing projects, have provided occasions for academic debates. See, e.g., Charles M. Haar and Lance Liebman, *Property and Law*, 2d ed. (Boston: Little, Brown, 1985), pp. 436–82, a case study of institutional reform litigation involving public housing.

[25]Mnookin, *In the Interests of Children*, pp. 25–42.

[26]See Deborah Rhode, "The Woman's Point of View," *J. Legal Educ.* 38 (1988), 39.

tween right and remedy and justification of new action in terms of precedent; in these ways, courts retain their distinct role of enunciating and enforcing rights after reasoned argument. Finally, the courts' rules themselves provide authority for all the innovations that characterize the test cases; for example, rules approved by Congress authorize courts to involve multiple parties and to modify judicial remedies in light of changing circumstances.[27] Abram Chayes has argued that the complaint against judicial action in public-interest cases rests on an outmoded conception of adjudication. Congress has authorized flexible mechanisms enabling courts to gather facts and devise remedies in complex, institutional reform litigation. These competencies, in turn, demonstrate the legitimacy of judicial action.[28]

Another way to address the questions about judicial legitimacy in test case litigation is to examine the assumptions behind the questions themselves. The questions seem to assume that there are clear boundaries dividing the branches of government and that tasks assigned to one branch are denied to another. These assumptions neglect a contrary view: that boundaries depend on relationships and that continuing processes allowing renegotiation of boundaries better describe the relationships between the branches of government established by the Constitution. According to this view, boundaries for organs of government are not intrinsic or predetermined but are constructed through a continual process of interaction, conflict, and temporary resolution. The alternative, wooden notion of bounded, separated branches and levels of government rests on the same faulty view of boundaries between people that mars the debate over rights. The usual discussion of the powers of the branches uses the idea of competencies: each branch is competent to perform only its own functions and incompetent beyond those functions. This locution bears an odd resemblance to the conception of individual persons as separate and to the idea that differences and competencies are intrinsic traits of individuals rather than features that may come to matter in people's relationships.

Among legal scholars expert in the doctrines governing the separation of governmental powers, it is commonplace to discuss the mutually defining nature of the branches. The language of the Constitution defies assignment of distinct functions to each branch, though their competence and legitimate boundaries are often monitored on these grounds. Professor Philip Kurland put it this way: "If we take the basic arguments usually asserted that it is for the legislature to make the rules governing conduct, for the executive to enforce those rules, and for the judiciary to apply those rules in the resolution of justiciable contests, it soon becomes apparent that it is necessary to government that sometimes the executive and sometimes the judiciary has to create rules, that sometimes the legislature and sometimes the judiciary has to enforce rules, and sometimes the legislature and sometimes the executive has to resolve controversies over rules."[29]

[27]Mnookin, *In the Interests of Children,* pp. 37–41, 59–61, 61–63.
[28]Chayes, "The Role of the Judge," p. 1281.
[29]See Philip Kurland, "The Rise and Fall of the 'Doctrine' of Separation of Powers," *Mich. L. Rev.* 85 (1986), 603.

Others similarly argue that a functional approach to the separation of powers neglects the checks and balances contemplated by the doctrine.[30] The innovation of the United States Constitution is its model not merely of divided power but also of checks and balances.[31] In defending this structure, James Madison wrote in the *Federalist Papers* (No. 51) that the only answer to the problem of dividing the powers of the government is "by so contriving the interior structure of the government as that its several constituent parts may, by their mutual relations, be the means of keeping each other in their proper places."

Madison himself drew an analogy between this conception of the branches of government and the conception of individuals, each self-interested, positioned so that "the private interest of every individual may be a sentinel over the public rights." Recently, law-and-economics advocates have located within the Constitution the same assumptions about individual self-interest pursued through voluntary exchange which undergirds economic theory.[32] Other scholars maintain that the Constitution's framers did not completely reject notions of virtue and communal governance in their acknowledgment of the powerful motives of self-interest.[33] To pursue fully the analogy to

---

[30]See Peter L. Strauss, "The Place of Agencies in Government: Separation of Powers and the Fourth Branch," *Colum. L. Rev.* 84 (1984), 573, 577–79; Thomas Sargentich, "The Contemporary Debate about Legislative-Executive Separation of Powers," *Cornell L. Rev.* 72 (1987), 433–44. See Martin Shapiro, "Stability and Change in Judicial Decision-Making: Incrementalism or State Decision?" *Law Transition Quarterly* 2 (1965), 134: "[Courts] are part of the government, they make public policy, and they are an integral part of the law-making and enforcement process which is the central focus of political activity. If legislatures are political and executives are political, then courts must be political since all three are inextricably bound together in a process of making law, and each sometimes performs the functions that each of the others performs at other times."

[31]See also Kurland, "Rise and Fall," pp. 592, 593: "Checks and balances suggested the joinder, not separation, of two or more governmental agencies before action could be validated—or the oversight of one by another"; and Richard Posner, "The Constitution as an Economic Document," *Geo. Wash. L. Rev.* 56 (1987), 10–12, exploring the increase in transaction costs, alongside division of labor, in the Constitution's particular form of separation of powers.

[32]E.g., Jonathan E. Macey, "Competing Economic Views of the Constitution," *Geo. Wash. L. Rev.* 56 (1987), 50, 54.

[33]Thus, there seems little to support the view advanced by Edwin Meese, attorney general under Ronald Reagan: "The Founding Fathers could not anticipate all the problems with which the government would eventually grapple, but they could do at least two things: they could count and they could divide. They created a federal government of *three* well-defined branches. And they carefully enumerated the powers and responsibilities of each. With a few exceptions, such as the veto and impeachment powers, they vested the legislative power *solely* in the Congress, the executive power *solely* in the President, and the judicial power *solely* in the courts" ("The Federal Bar Association," speech of Sept. 13, 1985), pp. 2–3, quoted in Alfred C. Aman, Jr., "Symposium: Bowsher v. Synar—Introduction," *Cornell L. Rev.* 72 [1987], 428). It is a punchy statement, but one with little connection to constitutional history or doctrine. The framers did fear concentrations of governmental power; therefore, they adopted a structure of divided powers. But the divisions were hardly straightforward or neat; the Constitution adopted a hybrid notion, assigning tasks to each branch that overlapped with the functions of each other branch. See *Federalist Papers* No. 51. See also Gordon S. Wood, *Creation of the American Republic, 1776–1787* (Chapel Hill: University of North Carolina Press, 1969), p. 604: the American notion of separation of powers is *sui generis*, not traceable to prior theories; M. J. C.

relationships between individuals, the conception of governmental powers should acknowledge that each person develops a sense of autonomy only through connection with others. The very construction of boundaries— between persons or between branches of government—depends on sufficient concern for the continued vitality of others. Madison's view emphasized the mutual relations of the branches necessary to their mutual checking function. The legal regulation of separation of powers requires a continuing process of mutual action and interaction.

Many scholars maintain that context is essential to the evaluation of whether a particular governmental action strains the necessary balance of powers.[34] The historical moment, the substantive issue at stake, the responsiveness of other branches to that issue, and their abilities to reassert their roles in the balance of power are more central than a remote theory of the distinct functions of each branch. Transformative periods in American political history have often culminated in public debates over the relationships between the branches, in light of specific historical events.[35] Evaluation of the

Vile, *Constitutionalism and the Separation of Powers* (Oxford: Clarendon Press, 1967): the U.S. Constitution rejected a pure separation and adopted a hybrid form; Jesse H. Choper, *Judicial Review and the National Political Process: A Functional Reconsideration of the Role of the Supreme Court* (Chicago: University of Chicago Press, 1980), p. 260. Thus, it is no minor exception but a central feature of the constitutional conception that assigns to the Senate the advise-and-consent responsibility in executive nominations. Similarly critical are the president's power to veto legislation and the courts' power to review legislative and executive action. See Strauss, "The Place of Agencies in Government," p. 579. See also Peter L. Strauss, "Formal and Functional Approaches to Separation-of-Powers Questions—A Foolish Inconsistency?" *Cornell L. Rev.* 72 (1987), 488, 492: "Virtually every part of the government Congress has created—the Department of Agriculture as well as the Securities and Exchange Commission—exercises *all three* of the governmental functions of the Constitution so carefully allocated among Congress, President, and Court."

[34]See, e.g., Russell K. Osgood, "Governmental Functions and Constitutional Doctrine: The Historical Constitution," *Cornell L. Rev.* 72 (1987), 553; Kurland, "Rise and Fall." See generally Laurence A. Tribe, *American Constitutional Law,* 2d ed. (Mineola, N.Y.: Foundation Press, 1988), pp. 1–400. A classic judicial statement appears in Justice Jackson's concurring opinion in Youngstown Sheet & Tube Co. v. Sawyer, 343 U.S. 579, 634–35 (1952), when the Supreme Court refused President Eisenhower the power to seize the steel mills in order to avert a strike during the Korean War: "The actual art of governing . . . cannot conform to judicial definitions of the power of any [branch] . . . torn from context"—the context of modern governmental needs. "While the Constitution diffuses power the better to secure liberty, it also contemplates that practice will integrate the disposed powers into a workable government. It enjoins upon its branches separateness but interdependence, autonomy by reciprocity."

[35]Similarly, Peter Strauss ("The Place of Agencies in Government," p. 667) has argued that the bureaucracies created under the executive must "permit, even encourage, the continuation of rivalries and tensions among the three named heads of government, in order that no one body become irreversibly dominant and thus threaten to deprive the people themselves of their voice and control." In addition, he argued that the checks-and-balances idea eliminates the illusion that executive agencies should be evaluated in terms of their placement in the executive branch; instead, their relationship to other governmental activities and their role in the continuing process of readjusting the balance of power are critical (p. 669). Strauss urges analysis of separation of powers in light of "the quality of relationships between an agency and each of the three named heads of government rather than categorical approaches" ("Formal and Functional Approaches," p. 494). See also Aman, "Symposium," p. 443: the complex interaction of branches contemplated by checks and balances "presumably requires some blending of the tasks of governance among supposedly distinct branches."

legitimacy of judicial conduct depends largely on the responsiveness of the other branches. Questions of the separation of powers concern not so much whether one branch has invaded the prerogatives of another as whether the branches all remain able to participate in the process of mutually defining their boundaries. Vigilant judicial review of the boundary disputes among all three branches itself may seem to enlarge the power of the courts, yet without this activity the purpose of balancing governmental powers could be defeated.[36]

Let's see if these ideas help—or deserve reconsideration—in light of a specific case.

Willowbrook

A case highlighting issues of judicial competence involved a ten-year effort to close down the Willowbrook State School, a New York institution for mentally retarded persons.[37] Even in the context of dramatic institutional reform litigation in that case, the court remained relatively weak, compared with other governmental actors. The court's special contribution was to help people with less power or influence get their issue on the public agenda.

Willowbrook in 1972 was overcrowded and understaffed, filthy, rotten-smelling, and dangerous to the health and safety of its 5,400 mentally retarded residents. Over 75 percent of the residents were classified as "profoundly retarded." Lacking supervision, many injured themselves and others. They lived in wards with little furniture or clothing. Several staff members tried to improve the conditions and sought larger appropriations—without success. They then tried to organize a group of parents of Willowbrook residents, and the parents did participate in protest marches. The administration fired the staff members who had met with the parents. William Bronston, one of those dismissed, had a friend who worked for ABC television. Through that connection this story was made the subject of a television exposé and then a subject of newspaper editorials and investigations. Willowbrook became a scandal.

The New York Civil Liberties Union, the Mental Health Law Project, and the Staten Island Legal Aid Society filed suits on behalf of Willowbrook residents. The suits charged violations of the residents' rights to privacy, dignity, treatment, or habilitation. They also charged that the institution inflicted cruel and unusual punishment on its residents.[38] The suits de-

[36]See Sargentich, "Contemporary Debate," p. 444 n.6; and Kurland, "Rise and Fall," p. 611.
[37]See David J. Rothman and Sheila M. Rothman, *The Willowbrook Wars: A Decade of Struggle for Social Justice* (New York: Harper & Row, 1984). The litigation was named New York State Ass'n for Retarded Children, Inc. v. Rockefeller, and published opinions appeared at 357 F. Supp. 752 (E.D. N.Y. 1973); 393 F. Supp. 715 (E.D. N.Y. 1975) (mem.) (consent decree guaranteeing residents of the state facility a stipulated level of care). I rely on Rothman and Rothman, *The Willowbrook Wars*, for much of this account.
[38]Ibid., p. 64. The complaint alleged violations of the first, fourth, fourteenth, and eighth amendments.

manded that the court declare the institution unacceptable, take it over, and shut it down, while presiding over the establishment of decent community facilities. The plaintiffs' lawyers accumulated vivid details of the actual conditions at Willowbrook. Although everyone conceded that the institution was a hellhole, the state took an adversarial stance. Its attorneys argued that the courts had no proper role in the case, since the residents could leave voluntarily and since the executive and legislative branches of state government had authority over the allocation of public resources. The judge found many reasons to avoid granting the relief requested. Why should a federal judge intrude upon a state institution? How could a judge tell the state legislature to spend more money on the care of its residents? How could a judge supervise the details of improving their care? In short, the legitimacy and competency of the court's involvement became real issues for Judge Orrin Judd.

Judge Judd ultimately ruled for the plaintiffs, maintaining that the residents had a right to protection from harm. He granted preliminary relief and set in motion a process of argument and negotiation that resulted in a "consent decree"—a settlement reached by the parties and backed by the court's enforcement powers. Using standards for residential facilities developed by a national accreditation committee and a federal agency,[39] the consent decree included precise details of acceptable conditions and services within the institution, which the state thereby promised to provide. The decree also included a commitment to move residents, where possible, to community placements. The agreement established its own monitoring mechanism: a seven-person review panel that would hire a professional staff to investigate and evaluate the state's progress in implementing the decree, resolve disagreements in interpreting it, and report periodically to the judge, who would retain jurisdiction and power to hold the state in contempt for noncompliance. The state no doubt agreed to sign the decree because it was in the midst of a change in administrations. The outgoing governor found signing the decree a solution to a scandal that had occurred during his administration, and the incoming governor wanted to signal a change in attitude and approach to distinguish his new administration.[40]

The state proceeded to implement the decree, pushed by the review committee. State administrators struggled to locate community placements, despite the reluctance of all possible providers in the community. A few imaginative administrators worked to organize group homes and, over the course of several years, produced enough decent community-based settings to fulfill basic human needs for food and shelter for 50 percent of the Willowbrook residents.[41] The state also responded to the resistance of the unionized

[39]Joint Commission for the Accreditation of Hospitals, *Standards for Residential Facilities for the Mentally Retarded;* and Department of Health, Education and Welfare, *Guidelines for Facilities for the Mentally Retarded.* See Rothman and Rothman, *The Willowbrook Wars,* p. 114.

[40]See Rothman and Rothman, *The Willowbrook Wars,* pp. 118–24, discussing Nelson Rockefeller and Hugh Carey.

[41]Ibid., p. 200. Not always treatment or habilitation, though.

workers to deinstitutionalization by finding many of them jobs in the community placements.[42]

Up to this point, the Willowbrook case demonstrated an effective use of the judiciary to challenge definitions of the "differences" of mentally retarded persons which had contributed to their having been warehoused and neglected. The litigation provided ways to solicit contrasting perspectives about the people housed in Willowbrook and prompted a dramatic set of efforts to remake the meanings of disabilities when people with those disabilities were offered care in different settings. But the Willowbrook case also provoked persistent disputes—among those involved in the case and among those watching it—about the proper role of the judiciary in a legal system committed to separating the powers of government.

Four years after the case began, Orrin Judd died. Judge John Bartels, who replaced him, indicated his full support for the decree and his confidence that he could manage the boundary between the court and other branches: "I don't want anybody to feel that the Federal court . . . [is] invading the field of the executive branch. . . . I am perfectly cognizant of what does happen in the various social and economic fields . . . by the decisions of federal courts . . . so I really don't want any of you to get any feeling that I am very anxious to come in here . . . and interfere with the Department of Mental Health. I'm not. . . . But I do have an obligation . . . a legal and moral obligation . . . and I do feel strongly about the care and health and future of these children."[43]

Yet new fights began, eight years after the initial exposé, as the review panel focused on some of the most disabled residents, and as the financial and political environment changed.[44] The panel was unable to settle disputes between the plaintiffs' lawyers and the state over certain placements, and the case came back to court. The state's fiscal burdens were mounting. A new state administrator proved less willing than his predecessor to reach agreements with the plaintiffs, while seeking also to speed up the community placement process. To plaintiffs' lawyers, this spelled their worst fear: the state would begin to "dump" Willowbrook residents in undesirable and inadequate settings rather than pursue the painstaking process of constructing quality community placements.

Then the legislature denied renewed funding for the review panel that had been established to monitor the implementation process. For the plaintiffs this was a major blow. Without the review panel the state could proceed quickly to place remaining residents with no monitoring agent to guard against dumping. In their book on the case, David and Sheila Rothman demonstrate that the governor's staff publicly opposed this measure but privately took credit for the maneuver as one that would eliminate a growing source of friction and constraint on their policies. Judge Bartels ordered the state to fund the panel, but the appellate court reversed,[45] citing separation-

[42]Ibid., p. 217.
[43]Bartels, quoted in ibid., p. 149.
[44]Ibid., pp. 299–300.
[45]Ibid., pp. 319–20.

of-powers concerns. It ruled that the governor had complied with the consent decree: the legislature had not declined funds to implement the decree, and the district court could not command financing of the panel simply to avoid future but as yet unproven harms. Thus, once the executive and administrative participants grew resistant to the restraints established by the review panel, the courts sensed—and then declared—a limit in the judiciary's ability to shape events. The court of appeals advised those concerned to lobby the legislature for funds.

In a subsequent review of another district court ruling in the case, the court of appeals also approved the state's decision to use some fifty-bed institutions rather than move all Willowbrook residents to small-scale community placements.[46] The period of gross abuses and massive deprivations within the institution was over; the urgency of judicial involvement had passed; and resolving disagreement about the number of beds appropriate for an acceptable placement was not something courts should do, reasoned the court of appeals. In other words, the judges directed the trial court to devise its own limits, now that the disagreements centered on details of implementing the consent decree. The court had more power than it ever used in the case; for example, it had never used its contempt power.[47] And the court never reasserted a role in construing the consent decree's commitment to community placements. The appellate judges set limits on the judicial involvement in institutional reform, once the parties could no longer agree on guidelines.

The court's involvement should not be construed as an intrusion on legislative tasks. The lawsuit brought the state bureaucracy to court, a bureaucracy insulated from both legislative and executive control by its civil service and its byzantine practices. And in a real sense the courts enabled the other branches to become more effective in the bureaucratic arena of mental health and social services. The judicial involvement took the public scandal and made it an issue for public policy. The judicial inquiry pressured for a settlement and then elicited professional innovations, creating community-based services for people once abandoned to the cesspool of a neglectful and abusive institution. If professionals in the field had previously assumed that foster care and other community placements were impossible for mentally retarded persons, the judicial action made them reconsider that view. Instead of treating existing placements as the norm, against which the mentally retarded individuals would be judged compatible or incompatible, the pressure of the consent decree induced state officials to adjust the placements to work for those individuals. The judicial finding of the plaintiffs' rights to protection from harm and the consent decree to enforce those rights encapsulated the perspective of the "different" person. From that perspective, some new alternatives could and would be created.

Even more practically, the court's action helped create constituencies with the ability to pressure elected officials to establish and then maintain com-

---

[46]Ibid., p. 350.
[47]Ibid., p. 354.

munity services. Rothman and Rothman observe that before the consent decree, few people had a stake in such community-based programs, "but the dynamic of implementation fostered a coalition that included voluntary agencies, religious organizations, parent groups, and even some real estate agents." Shifting demographic patterns during the decade actually left fewer numbers of "normal" foster children for existing agencies to handle, and the Willowbrook case helped to match the agencies with a new clientele that would keep them in business.[48]

As its own actions created resistance, the district court could back off and leave the next round of debate to political battles in the other branches.[49] At least 50 percent of those residents of Willowbrook found decent community placements that actually promoted their own personal development. The professional investment in improving their treatment was well in place. Public understanding and concern about their situation had dramatically increased. And in this context, the judiciary played an important though not permanent role in a continuing process.

The Partial Approach of Litigation

Some might criticize judicial involvement in cases that challenge the treatment of "different" people because the courts do not do enough; they address only parts of the problems. It is fair to describe judicial responses to complicated problems as a process of narrowing through translation, a process that leaves many aspects of the underlying problems not only untouched but also unacknowledged. Narrowing the issues behind racial segregation to the enrollment and curricular programs at one junior high school did not address the wider patterns of housing, jobs, and social attitudes behind the problem.[50] Moving people out of one state institution leaves in place other state institutions and the financial and social arrangements that lead people to send their seriously disabled relatives to institutions in the first place.

Restating each of these problems in litigative terms converts factual descriptions to issues of rights. The problems shift from complicated, general societal questions—such as how children who are not cared for by their parents should be treated when they come into state custody—to specific questions about the legality of particular existing arrangements. Restating the issues for judicial consideration transforms them from open-ended questions about the array of possible governing rules to yes-or-no questions about

---

[48]Ibid., pp. 356, 357.

[49]Rothman and Rothman concluded: "A dialectic appears to operate in judicial reform in which action sparks reaction. A court may ably serve in the first instance as an antidote to politics, rectifying obvious legislative failures, like Willowbrook in 1972. But to the degree its interventions are successful, to the degree that it reorders priorities to correct wrongs, it sooner or later generates a hostile political response" (ibid., p. 361).

[50]See generally William Julius Wilson, *The Truly Disadvantaged: The Inner City, the Underclass, and Public Policy* (Chicago: University of Chicago Press, 1987).

whether particular rights have been violated. Unlike the open-ended questions, these questions seem capable of being answered relatively quickly. Yet there are drawbacks: in order to pose a question capable of a yes-or-no answer, the problem may be so simplified, narrowed, and abstracted that the meaning of the answer, outside the legal doctrine, is difficult to assess—except for the conclusion that the legal solution leaves much of the problem untouched. Courts' solutions are especially limited when it comes to remaking daily relationships between people, although courts may establish the ground rules for doing so.[51]

The partial nature of legal solutions is all the more obvious when the issues of race, class, disability, and other differences are tracked through each of the problems. Litigation initiated on behalf of children, in particular, often reaches quickly into the other differences used in society's structures for social order. Like Progressive era reformers, many contemporary child advocates focus on children in order to attack interconnected patterns of poverty, discrimination, urban overcrowding, and indecent housing and working conditions. The focus on children seemed—and seems—a way to break intergenerational cycles of despair. The innocence and vulnerability of children can increase support for reforms that ultimately point to deeper social patterns. But although the interests of children provide a hopeful avenue for reformers who seek to tackle deep problems in society, it should not be surprising that even victories in the name of children do not necessarily reach the root of their problems.

The trouble with judicial solutions from this vantage point is not that judges do too much but that judicial action is too partial to attack the broad and deep origins of poverty and invidious discrimination. The courts take too small a slice of the problem.[52] But the courts would not operate effectively in relation to the other branches if they took on still more. The more powerfully legal claims on behalf of children push for change at the deeper, structural level, the more likely are there to be objections, from many quarters, to this use of law to reform society.

Are children, or other "different people," made worse off when courts address a small slice of a complex problem? This is the kind of question that deserves another question as an answer: What are the alternatives? One likely alternative is legislative indifference. Few powerful constituencies place the needs of "different" people high on their demands. Another alternative is merely symbolic legislative response. Appointing a study commission, declaring a day to honor the handicapped—these are easy, superficial measures

---

[51]E.g., a court can issue restraining orders against domestic violence that trigger judicial sanction if violated or even order the offending party to vacate the premises. A court can also issue orders requiring a halt to prison violence and supervise processes of reform within institutions so that they can come to reform themselves. See Note, "Mastering Prison Intervention," *Yale L.J.* 88 (1979), 1062.

[52]In another context, Michael Polanyi, *The Study of Man*, (Chicago: University of Chicago Press, 1959), p. 29, noted: "We cannot comprehend a whole without seeing its parts, but we can see the parts without comprehending the whole."

that make little difference to the "different." Legislatures or agencies may adopt demonstration programs to improve services and treatment and then watch these programs become easy targets for legislative reaction or executive budget cuts. Reformers may work for the election of new executives and hope that new programs will follow. But new administrative programs may be no better than the practices they are supposed to remedy.[53]

Given these alternatives, even the partial solutions reached by the courts provide an opportunity to improve public debate. Framing questions as alleged violations of legal rights which deserve judicial remedies can secure at least enough official attention to make the claim. The courts, of course, can deny the claim, but in the meantime the judge has to pay attention, and the fact of judicial attention itself can help mobilize concern in other arenas. Litigators can press further and urge courts to identify the shortcomings in current knowledge and the conflicts in values behind the societal treatment of "difference." On occasion, in particular situations, courts can orchestrate a conversation among many participants about how, temporarily, to address hidden assumptions that hinder mutual understanding. By moving back and forth between the parts that courts can answer and the wholes that elude judicial treatment, advocates can make "difference" a subject for renewed imagination.

The judicial case can be seen "as a means for complicating clichés and first attitudes into deeper understanding and for extending imaginative sympathy to those differently situated from ourselves; and finally, as a way of making a place of coherence in a process of cultural change."[54] Litigation provides opportunities to challenge the assumption that differences reside in the "different" persons rather than in social relationships that may express imbalances of power. Litigation also allows a chance to challenge dominant perspectives by identifying competing perspectives and by demanding justifications for what has been taken for granted as the way things have to be. Judicial action is one among many tools for making government more responsive. The tool is as good, or as bad, as the people involved. And the courts stand always in relationship with the other branches of government, which may be mobilized to counter or constrain judicial action.

Courting Change

Progressive era reformers and proponents of the New Deal viewed courts as enemies; after all, the courts repeatedly rejected, in the name of property rights, general welfare and health and safety legislation designed to protect children, women, and workers. But the civil rights movement and movements for rights of women, children, and disabled persons have often treated courts as the major branch of government. For many years the federal

[53]See Gilbert Steiner, *The Futility of Family Policy* (Washington, D.C.: Brookings Institution, 1981).

[54]James Boyd White, *When Words Lose Their Meaning: Constitutions and Reconstitutions of Language, Character, and Community* (Chicago: University of Chicago Press, 1984), p. 274.

judiciary in particular has served as a protector for people disfavored elsewhere in the society. Both views of courts—as enemies and as protectors—reflect the perspectives of particular groups in particular historical contexts.[55] Both, stated in the abstract, are faulty.[56]

This chapter has argued that separation of powers necessarily involves continuous relationships between the branches rather than confining each to entirely distinct fields of competence. Respect for these vital relationships requires judges to remain sensitive to the prerogatives and reactions of the other branches and to the particular balance of power and equities in the given situation. Judicial inaction, as well as judicial action, may impair relationships with the other branches and undermine the government's overall obligation to respect persons.

The risks of erroneous judicial inaction are serious. Courts have developed a panoply of methods for asserting their own passivity.[57] They may defer to other branches or levels of government or to professional or military judgment. When a court defers to the legislature, the executive, a state government, or a private actor, the judges are saying, "Let's not make a decision; let's leave it to others," or, "Let's endorse the freedom or respect the power of others." It is surely important for judges to understand their relationships with other people and institutions. But such understanding is quite different from ceding responsibility for what ensues. The courts' own responsibilities to the parties before them cannot be acquitted simply by asserting deference to other branches. As Frank Michelman put it, attention to other branches of government "cannot mean deference, or talismanic invocation of authority. The norm of justice to parties itself commands that no other norm should ever take a form that preempts questions or exempts from reason-giving."[58] The reasons a court gives for declining to respond to a complaint are inadequate if they merely state routine respect or deference for another governmental entity. The courts' special obligation to act arises where one party lacks sufficient political power to be taken seriously by the electoral branches—or by the bureaucracy.[59]

Courts also sometimes try to circumvent their own responsibilities by rou-

[55]One important contextual factor is the political orientation of the judges. Although the appointing executive has no control over the future decisions of a judge with life tenure, Reagan's appointment of more than 50 percent of the currently sitting federal judges is bound to influence the future participation of courts in litigation challenging the legal treatment of women, children, and members of varied minority groups.

[56]A distinct question is whether the adversarial process of litigation will help or undermine efforts by people in continuing relationships to work through a difficult problem. Thus, alternatives to court—such as administrative rulemaking, mediation, and informal counseling—may be preferable for handling conflicts over medical treatment decisions.

[57]See e.g., Tribe, *American Constitutional Law*, pp. 67–155, discussing "justiciability" doctrines through which a court may find a case "unripe," or "moot," or "a political question," or asserted by a party without "standing," and thereby avoid deciding the case. See also Fleming James, Jr., and Geoffrey Hazard, Jr., *Civil Procedure* 3d ed. (Boston: Little, Brown, 1985), p. 7, discussing judicial self-restraints on exercising jurisdiction.

[58]Frank Michelman, "The Supreme Court 1985 Term—Foreword: Traces of Self-Government," *Harv. L. Rev.* 100 (1986), 1, 76.

[59]See generally John Ely, *Democracy and Distrust: A Theory of Judicial Review* (Cambridge, Mass.: Harvard University Press, 1980).

tinely relying on doctrinal boundaries and categories—created by courts—
to resolve the case at hand. Of course, many problems fit neatly within an
existing category, which allows the court to resolve the case efficiently—
unless the lawyers can persuade the court to reconsider the rule altogether.
Yet many cases arise because the parties themselves can see that the case does
not fit a preexisting category, or because an injury is so great that a new
category seems needed. Legislatures and executives may, over time, respond
to a whole class of such cases, but they also may not. A given person or group
retains the power to bring to court a complaint that falls through the cracks
of preexisting legal doctrines.[60] When a court responds by taking the boundaries between doctrines as given, it obscures the moment of choice it has been
presented.

The culture of lawyering may contribute to this problem. By the time a case
reaches an appellate court, the adversaries have so focused on specific issues
of doctrinal disagreement that the competing arguments have come under
one framework, not under competing theories. Opposing arguments become
counters in a game rather than efforts to craft new understandings of a
difficult problem.[61] Legal analogies become narrow references to precedents,
telescoping the creative potential of a search for surprising similarities into a
limited focus on prior rulings that could "control" the instant case.[62] As a result, fabricated categories assume the status of immutable reality. Of course,
law would be overwhelming without doctrinal categories and separate lines
of precedent. But by holding to rigid categories, the courts deny the existence
of tensions and portray a false simplicity amid a rabbit warren of complexity.

Strict segregation of doctrines cloisters lines of thought and insight and
thereby restricts the use of larger or competing frames of judgment. Legal
precedents addressing problems of difference in the context of religion are
usually ignored in a case involving gender. This sequestering of precedents is
especially unfortunate because some judges may better glimpse missing perspectives about difference than others, and borrowing procedures across
contexts could enrich judicial appreciation for the perspectives of the "different" person.

Lon Fuller once explained that "the trouble with the law does not lie in its
use of concepts, nor even in its use of 'lump concepts.' The difficulty lies in

---

[60]Yet gaining access to court is no small problem, not just for poor people but also for middle-
class people who are not eligible for publicly subsidized legal services. Constitutional guarantees
of access are quite limited; see Tribe, *American Constitutional Law*, p. 1462. For this and other
reasons, judicial doctrines affecting the ability of any private person to represent the interests of
others—and to serve as a private attorney general to address wrongs neglected by government
officials, are quite important but have also been restricted by costs and by ideological concerns.
See Bryant Garth, Ilene Nagel, and S. Jay Plager, "The Institution of the Private Attorney
General: Perspectives from an Empirical Study of Class Action Litigation," *S. Cal. L. Rev.* 61
(1988), 353.

[61]See Karl Llewellyn, "Impressions of the Conference," *U. Cin. L. Rev.* 14 (1940), 343.

[62]The classic legal-realist statement of this view is Felix Cohen's "Transcendental Nonsense
and the Functional Approach," *Colum. L. Rev.* 35 (1935), 809. See also Ellen Peters, "Coping
with Uncertainty in the Law," *Conn. L. Rev.* 19 (1986), 1, 4.

part in the fact that we have sometimes put the 'lumps' in the wrong places, and in part in the fact that we have often forgotten that the 'lumps' are the creations of our minds."[63] The legal realists called for using reason to connect real-world causes and effects rather than conceptual analysis of an internally self-sufficient legal system.[64] It would be a mistake to pretend that the concepts of cause, effect, or any other notions used in argument avoid "lumps" in simplifying perceptions and judgments; these notions simply place the lumps in different places. Courts cannot "get it right" or even enunciate rights for all times, because rights are not preformed, platonic conceptions but articulations of the qualities of relationships that themselves shift over time. Moral and legal judgments require a process of responding, with reasons, to particular situations.[65] The judicial enunciation of rights may be most important in nurturing hope and a sense of entitlement that individuals can assert in other settings, at other times.[66]

Rather than relying on old "lump concepts" without thinking about them, those who use legal arguments should explore the relationships between concepts and think up analogies that break out of ill-fitting conceptual schemes. One observer of creative processes in art, science, and philosophy has commented that "in the history of human thinking the most fruitful developments frequently take place at those points where two lines of thought meet."[67] By seeing something in a new light, seeing its similarity to something else once thought quite different, we are able to attribute different meanings and consequences to what we see.[68] Recognizing the mutable meanings of legal categories—and the chance to remake them in each new case—would help people acknowledge, and debate, the realm of legal choice that persists, despite our classification schemes. Anthropologist Mary Douglas notes that although our categories reinforce our social choices, "mercifully, the system

[63]Lon Fuller, *Legal Fictions* (Stanford, Calif.: Stanford University Press, 1967), p. 136.

[64]See John Dewey, "Logical Method and Law," *Cornell L.Q.* 10 (1924), 17; Karl Llewellyn, "Some Realism about Realism—Responding to Dean Pound," *Harv. L. Rev.* 44 (1931), 1222. A current approach emphasizes the task of legal argument—in and out of courts—as crafting stories, woven from particular facts, to move the listener and convey a coherent, powerful reality. See Gerald López, "Lay Lawyering," *U.C.L.A. L. Rev.* 32 (1984), 2. Especially stories about actual human consequences of judicial decisions can help judges break out of the abstractions of their categories.

[65]See Charles Larmore, *Patterns of Moral Complexity* (Cambridge: Cambridge University Press, 1987), p. 20.

[66]See *The Constitution and American Life*, ed. David Thelen (Ithaca: Cornell University Press, 1988), a collection of essays addressing rights consciousness in American history.

[67]Werner Weisenberg, quoted in Fritjof Capra, *The Tao of Physics* (Boulder, Colo.: Shambhala, 1984), p. xii.

[68]Thinking through analogy and thinking through argument bear striking similarities to the virtues of reasoning in dialogue. The dialogue form puts the student in a position to follow the connections and divergences in the debate and to invent ways to think anew, rather than simply internalizing the monologue of inherited categories. See Barbara Johnson, *A World of Difference* (Baltimore, Md.: Johns Hopkins University Press, 1987), p. 83: "Learning seems to take place most rapidly when the student must respond to the contradictions between *two* teachers. And what the student learns in the process is both the power of ambiguity and the non-innocence of ignorance."

of classification never fits. When there is non-fit, there is choice. The classification can either be clamped down more firmly, and the misfit removed in the name of purity, or the classification can be softened."[69]

These ideas about breaking out of rigid legal categories bear special relevance to the problems of people who are labeled "different" in social and legal discourse. These ideas about breaking out of rigid legal categories also apply to conceptions of courts, compared with other branches of government. In each instance, it may be easier to try to put ideas into boxes than to think about relationships. It may be easier for a court to treat labels of "difference" as part of an ineluctable reality rather than as social constructions comparing people—constructions that require rejection, absent justifications. It may be easier to conceive of courts as too limited or too "incompetent" to resolve certain kinds of legal questions that spill over into public controversy. Thinking about the relationships between engines of government and the requisites of continuing interplay requires more flexibility; it requires resistance to ready categories in deciding when a court should or should not act. Similarly, thinking about relationships between people and about each person's need for enabling and supporting connections yields less certainty about the limits of each person's responsibilities to others than do conceptions of two classes of persons, the incompetent and the competent. But the focus on interrelationships—among branches of government, among people, and even among categories for understanding— provides a steady reminder of the choices we do have and our chances to make a difference.

[69]Mary Douglas, "Heathen Darkness," in *Implicit Meanings: Essays in Anthropology* (London: Routledge & Kegan Paul, 1975), pp. 226–27.

Different Beginnings:
Making All the Difference

> Knowledge is like a staircase built in such a way that every
> landing offers a view of yet another one, to which one can't help
> wanting to ascend. No one will ever be totally satisfied because
> knowledge is also an endless spiral.
>
> —Albert Memmi, *Dependence*

> Well, son, I'll tell you:
> Life for me ain't been no crystal stair.
> It had tacks in it,
> And splinters,
> And boards torn up,
> And places with no carpet on the floor—
> Bare.
> But all the time
> I'se been a-climbin' on,
> And reachin' landin's,
> And turnin' corners,
> And sometimes goin' in the dark
> Where there ain't been no light.
>
> —Langston Hughes, "Mother to Son"

The use of anesthesia in surgery spread quickly once it had been
discovered.[1] Nineteenth-century doctors who adopted anesthesia selected
which patients needed it and which deserved it; they thought some people's
pain more serious than others; some people were thought to be hardy enough
to withstand pain. Both the medical literature and actual medical practices

First epigraph: Copyright © 1984 by Beacon Press. Translated by Philip A. Facey from *La
Dependance*, © Editions Gallimard, 1979. Reprinted by permission of Beacon Press. Second
epigraph: Copyright 1926 by Alfred A. Knopf, Inc. and renewed 1954 by Langston Hughes.
Reprinted from *Selected Poems of Langston Hughes*, by permission of Alfred A. Knopf, Inc.
[1]Martin S. Pernick, *A Calculus of Suffering: Pain, Professionalism, and Anesthesia in
Nineteenth-Century America* (New York: Columbia University Press, 1985), pp. 3–4.

during the nineteenth century distinguished people's need for painkillers on the basis of race, gender, ethnicity, age, temperament, personal habits, and economic class. Women, for example, were thought to need painkillers more than men; the rich and educated more than the poor and uneducated. How might we, today, evaluate these distinctions? What differences between people should matter, and for what purposes?

The endless variety of our individualism means that we suffer different kinds of pain and may well experience pain differently. But when professionals use such categories as gender, race, ethnicity, and class to presume real differences in pain and entitlement to help, I worry. I worry that a difference assigned by someone with power over another will become endowed with an apparent reality, despite competing versions of that reality. If no one can really know another's pain, who shall decide to treat pain, and according to what calculus? These are questions of justice, not science. These are questions of complexity, not simple opportunities to categorize. And these are questions that demand answers, for failing to notice another's pain is an act with significance.

There is a certain paradox in even asking, "What's the difference?" That question can signal either a sincere request for information or a casual shrug. In an episode of the television show *All in the Family*, Edith Bunker asks whether her husband would like the laces of his bowling shoes laced under or over the holes. Her husband, Archie, replies, "What's the difference?" Edith begins to explain the difference meticulously, but Archie explodes; he had meant, by his reply, "Who cares?"[2]

I think we must think seriously about difference. Otherwise, its meanings—embedded in unstated norms, institutional practices, and unspoken prejudices—will operate without examination or justification. Not long ago Alice Jardine wrote: "At this point it seems impossible to think difference without thinking it aggressively or defensively. But think it we must, because if we don't it will continue to think us, as it has since Genesis at the very least."[3] In particular, a commitment to equality—to treating likes alike—will remain caught in contradiction.

It is not only official judges or people in visible positions of power who assign and judge difference; we all do. Labeling and stereotyping others as different carries consequences in private and even intimate settings as well as public ones. You have the power to label others "different" and to treat them differently on that basis. Even if you mean only to help others, not hurt them, because of their difference, you may realize the dilemma. By taking another person's difference into account—in a world that has made difference matter—you may recreate and reestablish both the difference and its negative implications. Any remedy for discrimination that departs from neutrality seems a new discrimination and risks a new source of stigma. Yet you cannot

[2]Thus, asking "What's the difference?" signals two mutually exclusive meanings: the literal meaning asking about the concept (difference), whose existence is denied by the figurative meaning. See Paul de Man, "The Epistemology of Metaphor," *Critical Inquiry* 5 (1978), 13.

[3]Alice Jardine, "Prelude: The Future of Difference," in *The Future of Difference*, ed. Hester Eisenstein and Alice Jardine (Boston: G. K. Hall, 1980), p. xxvi.

avoid trouble through ignoring difference; you cannot find a solution in neutrality. Ours is a world that has made difference matter. Being neutral about this past and ignoring someone's difference assigns remaining burdens of difference to that person. Treating Chinese-speaking students as though they were just like their classmates ignores their lack of English proficiency while judging them by standards that presume such proficiency. This is the effect of the unstated assumptions in schools, workplaces, and other social institutions that make difference matter.

We have seen the assumptions about difference deeply entrenched in our social institutions, and in the legal rules that govern them. One assumption treats difference as inherent in the "different" person rather than a function of comparisons; another assumption establishes as the norm for comparison the experience of only some people, such as English-speaking students, or white men, or able-bodied persons; a third assumption imagines an "objective" observer who can see without a perspective, uninfluenced by situation or experience. Differences perceived by judges, employers, and school administrators seem natural and inevitable; there seems no need to seek out contrary perspectives. Finally, the way things are seems given and immutable. All these assumptions make difference seem a dilemma. They so inscribe one point of view as natural and orderly that any conscious decision to seek other points of view seems irrelevant or strange; similarly, any effort to notice difference seems to violate neutrality, even while failure to notice difference undermines equality.

The dilemma becomes less paralyzing if we question these assumptions and try to look at the issues from another point of view. This is what Justice Stevens did when he assessed a zoning restriction excluding group homes for mentally retarded people by trying to imagine what someone in that group would think of the city ordinance.[4] This is what Justice Douglas did when he asked about the experience of non-English-speaking students sitting in a public classroom conducted entirely in English.[5]

From this different perspective, we may glimpse how our patterns for organizing the world are both arbitrary and effective in foreclosing their own reconsideration. We may find that the categories we usually take for granted do not highlight features that we do not know. We may now see an injury that we had not noticed, or take more seriously a harm that we had otherwise

[4]"I cannot believe that a rational member of this disadvantaged class could ever approve of the discriminatory application of the city's ordinance in this case": City of Cleburne v. Cleburne Living Center, 473 U.S. 432, 455 (July 1, 1985) (Stevens, J., concurring).

[5]Lau v. Nichols, 414 U.S. 563, 566 (January 21, 1974): "There is no equality of treatment merely by providing students with the same facilities, textbooks, teachers, and curriculum; for students who do not understand English are effectively foreclosed from any meaningful education." A sadly contrasting case is Justice Felix Frankfurter's statement in West Virginia State Board of Education v. Barnette, 319 U.S. 624, 646–67 (June 14, 1943) (Frankfurter, J., dissenting), in which he referred to his own Jewish background as a basis for his sensitivity to minority experiences yet rejected the argument that members of a minority religion could be exempt from the requirement that school children must pledge allegiance and salute the flag. For a provocative explanation of his discomfort with his own minority identity and his desire to conform and to become an "insider," see H. N. Hirsch, *The Enigma of Felix Frankfurter* (New York: Basic Books, 1981), pp. 23–24.

discounted. It was only when a friend of mine became the father of a daughter that he took offense at the use of "he" by the expert books on baby care; only then was the affront to his daughter's particularity as a "she" palpable to him.[6] Shifting to the standpoint of a historically marginalized person can reveal truths obscured by the dominant view. Making this shift may be disorienting or irritating, but if we treat other points of view merely as irritants in the way of our own vision, we are still hanging on to a faulty certainty. Even admitting the limits of our viewpoint is not enough if we treat our ignorance merely as a gap within the unchanging framework we already know.[7] Opening up to another point of view means at least entertaining the possibility that our prior categories and assumptions need revision. Opening up to another point of view could allow us to see how we are *all* different from one another and also how we are all the same. It depends upon how we look at it—and we all reflect the partiality of our own perspective.

Claiming that we are already impartial is insufficient if we do not consider changing how we think. Impartiality is the guise that partiality takes to seal bias against exposure. It looks impartial to apply a rule denying unemployment benefits to anyone who cannot fulfill the work schedule, but it is not impartial if the work schedule was devised with one religious Sabbath, and not another, in mind. The rule does not seem impartial to the employee who belongs to a minority religion. Until we try to imagine the point of view of someone unlike ourselves, we will not depart from our own partiality.

The point is not to find the new, true perspective; the point is to strive for impartiality by admitting our partiality.[8] The perspective of those who are labeled "different" may offer an important challenge to those who imposed the label, but it is a corrective lens, another partial view, not the absolute truth.[9] It is the complexity of our reciprocal realities and the conflict between the realities that constitute us which we need to understand.[10]

[6]See also George Eliot's *Daniel Deronda* (1874–76), ed. Graham Handley (Oxford: Clarendon Press, 1984), p. 155, which captures the impact of perspective on the meaning of harm: Eliot notes a moment when Daniel "was feeling the injury done him as a maimed boy feels the crushed limb which for others is merely reckoned in an average of accidents."

[7]See Barbara Johnson, *A World of Difference* (Baltimore, Md.: Johns Hopkins University Press, 1987), p. 16: "If I perceive my ignorance as a gap in knowledge instead of an imperative that changes the very nature of what I think I know, then I do not truly experience my ignorance. The surprise of otherness is that moment when a new form of ignorance is suddenly activated as an imperative."

[8]We cannot come close to the ideal of a government of laws rather than of *men* without recognizing that it is particular human beings, with particular situated perspectives, who govern and whose perspectives must be made subject to challenge.

[9]See Carol Gilligan, *In a Different Voice: Psychological Theory and Women's Development* (Cambridge, Mass.: Harvard University Press, 1982), pp. 151–74: maturity involves a complementary and productive tension between the (feminine) ethos of care and the (masculine) ethic of rights. Elevating the view from the margin as the new truth is problematic at least in part because doing so would reconfirm the underlying scheme, defined by the dominant view, about what lines of difference matter. See Fran Olsen, "The Sex of Law" (University of California, Los Angeles, Law School, unpublished manuscript), rejecting both the strategy of claiming that women are like men and the strategy of trying to elevate traditional female virtues as each falling into the trap of reconfirming categories defined by men.

[10]See Martha Nussbaum, *The Fragility of Goodness: Luck and Ethics in Greek Tragedy and Philosophy* (Cambridge: Cambridge University Press, 1986), pp. 311–14.

Shifting perspectives exposes how a "difference" depends on a relationship, a comparison drawn between people with reference to a norm. And making this reference point explicit opens up debate. Maybe the reference point itself should change. Employers do not have to treat pregnancy and parenthood as disabilities; instead, they could treat them as part of the lives of valued workers. It is possible to replace a norm that excludes with a norm that includes. Renovating the sidewalks to make them accessible to people in wheelchairs takes their needs as the norm but does not exclude others. Indeed, this renovation may yield unexpected benefits for people pushing baby strollers or riding bicycles.[11] Designing hospital procedures to treat every patient as potentially HIV-positive—"universal isolation"—protects the staff without stigmatizing a subset of the patient population. And teaching sign language to the entire class of hearing students so that they all may communicate with the hearing-impaired student, and she with them, enlarges and enriches everyone's education while according her some measure of equality. Changing the ways we classify, evaluate, reward, and punish may make the differences we had noticed less significant, irrelevant, or even a strength. The way things are is not the only way things could be. By aligning ourselves with the "different" person, for example, we could make difference mean something new; we could make *all* the difference.

Unstated norms, against which we "find" difference, remain powerful, however.[12] A good example appears in the legacy of the abnormal-persons approach to the legal treatment of difference. A legacy left by feudal traditions continues to assign a dependent status to some people and continues to seem rational and foreordained. Even after the revolution of liberalism accorded rights of equality and liberty to all "competent" persons, some people—people now called incompetent—remained "different." They were defined as having legal disabilities that removed them from the sphere of rights and subjected them to dependent relationships with those entrusted with their care and protection. Successive reform efforts challenged such treatment of married women, blacks, and, at times, children and mentally disabled persons. Yet the rhetoric of rights, deployed in these reforms, reaffirmed a conception of difference by rejecting only those legal deprivations for people shown to be the same as the unstated norm. "Real differences" still justified different legal treatment.

Rights analysis may challenge the exclusion of "different" people from schools and workplaces, but it fails to supply a basis for remaking those institutions to accommodate difference. Integrated into institutions not designed with them in mind, formerly marginalized people may simply become newly marginalized or stigmatized. They may well fail within the terms set by

---

[11]Innovations initially designed for disabled people often yield benefits for others. The Sorbothane Grip Strengthener (from Spectrum Sports in Twinsburg, Ohio), originally designed for physically disabled children, has been found useful for any persons who want to strengthen their grip: additionally, using it appears to reduce levels of stress.

[12]Some have called this the baseline problem. See Cass Sunstein, "Lochner's Legacy," *Colum. L. Rev.* 87 (1987), 873–919; Seth Kreimer, "Allocational Sanctions: The Problem of Negative Rights in a Positive State," *U. Pa. L. Rev.* 132 (1984), 1293–1397.

the institutions, thus seeming to confirm the judgment that they are different. Rights analysis particularly tends to preserve status quo arrangements and shield them from reevaluation when it comes to private, rather than public power. Husbands, parents, guardians, and state institutions serving as caretakers long enjoyed the mantle of privacy that shielded their treatment of dependents from review and from the disciplining power of individual rights. Thus, even as rights analysis trumpets its sensitivity to power and threats to liberty, it has often manifested a limited perspective about whose liberty matters. Philosophical theories of rights, based on the traditions of social contract and natural rights, similarly mistake the freedom of a "normal," competent adult for the freedom of all and neglect their own contributions to the creation of a second track of treatment for people who do not fit the norm. Legal theorists who claim to challenge rights traditions—scholars of the legal-process and law-and-economics schools—deploy the same assumptions. Some leverage for change is offered by individual members of the movement for critical legal studies, but even these theorists remain mesmerized by the dichotomy contrasting autonomy and dependence, with no further alternatives.[13]

It is difficult, in fact, to relinquish the idea that there are real differences that should distinguish competent and incompetent people. There are, of course, physical differences between people; there are also differences in mental capacity and ability. Yet the persistence of labels to describe people who differ from the majority in these traits tends to deny traits they all share. Labels tend to express and freeze in place fears about what may seem strange. Perhaps the assignment of a fixed place of difference helps people to manage fears about glimpses of dependence and "difference" in themselves.[14] We forget that things may appear frightful only because they are unfamiliar. We look at people we do not know and think they are different from us in important ways. We forget that even if they are "different," in ways that matter to them too, they also have a view and experience of reality, and ours is as different from theirs as theirs is from ours.

We all tend to forget that our conceptual schemes are simplifications, serving some interests and uses rather than others. We forget because our minds—and probably our hearts—cannot contain the whole world.[15] We reduce the world to shorthand that we can handle. Our shorthand, because it

---

[13]Alan Freeman, and many of the feminist theorists who also participate in critical legal studies, notably avoid most of these problems and more consistently seek discussion of the excluded or marginalized perspectives.

[14]See Sander Gilman, *Difference and Pathology: Stereotypes of Sexuality, Race, and Madness* (Ithaca: Cornell University Press, 1985), pp. 239–42.

[15]This familiar imagery, distinguishing head and heart, unfortunately depends on a kind of shorthand itself, one reinforcing a particular philosophic tradition that treats thought and emotion as importantly and necessarily separate. For contrasting views, see Lynn Henderson, "Dialogue of Head and Heart," *Cardozo L. Rev.* 10 (1988), 123–48; Martha Minow and Elizabeth V. Spelman, "Passion for Justice," *Cardozo L. Rev.* 10 (1988), 37; Joseph William Singer, "Radical Moderation" (Review Symposium on Ackerman's *Reconstructing American Law*), *Am. B. Found. Res. J.* 1985 (1985), 329, 343–44.

is *our* shorthand, reflects what we think we need, where we stand, and who we are. We do not see that our divisions of the world embody our early experiences of discovering how we are both the same as and different from our parents. We forget how we learned from them to encode the world into the same classifications they used to serve their own needs.[16]

The more powerful we are, the less we may be able to see that the world coincides with our view precisely because we shaped it in accordance with our view. Catharine MacKinnon has observed: "When Justice [Potter] Stewart said of obscenity, 'I know it when I see it,' that is even more interesting than it is usually taken to be, if viewed as a statement connecting epistemology—what he knows through his way of knowing, in this case, seeing—with the fact that his seeing determines what obscenity is in terms of what he sees it to be, because of his position of power."[17] Saying that the world is how we see it is just one of our privileges. Another is that we are able to put and hear questions in ways that do not question ourselves.[18] In contrast, the more marginal we feel in the world, the more likely we are to glimpse a contrast between some people's perceptions of reality and our own.[19] Yet we may still slip into the world view of the more powerful, because it is more likely to be validated. We prefer to have our perceptions validated; we need to feel acknowledged and confirmed. But when we fail to take the perspective of another, we deny that very acknowledgment and confirmation in return.

Learning to take the perspective of another is an opening wedge for an alternative to traditional legal treatments of difference. I call this alternative the approach of social relations in order to emphasize the basic connectedness between people and the injuries that result from social isolation and exclusion. The relational focus also assists an understanding of difference as a function of comparisons between people. This approach especially rejects distinctions drawn between people which express or confirm the distribution of power in ways that harm the less powerful. The social-relations approach

[16]Sometimes we realize that our perceptions and desires are influenced by others; sometimes we recognize that television, radio, school classes, or the attitudes of people who matter to us affect our inclinations. Every time we wear an item of clothing that we now think is fashionable but used to think was ugly, we brush up against the outside influences on what we think inside— yet we think we think independently. We forget that widely held beliefs may be the ones most influenced from the outside. See, e.g., Karl Mannheim, *Ideology and Utopia*, trans. Louis Wirth and Edward Shils (New York: Harcourt, Brace, 1936), pp. 84–87.

[17]Catharine MacKinnon, "Pornography, Civil Rights, and Speech," *Harv. C.R.–C.L. L. Rev.* 20 (1985), pp. 1, 3, quoting Jacbellis v. Ohio, 378 U.S. 184, 197 (1964) (Stewart, J., concurring).

[18]This idea is captured by the etymology of privilege, which "comes from the Latin words *privus* (single, one's own), and *lex* (law), as if there could be a 'law for one,' a law that addresses itself to the single person and the unique set of circumstances, rather than to the abstract generality of mankind and circumstance"; see Michael Denneny, "The Privilege of Ourselves: Hannah Arendt on Judgment," in *Hannah Arendt: The Recovery of the Public World*, ed. Melvyn A. Hill (New York: St. Martin's Press, 1979), pp. 245, 268.

[19]See, e.g., Paula Giddings, *When and Where I Enter: The Impact of Black Women on Race and Sex in America* (New York: William Morrow, 1984); Robert Bogdan and Steven Taylor, "The Judged, Not the Judges: An Insider's View of Mental Retardation," in *An Alternative Textbook in Special Education*, ed. Burton Blatt, Douglas Biklen, and Roger Bogdan (Denver, Colo.: Love, 1977), p. 217.

has roots in a dramatic shift of attention during the twentieth century—across the sciences, social sciences, and humanities—toward relationships rather than to the discrete items under observation. For many, this shift has brought a new focus on relationships between people within which individuals develop a sense of autonomy and identity. For others, the shift turns to the relationship between the knower and the known—the impact of the observer's situated perspective on what can be observed, and the part played by the observed in constituting the observer. Another topic of attention is the relationship between parts and wholes, and still another is the mutual dependence of theory and context. From work in relativity theory and the indeterminacy principle in physics to deconstructive strategies in literary interpretation, these relational concerns are occupying scholars in challenges to the assumptions of their fields of study.

I have been most helped by the elaboration of these strategies in the work of feminist scholars.[20] In biology, history, moral theory, literary criticism, and a variety of social sciences, feminists have exposed the dominance of conceptions that take men as the reference point and treat women as "other." By naming the power of naming, feminist work explores the relationship between observer and observed. By exposing the assignment of difference based on a limited norm, feminists have made vivid the interactions between theory and context, parts and wholes. Feminist work shows the power of connections, alongside distinctions, and welcomes the sometimes frightening recognition of our mutual implication in what we study and in one another. Feminist work thus offers interlaced strategies for interpreting and for critiquing prevailing practices and ways of knowing.

Holding on to these relational strategies is difficult to do, given the grip of modes of analysis that sort by categories. Relational strategies may be easily misunderstood and trigger opposition from seemingly contrary sources. Some critics object that conceiving of people as mutually implicated, rather than as autonomous, threatens limitless responsibility for others and invasions of private, bounded individualism. Others warn that relational thought initiates relativism, or suspended judgments about what is right and what is wrong.[21] Some may fear being overwhelmed or too moved by the world. Others fear being powerless before it.

The philosophic investigations of the American pragmatists help frame responses to these fears. The pragmatists, too, urged relational commitments to connect theory and practice, parts and wholes, observer and observed, as well as persons and persons. The pragmatists remain controversial, but their theories match up with my sense of how we really know and decide. We seek

---

[20]I am also helped by some work of the "postmodernists," who often seek out suppressed or marginal views. But the fascination of postmodernist theorists with abstraction and with the invention of new and inaccessible vocabulary reduces their helpfulness for my consideration of the legal treatment of difference. I have elaborated these views in "Partial Justice" (lecture presented at Amherst College, April 1988).

[21]The very contradiction between these warnings of increased moral authority and weakened moral judgments suggests that the problems lie outside these strategies.

contextual approaches to problems, based on a continual process of testing theory against practice and practice against theory. We make commitments when we make decisions. We reconfirm or remake current understandings by reflecting about a new situation. Sometimes, on reflection, we challenge presumptive solutions. Instead of trying continually to fit people into categories and to enforce or deny rights on that basis, we can and do make decisions by immersing ourselves in particulars to renew our commitment to a fair world. Martha Nussbaum describes such a process of decision this way:

> We reflect on an incident not by subsuming it under a general rule, not by assimilating its features to the terms of an elegant scientific procedure, but by burrowing down into the depths of the particular, finding images and connections that will permit us to see it more truly, describe it more richly; by combining this burrowing with a horizontal drawing of connections, so that every horizontal link contributes to the depth of our view of the particular, and every new depth creates new horizontal links.[22]

We can and do make judgments about right and wrong, but we do so in context and in light of particularized assessments of the patterns of power and meaning. We can and should confront our involvement in and responsibility for what happens when we act in a reality we did not invent but still have latitude to discredit or affirm.[23] We should strive for the standpoint of someone committed to the moral relevance of contingent particulars.[24] Judgments about right and wrong depend not on a fixed certainty. Justice, like philosophy, remarked Charles Sanders Peirce, ought "to trust rather to the multitude and variety of its arguments than to the conclusiveness of any one. Its reasoning should not form a chain which is no stronger than its weakest link, but a cable whose fibers may be ever so slender, provided they are sufficiently numerous and infinitely connected."[25]

This all sounds lovely, you may say, but awfully abstract. What actually happens? Don't people with power continue to ignore or misunderstand those without it, and won't these relational moves undermine the certain effectiveness of legal rules in checking power, especially when exercised in

[22]Nussbaum, *The Fragility of Goodness*, p. 69. Nussbaum uses Heraclitus's image of a spider in a web, "able to feel and respond to any tug in any part of the complicated structure." It is a vivid image of responsiveness to complexity in a world of practical choice. See, e.g., E. B. White, *Charlotte's Web* (New York: Harper, 1952), pp. 92–104, in which a spider acts as a sensitive and involved creature, using her web to spell an important message.

[23]See Robert Cover, *Justice Accused: Antislavery and the Judicial Process* (New Haven, Conn.: Yale University Press, 1975), pp. 1–7, 25–30, 119–58, 236–38, 257–59; John Thomas Noonan, *The Antelope: The Ordeal of the Recaptured Africans, in the Administrations of James Monroe and John Quincy Adams* (Berkeley: University of California Press, 1977), p. 159; John Thomas Noonan, *Persons and Masks of the Law: Cardozo, Holmes, Jefferson, and Wythe as Makers of the Masks* (New York: Farrar, Straus & Giroux, 1976), pp. 3–28.

[24]Nussbaum, *The Fragility of Goodness*, p. 314. See also Charles Larmore, *Patterns of Moral Complexity* (Cambridge: Cambridge University Press, 1987), p. 20.

[25]C. S. Peirce, "Some Consequences of Four Incapacities," in *Collected Papers*, ed. Charles Hartshorne and Paul Weiss (Cambridge, Mass.: Harvard University Press, 1931), p. 157.

the name of benevolence? Certainly, people do tend to forget their own partial perspectives and enlarge their own power by pretending to speak for others. Contemporary feminists, for example, too often claim to speak for all women while ignoring differences of race, religion, disability, and political identity and the other perspectives embraced by at least some women. And a study of elements of the Progressive movement's reforms during the early part of this century also shows the impact of the reformers' self-interests, political backlash, and failures to limit bureaucratic power. The juvenile court, for example, supplanted the legal rights of the criminal court with paternalist rhetoric that spawned sprawling empires of regulatory services and incarceration facilities, restraining more people for longer periods without noticeable results but with notable inequities and unpredictability. Don't these dangers of presumptive and oppressive power call for the stringent restraints of a system of individual rights, announced and enforced by the state?

My response: Of course, but that does not tell us what the rights should contain, and that does not mean rejecting relational strategies. Many of the failures of Progressive reform, like the short-sighted presumptions of contemporary feminism, grew from inadequate attention to relational concerns rather than overindulgence in them. Current feminists need more, not less, attention to relationships (as do rights theorists) to remind us to consult, debate, and explore—with people we think different from ourselves—the hidden assumptions about unstated norms that we retain. Turn-of-the-century Progressives manifested mixed motives, and often acted out of a desire to control the people they said they wanted to help. Here, too, failures of consultation, and failures of flexible responses when contexts defeated theories, were much at work. Then, as now, the power of dominant institutional arrangements set the ground rules for what people could imagine even in their efforts to bring about change. To battle these dominant arrangements, the language of rights offers methods to interrogate prevailing practices and offers images of change to lift people from current assumptions. But to treat existing arrangements and assumptions as the baseline for rights is to consign persons to an often unfair and prejudicial status quo.[26]

It is only contradictory to defend both rights and relational strategies in a conceptual framework that poses either/or solutions and reads any focus on human interconnection as a retreat from liberalism to feudalism. We are more inventive than that. It is a mistake to infer that relational strategies are inconsistent with rights. An emphasis on connections between people, as well as between theory and practice, can synthesize what is important in rights with what rights miss. Especially when located as a historical response to patterns of assigned status, rights present an important critical tool to challenge persistent relationships of unequal power. The shortfalls in traditional rights analysis, for those who question assignments of difference and legacies of stigma, are its insistence on proof of similarity with a given

[26]"To settle for the constitutionalization of the status quo is to bequeath a petrified forest" (Aviam Soifer, "Complacency and Constitutional Law," *Ohio St. L.J.* 42 [1981], 383, 409).

"norm" and its defense of the private power of people entrusted with the care of others. Here, relational strategies can help. Rights can be reconceived as a language for describing and remaking patterns of relationships. Rights can be understood as communally recognized rituals for securing attention in a continuing struggle over boundaries between people. Especially in struggles to secure greater respect for those—such as women, children, and mentally disabled persons—who remained dependent after others had secured rights for autonomous action, rights provide a rhetoric for naming and scrutinizing both private and public power. The work of the legal realists, themselves influenced by American pragmatism and by relational theories in science and social science, offers a lever to challenge the private power that traditional rights analysis shielded. Rescuing rights for new purposes will remake what rights mean; rights asserted by children, for example, will take new forms. Rights provide not an ultimate language but one of many for constituting collective and individual lives. Infused with attention to relations between theory and context, parts and wholes, selves and others, and observer and observed, the language of rights can enable rich contests over whose version of reality should prevail, for now.[27]

This resolution is not a solution but a shift in assumptions. From here, what we need to do is work, in specific contexts, on the problems of difference. There is no ultimate resting place but instead an opportunity for dialogue, conversation, continuing processes of mutual boundary setting, and efforts to manage colliding perspectives on reality. It is not even enough to imagine the perspective of the other; we must also try to share deliberations with the other person. History should remind us that none of us can resolve dilemmas of difference alone. None of us should rest confident that we have found the correct version of reality once and for all, or that we may fully trust the exercise of power.[28]

If we plunge into a specific debate over whether a court should order medical treatment for a severely disabled newborn whose parents decline to authorize treatment, we will discover a complex world of conflicting principles, polarized emotions, and overlapping spheres of decision-making. The language of rights contributes one of many themes in this world. The understanding of relationships affords a way to knit together seemingly antagonistic principles, a way to place parents, state officials, and medical personnel on the same rather than opposing sides of the decision. Attention to relationships helps to locate the medical treatment decision in the context of the social meanings of disability and the relationships that can alter those meanings for the child involved.[29]

[27]See also Jeffrey Stout, *Ethics after Babel: The Languages of Morals and Their Discontents* (Boston: Beacon Press, 1988), defending a pragmatic conception of the multiple languages currently found in ethical debates.

[28]"*In matters of power, the end of doubt and distrust is the beginning of tyranny*" (Laurence H. Tribe, *Constitutional Choices* [Cambridge, Mass.: Harvard University Press, 1985], p. 7, original emphasis).

[29]To make matters even more complicated, a broader context for the decision involves resource allocation: how to balance the cost of heroic efforts on behalf of severely disabled

Attention to relationships can also reformulate arguments about the proper role of each branch of government—especially given debates over the legitimacy of judicial action on behalf of "different" people. Although the governing doctrine is commonly called separation of powers, we can invigorate the idea of separateness by locating boundaries within relationships of mutual dependence. This is the notion behind "checks and balances." The Constitution set in motion a continual process of struggle between the branches rather than fixed categories for their actions. A case study of an aggressive judicial initiative to decide whether a plaintiff group is an "Indian tribe" exposes limitations in the adversarial process of a court removed from broad-based political participation. Another case study of a dramatic litigative challenge to the institutionalized treatment of mentally retarded persons shows how other branches came into the process, once the rights-based argument in court put the issue on public agendas. The partiality of judicial relief must be acknowledged, given the whole problems of difference which remain. The courts cannot address these problems alone.[30]

Addressing relationships, in the senses developed here, means rejecting the assignment of labels that have historically degraded the treatment of children, women, disabled persons, and members of racial, ethnic, religious, and language minorities in families, schools, and workplaces. Inquiry into relationships does not establish concepts or rules or new categories for confining disputes. Instead, such inquiry launches a way of removing the removal of ourselves from the problems of difference we see. If the institutional arrangements we take for granted are part of the problem in assigning the burdens of difference to those who depart from the norm, then we should explore ways to adjust them, ways in which the institutions themselves could change.

The issues of difference have never been more important.[31] The AIDS virus assures that each community will confront an enormous challenge. Will we respond with fear, seeking to exclude from our worlds those who contract the virus?[32] A deadly contagious disease may highlight what frightens us

---

newborns with the funds needed for prenatal care to reduce the risks of such disabilities. Compartmentalized decision processes obscure the connections between these and other allocation decisions; it will be a distant day when such connections become part and parcel of everyday politics.

[30]By ending the book with a chapter on courts, I do not mean to suggest that courts are the destiny of all problems of difference. I do mean that when judges hear these problems, there are good reasons for them to respond.

[31]The multiple and interlapping identities of difference complicate all efforts to understand it. See Elizabeth V. Spelman, *Inessential Woman: Problems of Exclusion in Feminist Thought* (Boston: Beacon Press, 1988), discussing the occlusion of racial, religious, and other variations among women by both traditional and feminist political theory. See also Alice Walker, "Advancing Luna—For Ida B. Wells," in *Midnight Birds: Stories by Contemporary Black Women Writers,* ed. Mary Helen Washington (Garden City, N.Y.: Anchor Books, 1980), p. 63, depicting the complexity of emotions and perceptions of reality in a relationship between a black woman and a white woman who claims to have been raped by a black man.

[32]Some have proposed reopening leper colonies, creating the equivalent of internment camps, or tattooing individuals whose test results are positive. Our history in dealing with fear by isolating the people we fear is not an admirable one. See Korematsu v. United States, 323 U.S. 214 (1944); Mari Matsuda, "Looking to the Bottom: Critical Legal Studies and Reparations," *Harv. C.R.–C.L. L. Rev.* 22 (1987), 323, 363–68.

most about difference. Those who have it live in a different time frame, shaped by physical pain and continual loss. But they were once like the rest of us—and we could be like them. That the risk groups seem discrete, and seem to overlap with other "differences" we have stigmatized in the past,[33] may lull some into thinking that there is a real difference between victims and "innocents"—but that is a conclusion enabled only by faulty categorical thinking. Communities have shut down public schools rather than allow their children to attend with a child who is HIV positive;[34] employers and landlords dismiss victims; medical systems refuse care. How we handle this difference will in no small measure constitute what, and who, we are.

Religious differences have grown more intense in many areas and pose profound questions for such institutions as public schools. Does accommodating members of different groups require abandoning the commitment to a shared public education in the values of secular culture and democracy?[35] A paradox of tolerance arises: should tolerance tolerate those who reject tolerance? The paradox is especially poignant for schools, whose mission is to provide for each generation a foundation of shared experience and language to enable self-governance across conflicting affiliations. Legal norms and processes in a heterogeneous, diverse society have been critical to that foundation. When public schools try to teach values without violating the Constitution's ban against establishing religion or favoring one religion over another, they generally turn to the civic values of freedom, tolerance, and participation.[36] If legal norms are themselves contested and embody a kind of intolerance for difference, it is difficult to imagine any shared normative endowment.

Some would cite affirmative action as a crisis of difference, an abandonment of commitments against discrimination in the name of fighting discrimination. Relational strategies demand contextual analyses: against what backdrop of institutional practices was the affirmative action plan adopted? If the plan was a voluntary adjustment of the selection procedures used by a school or an employer that in the past had effectively excluded members of particular minority groups, or white women, that plan may importantly and justifiably correct for faulty assumptions used to assign difference.[37] If the plan is ordered by a court to remedy demonstrated discrimination in the past,

---

[33]Homosexuals and intravenous drug users fit this description, but children who contract the disease from their parents, patients who get it through blood transfusions, and immigrants from particular danger spots in the world may not. Nonetheless, there is plenty of degradation to go around.

[34]Those school systems that have developed policies before a crisis, and educated parents ahead of time, have had greater success in preserving the ongoing operation of the schools while also including the AIDS student or teacher. See David L. Kirp, *Learning by Heart: AIDS and Schoolchildren in America's Communities* (New Brunswick, N.J.: Rutgers University Press, 1989). Schools must also plan now for children disabled by their parents' drug and alcohol abuse.

[35]See Mozert v. Hawkins County Public Schools, 647 F. Supp. 1194 (E.D. Tenn. 1986) (upholding a challenge by fundamentalist parents who objected to secular humanism in public school textbooks), rev'd, 827 F.2d 1058 (6th Cir. 1987), cert. denied, 108 S.Ct. 1029 (1988).

[36]See, e.g., Sanford Levinson, *Constitutional Faith* (Princeton, N.J.: Princeton University Press, 1988).

[37]See Regents of the Univ. of California v. Bakke, 438 U.S. 265 (1978).

it similarly can be justified as a corrective for distorted practices. Yet some object that these remedies impose new harms of discrimination by hurting white or white male applicants who were not themselves at fault. The very concept of fault, however, implies that only a few blameworthy individuals caused the prejudicial treatment of minority groups, rather than acknowledging the collective, institutional practices that accomplished that end— and, reciprocally, benefited the majority.[38] The question, thus, cannot be whether the selection process departs from neutrality, for "neutrality" could itself be harmful if it merely reiterated past injuries.[39] To conclude otherwise would be to create, and preserve, an entitlement for the majority to enjoy privileged access to the most sought-after jobs and schooling.[40]

Moreover, as even opponents of affirmative action plans acknowledge, selection criteria are seldom "neutral"; schools have long taken into account many factors besides individual merit, such as alumni parents, special musical or athletic talents, and geographic diversity.[41] Even standardized tests may implement a faulty norm by testing for the knowledge cultivated by a particular cultural subgroup—such as those exposed to opera—rather than for academic skills.[42] It should hardly be a defect for an institution now to conclude that it values racial diversity and gender balance in order to usher in a vision of an integrated future.[43] Selection criteria may well value the presence of members of previously excluded or underrepresented groups, as models for other applicants and as contributors who can help shape new understandings of difference within the school or workplace. To equate this with past preferences for whites or for men is to ignore the context of power and relationships that has made differences matter in the past.

Affirmative action may look most objectionable for abandoning the ideal of individualized treatment and justifying group membership as a criterion for selection. Certainly, the ideal of individualized treatment has proved a potent solvent for some bonds of assigned status and historic prejudice. But

[38]See Alan D. Freeman, "Legitimizing Racial Discrimination through Antidiscrimination Law: A Critical Review of Supreme Court Doctrine," *Minn. L. Rev.* 62 (1978), 1049, 1054.

[39]See Laurence Tribe, *American Constitutional Law,* 2d ed. (Mineola, N.Y.: Foundation Press, 1988), pp. 1521–44. Justice Lewis Powell articulated this view in his opinion for a plurality of the Supreme Court in Wygant v. Jackson Board of Educ., 106 S.Ct. 1842 (1986) (Powell, J., joined by Burger, C. J., and Rehnquist, J.): "As part of this Nation's dedication to eradicating racial discrimination, innocent persons may be called upon to bear some of the burden of the remedy."

[40]See Derrick Bell, "A Property Right in Whiteness" (Harvard Law School, unpublished draft, 1988); Kathleen M. Sullivan, Comment, "Sins of Discrimination: Last Term's Affirmative Action Cases," *Harv. L. Rev.* 100 (1986), 78–98. See also Richard H. Fallon, "To Each According to His Ability, From None According to His Race: The Concept of Merit in the Law of Antidiscrimination," *B.U.L. Rev.* 60 (1980), 815, 864–76.

[41]See Joseph Berger, "Impact of Bakke Case 10 Years Later," *New York Times,* July 13, 1988, p. 25, discussing the views of the American Jewish Committee and white ethnic associations.

[42]Moreover, standardized tests often predict only the student's first year grades, not subsequent grades or performance. See Barbara D. Underwood, "Law and the Crystal Ball: Predicting Behavior with Statistical Inference and Individualized Judgment," *Yale L.J.* 88 (1979), 1413 n.12.

[43]See Sullivan, "Sins of Discrimination."

individualized approaches leave in place the norms and institutional practices that prefer only one kind of person but pretend impartiality, making a mockery of the ideal of individualized treatment. Moreover, there is a conceptual flaw in an imagined jurisprudence of individualism that would never treat any individual as a member of a group. Resonant as it is with many American traditions, individualization of this sort is a delusion. Because our language is shared and our categories communally invented, any word I use to describe your uniqueness draws you into the classes of people sharing your traits. Even if ultimately I produce enough words so that the intersection of all classes you belong in contains only one member—you—we understand this through a language of comparison with others. This language, however, risks treating differences as features of individuals rather than as comparisons and relationships.

It is intriguing to trace early meanings of "individual," for this shows the twists and turns meanings can take even in communal language. Raymond Williams's research concludes that "individual" originally meant "indivisible, or necessary connection," as in the elements of the divine Trinity or the relation between husband and wife. In the seventeenth century people started to use the term to describe some idiosyncrasy or eccentric departure from common human nature. Only with the crumbling of medieval order did individuality come to signify "a man's personal existence over and above his place or function in a rigid hierarchical society."[44] Even with this meaning, individuality demands a larger whole within which the individual is recognized, and patterns of relationships within which the boundaries of people can be negotiated and acknowledged.[45] This larger context of relationships, within which we negotiate our individual boundaries, is made more palpable through relational strategies.

Despite its association with liberal individualism, the law of contracts is traveling a route that parallels the changing historical meanings of individualism. In feudal society, precursors of contract law governed the agreements of mutual aid that established relationships between inferior and superior lords, between lords and masters, and even between husbands and wives. Postfeudal liberalism crafted contract as the model for agreements between free and consenting competent adults, agreements establishing relationships removed from assigned status or coercion. Reaching its heyday in this country between 1870 and 1920, the classical theory of contract rejected the imposition of obligations beyond the formalities of contractual agreements, and it constricted obligations based on role or relationships except in reference to "abnormal" dependent people. This was the theory that courts used to reject popular legislation passed to protect women, children, and laborers

---

[44]Raymond Williams, *Keywords: A Vocabulary of Culture and Society* (New York: Oxford University Press, 1976), pp. 133–36. The new meanings also were informed by developments in science and math and, ultimately, utilitarian ethics.

[45]The paradoxical yearnings for individual uniqueness and communal connection appear in posters plastered on dormitory walls: some announce "I march to a different drummer"; others pronounce, "No man is an island."

in new industrial settings; this was the theory that pretended that the ideal of free and equal bargaining was a reality instead of a practice favoring the new industrialists.

The legal realists provided intellectual fuel alongside the political ferment that helped remake these understandings during the twentieth century. In the context of industrial labor relations the classical theory of contract simply defeated labor organizing and health and safety legislation. The relationships within which contracts arose became, for reformers, a critical context for evaluating and revising the law of contract. More recent reformers have adopted similar analyses in seeking reforms in marriage and divorce laws. The conception of individual rights exemplified by classical contract law neglected patterns of unequal power—called private but reinforced by public authority—which defeated any ideal of free and equal relationships. Rescuing that ideal, today, means reexamining the relationships within which individuals find and make their own boundaries.[46] Scholars have started to urge acknowledgment of people's mutual reliance and dependence, and recognition of obligations growing from these relationships.[47]

Similarly, public laws adopted by legislatures and rules announced by courts have sought and can continue to seek inclusive solutions to problems that have divided us. There are strategies to illuminate the variety of our differences rather than herding us into groups of the privileged and groups of the degraded. We can choose how to characterize our shared and divided lives; we can decide to emphasize what we have in common or where we diverge; we can pool our resources to share the burdens of our differences, or we can assign those burdens to the people with the least ability to protest. Our very self-conceptions are mutable, depending upon which alternative we adopt.

In Julio Cortázar's story about an enormous traffic jam on the highway to Paris, automobiles were stuck, immobilized, for miles. The congestion was so impacted that first one day went by with no movement, and then another. Gradually, drivers and passengers ventured out from their own automobiles. Some simply commiserated; others made friends. Some took on the job of trying to coordinate and redistribute resources such as food and blankets. An old person died. A young man developed a crush on a woman in another car. Little subcommunities of mutual aid sprang up. And then, on the third day, traffic started moving again, and the tendrils of connection, pockets of community, and lines of affection dissolved.[48] Perhaps, as in the story, we

---

[46]See also Stewart Macaulay, "Non-Contractual Relations in Business: A Preliminary Study," *American Sociological Review* 28 (1963), 55; Todd D. Rakoff, "Contracts of Adhesion: An Essay in Reconstruction," *Harv. L. Rev.* 96 (1983), 1174–1284.

[47]See Joseph William Singer, "The Reliance Interest in Property," *Stan. L. Rev.* 40 (1988), 611–751; Margaret F. Brinig and June Carbone, "The Reliance Interest in Marriage and Divorce," *Tulane L. Rev.* 62 (1988), 855–905.

[48]Julio Cortázar, "The Southern Thruway," in *All Fires the Fire and Other Stories*, trans. Suzanne Jill Levine (New York: Pantheon Books, 1973), pp. 3–26.

have at best temporary ties with one another. But the ways we think about one another affect our likelihood of connection when the opportunity does arise.

In their massive study of people who did and people who did not seek to rescue Jews in Nazi Europe, Samuel and Pearl Oliner found most strikingly that the rescuers were not individuals of unusual moral courage; like those who did not try to help, they were ordinary people. Yet the rescuers did differ from those who did not rescue: they were more likely to be members of vital communities, bound by religious, familial, or affective ties. Rescuers were more likely to have grown up in families that emphasized the commonalities of all humankind; they had had less exposure to anti-Semitic and other labels marking some groups as inherently worse than others.[49] The Oliners' study suggests that moral action may be shaped by the relationships people enjoy and by the messages they receive about their relationships with others.

In the search for commonalities and connections between people, the real divisions, conflicts, and disagreements must not be overlooked. The language of rights enables individuals and groups to demand attention from others for points of view that have been neglected. Locating rights within relationships protects against the faulty pretense that people are already equal and free. In communal contexts summoned by an invocation of rights, the public arena registered by claims of rights, we can make law a medium through which particular people engage in the continuous work of making justice.

Law "is part of a distinctive manner of imagining the real," says Clifford Geertz.[50] Legal decisions engrave upon our culture the stories we tell to and about ourselves, the meanings that constitute the traditions we invent, the dialogue through which we remake the normative endowment that shapes current understandings. Searching for words to describe realities too multiple and complex to be contained by any one language, litigants and judges struggle over what will be revealed and what will be concealed in the inevitable partiality of human judgment.

Through deliberate attention to our own partiality, we can begin to acknowledge the dangers of pretended impartiality. By taking difference into account, we can overcome our pretended indifference to difference and our tendency to sort the world into "same" and "different," familiar and unfamiliar, equal and unequal. As we make audible the struggles over which version of reality will secure power, we disrupt the silence of one perspective, imposed as if universal. Admitting the partiality of the perspective that temporarily gains official endorsement may embolden resistance to announced rules. But only by admitting that rules are resistible—and by justifying to the governed their calls for adherence—can justice be done in a democracy.

---

[49]Samuel P. Oliner and Pearl M. Oliner, *The Altruistic Personality: Rescuers of Jews in Nazi Europe* (New York: Free Press, 1988).

[50]Clifford Geertz, *Local Knowledge: Further Essays in Interpretive Anthropology* (New York: Basic Books, 1983), p. 184.

Boundaries and categories of some form are inevitable. They are necessary to our efforts to organize perceptions and to form judgments. But boundaries are also points of connection. Categories are humanly made, and mutable. The differences we identify and emphasize are expressions of ourselves and our values. What we do with difference, and whether we acknowledge our own participation in the meanings of the differences we assign to others, are choices that remain.[51] The experts in nineteenth-century anesthesiology did not stop to ask whether they properly understood the pain of others. We can do better. As Nancy Hartsock observes: "It is only through the variety of relations constructed by the plurality of beings that truth can be known and community constructed."[52] Then we can constitute ourselves as members of conflicting communities with enough reciprocal regard to talk across differences. We engender mutual regard for pain we know and pain we do not understand.

[51]"Sesame Street," which asks children to answer, "which one of these things is not like the other?" has recently changed its reply. If, for example, the question points to a chair, a table, a book, and a bed, the television program no longer gives only one answer but instead identifies different answers based on a choice of conceptual schemes. Perhaps the book is the anomaly, since the other items are articles of furniture. Perhaps the bed is the oddball, if the category selected looks to what belongs in a study. The program thus shows that the choice of categories is a choice of purposes; differences are not intrinsic but relative to chosen ends.

[52]Nancy Hartsock, *Money, Sex, and Power: Toward a Feminist Historical Materialism* (New York: Longman, 1983), p. 254, describing the view of Hannah Arendt.

Table of Cases

Index

Abbott, Grace, 246, 248
Abnormal-persons approach: elements of, 105–7, 119; history of, 125–30; legacy of, 377; legal boundaries and, 8; obligations and, 223–24; paternalism and, 169; reality of, 96, 142; rights-analysis approach and, 131–45; solutions of, 214–16
Abortion: debate over, 323; family law and, 277, 302; minors and, 277, 284, 292; women's concerns and, 197, 204
Abstract principles, 322–23
Accidents, law of. See Tort law
Accommodation: neutrality and, 21, 45; rights language and, 377–78; of workplace to parenting, 87–90
Addams, Jane, 14, 199, 243–47, 261, 263n, 265
Addelson, Kathryn Pyne, 323n
Adolescence, 283–84
Adversarial relations: between children and adults, 290–92; medical treatment decisions and, 333–37, 369n; welfare system and, 291n
Affirmative action: dilemma of difference and, 47, 49n, 76; legal approaches and, 11n; observer's perspective and, 63–64; relational strategies and, 385–87; social attitudes and, 73
AIDS, 48, 96, 337, 377, 384
American Academy of Pediatrics, 331–32
American Medical Association (AMA), 249
Amish community, 69
Analogical thinking, 1–3, 370
Anesthesia, 373–74
Animal welfare, 4–5
Anthropology, 184–86

antidiscrimination principle, 315n, 318, 332n
Appelby, Joyce, 310n
Argument, 8, 295, 238–39
Aristotle, 70
Assumptions, unstated: childrens' rights and, 297–98; difference dilemma and, 50–74, 174, 375–78; effects of, 74–78; feminist critiques of, 229–39; institutional definition of, 79–80; reformers and, 259; twentieth-century scholarship and, 177–81
Automobile accidents. See No-fault approach; Tort law
Autonomous individualism: children's rights and, 299–306; competence-incompetence distinction and, 125–28; as concept, 129; critical legal studies and, 169–70; dangers of, 268; family law and, 270, 273; feminist criticism of, 194; groups historically excepted from, 124; legal process theory and, 159; liberal theory of, 124; natural rights tradition and, 155–56; Progressive reform attempts and, 258–60; rhetoric of, 267n; rights-analysis approach and, 147; social contract theory and, 148, 150–54; social experience and, 183–84; vs. socialism, 242–43; social welfare legislation and, 249–50
Autonomy. See Autonomous individualism

Baby Jane Doe case, 329–31
Ball, Milner, 295
Bathrooms, 118n
Baudelaire, Charles, 204–5
Becker, Howard, 174
Becker, Phillip, 341–50

Library of Congress Cataloging-in-Publication Data

Minow, Martha, 1954–
    Making all the difference/ Martha Minow.
        p.   cm.
    ISBN 0-8014-2446-1 (alk. paper)
    1. Status (Law)—Interpretation and construction. 2. Personality (Law)—Interpretation and
construction. 3. Equality before the law—Interpretation and construction. 4. Sociological
jurisprudence. 5. Social groups. I. Title.
K627.M56 1990
346.01'3—dc20
[342.613]   90-1754